Professional Stage

Module E

Accounting
and
Audit Practice

ACCA Textbook

0246/J99

British Library Cataloguing-in-Publication Data

A catalogue record for this book is available from the British Library.

Published by AT Foulks Lynch Ltd
Number 4
The Griffin Centre
Staines Road
Feltham
Middlesex
TW14 0HS

Printed in Great Britain by Ashford Colour Press, Gosport, Hants.

ISBN 0 7483 4024 6

Acknowledgements

We are grateful to the Association of Chartered Certified Accountants, the Chartered Institute of Management Accountants and the Institute of Chartered Accountants in England and Wales for permission to reproduce past examination questions. The answers have been prepared by AT Foulks Lynch Ltd.

CONTENTS

PREFACE

This Textbook is the ACCA's official text for paper 10, Accounting and Audit Practice, and is part of the ACCA's official series produced for students taking the ACCA examinations. It has been produced with direct guidance from the examiner specifically for paper 10, and covers the syllabus and teaching guide in great detail giving appropriate weighting to the various topics.

This Textbook is, however, very different from a reference book or a more traditional style textbook. It is targeted very closely on the examinations and is written in a way that will help you assimilate the information easily and give you plenty of practice at the various techniques involved. Particular attention has been paid to producing an interactive text that will maintain your interest with a series of carefully designed features.

- **Introduction with learning objectives**. We put the chapter into context and set out clearly the learning objectives that will be achieved by the reader.

- **Definitions**. The text clearly defines key words or concepts. The purpose of including these definitions is **not** that you should learn them - rote learning is not required and is positively harmful. The definitions are included to focus your attention on the point being covered.

- **Brick-building style**. We build up techniques slowly, with simpler ideas leading to exam standard questions. This is a key feature and it is the natural way to learn.

- **Activities**. The text involves you in the learning process with a series of activities designed to arrest your attention and make you concentrate and respond.

- **Conclusions**. Where helpful, the text includes conclusions that summarise important points as you read through the chapter rather than leaving the conclusion to the chapter end. The purpose of this is to summarise concisely the key material that has just been covered so that you can constantly monitor your understanding of the material as you read it.

- **Self test questions**. At the end of each chapter there is a series of self test questions. The purpose of these is to help you revise some of the key elements of the chapter. The answer to each is a paragraph reference, encouraging you to go back and re-read and revise that point.

- **End of chapter questions**. At the end of each chapter we include examination style questions. These will give you a very good idea of the sort of thing the examiner will ask and will test your understanding of what has been covered.

Complementary Revision Series, Lynchpins and Audio Tapes

Revision Series - The ACCA Revision Series contains all the relevant current syllabus exam questions from June 1994 to December 1998 with the examiner's own official answers, all updated in January 1999.

What better way to revise for your exams than to read and study the examiner's own answers!

Lynchpins - The ACCA Lynchpins, pocket-sized revision aids which can be used throughout your course, contain revision notes of all main syllabus topics, all fully indexed, plus numerous examples and diagrams. They provide invaluable focus and assistance in keeping key topics in the front of your mind.

Audio Tapes - Our new 'Tracks' audio tapes are fully integrated with our other publications. They provide clear explanations of key aspects of the syllabus, invaluable throughout your studies and at the revision stage.

FORMAT OF THE EXAMINATION

The format of the paper will be as follows:

	Number of marks
Section A: 2 (out of 3) questions on Financial Accounting	50
Section B: Compulsory integrated accounting and auditing question	30
Compulsory auditing question	20
	100

Time allowed: 3 hours

The financial accounting content will account for approximately 65% of the marks and will be examined in Section A and part of Section B. The auditing content will account for the remaining 35% of the marks and will be examined in Section B.

SYLLABUS

Professional stage - Module E Paper 10: ACCOUNTING AND AUDIT PRACTICE

Introduction

Paper 10 builds on the overview of financial accounting from paper 1, and develops the auditing knowledge outlined in paper 6. The financial accounting content has a weighting of 65% and the auditing content has a weighting of 35%.

Chapter reference

(1)   THE THEORETICAL AND REGULATORY ACCOUNTING FRAMEWORK

      (a)   The interpretation and application of the following theories and principles   6, 7, 21

            (i)   theories of accounting in relation to the measurement of

- income
- capital maintenance
- valuation of assets and liabilities

            (ii)   principles of accounting for price level changes
            (iii)   accounting conventions
            (iv)   the recognition of revenue
            (v)   the recognition of assets and liabilities.

      (b)   The objectives of financial statements   1

            (i)   criteria of useful information
            (ii)   usefulness for particular purposes.

      (c)   The interpretation and application of all extant SSAPs and FRSs.   9 - 16, 20

      (d)   The appreciation of the role of the legal and regulatory framework of accounting.   1, 7

(2)   PREPARING FINANCIAL STATEMENTS

      (a)   The preparation and presentation of financial statements, under conditions of stable prices, for   2-5, 8-15, 20

            (i)   conversion of partnership to a limited company

            (ii)   branches

            (iii)   limited companies, within the legal and regulatory requirements including the application of all extant SSAPs and FRSs

- profit and loss accounts
- balance sheets
- cash flow statements
- directors' reports.

(b)   Calculation and accounting treatment of   6

      (i)   pre-incorporation profits
      (ii)   distributable profits
      (iii)   purchase of own shares.

(c)   Groups of companies   3, 17, 18, 19

      (i)   explaining statutory and professional requirements relating to the preparation for publication of consolidated accounts

      (ii)   accounting for the following organisational situations

- joint ventures
- associated undertakings
- simple groups

      (iii)   evaluating the following alternative group accounting methods

- equity accounting
- proportional consolidation
- acquisition accounting
- merger accounting.

(3)   ANALYSING AND APPRAISING FINANCIAL AND RELATED INFORMATION   22

(a)   Interpreting and analysing financial statements for indications of business performance, using inter-firm and inter-temporal methods.

(b)   Assessing information weaknesses in the financial statements.

(4)   COMMUNICATING TO USERS   22

Producing reports as specified to meet the needs of internal and external users, supported by appropriate accounts and financial statements, which include information on and, where necessary, explanations of

(i)   the results of operations and the state of affairs
(ii)   projected results
(iii)   accounting policies and practices used
(iv)   main assumptions on which the reports are based
(v)   significant departures from accounting standards, concepts and conventions
(vi)   any other material considerations.

(5)   ADVANCED AUDITING PRACTICES AND PROCEDURES

(a)   Controlling the audit, including advanced aspects of audit planning, audit programme design and testing, statistical sampling and sampling methods, evaluation of audit risk and test results.   23-26

THE OFFICIAL ACCA TEACHING GUIDE

Paper 10 - Accounting and Audit Practice

	Syllabus reference	*Chapter reference*

Session 1   *Review of Basic Concepts*

	Syllabus reference	*Chapter reference*
◆ a thorough knowledge of the ASB's Statement of Principles	1a, b	1
◆ discuss the characteristics of useful accounting information and financial accounting conventions		
◆ explain the regulatory system of accounting		
◆ discuss the notion of GAAP and a conceptual framework		

Self Study
- ◆ revise SSAP 2 included in the paper 1 syllabus
- ◆ prepare the final accounts of a simple business organisation

Session 2   *Partnership conversion to a limited liability company*

	Syllabus reference	*Chapter reference*
◆ close off the partnerships books on conversion to a limited company	2a	2
◆ open appropriate accounts in the company's records		
◆ prepare final accounts covering the year in which conversion takes place		
◆ describe the implications of partnerships converting to limited liability status (including aspects of legislation, tax and auditing)		

Session 3   *Branch Accounts*

	Syllabus reference	*Chapter reference*
◆ explain the nature of selling branches and the need for controls in the accounting system	2a	3
◆ explain the nature of independent branches and the requirements of the accounting system		
◆ prepare the final accounts of a business trading through independent branches		
◆ prepare branch accounts of the combined business possibly in the form of published financial statements		
◆ explain the audit problems of branches		

Note. Foreign branches are not examinable.

Self Study
- ◆ record a set of transactions in the accounts of the head office relating to a selling agency branch

Session 4   *Joint Ventures*

	Syllabus reference	*Chapter reference*
◆ explain the following different methods of conducting business in the form of a joint venture: a joint arrangement that is not an entity a structure with the form but not the substance of a joint venture a jointly controlled entity	2a, c(ii)	4
◆ prepare appropriate accounting statements as contained in FRS 9 'Associates and joint ventures' for each of the above forms of business		
◆ explain the audit problems of joint ventures		

Session 5   **Hire Purchase and Leasing**

- explain and distinguish between credit sale agreements, hire purchase agreements, operating leases and finance leases   2a   5
- describe the effect in the financial statements of treating a lease either as a finance lease or an operating lease
- record the ledger entries for credit sale, hire purchase, and operating leases
- outline the principles and disclosure provisions of SSAP 21
- record finance leases in the books of the lessor/lessee
- discuss the audit verification of leased assets

Session 6   **Recognition of Revenue, Distributable Profits and Purchase/Redemption of Shares**

- outline the principles of revenue recognition and the audit implications thereof   1a   6
- discuss the rules relating to the distribution of profits   2b
- explain how shares may be redeemed, and record the transactions involving the redemption of shares
- explain the power of companies to purchase their own shares, and record the transactions involving the purchase in the accounting records
- discuss the advantages of companies being able to redeem shares

Session 7   **Regulatory Framework**

- discuss the aims and operating process of the Accounting Standards Board (ASB), Financial Reporting Council (FRC) and Financial Reporting Review Panel (FRRP)   1a,d   7
- describe the role of the Urgent Issues Task Force (UITF)
- discuss current perceptions of the ASB and its performance
- discuss the politicisation of the standard setting process
- describe the intended role of the ASB Statement of Principles
- explain the significant features of the ASB Statement of Principles, and their current status
- evaluate the likely usefulness of the ASB Statement of Principles
- outline the principal requirements of the UITF Abstracts 4, 5, 7 and 16

Session 8   **Preparation of Published Financial Statements (Companies Act requirements)**

- explain the legal background to limited companies   2a   8
- state the requirements of Company law regarding the duty to prepare annual accounts and the use of prescribed formats
- describe the content and effect of the main provisions of Company law including the accounting rules
- prepare the financial statements of limited companies in accordance with the prescribed formats
- state the criteria used to distinguish between small and medium companies and the nature of the resulting modifications to the annual financial statements
- discuss other criteria that may be used to identify a small business enterprise and the future impact this may have on the applicability of accounting standards
- describe the requirements of the Financial Reporting Standard for Smaller Entities (FRSSE)

Session 9   *Accounting Standards*

- explain the key elements of SSAP 9 relating to long-term contracts including the disclosure requirements
- calculate the amounts to be shown in financial statements regarding long-term contracts, and the accounting entries thereof
- discuss the audit problems relating to compliance with SSAP 9
- prepare a cash flow statement for an individual company in accordance with FRS 1 (revised)
- appraise the usefulness of, and interpret the information in, a cash flow statement

1c
2a   9, 15

Self Study
- revise the requirements of the following SSAPs covered at paper 1: 9 (except as referred to above), 12, 13 and 17

Session 10   *Accounting Standards*

- explain the principles of FRS 12 'Provisions, contingent liabilities and contingent assets'
- discuss the relationship between FRS 12, the Statement of Principles and the concept of prudence and matching
- apply the requirements of FRS 12 to specified circumstances (refer to appendix III of the FRS for examples)

1(a)(v),
(c)   9

Self Study
- revise the requirements of the following SSAPs covered at paper 1: 9 (except as referred to above), 12, 13 and 17

Session 11   *Accounting for Taxation and Deferred Taxation*

- record entries relating to corporation tax in the accounting records
- explain the accounting treatment and record the accounting transactions of investment income and unfranked receipts and payments
- demonstrate and explain the effect of timing differences on accounting and taxable profits
- explain the deferral and liability methods of accounting for deferred taxation
- outline the requirements of SSAP 15 and the Companies Acts requirements relating to deferred tax
- record entries relating to deferred tax in the accounting records
- discuss the advantages and disadvantages of the full provision method compared to the partial provision method of accounting for deferred taxation
- discuss the problems of SSAP 15 and how it might be improved
- discuss the audit problems associated with SSAP 15

1c, 2a   10, 11

Self Study
- apply and review the disclosure requirements for VAT under SSAP 5

Session 12   *Earnings Per Share*

- explain the need for a standard for earnings per share and the problems in determining the earnings of a company
- describe the requirements of FRS 3 regarding the computation of EPS
- explain the implications of FRS 3 for the disclosure of EPS
- calculate the EPS in accordance with FRS 14 where there have been issues of shares during the year and circumstances that will give rise to a future dilution of the EPS

1c
2a   13

- explain the significance of the different figures for EPS that a company may disclose
- describe the requirements of FRS 14 regarding EPS

Session 13   *Financial Performance*

• discuss the requirements of FRS 3	1c	12
• explain the problems associated with the definitions of extraordinary items and discontinued activities and the implications for the auditors	2a	
• prepare accounts in accordance with FRS 3		
• discuss the usefulness and problems associated with segmental information		
• prepare segmental reports in accordance with SSAP 25		
• discuss the implications of the above for the auditors		
• outline the principal requirements of UITF Abstract 14		

Session 14   *FRS 4 and FRS 5*

• explain why FRS 4 and FRS 5 were introduced	1c	14
• discuss the objectives and principal requirements of FRS 4 and FRS 5		
• outline the basic principles underlying the classification of capital instruments		
• show how the costs of capital instruments should be dealt with		
• show the accounting treatment of debt instruments and share capital, including convertible debt		
• explain disclosure requirements of FRS 4		
• explain and apply the principles of recognition and derecognition of assets and liabilities as in FRS 5		
• explain at an introductory level the potential problems relating to derivatives. (*Note:* a detailed knowledge of FRS 13 is NOT required)		

Session 15   *Further Fixed Asset Accounting*

• describe alternative feasible ways of treating capital-based government grants received	1c	16
• explain and apply the provisions of SSAP 4	2a	
• explain why investment properties may need an accounting treatment different from other properties		
• explain and apply the SSAP 19 'Accounting for investment properties' requirements for the treatment of investment properties (as amended by FRS 3)		
• discuss the validity and legality of SSAP 19		
• discuss the way the auditor ensures compliance with the above standards		

Session 16   *Goodwill and Intangible Assets*

• describe the nature and possible accounting treatments of goodwill including negative goodwill	1c	16
• discuss the advantages and disadvantages of the above from the viewpoint of both management and the users of financial statements	2a	
• explain the requirements of FRS 10 regarding goodwill and intangibles		
• outline the issues raised in recent years by the brand and other similar assets valuation controversy		
• discuss the problems that the recent requirements relating to goodwill are likely to pose for auditors		
• discuss the requirements of FRS 11 on the impairment of fixed assets and goodwill		

Session 17   **Group Accounting - 1**

- explain the different methods which could be used to prepare group accounts   2c   17, 18, 19
- explain the requirements of the Companies Acts and FRS 2 regarding groups of companies
- prepare a consolidated balance sheet for a simple group (ie, not for a mixed or vertical group)
- show the effect on a consolidated balance sheet of an acquisition of a subsidiary
- understand the basic principles and disclosure requirements relating to the fair values of identifiable assets and liabilities on acquisition as set out in FRS 7
- understand and perform simple fair value calculations including their effect on consolidated goodwill
- outline the principal requirements of UITF Abstract 15

Session 18   **Group Accounting - 2**

- prepare a consolidated profit and loss account for a simple group (ie, not for a mixed or vertical group)   2c   18, 19
- demonstrate the equity and gross equity method of accounting and the accounting treatment of associates and joint ventures (as prescribed by the Companies Act and FRS 9)
- account for the effects of intra-group trading and other transactions including unrealised profits and intra-group dividends (in the profit and loss account and balance sheet)

Session 19   **Group Accounting - 3**

- discuss the criteria for determining whether a business combination should be treated as a merger or an acquisition   2c   19, 28
- explain the rationale for accounting for a merger in the manner set out in FRS 6
- prepare the financial statements applying merger accounting
- describe the impact on the financial statements of applying merger accounting compared with acquisition accounting
- discuss the audit problems relating to the correct classification of the status of investments in companies
- understand the significance of related party transactions
- explain the potential significance of related party transactions and the requirements of FRS 8

Session 20   **Sundry Accounting Standards**

- explain and distinguish foreign currency conversion and translation   1c
- state the requirements of SSAP 20 regarding individual companies and discuss the validity of their effect on reported earnings   2a   20
- describe a defined contribution pension scheme and a defined benefit pension scheme
- explain how deficiencies and surpluses of a pension scheme arise, and how they should be treated
- outline and apply the requirements of SSAP 24 'Accounting for Pension Costs'

  Self Study
- discuss the audit implications of the above standards

Session 21   **Theoretical Matters**

- outline the concepts of economic income, entry and exit values, deprival value   1a   21
- explain the concepts of current purchasing power and current cost accounting (note: detailed calculations on the preparation of CCA and CPP financial statements are NOT examinable)
- outline the principles of agency theory and the efficient markets hypothesis
- distinguish between positive and normative accounting concepts
- define economic consequences and discuss its implications for financial reporting

Self Study
- review the methods used to reflect the CPP and CCA methodologies in financial statements

Session 22   **Interpretation of Financial Statements**

- calculate useful financial ratios from company or group financial statements   3, 4   22
- analyse and discuss the implications of changes in accounting policies and management discretion in the choice of accounting policy
- production of written reports on the position and progress of companies including inter firm and inter temporal comparisons
- discuss how comparability may be improved
- discuss how the interpretation of current cost accounts or current purchasing power accounts would differ to the interpretation of historic cost accounts

Please note that the content of reports will draw upon knowledge required in other sessions. This session will concentrate on the preparation of reports and report writing skills.

Session 23   **Risk and Audit Sampling**

- explain the logic of assessing audit risk and risk based audits   5a, g   23, 24
- describe how the auditor assesses inherent risk and control risk in establishing the detection risk for a particular audit test
- explain how the audit programme reflects the application of audit objectives
- explain the use of audit sampling in the conduct of an audit

Self Study
- explain the nature, purpose and scope of an audit
- explain the regulatory framework of auditing
- identify the fundamental principles and concepts which affect auditing
- outline the nature of the audit process
- outline the importance of audit evidence

Session 24   ***Substantive Testing and Analytical Review***

♦ discuss the nature of substantive testing and substantive analysis	5a	25
♦ discuss the use of substantive testing in the verification of financial statements		
♦ formulate conclusions on substantive tests in line with critical audit objectives, risk evaluation and materiality levels		
♦ explain the relationship between substantive analysis and analytical review		
♦ describe the major analytical review techniques		
♦ describe how analytical review techniques can be used in audit planning and risk assessment		
♦ describe the uses of analytical review in the review of the financial statements		

Session 25   ***Computer Auditing***

♦ discuss the use of computers in the audit process (including the use of microcomputers for audit purposes)	5a 6b	26
♦ discuss the audit implications of the computerisation of a client's records		
♦ describe the use of CAATs (computer assisted auditing techniques) including the use of expert systems and audit enquiry programs		
♦ evaluate the usefulness of CAATs in the audit process		
♦ describe the importance of the audit procedures relating to systems development, acquisition and maintenance, and their resource implications		
♦ describe the trends in Information Technology and their impact on auditors		

Session 26   ***The Final Audit***

♦ explain the importance of the review of audit working papers	5c,d,e,f	27
♦ explain the ways in which the auditor reviews the financial statements		
♦ explain the importance of representations by management, audit completion checklists and other final audit matters		
♦ explain the audit responsibility for opening balances and comparatives		
♦ describe the auditors' role to consider client compliance with law and regulations		
♦ explain the audit implications of other information in documents containing audited financial statements		
♦ describe the tests conducted to discover pending legal action and other post balance sheet events and contingencies		
♦ describe the auditor's responsibilities for establishing the going concern status of the client		

Self Study

♦ describe any recent changes in legislation or case law which may affect the auditor

♦ describe the changing role of the auditor

Session 27   Group Audits

♦   explain the organisation, planning and managing of complex audit   5b,d   28
        situations

♦   explain the special considerations of the planning and controlling of a
        group audit

♦   discuss the regulatory requirements of accounting for groups of
        companies and the auditing implications thereof

♦   explain the relationship between principal and other auditors, and using
        the work of an expert

♦   explain the problems of auditing a foreign subsidiary

♦   describe the audit implications of related party transactions

Self Study

♦   explain the auditor's duties regarding directors' remuneration and
        transactions involving directors

**Session 28   *Audit Reporting, Auditor's Liability and Managing Audit
        Relationships***

♦   describe the content and meaning of unqualified and qualified audit   5c,f,g   29
        reports, as specified in SAS 600 'Auditors' reports on financial   6a
        statements'. (Students would not be expected to reproduce an audit
        report in full)

♦   describe the content and meaning of unqualified and qualified audit
        reports

♦   prepare audit reports to meet different specified situations

♦   describe the extent to which users understand the audit report

♦   discuss the ways in which the audit report could be improved

♦   discuss how audit qualifications may be avoided by negotiations with
        management

♦   describe and apply the ACCA rules of professional conduct and ethical
        responsibilities

♦   describe the current position on the legal liability of the auditor and the
        relationship with indemnity insurers

♦   describe the implications and principles involved when undertaking
        common forms of non-audit and related services engagements eg,
        consultancy work, reporting on forecast information

Self Study

♦   describe any recent changes in legislation which affect the auditor

ACCOUNTING STANDARDS

ABSTRACTS

No	Title	Issue date	Page
UITF Abstract 4	Presentation of long-term debtors in current assets	July 1992	118
UITF Abstract 5	Transfers from current assets to fixed assets	July 1992	119
UITF Abstract 7	True and fair view override disclosures	Dec 1992	119
UITF Abstract 14	Disclosure of changes in accounting policy	Nov 1995	119
UITF Abstract 15	Disclosure of substantial acquisitions (revised)	Feb 1999	120
UITF Abstract 16	Income and expenses subject to non-standard rates of tax	Feb 1997	120
UITF Abstract 20	Year 2000 issues: Accounting and disclosures	March 1998	120

OTHER STATEMENTS

Title	Issue date	Page
Operating and Financial Review	July 1993	185

EXPOSURE DRAFTS

Title	Issue date	Page
Statement of Principles for Financial Reporting	March 1999	2, 9, 122

Students should note that Chapters 1 and 3 of the Exposure Draft on the Statement of Principles are examinable in paper 1. At paper 10, students are expected to be aware of the issues/reasons which have led to the publication of the Statement of Principles, and to be able to discuss the main thrust of these documents.

AUDITING STANDARDS AND GUIDELINES

Statements of Auditing Standards (SASs) (issued by APB)

			Issue date	Page
Series	001/099	**Introductory matters**		
	010	The scope and authority of APB pronouncements	May 1993	550, 702
Series	100/199	**Responsibility**		
	100	Objective and general principles governing an audit of financial statements	March 1995	552
	110	Fraud and error	Jan 1995	682, 706
	120	Consideration of law and regulations	Jan 1995	682
	130	The going concern basis in financial statements	Nov 1994	657
	140	Engagement letters	March 1995	566
	150	Subsequent events	March 1995	649, 654
	160	Other information in documents containing audited financial statements	March 1995	653
Series	200/299	**Planning, controlling and recording**		
	200	Planning	March 1995	576
	210	Knowledge of the business	March 1995	565
	220	Materiality and the audit	March 1995	554, 595
	230	Working papers	March 1995	640
	240	Quality control for audit work	March 1995	641
Series	300/399	**Accounting systems and internal control**		
	300	Accounting and internal control systems and audit risk assessments	March 1995	569

1 REVIEW OF BASIC CONCEPTS

INTRODUCTION & LEARNING OBJECTIVES

This chapter revises the issues of the characteristics of accounting information, financial accounting conventions and accounts preparation.

When you have studied this chapter you should be able to do the following:

- Discuss the characteristics of useful accounting information and financial accounting conventions.
- Explain the regulatory system of accounting.
- Prepare final accounts in a simple situation.

1 ACCOUNTING INFORMATION AND FINANCIAL ACCOUNTING CONVENTIONS

1.1 Desirable characteristics of published financial statements

Three reports published during the 1970s attempted to identify the desirable characteristics of published financial statements.

(a) **The Corporate Report** said that reports should be relevant, understandable, reliable, complete, objective, timely and comparable.

(b) **The Sandilands Report** ('Report of the Inflation Accounting Committee' 1975) suggested similar characteristics, ie, they should be realistic, consistent, prudent and with economy of presentation.

(c) In the USA, **The Trueblood Report** ('Report of the study group on the objectives of financial statements' 1973, issued by the American Institute of Certified Public Accountants) suggested that reports should be understandable, objective, comparable, with 'form and substance', relevant, reliable and consistent.

The above reports identified common characteristics:

(a) **Relevance**

Relevance implies that the information provided seeks to meet the needs of a user group. The needs of a particular user group will be dependent upon the type of decisions they make. The provision of relevant information may require a knowledge of how a user group makes a decision. The information provided must be capable of influencing the user group's decision.

(b) **Understandability**

The reporting of understandable information implies a knowledge of the ability of the reader. Such a person may be defined as the 'reasonably instructed reader'. Appropriate presentation of information may improve the comprehension of the reader.

(c) **Reliability**

The user of financial statements may have greater confidence in the information if it appears reliable. Audited statements improve reliability. Where information is not capable of verification, for example forecasts, the user should be able to assess the degree of confidence he may place in that data. This may be achieved by reporting the underlying assumptions.

(d)   **Completeness**

All accounting information that is material to the user's decision should be provided. Immaterial and irrelevant information should be excluded as this may cause confusion and the incorrect decision to be made. The boundary between complete and irrelevant information needs careful attention.

(e)   **Objectivity**

This implies that the accounting information should be free from any bias on behalf of the person producing this information. Since the information may be used by several user groups, whose needs may vary, the inclusion of some subjective judgements cannot be avoided.

(f)   **Comparability**

In order to be able to compare one company's performance against another's, the reports of both companies must be prepared using similar methods. Unless accounting practice is made standard such comparability is unlikely to occur.

1.2   The Statement of Principles

More recently the Accounting Standards Board (ASB) has issued a Statement of Principles in draft form. One of the chapters of this statement is concerned with the qualitative characteristics of financial information and this will be covered in detail later.

It states that the primary qualitative characteristics are relevance, reliability, comparability and understandability.

1.3   Accounting conventions

[Definition]   Financial accounting conventions are assumptions which are used to prepare and disclose items in the financial statements.

They are also referred to as **concepts** or **principles**.

Some of the conventions are referred to in Statement of Standard Accounting Practice 2 (SSAP 2) but there are others. Both sets are covered here.

1.4   Fundamental accounting concepts

[Definition]   Fundamental accounting concepts are the broad basic assumptions which underlie the periodic financial accounts of business enterprises.

There are many such assumptions, but the four defined in *SSAP 2* are discussed here.

(a)   **Going concern concept**

Sometimes referred to as the **continuity of existence** assumption. In the absence of information to the contrary, it is assumed that the business has an indefinite life. The going concern concept clearly excludes situations where the business is, or may be, going into liquidation in the near future, or where its operations are to be drastically reduced in scope.

(b)   **Accruals concept**

Sometimes referred to as the **matching concept**, as it refers to the matching of costs and revenues. Revenue is usually recognised when it is **realised**. The **realisation** of revenue is usually taken to mean the date of sale rather than the date when the cash relating to the sale is received. It is thus logical to compare revenue reported in the period with the costs or expenses of earning that revenue. The operating profit determined in this way is supposed to indicate how efficiently the resources of the business have been utilised.

(c) **Consistency concept**

A business should be consistent in its accounting treatment of similar items, both within a particular accounting period, and between one accounting period and the next.

(d) **Prudence concept**

Revenues and profits are not reported and recognised in financial statements unless realised. Revenues and profits are not deemed realised until the likelihood of conversion to cash is high. In most cases, this means the date of sale. A business can provide for anticipated bad debts on credit sales as a separate exercise. By way of contrast, immediate provision is made for anticipated losses, even if such losses are unrealised. An example of the prudence concept is the valuation of stock at the lower of cost and net realisable value.

Where the prudence concept conflicts with the treatment required by another concept, it is the former which prevails. In particular, the accruals principle requires expenditure to be carried forward to be matched with related future income. Where there is significant uncertainty surrounding the realisation of this income, the prudence principle applies, and the related expenditure is written off in the period in which it arises.

1.5 Activity

A company has stock in hand at 31 December 19X3 with an original cost of £500.

Describe the accounting treatment of this stock if its net realisable value at the same date is

(a) £600
(b) £450.

1.6 Activity solution

(a) Under current practice, the stock would be stated in the balance sheet at 31 December 19X3 at £500 (the lower of cost and net realisable value). The unrealised gain of £100 would not be reported in the 19X3 profit and loss account. If the stock was realised for £600 in 19X4, the realised gain or profit of £100 would be recognised and reported in the 19X4 profit and loss account.

(b) Under current practice, the unrealised loss of £50 would be reported in the 19X3 profit and loss account, so that the stock would be stated at £450.

| Conclusion | SSAP 2 lays down four accounting concepts which published accounts must comply with. In the event of a conflict between the accruals concept and the prudence concept it is the latter that prevails.

1.7 Accounting principles: Companies Act 1985

The *SSAP 2* concepts are embodied in the *Companies Act 1985* as four of the five 'Accounting Principles'. The fifth principle states that in determining the aggregate amount of any item the amount of any individual asset or liability that falls to be taken into account shall be determined separately. For example, when stock is valued at the lower of cost and net realisable value the value must be determined for separate types of stock and then aggregated. In this way anticipated losses on one type of stock will not be offset against expected gains on another.

1.8 Further principles or conventions

(a) **Entity or accounting unit convention**

The term **entity** or **accounting unit** usually refers to the business enterprise, but may also refer, for example, to charities and trusts. The business for accounting purposes is a separate entity quite apart from the owners or proprietors of the business. Separate accounts are maintained for the entity.

(b)   **Accounting period convention**

For accounting purposes, the lifetime of the business is divided into arbitrary periods of a fixed length, usually one year. At the end of each arbitrary period, usually referred to as the accounting period, two financial statements are prepared:

(i)   The **balance sheet**, showing the position of the business as at the end of the accounting period, usually on a historical cost basis.

(ii)   The **profit and loss account** for the accounting period. Profit or loss is arrived at on the basis of the **matching** concept mentioned in *SSAP 2*.

Some accountants argue that profit can only be meaningfully measured over the lifetime of a business, ie, the period starting with the date the business is formed and ending with the date the business goes into liquidation. This is because by avoiding the use of arbitrary accounting periods the problem of matching does not arise. There is also certainty of income and expenditure.

In spite of the arbitrary nature of the accounting period convention, it is necessary to strike a compromise between theoretical accuracy and the needs of the financial community. These needs require periodic financial statements which will form the basis of subsequent financial decisions.

(c)   **Stable standard of measurement convention**

Business activity involves the undertaking of all types of transactions. These diverse transactions are expressed in terms of a common unit of measurement, namely the monetary unit. Financial statements prepared on a historical cost basis make the assumption that the pound sterling is a stable monetary unit. This means, therefore, that 19X1 £s can be added to 19X9 £s and a meaningful result obtained.

Example 1

A company balance sheet states its plant and machinery at **cost less aggregate depreciation**, made up as follows:

	Cost £	Aggregate depreciation £	Net book value £
Assets acquired 19X1	80,000	24,000	56,000
Assets acquired 19X2	100,000	20,000	80,000
Assets acquired 19X3	60,000	6,000	54,000
	240,000	50,000	190,000

If the pound sterling is a stable unit of measurement, the above aggregation is meaningful. The problem arises, however, that even in periods of gradual inflation, the pound sterling is not a stable unit of measurement. The purchasing power of a 19X2 £ is quite different from that of a 19X1 or 19X3 £. This is a severe criticism of accounts prepared on a conventional or historical cost basis.

(d)   **Materiality convention**

Financial statements should have regard to the materiality of various items, either individually or collectively. The materiality of an item refers basically to the relative importance of the item in the overall context of the final accounts. An item of expenditure of £10,000 may well be material to a company which makes an annual profit of £50,000, but not to a company making an annual profit of £50m.

(e)   **Objectivity convention**

Financial statements should be as objective as possible. Transactions are to be recorded objectively as historical events. This is the main basis of historical cost accounting. Certain aspects of historical cost accounting do, however, represent departures from the objectivity convention. For example, although the depreciation charge is often based on the original cost of an asset (objective) it depends also on the estimated useful life and estimated scrap value at the end of that useful life (subjective).

(f)   **Substance over form convention**

Financial Reporting Standard 5 (FRS 5) requires that normally the economic substance of a transaction should be reflected in the accounts, rather than simply its legal form.

A good example is that of assets acquired on hire-purchase terms or under finance leases. Despite the fact that such assets are not owned by the user, a fixed asset is recorded in his accounts.

2   THE LEGAL AND REGULATORY SYSTEM OF ACCOUNTING

2.1   Introduction

The regulatory framework of accounting is affected by a number of legislative and quasi-legislative influences. This section provides an overview of these influences which can be listed as

(a)   Company law
(b)   Accounting standards
(c)   EC Directives
(d)   The Stock Exchange.

2.2   Company law

The regulatory framework of accounting is affected by company law in a number of areas.

(a)   Financial statements of companies must show a 'true and fair view'.

(b)   Accounting standards issued by the ASB are given legal authority as recognised accounting standards.

(c)   Prescribed formats for the profit and loss account and balance sheet are required.

(d)   Detailed disclosures of information are required.

(e)   A company is limited in the amounts of profits it can distribute to its shareholders.

(f)   Various provisions have to be satisfied if a company wishes to increase or reduce its share capital.

Items (a) and (b) are dealt with in this chapter. The others are dealt with later.

2.3   The true and fair view

With regard to accounts of companies prepared under the Companies Act, there is the overriding requirement that those accounts show a true and fair view.

There is no universal definition of 'true and fair', which is a concept that has dominated UK company accounting since 1948. Effectively it is a concept which has been adapted as the years have passed, in the sense that what was true and fair in 1948 might not be said to be so today, but it remains a concept nonetheless, and a concept of critical importance.

2.4   The introduction of accounting standards

The Accounting Standards Committee was set up in 1970 as a result of considerable criticism during the 1960s of the scope allowed for manipulation of published accounts by the variety of acceptable bases. From its formation, the ASC attempted to build up a definitive body of rules to govern the presentation of published accounts.

Before a standard was introduced, it was first published by the ASC in the form of an Exposure Draft (ED). This was purely a discussion document. Once the discussion (or exposure) period elapsed, the document, amended in the light of the results of that discussion, was issued in the form of a Statement of Standard Accounting Practice (SSAP).

Such statements had binding effect immediately after the operative date (determined by the Consultative Committee of Accountancy Bodies (CCAB)). The CCAB consists of the six UK and Irish professional accountancy bodies.

In 1987 the CCAB appointed a committee under the chairmanship of Sir Ron Dearing to review and make recommendations on the standard-setting process.

2.5   Application in the Companies Act 1989

Some of the proposals of the Dearing Report were implemented in the CA 1989. In particular:

(a)   There is a power under the Act for grants to be made to the Financial Reporting Council.

(b)   Accounts must now state that they have been prepared in accordance with applicable accounting standards. The Secretary of State had power to introduce this requirement for different classes of companies and it was introduced for plcs and large private companies.

(c)   The Secretary of State or other 'authorised persons' may apply to the courts to order the revision of defective accounts. There is a procedure whereby a company may revise its defective accounts voluntarily without involving the courts.

2.6   The current standard setting process

Many of the recommendations of the Dearing Report are reflected in the current standard setting process which came into effect in August 1990.

(a)   **The Financial Reporting Council (FRC)**

The FRC comprises around 25 members drawn from the users and preparers of accounts and auditors. It has two operating bodies – the Accounting Standards Board (ASB) and the Review Panel.

The FRC is responsible for guiding the ASB on its planned work programme.

(b)   **The Accounting Standards Board (ASB)**

The ASB has approximately ten members, including a full-time chairman and a full-time technical director. Part-time members are encouraged to give more of their time to the task than ASC members could reasonably expect to do. The part-time members are all well versed in accounting and financial matters.

(c)   **The Financial Reporting Review Panel**

The Review Panel has about fifteen members and is concerned with the examination and questioning of departures from accounting standards by large companies.

(d)   **The Urgent Issues Task Force (UITF)**

This is an offshoot of the ASB. Its function is to tackle urgent matters not covered by existing standards and for which, given the urgency, the normal standard-setting process would not be practicable.

The differences between the old and the new structure are:

(a)   The FRC contains a much wider field of interested parties than the CCAB (which used to oversee the old ASC).

(b)   The ASB can issue standards on its own authority (unlike the ASC). The CCAB bodies are not now responsible for approving standards.

(c)   Under the CA 1989 the accounting standards issued by the ASB are recognised as 'accounting standards' for the purposes of the Act. Directors of public companies are under a statutory duty to disclose whether there has been a material departure from accounting standards.

The authority for SSAPs under the ASC system was derived only from the fact that the six professional accountancy bodies expected their members to observe them.

(d)   The Review Panel has an ultimate legal backing to its review; it can apply to the court following a material departure by a public company from an accounting standard. The court may, as a result, order the company concerned to prepare revised accounts.

2.7   Current and prospective Accounting Standards

In order to avoid the confusion that might result from accounting standards having different sources of authority because they were/are issued by the ASC or the ASB, the ASB formally adopted the 22 SSAPs issued by the ASC which were still in issue as its own SSAPs. They are thus 'accounting standards' under the CA 1989.

In June 1993 the ASB issued a **Foreword to accounting standards** in which the scope and application of accounting standards was made clear, and the procedure for issuing standards was laid down. Accounting standards are applicable to all financial statements intended to give a true and fair view, but need not be applied to immaterial items.

All extant SSAPs and FRSs are required knowledge at this level of accounting.

2.8   International Accounting Standards (IASs)

The International Accounting Standards Committee (IASC) came into existence in 1973 as a result of an agreement by the leading accountancy bodies of several countries.

The objectives of the IASC are to

(a)	formulate and publish, in the public interest, accounting standards to be observed in the presentation of audited financial statements and to promote their worldwide acceptance and observance.
(b)	work generally for the improvement and harmonisation of regulations, accounting standards and procedures relating to the presentation of financial statements.

The 1993 **Foreword to accounting standards** states the attitude of the ASB to international accounting standards.

> FRSs are formulated with due regard to international developments. The ASB supports the IASC in its aim to harmonise international financial reporting. As part of this support an FRS contains a section explaining how it relates to the International Accounting Standard (IAS) dealing with the same topic. In most cases, compliance with an FRS automatically ensures compliance with the relevant IAS. Where the requirements of an accounting standard and an IAS differ, the accounting standard should be followed by entities reporting within the area of application of the ASB's accounting standards.

2.9   EC Directives

It is the aim of the European Union (EU) that its member states will eventually become parts of a single economic entity. To achieve this goal businesses must operate under the same legal and accounting requirements.

The Fourth Directive resulted in accounts formats and detailed disclosure requirements being contained in Sch 4 CA 1985. Other EU members have passed similar legislation.

The Seventh Directive on group accounts was passed by the EC Council in June 1983. The provisions are contained in CA 1989.

2.10   The Stock Exchange

The Stock Exchange is a market place for trading in the securities of companies. The purpose of The Listing Rules publication (known as the 'Yellow Book') is to set out and explain the requirements which apply to applicants for 'listing' (ie, admission to the Official List of the Stock Exchange), the manner in which any proposed marketing of securities is to be conducted and the continuing obligations of the issuers.

A most important condition for listing is acceptance of the continuing obligations which will apply following admission. These obligations form the basis of the relationship between the issuer and the Stock Exchange, governing the disclosure of information necessary to protect investors and maintain an orderly market.

3   THE NOTION OF GAAP AND A CONCEPTUAL FRAMEWORK

3.1   Generally Accepted Accounting Practice (GAAP)

In the UK published accounts of companies should be 'true and fair'. In the US the equivalent requirement is 'fair presentation in conformity with GAAP'.

As a consequence references to GAAP are rarely found in the UK literature and, where it is used, the term is loosely defined.

Broadly, GAAP is accounting practice which has substantial authoritative support amongst users of financial information. Accounting standards will generally represent GAAP but there may be a GAAP which is not reflected in an accounting standard.

Accordingly the boundaries of UK GAAP extend beyond the principles contained in accounting standards. It includes the requirements of the Companies Act, the Stock Exchange and other acceptable accounting treatments not incorporated in legislation or quasi-legislation.

3.2   A conceptual framework

> **Definition**   A conceptual framework is a coherent system of inter-related objectives and fundamentals that can lead to consistent standards and that prescribes the nature, function and limits of financial accounting and financial statements.

The basic objective and need for a conceptual framework is to enable accounting standards and GAAP to be developed which are less likely to be attacked as they would fit within the agreed principles of a conceptual framework. A conceptual framework would thus avoid what has been termed the 'fire fighting' approach of standards issued by the ASC ie, a problem is seen in a particular area and a standard is issued to counter the immediate problem. The end result is a set of standards developed on a piecemeal basis with little overall consensus.

3.3   Statement of principles

In order to provide a coherent framework for the issue of FRSs, the ASB is developing a statement of principles.

Much work has been published on the principles underlying accounting and financial reporting - notably in the USA by the Financial Accounting Standards Board (FASB), which carried out the pioneering work on a conceptual framework in the late 1970s and early 1980s. More recently the International Accounting Standards Committee (IASC) published its Framework for the Preparation and Presentation of Financial Statements which sets out the principles of accounting in an international context.

The Statement of Principles will not itself be an accounting standard. It will set out the concepts that underlie the preparation of financial statements for external users. Its purpose is, among other things, to assist the ASB in the development and review of accounting standards and to provide those interested in its work with an understanding of the ASB's approach to the formulation of accounting standards. The contents of the ASB's draft statement are considered in detail later in this text.

4   PREPARATION OF THE FINAL ACCOUNTS OF A SIMPLE BUSINESS ORGANISATION

4.1   Revision of key areas and terms used in basic financial statements

Accounts preparation is extensively covered in Paper 1 and the accounts preparation at this level of accounting needs a clear understanding of the techniques learned at the earlier stage.

Layout of the final accounts is important and the correct terminology should be used. Headings such as fixed assets and current assets need to be shown in their correct place on the normal presentation of a balance sheet. The layout and terms used in a profit and loss account can vary more due to the type of business and thus the types of income and expenses which it has.

You can revise the terminology by working through the example which follows. The example shows the preparation of financial statements from a trial balance. Other information is given regarding such items as accruals and prepayments, depreciation, stock and bad and doubtful debts.

4.2   Revision question

The following is the trial balance extracted from the books of Delta at 31 December 19X9:

	£	£
Capital at 1 Jan 19X9		20,000
Loan account, Omega		2,000
Drawings	1,750	
Freehold premises	8,000	
Furniture and fittings	500	
Plant and machinery	5,500	
Stock at 1 Jan	8,000	
Cash at bank	650	
Provision for doubtful debts		740
Purchases	86,046	
Sales		124,450
Bad debts	256	
Bad debts recovered		45
Trade debtors	20,280	
Trade creditors		10,056
Bank charges	120	
Rent	2,000	
Returns inwards	186	

Returns outwards		135
Salaries	3,500	
Factory wages	8,250	
Travelling expenses	1,040	
Carriage inwards	156	
Carriage outwards	546	
Discounts allowed	48	
Discounts received		138
General expenses	2,056	
Gas, electricity and water	2,560	
Travellers' salaries and commission	5,480	
Printing and stationery	640	
	157,564	157,564

You are required to draw up the trading, profit and loss account for the year to 31 December 19X9 and the balance sheet at that date, after taking into account the following:

(a)   stock at 31 December 19X9 £7,550;

(b)   interest on the loan at 5% pa had not been paid at 31 December;

(c)   rent includes £250 for premises paid in advance to 31 March next;

(d)   depreciate plant and machinery by 10% pa;
       depreciate furniture and fittings by 5% pa;

(e)   adjust the provision for doubtful debts to 5% of trade debtors;

(f)   show wages as part of cost of sales.   **(20 marks)**

4.3   Solution

Delta
Trading and profit and loss account for the year to 31 December 19X9

	£	£	£
Sales			124,450
Less: Returns			186
			124,264
Opening stock		8,000	
Add: Purchases	86,046		
Less: Returns	135		
	85,911		
Carriage inwards	156		
Wages	8,250		
		94,317	
Less: Closing stock		(7,550)	
			94,767
Gross profit			29,497
Discount received			138
			29,635

Salaries	3,500	
Travellers' salaries	5,480	
Travelling expenses	1,040	
Discounts allowed	48	
General expenses	2,056	
Gas, electricity and water	2,560	
Rent (2,000 − 250)	1,750	
Carriage outwards	546	
Printing and stationery	640	
Bad debts (W2)	485	
Loan interest (5% × 2,000)	100	
Depreciation (W1)	575	
Bank charges	120	
	———	
		18,900
Net profit		10,735

Balance sheet as at 31 December 19X9

	Cost £	Dep'n £	£
Fixed assets			
Premises	8,000	-	8,000
Plant and machinery	5,500	550	4,950
Furniture and fittings	500	25	475
	———	———	———
	14,000	575	13,425
	———	———	
Current assets			
Stock		7,550	
Debtors	20,280		
Less: Provision (W2)	1,014		
	———		
		19,266	
Prepayments		250	
Cash at bank		650	
		———	
		27,716	
Current liabilities			
Creditors	10,056		
Accruals - loan interest	100		
	———		
		10,156	
Net current assets		———	17,560
			———
			30,985
Loan - Omega			2,000
			———
			28,985
Capital: Balance at 1 Jan 19X9			20,000
Add: Profit for the year			10,735
Less: Drawings			(1,750)
			———
			28,985

WORKINGS

(W1)   Depreciation

Plant and machinery 10% × £5,500	550
Furniture and fittings 5% × £500	25
	575

(W2)   Bad debts

Bad debts account

	£		£
Balance b/d (per trial balance)		Balance b/d (per trial balance)	
Bad debts	256	Bad debts recovered	45
Provision for doubtful debts	274	Profit and loss account	485
	530		530

Provision for doubtful debts account

	£		£
Balance required c/d		Balance b/d (per trial balance)	740
5% × £20,280	1,014	Bad debts account	274
	1,014		1,014

5   CHAPTER SUMMARY

Financial statements should possess certain characteristics if they are to be of use to the users of the accounts. They also need to be prepared using accepted conventions.

The standard setting machinery was changed in 1990. The constituent bodies and their functions need to be understood.

6   SELF TEST QUESTIONS

6.1   What is relevance? (1.1)

6.2   What is objectivity? (1.1)

6.3   What is an accounting convention? (1.3)

6.4   What are the four fundamental accounting concepts? (1.4)

6.5   What report changed the UK accounting standard setting machinery? (2.5)

6.6   What does FRC stand for? (2.6)

6.7   What does UITF stand for? (2.6)

6.8   What are the objectives of the IASC? (2.8)

6.9   What is a conceptual framework? (3.2)

7   EXAMINATION TYPE QUESTION

7.1   Leila

You are provided with the following trial balance of Leila as at 31 December 19X8.

	£	£
Capital account at 1.1.X8		22,607
Purchases	194,100	
Sales		261,450
Office wages and salaries	16,720	
Rent and rates	4,930	
Debtors	36,150	
Sundry expenses	2,071	
Bad debts written off	942	
Drawings	4,751	
Provision for doubtful debts		1,851
Cash at bank	1,408	
Creditors		17,154
Cash in hand	167	
Stock	41,062	
Motor car - cost	3,600	
Motor car - depreciation (at 31.12.X7)		1,050
Discounts received		974
Carriage inwards	436	
Commissions received		1,251
	306,337	306,337

You are provided with the following additional information for the purposes of preparing the final accounts:

(1)   Closing stock has been valued at £49,678.

(2)   The rent of the premises is £3,200 pa payable half-yearly in advance on 31 March and 30 September.

(3)   Rates for the year ending 31 March 19X9, amounting to £744 were paid on 11 April 19X8.

(4)   Depreciation on the car is to be provided using the straight line method at a rate of 20% pa.

(5)   The provision for doubtful debts (£1,851) was the general provision which appeared in last year's accounts. During the current year, bad debts of £942 were written off against the accounts of specific customers. It has now been agreed that further debts amounting to £710 are to be written off against specific customers, and closing provision is to be adjusted to 5% of the revised debtors figure.

(6)   Wages and salaries to be accrued amount to £1,506.

You are required to prepare:

(a)   The trading and profit and loss account for the year ended 31 December 19X8.
(b)   The balance sheet as at 31 December 19X8.   **(22 marks)**

8   ANSWER TO EXAMINATION TYPE QUESTION

8.1   Leila

(a)   **Trading and profit and loss account for the year ended 31 December 19X8**

	£	£
Sales		261,450
Opening stock	41,062	
Purchases	194,100	
Carriage inwards	436	
	235,598	
Less: Closing stock	49,678	
		185,920
Gross profit		75,530
Commissions received		1,251
Discounts received		974
		77,755
Depreciation (20% × £3,600)	720	
Wages and salaries (16,720 + 1,506)	18,226	
Sundry expenses	2,071	
Rent and rates (4,930 − 986 (W1))	3,944	
Bad debts (W2)	1,573	
		26,534
Net profit		51,221

(b)   **Balance sheet as at 31 December 19X8**

	£	£	£
Fixed assets			
Motor car - cost			3,600
- depreciation (1,050 + 720)			1,770
			1,830
Current assets			
Stock		49,678	
Debtors (36,150 − 710)	35,440		
Less: Provision for doubtful debts	1,772		
		33,668	
Prepayments (W1)		986	
Cash at bank		1,408	
Cash in hand		167	
		85,907	
Current liabilities			
Creditors	17,154		
Accrued expenses	1,506		
		18,660	
Net current assets			67,247
			69,077

Capital account

Balance at 1.1.X8	22,607
Net profit	51,221
	73,828
Drawings	(4,751)
	69,077

WORKINGS

(1) **Rent and rates**

Closing prepayments: Rent ($\frac{3}{12} \times$ £3,200) + Rates ($\frac{3}{12} \times$ £744) = £986

(2) (a) **Provision for doubtful debts a/c**

	£		£
Bad debts a/c (bal fig)	79	Balance b/d	1,851
Balance c/d			
5% × £35,440	1,772		
	1,851		1,851

(b) **Bad debts a/c**

	£		£
Trial balance	942	Provision a/c	79
Debtors (see note (5))	710	P&L a/c (bal fig)	1,573
	1,652		1,652

2 PARTNERSHIP CONVERSION TO A LIMITED LIABILITY COMPANY

INTRODUCTION & LEARNING OBJECTIVES

Most aspects of accounting for partnerships were examined in paper 1 and you are assumed to be familiar with simple partnership accounts.

This chapter covers a further area which is new to this stage in the examinations.

This topic provides good practice of your double entry techniques.

When you have studied this chapter you should be able to do the following:

- Account for the conversion of a partnership into a limited company.

1 PARTNERSHIP TRANSFERRED TO A COMPANY

1.1 Introduction

This is a fairly common situation since it covers the conversion of a partnership into a limited company as well as a direct sale to outside parties. Often the limited company will be entirely owned by the old partners ie, they will be given shares in the company as part or all of the consideration for their share in the partnership. A partnership will often be 'converted' into a limited company when the business becomes quite large.

1.2 Closing off a set of partnership books on sale or conversion to a limited company

Accounting is for two basic operations:

(a) **The sale of the assets to the company**

Normally, all or most of the assets are sold to the company, but some assets might be sold to third parties or taken over by individual partners. Assets transferred to the company might include some or all of the cash.

The assets transferred to the company are not sold for cash alone, but for a mixture of shares, debentures and cash.

(i) Open a realisation account. This acts as a profit and loss account for the disposal. The assets are debited to the realisation account at their book values. The purchase consideration or agreed take-over values are credited to the account. The balance remaining represents the profit or loss on disposal, which is transferred to the partners' accounts in the profit sharing ratio.

(ii) The purchase consideration payable by the company is in effect the sale proceeds. This must be computed - when shares are issued they are always valued at their issued price not the nominal value. As the contract with the company may be agreed before the purchase consideration is received, it is normal to open a personal account for the purchaser ie, the new company.

Dr   New company account   with the purchase consideration
      Cr   Realisation account

The balance on the realisation account is credited/debited to the partners' accounts. (Note that the capital/current account distinction has become meaningless, so that these accounts can be combined together into one single account.)

(iii)   When the company pays the purchase consideration:

Dr   Cash
Dr   Shares in new company (at issue value)
      Cr   New company account

- this is merely the discharge of a debt.

(b)   **The distribution of the purchase consideration between the partners**

(i)   Transfer shares and debentures to partners in the agreed proportions.

Dr   Partners' accounts
      Cr   Shares in new company (at issue value)
      Cr   Debentures in new company (at issue value)

(ii)   Finally transfer cash in or out to close down the partnership books.

1.3   Opening appropriate accounts in the company's records

The company will place values on the assets it acquires. If the purchase consideration exceeds the value of the net tangible assets, the surplus will be treated as goodwill because it represents the premium paid to acquire those assets.

The accounting treatment centres around a personal account for the vendor ie, the old partnership and again comprises two basic operations:

(a)   The purchase of the assets:

Dr   Sundry assets at agreed values
      Cr   Vendor (partnership) account

(b)   The discharge of purchase consideration:

Dr   Vendor (partnership) account with elements of purchase consideration
      Cr   Share capital, share premium,
            debentures, cash, etc.

Any balance on the vendor's account is then transferred to goodwill.

1.4   Preparing final accounts covering the year in which sale or conversion takes place

A and B trade as partners sharing profits 3 : 2 and decide to sell their business to X Ltd which agrees to pay £16,000 in the form of:

5,000 £1 shares at a premium of 20p
6,000 £1 8% debentures issued at 90,
cash of £4,600

X Ltd is to acquire all the net assets of the partnership with the exception of the cash and the two motor vehicles which A and B are to take over at values of £900 and £600 respectively.

A and B agree that their accounts are to be settled so that:

(a)   they take the ordinary shares in X Ltd in their profit sharing ratio;
(b)   the debentures are to be taken in the ratio of their capital accounts;
(c)   balance settled by cash transfer.

Balance sheet of A and B at date of take-over

	Cost £	Dep'n £	NBV £
Fixed assets:			
Freehold property	4,000		4,000
Fixtures and fittings	1,000	500	500
Motor vehicles	2,500	500	2,000
	7,500	1,000	6,500
Current assets:			
Stock		4,000	
Debtors	2,100		
Less: Provision	100		
		2,000	
Cash		1,000	
		7,000	
Current liabilities		1,500	
			5,500
			12,000
Capital accounts:			
A		6,000	
B		3,000	
			9,000
Current accounts:			
A		1,500	
B		1,500	
			3,000
			12,000

You are required:

(a)   to show the ledger accounts reflecting the above transactions in the books of A and B;

(b)   to show the journal entries in the books of X Ltd to reflect the take-over assuming that the partnership assets are taken over at book value with the exception of the freehold which is to be valued at £7,000 and the debtors at £1,800;

(c)   to construct the opening balance sheet of X Ltd.

1.5   Solution

Numbers in brackets refer to sequence of entries.

(a)   **Books of A and B**

Realisation account

	£	£		£	£
(1) Freehold property		4,000	(2) Trade creditors		1,500
(1) Fixtures and fittings		500	(3) X Ltd account -		
(1) Motor vehicles		2,000	monetary value		
(1) Stock		4,000	of purchase		
(1) Debtors		2,000	consideration:		
Partners accounts -			Shares		
profit on sale:			5,000 at £1.20	6,000	
(5) A (3)	3,900		Debentures		
(5) B (2)	2,600		6,000 at 90p	5,400	
		6,500	Cash	4,600	
					16,000
			Partners' accounts		
			- motor vehicles		
			taken over:		
			(4) A	900	
			(4) B	600	
					1,500
		19,000			19,000

Partners' accounts

	A £	B £		A £	B £
(4) Realisation account -			Balances b/d:		
motor vehicles taken			Capital accounts	6,000	3,000
over	900	600	Current accounts	1,500	1,500
X Ltd account -				7,500	4,500
discharge of					
purchase			(5) Realisation		
consideration:			account - profit		
(6) Shares 3 : 2	3,600	2,400	on sale	3,900	2,600
(6) Debentures 2 : 1	3,600	1,800			
(8) Cash	3,300	2,300			
	11,400	7,100		11,400	7,100

Cash account

	£		£
Balance b/d	1,000	Final settlement to close	
(7) X Ltd	4,600	down books:	
		(8) A	3,300
		(8) B	2,300
	5,600		5,600

New company's account - X Ltd

	£			£
(3) Realisation account - monetary value of purchase consideration	16,000		Discharge of purchase consideration to partners' accounts:	
		(6)	Shares in X Ltd	6,000
		(6)	Debentures in X Ltd	5,400
		(7)	Cash	4,600
	16,000			16,000

(b)   **X Ltd Journal**

	Dr £	Cr £
Freehold property	7,000	
Fixtures and fittings	500	
Stock	4,000	
Debtors	2,100	
Bad debt provision		300
Trade creditors		1,500
A and B partnership account		16,000
Goodwill - balancing figure (see note)	4,200	
	17,800	17,800

Purchase of £11,800 specific net assets from A and B for £16,000, giving rise to £4,200 goodwill.

A and B partnership account	16,000	
Debenture discount	600	
Ordinary share capital		5,000
Share premium account		1,000
8% debentures		6,000
Cash - bank overdraft		4,600
	16,600	16,600

Discharge of purchase consideration, being:
- 5,000 ordinary £1 shares issued at a premium of 20p per share
- 6,000 £1 8% debentures issued at 90
- £4,600 in cash

(Tutorial note: the 'goodwill' arising in the new limited company's accounts is simply the excess of the purchase consideration over the fair values placed on the net tangible assets taken over. This should be contrasted with the 'profit on realisation' in the partnership books, which is the surplus of the sale proceeds over the book values of the assets sold. The two figures will thus not necessarily be the same.*)*

(c)   **X Ltd opening balance sheet**

	£	£	£
Fixed assets:			
Goodwill			4,200
Freehold property at valuation			7,000
Fixtures and fittings at valuation			500
			11,700

Current assets:

Stock		4,000
Debtors	2,100	
Less: Provision	300	
		1,800
		5,800

Less: Creditors (amounts due within one year):

Trade creditors	1,500	
Bank overdraft	4,600	
		6,100

	(300)
	11,400

Creditors (amounts due in more than one year):

8% debentures	(6,000)
	5,400

Capital and reserves:

Ordinary shares of £1, fully paid		5,000
Share premium account	1,000	
Less: Debenture discount written off	600	
		400
		5,400

(Tutorial note: partner A now owns 60% of the company's shares and partner B owns 40%. They are effectively still acting as a partnership but through the medium of a company.*)*

1.6   Activity

The AB partnership sells net assets with a book value of £40,000 to Z Ltd for consideration of 45,000 £1 shares issued at par. Z Ltd values the net assets at £38,000.

(a)   What is the profit on realisation to be shared between the partners?

(b)   What value will be placed on goodwill in Z Ltd's books?

(c)   If the shares in Z Ltd were issued at a premium of 25p, how many shares would have to be issued?

(d)   What accounting entries would be required in Z Ltd's books to record the transfer (assuming shares issued at £1.25)?

1.7   Activity solution

(a)   £5,000 (45,000 – 40,000)

(b)   £7,000 (45,000 – 38,000)

(c) $\dfrac{45,000}{1.25} = 36,000$ £1 shares

				£	£
(d)	Dr	Sundry assets		38,000	
	Dr	Goodwill		7,000	
		Cr	AB partnership account		45,000
	Dr	AB partnership account		45,000	
		Cr	Share capital		36,000
		Cr	Share premium		9,000

1.8 Books carried on without a break

The above example of X Ltd assumes that the partnership books are closed off, and new books are opened up for the company. In practice very often the old books are carried on without a break and amended at the end of the accounting period to reflect the conversion into a company. In this situation the necessary adjusting entries can be made through the partners' accounts since they represent the net assets of the partnership at their existing book values. Hence:

(a)   Any assets or liabilities not taken over must be written out of the books by transfer to the partner concerned ie,

        (i)   Assets not taken over:

                Dr   Partner's account
                      Cr   Asset account

        thus reducing both the balance due to the partner and the net assets taken over.

        (ii)   Liabilities not taken over:

                Dr   Liability account
                      Cr   Partner's account

        thus extinguishing the liability and increasing the net assets taken over.

(b)   The remaining assets (including goodwill) and liabilities must be increased or reduced to their agreed take-over values. The profit or loss arising will be credited or debited to the partners' accounts in profit sharing ratio. A revaluation account may be used for this purpose if several adjustments are required.

(c)   Open up accounts for each element of the purchase consideration and debit each partner's share to his partner's account.

(d)   Any balances remaining on the partner's accounts will be settled by cash transfers into or out of the business.

(e)   A company cannot distribute profits made prior to the date of its incorporation. Consequently any pre-incorporation profits should be transferred to a non-distributable reserve.

1.9 Debtors and creditors not taken over

Often the purchaser of a business will not take over the existing debtors and creditors (for tax reasons). He may however agree to collect the debts and pay off the liabilities on behalf of the vendor, so that the existing purchase and sales ledgers are carried on. The transactions affecting the vendor are recorded by means of suspense accounts. The necessary entries would be made as follows:

Debtors

(a)   Debts to be collected   Dr   Debtors' account
                                                    Cr   Debtors' suspense account

(b)   Cash collected   Dr   Cash
                                                    Cr   Debtors' account

(c)   Bad debts incurred or
        discounts allowed   Dr   Debtors' suspense account
                                                    Cr   Debtors' account

(d)   Amount due to vendor   Dr   Debtors' suspense account
                                                    Cr   Vendor's account

Creditors

(a)   Creditors to be paid   Dr   Creditors' suspense account
                                                    Cr   Creditors' account

(b)   Cash paid   Dr   Creditors' account
                                                    Cr   Cash

(c)   Discounts received   Dr   Creditors' account
                                                    Cr   Creditors' suspense account

(d)   Amount due from vendor   Dr   Vendor's account
                                                    Cr   Creditors' suspense account

1.10   Activity

When taking over the business of Generous & Co, Generous Ltd agreed to collect the debtors of £7,700 and pay off the creditors of £5,600 on behalf of the former partners. The debts were collected subject to a bad debt of £320 and discount allowed of £150 and out of the proceeds the creditors were paid subject to discount received of £95.

Record the entries in the books of the company to show the final amount payable to the partners.

1.11   Activity solution

Debtors' account

	£		£
Debtors' suspense account	7,700	Cash (bal fig)	7,230
		Debtors' suspense account:	
		Bad debt	320
		Discount allowed	150
	7,700		7,700

Debtors' suspense account

	£		£
Debtors' account:		Debtors' account	7,700
Bad debt	320		
Discount allowed	150		
Vendor's account (bal fig)	7,230		
	7,700		7,700

Vendor's account

	£		£
Creditors' suspense account	5,505	Debtors' suspense account	7,230
Balance c/d	1,725		
	7,230		7,230

Creditors' account

	£		£
Cash (bal fig)	5,505	Creditors' suspense account	5,600
Creditors' suspense account			
- discount received	95		
	5,600		5,600

Creditors' suspense account

	£		£
Creditors' account	5,600	Creditors' account - discount received	95
		Vendor's account (bal fig)	5,505
	5,600		5,600

The balance remaining on the vendor's account represents the final amount payable to the partners.

Note: for balance sheet purposes any balances on the suspense accounts will cancel out with the corresponding balances on the debtors' and creditors' accounts.

2 THE IMPLICATIONS OF PARTNERSHIPS CONVERTING TO LIMITED LIABILITY STATUS

2.1 Legal aspects

There are several differences between the law as it applies to partnerships and the law as it applies to limited companies. Limited companies are subject to the requirements of the Companies Acts 1985 and 1989, while partnerships are subject to the requirements of the much simpler Partnership Act 1890.

(a)   Partners are jointly and severally liable for all the debts of the partnership. This means that their personal assets, as well as the partnership's assets, may be at risk in a liquidation or if the partnership is sued. Shareholders of a limited company are liable only for the amount paid up on their shares.

(b)   Limited companies normally have greater access to finance than partnerships. Limited companies may have any number of shareholders, while partnerships are normally limited to twenty partners.

(c)   The Companies Acts impose restrictions on issues and particularly on reductions of capital. A partnership can increase or withdraw its capital whenever the partners wish.

(d)   Limited companies must prepare annual accounts in prescribed formats and these accounts must give 'a true and fair view' of the state of affairs of the company at the balance sheet date and of its results for the year. This means that the accounts must also comply with the requirements of accounting standards. In practice, these requirements may be onerous and costly for a small company. Company accounts must also be filed with the Registrar of Companies and in theory anybody (including competitors) may have access to them. There is no requirement to publish or file partnership accounts.

(e) A limited company is a separate legal personality and continues to operate regardless of the identities of its individual shareholders. A partnership technically ceases and a new partnership starts when a partner is admitted or retires.

2.2 Tax aspects

Limited companies are a separate legal personality and are liable for tax in their own right. Tax is treated as an appropriation of limited company profit. This contrasts with partnerships, where the partners are each personally liable to tax on their share of the partnership profit.

The tax regime for companies is often seen as more favourable than the tax regime for partnerships. Limited companies are generally liable to pay corporation tax nine months after their year end, whereas partners must pay tax on account before the end of the accounting period. The basic rate of corporation tax is also lower (currently 30%) than the higher rate of tax for individuals (currently 40%).

2.3 Audit

The accounts of larger limited companies must be audited, whereas partnership accounts need not be audited. The requirement for an audit is normally seen as a disadvantage of incorporation, mainly on grounds of cost.

3 CHAPTER SUMMARY

The conversion of a partnership business to a limited company effectively involves the dissolution of the partnership. The assets are transferred to the company in exchange for an issue of shares and loan stock. Goodwill arises where the value of the purchase consideration exceeds the fair value of the tangible net assets acquired.

4 SELF TEST QUESTIONS

4.1 What does a realisation account act as? (1.2)

4.2 Is a realisation account debited or credited with the book values of the partnership assets? (1.2)

4.3 What is the entry for the purchase consideration from a company for the partnership assets? (1.2)

4.4 Where does the balance on the realisation account go? (1.2)

4.5 In the company's books where does the balance on the vendor account go? (1.3)

4.6 Do partnership accounts have to be audited? (2.3)

5   EXAMINATION TYPE QUESTION

5.1   John, Keith and Len

John, Keith and Len are in partnership sharing profits in the ratio of 3:2:1 respectively.

A balance sheet for the partnership as at 31 March 19X3 is shown below:

	£			£
Fixed assets		Capital accounts		
Premises	100,000	John		100,000
Plant	52,000	Keith		80,000
Office furniture	27,000	Len		40,000
	179,000			220,000
			£	
Current assets		Current accounts		
Stock	29,500	John	6,450	
Debtors	51,500	Keith	14,978	
Cash	10,412	Len	(2,636)	
				18,792
		Trade creditors		31,620
	270,412			270,412

Len retired on 31 March 19X3, and John and Keith formed a company, Jake Ltd, to take over the business on that date.

Details of the changes agreed were as follows:

(a)   The assets of the business, other than cash, were to be taken over by the company at a valuation of £284,000, but the tangible assets were to be recorded in the books of Jake Ltd at the same book value as in the partnership books. Trade creditors were to be paid by the partnership.

(b)   The authorised capital of Jake Ltd was

> 135,000 ordinary shares of £1 each
> 65,000 12% preference shares of £1 each.

(c)   The company raised a 16% debenture loan of £70,000 from a merchant bank.

(d)   Jake Ltd paid for its acquisition as follows:

> (i)   135,000 ordinary shares issued to John and Keith to satisfy their capital accounts;
> (ii)   16% debentures issued to John, Keith and Len to repay their current accounts;
> (iii)   the balance in cash.

(e)   The profit/loss on realisation is to be transferred to the current accounts.

You are required:

(a)	to prepare the current accounts of the partners.	**(4 marks)**
(b)	to draft journal entries to record these transactions in the books of Jake Ltd.	**(8 marks)**
(c)	to prepare the cash account of the partnership.	**(3 marks)**
(d)	to prepare a balance sheet for Jake Ltd as at 1 April 19X3.	**(5 marks)**
		(Total: 20 marks)

6   ANSWER TO EXAMINATION TYPE QUESTION

6.1   John, Keith and Len

(a)

Current accounts

	John £	Keith £	Len £		John £	Keith £	Len £
Balance b/d			2,636	Balance b/d	6,450	14,978	
16% Deben-				Realisation a/c	12,000	8,000	4,000
tures	18,450	22,978	1,364				
	18,450	22,978	4,000		18,450	22,978	4,000

The 16% Debentures issued to partners total £42,792.

(b)

Journal entries

	Dr £	Cr £
Goodwill (bal fig)	24,000	
Premises	100,000	
Plant	52,000	
Furniture	27,000	
Stock	29,500	
Debtors	51,500	
Vendors - the partnership		284,000

Assets purchased from the partnership
and goodwill as the excess of price over
book value of assets acquired.

	Dr £	Cr £
Vendor	284,000	
Ordinary shares of £1 each		135,000
Share premium account (W2)		45,000
16% debentures (see (a))		42,792
Cash (bal fig)		61,208

Being payment to the vendor.

	Dr £	Cr £
Cash	70,000	
16% debentures		70,000

Being debentures issued for cash

(c)

Cash account (partnership)

	£		£
Balance b/d	10,412	Creditors	31,620
Cash from Jake Ltd	61,208	Len's capital account	40,000
	71,620		71,620

(d)

Jake Ltd Balance sheet as at 1 April 19X3

	£	£
Fixed assets		
Goodwill		24,000
Tangible assets		
- Premises	100,000	
- Plant	52,000	
- Furniture	27,000	
		179,000
Current assets		
Stock	29,500	
Debtors	51,500	
Cash	8,792	
		89,792
Total assets less current liabilities		292,792
16% debentures (70,000 + 42,792)		112,792
		180,000

Capital	Authorised	Issued and fully paid
	£	£
Share capital		
- Ordinary shares of £1 each	135,000	135,000
- 12% preference shares of £1 each	65,000	
		-
Share premium account		45,000
		180,000

WORKINGS

(W1)

Realisation account

	£	£		£
Book value of:			Consideration	284,000
Fixed assets		179,000		
Stock		29,500		
Debtors		51,500		
Profit on realisation				
John 3	12,000			
Keith 2	8,000			
Len 1	4,000			
		24,000		
		284,000		284,000

(W2)   Issue of shares - 135,000 shares satisfies balances on John and Keith's accounts

	£
Balance on capital accounts	180,000
Nominal value of shares issued	(135,000)
Share premium	45,000

3 BRANCH ACCOUNTS

INTRODUCTION & LEARNING OBJECTIVES

One of the functions of accountancy is to control by means of records the movements of people and materials. This control becomes more complicated where the people and materials are located in more than one place eg, where there is a head office in one location and branches in others. If the central management at head office is to supervise branch activities properly, it must be supplied with regular returns on a daily or weekly basis from the outlying branches. Such branch accounting is normally considered under two heads:

(a)   where all the bookkeeping is done at the head office on the basis of daily returns of banking and sales from each branch;

(b)   where each branch keeps books of account and thus controls its own activities.

Either (a) or (b) can be the subject of a complete question.

When you have studied this chapter you should be able to do the following:

- Account for the activities of branches recorded in a single set of accounting records.
- Account for the activities of branches where each branch maintains its own distinct accounting records.
- Explain the audit problems of branches.

1 BRANCH ACCOUNTS - SELLING AGENCY

1.1 The nature of selling agency branches

A selling agency type of branch is a place where sales are made for the business for a particular geographical area. It also has some of its own costs such as rent and rates and wages and thus it is appropriate to look upon the branch as a profit centre. A branch could be any retail outlet of the organisation using the term retail in its widest sense. Thus a branch could be an off licence or a shoe shop but it could alternatively be a bank, estate agent or travel agent.

Where a company owns a chain of off-licence or shoe shops it is very unlikely that it will be considered worthwhile to employ a bookkeeper at each shop in order to record the activities of that shop. More sensibly, the shop manager will be required to bank his takings daily, forwarding the bank paying-in slip to his head office together with a return showing stocks, sales, payments out of sales for local purchases, etc. From these daily returns the head office accountant must keep records which will:

(a)   ensure that branch staff do not steal or lose cash or stocks;

(b)   show the profitability of each branch.

1.2 Recording a set of transactions in the head office accounts relating to a selling agency branch

There are a number of ways of doing this, none of which is entirely satisfactory. The most popular is to put each branch onto a sort of 'imprest system'. Stocks are purchased at head office and invoiced to the branch at selling price. Then at any moment of time the invoice price of the stock in the branch shop plus the bankings since the imprest was last 'topped up' should equal the amount of the 'imprest' (say £10,000). Where stock is particularly attractive to staff eg, in the liquor trade, it is customary to have a team of travelling stock-takers who arrive unannounced at branches and check the stocks plus bankings against the imprest total.

The problem with invoicing branches at selling price is that when the annual accounts are prepared the stock at branches must be included at cost price and not selling price, and the 'profit' to the head office of invoicing stock not yet sold by the branch must be eliminated. This is a rather 'untidy' accounting adjustment.

1.3   Stock invoiced at selling price with a 'mark-up' account

In this method three special accounts are opened at the head office for each branch or shop. They are prepared with the aid of the daily or weekly returns from each branch.

(a)   **Branch X stock control account**

This account is charged by the head office with all goods sent to Branch X at selling price. The proceeds of sale by Branch X are credited to the account so that at any moment of time the balance on this account is the sales value of stocks at Branch X. This gives good stock control.

(b)   **Branch X mark-up account**

This account shows the mark up or gross profit on all the stocks sent by the head office to Branch X. At the end of the period, if the 'profit' in the closing stock at branch is carried down to the new period, the balance on the account is the gross profit of Branch X which may be taken to the general profit and loss account. The profit in the closing branch stock may be deducted from the balance of stock at selling price on the Branch X stock control account to give the closing stock at Branch X at cost. This figure will then be included on the company's balance sheet. Thus the gross profit of each branch is recorded.

(c)   **Goods sent to Branch X account**

This account is a 'pending tray'. When the head office sends goods to Branch X it will debit the Branch X stock control account with the selling price of the goods and credit:

(i)   the 'profit' to the Branch X mark-up account; and
(ii)   the 'cost price' to the Goods sent to Branch X account.

At the end of the period the total of the Goods sent to Branch X account is credited to (ie, reduces) Purchases account. This means that the balance on the Purchases account consists only of those purchases not sent to the branches and is therefore part of the cost of sales of the head office.

1.4   Example

C Ltd opened a new branch shop on 1 January. All goods for sale at the shop are purchased by the head office and charged to the branch at retail selling price which is cost plus one-third. The branch banks its takings, without deduction, for the credit of the head office. Although it is a cash business the branch manager is allowed to give credit in a few special cases.

The following information is relevant for the three months to 31 March:

	£
Purchases	10,550
Sales at head office	1,600
Goods sent by head office to branch at selling price	12,000
Cash sales at branch	8,000
Credit sales by branch	2,000
Goods returned to head office at selling price	600
Cash collected from branch debtors	1,800
Branch expenses	1,000
Head office expenses	200

Show, by means of ledger accounts, the above transactions in the head office books where all the records are kept. Prepare C Ltd's trading and profit and loss account and balance sheet extract.

Closing stock at branch was £1,380 at invoice price. Closing stock at head office was £800 at cost.

1.5   Solution

Books of C Ltd

(Numbers in brackets refer to sequence of entries in key accounts).
SC = Stock control account; MU = Mark-up account; GS = Goods sent account.

New branch stock control account (SC)

			£	£					£	£
(1)	1 Jan	New branch			(3)	1 Jan	Cash (sales)			8,000
	to	MU – Profit	3,000			to				
(2)	31 Mar	Goods sent to			(4)	31 Mar	Debtors			2,000
		new branch			(6)		New branch			
		cost	9,000				MU		150	
				12,000	(7)		Goods sent to			
							new branch		450	
										600
						31 Mar	Balance c/d			
							being			
					(8A)		closing stock			
							at selling price			1,380
					(9)		New branch MU			
							– normal loss			
							(Bal fig after			
							(8A) is inserted)			20
				12,000						12,000
(8A)	1 Apr	Balance b/d		1,380						

New branch mark-up account (MU)

			£				£
(6)	1 Jan.	New branch		(3)	1 Jan.	New branch	
	to	SC – Returns	150		to	SC – Profit	3,000
	31 Mar.				31 Mar.		
(9)	31 Mar.	New branch SC					
		– stock					
		difference	20				
	31 Mar.	Balance c/d:					
(8B)		Profit in stock					
		of £1,380	345				
(10)		Profit and loss					
		account (bal					
		fig)	2,485				
			3,000				3,000
				(8B)	1 Apr.	Balance b/d	345

Goods sent to New branch account (GS)

			£				£
(1)	1 Jan.	New branch SC		(2)	1 Jan.	New branch SC	
	to	– Returns	450		to	– cost	9,000
	31 Mar.				31 Mar.		
(11)	31 Mar.	Purchases	8,550				
			9,000				9,000

Purchases

			£				£
1 Jan.	Sundries	10,550	(11)	31 Mar.	Goods sent to new branch	8,550
				31 Mar.	Trading account	2,000
		10,550				10,550

Head office sales

		£				£
31 Mar.	Trading account	1,600	1 Jan. to 31 Mar.	Sundries	1,600

New branch debtors

			£				£
(4)	1 Jan. to 31 Mar.	New branch SC – Sales	2,000	(5)	1 Jan. to 31 Mar.	Cash	1,800
						Balance c/d	200
			2,000				2,000
	1 Apr.	Balance b/d	200				

Head office stocks

		£		£
31 Mar.	Trading account	800		

New branch expenses

		£			£
1 Jan. to 31 Mar.	Sundries	1,000	31 Mar.	Profit and loss account	1,000

Head office expenses

		£			£
1 Jan. to 31 Mar.	Sundries	200	31 Mar.	Profit and loss account	200

Head office trading account for the three months ended 31 March

	£	£
Head office sales		1,600
Opening stock	-	
Purchases of head office	2,000	
Less: Closing stock	800	
Cost of head office sales		(1,200)
Gross profit		400
New branch gross profit		2,485
New branch expenses	1,000	
Head office expenses	200	
		(1,200)
Net profit		1,685

Balance sheet at 31 March (extract)

	£	£	£
Current assets:			
Stock at cost:			
Stock at head office		800	
Stock at new branch	1,380		
Less: Profit therein	345		
		1,035	
			1,835
Debtors:			
Head office		X	
New branch		200	
			200
Reserves:			
Profit and loss account			1,685

Note: the treatment of the stock difference. When the closing stock at selling price of £1,380 is inserted in New branch control account, there is found to be a loss of stock of £20 at selling price. This is considered to be a 'normal' difference and has therefore been written off against the New branch gross profit by charging the Mark-up account with the full £20. A 'normal' loss is an expected loss and this is charged fully in arriving at branch gross profit. An 'abnormal' loss is an unexpected loss. The cost of this appears separately in the profit and loss account.

For example, if stock were stolen:

Dr	Pilferage account	Cost of stock lost, to profit and loss account
Dr	Branch mark-up account	Profit margin on stock lost
Cr	Branch stock control account	SP of stock lost

The main difficulty with this method of accounting for branches is the 'split posting' which is necessary when sending goods to the branch and in the treatment of differences.

1.6   Activity

Octopus Ltd, with its head office at Cardiff, operates a branch at Swansea. All goods are purchased by head office and invoiced to and sold by the branch at cost plus one-third.

Other than the sales ledger kept at Swansea, all transactions are recorded in the books at Cardiff.

The following particulars are given of the transactions at the branch during the year ended 28 February 19X7:

	£
Stock on hand, 1 March 19X6, at invoice price	4,400
Debtors on 1 March 19X6	3,946
Stock on hand, 28 February 19X7, at invoice price	3,948
Goods sent from Cardiff during the year at invoice price	24,800
Credit sales	21,000
Cash sales	2,400
Returns to head office at invoice price	1,000
Invoice value of goods stolen	600
Bad debts written off	148
Cash from debtors	22,400
Normal loss at invoice price due to wastage	100
Cash discount allowed to debtors	428

You are required to write up the Branch stock account, Branch total debtors account and Branch stock adjustment account (otherwise known as the mark-up account) for the year ended 28 February 19X7, as they would appear in the head office books.

1.7   Activity solution

Cardiff books relating to Swansea branch – year ended 28 February 19X7

Branch stock account (at selling price)

	£		£
Opening stock	4,400	Sales:	
Goods sent to branch	24,800	Credit	21,000
		Cash	2,400
		Returns to Cardiff	1,000
		Stock stolen	600
		Normal loss	100
		Apparent loss (bal fig)	152
		Closing stock	3,948
	29,200		29,200

Branch total debtors account

	£		£
Opening debtors	3,946	Cash received	22,400
Credit sales	21,000	Cash discount	428
		Bad debts written off	148
		Closing debtors	1,970
	24,946		24,946

Branch stock adjustment account

	£		£
Mark up on:		Opening provision for unrealised	
Returns to Cardiff	250	profit ($1/4 \times £4,400$)	1,100
Stock stolen	150	Mark up on goods sent	6,200
Normal and apparent losses	252		
Gross profit (bal fig)*	5,661		
Closing provision			
($1/4 \times £3,948$)	987		
			7,300
	7,300		

* The gross profit figure is obtained as a balancing figure, but can be calculated as follows:

		£
Gross profit		
on sales ($1/4 \times £23,400$)		5,850
Less: Cost of losses:		
Normal	100	
Apparent	152	
	$252 \times 3/4 =$	189
		5,661

Note: since no indication is given as to the nature of the difference in the Branch stock account (it could represent reductions in selling prices, loss of stock or loss of cash), the whole amount has been written off against the branch gross profit ie, treated as a normal loss.

2   INDEPENDENT BRANCHES

2.1   The nature of independent branches and the requirements of the accounting system

An independent branch may have the following characteristics:

(a)   It may finance its own working capital needs ie, the cash is not remitted to head office on a daily basis and some creditors are paid locally.

(b)   It may have control of a wide range of assets rather than just assets originally bought by head office.

(c)   It may purchase some of its own trading supplies.

In summary an independent branch is best thought of as a separate company from the head office, but for various reasons the head office prefers an arrangement where the branch does not constitute a separate legal entity.

The requirements of the accounting system will be as follows:

(a)   The net profitability of the branch can be computed. With a selling agency, the system computes gross rather than net profit.

(b)   Return on capital employed can be computed as the assets are also within the branch accounting system.

(c)   The system must be compatible with the head office system as at various points the two sets of data need to be consolidated to show the overall financial position of the organisation. Also head office may still transfer a lot of goods for resale to the branch ie, the head office, as in a selling agency arrangement, may act as a central purchaser. Accounting for such transfers must be consistent in order to be able to eliminate the contra entries when the two sets of financial data are consolidated.

2.2   Preparation of the final accounts of a business trading through independent branches

Each branch will control its own assets and compute its own profit.

It is not then necessary for the head office to keep branch stock control accounts or to compute branch gross profit. However, new accounting problems do arise at the end of the accounting period. These problems are very similar to the preparation of group accounts.

2.3   The preparation of final accounts on working papers

The accounts which could be prepared from the set of books kept at head office would only show details of head office income and expenditure and head office assets (including advances to each branch). This would not be very meaningful. The accounts of the organisation as a whole should show the total assets and liabilities and the income and expenditure of the head office and all the branches. These items must be garnered from two or more sets of books. This is done by the accountant on working papers prepared, normally at head office, from total balances sent in by the branch accountants. A number of balances in the different sets of books are equal and opposite and must be contra'd out in the working papers.

In this text we look at the position of undertakings with one branch but in practice there may be a hundred or so. The following accounts must be made to contra:

In head office books	*In branch books*
Branch current account (debit – an investment)	Head office account (credit – this is the branch's 'capital' account)
Goods sent to branch account (credit)	Goods from head office account (debit)

When the trial balances arrive at head office these four accounts may not be equal and opposite. The head office accountant must examine the make-up of the balances concerned and where necessary amend his books so that the contra can be made. The normal reason for differences is that goods or cash are, at the accounting date, in transit between head office and branch. They will then have been entered in the books of the despatching party at the balance sheet date but will not be recorded by the receiving party until the early days of the new accounting period. The head office accountant must adjust for this by opening 'in transit' accounts in his books.

Another complication arises where head office invoices stock to its branches at a profit to itself. Where the stock is unsold at the balance sheet date the head office must make proper provision for this unrealised profit. This provision will be created in the head office books as it is in those books that the 'paper' profit has been taken. When the accounts of head office and branch are prepared, this provision in the head office books can be conveniently deducted from the closing stock at branch to reduce it to 'cost' price.

The preparation of the accountant's working papers is something with which you must be familiar. The method is indicated in the following sections.

2.4   The balance sheet

The balance sheet of a head office and its branch as at the same date look as follows:

(a)   **Head office books**

Head office – Balance sheet

	£	£
Fixed assets		80
Branch account		40
Current assets	30	
Current liabilities	10	
	—	
		20
		—
		140
		—
Capital		100
Profit and loss account		40
		—
		140
		—

(b)   **Branch books**

Branch – Balance sheet

	£	£
Fixed assets		30
Current assets	20	
Current liabilities	10	
	—	
		10
		—
		40
		—
Head office account		40
		—

(c)   **Combined balance sheet**

Head office and branch – Balance sheet

	£	£
Fixed assets		110
Current assets	50	
Current liabilities	20	
	—	
		30
		—
		140
		—
Capital		100
Profit and loss account		40
		—
		140
		—

Notes:

(a)   The branch account (in head office books) and the head office account (in branch books) represent the two records of the one current account. **The balances on the two accounts should be equal and opposite.** Provided that they are so, preparation of the combined balance sheet is simple:

    (i)   contra branch and head office accounts;
    (ii)   combine all other items.

(b)   The branch account (in head office books) should always show a debit balance.
It represents the investment by the head office in the branch.
It records all transactions between head office and branch.

(c)   The head office account (in branch books) should always show a credit balance.
It represents the capital of the branch.
It records all transactions between branch and head office.

(d)   The head office may be a sole trader, partnership or limited company. A knowledge of the correct accounting treatment of each type of business unit will therefore be required in this sort of problem.

(e)   To save time an alternative presentation of the three balance sheets would be in column form.

(f)   Any provision for unrealised profit on branch stock that will be raised in head office books if goods are invoiced to branch at more than cost price (see below) will appear in the head office balance sheet under current liabilities, but will be deducted from stock in the combined balance sheet. This will reduce branch stock to cost for the purpose of the combined balance sheet.

(g)   The balances on the branch and head office accounts may not agree at any date if there are, at that date, items in transit between head office and branch. The accounts must be brought into agreement before combined final accounts can be produced:

Cash in transit:

Dr   Cash in transit
Cr   Branch account

Goods in transit:

Dr   Goods sent to branch
Cr   Branch account   – at invoice price

Also add these goods to head office closing stock **at cost**.

It should be noted that the treatment of items in transit is **always** in the head office books, the treatment of cash in transit introducing a new asset for balance sheet purposes. The treatment of goods in transit **reverses the original entry** when the goods were invoiced to the branch. Thus the assumption is made that goods in transit at the year end have never left head office. To complete this reversal the goods concerned must be added to head office closing stock, valued at cost.

2.5   Trading and profit and loss accounts

(a)   Head office trading and profit and loss account will show, in addition to sales, goods sent to branch at invoice prices. These goods may be invoiced at cost which raises no problems, or at cost plus some profit (usually equivalent to wholesale price). To the extent that goods invoiced to branch at wholesale price remain unsold at the year end, the head office will have taken credit for unrealised profit. This amounts to the mark-up on those goods sent from head office that form part of branch closing stock. Therefore:

Dr   Head office profit and loss account
Cr   Provision for unrealised profit on branch stock account

with the amount needed to adjust the opening provision to the 'profit mark up' in branch closing stock.

(b)   Branch trading and profit and loss account will add to outside purchases the goods received from head office at invoice price to the branch.

(c)   Combined trading and profit and loss account must relate to the business as a whole, ignoring goods transferred between branch and head office, and removing profits earned by such transfers. Therefore:

(i)   Goods sent to branch and goods received from head office contra out.

(ii)   Opening stock figures for branch and head office; and
closing stock figures for branch and head office; and
gross profit figures for branch and head office
will not cross-cast to the combined figures **if** goods are invoiced at cost plus.

(iii)   Net profits must cross-cast.

2.6   Example

	Head office £	Head office £	Branch £	Branch £	Adj £	Combined £	Combined £
Sales		45,000		14,000			59,000
Goods sent to branch		9,000			contra		
Opening stock	10,000		3,000		(1,000)	12,000	
Purchases	50,000		-			50,000	
Goods from head office			9,000		contra		
Closing stock	(12,000)		(4,500)		1,500	(15,000)	
		48,000		7,500			47,000
Gross profit		6,000		6,500	(500)		12,000
Office expenses	1,000		500			1,500	
Provision for unrealised profit	500**		-		(500)	-	
		1,500		500			1,500
Net profit		4,500		6,000			10,500

Goods have been consistently invoiced to the branch at wholesale price, cost plus 50% ie, extra provision is $1/3 \times (4,500 - 3,000) = £500$**. The unrealised profit in opening stock is $1/3 \times £3,000$ and closing stock is $1/3 \times £4,500$.

2.7   Example of final accounts

In the examination, you may be required to prepare the accounts of the combined head office and branch in the form of limited company published accounts. You have already covered the basic Companies Act formats for the limited company profit and loss account and balance sheet as part of your studies for Paper 1. The preparation of limited company accounts for publication is covered in more detail in a later chapter.

This example requires the preparation of basic limited company accounts for publication.

The trial balances at 31 December 19X9 of the head office of Court Ltd and of its branch in Sutton are as follows:

	Dr Head office £	Dr Branch £	Cr Head office £	Cr Branch £
Share capital			10,000	
Profit and loss account			9,100	
Stock	15,000	7,000		
Creditors			6,300	1,500
Debtors	11,000	5,000		
Sales			90,000	40,000
Purchases	60,000	20,000		
Office expenses	19,000	4,400		
Fixtures and fittings:				
Cost	10,000	6,000		
Depreciation			4,000	1,200
Goods sent to branch			12,200	
Goods from head office		10,000		
Cash and bank	4,000	1,000		
Branch account	12,900			
Head office account				10,700
Provision for unrealised profit			300	
	131,900	53,400	131,900	53,400

The following information is given:

(a)   Goods are invoiced by head office to the branch at cost plus 10%.

(b)   Stocks at 31 December 19X9 are head office £12,000; branch £8,000 (including goods from head office at invoice price £5,500).

(c)   Branch opening stock includes goods from head office at invoice price £3,300.

(d)   Goods at invoice price £2,200 are in transit from head office to branch at the year end.

(e)   Fixtures and fittings are depreciated at 10% pa on cost.

You are required:

(a)   to prepare the trading and profit and loss account, in columnar form, for head office, branch and Court Ltd for the year ended 31 December 19X9; and

(b)   to prepare the profit and loss account of Court Ltd for the year ended 31 December 19X9 and the balance sheet at that date in a form suitable for distribution to the shareholders. (*Note:* if you are not familiar with the statutory formats for the profit and loss account and balance sheet, you may wish to return to this question after studying the formats later in this text.)

2.8   Solution

(a)

	Head office		Branch		Adj	Combined	
	£	£	£	£	£	£	£
Sales		90,000		40,000			130,000
Goods sent to branch (W1)		10,000					
Opening stock (W3)	15,000		7,000		(300)	21,700	
Purchases	60,000		20,000			80,000	
Goods from head office			10,000				
Closing stock (W3)	(14,000)		(8,000)		500	(21,500)	
		61,000		29,000			80,200
Gross profit		39,000		11,000	(200)		49,800
Office expenses	19,000		4,400			23,400	
Depreciation	1,000		600			1,600	
Provision for unrealised profit (W2)	200		-		(200)	-	
		20,200		5,000			25,000
Net profit		18,800		6,000			24,800

(b)

Court Ltd

Profit and loss account for the year ended 31 December 19X9

	£
Turnover	130,000
Cost of sales	(80,200)
Gross profit	49,800
Administrative expenses	(25,000)
Net profit	24,800
Profit and loss account brought forward	9,100
Profit and loss account carried forward	33,900

Court Ltd

Balance sheet as at 31 December 19X9

	£	£
Fixed assets		
Tangible assets (16,000 − 5,200 − 1,600)		9,200
Current assets		
Stocks	21,500	
Debtors	16,000	
Cash at bank and in hand	5,000	
	42,500	

Creditors: amounts falling due within one year	(7,800)	
Net current assets		34,700
		43,900
Capital and reserves		
Called up share capital		10,000
Profit and loss account		33,900
		43,900

WORKINGS

(W1)   Ensure agreement of:

(i)   branch and head office accounts;

(ii)   goods sent to branch account and goods from head office account.

Make any adjusting entries required in the head office books.

Branch account

	£		£
Balance b/d	12,900	Goods sent to branch account	2,200
		Balance c/d	10,700
	12,900		12,900

Goods sent to branch account

	£		£
Branch account	2,200	Balance b/d	12,200
Balance c/d	10,000		
	12,200		12,200

The stock is treated as if it had not left head office and therefore included in head office closing stock at cost:

$$\frac{100}{110} \times 2{,}200 = £2{,}000$$

(W2)   Increase in provision for unrealised profit in stock held at branch:

		£
Closing	$\frac{10}{110} \times 5{,}500$	500
Opening	$\frac{10}{110} \times 3{,}300$	300 (as shown in trial balance)
Profit and loss for year		200

(W3)   Stock:

	Opening £	Closing £
Per head office	15,000	12,000
Stock in transit at cost	-	2,000
Total for head office	15,000	14,000
Total for branch	7,000	8,000
	22,000	22,000
Less: Unrealised profit per (2) above	300	500
Combined total at cost	21,700	21,500

2.9   Introduction of branch profit into head office books

Although the accounts of the undertaking would be prepared on working papers as shown in the previous sub-section, the closing entries must be made in head office and branch books as follows:

(a)   **Branch books**

The branch profit and loss account is prepared in the branch ledgers and the profit thereon transferred to the branch's capital account ie, Head office account in the branch books. The branch books are now ruled off but the Head office account will exceed the Branch account in head office books by the branch profit.

(b)   **Head office books**

The branch profit is introduced into the head office books:

Dr   Branch account   (say) £6,000
Cr   Profit and loss account   (say) £6,000

being branch profit for the year.

Profit and loss account

£		£
	Head office profit b/d	18,800
	Branch profit	6,000
	Combined profit per working papers	24,800

(see example of final accounts above)

The head office account now agrees with the branch account and the profit and loss account in the head office books shows the combined profit of head office and branch.

2.10 Summary of bookkeeping for branch transactions

	Item	Head office books		Branch books	
1	Goods from head office to branch	Debit	Branch account	Debit	Goods from head office
		Credit	Goods sent to branch account	Credit	Head office account
2	Cash from branch to head office	Debit	Cash book	Debit	Head office account
		Credit	Branch account	Credit	Cash book
3	Profit of branch for period	Debit	Branch account	Debit	Profit & loss account of branch
		Credit	Profit & loss a/c of head office	Credit	Head office account
4	Items in transit at end of period	Debit	Goods sent to branch a/c	NO ENTRY	
		Debit	Cash in transit account		
		Credit	Branch account		
5	Expenses paid by head office on behalf of branch	Debit	Branch account	Debit	Expense account
		Credit	Cash book/creditor	Credit	Head office account

2.11 Activity

(a)   What accounting entry is required in head office books for goods sent to branch?

(b)   What increase in the provision for unrealised profit in head office books is required in the following cases?

	(i) £	(ii) £
Branch opening stock of goods from head office	12,600	99,000
Branch closing stock of goods from head office	15,000	112,500

assuming that stock is consistently invoiced to branch at cost + 20%.

(c)   What does the closing balance on branch account in the head office books represent?

2.12 Activity solution

(a)   Dr   Branch current account
       Cr   Goods sent to branch

(b)   (i) $\dfrac{20}{120} \times (15,000 - 12,600) = £400$

       (ii) $\dfrac{20}{120} \times (112,500 - 99,000) = £2,250$

(c)   The net assets of the branch.

3   THE AUDIT PROBLEMS OF BRANCHES

3.1   Planning of work

The number and types of branches will vary from organisation to organisation. In some organisations the branch network may be extensive with all the sales being conducted through selling agency branches. In other organisations there may only be one branch but of a large and independent nature. The auditor must therefore in his planning of work, assess the need for visits to branches.

He does not however have to visit all branches. If there are many branches which are similar in form such as found in a national chain of shoe shops, the auditor can visit a sample with the sample being chosen by reference to any particular audit risks that may be perceived to exist.

3.2   Audit procedures at branch visited

Audit work that may need to be carried out at a selling agency branch includes normal audit procedures covering such areas as stocktaking, cash and bank procedures, sales and petty cash.

For an independent branch, the work is more likely to cover the full range of procedures that would be conducted on a single entity. The branch may be, after all, equivalent to a sizeable 'company' in its own right.

3.3   Audit work on all branches

The auditor has a specific statutory responsibility to determine that proper accounting records have been kept and proper returns adequate for the audit have been received from branches not visited by him.

The auditor must therefore perform some work on all branches and the emphasis will be on analytical review procedures. Branch returns can be compared with expected results, with each other and with returns from previous years.

4   CHAPTER SUMMARY

In this chapter we have looked at the problems of preparing accounts for a business which conducts its activities through one or more branches. You need to be familiar both with the case where all accounting records are maintained by head office, and with the case where individual branches maintain their own accounts.

5   SELF TEST QUESTIONS

5.1   Where all the accounting entries are made in the head office books, what three ledger accounts must the head office open for each branch? (1.3)

5.2   What is represented by the closing balance on the branch mark-up account? (1.3)

5.3   Where each branch keeps its own books of account, what is represented by the balance on the 'current account with branch' account in the head office books? (2.4)

5.4   Why might a provision for unrealised profit be necessary when combining the head office and branch accounts? (2.4)

5.5   Name two items that might explain the balances on the head office and branch accounts not being equal and opposite. (2.4)

5.6   What is the double entry in the head office books at the year end for expenses paid by the head office on behalf of the branch? (2.10)

5.7   What is the double entry in the branch books at the year end for cash still in transit to the head office? (2.10)

6   EXAMINATION TYPE QUESTION

6.1   H Ltd

H Ltd operates through a head office and an autonomous branch. All purchases are made by the head office, which invoices the branch at cost plus 25%. The trial balances of the head office and branch as at 30 September 19X1 are shown below:

	Head office		Branch	
	£	£	£	£
Sales		250,000		120,000
Goods sent to branch		70,000		
Stock at 30 September 19X0	18,000		8,000	
Purchases	264,000			
Goods from head office			66,000	
Provision for unrealised profit		1,600		
Wages	24,000		18,000	
Rates	6,000			
Insurance	2,000			
Electricity	1,300		900	
Fixed assets				
Cost	80,000		50,000	
Depreciation		35,000		22,000
Debtors	23,000		9,000	
Bank	500		40	
Creditors		27,400		
Share capital		40,000		
Profit and loss (brought forward)		9,490		
Current accounts	14,690			9,940
	433,490	433,490	151,940	151,940

Notes:

(1)   The head office despatched goods valued at £4,000 to the branch on 27 September 19X1. These did not arrive until 4 October 19X1.

(2)   The branch sent a cheque to head office for £750 on 25 September 19X1. This was not received until 2 October 19X1.

(3)   All bills for rates and insurance are directed to the head office. At the year end, the head office has decided to charge 25% of the cost of these expenses to the branch.

(4)   The head office valued their closing stock at £22,000 (cost) at the year end. The branch staff valued their stock at £10,000 (transfer price).

(5)   Fixed assets are to be depreciated by 20% using the reducing balance method.

(6)   The branch manager is entitled to a bonus of 2% of the net profit made by the branch. (This calculation should be based on net profit **before** the calculation of bonus).

(7)   Ignore taxation.

You are required:

(a)   to prepare columnar profit and loss accounts for the year ended 30 September 19X1 for the head office, the branch and the combined business;   **(7 marks)**

(b)   to show the current accounts for the branch and head office;   **(4 marks)**

(c) to prepare, in a form suitable for distribution to the shareholders, the profit and loss account for H Ltd for the year ended 30 September 19X1 and a balance sheet as at that date.   **(12 marks)**

(Total: 23 marks)

7   ANSWER TO EXAMINATION TYPE QUESTION

7.1   H Ltd

(a)   **Profit and loss accounts**

	Head office £	Head office £	Branch £	Branch £	Combined £	Combined £
Sales	250,000			120,000		370,000
Sales to branch	70,000					
		320,000				
Opening stock	18,000		8,000		24,400 (W2)	
Purchases	264,000				264,000	
Goods from head office			66,000			
	282,000		74,000		288,400	
Closing stock	22,000		10,000		33,200 (W3)	
Cost of sales		260,000		64,000		255,200
Gross profit		60,000		56,000		114,800
Provision for unrealised profit (W1)	1,200					
Wages	24,000		18,000		42,000	
Rates	4,500		1,500		6,000	
Insurance	1,500		500		2,000	
Electricity	1,300		900		2,200	
Depreciation	9,000		5,600		14,600	
		41,500		26,500		66,800
Net profit (before bonus)				29,500		
Manager's bonus				590		590
Net profit		18,500		28,910		47,410
Balance brought forward		9,490				9,490
		27,990		28,910		56,900

(b)   **In the books of head office**

Branch current account

	£		£
Balance b/d	14,690	Stock	4,000
Rates and insurance	2,000	Cash	750
P&L a/c	28,910	Balance c/d	40,850
	45,600		45,600
Balance b/d	40,850		

In the books of the branch

Head office current account

	£		£
Balance c/d	40,850	Balance b/d	9,940
		Rates and insurance	2,000
		P&L a/c	28,910
	40,850		40,850
		Balance b/d	40,850

(c)

H Ltd
Profit and loss account for the year ended 30 September 19X1

	£
Turnover	370,000
Cost of sales	(255,200)
Gross profit	114,800
Administrative expenses	(67,390)
Net profit	47,410
Profit and loss account brought forward	9,490
Profit and loss account carried forward	56,900

H Ltd
Balance sheet as at 30 September 19X1

	£	£
Fixed assets		
Tangible assets (130,000 − 57,000 − 14,600)		58,400
Current assets		
Stocks (22,000 + 8,000 + 3,200)	33,200	
Debtors	32,000	
Cash at bank and in hand (540 + 750)	1,290	
	66,490	
Creditors: amounts falling due within one year		
Creditors	27,400	
Accrued bonus payable	590	
	27,990	
Net current assets		38,500
		96,900
Capital and reserves		
Called up share capital		40,000
Profit and loss account		56,900
		96,900

WORKINGS

(W1)   Head office books

Provision for unrealised profit

	£		£
Balance c/d	2,800	Balance b/d	1,600 *
		∴ HO profit and loss	
		(bal fig)	1,200
	2,800		2,800
		Required balances b/d	
		on goods in transit	
		$^{25}/_{125} \times 4,000$	800
		on branch's closing	
		stock	
		$^{25}/_{125} \times 10,000$	2,000

* being the head office's provision for unrealised profit on the branch's opening stock

$$^{25}/_{125} \times 8,000 = 1,600$$

(W2)   The opening stock in the combined column must be stated at the cost to H Ltd and will comprise head office stock and branch stock (but at cost to H Ltd not the branch ie, net of the provision for unrealised profit).

$$18,000 + (8,000 - 1,600) = 24,400.$$

(W3)   The closing stock in the combined column must be stated at the cost to H Ltd and will comprise head office stock, and branch stock (but at cost to H Ltd) and the goods in transit (again only at the cost to H Ltd).

$$22,000 + (10,000 - 2,000) + (4,000 - 800) = 33,200.$$

4 JOINT VENTURES

INTRODUCTION & LEARNING OBJECTIVES

Joint ventures are a form of partnership between two different enterprises, normally restricted to the length of a particular project. The partners, or 'venturers', typically each take responsibility for defined costs and share an eventual profit, if any, in a pre-determined ratio. Joint ventures are becoming increasingly common in business, for a number of reasons.

This chapter covers accounting for joint ventures in the accounts of the individual venturers and the preparation of accounts for the joint venture as a whole. This is partly a test of double entry bookkeeping, but it is very important that you understand the procedures, rather than simply learning them by rote.

When you have studied this chapter you should be able to do the following:

- Understand the nature of a joint venture.
- Account for simple joint ventures.

1 THE NATURE OF A JOINT VENTURE

1.1 Introduction

The term 'joint venture' has two common meanings in use. It can refer to a **joint project** or to an **entity** set up to carry out the joint project.

> **Definition** A **joint venture** is a contractual arrangement whereby two or more parties undertake an economic activity which is subject to joint control.

> **Definition** A **joint venture** is an entity that, as a result of a contractual arrangement, is jointly controlled by the reporting entity and other venturers.

FRS 9 *Associates and joint ventures* defines a joint venture as the second of these definitions (ie, requires a joint venture to be an entity), while the first of the definitions is described as a 'joint arrangement that is not an entity'. However in day-to-day parlance, both situations are described as joint ventures.

In both cases, joint control is the determining factor.

> **Definition** **Joint control** is the contractually agreed sharing of control over an economic activity.

In practice, joint control means that none of the parties alone can control the activity, but all together can do so. Important decisions on financial and operating policy require each venturer's consent. Control is the power to govern the financial and operating policies of an economic activity (or an entity) so as to obtain benefits from it.

The contract which establishes the joint venture usually deals with the following matters:

- the activity and duration of the venture
- voting rights of venturers
- capital contributions
- profit sharing arrangements
- the appointment of operators or managers
- the policy decisions which require the consent of all venturers.

A joint venture can be entered into by individuals, partnerships or companies. One common use of a joint venture in practice is when a UK company wants to start operations in an overseas country. Rather than build up a new company on its own from scratch, the UK company can enter into a joint venture with a local company which is already operating in the overseas country. The foreign company should be able to contribute local expertise to the venture to increase its chances of success.

1.2   Types of joint venture

There are three basic types of joint venture:

(a)   **Jointly controlled operations**

A jointly controlled operation is a joint venture which involves the use of the assets and other resources of the venturers rather than the establishment of an entity which is separate from the venturers themselves. Each venturer uses its own assets and incurs its own expenses and liabilities. Profits are shared among the venturers in accordance with the contractual agreement.

Example

A and B decide to enter into a joint venture agreement to produce a new product. A undertakes one manufacturing process and B undertakes the other. A and B each bear their own expenses and take an agreed share of the sales revenue from the product.

(b)   **Jointly controlled assets**

A jointly controlled asset is a joint venture in which the venturers control jointly (and often own jointly) an asset contributing to or acquired for the purpose of the joint venture. The venturers each take a share of the profit or income from the asset and each bears a share of the expenses involved.

Example

C and D together buy a house which they let to tenants. C is responsible for the initial refurbishment and maintenance of the house and D finds the tenants and collects the rents. C and D each take an agreed share of the rental income from the house.

(c)   **Jointly controlled entities**

A jointly controlled entity is a joint venture which involves the establishment of a company, partnership or other entity in which each venturer has an interest. The agreement between the venturers provides for their joint control over the entity. Otherwise, a jointly controlled entity operates in the same way as any other enterprise. Each venturer is entitled to a share of the entity's results. This is the strict FRS 9 definition of a joint venture.

Example

E and F enter into a joint venture agreement to manufacture and sell a new product. They set up a company which carries out these activities. E and F each own 50% of the equity share capital of the company and are its only directors. They share equally in major policy decisions and are each entitled to 50% of the profits of the company.

2   ACCOUNTING IMPLICATIONS OF JOINT VENTURES

There are three different aspects of accounting for joint ventures:

(a)   the accounts of the joint venture
(b)   the individual accounts of each individual venturer
(c)   the consolidated (group) accounts of each individual venturer.

This chapter will look at the accounts of the joint venture and at the treatment of the joint venture in the accounts of each individual venturer. A later chapter will consider the treatment of joint ventures in consolidated accounts (which only applies to jointly controlled entities and is the subject of FRS 9).

3   JOINTLY CONTROLLED OPERATIONS

3.1   The accounts of the joint venture

(a)   **Separate books**

Where the venture has a full set of books, the transactions are recorded in exactly the same way as for an ordinary partnership. A separate profit and loss account can be extracted from which each venturer will be credited or debited with his agreed share of the profit or loss.

In theory it is possible for a jointly controlled operation to have a full set of books, but this is extremely rare in practice.

(b)   **No separate books**

Often (and certainly in examination questions), due to the short life time or size of the joint venture, it is not considered worthwhile opening a new set of books to record what may only be a few transactions. In this case each venturer will record transactions on behalf of the venture in his own books, alongside his other business dealings. There are two alternative methods of achieving this:

(i)   Each venturer records only those transactions which affect him. The profit and loss account must then be prepared in MEMORANDUM fashion.

or

(ii)   One (or each) venturer can record **all** the transactions in his own books, in which case the profit and loss account can be prepared in DOUBLE ENTRY fashion. This method is covered for the sake of completeness, but is now rarely used in practice.

3.2   Method (i) – using a memorandum profit and loss account

Each venturer will keep a joint venture account in which to record the transactions into which he enters. This represents a personal account with the joint venture, and is therefore debited and credited with amounts due to and from the venture in the form of purchases, sales, expenses, stock taken over, profit shares, etc.

At the end of the venture each party will render a statement of his transactions to the other, so that they can be combined into a memorandum profit and loss account, outside the books.

Each party will then take up his profit share into his own books, and the balances remaining on the joint venture accounts settled by cash transfers.

3.3   Example

A and B undertake a joint venture sharing profits in the ratio 2 : 1. A makes purchases of £4,700 and cash sales of £5,000. B makes purchases of £5,300 and cash sales of £5,800. At the end of the venture the unsold stock is taken over by A at an agreed valuation of £400.

3.4   Solution

A's books

Joint venture with B account

Note: this is a personal account with the joint venture itself, NOT a personal account with B.

Amounts due from venture	£	Amounts due to venture	£
Purchases	4,700	Cash sales	5,000
Profit share	800	Stock	400
		Cash received from B (balance)	100
	5,500		5,500

B's books

Joint venture with A account

Note: again this is a personal account with the venture, NOT A.

Amounts due from venture	£	Amounts due to venture	£
Purchases	5,300	Cash sales	5,800
Profit share	400		
Cash paid to A (balance)	100		
	5,800		5,800

Nobody's books

Memorandum joint venture profit and loss account

	£	£
Sales £(5,000 + 5,800)		10,800
Purchases £(4,700 + 5,300)	10,000	
Less: Closing stock	400	
Cost of sales		9,600
Gross profit		1,200
A – two-thirds		800
B – one-third		400

Notes:

(1)   The profit is computed outside the books – it represents the extra wealth generated by the venture which is due to the venturers. Each will take his share up into his own books by:

   Dr   Joint venture account
   Cr   Profit and loss account (ie, his own profit and loss account)

(2)   Where a venturer takes over a venture asset (eg, stock) he is effectively buying it from the venture and must therefore credit his joint venture account:

   Dr   Purchases/fixed asset account
   Cr   Joint venture account

(3)   The physical movement of joint venture stock between venturers NEVER gives rise to any accounting entries. Stock only appears in the books if it is taken over by a venturer.

(4)   The balances remaining on the joint venture accounts represent the cash due respectively to and from the joint venture. Rather than being treated as a direct settlement between the parties, it should be considered as a payment into the venture by one, which is then passed over to the other ie,

A ⟨ | Joint venture | ⟨   B

This represents the true accounting position.

(5)   If a separate bank account is opened for the joint venture, transactions with third parties will not be recorded in the double entry books since each venturer will only enter the receipts and payments which affect him personally. Instead, a memorandum joint venture cash book must be used.

3.5   Method (ii) – all transactions recorded in double entry form

With the first method, the two sets of books needed to be looked at together to obtain a complete picture of the joint venture. The main feature of the second method is that each venturer incorporates all the transactions into his own books by means of two double entry accounts:

(a)   joint venture account – this acts as a profit and loss account;

(b)   personal account with the other venturer.

3.6   Example

Using the same facts as in the previous example.

A's books

Joint venture profit and loss account

	£		£
Purchases	4,700	Sales	5,000
B's purchases	5,300	B's sales	5,800
Profit c/d	1,200	Stock taken over	400
	11,200		11,200
General profit and loss account two-thirds	800	Profit b/d	1,200
B's account one-third	400		
	1,200		1,200

B's personal account

	£		£
Joint venture profit and loss account Sales	5,800	Joint venture profit and loss account:	
		Purchases	5,300
		Profit share	400
		Cash to A (balance)	100
	5,800		5,800

In B's books a similar joint venture profit and loss account would appear, and a personal account with A.

Notes on accounting treatment in A's books

(1)   The venture profit is appropriated by:

        Dr   Joint venture profit and loss account
        Cr   Profit and loss account – A's share
        Cr   B's account – his share

(2)   Any stock or fixed asset taken over would be treated in the books of A as follows:

    (i)   By A:

        Dr   Purchases/fixed asset
        Cr   Joint venture profit and loss account

    (ii)   By B:

        Dr   B's account
        Cr   Joint venture profit and loss account

    in both cases with agreed take-over value.

(3)   As before, NO entries are made where stock merely changes its location.

(4)   B's personal account is cleared by a cash payment.

(5)   If a separate bank account is opened for the joint venture, each venturer would keep a joint venture cash book within his double entry books of account.

3.7   Activity

(a)   Why is a memorandum joint venture profit and loss account so called?

(b)   X and Y terminate their joint venture and X agrees to take over unsold stock at a value of £900. What accounting entry is required in X's books?

3.8   Activity solution

(a)   See 3.2 for explanation.

(b)   Solution: Dr   Purchases account
                Cr   Joint venture account
    or   Cr   Joint venture profit and loss account

3.9   The individual accounts of the venturers

In its separate financial statements each individual venturer recognises:

(a)   the assets that it controls and the liabilities that it incurs; and

(b)   the expenses that it incurs and its share of the revenue that it earns from the sale of goods or services by the joint venture.

3.10   Example

A and B undertake a joint venture. Each venturer bears their own expenses, but income is shared equally. A makes purchases of £9,400 and cash sales of £10,000. A also takes out a short-term loan of £5,000 in order to finance its part of the venture. B makes purchases of £10,600 and cash sales of £11,600. At the end of the venture the unsold stock is taken over by A at an agreed valuation of £600.

How do these transactions appear in the accounts of A?

3.11   Solution

<h3 align="center">Profit and loss account (extracts)</h3>

	£	£
Sales (10,000 + 11,600) × ½		10,800
Purchases	9,400	
Less: closing stock	(600)	
		(8,800)
Profit		2,000

<h3 align="center">Balance sheet (extract)</h3>

Current assets:	
Stocks	600
Debtor (joint venture with B)	200
Creditors: Short term loan	(5,000)

WORKING

<h4 align="center">Joint venture with B</h4>

	£		£
Share of income	10,800	Cash sales	10,000
		Stock	600
		Balance c/d	200
	10,800		10,800

4   JOINTLY CONTROLLED ASSETS

4.1   The accounts of the joint venture

It is extremely unlikely that separate accounting records will be kept for this type of joint venture. In practice, the accounting treatment of a jointly controlled asset is very similar to that of a jointly controlled operation:

(a)   the individual venturers may set up joint venture accounts in their own books to record income and expenses directly incurred as part of the venture (the balance on the account represents the amount receivable from or payable to the venture);

(b)   a memorandum profit and loss account is prepared periodically in order to calculate the shares of income and expenses due to/from the individual venturers (this may also be used to assess the performance of the venture).

The extent of the accounting records kept will normally depend upon the exact terms of the agreement. In some cases, all that is necessary is an annual statement of joint expenses.

4.2   The individual accounts of the venturers

A jointly controlled asset may have a considerable impact on the accounts of the individual venturers.

In its separate financial statements, each venturer should recognise the following:

(a)   its share of the jointly controlled asset, classified according to its nature (eg, plant and equipment);

(b)   any liabilities which it has incurred;

(c)   its share of any liabilities incurred jointly with the other venturers in relation to the joint venture;

(d)   any income from the sale or use of its share of the output of the joint venture; and

(e)   any expenses which it has incurred in respect of its interest in the joint venture.

4.3   Example

On 1 January 19X1 C and D entered into a joint venture to construct and operate an oil pipeline. Each was to contribute equally to the cost of constructing the pipeline. C would be responsible for carrying out the work to maintain the pipeline once construction was complete. Both C and D would use the pipeline for their own separate operations. All maintenance expenses and any income arising from third parties using the pipeline was to be shared in the ratio 3:2.

The pipeline became operational on 1 July 19X1 and was expected to have a useful economic life of 10 years. In the year to 31 December 19X1 C incurred construction costs of £450,000 and maintenance costs of £50,000. D incurred construction costs of £550,000 and collected income of £20,000 from a third party. In order to complete the work on the pipeline the venturers raised a joint loan of £500,000 on which D paid interest of £40,000 for the year to 31 December 19X1 (at which date the loan was still outstanding).

Prepare the memorandum accounts of the joint venture for 19X1 and the entries that would be made in each venturer's individual accounts.

4.4   Solution

Memorandum accounts of the joint venture

	£'000	£'000
Cost of construction:		
C	450	
D	550	
	1,000	
Interest	40	
		1,040
Shared 1:1:		
C		520
D		520
Net expenses:		
C	50	
D	(20)	
		30
Shared 3:2:		
C (3/5)		18
D (2/5)		12

Accounts of the individual venturers

	C	D
	£'000	£'000

Profit and loss accounts for the year ended 31 December 19X1 (extracts)

	C	D
Income (3:2)	12	8
Depreciation $(1,000 \times 10\% \times 6/12)$	(25)	(25)
Maintenance costs (3:2)	(30)	(20)
Interest (on joint loan)	(20)	(20)

Balance sheets at 31 December 19X1 (extracts)

	C	D
Tangible fixed assets:		
Plant and equipment (1,000 - 50)	475	475
Current assets:		
Debtors (W)	-	38
Creditors: amounts falling due within one year (W)	38	-
Creditors: amounts falling due after more than one year		
Loan	250	250

WORKINGS

In C's books:

Joint venture account with D

	£'000		£'000
Construction costs	450	Share of construction costs	520
Maintenance costs	50	Share of maintenance costs	18
Balance c/d	38		
	538		538

In D's books:

Joint venture account with C

	£'000		£'000
Construction costs	550	Income	20
Interest	40	Share of construction costs	520
		Share of maintenance costs	12
		Balance c/d	38
	590		590

5   JOINTLY CONTROLLED ENTITIES

5.1   The accounts of the joint venture

A jointly controlled entity keeps its own accounting records and prepares and presents accounts in the same way as any other enterprise.

5.2   The individual accounts of the venturers

Each venturer usually contributes cash or other resources to the jointly controlled entity. For example, if the entity is a limited company a venturer normally exchanges cash or other assets for equity shares.

The venturers' interests in the joint venture are interests in the entity as a whole, not in its individual assets and liabilities. Therefore a venturer's interest in a jointly controlled entity is recognised in its own accounts as a fixed asset investment at cost, less any amounts written off, or at valuation.

5.3 Example

E Ltd and F Ltd set up a limited company, G Ltd, to carry out a joint venture. E Ltd transfers fixed assets with a net book value of £140,000 to the new company and F Ltd transfers stocks at a cost of £95,000.

G Ltd has an issued share capital of 200,000 £1 ordinary shares. E Ltd and F Ltd each subscribe for 50% of these shares at £1.50 each. The cost of the assets transferred to G Ltd is counted as part of the purchase consideration and the balance is paid in cash. The fair values of the tangible fixed assets and stock may be taken to be equal to their book values.

Prepare the opening balance sheet of G Ltd and show how the investment in the joint venture will be recorded in the separate accounts of E Ltd and F Ltd.

5.4 Solution

Balance sheet of G Ltd

	£	£
Tangible fixed assets		140,000
Current assets:		
Stocks	95,000	
Cash (balancing figure)	65,000	
		160,000
		300,000
Share capital		200,000
Share premium		100,000
		300,000

Investment in G Ltd

This will be shown in the separate accounts of E Ltd and F Ltd:

	£
Fixed assets:	
Investments (at cost) (300,000 × 50%)	150,000

6 THE AUDIT PROBLEMS OF JOINT VENTURES

A jointly controlled entity will be subject to the law in which it was established and in which it operates. For example, a joint venture established as a jointly controlled limited company incorporated in the UK is subject to the provisions of the Companies Acts, and an annual audit will be required unless the minimum size criteria are satisfied.

Where a joint venture is operated as jointly controlled operations or jointly controlled assets, the accounting entries for the venture will be made in the venturers' own books, so these entries will be subject to audit if the venturer itself is audited.

The main problem in auditing joint ventures is in getting full and timely access to the relevant financial information. The overall profitability of a venture will not be known until each venturer has provided information on its dealings with the venture, so it will take time to gather all the relevant information, particularly if the venturers are situated in disperse regions of the world.

Furthermore, foreign joint ventures may prepare accounts in overseas currencies and using accounting policies different from UK GAAP. The auditor's problems are therefore a combination of gathering sufficient audit evidence concerning the joint venture, and deciding whether the information in the financial statements does present a true and fair view of the result and state of affairs.

7   CHAPTER SUMMARY

In this chapter we have looked at the nature of joint ventures. We have also looked at the problems of preparing accounts for joint ventures and of reflecting joint ventures in the separate accounts of the individual venturers.

There are three different types of joint venture: jointly controlled operations, jointly controlled assets and jointly controlled entities. You need to understand the differences between them. It is also important that you are able to account for all three types of joint venture.

8   SELF TEST QUESTIONS

8.1   What is a joint venture? (1.1)

8.2   What is a jointly controlled asset? (1.2)

8.3   How are transfers of stock between joint venturers recorded in the accounts? (3.4)

8.4   How are jointly controlled operations accounted for in the separate accounts of the individual venturers? (3.9)

8.5   How are joint venture accounts prepared for a jointly controlled asset? (4.1)

8.6   How does an individual venturer record its interest in a jointly controlled entity in its own accounts? (5.2)

9   EXAMINATION TYPE QUESTION

9.1   Trilby and Bowler

Trilby and Bowler entered into a joint venture agreement for the purchase and sale of hats on 1 June 19X1. Transactions were as follows:

19X1

1 June	Trilby purchased hats for £6,000. To finance the purchase he took out a loan of £2,000 with Cromby and paid the balance in cash.
15 June	Trilby sent to Bowler hats costing £2,400 and paid carriage charges of £280 in that connection.
25 July	Bowler sold all his hats for £5,000 and paid Cromby £2,030 in full settlement of the latter's loan with Trilby.
31 July	Trilby paid insurance of £600. Bowler paid £40 for rent of a garage for storing the hats.
3 August	Bowler paid £1,000 to Trilby.
6 August	Trilby sold part of the hats in his possession for £8,000. He agreed to take over the remaining hats personally at a cost of £1,800.

Each party is entitled to a commission of 5% on his own gross sales. The balance of profits is to be shared, Trilby seven-tenths, Bowler three-tenths. Final cash settlement between the partners was made on 31 August.

You are required to record the above transactions on the basis that:

(a)   each party to the venture keeps a joint venture account in his own books; and

(b)   all transactions are recorded in the books of Trilby.   **(15 marks)**

10   ANSWER TO EXAMINATION TYPE QUESTION

10.1   Trilby and Bowler

(a)   **Books of Trilby**

Joint venture with Bowler

	£		£
Purchases:		Cash from Bowler	1,000
Bank	4,000	Sales	8,000
Loan account	2,000	Purchases – stock	
Carriage	280	taken over	1,800
Insurance	600	Loan account – paid	
Commission – 5% × £8,000	400	direct by Bowler	2,000
Share of profit	5,040		
Balance – cash to Bowler	480		
	12,800		12,800

Books of Bowler

Joint venture with Trilby

	£		£
Loan repaid	2,000	Sales	5,000
Loan interest	30	Balance – cash from	
Rent	40	Trilby	480
Cash to Trilby	1,000		
Commission – 5% × £5,000	250		
Share of profit	2,160		
	5,480		5,480

Memorandum joint venture account

	£	£		£
Purchases		6,000	Sales	13,000
Carriage		280	Trilby – stock taken over	1,800
Insurance		600		
Rent		40		
Loan interest		30		
Commission		650		
Net profit:				
Trilby (7/10)	5,040			
Bowler (3/10)	2,160			
		7,200		
		14,800		14,800

*(**Tutorial note:** as the Joint Venture account is memorandum only, there is no need to display it as a ledger account.)*

(b)   **Books of Trilby**

Joint venture account

	£	£		£
Purchases:			Sales	8,000
Bank		4,000	Purchases – stock	
Loan account		2,000	taken over	1,800
Carriage		280	Bowler – sales	5,000
Insurance		600		
Commission:				
Trilby		400		
Bowler		250		
Bowler:				
Interest		30		
Rent		40		
		–––––		
		7,600		
Balance – profit:				
Trilby (7/10)	5,040			
Bowler (3/10)	2,160			
	–––––			
		7,200		
		–––––		–––––
		14,800		14,800
		–––––		–––––

Bowler

	£		£
Joint venture account –		Loan account – repaid	2,000
sales	5,000	Joint venture account:	
Bank – cash to Bowler	480	Interest	30
		Rent	40
		Bank account – cash from	
		Bowler	1,000
		Joint venture account:	
		Commission	250
		Profit	2,160
	–––––		–––––
	5,480		5,480
	–––––		–––––

5 HIRE PURCHASE AND LEASING

INTRODUCTION & LEARNING OBJECTIVES

This chapter covers the appropriate accounting treatment for assets which are used by a business but payment for the asset is spread over time. In some cases, such as finance leases, the user of the asset will probably never become the owner of the asset.

There is a fair amount of new terminology and accounting entries for you to consider. It is easy to get lost at times in the details of the entries but the main principle for most of these situations should be returned to when this happens. That is, we treat most of these transactions as if the business has purchased an asset and taken on a loan to finance the purchase.

The chapter also covers the transactions from the point of view of the business providing the asset - the lessor or HP trader. This area may be new to you and should be studied carefully. Most exam questions however concentrate on the user of the asset and not the supplier.

When you have studied this chapter you should be able to do the following:

- Explain the various types of agreements that may exist
- Account for HP and leasing transactions in the books of the lessor and lessee.

1 EXPLANATION OF CREDIT AND LEASING AGREEMENTS

1.1 Legal background

It is important to distinguish between the different types of agreements whereby payment can be made on extended terms so that the appropriate means of accounting can be considered.

1.2 Hire purchase

 Under a hire purchase agreement, goods are supplied on hire to customers on terms that, once an agreed number of instalments have been paid, they may exercise an option to purchase the goods for a nominal sum. Until the option is exercised, the goods remain the legal property of the supplier.

As the goods remain the property of the seller until the option to purchase is exercised, the seller may repossess the goods for non-payment of instalments, although a court order is required for repossession once one-third of the hire purchase price has been paid.

Thus if we accounted for the legal form of the transaction, the asset would not be treated as such in the accounts of the user of the asset until all payments had been made. However as the substance of the transaction is the purchase of an asset financed over time, an HP item is recorded as an asset from the date of the agreement in the books of the 'buyer'. In the books of the 'seller' the accounting treatment is more complex but for now it is sufficient to know that the treatment will normally be the same as for a finance lease (see below).

Treating the goods as a fixed asset in the books of the buyer creates an accounting problem in that the total amounts payable under the agreement exceed the price which would have been paid on a normal sale for credit or cash.

The solution for the buyer is to record the asset at its 'cash price' and any excess is treated as interest which is charged to profit and loss account over the life of the agreement.

1.3   Credit sale agreement

Definition   A credit sale agreement is a contract for the sale of goods, whereby the price is paid by five or more instalments. Since ownership passes on delivery to the buyer, the seller's only remedy on default by the buyer is to sue for the outstanding instalments; he cannot recover the goods.

Credit sale agreements are treated in a similar way to hire purchase in the books of the buyer.

In the books of the seller, the transaction is treated as a sale at the date of the agreement, but the proceeds need to be split between 'normal' proceeds ie, those that would have been receivable on a cash sale, and the interest element. The difference between 'normal' proceeds and cost is a trading profit which is taken to profit and loss account in the accounting period in which the agreement is entered into. The interest element is spread over the life of the agreement to the profit and loss account and recorded as interest receivable.

1.4   Lease agreements

Definition   Under a lease agreement, a customer agrees to hire goods, normally for a fixed minimum period with rights of renewal. The goods remain the property of the hirer throughout the period. Lease agreements can involve a finance lease, where the rights and responsibilities in the asset pass to the user (lessee) or an operating lease, where such rights remain with the owner (lessor).

In substance a finance lease is similar to a hire purchase transaction as the lessee treats the asset as if it is his own property. The lease is recorded as a fixed asset in the lessee's books. We will see later how this is achieved.

The lessor will treat the transaction as if he has made a loan to the lessee which, initially, will be represented by the cost in providing the asset for the use of the lessee. This loan will be reduced over a period of time by the 'capital' element of the rental payments made by the lessee. The 'income' elements of the rentals will constitute interest income to be recorded in the profit and loss account over the period of the 'loan'.

An operating lease will however be treated as a fixed asset in the books of the **lessor** as it is contemplated that the lessor will be hiring out the asset to more than one person. The lessee does not treat the asset as a fixed asset and the rentals paid are expenses to be charged in the profit and loss account.

Conclusion   Of all the agreements which require payment for the use of an asset over a period of time, it is only operating leases in which the user of the asset does not record the asset as a fixed asset in his books.

2   LEDGER ENTRIES FOR CREDIT SALE, HIRE PURCHASE AND OPERATING LEASES

2.1   Introduction

In this section we look at the accounting entries made by the user of an asset which is being paid for under any of the above types of agreements.

Credit sale and hire purchase agreements are treated in exactly the same way except for one area (repossessed goods which are covered later in the section) and thus the term hire purchase in this section should be read as applying to credit sale agreements as well.

Operating leases are the easiest to deal with and this area is covered first.

2.2   Operating lease

The ledger accounts for recording an operating lease in the books of the user will only require the opening of an expense account with an appropriate heading such as operating lease rentals. Payments, which are generally monthly or every three months for longer term operating leases or one off payments for short term hire, are debited to the expense account and credited to cash. The expense account is closed off to the profit and loss account at the end of the accounting period.

2.3   Hire purchase – Accounting in the books of the buyer

It is useful first to distinguish between:

(a)   the cash purchase price; and

(b)   the hire purchase price.

2.4   Activity

Julby is about to acquire a new car. If he buys it outright it will cost £6,000, but he can acquire it under hire purchase if he pays a deposit of £1,500 plus twenty monthly instalments of £300 each.

How much interest is charged over the life of the agreement?

2.5   Activity solution

	£	£
Cash purchase price		6,000
Hire purchase price:		
Deposit	1,500	
Instalments 20 × £300	6,000	
	———	
		7,500
		———
Therefore, hire purchase interest		1,500
		———

The simplest assumption to make is that interest is spread on a straight line basis over the life of the agreement (other possibilities will be discussed later). On this basis, each instalment of £300 is treated as containing £1,500 ÷ 20 ie, £75 interest.

The bookkeeping entries are outlined below:

(a)   On signing the hire purchase agreement and taking possession of the asset:

	Dr	*Cr*	*With*
(1)	Fixed asset account	HP vendor's account (personal account with HP company)	Cash price

(b)   On payment of the deposit or an instalment:

	Dr	*Cr*	*With*
(2)	HP vendor's account	Cash account	Deposit or instalments paid

(c)   At the year end, transfer the hire purchase interest included in the instalments paid to profit and loss account:

	Dr	*Cr*	*With*
(3)	Profit and loss account	HP vendor's account	Interest (as calculated)

Conclusion   (a)   There are various ways of calculating the interest in (c). If the straight line approach is followed (as illustrated above), the charge in the profit and loss account is simply the number of instalments paid times the interest portion per instalment.

(b)   The balance remaining on the hire purchase vendor's account represents the unpaid portion of the cash price. It is disclosed as a liability in the balance sheet.

(c)   The fixed asset is depreciated in the usual way, the depreciation charge being based on the cash price.

2.6   Activity

On 1 January 19X5 Ramsey acquired a motor car on hire purchase for use in his business. He paid a deposit of £1,920 and agreed to pay thirty-six monthly instalments of £100, payable on the last day of each month. The cash price was £4,800. He prepares his accounts annually to 30 September, and depreciates his car at 25% pa on the reducing balance.

Show the necessary ledger accounts for the two years to 30 September 19X6, and the balance sheet extracts at each year end. Assume that interest is spread evenly over the life of the agreement.

2.7   Activity solution

Step 1   Calculate the amount of HP interest.

	£
Deposit	1,920
Instalments 36 × £100	3,600
	———
Hire purchase price	5,520
Less: Cash price	4,800
	———
Hire purchase interest	720
	———

Step 2   Analyse each instalment between interest charge and capital repayment.

Each instalment represents:

	£
Interest £720 ÷ 36	20
Capital (bal fig)	80
	———
	100
	———

Step 3   Open up ledger accounts: vendor's account, asset account and provision for depreciation account.

Hire purchase vendor's account

19X5		£	19X5		£
1 Jan.	Cash – deposit	1,920	1 Jan.	Motor car account	
	Cash – instalments			(cash price)	4,800
	9 × £100	900	30 Sep.	Profit and loss account	
30 Sep.	Balance c/d	2,160		– HP interest 9 × £20	180
		4,980			4,980
			1 Oct.	Balance b/d	2,160
19X6			19X6		
	Cash – instalments		30 Sep.	Profit and loss account	
	12 × £100	1,200		– HP interest 12 × £20	240
30 Sep.	Balance c/d	1,200			
		2,400			2,400

Note: the balance c/d of £1,200 represents fifteen outstanding instalments, each including a capital content of £80 per instalment.

Motor car account

19X5		£	19X5	£
1 Jan.	HP vendor's account	4,800		

Provision for depreciation account

19X5		£	19X5		£
	Balance c/d	900	30 Sep.	Profit and loss account – depreciation charge	
				25% × 9/12 × £4,800	900
			1 Oct.	Balance b/d	900
19X6			19X6		
30 Sep.	Balance c/d	1,875	30 Sep.	Profit and loss account – depreciation charge	
				25% × £(4,800 – 900)	975
		1,875			1,875

Step 4   The balance sheet extracts can now be prepared.

Balance sheet extracts at 30 September

	19X5		19X6	
	£	£	£	£
Fixed assets:				
Motor car, at cost	4,800		4,800	
Less: Depreciation	900		1,875	
		3,900		2,925
Liabilities:				
Amount outstanding on HP agreement		2,160		1,200

Note: under the above method no record is kept in the ledger account of the outstanding hire purchase interest at the balance sheet date. There is an alternative method – the suspense account method – which rectifies this. On the basis of recent questions, it is unlikely that the examiners would specify a particular method.

2.8   Amount outstanding on HP agreement

In the previous example the balance c/d in the HP vendor's account each year end is shown as one sum under liabilities. If the instalments are payable over a period greater than twelve months from the balance sheet date the liability should be split into two elements: a **current** liability (amounts payable within 12 months) and a **non-current** liability. This division is of most importance in the preparation of published accounts for a company when creditors are required to be split.

The split can be calculated quite easily provided the vendor's account is written up for the full life of the HP agreement (ie, in advance). A balance c/d in the following year's ledger represents the non-current element.

In the previous example the total liability at each balance sheet date has been calculated. At 30 September 19X5 £2,160 is outstanding. Of this sum £1,200 is outstanding at 30 September 19X6. This £1,200 is non-current at 30 September 19X5. The balance (£2,160 – £1,200) £960 is a current liability.

The more detailed balance sheet extracts are thus:

	19X5 £	19X6 £
Current liability		
Amount outstanding on HP agreement		
(£2,160 – £1,200)	960	
(£1,200 – £240)		960
Non-current liability		
Amount outstanding on HP agreement		
(look at next year's balance c/d)	1,200	240 (Working)

WORKING

Hire purchase vendor's account (19X7)

	£			£
		1 Oct. 19X7	Balance b/d	1,200
Cash instalments	1,200	30 Sep.	Profit and loss account	
Balance c/d	240		HP interest 12 × 20	240
	1,440			1,440

3   APPORTIONMENT OF HIRE PURCHASE INTEREST

3.1   Introduction

There are three main methods of calculating the way in which the interest charge is to be spread over the life of the agreement.

3.2   The straight line method

This is the method that has been used so far. Its main advantage is that of simplicity. From a theoretical viewpoint it can be argued that the earlier instalments contain a greater proportion of interest than the later instalments, on the grounds that the capital debt outstanding reduces over the life of the agreement. This factor is taken into account by the two methods below.

3.3 The sum of the years' digits method

The total interest charge contained in the agreement is distributed over the life of the agreement arithmetically in proportion to the reducing balances outstanding.

3.4 Activity

£234 interest is charged on a hire purchase agreement spread over twelve instalments.

Calculate the interest charge included in each instalment, using the sum of the years' digits method.

3.5 Activity solution

The sum of the years' digits for twelve instalments is:

$$12 + 11 + 10 + 9 + 8 + 7 + 6 + 5 + 4 + 3 + 2 + 1 = 78$$

The interest is spread as follows:

Instalment No.	Relevant fraction		Interest charge per instalment
			£
1	12/78		36
2	11/78		33
3	10/78		30
4	9/78		27
5	8/78		24
6	7/78	× £234	21
7	6/78		18
8	5/78		15
9	4/78		12
10	3/78		9
11	2/78		6
12	1/78		3
Total	1		234

This is a very satisfactory method of apportioning interest.

The sum of digits can be computed by using the formula:

$$\frac{N(N+1)}{2}, \text{ where N = number of instalments.}$$

For twelve instalments: $\frac{12(13)}{2} = 78$

The formula is sometimes referred to as the **rule of 78** (quite why is shrouded in mystery: it is only a rule of 78 if the numbers from 1 to 12 are aggregated.)

3.6 The actuarial method

Actuarial tables or interest tables are used to allocate the interest charges to particular periods. This method is the most accurate method of calculating interest and SSAP 21 recommends its use. The method is unlikely to be tested in detail due to the amount of calculation work required.

If it is tested, the relevant rate of interest will be given and you will need to construct a table in order to calculate the interest.

3.7   Example

An asset with a cash selling price of £5,710 is acquired under an HP agreement on 1 January 19X2 requiring 4 annual payments of £2,000 in arrears. The rate of interest is 15% pa.

3.8   Solution

The total finance charge is £(8,000 – 5,710) = £2,290. The allocation of this to each rental payment and the consequent capital sum outstanding is calculated as follows:

Period (year ended 31 December)	Capital sum at start of period	Finance charge at 15% pa	Sub-total	Rental paid	Capital sum at end of period
	£	£	£	£	£
19X2	5,710	856	6,566	(2,000)	4,566
19X3	4,566	685	5,251	(2,000)	3,251
19X4	3,251	488	3,739	(2,000)	1,739
19X5	1,739	261	2,000	(2,000)	-
		2,290		(8,000)	

Note: that if the rental is payable in advance the rental paid column should be located **before** the calculation of the finance charge column so that the correct finance charge is computed.

Conclusion   Both the straight line method and the sum of the years' digits method may be important from the viewpoint of the examination. Generally speaking, the straight line method is easier, but you should be prepared to apply the sum of the years' digits method and actuarial methods if required to do so. It is important to remember that the sequence of double entries is unaffected by the method chosen.

4   COMPLICATIONS

4.1   Complication 1 - Early completion by the hirer

The hirer may terminate the agreement before the due date of completion by making a lump sum payment to the finance company. Early completion often arises as a result of an asset destroyed in an accident. In this case the asset must be written out of the books, using the insurance claim as the disposal proceeds.

4.2   Activity

Turn to the earlier example of the motor car acquired by Ramsey. Suppose that on 3 October 19X6 the car was involved in a road accident and became a total write-off. The insurance company agreed the claim at £2,700, and the finance company accepted £1,360 in full settlement of the agreement.

Show the necessary entries in Ramsey's books.

4.3   Activity solution

Hire purchase vendor's account

19X6		£	19X6		£
3 Oct.	Cash	1,360	1 Oct.	Balance b/d	1,200
			3 Oct.	Profit and loss account termination charge (bal fig)	160
		1,360			1,360

Motor car disposal account

19X6		£	19X6		£
3 Oct.	Cost transferred from fixed asset account	4,800	3 Oct.	Accumulated depreciation transferred from depreciation provision account	1,875
			3 Oct.	Cash – Insurance claim	2,700
			3 Oct.	Profit and loss account – under-provision for depreciation (bal fig)	225
		4,800			4,800

Conclusion   The key point to note is that **the accounting for the asset disposal is entirely separate from the repayment to the finance company.**

4.4   Complication 2 – Repossession of the goods by the vendor

Suppose the hirer defaults with his payments. This automatically terminates the hire purchase agreement and the vendor repossesses the goods. This is treated as an unusual disposal in the hirer's books. In effect, the extinguishing of the debt by the vendor is the consideration for the 'disposal' of the asset.

Note that repossession cannot be made under a credit sale agreement and this complication will not arise.

4.5   Activity

Suppose that, instead of being written off, Ramsey's car was repossessed by the finance company on 3 October 19X6.

Show the motor car disposal account as it would appear in the books of Ramsey.

4.6   Activity solution

Motor car disposal account

19X6		£	19X6		£
3 Oct.	Cost transferred from motor car account	4,800	3 Oct.	Accumulated depreciation transferred from depreciation provision account	1,875
			3 Oct.	Balance transferred from HP vendor's account	1,200
			3 Oct.	Profit and loss account loss (bal fig)	1,725
		4,800			4,800

5   THE PRINCIPLES AND DISCLOSURE PROVISIONS OF SSAP 21

5.1   Lease agreements

The impetus for the issue of SSAP 21 was the need to change the accounting treatment of leases.

As mentioned at the beginning of this chapter, lease agreements can be either finance leases, where the rights and responsibilities of ownership (though not the legal title) pass to the user, or operating leases where such rights remain with the owner.

A finance lease is required by SSAP 21 *Accounting for leases and hire purchase contracts* to be dealt with in the same way as a hire purchase agreement. The lessee (user) treats the 'fair value' of the asset as a fixed asset and sets up a liability for this amount. Payments made are split between payment of this capital amount and payment of finance charges, with the latter debited to profit and loss account.

Payments made under an operating lease are debited to profit and loss account and no asset is shown in the books of the lessee. This used to be the treatment for finance leases as well.

5.2   Substance over form

Finance leases give rights over the use of assets for a period which covers all or a substantial part of their useful life. Such leases are effectively an alternative to hire purchase and loan financing. Hence failure to capitalise such leases would give rise to a disparity of accounting treatment which could distort comparisons between companies. In particular, comparisons of:

(a)   return on capital employed;

(b)   debt/equity ratio

could be misleading.

The treatment of finance leases is an example of the application of substance over form.

Substance over form requires that transactions and other events should be accounted for and presented in accordance with their substance and financial reality and not merely with their legal form. Substance over form is at the heart of *SSAP 21*:

(a)   Under a finance lease, the lessee acquires substantially all the benefits of use of an asset for the substantial majority of its useful economic life. The lessee also takes on the risks of ownership – repairs, maintenance and insurance. A finance lease is therefore similar to the purchase of an asset on credit terms.

(b)   Under a finance lease, the lessor is providing finance and obtaining a return on his investment.

5.3   Finance leases - identification

A finance lease is defined as a lease that transfers substantially all the risks and rewards of ownership of an asset to the lessee. To decide whether there is a presumption of transfer of risks and rewards of ownership it is necessary to complete the following steps:

	Step	*Comment*
(1)	Calculate minimum lease payments (MLPs) inclusive of initial payment.	MLPs = minimum payments plus any residual amounts guaranteed by lessee.
(2)	Discount (1) to determine present value of MLPs.	Discount factor is either: (i) rate of interest implicit in lease (if known) or (ii) a commercial rate of interest (for a similar lease)
(3)	Calculate fair value of asset at beginning of lease.	Fair value = arm's length price less any government grants receivable by lessor.
(4)	Presumption is satisfied if (2) amounts to 90% or more of (3).	

5.4   Disclosure provisions

The disclosure provisions of SSAP 21 are extensive and are illustrated after we have shown how leases are recorded in the books of the lessor and lessee.

6   RECORDING FINANCE LEASES IN THE BOOKS OF THE LESSEE

6.1   Finance leases – initial entries

At the start of the lease:

(a)   the present value of the MLPs should be included as a fixed asset, subject to depreciation;

(b)   the obligation to pay rentals should be included as a liability.

In practice the fair value of the asset or its cash price will often be a sufficiently close approximation to the present value of the MLPs and therefore can be used instead.

6.2   Finance leases – depreciation

The related fixed asset should be depreciated over the shorter of:

(a)   the useful economic life of the asset (as in FRS 15); and

(b)   the lease term.

The lease term is essentially the period over which the lessee has the use of the asset. It includes:

(i)   the primary (non-cancellable) period; plus

(ii)   any secondary periods during which the lessee has the contractual right to continue to use the asset, provided that it is reasonably certain at the outset that this right will be exercised.

6.3   Finance leases – allocation of finance charges

(a)   Over the period of the lease, the total finance charge is the amount by which the rentals paid to the lessor exceed the present value of the MLPs.

(b)   Each individual rental payment should be split between:

(i)   finance charge (P/L account item); and

(ii)   repayment of obligation to pay rentals (thus reducing the balance sheet liability).

(c)   How should finance charges be allocated over the term of the lease? The basic aim is to allocate the charge in such a way as to produce a reasonably constant periodic rate of return on the remaining balance of liability. There are three main methods:

(i)   actuarial method;

(ii)   sum of the digits (rule of 78) method;

(iii)   straight-line method.

Of the above methods the actuarial method gives the most accurate result.

6.4   Example of the actuarial method

A company has two options. It can buy an asset for cash at a cost of £5,710 or it can lease it by way of a finance lease. The terms of the lease are as follows:

(1)   primary period is for four years from 1 January 19X2 with a rental of £2,000 pa payable on the 31 December each year;

(2)   the lessee has the right to continue to lease the asset after the end of the primary period for an indefinite period, subject only to a peppercorn (nominal) rent;

(3)   the lessee is required to pay all repair, maintenance and insurance costs as they arise;

(4)   the interest rate implicit in the lease is 15%.

The lessee estimates the useful economic life of the asset to be eight years. Depreciation is provided on a straight-line basis.

6.5   Solution

Step 1   Is the lease a finance lease?

Referring to the steps in paragraph 5.3:

(1)   MLPs = 4 × £2,000 = £8,000

(2)   Present values of MLPs:

From discount tables – present value of four annual sums – first receivable at the end of the first year:

£2,000 × 2.855 = £5,710

(3)   Fair value of asset is £5,710.

(4)   Present value of MLPs is more than 90% of fair value of asset.

The lease is therefore a finance lease.

Step 2   The asset is shown in the balance sheet at £5,710 (subject to depreciation).

Depreciation is over eight years (presumably no residual value to the asset at the end of eight years).

Annual depreciation charge = 1/8 × £5,710 = £714

Step 3   The liability is shown in the balance sheet at £5,710 but subsequently reduced by the capital portion of the leasing payments.

The total finance charge is £(8,000 – 5,710) = £2,290. The allocation of this to each rental payment and the consequent capital sum outstanding is calculated as follows:

Period (year ended 31 December)	Capital sum at start of period	Finance charge at 15% pa	Sub-total	Rental paid	Capital sum at end of period
	£	£	£	£	£
19X2	5,710	856	6,566	(2,000)	4,566
19X3	4,566	685	5,251	(2,000)	3,251
19X4	3,251	488	3,739	(2,000)	1,739
19X5	1,739	261	2,000	(2,000)	-
		2,290		8,000	

Step 4   The effect on the financial statements of the lessee may be summarised as follows:

Year ended 31 December	*Profit and loss account*		*Balance sheet*			
	Finance charge	Dep'n.	Fixed asset (NBV)	Obligation		
				Total	Non-current	Current
	£	£	£	£	£	£
19X2	856	714	4,996	4,566	3,251	1,315
19X3	685	714	4,282	3,251	1,739	1,512
19X4	488	714	3,568	1,739	-	1,739
19X5	261	714	2,854	-	-	-
19X6	-	714	2,140	-	-	-
19X7	-	714	1,426	-	-	-
19X8	-	714	712	-	-	-
19X9	-	712	-	-	-	-
	2,290	5,710				

The finance charge each year is a constant periodic rate of return (15%) on the remaining balance of liability eg, £856 is 15% of £5,710, etc.

6.6   Operating leases

Rentals under operating leases should be charged to the profit and loss account on a straight-line basis over the term of the lease unless another systematic and rational basis is more appropriate. Any difference between amounts charged and amounts paid should be adjusted to debtors or creditors.

6.7   Disclosure – finance leases and hire purchase contracts

For disclosure purposes finance leases and hire purchase agreements are treated as one group.

(a)   **Balance sheet: assets**

There is a choice of disclosure for assets. Either:

(i)   show by each major class of asset the gross amounts of assets held under a finance lease and related accumulated depreciation; or

(ii)   integrate the finance lease assets with owned fixed assets and disclose the **net** amount of assets held under finance leases.

(b)   **Balance sheet: obligations under finance leases**

The amounts of obligations related to finance leases (net of finance charges allocated to future periods) should be disclosed separately from other obligations and liabilities, either on the face of the balance sheet or in the notes to the accounts.

These net obligations under finance leases should then be analysed between amounts payable in the next year, amounts payable in the second to fifth years inclusive from the balance sheet date, and the aggregate amounts payable thereafter. This analysis may be presented either:

(i)   separately for obligations under finance leases; or

(ii)   where the total of these items is combined on the balance sheet with other obligations and liabilities, by giving the equivalent analysis of the total in which it is included.

If the analysis is presented according to (i) above, a lessee may, as an alternative to analysing the net obligations, analyse the gross obligations, with future finance charges being separately deducted from the total.

(c)   **Profit and loss account**

The total depreciation charge and the aggregate finance charges for the period in respect of finance leases should be disclosed.

6.8   Disclosure - Operating leases

(a)   **Balance sheet: obligations under operating leases**

In respect of operating leases, the lessee should disclose the payments which he is committed to make during the next year, analysed between those in which the commitment expires within that year, in the second to fifth years inclusive and over five years from the balance sheet date, showing separately the commitments in respect of leases of land and buildings and other operating leases.

(b)   **Profit and loss account**

Total operating lease rentals charged as an expense in the profit and loss account - split between hire of plant and machinery rentals and other operating leases.

6.9   Illustration of disclosure requirements – finance leases

Using the earlier illustration and the calculations under the actuarial method the following disclosure would be appropriate:

Extracts from balance sheet

	31 Dec. 19X2
	£
Assets:	
Leased property under finance leases	5,710
Less: Accumulated depreciation	714
	4,996

Alternatively, the above figures could be included within the overall totals of fixed assets and disclose merely the NBV of £4,996.

Extracts from balance sheet

	£
Liabilities:	
Non-current obligations under finance leases	3,251
Current obligations under finance leases	1,315
	4,566

The above figures may be disclosed separately on the face of the balance sheet or aggregated with other items (eg, bank loans and overdrafts). In the latter situation the notes to the accounts would reveal the above figures.

Notes to the accounts – Obligations under finance leases

The future minimum lease payments to which the company is committed as at 31 December 19X2 are:

	£
Amounts payable next year	2,000
Amounts payable in the second and third years	4,000
	6,000

Less: Finance charges allocated to future periods	1,434
	4,566

An alternative disclosure would be:

The future net obligations to which the company is committed as at 31 December 19X2 are:

	£
Amounts due within one year	1,315
Amounts due in the second and third years	3,251
	4,566

Notes to the accounts – Profit and loss account

Profit is stated after charging:

	£
Depreciation of owned assets	X
Depreciation of assets held under finance leases	
(and hire purchase contracts – if relevant)	714
Finance charges payable:	
Finance leases (and hire purchase contracts)	856
Hire of plant and machinery – operating leases	X
Hire of other assets – operating leases	X

Extract from statement of accounting policies

Where assets are financed by leasing agreements that give rights approximating to ownership ('finance leases'), the assets are treated as if they had been purchased outright at the present value of the total rentals payable during the primary period of the lease. The corresponding leasing commitments are shown as obligations to the lessor.

Charges are made to profit and loss account in respect of:

(a)   depreciation – which is provided on a straight-line basis over the economic useful life of the asset;

(b)   the total finance charge is allocated over the primary period of the lease using the actuarial method.

6.10   Illustration of disclosure requirements - operating leases

The commitments should be analysed as follows:

At 31 December 19X2 the company had annual commitments under non-cancellable operating leases as set out below:

	Land and buildings	Other
	£	£
Operating leases which expire:		
Within one year	x	x
In the second to fifth years inclusive	x	x
Over five years	x	x

This disclosure is not requiring the total sums which will actually be paid in future, but merely for how long a particular lease will require payments. For example, a company uses two offices, both leased:

Lease A expires in three years   –   Annual rental £30,000
Lease B expires in forty five years –   Annual rental £20,000

The disclosure would be:

	Land and buildings £
Operating leases which expire:	
In the second to fifth years inclusive	30,000
Over five years	20,000
	———
Total annual commitment as at the current year-end	50,000
	———

6.11   Activity

P Ltd entered into a five year lease on 1 January 19X3 for a machine with a fair value of £20,000. Rentals are £5,200 pa payable in advance and the residual value at the end of the lease is calculated as £4,200 which will be returned to P Ltd.

P Ltd is responsible for insurance and maintenance costs. The rate of interest implicit in the lease is 15.15%. You are required to show the allocation of finance charges on a sum of the digits basis and on an actuarial basis and comment on the result.

6.12   Activity solution

Step 1   Calculate the finance charge.

	£
5 × £5,200	26,000
Fair value	20,000
	———
Finance charge	6,000
	———

Step 2   Allocate finance charge on a sum of the digits basis.

$$\text{Finance charge pa} = \frac{\text{Number of rentals not yet due} \times \text{total finance charge}}{\text{Sum of number of rentals}}$$

Year	*No of rentals not yet due*			*Finance charge*
19X3	4			2,400
19X4	3	$6,000$		1,800
19X5	2	$\overline{10}$		1,200
19X6	1			600
19X7	-			———
	—			6,000
	10			———
	—			

Allocate finance charge on an actuarial basis.

Year	Capital £	Lease payment £	Capital outstanding £	Finance charge £	Capital at year end £
19X3	20,000	5,200	14,800	2,242	17,042
19X4	17,042	5,200	11,842	1,794	13,636
19X5	13,636	5,200	8,436	1,278	9,714
19X6	9,714	5,200	4,514	686	5,200
19X7	5,200	5,200	-	-	-

Conclusion   Where the lease term is relatively short and the interest rate is not high the two methods of interest allocation produce very similar results.

7   RECORDING FINANCE LEASES IN THE BOOKS OF THE LESSOR

7.1   Introduction

From the viewpoint of the lessor, the substance over form argument regards a finance lease as being equivalent to the provision of finance, rather than the hiring out of a fixed asset. Conversely an operating lease should be accounted for by capitalising and depreciating the leased asset.

The two types of lease may be compared as follows:

	Finance leases	*Operating leases*
Balance sheet	Net investment in finance lease (ie, a debtor)	Property held for operating leases (cost - depreciation)
Profit and loss account	Finance charge (allocated on basis which gives constant periodic return on net cash investment)	Rental income (straight-line basis) Depreciation

7.2   Accounting for finance leases

SSAP 21 deals with calculation of the carrying value of the finance lease receivables and with lessors' profit recognition. It requires the receivables to be carried on a balance sheet at an amount based on the net investment in the lease. Conversely, it requires that profit recognition should normally be based on the lessor's net *cash* investment.

The net investment in a lease is initially the cost of the asset to the lessor, less any government or other grants receivable (ie, the fair value).

The rentals paid by the lessee should be apportioned by the lessor between (a) gross earnings (ie, the lessor's interest earned) and (b) a repayment of capital.

Over the period of the lease the net investment in the lease (ie, the carrying value of the receivables) will therefore be the fair value of the asset less those portions of the rentals which are apportioned as a repayment of capital.

For the purposes of profit recognition, however, the total gross earnings should normally be allocated to accounting periods to give a constant periodic rate of return on the lessor's net **cash** investment (NCI) in the lease in each period. The NCI is based on the funds which the lessor has invested in the lease. The amount of funds invested in a lease by a lessor is different from the net investment in the lease because there are a number of other cash flows which affect the lessor in addition to those which affect net investment. In particular, tax cash flows are an important component of the NCI.

The standard permits a reasonable approximation to be made in arriving at the constant period rate of return. Hence there are a number of different methods of profit recognition which may comply with the standard. The two most precise methods (the 'after tax' methods) are the actuarial method after tax and the investment period method, but the calculations involved are rather complicated and these two methods are therefore unlikely to be examined. Instead the 'pre tax' methods already looked at in lessee accounting (ie, the straight line method, the sum of the digits method and the actuarial method) will usually give an acceptable answer for lessor accounting as well.

A particular exam question will specify the method to be used, but it will help if you think of lessor accounting as being the mirror image of the entries made in the lessee's accounts.

7.3   Illustration of lessor accounting for a finance lease

The lessor in the example in paragraph 6.4 above will account for the leased asset as follows:

(a)   Confirm that the terms of the lease satisfy the conditions to be a finance lease. This is the same as in 6.5 above.

(b)   Recognise the £5,710 value of the asset as a receivable (debtor), 'investment in finance lease'.

(c)   Recognise the finance income receivable each year on the same basis that the lessee recognised the finance charge payable:

Year	Finance income receivable £
19X2	856
19X3	685
19X4	488
19X5	261
	2,290

(d)   At the end of the primary period of the lease, the total lease payments received (4 × £2,000) will exactly equal the original receivable (£5,710) plus the total finance income recognised (£2,290).

7.4   Accounting for hire purchase contracts

In the case of hire purchase, profit recognition should also, in principle, be based on net cash investment. However, since the capital allowances under a hire purchase contract accrue to the hirer, the finance company's net cash investment is often not significantly different from its net investment; hence, again, the allocation of gross earnings (ie, finance charges) based on net investment will in most cases be a suitable approximation to allocation based on net cash investment.

This will have the result that, again, the entries in the finance company's accounts will be a mirror image of the entries in the hirer's accounts if the hirer is using the actuarial method before tax.

7.5   Presentation in accounts

The standard requires disclosure of the net investment in (a) finance leases and (b) hire purchase contracts at each balance sheet date. The amounts should be described as receivables. Whereas in lessee accounting the figures in respect of leases and hire purchase contracts may be aggregated, in the case of lessors and finance companies the amounts in respect of each should be shown separately.

For companies subject to *Sch 4 CA85* the net investment in finance leases and hire purchase contracts should be included in current assets under the heading 'debtors' and described as 'finance lease receivables' and/or 'hire purchase receivables' as appropriate. It should be analysed in the notes to the accounts between those amounts receivable within one year and those amounts receivable thereafter.

A suitable form of disclosure would be:

Balance sheet as at 31 December 19X7

	£	*19X6* £
Current assets:		
Finance lease and hire purchase receivables	1,200	1,100

Notes to the accounts

(1)   The amounts receivable under finance leases and hire purchase contracts comprise:

	£	*19X6* £
Finance leases	900	820
Hire purchase contracts	300	280
	1,200	1,100

Included in the totals receivable is £900 (19X6 £850) which falls due after more than one year.

The standard requires that the gross amounts (ie, original cost or revaluation) and accumulated depreciation of assets held for use in operating leases should be disclosed. This information could be incorporated into tables showing the amounts for other fixed assets or could be shown as a separate table. It is recognised that, for banks, assets held for use in operating leases are different in nature from a bank's infrastructure (eg, its own premises). Hence it may not be appropriate to combine assets held for use in operating leases with a bank's infrastructure for capital adequacy purposes.

7.6   Manufacturer/dealer lessor

A manufacturer or dealer may offer customers the option of either outright purchase or rental of an asset. The rental option is thus a means of encouraging sales and may be packaged to appear attractive, eg, cars sold with 0% finance option.

The question then arises as to whether the total profit on a transaction is split into a trading profit (and thus recognised at the date the agreement is signed) and finance income (spread over the lifetime of the agreement).

SSAP 21 states 'A manufacturer or dealer/lessor should not recognise a selling profit under an operating lease. The selling profit under a finance lease should be restricted to the excess of the fair value of the asset over the manufacturer's or dealer's cost less any grants receivable by the manufacturer or dealer towards the purchase, construction or use of the asset.'

The fair value of the asset can be taken to be the cash selling price as long as the credit terms reflect a reasonable level of interest. However where, for example, a car dealer is offering 0% finance deals it is not reasonable to record all the profit as trading profit and no finance income. Clearly the trader in this situation is reducing the fair value of the car. An approach that could be taken in this situation is to discount the lease payments using a reasonable estimate of the implicit rate of interest. The PV of the MLPs thus becomes the fair value for determining trading profit.

7.7   Amendment to SSAP 21: Tax free grants

Lessors may be able to obtain tax free grants against the purchase price of assets acquired for leasing.

One possible method of accounting for tax free grants is 'grossing up'. The pre-tax profit and the tax charge are changed by the same amount so that a standard tax charge is reported.

'Grossing up' fails to reflect the true nature of the transactions that have occurred in the period.

SSAP 21 has been amended to prohibit the grossing up of tax free grants to lessors. SSAP 21 now requires that such grants should be spread over the period of the lease. The grant is treated as non-taxable income.

8   THE AUDIT VERIFICATION OF LEASED ASSETS

8.1   Split of leases

The main problem in the audit of leased assets in the books of the user of the asset is to ensure that a proper split has been made between assets under an operating lease and assets under a finance lease. It should be recognised that there may be a high risk in this area due to the client preferring the asset to be recognised as an operating lease as this will keep the 'debt' off the balance sheet.

The calculations used to determine whether a lease is a finance lease can be quite complex and thus the auditor must ensure that he understands the principles behind the calculations and that the assumptions used (eg, the implicit rate of interest) are reasonable. Having understood the principles, a sample of the calculations need to be checked for **all** leases ie, including those which the client has designated as operating leases.

8.2   Audit procedures for accounting transactions

For the leases which have been classified as finance leases, a sample needs to be checked for the following matters.

(a)   Check method used to split interest and capital.

(b)   Check the method is correctly applied to lease payments.

(c)   Check depreciation is based on the shorter of the lease term and the useful life of the asset to the lessee.

In addition 'normal' audit tests apply to verification of the asset as for any other fixed asset.

If the lease has been classified as an operating lease, then a check is required of the manner in which the rentals have been charged to the profit and loss account. A check should also be made on the physical existence of the asset if, at the time of the audit, the lease is still in existence.

Finally regard should be had to the possibility of assets being held under leases also being shown in normal fixed assets in the balance sheet. This is particularly relevant to operating leases where the existence of a physical asset at the balance sheet date may be used to support the inclusion of the asset in the fixed asset account.

9   CHAPTER SUMMARY

Assets acquired under hire purchase or finance leases in law remain the property of the owner/lessor. However, for accounting purposes they are treated as though they belonged to the user. The consequences of this are that:

(a)   the owner/lessor in effect accounts for the transactions as a sale and the main accounting problem is to allocate the finance charges across the relevant accounting periods; and

(b)   the user in effect accounts for the transactions as a purchase and discloses the asset in his balance sheet.

10 SELF TEST QUESTIONS

10.1 What is the difference between a hire purchase agreement and a lease? (1.2, 1.4)

10.2 What is the double entry in the purchaser's books when he takes possession of an asset under a hire purchase agreement? (2.5)

10.3 Explain how the sum of the digits method works in apportioning HP interest. (3.3)

10.4 Distinguish between a finance lease and an operating lease. (1.4, 5.1)

10.5 What is a minimum lease payment? (5.3)

10.6 Which method of spreading interest gives the lessee the most accurate result? (6.3)

10.7 What should be disclosed in the notes to the balance sheet for operating leases? (6.8)

10.8 Is it the net investment or the net cash investment which is recorded on the balance sheet of a lessor? (7.2)

11 EXAMINATION TYPE QUESTIONS

11.1 Morris

Morris, a general dealer making his accounts up annually on 31 December purchased two vehicles on hire purchase. The details are as follows:

	Vehicle A	Vehicle B
Date of purchase	1 July 19X6	1 April 19X7
Cost	£7,500	£10,000
Deposit paid at date of purchase	£3,500	£4,000
Hire purchase monthly repayments 24@	£200	£300

Vehicle A was sold for £4,000 cash on 1 October 19X8.

Depreciation is provided by means of the straight line method based on a five year life, a full year's depreciation provided in the year of purchase but none in the year of sale. The charge for interest is to be spread evenly over the period of the loan pro rata to time, and the first monthly repayment is due on the last day of the month of purchase.

You are required to show for each of the years ended 31 December 19X6, 19X7, 19X8 and 19X9:

(a) the relevant entries as regards hire purchase and motor vehicles in the profit and loss account of Morris; and

(b) the suggested drafting of the items 'motor vehicles' and 'HP creditor' as they might appear in the balance sheet. **(15 marks)**

11.2 Jones plc

Jones plc is considering acquiring on 1 January 19X7 the use of a major piece of heavy agricultural plant, the Vinnie, which has a useful economic life of 8 years. The cost of the Vinnie would be £600,000 if it were bought for cash. Jones plc has employed a firm of consultants, Cly Vallon and Co, who are experienced in high value purchases of this type, to recommend a range of financing options. Their suggestions are as follows, all transactions being with Backward or Bust plc.

Option A

Enter an HP agreement for the Vinnie. The rentals would be £100,000 per annum for four years, with a deposit of £100,000 payable immediately. At the end of the four year period, Jones plc would have the option to purchase the Vinnie for £200,000.

Option B

Enter an 8 year lease for the Vinnie, with lease rentals of £110,000 payable annually in advance.

Option C

Enter a four year lease for the Vinnie, with lease rentals of £150,000 payable annually in advance, and with an optional secondary period of three years at rentals of 60%, 40% and 20% of the annual rental in the primary period.

Maintenance and insurance are to be the responsibility of Jones plc but Backward or Bust plc has negotiated a guaranteed trade-in with the manufacturer at £166,000 if Jones plc returns the Vinnie after 4 years and does not take up the secondary period. The rate of interest implicit in the lease is 13.5%. The Vinnie would be worthless at the end of the secondary lease period if it was taken up.

You are required:

(a)   to prepare a memorandum for the finance director of Jones plc setting out the amounts to be included in the balance sheet and profit and loss account of Jones plc at 31 December 19X7 under each of the three alternatives, explaining briefly the justification for the treatments you have adopted.   **(10 marks)**

(b)   to state briefly (without calculations) how the three alternatives would be treated in Backward or Bust plc's accounts for the year ended 31 December 19X7.   **(4 marks)**
    (Total: 14 marks)

12   ANSWERS TO EXAMINATION TYPE QUESTIONS

12.1   Morris

(a)   **Profit and loss account (extracts)**

	Year ended 31 December			
	19X6	*19X7*	*19X8*	*19X9*
	£	£	£	£
(W4) Hire purchase interest	200	850	800	150
(W2) Loss on disposal of vehicle	-	-	500	-
(W1) Depreciation	1,500	3,500	2,000	2,000

(b)   **Balance sheet (extracts)**

				At 31 December				
	19X6		*19X7*		*19X8*		*19X9*	
	£	£	£	£	£	£	£	£
Fixed assets:								
Motor vehicles								
Cost	7,500		17,500		10,000		10,000	
(W1) Less: Depreciation	1,500		5,000		4,000		6,000	
		6,000		12,500		6,000		4,000
(W4) HP creditor within one year		2,000		4,000		750		—
(W4) HP creditor more than one year		1,000		750		—		—

WORKINGS

(W1)
Provision for depreciation

	£			£
		19X6		
		31 Dec	P & L account: Vehicle A	1,500
		19X7		
		31 Dec	P & L account:	
19X7			Vehicle A	1,500
31 Dec Balance c/d	5,000		Vehicle B	2,000
	5,000			5,000
19X8		*19X7*		
1 Oct Motor vehicle disposals account: Vehicle A	3,000	31 Dec Balance b/d		5,000
		19X8		
31 Dec Balance c/d	4,000	31 Dec	P & L account: Vehicle B	2,000
	7,000			7,000
		19X8		
		31 Dec Balance b/d		4,000
19X9		*19X9*		
31 Dec Balance c/d	6,000	31 Dec	P & L account: Vehicle B	2,000
	6,000			6,000

(W2)
Motor vehicles disposals

	£			£
19X8		*19X8*		
1 Jul. Motor vehicles Vehicle A	7,500	1 Oct. Provision for depreciation		3,000
			Bank	4,000
			P & L account – loss	500
	7,500			7,500

(W3)   **Hire purchase interest**

		Vehicle A £		Vehicle B £
Deposits		3,500		4,000
Instalments	(24 × £200)	4,800	(24 × £300)	7,200
		8,300		11,200
Less: Cash price		7,500		10,000
Total interest spread over two years		800		1,200

Official ACCA *Textbook, published by AT Foulks Lynch*

(W4)   **HP creditors**

P&L charge			A £	B £	Total £
		Cash price of asset	7,500	10,000	
		Less: Deposit	3,500	4,000	
			4,000	6,000	
	19X6	Paid 6 @ 200	(1,200)		
200		Interest 6/24 × 800	200		
			3,000		3,000
	19X7	Paid 12 @ 200	(2,400)		
		Paid 9 @ 300		(2,700)	
850		Interest 12/24 × 800	400		
		9/24 × 1,200		450	
			1,000	3,750	4,750
	19X8	Paid 6 @ 200	(1,200)		
		Paid 12 @ 300		(3,600)	
800		Interest 6/24 × 800	200		
		12/24 × 1,200		600	
			NIL	750	750

12.2   Jones plc

(a)

MEMORANDUM

To: Finance Director, Jones plc

From: ABC, Accountant

Date: XX-XX-XX

Accounting for lease/hire of 'Vinnie'

Option A

Owing to the size of the option to purchase, and to the fact that the hire term is substantially shorter than the Vinnie's useful economic life, SSAP 21 dictates that this arrangement (unusually for an HP agreement) should be accounted for as an operating lease.

Amounts in the financial statements should therefore be as follows

(i)   **Profit and loss account**

	£
Hire of plant and machinery (W1)	125,000

(ii)   **Balance sheet**

Prepayment and accrued income (W1)	75,000

Option B

The primary period of this lease is for the whole of the Vinnie's useful economic life. This lease must therefore be accounted for as a finance lease, as the risks and rewards of ownership have passed totally to the lessee. The sum of digits method of allocating finance charges has been adopted. A straight line method would have been unacceptable due to the size of the lease, while actuarial methods could have been used as an alternative to sum of digits.

Amounts in the financial statements should therefore be as follows

(i)   **Balance sheet**

        Creditors: amounts falling due

	within one year £	*after one year* £
Net obligation under finance leases (W2)	40,000	450,000
Accruals and deferred income (W2)	70,000	

        Fixed assets, tangible

        Plant held under finance leases:

Cost	600,000
Depreciation $\dfrac{(600,000)}{8}$	75,000

(ii)   **Profit and loss account**

Depreciation on plant held under finance leases	75,000
Finance charges under finance leases (W2)	70,000

Option C

The contracted lease term is only for half of the useful economic life of the Vinnie and thus the risks and rewards of ownership have not passed to the lessee. Accordingly, Jones plc should account for this lease as an operating lease.

Amounts in the financial statements should therefore be

Profit and loss account

	£
Hire of plant and machinery	150,000

(b)   **Accounting treatments in Backward or Bust plc's books**

Option A

The transaction would be treated as an operating lease. Therefore the balance sheet would show the plant as a tangible fixed asset, and the rentals receivable would be credited to profit and loss account. The deposit would be credited to profit and loss account over the four year period on a straight-line basis.

Option B

The transaction would be treated as a finance lease. Thus the balance sheet would show as a current asset the capital amount outstanding under the lease, and the profit and loss account would be credited with the interest element of the lease rentals received.

Option C

All residual amounts are guaranteed to Backward or Bust plc, although not necessarily by Jones plc. Backward or Bust plc should therefore account for this transaction as a finance lease.

WORKINGS

(W1)   **Option A**   £

Payment over lease term   500,000
                                                                                   ‾‾‾‾‾‾‾‾
Profit and loss charge per annum (4 years)   125,000
Amount paid 19X7   200,000
                                                                                   ‾‾‾‾‾‾‾‾
Prepayment 31.12.X7   75,000
                                                                                   ‾‾‾‾‾‾‾‾

(W2)   **Option B:** net obligation   £

Capitalised amount (fair value)   600,000
Rentals 19X7   (110,000)
                                                                                   ‾‾‾‾‾‾‾‾
                                                                                490,000
Finance charges in 19X7 rentals (as in advance)   -
                                                                                   ‾‾‾‾‾‾‾‾
Net obligation   490,000
                                                                                   ‾‾‾‾‾‾‾‾

Of which due within one year Instalment 19X8   110,000
Less finance charges 19X7   (70,000)
                                                                                   ‾‾‾‾‾‾‾‾
                                                                                 40,000
                                                                                   ‾‾‾‾‾‾‾‾

Finance charges

                                                                                    £

Minimum lease payments (8 × £110,000)   880,000
Fair value   (600,000)
                                                                                   ‾‾‾‾‾‾‾‾
Total   280,000
                                                                                   ‾‾‾‾‾‾‾‾

Allocated to 19X7 (sum of digits) $= \dfrac{7}{8(8-1)(\frac{1}{2})} \times £280,000$

                                     $= \quad £70,000$

(Tutorial notes:

(1)   To charge the full £200,000 paid under Option A to profit and loss account in 19X7 would be inappropriate as it would not follow the matching concept set out in SSAP 21 for operating leases.

(2)   The '90% test' is totally unnecessary in Option B (which is just as well, as no information is given) because the risks and rewards of ownership ie, the rights to the undivided enjoyment of the leased asset, have passed to the lessee.

(3)   The '90% test' could have been applied under Option C, but this would have been a waste of time as the lease is clearly an operating lease from useful economic life considerations. The maintenance and insurance are of peripheral importance.*)

For information:

Fair value = £600,000
PV of minimum lease payments = £501,188 (ie, 83.5% of fair value)

6 RECOGNITION OF REVENUE, DISTRIBUTABLE PROFITS & PURCHASE & REDEMPTION OF SHARES

INTRODUCTION & LEARNING OBJECTIVES

This chapter covers the various changes in share capital that are examinable at this level, and the calculation of distributable profits. Company law has an important part to play in these areas. It provides a legal framework for the issue and redemption of shares within which the accounting entries must operate.

It is however important to appreciate the commercial reasons for companies to make changes to their capital structure. The legal provisions would be of little importance if companies had no commercial reasons for issuing and redeeming shares.

The chapter looks at distributable profits, initially considering the meaning of revenue in accounting theory terms. Later, we consider the extent to which changing prices should make companies restrict their distribution of profits in order to maintain capital. This chapter, however, concentrates on the legal provisions which, in the main, take the accounting profits as a starting point.

When you have studied this chapter you should be able to do the following:

- Outline the principles of revenue recognition.
- Discuss the rules relating to the distribution of profits.
- Explain the various provisions for changing capital and record the accounting entries.

1 THE PRINCIPLES OF REVENUE RECOGNITION

This section is concerned with the question of when revenue and expenses should be recognised in the profit and loss account.

1.1 Meaning of revenue

The term revenue could apply in any of the following situations

(a)   the supply of goods on cash or credit sale terms
(b)   the provision of services on cash or credit terms
(c)   rent received from equipment or property hired out, or
(d)   interest or dividends received on a trade investment.

1.2 Measurement of revenue

 Revenue is measured by the immediate exchange value of the goods or services involved.

(a)   If the sale is a cash sale, then the revenue is the immediate proceeds of sale. Provision may be made for expected returns and allowances.

(b)   If the sale is a credit sale ie, a sale for a claim to cash, then anticipated cash is revenue.

Provisions for bad debts, returns and allowances are usually computed as a separate exercise and disclosed separately. If the anticipated collectable value on sales of £1,000 is £950, some accountants would argue that this should be shown as £950 revenue. Current practice, however, would show £1,000 in the trading account as revenue, and £50 as an expense in the profit and loss account.

1.3   Timing of revenue recognition

Definition   Timing of revenue recognition refers to the accounting period in which the revenue is reported. The most common problem is when to recognise revenue on a sale.

Traditionally, there are two conditions required before revenue is recognised and reported in the profit and loss account:

(a)   The revenue must be earned ie, the activities undertaken to create the revenue must be substantially completed.

(b)   The revenue must be realised ie, an event has occurred which significantly increases the likelihood of conversion into cash. Also, the revenue should be capable of being verifiably measured.

1.4   Earning of revenue

In reality, revenue is earned over a period of time. The traditional approach to the timing of revenue recognition may mean that revenue is reported in one period, even though it was substantially earned in an earlier period.

Furthermore, the earning of revenue is not a uniform process. Some activities of the business are more efficient than others. In addition, there is the problem of internal transfers (eg, stocks and materials) within an organisation.

1.5   Realisation of revenue

This is an important principle in accounting. In most practical cases, realisation is deemed to occur on the date of sale. This follows one definition of realisation, namely that an event has occurred (the sale transaction) which has made the conversion of an asset (stock) into cash highly probable.

The stock may have been turned into cash or into a highly liquid asset (trade debtor). Thus, the date of the sale transaction is the moment that the revenue is recognised in the financial statement.

A further definition of realisation is that a change in an asset or liability has become sufficiently definite and objective to warrant recognition in the accounts. The ASB's draft Statement of Principles (discussed in the next chapter) links the recognition of revenue with the recognition of assets and liabilities.

1.6   Criticisms of the principle of realisation

The following are some of the criticisms of the realisation principle:

(a)   Revenue is recognised in the period of sale rather than the period during which it is earned.

(b)   The realisation of revenue principle conflicts with the continuity of existence (or going concern) concept. Revenue-earning is a continuous process.

1.7   Bases of timing of revenue recognition

(a)   **Sales basis**

This is the simplest and most common approach. It can apply to a cash sale or to a credit sale. The following points can be claimed in favour of this method:

(i)   Physical delivery of the goods is an identifiable event.

(ii)   When the title passes, the risk of destruction of goods or a fall in market prices passes from the seller to the buyer.

(iii)   The revenue can be easily measured.

(iv)   The earning process is almost completed.

(v)   The revenue is realised, as the event results in cash (cash sale) or a claim to cash (credit sale).

(vi)   At this stage, the expenses of sale can be calculated and thus profit determined.

This method assumes that revenue is both earned and realised at the moment of sale. In reality, revenue is earned over a period of time rather than at one point in time, but the approach is easier in practice.

While the sale basis approach has clear practical advantages, it may be criticised on the grounds that revenue may possibly be allocated to the wrong accounting period (ie, by reference to the date it was realised rather than the period over which it was earned).

(b)   **Cash collection basis**

This is generally only acceptable in the case of cash sales (in effect already considered above under sales basis) where the receipt of cash is accompanied by delivery of goods or performance of the service.

The two other possibilities are:

(i)   Cash received after the date of sale - this is unacceptable since it does not comply with the accruals basis of accounting.

(ii)   Cash received before the date of sale - revenue would not usually be recognised until the date of sale.

It should be emphasised that the cash collection basis only refers to when revenue is recognised. The matching principle is still applied - in other words when the revenue is recognised it is matched with the expenses of earning that revenue.

(c)   **Production basis - while production is in progress**

Revenue is recognised in accordance with production.

If production is interpreted to include services as well as goods, then this basis could be important in the following situations:

(i)   Service revenues such as interest and rent - revenues are apportioned or prorated over the period to which the revenue relates, often on a time apportionment basis. Frequently, there is some form of agreement or contract specifying terms. Performance of a service thus gives the company a claim on the customer. Revenue can thus be said to be both earned and realised.

(ii)   Long-term contracts - the production for the contract may extend over several accounting periods. It might be argued that revenue should be recognised on the placing of the order. This would entail estimating future costs in order that they could be matched with revenue. Prudent accounting would consider that there were too many uncertainties. Accordingly, current practice does not take account of any profit until the contract is sufficiently advanced to indicate profitability.

The alternative procedure of recognising no profit until the contract was complete could lead to distortion of results as between particular accounting periods.

(d)   **Order basis**

Assume that no cash is received with the order. The receipt of an order is not normally regarded as an event which justifies the recognition of revenue and subsequent matching of anticipated expenditure. An important reason is that orders may be cancelled with no subsequent claim on the cancelling company. There may be an economic justification in permitting orders to affect business profits, in that an order may change the value of a firm, provided there is a very high likelihood of an order being converted into a sale. However, while the state of the order book is clearly important to a business at a point in time, conventional accounting practice does not permit orders to affect business profits for an accounting period.

1.8   Definition of expenses

Definition   Expenses may be defined as the flow of resources or service potentials consumed during production. Service potential may be defined as the potential future output of goods or services from an asset.

Two essential features of assets are:

(a)   the existence of service potential and
(b)   the right to receive those benefits or service potentials.

For example, a lease on a building would satisfy conditions (a) and (b) and thus be classed as an asset.

Amortisation of a lease is an attempt to measure the extent of service potential consumed.

1.9   Measurement of expenses

Expenses are measured as the value of resources or service potentials consumed. This measurement may be by reference to either of the following

(a)   **Expenses measured by reference to original cost**

The advantage is objectivity. The extent to which expense measurement may be influenced by subjective opinions is kept to a minimum. The difficulty is that there is a considerable degree of expenditure which confers benefits which will extend over more than one accounting period. Thus, even if the amount of the original expenditure is a verifiable objective fact, subjective opinion may be necessary to allocate this expenditure over the various accounting periods. A major disadvantage of the historical cost approach to cost measurement is that such expenses may bear little relation to current expenses. Historical expenses are thus matched against current revenues.

(b)   **Expenses measured by reference to current cost or value**

This approach attempts to compare like with like by matching current expenses against current revenues. Although the expense is not computed by reference to a verifiable historical transaction, it has the advantage, in theory, of arriving at a meaningful profit figure. This area is considered later in the text.

1.10   Timing of expense recognition

The purpose of profit measurement is to give an indication of the efficiency with which the resources of the business have been utilised during the period. This can only be achieved if related revenues and expenses are matched together. Basically, expense recognition is a function of revenue recognition, since it is the expenditure which gives rise to the revenue. Once it has been decided when to recognise the revenues, the cost and expense of earning that revenue is determined and matched with the revenue. The concept is easy to apply to expenses which bear some relationship to revenue, but clearly many expenses bear little or no relationship to revenue and are thus allocated to accounting periods on an arbitrary basis.

An example of an expense which bears a strong relationship to revenue is the cost of goods sold.

1.11   Types of costs and expenses

(a)   Direct product costs

These include costs such as materials and direct labour. All these costs can be linked to particular goods.

These costs or expenses are recognised when the revenue from the related product is realised. In other words, the first step is to determine the timing of revenue recognition. The direct costs can then be linked to this revenue.

(b)   Direct non-product costs or indirect expenses

These can be linked to production in general but not to particular units of output.

They include items such as salesmen's commission, promotion expenses and warranty expenses. Indirect expenses should be matched against the revenues of the accounting periods which benefit from these expenses.

(c)   Periodic costs or expenses

These include items such as rent, insurances and rates. They are allocated to the profit and loss account on a time basis ie, as the expenses are incurred.

1.12   Other costs and expenses

Items such as capital expenditure, taxation and research and development expenditure present particular problems.

They are costs, which may need to be allocated to revenue in several accounting periods. Also, on the grounds of prudence some of these costs may need to be written off in the year of expenditure rather than carried to be matched with potential revenue.

1.13   The audit implications

The auditor's prime concern will be that revenue and expenses are recognised in the correct accounting period. To the extent that they are not so recognised, there may be a material misstatement in reported profit. The correct allocation of income and expenses will be tested in many areas with the main test being that cut off procedures have been correctly applied. The physical verification of stock for example will involve checking cut off for stock, and hence cost of sales, purchases and sales.

Special types of purchases and sales will need to be considered by reference to accounting principles. Examples include:

(a)   goods sold subject to 'reservation of title'

(b)   sale or return

(c)   sales made via agents with the agents holding supplies (and hence stock) for onward sale to customers.

The principles of FRS 5 *Reporting the substance of transactions* will be important in this regard (see later).

1.14   Activity

(a)   What do you understand by the term 'revenue recognition'?

(b)   Briefly outline a suitable policy on revenue recognition for each of the following

     (i)   magazine subscriptions received by a publisher
     (ii)   the sale of cars on credit terms
     (iii)   work-in-progress on a long term contract.

1.15   Activity solution

(a)   Revenue recognition is concerned with the point in time at which income should be included in the profit and loss account.

There are two general principles in recognising revenue.

     (i)   The revenue must be earned - services have been undertaken or goods provided.

     (ii)   The revenue must be realised - realisation occurs when cash has been received or when the likelihood of a cash receipt is a probable expectation.

Revenue may be earned over a period of time. For example, whisky may take some years to produce. As the earning of revenue will often precede the realisation of revenue, the realisation principle normally determines when revenue is recognised.

However, in some cases a customer may pay in advance of the goods/services being provided and thus the income should not be recognised until the revenue has been earned.

(b)   (i)   Magazine subscriptions are normally paid in advance - typically for 12 months. The revenue is partially earned when each magazine is supplied. A proportion of the subscriptions should thus be deferred at the year end. What proportion will depend on the relative costs of producing each magazine and the possibly heavy initial advertising expenditure that was incurred at the start of the subscription period.

     (ii)   The sale of a car on credit terms gives rise to two different types of revenue - trading profit and finance income. If the credit agreement is such that the user of the car becomes immediately or eventually the legal owner, then the trading profit can be regarded as being earned at the date the agreement is signed. The finance income will be spread over the duration of the agreement.

          If the 'sale' is a lease whereby the user does not become the owner of the asset, it may be appropriate to spread the whole of the income over the lease period. There would, however, still be a strong argument for deeming the lease to comprise two types of profit.

     (iii)   Work on a long term contract may extend over several accounting periods. Thus revenue is earned over several periods as the services are being performed.

          Cash is often received in part payments over the life of the contract, thus reinforcing the need to recognise before the contract is finished.

          Accordingly some revenue should be recognised in each accounting period. However, the recognition of revenue then requires a matching of costs. SSAP 9 does not allow any revenue to be recognised which exceeds costs charged to the profit and loss account in the early stages of a contract, as it will not usually be clear that a profit will eventually be made.

2   THE RULES RELATING TO THE DISTRIBUTION OF PROFITS

2.1   Distributable profit

It is a basic principle of company law that a company with limited liability may not return capital to members except by the proper and strictly regulated procedure of reduction of capital or a liquidation. The principle is designed to safeguard the rights of creditors to be paid what is owing to them before capital is returned to members.

The principle underlies many specific rules such as the treatment of share premiums as a capital reserve, the rule that the redemption of redeemable shares is possible only out of the proceeds of a fresh issue of new shares or from distributable profits and the restrictions imposed on the purchase by a company of its own shares (these matters are dealt with later in the chapter).

Apart from the legal rules imposed on companies by the CA85 there are a number of practical constraints on dividend policy.

(a)   If the company becomes insolvent and goes into liquidation, the directors and others may be liable for defrauding creditors.

(b)   Dividends require cash. There are practical limits on what can be borrowed to finance dividend payments. The accounts will, after the event at least, reveal the depletion of liquid assets.

(c)   The articles of association may restrict payment of dividends eg, by limiting distributions to trading profit (thereby excluding profits arising from sale of fixed assets).

(d)   The commercial standing and credit rating of a company depend to some extent on financial prudence and some retention of profits for expansion.

It follows from the principle of conservation of subscribed capital that dividends may only be paid out of profits. The principle cannot, of course, safeguard the company from a loss of capital by unprofitable trading or unwise investment.

2.2   Profits available for dividend: rules for all companies

All companies, including private companies, are prohibited from paying dividends (making a distribution) except out of profits available for that purpose.

Profits available for dividend are:

Definition   Accumulated, realised profits, so far as not previously utilised (whether by distribution or capitalisation), less the accumulated, realised losses, so far as not previously written off: S263 (3) CA85.

This definition permits the distribution as dividend of a capital profit ie, a surplus over book value realised on sale of a fixed asset. But the key words are:

(a)   Accumulated - which means that the balance of profit or loss from previous years must be brought into account in the current period, and

(b)   Realised - which prohibits the inclusion of unrealised profits arising from eg, the revaluation of fixed assets retained by the company.

There are the following detailed rules in CA85.

(a)   A provision made in the accounts is a realised loss.

(b)   A revaluation surplus is an unrealised profit.

(c)   If fixed assets are revalued and as a result more has to be provided for depreciation than would have been necessary if the original value had been retained, the additional depreciation may be treated as part of the realised profit for dividend purposes. This effectively means the depreciation based on the revaluation surplus can be added back notionally to the profit and loss account for the determination of realised profits. This adjustment can be put through the accounts as a transfer between reserves.

(d)   On the disposal of a revalued asset any unrealised surplus or loss on valuation immediately becomes realised.

(e)   If there is no available record of the original cost of an asset, its cost may be taken as the value put on it in the earliest available record.

(f)   If it is impossible to establish whether a profit or a loss brought forward was realised or unrealised, any such profit may be treated as realised and any such loss as unrealised.

2.3   Activity

A Ltd purchased freehold land and buildings on 30 June 19X4 for £200,000 (land £60,000, buildings £140,000). The net book value of the buildings at 31 December 19X7 is £121,386. On 1 January 19X8 the land was revalued to £75,000 and the buildings to £135,000. Depreciation on buildings is computed at 4% reducing balance. Accounts are prepared on a calendar year basis.

Show the revaluation reserve for the year to 31 December 19X8.

2.4   Activity solution

The entries to the revaluation reserve should be

	£
Re land	15,000
Re buildings £(135,000 − 121,386)	13,614
	£28,614

The depreciation charge for the year ended 31 December 19X8 = 4% × £135,000 = £5,400. This amount is the charge to P&L account (FRS 15) although CA85 requires only the HC depreciation (4% × £121,386 = £4,855).

However, to show the realised part of the revaluation reserve a transfer from the reserve to distributable reserves may be made.

Revaluation reserve

	£
Balance at 1 January 19X8	28,614
Transfer to distributable reserves	
£(5,400 − 4,855)	545
Balance at 31 December 19X8	£28,069

2.5   Revaluation deficits

Company legislation has enshrined in law the principles of distributable profits and losses decided in a series of court cases in the late nineteenth and early twentieth centuries. These principles were, in part, based on sound accounting concepts. However, in the treatment of provisions for losses on assets, the judgements of the courts were very difficult to reconcile with any accounting principles.

The CA85 stipulates the following

(a)   A provision made in the accounts is a realised loss. A revaluation deficit is a provision for a loss in value and is therefore a realised loss.

(b)   If a revaluation deficit arises on a revaluation of all fixed assets (or on a revaluation of all fixed assets except for goodwill) the revaluation deficit is an unrealised loss.

   Consequently, where a company undertakes a partial revaluation of fixed assets, a deficit on one asset is a realised loss and cannot therefore be offset against a surplus on another asset (an unrealised profit) for the purposes of arriving at distributable profits. This is despite the fact that all surpluses and deficits can be accounted for in the revaluation reserve.

(c)   A partial remedy to this problem is contained in the CA85. Deficits arising on an asset where there has been a partial revaluation of the assets are to be treated as unrealised losses provided that

   (i)   the directors have 'considered' the aggregate value of the fixed assets which have not been revalued at the date of the partial revaluation, and

   (ii)   the directors are satisfied that the aggregate value is not less than their aggregate book value, and

   (iii)   a note to the accounts states the above two facts.

2.6   Example

X Ltd has the following balance sheet

	£'000
Net assets	
Share capital	100
Share premium	50
Revaluation reserve	70
Profit and loss account	80

Two of the company's assets were revalued during the year, one giving rise to a surplus of £100,000, the other a deficit of £30,000.

The profits available for dividend are

	£'000
Net realised profits - profit and loss account	80
Less: Realised losses - revaluation deficit	30
	50

If all the company's assets had been revalued or the directors had 'considered' the value of the assets not revalued, the revaluation deficit would be unrealised and therefore the profits available for distribution would be £80,000.

2.7   Revaluation surpluses

Revaluation surpluses are unrealised profits in the accounting period in which the revaluation takes place. The only exception to this rule is where the same asset was

(a)   previously revalued giving rise to a deficit, and

(b)   the deficit was treated as a realised loss. In such a case, the revaluation surplus will be a realised profit to the extent that it makes good the realised loss. It should be noted that company law does not specify this but best accounting practice would require this treatment.

It should also be remembered that revaluation surpluses can eventually become realised profits when the asset is either depreciated or sold.

2.8   Development expenditure

The CA85 has special rules for development costs if they are not written off in the year in which the expenditure is incurred but carried forward as intangible assets. Whilst the legislation allows such intangible expenditure to be carried forward, on the grounds of prudence S269 CA85 states that development costs shown as an asset in the accounts are to be treated as a realised loss.

Therefore, they must be deducted from the accounting profits.

However, the legislation allows an exception to this, if

(a)   there are special circumstances justifying the directors in deciding that the amount is not to be treated as a realised loss and

(b)   the note to the accounts required by paragraph 20 Schedule 4 (reasons for showing development costs as an asset) states that the amount is not to be so treated and explains the circumstances relied upon to justify the decision of the directors to that effect.

The special circumstances are satisfied if the expenditure is carried forward under the provisions of SSAP 13.

In conclusion, the only practical effect of this provision is to require a statement in the notes to the accounts. It should also be noted that if the expenditure is not treated as a realised loss in the year of expenditure it will be a realised loss when written off in future years.

2.9   Profits available for dividend: additional rules for public companies

In addition to the rules set out above, a public company may not pay a dividend unless its net assets are at least equal to the aggregate amount of its called-up share capital and undistributable reserves. It may not pay a dividend so as to reduce its net assets below that aggregate amount: S264 CA85. It must maintain its called-up share capital and undistributable reserves.

Definition   Undistributable reserves are

(a)   Share premium account

(b)   Capital redemption reserve

(c)   Unrealised profits (less unrealised losses unless previously written off)

(d)   Any other reserve which the company is prohibited from distributing by any statute or by its memorandum or articles of association.

The effect of this provision is that any excess of unrealised losses over unrealised profits must be deducted from realised profits in arriving at the amount available for distribution.

Example

		£'000
eg,	Share capital	100
	Unrealised profits	60
	Unrealised losses	(80)
	Realised profits	35
		115
	Net assets	115

Net assets must not be reduced below

Share capital	100
Undistributable reserves	-
	100

ie, maximum distribution is £15,000 being

Realised profits	35
Less: Excess of unrealised losses over unrealised profits	(20)
	15

For a private company the maximum distribution would be £35,000.

2.10   Distributable profit of investment companies

There are special rules for certain types of investment companies, due to the restrictions they are required to place upon themselves as to the distribution of profits.

For the purposes of the special distribution rules an investment company is a public company which has complied with the following requirements:

(a)   that the business of the company consists of investing its funds mainly in securities, with the aim of spreading investment risk and giving members of the company the benefits of the results of the management of its funds

(b)   that none of the company's holdings in companies (other than those which are for the time being in investment companies) represents more than 15% by value of the investing company's investments

(c)   that distribution of the company's capital profits is prohibited by its memorandum or articles of association

(d)   that the company has not retained in any accounting reference period more than 15% of the income it derives from securities.

The key part of the requirements is point (c): an investment company is precluded from distributing all capital profits (including realised). Thus, if the company had to maintain capital in the same way as any other public company, this would result in a deficit on revaluation of the investments (an unrealised loss) reducing the profit available for distribution, without the benefit of capital profits being taken into account.

Investment companies may make a distribution on the basis of the capital maintenance test for public companies (excluding capital profits) or on the basis of an asset ratio test.

Under the asset ratio test distribution can be made up to the total of

Accumulated realised revenue profits
Less: Accumulated revenue losses (whether realised or not)
    provided that after the distribution
Total assets exceed 150% of liabilities.

Example

The balance sheets of two investment companies are as follows

	A plc £	B plc £
Share capital	100	100
Unrealised capital profits	100	
Unrealised capital losses		(70)
Unrealised revenue profits		30
Unrealised revenue losses	(50)	
Realised capital profits	100	
Realised capital losses		(120)
Realised revenue profits	200	250
	450	190
Assets	800	400
Liabilities	(350)	(210)
	450	190

Capital maintenance test		
'Private company' rules		
Net realised profits (not capital profits)		
(250 – 120)	200	130
'Public company' rules		
Less: Unrealised losses	50	40 (70 – 30)
	150	90

Asset ratio test		
A plc £(200 – 50)	150	

(Assets would fall to £650 which is more than
one-and-a-half times liabilities, so distributable
profit is £150.)

B plc		250

(Assets would fall to £150 which is less than
one-and-a-half times liabilities. One-and-a-
half times liabilities is £315, thus assets may
only fall by £85 so distributable profit is £85
on this basis. Thus B plc will not opt for the
asset ratio test. It can make the distribution on
the capital maintenance test of £90.

2.11   Relevant accounts: S270 CA85

The basis of calculation of what is available for dividend is the relevant accounts.

(a)   Usually the relevant accounts are the latest audited annual accounts laid before the company in general meeting as required by S270 CA85.

When the annual accounts are the basis of calculation the rules are

(i)   The accounts must have been properly prepared and also audited

(ii)   The report of the auditors must either be unqualified or, if qualified, accompanied by a statement by the auditors as to whether in their opinion the subject of their qualification is material to the determination of distributable profits. In this context an unqualified report is one which states without qualification that the accounts have been properly prepared.

(b)   If figures, derived from the latest annual accounts would preclude the payment of a dividend, interim accounts may be used but they must be such as are necessary to enable a reasonable judgement to be made.

(c)   If the company has not yet produced its first annual accounts, interim accounts (as described in (b) above) may be used.

When annual accounts are used under (a) or interim accounts are used under (b) or (c) above, they must be properly prepared ie, they must comply with the various rules on statutory accounts and they must give a true and fair view. It is not necessary, however, that they should deal with matters which are not material to the dividend rules. In case (c) the auditors must report whether in their opinion the accounts have been properly prepared.

2.12   Pre-incorporation profits

Pre-incorporation profits are profits made by a company before it is legally incorporated. This may arise because the shareholders/directors who form the company are slow in sorting out the necessary paperwork and commence trading prior to incorporation.

In such a situation any profits made by the company are not distributable as legally the company did not exist. Profits however have been made and are due to the shareholders. They are thus put to a capital reserve ie, they increase the capital worth of the shareholders' investment.

For example, a company starts trading on the 1 January, is incorporated on 31 March and computes profits in the first year to 31 December as £60,000.

If we assume profits accrue evenly over the period, £15,000 is transferred from profit and loss account to capital reserve. £45,000 remains as distributable.

2.13   Activity

Scraper Ltd - balance sheet as at 30 November 19X3

	Cost/valuation £	Dep'n £	NBV £	£
Fixed assets				
Freehold properties	194,400	14,400	180,000	
Vehicles	300,000	60,000	240,000	
Fixtures and fittings	28,000	12,000	16,000	
				436,000
Current assets				
Stock		395,000		
Debtors		176,000		
Cash		232,000		
			803,000	
Creditors - amounts due less than 1 year				
Trade creditors		112,000		
HP creditors		89,100		
Bank overdraft		17,043		
			218,143	
Net current assets				584,857
Total assets less current liabilities				1,020,857

Creditors - amounts due more than 1 year		
10% debentures (convertible 19X6)	100,000	
Other creditors including tax	174,857	
		274,857
Net assets		746,000
Capital and reserves		
Share capital		400,000
Share premium account		50,000
Capital redemption reserve		100,000
Revaluation deficit		(130,000)
General reserve		70,000
Profit and loss account		256,000
		746,000

Note: the revaluation deficit results from a reappraisal on 30 November 19X3 of the fixed asset register of fixtures and fittings within one of the London properties. One of the properties was revalued from £30,000 to £124,400 on 1 December 19X2. There was no general programme of revaluation. The gain on the freehold has been netted off against the loss on revaluation of fixtures.

Depreciation on the freehold properties was £3,888 pa calculated at 2% of valuation cost.

The directors consider that the value of the assets not revalued is at least equal to their book value.

Calculate the distributable profits for Scraper Ltd as at 30 November 19X3

(a)   on the basis that Scraper Ltd is a private company and
(b)   on the basis that Scraper Ltd is a public company.

2.14   Activity solution

(a)   Distributable profits calculated on basis that Scraper Ltd is a private company.

	£	£
Profit and loss account		256,000
Add: Depreciation on revalued amount of:		
Freehold 2% of £194,400 =	3,888	
2% of cost £100,000 =	2,000	
		1,888
		257,888
General reserve		70,000
Available for distribution		327,888

(*Tutorial note:*

The revaluation deficit is an unrealised loss as although there was only a partial revaluation, the directors have 'considered' the value of all the assets.)

(b)   If Scraper was a public company

	£	£
'Private' company rules		327,888
Less excess unrealised losses over unrealised profits		
Revaluation deficit (130,000 + 94,400)	224,400	
Revaluation surplus (94,400 – 1,888)	92,512	
		131,888
Distributable profit		196,000

(*Tutorial note:*

The alternative calculation compares net assets to share capital and undistributable reserves and can be used as a check.

	£	£
Net assets before dividend		746,000
Share capital	400,000	
Share premium	50,000	
CRR	100,000	
		550,000
		196,000

)

3   THE ISSUE AND REORGANISATION OF CAPITAL

3.1   Introduction

In order to account properly for changes in the capital of a company or for the reorganisation of the existing capital, two areas need to be understood.

(a)   the relevant areas of company law

(b)   the commercial considerations which have brought about the need for change.

If this background is known, then the debits and credits are understandable.   Do not learn the provisions at this stage but refer back to this section when studying the examples in section 4.

3.2   Company law - capital changes

(a)   **Authorised, issued and called up capital**

The distinction between these terms is as follows

(i)   Authorised share capital is the amount of share capital which a company is authorised to issue eg, £100 divided into 100 shares of £1 each.

(ii)   Issued share capital is the nominal amount of the share capital actually issued at any time eg, £100 authorised capital of which 50 £1 shares have been issued.

(iii)   Called up share capital is the aggregate amount of the calls made on its shares (whether or not those calls have been paid), together with any share capital paid up without being called and any share capital to be paid on a specified future date under the terms of allotment.

The original authorised capital of a company is stated in its memorandum and articles of association.   Subsequently, the company may wish to increase or to reduce its authorised and/or issued capital.

(b)   **Increase of capital**

This expression covers two situations

(i)   Increase of the issued share capital up to the authorised amount. In the illustration above the issued share capital could be increased by allotting and issuing the available 50 unissued £1 shares. This is a simple operation which the company itself effects by the appropriate procedure.

(ii)   Increase of the authorised share capital which may be accompanied by an increase in the issued share capital. A company may increase its authorised share capital if so authorised by its articles.

The expression 'increase of share capital' usually denotes an increase of authorised share capital.

(c)   **Reduction of capital**

The company may cancel unissued shares in the same way (see above) as it can increase its unissued shares. But if it wishes to reduce its issued share capital, there are various means available.

- Capital reduction scheme: S135 CA85

- Power of a company to issue redeemable shares: Ss159 & 160 CA85

- Purchase by a company of its own shares: S162 CA85

- Redemption or purchase out of capital: S171 CA85.

Capital reduction schemes are not examinable at this level. The statutory provisions for the other three means of reducing capital are covered below.

3.3   How shares may be redeemed

Prior to the CA81 a limited company could issue and later redeem redeemable preference shares. The CA81 gave greater flexibility, as redeemable shares need no longer be preference shares.

The restrictions on the issue and redemption of redeemable shares are

(a)   the issue of redeemable shares must be authorised by the company's articles

(b)   redeemable shares can only be issued when there are other issued shares which are not redeemable

(c)   shares cannot be redeemed unless they are fully paid, and redemption may be made only out of profits otherwise available

(d)   these available profits are the accumulated appropriated profits; however redemption may also be paid for from the proceeds of a fresh issue of shares made for the purposes of the redemption, or a combination of both methods.

Where shares are redeemed wholly or partly out of profits available for appropriation, an amount equal to the excess of the nominal value of the shares redeemed over the proceeds of any fresh issue of shares must be transferred to a **capital redemption reserve.** This reserve may only be used to make a bonus issue of shares.

The capital redemption reserve does not have to replace any premium payable on redemption. Except as detailed below, any premium on redemption must be provided out of distributable profits.

Where the shares to be redeemed were issued at a premium and a fresh issue of shares is made for the purposes of the redemption, any premium payable on redemption may be charged against the share premium account. The premium so charged cannot exceed the lower of

(a)   the premium received on the issue of the shares now being redeemed, or

(b)   the current balance of the share premium account, including any premium on the new share issue, or

(c)   the proceeds of the fresh issue.

The premium on any redeemable preference shares issued before S160 CA85 came into effect may be charged against share premium account up to the balance on that account.

3.4   The power of companies to purchase their own shares

Any limited company may, if authorised to do so by its articles, purchase its own shares (including redeemable shares), subject to the same conditions as apply to the redemption of redeemable shares, except that the terms and manner of purchase need not be determined by the articles.

The procedure prescribed for the purchase of shares varies according to whether or not the purchase takes place through a recognised stock exchange.

(a)   **An off-market purchase**

An off-market purchase must be in pursuance of an interim contract of purchase, approved in advance by a special resolution of the company. The contract, or a memorandum thereof, must have been available for inspection by members for 15 days before the meeting and at the meeting at which it is approved.

(b)   **Market purchase**

A company cannot purchase its shares on a recognised stock exchange unless the purchase has been authorised by an ordinary resolution of the company. Such resolutions must specify the maximum number of shares that may be purchased, the maximum and minimum prices to be paid and the date the authority expires.

For both types of purchase there are detailed requirements for notice to the registrar and disclosure in the directors' report.

The main advantage to a company of being able to purchase its shares is that it provides a means of using surplus capital and enabling the remaining shareholders to acquire a larger percentage interest in the company. This could be particularly useful to private companies with a small number of shareholders where one of them dies, retires or leaves the service of the company. The other shareholders may be unable or unwilling to purchase his shares themselves, but can arrange for the company to do so.

3.5   Redemption or purchase out of capital

In addition to the above choices a private company may, if authorised by its articles, redeem or purchase its shares out of capital. However, this is only to the extent that the purchase or redemption price exceeds available distributable profits and the proceeds of a new share issue.

The Act refers to the permissible capital payment (PCP). This is the amount by which the purchase or redemption cost exceeds the amount of distributable profits plus the proceeds of any new share issue.

The difference between the PCP and the nominal value of the shares redeemed is dealt with as follows

(a)   if the total of PCP plus proceeds of share issue is less than the nominal value of the shares redeemed, the difference is transferred to capital redemption reserve

(b)   if the total of PCP plus proceeds of share issue is more than the nominal value of the shares redeemed, the excess may be used to reduce any of the following

    (A)   capital redemption reserve
    (B)   share premium account
    (C)   fully paid share capital
    (D)   revaluation reserve.

There are in addition elaborate safeguards both for members and for creditors

(a)   the purchase or redemption must be authorised by special resolution (with voting restrictions on intending vendors)

(b)   directors must make a statutory declaration specifying the amount of the payments and stating that in their opinion the company could pay all existing debts, after the capital payment, and will be able to pay its debts throughout the ensuing year.

(c)   the directors' declaration must be supported by the auditor stating that he has enquired into the company's affairs and considered that the amount specified in the declaration conforms to the requirements and that the opinion expressed by the directors is not unreasonable

(d)   the special resolution authorising payment must be passed within a week of the directors' statutory declaration, and the payment itself should be made not earlier than five nor later than seven weeks after the date of the resolution

(e)   details of the transaction must be published in the London Gazette and a national newspaper and a copy of the directors' statutory declaration, with the auditors' report attached, must be delivered to the Registrar of Companies

(f)   a member of the company or creditor has five weeks from the date of the resolution to apply to the court to set aside the resolution

(g)   if the company is wound up within one year of making the payment and is unable to pay its debts the payment may be recovered earlier from the person who sold or redeemed the shares or the directors signing the statutory declaration.

3.6   Reorganisation of the capital structure - commercial considerations

Companies undertake restructuring to improve both their mix of different types of capital and the timing of availability of funds.

This can be done without altering the total capital requirement. The specific objects of reorganisation may be one or more of the following

(i)   to reduce the net of tax cost of borrowing
(ii)   to repay borrowing sooner or later
(iii)   to improve security of finance
(iv)   to make security in the company more attractive
(v)   to improve the image of the company to third parties
(vi)   to tidy up the balance sheet.

3.7   The advantages of redeemable shares

There are many reasons why companies may wish to issue redeemable shares, or to purchase their own shares:

(a)   Reduction in share capital increases earnings per share and return on capital employed. This makes the company more attractive to potential lenders and investors.

(b)   Shares may be redeemed in order to buy out dissident shareholders.

(c)   Redeemable shares may be attractive to potential private company shareholders as they provide an opportunity to invest in a company without being committed to that investment in the long term. (There is normally a very limited market for private company shares.)

(d)   It enables companies to reduce total dividend payments while maintaining or increasing the level of dividend to individual shareholders. This means that more earnings are available for capital investment which leads to growth.

(e)   Many companies now operate employee share schemes. Redeemable shares may be bought back when employees leave the company.

(f)   Shares may be redeemed at a discount where the market price is low.

(g)   Redemption or purchase of own shares may be used to take the company out of the public market and back into private ownership.

(h)   Redemption or purchase of own shares provides an efficient means of returning surplus cash to the shareholders.

4   RECORDING THE TRANSACTIONS INVOLVING THE REDEMPTION/PURCHASE OF SHARES

The previous section has summarised the legal provisions for reorganising capital. Examples of the accounting implications are shown in this section.

4.1   Approach

The legal provisions in this area are complex but the accounting entries are more straightforward providing the redemption/purchase is tackled in a logical way. In summary the steps are as follows.

Step 1   If a private limited company, decide whether the redemption is out of profits or capital.

Step 2   If out of profits, account for the cash inflow from any issue of shares made to finance the redemption first.

This is necessary as the balance in share premium needs to be established before the redemption takes place.

Step 3   Account for the cash outflow for the redemption and the transfer of the nominal value of the shares redeemed through a redemption account.

Step 4   Decide whether any of the balance in the redemption account (the balance will represent the premium on redemption) can be charged against share premium.

Step 5   Calculate the required transfer to CRR.

4.2 Example

The summarised balance sheet of A plc is

	A plc
	£
Net assets	100,000
Ordinary shares of £1	20,000
Share premium	10,000
Revaluation reserve	15,000
Profit and loss account	55,000
	100,000

A plc purchases 5,000 of its shares on the stock market for £30,000 as it does not have suitable opportunities for investment of surplus funds and it regards its share price as being relatively low at the present time.

The shares were originally issued at a premium of 50p per share.

4.3 Solution

Steps 1 and 2 are not applicable (the company is a plc and there is no fresh issue).

Step 3		£
	Redemption price	30,000
	NV of shares redeemed	5,000
	Premium on redemption	25,000

Step 4 As no fresh issue, premium must go to profit and loss account.

Step 5	Transfer to CRR	£
	NV of shares redeemed	5,000
	Less: Proceeds of fresh issue of shares	Nil
		5,000

WORKING

Profit and loss account

	£
Original balance	55,000
Less: Premium on redemption	(25,000)
To CRR	(5,000)
	25,000

*(**Tutorial note:** the premium on redemption must come from distributable profits as there is no fresh issue of shares.)*

4.4 Reasons for provisions

The reason for these legal provisions is to protect the rights of creditors. Capital can be returned to shareholders provided that the fund of assets available to pay creditors (the creditors' buffer) is not reduced as a result of the redemption/purchase of shares.

Proof

	Before purchase of shares £	After purchase of shares £
Net assets	100,000	70,000
Less: Reduction of assets if maximum dividend paid to shareholders (balance on profit and loss account)	55,000	25,000
Creditors' buffer	45,000	45,000

Despite the return of capital the creditors' buffer remains the same amount because the legal provisions reduce the amount of distributable profits.

4.5   Example where shares originally issued at a premium

A plc redeems 25% of its ordinary shares for £30,000. It finances the redemption by issuing £30,000 10% Preference shares.

The shares were originally issued at a premium of 50p per share.

The balance sheet becomes

	£
Net assets £(100 + 30 − 30)	100,000
Ordinary shares £(20 − 5)	15,000
Preference shares	30,000
Share premium	7,500 (W2)
Revaluation reserve	15,000
Profit and loss account	32,500 (W3)
	100,000

WORKINGS

(W1)   Transfer to CRR

	£	£
NV of shares redeemed		5,000
Less: Proceeds of fresh issue of shares		30,000
∴ No transfer to CRR		

(W2)   Share premium account

	£	£
Original balance		10,000
Less: Lowest of		
Proceeds of fresh issue	30,000	
Original premium on shares now being redeemed 5,000 × 50p	2,500	
Current balance on share premium account	10,000	
		(2,500)
		7,500

Tutorial note: the premium offset against share premium is effectively the lowest of three figures

(a)   the proceeds of the fresh issue of shares

(b)   the original premium on issue

(c)   the balance on share premium ie, a negative balance on share premium account is not allowed.

(W3)   **Profit and loss account**

	£
Original balance	55,000
Less: Premium on redemption to the extent not set off against share premium £(25,000 – 2,500)	(22,500)
	32,500

As fresh capital of £30,000 has replaced old capital of £30,000 the creditors' buffer should be maintained without any transfers to CRR.

In this case the creditors' buffer actually increases as most of the premium on redemption reduces distributable profits even though new capital has come in to replace the old.

4.6   Redemption out of capital

Only private companies may redeem shares out of capital and even then the redemption will be firstly out of distributable profits and a fresh issue of shares. Therefore the first step is to consider whether a payment has or has not been made out of capital.

Example

Wessex Ltd issued 20,000 £1 ordinary shares and 6,000 £1 redeemable A ordinary shares several years ago at par. The A ordinary shares are now to be redeemed at a total cost of £7,000. Distributable reserves amount to £5,400. There is to be no new share issue.

Step 1   Is the payment out of capital?

	£
Total redemption cost	7,000
Distributable profits	5,400
PCP	1,600

As the redemption cost is greater than the available distributable profits, the redemption is partly out of capital.

The journal entries are

		Dr £	Cr £
(1)	A ordinary share capital	6,000	
	Distributable profits	1,000	
	Bank		7,000

Being redemption of A ordinary shares at a premium totalling £1,000.

		Dr £	Cr £
(2)	Distributable profits	4,400	
	Capital redemption reserve		4,400

Being transfer to capital redemption reserve of excess of nominal value of shares over permissible capital payment.

Share capital and non-distributable reserves consist of

	Before redemption £	After redemption £
Ordinary shares	20,000	20,000
A ordinary shares	6,000	
Capital redemption reserve		4,400
	26,000	24,400

The £1,600 reduction is the amount of the PCP.

Journal entry 2 can alternatively be calculated by reference to the PCP. The company law provisions (dealt with earlier) state that if the total of the PCP plus proceeds of a share issue is less than the nominal value of the shares redeemed, the difference is transferred to capital redemption reserve ie,

	£
Nominal value of shares redeemed	6,000
PCP	1,600
CRR	4,400

The main point to grasp with the payment out of capital provisions is that although a payment out of capital is allowed, the redemption must, to the extent that they are available, come out of the proceeds of a fresh issue of shares made to finance the redemption and distributable profits.

5   CHAPTER SUMMARY

Revenue recognition is the starting point for determining the profits which may legally be distributed as dividends as the law assumes 'normal' accounting conventions have been applied.

Distributable profits are maximised for private companies with public companies facing further restrictions. Certain types of investment companies have relieving provisions from the normal plc rules.

A company may redeem or purchase its shares. It must protect the right of creditors to maintained capital by creating a non-distributable reserve (the CRR) if there has been insufficient proceeds from new capital.

6   SELF TEST QUESTIONS

6.1   How is revenue measured for a credit sale? (1.2)

6.2   What are the bases of timing of revenue recognition? (1.7)

6.3   What is a definition of expenses? (1.8)

6.4   What are the profits available for a dividend for a limited company? (2.2)

6.5   Is a provision a realised or unrealised loss? (2.2)

6.6   If a company revalues some of its assets and there is a deficit on one of the assets, how do the directors act so that it is not treated as a realised loss? (2.5)

6.7   What are the restrictions on issue and redemption of redeemable shares? (3.3)

6.8   What is a PCP? (3.5)

6.9   What is a creditors' buffer? (4.4)

7   EXAMINATION TYPE QUESTION

7.1   Purchase of own shares

(a)   Set out below are the summarised balance sheets of A plc and B Ltd at 30 June 19X5.

	A plc £'000	B Ltd £'000
Capital and reserves		
Called up share capital		
£1 ordinary shares	300	300
Share premium account	60	60
Profit and loss account	160	20
	520	380
Net assets	520	380

On 1 July 19X5 A plc and B Ltd each purchased 50,000 of their own ordinary shares as follows:

A plc purchased its own shares at 150p each. The shares were originally issued at a premium of 20p. The redemption was partly financed by the issue at par of 5,000 10% redeemable preference shares of £1 each.

B Ltd purchased its own shares out of capital at a price of 80p each.

You are required to prepare the summarised balance sheets of A plc and B Ltd at 1 July 19X5 immediately after the above transactions have been effected.   **(7 marks)**

(b)   What advantages are there in allowing companies to purchase their own ordinary shares?

(8 marks)

(Total: 15 marks)

8   ANSWER TO EXAMINATION TYPE QUESTION

8.1   Purchase of own shares

(a)

	A plc £'000	B Ltd £'000
Capital and reserves		
Ordinary shares	250	250
10% preference shares	5	-
Share premium account	55	60
Capital redemption reserve	45	30
Profit and loss account	95	-
	450	340
Net assets	450	340

(*Tutorial notes:*

B Ltd's fixed capital has fallen from £360,000 to £340,000. This represents a PCP of £20,000 which could have been calculated as:

	£
Purchase price	40,000
Less: Profit and loss account	(20,000)
Less: Proceeds of new issue	-
	20,000
	)

WORKINGS

A plc

	Dr £	Cr £
Dr Cash	5,000	
Cr 10% preference shares		5,000

Being the new issue of shares

	Dr	Cr
Dr Ordinary shares	50,000	
Dr Share premium account	5,000	
Dr Profit and loss account	20,000	
Cr Cash		75,000

Being the purchase of own shares - with the amount of premium on purchase charged to the share premium being restricted to the lowest of premium originally received on issue (50,000 × 20p = £10,000), balance on share premium account (£60,000), and proceeds of new issue (£5,000).

Dr Profit and loss account	45,000	
Cr Capital redemption reserve		45,000

Being the difference between the nominal value of the shares purchased (£50,000) and the proceeds of the new issue (£5,000) transferred to the capital redemption reserve so as to maintain the company's fixed capital.

B Ltd

	£	£
Dr Ordinary shares	50,000	
Cr Cash		40,000
Cr Profit and loss account		10,000

Being a profit on the purchase of own shares

Dr Profit and loss account	30,000	
Cr Capital redemption reserve		30,000

Being the nominal value of the shares purchased (£50,000) restricted to available profits (£20,000 + £10,000 = £30,000).

(b)   Advantages in allowing companies to purchase their own shares include

(i)   a shareholder in an unlisted company can find a buyer.

(ii)   shares issued under an employees' share scheme may be purchased when employees leave the company.

(iii)   it may increase the attraction of shares since a company may grant an option to sell back to the company.

(iv)   a use for surplus cash if it arises.

(v)   maintenance of control over a family company when a member dies and other members do not have the funds to purchase the shares.

7 REGULATORY FRAMEWORK

INTRODUCTION & LEARNING OBJECTIVES

This chapter looks in more detail at the work of the bodies involved in the standard setting process. We have already summarised their work in chapter 1.

Much of the detail of this chapter is however concerned with the ASB's Statement of Principles. You may find reading this heavy going at first. It is better for you not to spend a lot of time on the contents for now but to return to the chapter from time to time as various theoretical concepts are covered in later chapters.

When you have studied this chapter you should be able to do the following:

- Discuss the aims and operating process of the bodies involved in the standard setting process.
- Describe the role and features of the Statement of Principles.

1 THE BODIES INVOLVED IN THE STANDARD SETTING PROCESS

1.1 Introduction

The duties and functions of the various bodies involved in the standard setting process were summarised in chapter 1. In this section we consider their aims and the way in which they operate in more detail.

1.2 The ASB

In July 1991 the ASB issued a short statement of its aims.

(a) **Aims**

The aims of the Accounting Standards Board (ASB) are to establish and improve standards of financial accounting and reporting, for the benefit of users, preparers, and auditors of financial information.

(b) **Achieving the aims**

The ASB intends to achieve its aims by:

(i) developing principles to guide it in establishing standards and to provide a framework within which others can exercise judgement in resolving accounting issues;

(ii) issuing new accounting standards, or amending existing ones, in response to evolving business practices, new economic developments and deficiencies being identified in current practice;

(iii) addressing urgent issues promptly.

(c) **Operating process**

The ASB follows certain guidelines in conducting its affairs:

(i) To be objective and to ensure that the information resulting from the application of accounting standards faithfully represents the underlying commercial activity. Such information should be neutral in the sense that it is free from any form of bias intended to influence users in a particular direction and should not be designed to favour any group of users or preparers.

(ii) To ensure that accounting standards are clearly expressed and supported by a reasoned analysis of the issues.

(iii) To determine what should be incorporated in accounting standards based on research, public consultation and careful deliberation about the usefulness of the resulting information.

(iv) To ensure that, through a process of regular communication, accounting standards are produced with due regard to international developments.

(v) To ensure that there is consistency both from one accounting standard to another and between accounting standards and company law.

(vi) To issue accounting standards only when the expected benefits exceed the perceived costs. The ASB recognises that reliable cost/benefit calculations are seldom possible. However, it will always assess the need for standards in terms of the significance and extent of the problem being addressed and will choose the standard which appears to be most effective in cost/benefit terms.

(vii) To take account of the desire of the financial community for evolutionary rather than revolutionary change in the reporting process where this is consistent with the objectives outlined above.

1.3 The FRC

The Financial Reporting Council (FRC) guides the standard setting process and ensures that its work is properly funded. It is ultimately responsible for the enforcement of standards, and achieves the enforcement by the use of the Review Panel.

It is the 'political' front to the bodies involved in the standard setting process and produces an annual review which summarises recent events and likely action by the ASB, the Review Panel and the UITF.

In the annual review published in December 1993, Sir Ron Dearing stated: "One of the most significant developments over the past three years is that financial accounting is now not seen as just the province of the finance director but rather as something that concerns all members of company boards."

A particular task to be continued in the future is the informal co-ordination of the timing of issue of new financial reporting proposals and requirements by various bodies. Those involved in the work are the Accounting Standards Board, the Auditing Practices Board, the various professional accounting bodies and the Hundred Group of Finance Directors.

1.4 The FRRP

In 1992 the Financial Reporting Review Panel (FRRP) started to issue statements about the accounts of individual companies. Its aim is to ensure that all accounts comply with relevant accounting standards and *Companies Acts* requirements.

For serious breaches the Review Panel has power to require companies to redraft the offending accounts. For minor faults it is more likely to ask the companies for an assurance that the rules will be complied with in the future.

Examples of public reports include:

(a)   **Trafalgar House plc**

In 1991 this company transferred a number of commercial properties from current assets to tangible fixed assets. If the properties had remained in current assets, they would have been valued at the lower of cost and net realisable value and this would have reduced pre-tax profits for the accounting period by £102 million.

The FRRP took the view that the accounts did not give a true and fair view and that Trafalgar House plc was therefore in breach of the Companies Act. Initially the directors refused to revise the accounts, but were finally forced to do so when the FRRP applied for a court order. UITF Abstract 5 *Transfers from fixed assets to current assets* was issued in 1992 in order to prevent companies from avoiding a charge to the profit and loss account by transferring unsold trading assets to fixed assets.

(b)   **Associated Nursing Services**

Associated Nursing Services (ANS) treated certain joint ventures as associated undertakings and also incorrectly accounted for a sale and leaseback transaction. The FRRP raised the issue of whether the accounting treatments reflected the substance of these transactions according to the requirements of FRS 5 *Reporting the substance of transactions.* ANS subsequently restated its accounts.

(c)   **Reckitt and Colman plc**

Reckitt and Colman plc was forced to alter its 1995 accounts because of inadequate disclosure following an acquisition. The FRRP held that Reckitt and Colman did not explain a valuation adjustment adequately and was therefore in breach of FRS 6 *Acquisitions and mergers* and FRS 7 *Fair values in acquisition accounting.*

(d)   **Burn Stewart**

Burn Stewart, a whisky producer, was forced to increase the disclosures in its 1996 accounts. The FRRP ruled that the company had not complied with FRS 5 *Reporting the substance of transactions.*

So far, all cases have been concluded by voluntary agreement with the directors of the companies concerned; it has not yet been necessary for the Panel to seek recourse to the Court.

1.5   Consensus pronouncements of the UITF

In July 1991 the UITF issued its first pronouncement together with a statement explaining the function of its **consensus pronouncements**. This statement has subsequently been incorporated into a *Foreword to UITF Abstracts.*

The main points in the statement are summarised below. Many of the pronouncements cover very detailed points and these are not required knowledge for the examination. You are required for this exam to be familiar with Abstracts 4, 5, 7, 14, 15, 16 and 20. These are covered after the explanatory statement. As at 31 May 1999 twenty-two Abstracts had been issued and most of these were still in force.

Summary of the foreword

(a)   **Introduction**

The Urgent Issues Task Force (UITF) is a committee of the ASB comprising a number of people of major standing in the field of financial reporting. Its purpose is to enlist the experience and influence of its members to assist the ASB in the maintenance and development of good accounting standards and best practice in financial reporting.

The UITF's main role is to assist the ASB in areas where an accounting standard or a Companies Act provision exists, but where unsatisfactory or conflicting interpretations have developed or seem likely to develop. In such circumstances it operates by seeking a voluntary consensus as to the accounting treatment that should be adopted. Such a consensus is reached against the background of the ASB's declared aim of relying on principles rather than detailed prescription. Thus within its remit the UITF is only concerned with serious divergences of current practice or with major developments likely to create serious divergences in the future.

Nothing in the abstracts issued by the UITF is to be construed as amending or overriding the accounting standards or other statements issued by the ASB.

(b)   **Scope and application**

Consensus pronouncements are applicable to financial statements of a reporting entity that are intended to give a true and fair view of its state of affairs at the balance sheet date and of its profit and loss (or income and expenditure) for the financial period ending on that date. Consensus pronouncements need not be applied to immaterial items.

(c)   **Compliance with consensus pronouncements**

Consensus pronouncements should be considered to be part of the corpus of practices forming the basis for determining what constitutes a true and fair view. Such pronouncements consequently may be taken into consideration by the Financial Reporting Review Panel in deciding whether financial statements call for review.

(d)   **Dissemination**

Consensus pronouncements are disseminated by means of published extracts. These include a discussion of the matter, the accounting issues identified, reference sources, and a summary of the UITF's deliberations, and clearly indicate what conclusion has been reached.

A consensus will have been attained where not more than two UITF members have voted against the proposed accounting treatment in question.

1.6   Examinable Abstracts

You are required to know the principles of Abstracts 4, 5, 7, 14, 15, 16 and 20. These are described below.

UITF - Abstract 4. Presentation of long-term debtors in current assets, July 1992

(a)   **The issue**

Both for liabilities and for debtors the *Companies Act* requires a distinction to be drawn between the amounts payable or receivable within one year and those due to be settled or received after more than one year. Although the distinction is disclosed in the notes for each of the items forming part of debtors, unlike in the case of liabilities it is not required to be carried through to the total of current assets nor to the significant Format 1 sub-total of net current assets (liabilities).

In consequence, there is a certain imbalance between the items that the formats require to be classified under current assets or current liabilities. Examples of long-term debtor items include much of the trade debtors of lessors and pension fund surpluses recognised as a prepayment.

(b)   **UITF consensus**

There will be some instances where the amount is so material in the context of the total net current assets that in the absence of disclosure of debtors due after more than one year on the face of the balance sheet, readers may misinterpret the accounts. In such circumstances the amount should be disclosed on the face of the balance sheet.

UITF - Abstract 5. Transfers from current assets to fixed assets, July 1992

(a)   **The issue**

Where it is decided to retain a current asset for use on a continuing basis in the company's activities, it becomes a fixed asset and the question arises as to the appropriate transfer value. Of particular concern is the possibility that companies could avoid charging the profit and loss account with write-downs to net realisable value by transferring the relevant assets from current assets to fixed assets at above net realisable value and then charging any subsequent write-down to revaluation reserve.

(b)   **UITF consensus**

Where assets are transferred from current to fixed, the transfer should be made at the lower of cost and net realisable value at the date of transfer. Fixed asset accounting rules then apply subsequent to the transfer.

UITF - Abstract 7. True and fair view override disclosures, December 1992

(a)   **The issue**

The Companies Act 1985 requires the directors to depart from any specific provision of the Act in the overriding interest that the individual accounts and group accounts shall present a true and fair view. Where the override is invoked, the Act requires that 'particulars of any such departure, the reasons for it and its effect shall be given in a note to the accounts'.

However in practice a variety of different approaches has been seen in the contents of this note; this Abstract seeks to clarify the required contents.

(b)   **UITF consensus**

Where the true and fair view override is being invoked, this should be stated clearly and unambiguously. The statutory disclosure requirement should be interpreted as follows:

(i)   Particulars - a statement of the treatment which the Act would normally require in the circumstances and a description of the treatment actually adopted.

(ii)   Reasons - a statement as to why the treatment prescribed would not give a true and fair view.

(iii)   Effect - a description of how the position shown in the accounts is different as a result of the departure, normally with quantification.

UITF - Abstract 14. Disclosure of changes in accounting policy, November 1995

(a)   **The issue**

Uncertainty has arisen concerning what is required to be disclosed by an organisation which has decided to change an accounting policy. FRS 3 requires that 'following a change in accounting policy, the amounts for the current and corresponding periods should be restated on the basis of the new policies' and requires the effect on the results for the preceding period to be disclosed where practicable. The question arises as to whether this is enough, or whether the effect on the current year's figures is also necessary.

(b)   **UITF consensus**

When a change in accounting policy is made, in addition to the disclosure of the effect required by FRS 3, an indication should also be given of the effect on the current year's results, where practicable.

UITF - Abstract 15 (revised). Disclosure of substantial acquisitions, February 1999

FRS 6 requires detailed disclosures in respect of substantial acquisitions arising during the accounting period. For listed companies FRS 6 defines 'substantial' by reference to Class 1 or Super Class 1 transactions under the Stock Exchange Listing Rules. These classify transactions by assessing their size relative to that of the company making the transaction. It does this by ascertaining whether any of a number of ratios (eg, the net assets of the target to the net assets of the offeror) exceeds a given percentage. UITF Abstract 15 was issued in order to clarify the definition of 'substantial' in respect of listed companies, as the Listing Rules have changed since FRS 6 was issued. An acquisition is now defined as substantial if it is a transaction in which any of the ratios set out in the London Stock Exchange Listing Rules defining Class 1 transactions exceeds 15%.

For other entities, an acquisition is 'substantial':

(a)   where the net assets or operating profits of the acquired entity exceed 15% of those of the acquiring entity, or

(b)   where the fair value of the consideration given exceeds 15% of the net assets of the acquiring entity.

For substantial acquisitions, the following information must be disclosed:

(a)   the summarised profit and loss account and statement of total recognised gains and losses of the acquired entity for the period from the beginning of its financial year to the effective date of acquisition, giving the date on which this period began; and

(b)   the profit after tax and minority interests for the acquired entity's previous financial year.

UITF - Abstract 16. Income and expenses subject to non-standard rates of tax, February 1997

(a)   **The issue**

Some transactions are structured so that some or all of the income or expenditure is non-taxable or taxable at a lower or higher rate than the standard rate. In some cases the transaction may result in a pre-tax loss or an after tax profit. Examples include some leasing transactions, advances and investments made by financial institutions.

(b)   **UITF consensus**

Income and expenses subject to non-standard rates of tax should be included in the pre-tax results on the basis of the income or expenses actually receivable or payable. There should be no adjustment ('grossing up') to reflect a notional amount of tax that would have been paid or received in respect of the transaction if it had been taxable on a different basis.

Both the Companies Acts and FRS 3 *Reporting Financial Performance* require disclosure of any special circumstances which affect the tax liability of an entity. Therefore users of the financial statements will be made aware of the effect of transactions subject to non-standard rates of tax, if this is material.

UITF - Abstract 20. Year 2000 issues: accounting and disclosures, March 1998

(a)   **The issue**

Many businesses need to adapt their computer software so that it can cope with dates in the next century. This Abstract addresses the accounting for external and internal costs of modifying existing computer equipment to achieve year 2000 compliance.

There are two main accounting issues:

(i)   Should the costs of Year 2000 compliance be capitalised (treated as part of fixed assets) or should they be written off as expenses as they are incurred?

(ii)   Should provisions be made for estimated future costs?

(b)   **UITF Consensus**

Costs incurred in rendering existing software year 2000 compliant should be written off to the profit and loss account except in those cases where:

(i)   the entity already has an accounting policy of capitalising software costs; and

(ii)   the expenditure clearly represents an enhancement of the software, rather than merely maintaining its service potential.

In some cases these costs may need to be treated as exceptional items in accordance with FRS 3 *Reporting financial performance*.

Entities should disclose significant commitments at the balance sheet date in respect of Year 2000 software costs (whether these are to be treated as capital or revenue). Following the issue of FRS 12 *Provisions, contingent liabilities and contingent assets* provisions can no longer be made unless the entity has an obligation to transfer economic benefits; an intention to incur expenditure is not sufficient.

The following disclosures should be made:

(i)   the risks and uncertainties associated with the year 2000 problem (or a statement that they have not been addressed);

(ii)   the entity's general plans to address the year 2000 issues relating to its business and operations;

(iii)   whether the total estimated costs of these plans, including amounts to be spent in future periods, have been quantified, and, where applicable, an indication of the total costs likely to be incurred.

These disclosures may either be made in the Directors' Report or in the Operating and Financial Review.

1.7   Current perceptions of the ASB and its performance

The ASB believes that it must be forceful in its approach so that preparers of accounting information follow its requirements. Many support the strong approach taken to reduce the incidence of creative accounting.

Most commentators see the sense of developing a statement of principles although there is also a feeling that the statement will not materially solve any problems. The USA has developed principles over a number of years and there are still significant problems with accounting standards.

Criticisms of the ASB include the following.

(a)   Standards need to be set by legislation.

The ASB despite its strong approach may not be powerful enough to issue and get enforced, certain required standards.

(b)   Standards should be set by non-accountants.

It is the users of accounting information who should set the framework and requirements as the information is being produced for their needs.

(c)   The ASB is too strict.

There are supporters of the more liberal regime that used to exist on the grounds that no one accounting treatment is necessarily relevant to all situations. The enforcement of rigid rules may be at the expense of the true and fair principle.

1.8   The politicisation of the standard setting process

Definition   Politicisation refers to the pressures put on a standard setting body by pressure groups.

The ASC was criticised that it was too open to external influence. Certain SSAPs eg, goodwill and merger accounting were changed partly in response to various pressure groups. Other SSAPs were issued in response to demands from pressure groupings eg, SSAP 19 was issued to allow property companies effectively to be exempted from charging depreciation on their investment properties.

There is general agreement that the ASB has been very much more effective than the ASC. Because it has been able to issue standards on its own authority, it has been less susceptible to pressure from special interest groups. Much of its output to date has been aimed at reducing the scope for 'creative accounting'. Its 'principles based' approach to developing accounting standards also means that it is less likely to be influenced by outside parties.

The ASB is committed to consultation, through Discussion Papers, Financial Reporting Exposure Drafts (FREDs) and on occasion, public hearings. However, the ultimate content of an FRS is determined by the Board's own judgement, based on research, public consultation and careful deliberation about the benefits and costs of providing the resulting information.

Parts of the draft Statement of Principles (discussed later in this chapter) have proved extremely controversial, so much so that the ASB has had to issue a second version of the Exposure Draft, rather than proceeding immediately to a final version. It could also be argued that some of the ASB's latest rules on accounting for goodwill and intangible assets have made significant concessions to some large companies. (These rules are discussed in a later chapter.)

Many commentators believe that during the next few years the greatest threat to the independence of the ASB will not come from interest groups in the UK, but from the movement towards international harmonisation. The ASB will be under increasing pressure to issue standards which bring UK financial reporting practice into line with international accounting standards (IASs) and US accounting standards.

2   THE STATEMENT OF PRINCIPLES

2.1   The intended role of the ASB Statement of Principles

The Statement of Principles has been considered in chapter 1 as an attempt to formulate a conceptual framework within which accounting standards can be issued.

In detail the intended role of the Statement is to:

(a)   assist the ASB in the development of future accounting standards and in its review of existing accounting standards;

(b)   assist the ASB by providing a basis for reducing the number of alternative accounting treatments permitted by law and accounting standards;

(c)   assist preparers of financial statements in applying accounting standards and in dealing with topics that do not form the subject of an accounting standard;

(d)   assist auditors in forming an opinion whether financial statements conform with accounting standards;

(e)   assist users of financial statements in interpreting the information contained in financial statements prepared in conformity with accounting standards; and

(f)   provide those who are interested in the work of the ASB with information about its approach to the formulation of accounting standards.

2.2   The significant features of the ASB Statement of Principles and their current status

The following topics are to be covered in the various chapters of the **Statement of Principles:**

1   The objective of financial statements
2   The reporting entity
3   The qualitative characteristics of financial information
4   The elements of financial statements
5   Recognition in financial statements
6   Measurement in financial statements
7   Presentation of financial information
8   Accounting for interests in other entities.

An Exposure Draft of the complete Statement was issued late in 1995. A revised version was issued in March 1999.

2.3   Scope of the Statement of Principles

The Statement of Principles will not be an accounting standard nor will it have a status that is equivalent to an accounting standard.

It is intended to be relevant to the financial statements of profit-oriented entities, including public sector profit-oriented entities, regardless of their size. The Statement is also relevant to not-for-profit entities, but some of the principles would need to be re-expressed and others would need changes of emphasis before they could be applied to that sector.

2.4   True and fair

The Introduction to the Statement of Principles states that it is not intended to be a definition or an explanation of the meaning of true and fair. Detailed legal requirements, accounting standards and other evidence of generally accepted accounting practice normally determine the content of financial statements intended to give a true and fair view.

However, the Introduction acknowledges that the concept of a true and fair view lies at the heart of financial reporting in the UK. Although the Statement of Principles does not discuss the true and fair view, that does not mean that the concept has been abandoned.

2.5   Standard setting and the ASB's objectives

There is widespread support for a conceptual framework. However, several aspects of the 1995 version of the draft Statement were controversial and the ASB was heavily criticised.

Before revising the Statement the ASB issued a progress paper which attempted to reply to specific concerns. Parts of this paper remain relevant as they clarify the ASB's intentions.

The standard setting process

The Statement of Principles is expected to play an important role in the ASB's development of standards. However, in setting standards the ASB will also take into account legal requirements, cost-benefit considerations, industry-specific issues, the desirability of evolutionary change and implementation issues.

The ASB's objectives

Many traditional accounting principles were originally devised for manufacturing companies with an emphasis on accounting for stocks and fixed assets. They are not adequate to cope with issues such as accounting for intangibles and complex financial instruments.

The ASB has set itself five principal objectives:

(i)   Exclude from the balance sheet items that are neither assets nor liabilities.

(ii)   Make 'off balance sheet' assets and liabilities more visible by putting them on the balance sheet wherever possible.

(iii)   Ensure that all gains and losses are reported prominently so that nothing can be overlooked.

(iv)   Reverse the 'bottom line' mentality by focusing performance reporting on the components of income.

(v)   Use up-to-date measures, where appropriate, if other measures such as historical cost are ineffective.

The ASB believes that implementing principles based on these objectives will result in evolutionary change in financial reporting, rather than revolutionary change.

2.6   The likely usefulness of the ASB Statement of Principles

The intention of the Statement is to provide a coherent basis for setting accounting standards. The principles are however, by definition, of a general nature. They may not therefore, in practice, reduce the options available.

A further problem may be that there will be disagreement as to the contents of the Statement in addition to the existing disagreements over certain accounting standards. Therefore the end effect may simply be to extend the amount of disagreement that exists. When FRS 3 was issued one of the members of the ASB could not support the issue of the standard as he considered that it conflicted with the draft Chapter 6 of the Statement.

Clearly the ASB considers that the Statement will be useful which is why it is continuing with its issue.

3   THE OBJECTIVE OF FINANCIAL STATEMENTS

3.1   Chapter 1 - The objective of financial statements

> **Definition**   The objective of financial statements is to provide information about an entity's financial performance and financial position, that is useful to a wide range of users for assessing the stewardship of management and for making economic decisions.

It can usually be presumed that this objective can be met by focusing exclusively on the information needs of the defining class of user, investors.

3.2   Users and their needs

Investors (providers of risk capital) are interested in information that is useful in assessing the stewardship of management and in taking decisions about their investment or potential investment in the entity. They are, as a result, concerned with the risk inherent in, and return provided by, their investments, and need information on the entity's financial performance and financial position that helps them to assess its cash generation abilities and its financial adaptability.

Not all the information needs of all users can be met by financial statements. However, all users have some interest in the entity's financial performance and financial position.

Other users of financial statements, and their information needs, include the following:

(a)   *Lenders* are interested in information that enables them to determine whether their loans will be repaid and the interest attaching to them paid, when due. Potential lenders are interested in information that helps them to decide whether to lend to the entity and on what terms.

(b)   *Suppliers and other creditors* are interested in information that enables them to decide whether to sell to the entity and to assess the likelihood that amounts owing to them will be paid when due.

(c)   *Employees* are interested in information about the stability and profitability of their employers. They are also interested in information that helps them to assess the ability of their employer to provide remuneration, employment opportunities and retirement benefits.

(d)   *Customers* are interested in information about the entity's continued existence. This is especially so when they are dependent on the entity (eg, if product warranties are involved or if specialised replacement parts may be needed).

(e)   *Governments and their agencies* are interested in the allocation of resources and, therefore, the activities of entities. They also require information in order to regulate the activities of entities, assess taxation and provide a basis for national statistics.

(f)   *The public* may be interested in information about the trends and recent developments in the entity's prosperity and the range of its activities. For example, an entity may make a substantial contribution to a local economy by providing employment and using local suppliers.

3.3   Information required by investors

Investors (and other users of the financial statements) require information that focuses on four key areas.

(a)   The **financial performance** of an entity comprises the return it obtains on the resources it controls, the components of that return and the characteristics of those components.

(b)   The **financial position** of an entity encompasses:

   (i)   the economic resources it controls;
   (ii)   its financial structure;
   (iii)   its liquidity and solvency; and
   (iv)   its capacity to adapt to changes in the environment in which it operates.

(c)   Information about the ways in which an entity **generates and uses cash** in its operations, its investment activities and its financing activities provides an additional perspective on its financial performance - one that is largely free from allocation and valuation issues.

(d)   An entity's **financial adaptability** is its ability to take effective action to alter the amount and timing of its cash flows so that it can respond to unexpected needs or opportunities.

3.4   Chapter 2 - The reporting entity

An entity should prepare and publish financial statements if there is a legitimate demand for the information that its financial statements would provide and it is a cohesive economic unit.

The boundary of the reporting entity is determined by the scope of its control. For this purpose, first direct control and, secondly, direct plus indirect control are taken into account.

An entity will have control of a second entity if it has the ability to direct that entity's operating and financial policies with a view to gaining economic benefit from its activities. Control will be evidenced in a variety of ways depending on its basis (for example ownership or other rights) and the way in which it is exercised (interventionist or not).

3.5   Chapter 3 – The qualitative characteristics of financial information

Definition   Qualitative characteristics are the attributes that make the information provided in financial statements useful to others.

The relationship between the qualitative characteristics is shown in the diagram below.

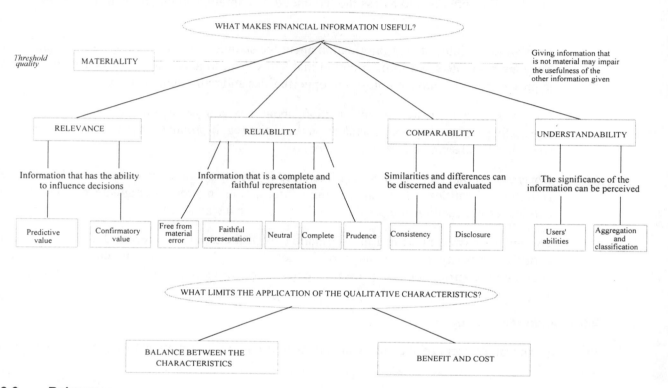

3.6   Relevance

Definition   Information is relevant if it has the ability to influence the economic decisions of users.

Information provided by the financial statements needs to be relevant. Where choices have to be made between mutually exclusive options, the option selected should be the one that results in the relevance of the information being maximised - in other words, the one that would be of most use in taking economic decisions.

Information that is relevant has predictive value or confirmatory value. It has predictive value if it enables users to evaluate or assess past, present or future events. It will have confirmatory value if it helps users to confirm or correct their past evaluations and assessments. Information may have both predictive and confirmatory value.

To have predictive value, information need not be in the form of an explicit forecast. The ability to make predictions from financial statements is enhanced, however, by the manner in which information concerning past transactions and events is displayed. For example, the predictive value of the income statement is enhanced if unusual, abnormal and infrequent items of income or expense are separately disclosed.

3.7   Reliability

Information provided by the financial statements must be reliable.

[Definition]   Information is reliable when:

(a)   it can be depended upon by users to represent faithfully what it either purports to represent or could reasonably be expected to represent;

(b)   it is free from deliberate or systematic bias (ie, it is neutral);

(c)   it is free from material error;

(d)   it is complete within the bounds of materiality; and

(e)   in conditions of uncertainty, a degree of caution (ie, prudence) has been applied in exercising judgement and making the necessary estimates.

(a)   **Faithful representation**

If information is to represent faithfully the transactions and other events that it purports to represent, it is necessary that they are accounted for and presented in accordance with their substance and economic reality and not merely their legal form.

(b)   **Neutrality**

Information must be neutral, that is, free from bias. Financial statements are not neutral if, by the selection or presentation of information, they influence the making of a decision or judgement in order to achieve a predetermined result or outcome.

(c)   **Completeness**

The information must be complete within the bounds of materiality and cost. An omission can cause information to be false or misleading and thus unreliable and deficient in terms of its relevance.

(d)   **Prudence**

The preparers of financial statements have to contend with the uncertainties that inevitably surround many events and circumstances, such as the collectability of debts. Prudence is the inclusion of a degree of caution in the exercise of the judgements needed in making the estimates required under conditions of uncertainty, such that assets or income are not overstated and liabilities or expenses are not understated. However, the exercise of prudence does not allow, for example, the creation of hidden reserves or excessive provisions, the deliberate understatement of assets or income, or the deliberate overstatement of liabilities or expenses.

3.8   Comparability

Users must be able to compare the financial statements of an entity over time to identify trends in its financial position and performance. Users must also be able to compare the financial statements of different entities to evaluate their relative financial performance and financial position. **Consistency** and **disclosures** are therefore required.

Users need to be able to identify differences between:

(a)   the accounting policies adopted from period to period;
(b)   the accounting policies adopted to account for like transactions and other events; and
(c)   the accounting policies adopted by different entities.

3.9   Understandability

Information needs to be understandable; users need to be able to perceive its significance.

Understandability depends on:

(a)   the way in which information is presented

(b)   the capabilities of users.

It is assumed that users have a reasonable knowledge of business and economic activities and are willing to study the information provided with reasonable diligence.

3.10   Materiality

Materiality is a threshold quality that is demanded of all information given in the financial statements.

Information that is material needs to be given in the financial statements and information that is not material need not be given.

> **[Definition]**   Information is **material** to the financial statements if its misstatement or omission might reasonably be expected to influence the economic decisions of users.

Whether information is material will depend upon the size and nature of the item in question judged in the particular circumstances of the case.

3.11   Constraints on the qualitative characteristics

Conflicts may arise between the key qualitative characteristics. In these circumstances a trade off needs to be found that still enables the objective of the financial statements to be met.

(a)   **Relevance and reliability**

Where there is a conflict, it is usually appropriate to use the information that is the most relevant of whichever information is available.

Conflicts may arise over timeliness. A delay in providing information can make it out of date and less relevant, but reporting on transactions and other events before all the uncertainties are resolved may make information less reliable. Financial information should not be provided until it is sufficiently reliable.

(b)   **Neutrality and prudence**

Neutrality involves freedom from bias. Prudence is potentially biased because it seeks to ensure that gains and assets are not overstated and losses or liabilities are not understated in conditions of uncertainty. It is necessary to find a balance that ensures that deliberate understatement of assets or gains and overstatement of liabilities or losses does not occur.

(c)   **Understandability**

Information that is relevant and reliable should not be excluded from the financial statements simply because it is too difficult for some users to understand.

4   CHAPTERS 4 AND 5

4.1   Chapter 4: The elements of financial statements

Seven elements of financial statements are identified, all of which are seen to be interrelated. In order for an item to be included in financial statements it must fall within one of the definitions of elements, but it must also meet the recognition criteria of Chapter 5.

(a)   **Assets**

Definition   Assets are rights or other access to future economic benefits controlled by an entity as a result of past transactions or events.

(i)   **'Rights or other access'**

For example property is only an asset because of the rights (shared or sole) deriving from ownership or the other rights of occupation and use.

(ii)   **'Future economic benefits'**

These are evidenced by the prospective receipt of cash. This could be cash itself, a debt receivable or any item which may be sold. Although, for example, a factory may not be sold (on a going concern basis) it houses the manufacture of goods. When these goods are sold the economic benefit resulting from the use of the factory is realised as cash.

(iii)   **'Controlled by an entity'**

Control is the ability to obtain the economic benefits and to restrict the access of others (eg, by a company being the sole user of its plant and machinery, or by selling surplus plant and machinery).

(iv)   **'Past transactions or events'**

The transaction or event must be 'past' before an asset can arise.

(b)   **Liabilities**

Definition   Liabilities are an entity's obligations to transfer economic benefits as a result of past transactions or events.

(i)   **'Obligations'**

These may be legal or not. For example, an entity may have no realistic alternative to refunding the price of goods that fail to meet the expectations of customers, even though there is no legal right to do so.

Obligation implies that the outflow of resources is **unavoidable**. Costs to be incurred in the future do not represent liabilities as long as the entity can choose to avoid the expenditure.

(ii)   **'Transfer economic benefits'**

This could be a transfer of cash, or other property, the provision of a service, or the refraining from activities which would otherwise be profitable.

(iii)   **'Past transactions or events'**

Similar points are made here to those under assets.

(c)   **Ownership interest**

Definition   Ownership interest is the residual amount found by deducting all liabilities of the entity from all of the entity's assets.

Owners invest in an entity in the hope of a return (for example, the payment of dividends). Unlike creditors, owners cannot insist that a transfer is made to them regardless of the circumstances. Their interest is in the assets of the entity after all the liabilities have been deducted.

(d)   **Gains and losses**

These are counted as two of the seven elements.

[Definition]   Gains are increases in ownership interest, not resulting from contributions from owners.

[Definition]   Losses are decreases in ownership interest, not resulting from distributions to owners.

(e)   **Contributions from owners**

[Definition]   Contributions from owners are increases in ownership interest resulting from transfers from owners in their capacity as owners.

Owners contribute to entities by transferring assets, performing services or accepting ownership interest in satisfaction of liabilities. Rights in the ownership interest are usually granted in return for a contribution from owners. For example, owners may provide cash (additional capital) to an entity in return for additional shares.

(f)   **Distributions to owners**

[Definition]   Distributions to owners are decreases in ownership interest resulting from transfers to owners in their capacity as owners.

Distributions to owners include the payment of dividends and the return of capital. For example, when a company purchases its own shares, this is reflected by reducing the amount of ownership interest.

4.2   Chapter 5: Recognition in financial statements

[Definition]   Recognition involves depiction of the element in words and by a monetary amount and the inclusion of that amount in the financial statement totals.

The recognition process has the following stages:

(a)   initial recognition, which is where an item is depicted in the primary financial statements for the first time (eg, the purchase of an asset);

(b)   subsequent remeasurement, which involves changing the amount at which an already recognised asset or liability is stated in the primary financial statements (eg, revaluation); and

(c)   derecognition, which is where an item that was until then recognised ceases to be recognised (eg, the sale of an asset).

All events that may have an effect on elements of the financial statements should be, as far as possible, identified and reflected in an appropriate manner in the financial statements.

Transactions are the most common form of such events. Other events that may result in recognition are:

(a)   discovery, growth, extraction, processing or innovation that results in new assets;
(b)   the imposition of a penalty by a court that may create a new liability;
(c)   events that damage assets (eg, fire); and
(d)   lapse of time that results in an obligation expiring.

4.3   Recognition and derecognition

If a transaction or other event has created a new asset or liability or added to an existing asset or liability, that effect is recognised if:

(a)   sufficient evidence exists that the new asset or liability has been created or that there has been an addition to an existing asset or liability; and

(b)   the new asset or liability or the addition to the existing asset or liability can be measured at a monetary amount with sufficient reliability.

An asset or liability is wholly or partly derecognised if:

(a)   sufficient evidence exists that a transaction or other past event has eliminated a previously recognised asset or liability; or

(b)   although an item continues to be an asset or liability, the criteria for recognition are no longer met.

4.4   Sufficient evidence

What constitutes sufficient evidence is a matter of judgement in the particular circumstances of each case. The main source of evidence is experience, including:

(a)   evidence provided by the event that has given rise to the item;

(b)   past experience with similar items;

(c)   current information directly relating to the item;

(d)   evidence provided by transactions of other entities in similar items.

4.5   Measurement

Items that are recognised must be capable of being measured at a monetary amount. This involves two steps: selecting a suitable measurement basis (eg, historical cost or current value) for the item and determining for the basis chosen an appropriate monetary amount.

4.6   Revenue recognition

The starting point for the recognition process is always the effect that the transaction or other event involved has had on the reporting entity's assets and liabilities. Assuming that no contribution from owners or transfer to owners is involved:

(a)   if net assets increase, a gain is recognised; and

(b)   a loss is recognised if, and to the extent that, previously recognised assets are reduced or eliminated.

However, applying the matching (accruals) concept will often help in identifying these effects.

When goods or services are sold, the recognition criteria are met on the occurrence of the critical event in the operating cycle involved. (This is usually, but not always, the delivery of the goods.)

5   CHAPTER 6: MEASUREMENT IN FINANCIAL STATEMENTS

5.1   Introduction

The earlier version of this Chapter concluded that practice should develop by evolving in the direction of greater use of current values to the extent that this is consistent with the constraints of reliability and cost. This conclusion was extremely controversial as many commentators interpreted it to mean that the ASB intended to reintroduce a form of current cost accounting.

The ASB denied that it intended to re-introduce current cost accounting and stated that it accepts that the existing modified historical cost system will be used for the foreseeable future.

5.2   The principles

The main points made in the revised version are set out below.

(a)   There is a choice between a measurement system that requires:

    (i)   a single measurement basis (eg, historic cost or current value) to be used for all assets and liabilities; or

    (ii)   the measurement basis to be selected separately for each category of assets or liabilities so that it fits the circumstances surrounding that particular category (for example, the 'modified historic cost' system where some fixed assets are stated at current value while the rest are stated at historic cost).

It is envisaged that the latter approach (the mixed measurement system) will be adopted.

(b)   A measurement basis (historic cost or current value) must be selected for each category of assets or liabilities. The basis selected should be the one that best meets the objective of financial statements and the qualitative characteristics of financial information (particularly relevance and reliability), bearing in mind the nature of the assets or liabilities concerned and the circumstances involved.

If only one of the measures available is reliable, it should be the one used if it is also relevant. If both historic cost and current value are reliable, the better measure to use is the one that is most relevant. Current value is not necessarily less reliable than historic cost.

(c)   The vast majority of assets and liabilities are measured at their transaction cost when they are initially recognised. Subsequent remeasurement may be needed to ensure that:

    (i)   assets measured at historic cost are carried at the lower of cost and recoverable amount;

    (ii)   monetary items denominated in foreign currency are carried at amounts based on up-to-date exchange rates; and

    (iii)   assets and liabilities measured on the current value basis are carried at up-to-date current values.

(d)   Remeasurements are only recognised if:

    (i)   there is sufficient evidence that the monetary amount of the asset or liability has changed; and

    (ii)   the new amount of the asset or liability can be measured with sufficient reliability.

(e)   The value to the business rule should be used to select from alternative measures of current value. The current value of an asset is the loss that the entity would suffer if it were deprived of it (deprival value). The rule can be portrayed diagrammatically as follows:

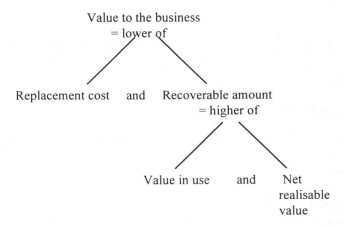

The value to the business rule is discussed in more detail in chapter 21 of this text.

(f)   When basing carrying amounts on future cash flows, those cash flows should be discounted.

(g)   Financial capital maintenance is not satisfactory when general or specific price changes are significant. In these circumstances it will be necessary to:

(i)   recognise profit only after adjustments for general price changes have been made to maintain the purchasing power of the entity's financial capital; and/or

(ii)   inform the user of the significance of specific price changes for the entity's financial performance and financial position.

Item (g) (i) is referring to 'real terms' capital maintenance which again, will be explained in more detail in chapter 21.

In later chapters you will be covering financial reporting standards on accounting for tangible and intangible fixed assets (FRSs 10, 11 and 15). These reflect the ASB's thinking on measurement, particularly on subsequent remeasurement (revaluation and impairment) and use of the value to the business model. As stated in the earlier version of the Statement of Principles, the ASB *does* favour greater use of current values, but a return to current cost accounting as such does not appear to be on the agenda. Notice, however, that it has not been completely ruled out (see point (g) above).

6   CHAPTER 7 – PRESENTATION OF FINANCIAL INFORMATION

6.1   The principles

Financial statements consist of primary financial statements and supporting notes. The primary financial statements are:

(a)   the statement(s) of financial performance (profit and loss account and statement of total recognised gains and losses)

(b)   the statement of financial position (balance sheet)

(c)   the cash flow statement.

The presentation of information on **financial performance** focuses on the components of financial performance and their characteristics.

The presentation of information on **financial position** focuses on the types and functions of assets and liabilities held and on the relationships between them.

The presentation of **cash flow information** shows the extent to which the entity's various activities generate and use cash. In particular it distinguishes between those cash flows that result from operations and those that result from other activities.

6.2   Presentation

Financial statements should communicate clearly and effectively and in as straightforward a manner as possible without loss of relevance or reliability and without significantly increasing the length of the financial statements.

Structure and aggregation

The mass of detail would obscure the message if financial statements reported every single aspect of every relevant transaction and event. Greater knowledge results from an orderly **loss** of information. Aggregating information:

(a)   conveys information that would otherwise have been obscured;

(b)   highlights significant items and relationships between items;

(c)   facilitates comparability between different entities; and

(d)   is more understandable to users.

The notes and primary financial statements form an integrated whole. The notes amplify and explain the financial statements by providing:

(a)   more detailed information on items recognised in the primary financial statements

(b)   an alternative view of items recognised in the primary financial statements (for example, by disclosing a range of possible outcomes for a liability that is in dispute, or by disclosing segmental information)

(c)   relevant information that it is not practicable to incorporate in the primary financial statements (for example, because of uncertainty).

Disclosure of information in the notes to the financial statements is not a substitute for recognition. It does not correct or justify any misrepresentation or omission in the primary financial statements.

Classification

Items that are similar should be presented together and distinguished from dissimilar items. Classification should consider the relationships between different classes of items, for example the relative sizes of profits and capital employed or debtors and sales.

Items that are similar or related should be presented in a manner that highlights that similarity or relationship. For example, different kinds of current assets are shown adjacent to each other and current liabilities are usually shown in a manner that highlights their relationship to current assets.

6.3   Accompanying information

Financial statements are often accompanied by other information, for example, five year trend information, operating and financial reviews, directors' reports and statements by the chairman. This information should not be inconsistent with the financial statements.

The more complex an entity and its transactions become, the more users need an objective and comprehensive analysis and explanation of the main features underlying the entity's financial performance and position. These disclosures (normally included in the operating and financial review) are best presented in the context of a discussion of the business as a whole.

7   CHAPTER 8 – ACCOUNTING FOR INTERESTS IN OTHER ENTITIES

7.1   The principles

These restate generally accepted accounting practice which is covered in the chapters on group accounts.

(a)   Single entity financial statements and consolidated financial statements present the reporting entity's interests in other entities from different perspectives.

(b)   In single entity financial statements, interests in other entities are dealt with by focusing on the income and capital growth arising from the interest (eg, dividends received and changes in market value).

(c)   In consolidated financial statements, the way in which interests in other entities are dealt with depends on the degree of influence involved.

-     An interest in another entity that involves control of that other entity's operating and financial policies is dealt with by incorporating the controlled entity as part of the reporting entity (ie, by consolidation).

-     An interest in another entity that involves joint control of, or significant influence over, that other entity's operating and financial policies is dealt with by recognising the reporting entity's share of that other entity's results and resources in a way that does not imply that they are controlled by the reporting entity (eg, by the equity method or gross equity method).

-     Other interests in other entities (simple investments) are dealt with in the same way as any other asset.

(d)   Consolidated financial statements are prepared from the perspective of the parent's shareholders.

(e)   Consolidated financial statements reflect the whole of the parent's investment in its subsidiaries, including purchased goodwill.

(f)   A business combination is reflected in the consolidated financial statements in accordance with its character. Therefore, a transaction that is in the character of:

-     an acquisition is reflected in the consolidated financial statements as if the acquirer purchased the acquiree's assets and liabilities as a bundle of assets and liabilities on the open market.

-     a merger is reflected in the consolidated financial statements as if a new reporting entity, comprising all the parties to the transaction, had been formed.

8   CHAPTER SUMMARY

The bodies involved in the standard setting process are centred around the issuing of standards by the ASB.

The ASB's Statement of Principles is an attempt to develop a conceptual framework within which accounting standards can be tested and developed.

9   SELF TEST QUESTIONS

9.1   How does the ASB intend to achieve its aims? (1.2)

9.2   What is the role of the FRC? (1.3)

9.3   What does politicisation mean? (1.8)

9.4   What are the six purposes of the Statement of Principles? (2.1)

9.5   What is the objective of financial statements? (3.1)

9.6   What are the qualitative characteristics of financial statements? (3.5)

10   EXAMINATION TYPE QUESTIONS

10.1   Conceptual framework

(a)   If a 'statement of accounting principles' is to be developed, what would its principal components need to be?   **(10 marks)**

(b)   List and explain the advantages and difficulties which could result from the development of a 'statement of accounting principles'.   **(10 marks)**

(Total: 20 marks)

10.2   Information

In financial reporting it is essential to ensure that information is communicated in a manner which can be understood by the recipients of the report. In addition, it is of the utmost importance that company statutory reports do not become over-burdened with unnecessary detail and that the costs of collecting and publishing the information are kept within reasonable bounds.

What is the reasoning behind this statement and what are the implications?   **(20 marks)**

11   ANSWERS TO EXAMINATION TYPE QUESTIONS

11.1   Conceptual framework

(*Tutorial note:* This should be answered with the Accounting Standards Board's proposed statement as a guide.)

(a)   A 'Statement of accounting principles' should set out the concepts that underlie the preparation of financial statements for external users. The statement could be expected to cover the following:

(i)   the objective(s) of financial statements, including details of the relevant user groups, their information needs and the financial statements required to meet those needs.

(ii)   the qualitative characteristics that make financial statements of value to users, eg, relevance, reliability.

(iii)   the elements of financial statements and how these elements interact to form a basis on which financial statements could present information in a structured manner; this would include definitions for assets, liabilities and ownership interest.

(iv)   the criteria that an item should attain if it is to be recognised, and therefore incorporated, in financial statements.

(v)   details of how elements of financial statements should be valued and measured.

(vi)   the need for suitable presentation of financial information in financial statements so that the objective of meeting users' information needs can be achieved.

(vii)   the principles governing which entities should have to publish their accounts.

(b)   The advantages of an agreed 'Statement of accounting principles' include the following:

(i)   it will assist the standard-setting body in the development of new accounting standards and in the review of existing standards.

(ii)   the standard-setting body will have a base when attempting to reduce the number of alternative accounting treatments permitted by law and by an accounting standard.

(iii)   preparers of financial statements will have some guidance in dealing with topics and transactions that do not form the subject of an accounting standard.

(iv)   assistance will be given to auditors in forming an opinion on whether or not financial statements comply with accounting standards.

(v)   users of financial statements may find it easier to interpret the information contained in financial statements prepared in conformity with accounting standards.

(vi)   it will provide those who are interested in the work of the standard-setting body with information about its approach to the formulation of accounting standards.

There are likely to be considerable difficulties in developing a statement of accounting principles that can be agreed by all relevant parties. Agreement will be difficult on who are the primary user groups and what are the information needs of those groups, and different people will have different ideas on what are the elements of financial statements. There is, for example, more than one definition of an asset.

A further difficulty with the statement will be in its application to the development of accounting standards. These standards often conflict with each other and are shaped by many forces. It is debatable whether a statement of accounting principles would overcome these problems.

11.2   Information

(*Tutorial note:*

Break down the statement down into distinct parts and make sure you cover the following:

-       data v information
-       reporting v communicating
-       simplification of financial statements
-       user needs and user decisions
-       cost v benefit analysis.)

The statement can be analysed as follows.

Part 1: In financial reporting it is essential to ensure that information is communicated ...

It is important that published financial accounts are not seen to be mere statements of data produced for no purpose. The accounts should include useful information that should be readily available to those who have a right to receive and use such information.

Part 2: ... in a manner which can be understood by the recipients of the report ...

If the financial reports are communicated to the relevant users it is essential that the reports are in a form such that their content can be readily understood. There is little point in sending to non-accountant users complicated financial statements containing details expressed in technical accounting jargon.   Such reports should be simplified, possibly by summarising the full accounts, with explanations in 'plain' language. This is particularly important when attempting to provide financial information to employees. A complicated report will go unused.

Part 3: In addition it is of the utmost importance that company statutory reports do not become over-burdened with unnecessary detail ...

With the development of Statements of Standard Accounting Practice under the Accounting Standards Committee and subsequently Financial Reporting Standards under the Accounting Standards Board, and with the increased amount of legislation in the Companies Acts, the financial reports of most companies have become formidable documents. Some believe that the statutory reports of companies have become so detailed that only those with an accounting background can use such documents. The development of the standard on cash flow statements and the reorganisation of the information contained in the profit and loss account can be considered as illustrations of detailed statements that may be considered to over-burden the reader.

However, the answer may not be to simplify such reports. What constitutes 'unnecessary detail' is a matter of subjective judgement and some vital information may be lost if detail is removed or - worse - the details provided could be misinterpreted or taken out of context. There is a fine dividing line between detailed statements that provide a true and fair view and over-detailed statements that a reader cannot use without a great deal of time and effort. As yet the optimum level of reporting has to be agreed, but the accounting profession is likely to continue in its endeavour to make 'corporate reports valuable' by meeting the various user needs.

Part 4: ... the costs of collecting and publishing the information are kept within reasonable bounds.

This is an application of the cost-benefit principle. The development of sending summary financial statements to shareholders is based on this idea, thereby reducing the not inconsiderable cost of printing and distributing full financial statements to all shareholders, many of whom cannot fully understand such statements and therefore derive no benefit from their receipt. It is unlikely that the cost of collecting the information is particularly relevant. Much of the detail is required for internal management reporting purposes; the incremental cost related to collecting information to meet additional external reporting requirements is not likely to be significant. Often the problem of confidentiality means that much more information is available internally than will ever be made available externally.

The development of more 'user-friendly' published accounts will continue and the accounting profession may be forced to change its current position if it is to have credibility as a useful, relevant profession in the future. The service provided by the publication of financial reports must be relevant to the environment in which it exists.

8 PREPARATION OF PUBLISHED FINANCIAL STATEMENTS (COMPANIES ACT REQUIREMENTS)

INTRODUCTION & LEARNING OBJECTIVES

This is a long chapter but one on which a regular and important type of question is set: the 'published accounts' question. This is likely to be a computational question which will also require knowledge of the effect of various accounting standards.

Do not be put off by the volume of detail in the chapter. You will gradually acquire the required knowledge by tackling published accounts questions later in your studies. Refer back to this chapter regularly and you will find that knowledge of the detailed provisions will become familiar to you.

When you have studied this chapter you should be able to do the following:

- State the requirements of company law regarding the use of formats.
- Prepare accounts in accordance with the formats.
- State the criteria for small and medium companies and their effect.
- List the contents of a directors' report.

1 COMPANY LAW

1.1 The legal background to limited companies

Fifty years ago, it was very difficult for shareholders to obtain an accurate assessment of a company's financial position, since very little information was required by statute to be disclosed to them. An attempt to remedy this situation was made in the Companies Act 1929, which required every company to produce financial accounts to the shareholders at regular intervals.

In 1948, a new Companies Act was passed which laid down detailed requirements concerning the presentation of company accounts and the disclosure of information to shareholders.

These requirements were subsequently amplified in the Companies Acts 1967 and 1981. As a result of the Companies Act 1967 all companies, except those registered as unlimited companies, had to disclose their financial affairs to the public by submitting audited accounts and a directors' report with their annual return to the Registrar of Companies. These three Acts, which regulated the form and content of all published accounts, together with the Companies Act 1976 and 1980 were consolidated in 1985 into four new Acts, the Companies Act 1985, Company Securities (Insider Dealing) Act 1985, Business Names Act 1985, and Companies Consolidation (Consequential Provisions) Act 1985.

The Companies Act 1989 amended various requirements of the Companies Act 1985. The following pages set out the minimum disclosure requirements of the Companies Act 1985 (as amended by the Companies Act 1989 and by later Statutory Instruments) in so far as they relate to the balance sheet, the profit and loss account and the directors' report. Some very detailed provisions have been omitted.

1.2 The duty to prepare annual accounts and the use of prescribed formats

The directors are responsible for presenting to the company in general meeting a profit and loss account and balance sheet within eighteen months of incorporation, and subsequently at least once in every calendar year. For a public company, the accounts must be made up to a date not more than seven months before the date of the meeting. Additionally, all such accounts laid before the company in general meeting must contain a report by the auditors in which they are required to state **(inter alia)** whether in their opinion the company's balance sheet and profit and loss account have been prepared in accordance with the provisions of the Companies Act 1985.

Until the CA81 there was no prescribed form of accounts laid down by law, and provided the statutory requirements on disclosure were met, there was allowed a certain latitude in the presentation of financial statements. Sch 4 CA85 allows a choice of format of one from two balance sheet formats and one from four profit and loss account formats. This text follows format 1 for each.

Balance sheet format 1 is a continuous vertical format; while format 2 sets out firstly all assets, followed by all liabilities, which would allow for a horizontal format.

The different profit and loss account formats give different information. Format 1 analyses on an operational basis; format 2 analyses costs by type of expenditure. Formats 3 and 4 allow the presentation of profit and loss accounts in horizontal form and will not be further considered here since they would not normally be used by UK companies.

The formats used in group accounts will be considered later in the text.

1.3   The main accounting provisions of Company law

The *SSAP 2* concepts are embodied in the *Companies Act 1985* as four of the five 'Accounting Principles'. The fifth principle states that in determining the aggregate amount of any item the amount of any individual asset or liability that falls to be taken into account shall be determined separately. For example, when stock is valued at the lower of cost and net realisable value the value must be determined for separate types of stock and then aggregated. In this way anticipated losses on one type of stock will not be offset against expected gains on another.

More detailed accounting provisions are also included in the legislation for certain items. These are detailed in later sections of this chapter when the relevant items are considered.

Accounting rules are contained in the *CA85*. They relate to the amount at which assets are stated in financial statements of companies. There are no statutory accounting rules for the measurement of liabilities.

Companies may use either HISTORICAL COST accounting rules or ALTERNATIVE accounting rules which are based upon current costs or market value. It is possible for a company to use a mixture of these rules as in the 'Modified Historical Cost Convention' when historical cost accounts are modified by the revaluation of certain fixed assets.

The accounting rules are contained in *Sch 4 CA85*. The table below summarises the rules.

ACCOUNTING RULES

Relate to amount at which ASSETS are stated in accounts

HISTORICAL COST ACCOUNTING RULES	ALTERNATIVE ACCOUNTING RULES
Assets should be stated at the PURCHASE PRICE or PRODUCTION COST	Any of the following assets may be stated at alternative amounts:
These terms are defined, but with alternative rules for the identification of stock and fungible assets.	FIXED ASSETS
Modifications to stating asset at purchase price/production cost:	(i) Tangible fixed assets. Market value (at last valuation date) or current cost.
FIXED ASSETS / **CURRENT ASSETS**	(ii) Intangible fixed assets (except goodwill). Current cost.
Reduce cost by provisions for depreciation with special rules for development costs and goodwill / Reduce cost to net realisable value.	(iii) Investments. Market value (at last valuation date) or any other appropriate basis.
	CURRENT ASSETS
	(i) Investments. Current cost.
	(ii) Stock. Current cost.
	Application of the alternative accounting rules for any of the assets may result in:
	(i) Amendment to the depreciation charge.
	(ii) Additional disclosure of information.
	(iii) Treatment of revaluations.

Definitions

Fungible assets: assets which are substantially indistinguishable from one another. Investments are specifically included within this term.

Purchase price: the actual price paid plus any expenses incidental to the acquisition.

Production cost: the total of the purchase price of the raw materials and consumables used and the amount of costs incurred which are directly attributable to the production of the asset. In addition there **may** be included a proportion of overhead expenditure and interest on capital borrowed to finance the production of the asset to the extent that it accrues in respect of the period of production.

2   THE BALANCE SHEET

2.1   The format

Format 1 (the vertical balance sheet) is reproduced below:

A	Called up share capital not paid (1)		
B	Fixed assets		
	I	Intangible assets	
		1	Development costs
		2	Concessions, patents, licences, trade marks and similar rights and assets (2)

	3	Goodwill (3)
	4	Payments on account

II   Tangible assets

	1	Land and buildings
	2	Plant and machinery
	3	Fixtures, fittings, tools and equipment
	4	Payments on account and assets in course of construction

III   Investments

	1	Shares in group undertakings
	2	Loans to group undertakings
	3	Participating interests
	4	Loans to undertakings in which the company has a participating interest
	5	Other investments other than loans
	6	Other loans
	7	Own shares (4)

C   Current assets

I   Stocks

	1	Raw materials and consumables
	2	Work in progress
	3	Finished goods and goods for resale
	4	Payments on account

II   Debtors (5)

	1	Trade debtors
	2	Amounts owed by group undertakings
	3	Amounts owed by undertakings in which the company has a participating interest
	4	Other debtors
	5	Called up share capital not paid (1)
	6	Prepayments and accrued income (6)

III   Investments

	1	Shares in group undertakings
	2	Own shares (4)
	3	Other investments

IV   Cash at bank and in hand

D   Prepayments and accrued income (6)

E   Creditors: amounts falling due within one year

	1	Debenture loans (7)
	2	Bank loans and overdrafts
	3	Payments received on account (8)
	4	Trade creditors
	5	Bills of exchange payable
	6	Amounts owed to group undertakings
	7	Amounts owed to undertakings in which the company has a participating interest
	8	Other creditors including taxation and social security (9)
	9	Accruals and deferred income (10)

F   Net current assets (liabilities) (11)

G   Total assets less current liabilities

H   Creditors: amounts falling due after more than one year

	1	Debenture loans (7)
	2	Bank loans and overdrafts
	3	Payments received on account (8)
	4	Trade creditors
	5	Bills of exchange payable
	6	Amounts owed to group undertakings
	7	Amounts owed to undertakings in which the company has a participating interest
	8	Other creditors including taxation and social security (9)
	9	Accruals and deferred income (10)

I   Provisions for liabilities and charges

    1   Pensions and similar obligations
    2   Taxation, including deferred taxation
    3   Other provisions

J   Accruals and deferred income (10)

K   Capital and reserves

    I   Called up share capital (12)

    II   Share premium account

    III   Revaluation reserve

    IV   Other reserves

        1   Capital redemption reserve
        2   Reserve for own shares
        3   Reserves provided for by the articles of association
        4   Other reserves

    V   Profit and loss account

Notes on the balance sheet formats

(1)   Called up share capital not paid
(Items A and C.II.5.)
This item may be shown in either of the two positions given.

(2)   Concessions, patents, licences, trade marks and similar rights and assets (Item B.I.2.)   Amounts in respect of assets shall only be included in a company's balance sheet under this item if either –

(a)   the assets were acquired for valuable consideration and are not required to be shown under goodwill; or

(b)   the assets in question were created by the company itself.

(3)   Goodwill

(Item B.I.3.)
Amounts representing goodwill shall only be included to the extent that the goodwill was acquired for valuable consideration.

(4)   Own shares

(Items B.III.7 and C.III.2.)
The nominal value of the shares held shall be shown separately.

(5)   Debtors

(Items C.II.1 to 6.)
The amount falling due after more than one year shall be shown separately for each item included under debtors.

(6)   Prepayments and accrued income

(Items C.II.6 and D.)
This item may be shown in either of the two positions given.

(7)   Debenture loans

(Items E.1 and H.1)
The amount of any convertible loans shall be shown separately.

(8)   Payments received on account

(Items E.3 and H.3)
Payments received on account of orders shall be shown for each of these items in so far as they are not shown as deductions from stocks.

(9)   Other creditors including taxation and social security

(Items E.8 and H.8)
The amount for creditors in respect of taxation and social security shall be shown separately from the amount for other creditors.

(10)   Accruals and deferred income

(Items E.9, H.9 and J.)
The two positions given for this item at E.9 and H.9 are an alternative to the position at J, but if the item is not shown in a position corresponding to that at J it may be shown in either or both of the other two positions (as the case may require).

(11)   Net current assets (liabilities)

(Item F.)
In determining the amount to be shown for this item any amounts shown under 'prepayments and accrued income' shall be taken into account wherever shown.

(12)   Called up share capital

(Item K.1)
The amount of allotted share capital and the amount of called up share capital which has been paid up shall be shown separately.

2.2   Comments on the balance sheet

(a)   The letters and numbers by each item do not have to be shown in the accounts, but they are relevant in determining which items have to be disclosed on the **face** of the balance sheet and which items may, in certain circumstances, be disclosed in the supporting notes.

(b)   Items with a capital letter or roman numerals must be shown on the face of the balance sheet and must be shown in the order in which they are dealt with in Format 1. There are, however, two exceptions to this:

(i)   Materiality. Para 86 states that amounts which are not material in the particular context of any provision of Sch 4 may be disregarded.

(ii)   Certain items, A, D and J, may be shown elsewhere and will thus have the status of items designated with an arabic numeral (see notes 1, 6 and 10).

(c)   The position of those items assigned arabic numerals is more complicated. These items **must** be rearranged or adapted where the special nature of the company's business requires it. In addition, these items **may** be combined if either:

(i)   the individual amounts are not material to assessing the state of affairs; or

(ii)   the combination of items facilitates that assessment.

In the case of the latter point, the individual amounts must be disclosed in a note to the accounts.

(d)   All assets must be shown under the head of fixed or current assets. Fixed assets are defined as those assets intended for use on a continuing basis in the company's activities. Any other asset is a current asset.

(e)   Miscellaneous:

   (i)   any item may be shown in greater detail;

   (ii)   additional headings may be added for items not otherwise covered;

   (iii)   corresponding amounts must be shown for the previous year, and these amounts must be comparable to the current year's figures.

2.3   The balance sheet – an example of presentation

In the example which follows, the financial statements for Seaton plc are given under the CA85 disclosure and accounting requirements. The example is annotated by tutorial notes (which would not, of course, appear in a set of published accounts) giving the full disclosure and accounting requirements of the Companies Act.

Seaton plc
Balance sheet at 31 December 19X4

	Notes	£'000	*19X3* £'000
Fixed assets			
Intangible assets	(3.2)	153	101
Tangible assets	(3.3)	1,986	1,753
Investments	(3.5)	29	33
		2,168	1,887
Current assets			
Stocks	(4.2)	1,637	1,598
Debtors	(4.3)	2,079	1,635
Investments	(4.4)	126	39
Cash at bank and in hand		75	41
		3,917	3,313
Creditors: amounts falling due within one year	(4.5)	3,010	2,980
Net current assets		907	333
Total assets less current liabilities		3,075	2,220
Creditors: amounts falling due after more than one year	(4.6)	910	495
Provisions for liabilities and charges	(4.7)	27	13
		937	508
		2,138	1,712

Capital and reserves

Called up share capital	(4.8)	1,500	1,500
Share premium account		23	23
Revaluation reserve		25	25
Other reserves	(4.9)	67	67
Profit and loss account	(4.9)	523	97
		2,138	1,712

The accounts were approved by
the directors on 3 March 19X5

Colyn Seaton

Director

2.4   Approval and signing of accounts

A company's individual (and consolidated) accounts must be approved by the board of directors and the company's individual **balance sheet** must be signed on behalf of the board by **a** director. The copy of the balance sheet which is sent to the registrar of companies must also be signed by **a** director but not necessarily the same director.

In addition, the directors' report must be approved by the board of directors and signed on behalf of the board by **a** director **or** the secretary of the company. (The directors' report is dealt with later.)

3   NOTES TO THE BALANCE SHEET - FIXED ASSETS

3.1   Introduction

Accounting policies are required to be stated where relevant. It should be stated whether the accounts have been prepared in accordance with applicable accounting standards and particulars of any material departure from those standards and reasons for it shall be given. The previous sentence does not apply to small or medium companies (defined later).

Assets are to be shown as fixed assets if they are intended for use on a continuing basis in the company's activities. All other assets are to be shown as current assets.

3.2   Intangible assets

		£'000	*19X3* £'000
(a)	Development costs	73	31
(b)	Concessions, patents, licences and trade marks	26	13
(c)	Goodwill	40	50
(d)	Payments on account for intangible assets	14	7
		153	101

(a)   Development costs

Development costs relate to a special project for the manufacture, design and marketing of a new range of seatons. Development commenced in 19X2 and was concluded during the year. Sales commenced during the current year. The costs are being written off over the five year expected life of the new product range.

	£'000
Cost:	
At 1 January 19X4	31
Additions	60
At 31 December 19X4	91

	£'000
Accumulated depreciation:	
At 1 January 19X4	-
Provision for the year	18
At 31 December 19X4	18
Net book amount at 31 December 19X4	73
Net book amount at 31 December 19X3	31

Give reasons for capitalising development costs and the period over which they are being written off.

(b)   **Concessions, patents, licences and trade marks**

	£'000
Cost or valuation:	
At 1 January 19X4	28
Additions	23
Disposals	(5)
At 31 December 19X4	46

	£'000
Accumulated depreciation:	
At 1 January 19X4	15
Provision for the year	9
Disposals	(4)
At 31 December 19X4	20
Net book amount at 31 December 19X4	26
Net book amount at 31 December 19X3	13

See rules for tangible assets.

(c)   **Goodwill**

	£'000
Cost:	
At 1 January 19X4 and 31 December 19X4	50
Accumulated depreciation:	
At 1 January 19X4	-
Provision for the year	10

At 31 December 19X4	10
Net book amount at 31 December 19X4	40
Net book amount at 31 December 19X3	50

The goodwill arose on the acquisition of the partnership business of Seapound & Co in 19X3 and was equal to three times the average profits of that partnership during its last five years of trading. It is being written off in equal instalments over five years, being its estimated useful economic life.

Goodwill is to be written off over a period not exceeding its useful economic life. The reasons for choosing the write-off period must be stated.

3.3   Tangible assets

	Land and buildings	Plant and machinery	Fixtures, fittings, tools and equipment	Payments on account and assets in course of construction	Total
	£'000	£'000	£'000	£'000	£'000
Cost or valuation:					
At 1 January 19X4	871	998	207	27	2,103
Additions	74	809	25	13	921
Disposals	-	(23)	(5)	-	(28)
At 31 December 19X4	945	1,784	227	40	2,996
Includes assets valued in 19X1:					
At 31 December 19X4	461	29	-	-	490
At 31 December 19X3	461	29	-	-	490
Accumulated depreciation:					
At 1 January 19X4	33	292	25	-	350
Provision for year	11	622	27	8	668
Disposals	-	(4)	(4)	-	(8)
At 31 December 19X4	44	910	48	8	1,010
Net book amount:					
at 31 December 19X4	901	874	179	32	1,986
at 31 December 19X3	838	706	182	27	1,753

The net book amount of land and buildings comprises:

	19X4 £'000	19X3 £'000
Freehold	629	555
Long leasehold	129	129
Short leasehold	143	154
	901	838

Accounting principles for fixed assets

These also apply to investments which are fixed assets.

(a)   Normally to be stated at purchase price or production cost, less provisions for depreciation or diminution in value where appropriate. Interest on capital borrowed to finance the manufacture of an asset may be capitalised. Current cost accounting or the revaluation of specific assets is, however, permitted, but historical cost equivalents must be shown in the notes.

(b)   The depreciable amount of assets with limited useful economic lives must be written off systematically over those lives.

(c)   Provision for diminution in value must be made if any reduction in value is expected to be permanent or written back to the extent that it is no longer necessary.

(d)   Tangible assets may be carried at a fixed amount where they are constantly being replaced and are neither material to the company nor subject to material variation in quantity or value (such as tools).

3.4   Disclosure of fixed assets

Movements on each of the four categories (may be shown in notes) giving cost or revalued amount (whichever is appropriate), additions, disposals, transfers and any revision of revalued amount. Movements on cumulative depreciation and provisions for diminution in value must also be shown, including provision for the year, the effect of disposals and any other adjustment.

(a)   **Valuation of fixed assets**

Where fixed assets are included at a valuation the notes must disclose:

(i)   The years (so far as they are known to the directors) in which the assets were valued and, for each year, the value of the assets involved;

(ii)   For assets which have been valued during the financial year, the names of the persons who valued them or particulars of their qualifications and, in either event, the bases of valuation adopted;

(iii)   All historical cost information that would be required if there were no valuation.

(b)   **Land and buildings**

There must be disclosure of the division between freehold and leasehold interests in respect of amounts shown in the balance sheet or its related notes in respect of land and buildings. Leasehold interest must be further sub-divided between long leases (unexpired terms of 50 years or more) and short leases (unexpired terms of less than 50 years).

3.5   Investments

	1 Jan. 19X4 £'000	Additions £'000	Disposals £'000	31 Dec. 19X4 £'000
Listed shares (market value £28,500) **(£31,000)**	24	1	5	20
Unquoted investments in shares	8	-	-	8
Loans	1	-	-	1
	33	1	5	29

Presentation of investments

The investments must be analysed into seven categories:

(a)   Shares in group undertakings;
(b)   Loans to group undertakings;
(c)   Participating interests;
(d)   Loans to undertakings in which the company has a participating interest;
(e)   Other investments other than loans;
(f)   Other loans;
(g)   Own shares.

Note: that in the example, only categories (e) and (f) are represented.

For each category of investments there must be disclosure of the book amount of listed investments.

The market value of listed investments in each category must be given by way of note where it differs from the balance sheet amount. The stock exchange value of any investment must be disclosed where a market value has been taken which is higher than the stock exchange value.

Accounting principles for investments

(a)   As for tangible assets, except that the purchase price of fungible assets (ie, those which are indistinguishable from one another) may be calculated using an appropriate method such as FIFO, LIFO or weighted average.

(b)   Provision for diminution in value may be made where an investment has fallen in value even though the fall may be temporary. Such a provision must be written back to the extent that it is no longer necessary.

Definitions of investments

(a)   Group undertakings are a parent company, subsidiary undertakings or fellow subsidiary undertakings.

(b)   A participating interest is an interest held in the shares of another undertaking, held for the long term, with a view to exercising control or influence to secure a benefit to the investor's own activities. Where an investor holds 20% or more of the shares there is a presumption that this is a participating interest.

4   NOTES TO THE BALANCE SHEET - CURRENT ASSETS & LIABILITIES

4.1   Accounting principles

General rules for current assets:

(a)   Stated at purchase price or production cost, except where net realisable value is lower.

(b)   Provisions to reduce to net realisable value must be written back if the reasons for which they were made have ceased to apply.

[Definition]   Purchase price is the actual price paid plus any expenses incidental to the acquisition and includes any consideration (whether in cash or otherwise) given in respect of an asset.

[Definition]   Production cost includes raw materials, consumables and direct production costs. A reasonable proportion of indirect production costs and interest on capital borrowed to finance production of the asset may also be included. In the case of a current asset, distribution costs may not be included in production costs.

4.2   Stocks

	£'000	*19X3* £'000
Raw materials and consumables	437	505
Work in progress	306	281
Finished goods and goods for resale	871	803
Payments on account	23	9
	1,637	1,598

Accounting principles

(a)   Purchase price or production cost may be determined by FIFO, LIFO, weighted average or some similar method. The method chosen must be one which appears to the directors to be appropriate in the circumstances of the company. However, the use of LIFO would not normally be permitted by accounting standards. Any material difference between cost calculated by one of these methods and market value or replacement cost or, if more appropriate, the most recent actual purchase price must be disclosed in the notes.

(b)   Stocks may be included at current cost.

(c)   Raw materials and consumables may be carried at a fixed amount where they are constantly being replaced and are neither material to the company nor subject to material variation in quantity or value.

Disclosure

Any material difference between the balance sheet amount of stocks and replacement cost or, if more appropriate, the most recent actual purchase price must be disclosed for each category of stocks.

4.3   Debtors

	£'000	*19X3* £'000
Trade debtors	1,327	1,191
Other debtors	408	250
Prepayments and accrued income	344	194
	2,079	1,635

Presentation

(a)   Amounts falling due after more than one year must be shown separately for each item.

(b)   There are six categories:

    (i)   Trade debtors;
    (ii)   Amounts owed by group undertakings;
    (iii)   Amounts owed by undertakings in which the company has a participating interest;
    (iv)   Other debtors;
    (v)   Called up share capital not paid;
    (vi)   Prepayments and accrued income.

Notes:

    (1)   Called up share capital not paid may be shown as the first item on the balance sheet, before fixed assets, if preferred.

(2)   Prepayments and accrued income may be shown as a separate category, after cash at bank and in hand, if preferred.

4.4   Investments

All investments disclosed as current assets are in shares listed on a recognised stock exchange and are shown at the lower of cost and market value. The aggregate market value is £143,000 (19X3 £45,000).

Presentation

There are three categories (these may be shown in notes):

(a)   Shares in group undertakings;
(b)   Own shares;
(c)   Other investments.

Accounting principles

(a)   As for current assets generally but purchase price of similar investments may be calculated using an appropriate method such as FIFO, LIFO or weighted average.

(b)   Investments may be stated at current cost.

Disclosure

In any case where cost is calculated using the methods appropriate for fungible assets, any material difference from market value or, if more appropriate, the most recent actual price must be disclosed.

4.5   Creditors: amounts falling due within one year

	£'000	*19X3* £'000
Debenture loans	200	-
Bank loans and overdrafts	20	20
Trade creditors	1,281	1,007
Taxation and social security	35	11
Proposed dividends	30	-
Other creditors	62	613
Accruals and deferred income	1,382	1,329
	3,010	2,980

Presentation

There are nine categories illustrated in the pro-formas in **CA85**. These are expanded as follows to include other items which, if they arose, would require to be shown separately:

(a)   Debenture loans (showing convertible loans separately);
(b)   Bank loans and overdrafts;
(c)   Other loans;
(d)   Payments received on account (if not shown as deductions from stocks);
(e)   Trade creditors;
(f)   Bills of exchange payable;
(g)   Amounts owed to group undertakings;
(h)   Amounts owed to undertakings in which the company has a participating interest;
(i)   Taxation and social security;
(j)   Proposed dividends;
(k)   Other creditors;
(l)   Accruals and deferred income.

Accounting principles

(a)   Where the amount owing to a creditor is greater than the value of the consideration received (eg, discount on issue of a debenture loan) the difference may be treated as an asset (rather than written off at once). The difference must be written off by a reasonable amount each year and be completely written off before repayment of the debt. The current amount not written off must be shown separately in the balance sheet or in the notes.

(b)   The accruals concept should be followed.

Notes:

(1)   Indicate loans which are secured on the company's assets without specifying which assets.

(2)   Provisions for deferred taxation should be shown separately from provisions for other taxation.

(3)   Show proposed dividends at the net cash amount payable to the shareholders.

4.6   Creditors: amounts falling due after more than one year

	£'000	*19X3* £'000
Debenture loans	100	300
Bank loans and overdrafts	29	115
Other loans	224	24
Taxation and social security	400	23
Deferred income	157	33
	910	495

(a)   **Debenture loans**

Interest is payable at a rate of 10% pa. The loans are redeemable in 19X9. £200,000 of the long-term debenture loans outstanding in 19X3 are redeemable during 19X5 and are included in arriving at net current assets.

(b)   **Other loans**

	£'000	*19X3* £'000
Medium-term (repayable within five years from the current balance sheet date)	15	15
Long-term	209	9
	224	24

The long-term loan is from Seascrew Finance plc. It is repayable on demand after 19X8, and carries a rate of interest of 18% pa. The loan is secured by a floating charge on the undertaking, property and assets of the company.

Notes:

(1)   Presentation should be as for current liability creditors, with a maximum of twelve categories.

(2)   Debentures and loan stocks:

Where debentures or any form of loan stock have been issued during a financial year, there must be shown:

(i)   The classes of debenture issued;

(ii)   For each class, the amount issued and the consideration received.

Where any of the debentures are held for the company by a nominee or trustee, the nominal amount of the debentures and the amount at which they are carried in the company's accounting records must be disclosed.

(3)   **All creditors**

For each item under creditors show the aggregate of both:

(i)   non-instalment debts that fall due for repayment after five years; and
(ii)   instalment debts some of which fall due for payment after five years.

The terms of repayment and the rate of interest payable should be shown for each debt which falls to be taken into account in the above disclosure. However, it will be sufficient to provide a general indication of repayment terms and interest rates if compliance with this requirement would result in a statement of excessive length.

For each category of creditors, there must be shown the amount for which security has been given and an indication of the nature of the security.

4.7   Provisions for liabilities and charges

		19X3
	£'000	£'000
Pensions and similar obligations	16	2
Taxation, including deferred taxation	8	8
Other provisions	3	3
	27	13

Pensions and similar obligations:	
At 1 January 19X4	2
Transfer from profit and loss account	14
At 31 December 19X4	16

The taxation provision is wholly in respect of deferred taxation. There has been no movement on this account during the year.

Notes:

(1)   Movements:

Where there is a movement on any provision for liabilities and charges (other than a transfer from a provision for the purpose for which it was established) there must be disclosure of the movements on that provision, consisting of:

(i)   The amount at the beginning and the end of the year;
(ii)   Transfers to or from the provision during that year;
(iii)   The source and application of the amounts transferred.

Corresponding amounts need not be given.

(2)   Pensions:

Particulars must be given of any pension commitments which have been provided for under 'provisions for liabilities and charges' and of any pension contributions for which no provision has been made. Separate particulars are required of any commitment which relates wholly or partly to pensions payable to past directors.

Definition   Provisions are amounts retained for any liability or loss which either is likely to be incurred, or certain to be incurred but uncertain as to amount or date on which it will arise.

Deferred taxation, which is not defined in the Act, is expected to be treated as a 'provision' since it is likely that there will be some uncertainty regarding either the amount required or the date on which timing differences may reverse. Other tax 'provisions' are likely to be classified as 'creditors' unless there is some uncertainty as to either the amount of the liability or the date on which it will arise.

4.8   Called up share capital

		19X3
	£'000	£'000
Allotted and fully paid:		
Ordinary shares of £1 each	1,200	1,200
6% cumulative preference shares of 50p each	300	300
	1,500	1,500

Disclosure

(a)   The amount of allotted share capital and the amount of called up share capital which has been paid up must be shown separately.

(b)   The authorised share capital and, where there is more than one class of shares, the number and aggregate nominal value of each class allotted must be disclosed.

(c)   Where shares have been allotted during a financial year there must be shown:

   (i)   the class of shares allotted;

   (ii)   for each class, the number allotted, their aggregate nominal value and the consideration received.

(d)   If there are any redeemable shares, there must be disclosed:

   (i)   The earliest and latest dates of redemption;
   (ii)   Whether the redemption is obligatory or at the option of the company;
   (iii)   Whether any premium is payable on redemption.

(e)   If any fixed cumulative dividends on shares are in arrears, there must be shown:

   (i)   The amount of the arrears;
   (ii)   The period for which the dividends are in arrears (by class of shares).

Definition   Called up share capital is the aggregate amount of calls made on shares, share capital paid up without being called and share capital to be paid on a specified future date under the terms of allotment.

Allotted share capital is not defined but is presumed to be the full nominal value of shares allotted.

4.9   Reserves

	Profit and loss account £'000
At 1 January 19X4	97
Currency translation differences	(28)
Amount set aside from profit for the financial year	454
At 31 December 19X4	523

The profit and loss account balance and the other reserves are wholly distributable.

Revaluation reserve

Presentation

An alternative name may be used such as current cost reserve.

Accounting principles

(a)   Surpluses or deficits which arise from stating assets at market value or current cost must be taken to the revaluation reserve.

(b)   An amount may be transferred from the revaluation reserve to the profit and loss account if the amount was previously charged to that account and represents realised profit.

(c)   An amount may be transferred from the revaluation reserve on capitalisation by means of a bonus issue of shares.

Disclosure

(a)   The treatment for tax purposes of amounts taken to revaluation reserve must be disclosed.

(b)   Movements on revaluation reserve are to be shown in notes.

Other reserves

There are four categories:

(a)   Capital redemption reserve;
(b)   Reserve for own shares;
(c)   Reserves provided for by the articles of association;
(d)   Other reserves.

All movements on reserve accounts must be shown. It is advisable to indicate whether reserves are considered to be distributable or otherwise.

4.10   Other balance sheet notes

(a)   Security for the indebtedness of others

Any charge on the assets of the company to secure the liabilities of another person must be disclosed, including, where practicable, the amount secured.

(b)   Contingent liabilities and financial commitments

For any contingent liability not provided for in the accounts, there must be shown:

(i)   The amount or estimated amount of the liability;
(ii)   Its legal nature;
(iii)   Details of any security provided in connection with the liability.

As regards commitments for capital expenditure, there must be shown the amount of contracts for capital expenditure which have not been provided for in the accounts.

Any other financial commitments which have not been provided for in the accounts and are relevant to an assessment of the company's state of affairs must be disclosed.

Any security, contingent liability or commitment which has been entered into on behalf of a group undertaking must be shown separately. Any such disclosure must distinguish between commitments on behalf of:

(i)   A parent company or a fellow subsidiary undertaking;

(ii)   A subsidiary undertaking.

(c)   **Transactions and arrangements in which directors have a material interest**

The name of the director and the nature of his interest must be disclosed, together with the value of the transaction or arrangement. Service contracts are excluded, and also transactions or arrangements which do not at any time exceed the lower of £5,000 and 1% of net assets as at the year end.

5   PREPARING ACCOUNTS IN ACCORDANCE WITH THE PRESCRIBED FORMATS

5.1   Approach to computational questions

Computational balance sheet disclosure questions do not generally specify a particular format to be used and thus Format 1 should be followed.

Allow a whole page for the balance sheet, a page for the notes and a separate page for the workings.

Few workings will be required as the notes to the accounts can often act as workings as well. For example a fixed asset note per the CA 85 requires an analysis of each major type of fixed asset showing brought forward figures, additions and disposals for both cost and depreciation. Thus the working out of the year end figures for fixed assets is effectively done by producing the note.

When presenting the balance sheet

(a)   write out a heading in full

(b)   use the same narrative as in the CA 85 format

(c)   leave some space between the various parts and allow for the later insertion of figures that you may have forgotten to include. The examiner will not deduct marks if there is a lot of 'white space'. He will deduct marks if the statement is so cramped as to be illegible.

Much use can be made of the combination provisions of the CA 85 to show a summarised balance sheet and the detailed figures in the notes. For example

Approach 1

Face of balance sheet

	£
Creditors: amounts falling due within one year	300,000

Notes to the accounts

Creditors: amounts falling due within one year:	
Bank overdraft	160,000
Trade creditors	120,000
Accruals	5,000
Proposed dividend	15,000
	300,000

Approach 2

Face of balance sheet

		£
Creditors:	amounts falling due within one year:	
	Bank overdraft	160,000
	Trade creditors	120,000
	Accruals	5,000
	Proposed dividend	15,000
		300,000

The advantages of approach 1 are

(a)   it is often neater and

(b)   it is easier to add missed out creditors without the end result being cramped.

The advantage of approach 2 is that less writing is involved.

The choice really depends on how tidy and methodical you are.

It is helpful to allow two or three columns for the figures on the balance sheet (comparative figures are rarely required). An example balance sheet (based on Seaton's that was introduced earlier) is reproduced below to show a suggested layout for examination purposes.

Seaton plc
Balance sheet at 31 December 19X4

	Notes	£'000	£'000
Fixed assets			
Tangible assets	(1)		2,139
Investments	(2)		29
			2,168
Current assets			
Stocks	(3)	1,637	
Debtors	(4)	2,079	
Investments	(5)	126	
Cash at bank and in hand		75	
		3,917	
Creditors: amounts falling due within one year	(6)	3,010	
Net current assets			907
Total assets less current liabilities			3,075
Creditors: amounts falling due after more than one year	(7)	910	
Provisions for liabilities and charges	(8)	27	
			937
			2,138

Capital and reserves

Called up share capital	(9)	1,500
Share premium account		23
Revaluation reserve		25
Other reserves	(10)	67
Profit and loss account	(10)	523
		2,138

The accounts were approved by
the directors on 3 March 19X5

Colyn Seaton

Director

5.2   Activity

Small plc is a quoted company with an authorised share capital of £250,000, consisting of ordinary shares of £1 each. The company prepares its accounts as on 31 March in each year and the trial balance, before final adjustments, extracted on 31 March 19X5 showed:

	£	£
Ordinary share capital, issued and fully paid		200,000
Retained profits as on 1 April 19X4		61,000
6% Debenture stock (secured on leasehold factory)		60,000
Leasehold factory:		
Cost at beginning of year	200,000	
Accumulated depreciation at beginning of year		76,000
Plant and machinery :		
Cost at beginning of year	80,000	
Accumulated depreciation		30,000
Additions in year	10,000	
Creditors and accrued expenses		170,000
Stock as on 31 March 19X5	160,000	
Debtors	100,000	
Prepayments	80,000	
Balance at bank	90,000	
Profit for the year (subject to any items in the following notes)		111,000
Sale proceeds of plant		12,000
	720,000	720,000

You ascertain that:

(1)   The debenture stock is repayable at par by six equal annual drawings starting on 31 December 19X5.

(2)   The lease of the factory has 56 years remaining at 31 March 19X5.

(3)   Annual depreciation is calculated as to:

> Leasehold factory   –   2% on cost

> Plant and machinery   –   20% reducing balance on NBV as at 31 March 19X4 plus additions less disposals in the year

(4)   Plant disposed of originally cost £16,000. Accumulated depreciation is £3,200.

(5)   Stock has been valued consistently at the lower of cost and net realisable value.

(6)   A dividend of 20% is proposed.

(7)   The directors have placed contracts for new plant costing £5,000. These have not been provided for, but should be disclosed.

You are required to prepare in a form suitable for publication and in conformity with the provisions of the Companies Act 1985, the balance sheet as on 31 March 19X5 together with accompanying notes.

5.3   Activity solution

Small plc

Balance sheet as at 31 March 19X5

	£	£
Fixed assets		
Tangible assets		157,760
Current assets		
Stocks	160,000	
Debtors	180,000	
Cash at bank and in hand	90,000	
	430,000	
Creditors: amounts falling due within one year	220,000	
Net current assets		210,000
Total assets less current liabilities		367,760
Creditors: amounts falling due after more than one year		50,000
		317,760
Capital and reserves		
Called up share capital		200,000
Profit and loss account		117,760
		317,760

The accounts were approved by the directors on ....

Signed A Director

Notes to the balance sheet

(a)   **Statement of accounting policies**

    (i)   The accounts have been prepared in accordance with applicable accounting standards.

    (ii)   Depreciation

        (1)   Leasehold factory - 2% on cost.

(2)   Plant and machinery - depreciation is calculated on the reducing balance method at a rate of 20% pa. Assets acquired during the year are charged with a full year's depreciation.

(iii)   Stock

Stock has been valued at the lower of cost and net realisable value.

(b)   **Tangible assets**

	Long leasehold property £	Plant and machinery £	Total £
Cost:			
At 1 April 19X4	200,000	80,000	280,000
Additions	-	10,000	10,000
Disposals	-	(16,000)	(16,000)
At 31 March 19X5	200,000	74,000	274,000
Aggregate depreciation:			
At 1 April 19X4	76,000	30,000	106,000
Eliminated on disposals		(3,200)	(3,200)
Amount provided	4,000	9,440	13,440
At 31 March 19X5	80,000	36,240	116,240
Net book value:			
at 31 March 19X5	120,000	37,760	157,760
at 31 March 19X4	124,000	50,000	174,000

Note: future capital expenditure

	£
Contracted for but not provided in the accounts	5,000

(Tutorial note: the note above is an example of some detailed disclosure requirements that can be tested (see the end of the section dealing with the balance sheet in the chapter). You will not fail an exam if you do not know such detailed points but the more that is known, the more 'bonus' marks you will pick up.*)*

(c)   **Debtors**

	£
Trade debtors	100,000
Prepayments and accrued income	80,000
	180,000

(d)   **Creditors: amounts falling due within one year**

	£
Debenture loan	10,000
Trade creditors	170,000
Proposed dividend	40,000
	220,000

(e)   **Creditors: amounts falling due after more than one year**

This consists of 6% debenture stock repayable at par by five equal annual drawings commencing 31 December 19X6. £10,000 is payable more than five years from the balance sheet date. The debenture stock is secured.

(f)   **Called up share capital**

	Authorised £	Allotted fully paid £
Ordinary shares of £1 each	250,000	200,000

(g)   **Profit and loss account**

	£
Retained profit as at 1 April 19X4	61,000
Add: Retained profit for the year (W3)	56,760
Retained profit as at 31 March 19X5	117,760

WORKINGS

(W1)	Depreciation		£	£
	Leasehold factory 2% of £200,000			4,000
	Plant and machinery			
	NBV b/d		50,000	
	Additions		10,000	
	Disposals at NBV		(12,800)	
	Depreciation 20% ×		47,200 =	9,440
				13,440

(W2)	Disposal of plant		
	Proceeds		12,000
	Cost	16,000	
	Less: Depreciation	3,200	
			12,800
			800

(W3)	Profit for year per TB			111,000
	Less: Depreciation	(4,000 + 9,440)	13,440	
	Loss on sale	(W2)	800	
	Proposed dividend	(20% × 200,000)	40,000	
				54,240
				56,760

6   THE PROFIT AND LOSS ACCOUNT – FORMATS

6.1   The formats

The two vertical formats are reproduced below. Format 1 is the 'operational' statement and format 2 is the 'type of expenditure' statement. Format 1 is the more common.

Profit and loss account - Format 1

1   Turnover
2   Cost of sales (14)
3   Gross profit or loss
4   Distribution costs (14)
5   Administrative expenses (14)
6   Other operating income
7   Income from shares in group undertakings
8   Income from participating interests
9   Income from other fixed asset investments (15)
10   Other interest receivable and similar income (15)
11   Amounts written off investments
12   Interest payable and similar charges (16)
13   Tax on profit or loss on ordinary activities
14   Profit or loss on ordinary activities after taxation
15   Extraordinary income
16   Extraordinary charges
17   Extraordinary profit or loss
18   Tax on extraordinary profit or loss
19   Other taxes not shown under the above items
20   Profit or loss for the financial year

Format 2

1   Turnover
2   Change in stocks of finished goods and in work in progress
3   Own work capitalised
4   Other operating income
5   (a)   Raw materials and consumables
        (b)   Other external charges
6   Staff costs:
        (a)   Wages and salaries
        (b)   Social security costs
        (c)   Other pension costs
7   (a)   Depreciation and other amounts written off tangible and intangible fixed assets
        (b)   Exceptional amounts written off current assets
8   Other operating charges
9   Income from shares in group undertakings
10   Income from participating interests
11   Income from other fixed asset investments (15)
12   Other interest receivable and similar income (15)
13   Amounts written off investments
14   Interest payable and similar charges (16)
15   Tax on profit or loss on ordinary activities
16   Profit or loss on ordinary activities after taxation
17   Extraordinary income
18   Extraordinary charges
19   Extraordinary profit or loss
20   Tax on extraordinary profit or loss
21   Other taxes not shown under the above items
22   Profit or loss for the financial year

Notes on the profit and loss account formats

(14) Cost of sales: distribution costs: administrative expenses
(Format 1, items 2, 4 and 5)
These items shall be stated after taking into account any necessary provisions for depreciation or diminution in value of assets.

(15) Income from other fixed asset investments: other interest receivable and similar income
(Format 1, items 9 and 10: Format 2, items 11 and 12)
Income and interest derived from group companies shall be shown separately from income and interest derived from other sources.

(16) Interest payable and similar charges
(Format 1, item 12: Format 2, item 14)
The amount payable to group companies shall be shown separately.

(17) Format 1
The amount of any provisions for depreciation and diminution in value of tangible and intangible fixed assets falling to be shown under item 7(a) in Format 2 shall be disclosed in a note to the accounts in any case where the profit and loss account is prepared by reference to Format 1.

6.2 Comments on the profit and loss account

(a) As there are no alphabetical or Roman numerals assigned to items in the profit and loss account none of these items have to be disclosed on the face of the profit and loss account. The items which must appear in a profit and loss account do not in fact appear in any of the formats but every profit and loss account must show:

(i) the company's profit or loss on ordinary activities before taxation

(ii) any amount set aside or proposed to be set aside to, or withdrawn or proposed to be withdrawn from, reserves and

(iii) the aggregate amount of any dividends paid and proposed, showing separately the amount of proposed dividends if this is not disclosed in a note.

(b) The extent to which items included in the formats need to be disclosed on the face of the profit and loss account is subject to the same principles as the balance sheet:

(i) items must be rearranged or adapted where the special nature of the company's business requires such adaptation

(ii) items may be combined if either (1) the individual amounts are not material to assessing the profit and loss of the company or (2) the combination of items facilitates the assessment of the profit and loss of the company.

In the latter case the individual amounts of the combined items must be disclosed in a note to the accounts.

(c) The information disclosed in Formats 1 and 2 is not exactly equivalent. For example gross profit is not shown in Format 2. It should be also noted that although Format 1 does not include items such as staff costs, such items are required to be disclosed as part of the general disclosure provisions (dealt with later).

(d) You should be aware from your earlier studies of FRS 3 that extraordinary items have now effectively been outlawed, so items 15 to 18 (format 1) and items 17 to 20 (format 2) in the statutory profit and loss accounts would not now be used.

(e)   The arabic numerals themselves are **not** disclosed in the profit and loss account.

6.3   The profit and loss account – An example of presentation

Seaton plc
Profit and loss account for the year ended 31 December 19X4

	Notes	£'000	19X3 £'000
Turnover	(7.1)	4,910	3,505
Cost of sales		(2,475)	(1,210)
Gross profit		2,435	2,295
Distribution costs		(716)	(946)
Administrative expenses		(756)	(1,198)
Other operating income		13	7
Income from fixed asset investments	(7.5)	4	6
Other interest receivable and similar income		15	5
Interest payable and similar charges	(7.6)	(85)	(57)
Profit on ordinary activities before taxation	(7.2)	910	112
Tax on profit on ordinary activities	(7.7)	386	22
Profit for the financial year		524	90
Dividends paid and proposed		70	-
Amount set aside to reserves		454	90

7   NOTES TO THE PROFIT AND LOSS ACCOUNT

Note: not all these notes are cross referenced directly to the profit and loss account.   Accounting policies are required where relevant.

7.1   Segmental information

	Turnover	
	19X4 £'000	19X3 £'000
Class of business:		
Seaton	2,378	1,650
Seatex	1,831	1,583
Seatan	701	272
	4,910	3,505

	Turnover	
	19X4 £'000	19X3 £'000
Geographical market:		
United Kingdom	2,490	2,112
United States of America	1,012	989
Europe	987	182
India	151	63
Australia	270	159
	4,910	3,505

Turnover and profit disclosure

(a) Notes must show turnover broken down by classes of business and by geographical markets, having regard to the manner in which the company's activities are organised, in so far as these classes and markets differ substantially.

(b) SSAP 25 contains additional requirements for larger companies to disclose the segmental breakdown of profits before tax as well as turnover.

(c) Classes or markets which do not differ substantially must be treated as one class or market. Immaterial amounts may be combined with those of another class or market.

(d) This segmental information may be omitted if disclosure would be seriously prejudicial to the company's interests. The fact that such information has not been disclosed must be stated in the notes.

7.2 Profit on ordinary activities before taxation

	£'000	£'000
Profit before taxation is stated after the following amounts:		
Depreciation and amortisation	701	450
Auditors' remuneration	28	22

Profit before taxation - presentation

Surprisingly this heading does not appear in any of the formats but, nevertheless, CA85 specifies that the amount of profit or loss on ordinary activities before taxation must be shown in the profit and loss account.

Note: CA85 specifies that cost of sales, distribution costs and administrative expenses must include any necessary provisions for depreciation or diminution in the value of assets.

(a) **Depreciation and other amounts written off tangible and intangible fixed assets**

Accounting principles

(i) The depreciable amount of assets with limited useful economic lives must be written off systematically over those lives.

(ii) Provision for diminution in value must be made if any reduction in value is expected to be permanent or written back to the extent that it is no longer necessary.

(iii) Goodwill is to be written off over a period not exceeding its useful economic life.

(iv) Development costs, where capitalised, are to be written off over a period which must be stated in those notes.

(b) **Auditors' remuneration**

Amounts must be disclosed both for fees (including expenses) paid to the auditors for audit work as well as fees for non-audit work.

7.3   Directors' emoluments

		19X3
	£'000	£'000
Aggregate emoluments	225	114
Gains made on exercise of share options	10	8
Amounts receivable under long-term incentive schemes	10	5
Company pension contributions to money purchase schemes	25	20
Compensation for loss of office	45	–
Sums paid to third parties for directors' services	–	3
	315	150

Retirement benefits are accruing to six directors under a money purchase pension scheme and to two directors under a defined benefit scheme.

The highest paid director received emoluments as follows:

		19X3
	£'000	£'000
Aggregate emoluments, gains on share options exercised and benefits under long-term incentive schemes	47	21
Company pension contributions to money purchase scheme	-	-
Defined benefit pension scheme:		
Accrued pension at end of year	20	17
Accrued lump sum at end of year	50	40

Disclosure

(a)   The aggregate amount of emoluments paid to or receivable by directors in respect of qualifying services (ie, services as a director of the company). Emoluments include salaries, fees and bonuses, taxable expense allowances, estimated money value of any other benefits and any amounts paid in respect of the director accepting office as a director.

(b)   The aggregate of the amount of directors' gains on the exercise of share options.

(c)   The aggregate of the following:

(i)   the amount of money paid to or receivable by directors under long term incentive schemes in respect of qualifying services; and

(ii)   the net value of assets (other than money and share options) received or receivable by directors under such schemes.

(d)   The aggregate value of any company contributions paid to a pension scheme in respect of directors' qualifying services.

(Unlisted companies do not have to disclose share option gains, but must show the number of directors who exercised share options and who received or became entitled to shares under long term incentive schemes.)

(e)   Number of directors who are accruing benefits under:

•   money purchase pension schemes
•   defined benefit pension schemes.

Where the combined total of directors' emoluments, gains on the exercise of share options and amounts receivable under long term incentive schemes is £200,000 or more the following additional information must be given in respect of the **highest paid director**:

(a)   Emoluments (including gains on the exercise of share options and amounts receivable under long term incentive schemes).

(b)   Company contributions paid to a pension scheme.

(c)   Accrued retirement benefits (where the highest paid director is a member of a defined benefit scheme).

Unlisted companies must also state whether the highest paid director exercised share options or became entitled to shares under long term incentive schemes.

7.4   Staff costs – employees

		19X3
	£'000	£'000
Staff costs:		
Wages and salaries	1,600	1,885
Social security costs	235	280
Other pension costs	187	125

The average number of people employed by the group during the year was:

		19X3
United Kingdom	55	82
United States of America	38	42
Europe	47	25
India	30	20
Australia	35	29

Disclosure

(a)   Staff costs

Disclose:

(i)   Wages and salaries;
(ii)   Social security costs;
(iii)   Other pension costs.

(b)   The average number of employees during the financial year.

(c)   The average number employed within particular categories, as determined by the directors.

The analysis above might alternatively have been given by class of business, or by qualification of employee. The average number is determined by summing the total number of employees each month throughout the year and dividing by 12.

7.5   Income from investments

Within the headings 'Income from other fixed investments' and 'Other interest receivable and similar income', the income and interest derived from group companies should be shown separately.

7.6   Interest payable and similar charges

		19X3
	£'000	£'000
Interest payable on bank loans and overdrafts	80	52
Interest payable on other loans	5	5
	85	57

Disclosure

Separate disclosure is required of the amount of interest payable on, or similar charges in respect of:

(a)   Bank loans and overdrafts;

(b)   Loans of any other kind, whether or not secured.

7.7   Tax on profit on ordinary activities

	£'000	*19X3* £'000
Taxation on the profit for the year:		
UK corporation tax at 30%	356	19
Relief for overseas tax	(15)	(10)
	341	9
Overseas tax	45	13
	386	22

The charge for taxation on the profit for the year has been reduced by £107,000 (19X3 £28,000) in respect of fixed asset timing differences for which no deferred taxation has been provided.

Disclosure

(a)   Special circumstances affecting the liability in respect of profits, income or capital gains for current year or succeeding years.

(b)   Amounts included in tax on profit or loss on ordinary activities for:

   (i)   UK corporation tax;

   (ii)   UK corporation tax before double taxation relief;

   (iii)   UK income tax;

   (iv)   Foreign taxes on profits, income and (if charged to revenue) capital gains.

7.8   Other items

(a)   **Appropriations**

Presentation

The profit and loss account must show two additional items:

●   Amounts transferred or proposed to be transferred to, or withdrawn or proposed to be withdrawn from, reserves.

●   Aggregate amount of dividends paid and proposed, showing separately the amount of proposed dividends if this is not disclosed in a note.

(b)   **Exceptional items**

[Definition]   Items within the normal activities of the business which require disclosure on account of their abnormal size or incidence eg, large bad debts, stock write-offs and losses on long-term contracts. These should be disclosed in arriving at the profit on ordinary activities.

(c)   **Prior period adjustments**

Definition   These are adjustments arising during the accounting period which apply to prior years. They arise fairly rarely, on a change of accounting policy and on the correction of fundamental errors. Their effect must be shown on the balance of retained profit brought forward.

7.9   Activity

Jot down notes explaining which of the items below would require to be disclosed in notes to the profit and loss account.

(a)   Audit fee – £6,000.
(b)   Auditors' expenses – £250.
(c)   Bad debts – £6,000.
(d)   Auditors' preparation of taxation computations – £200.
(e)   Rent of office accommodation – £1,000.
(f)   Capital expenditure of £20,000 authorised by directors, but no contract placed.

7.10   Activity solution

(a)
(b)   require disclosure in notes to the profit and loss account;

(c)   would require disclosure only if the amount were exceptional for the company concerned;

(d)   requires disclosure in notes to the profit and loss account;

(e)   does not require disclosure;

(f)   does not require disclosure.

Conclusion   The detailed disclosure requirements for the profit and loss account are best learnt by memorising the statutory formats and then using each caption as a mental 'peg' on which to hang the information disclosed by notes.

8   PREPARING ACCOUNTS IN ACCORDANCE WITH THE PRESCRIBED FORMATS

8.1   Approach to computational questions

Most computational questions do not specify a particular format to be used. Format 1 is generally the easiest to use.

Allow a whole page for the profit and loss account and a page for the notes to the profit and loss account. A working paper may also be needed to show how the various costs given in the question have been allocated to cost of sales, distribution costs and administrative expenses. There are no definitions in the Companies Acts of these cost headings and so, provided a working is submitted which is clear, any reasonable allocation of costs will be marked as correct.

It is important however, to keep the notes to the accounts on a separate page to the workings. In the note to the accounts, you are trying to reproduce information in a published document. The most common notes that are required are

(a)   Detailed expenses
(b)   Directors' emoluments
(c)   Details of tax charge
(d)   Earnings per share (see later).

When presenting the profit and loss account use the same principles as for the balance sheet

(a)   write out a heading in full

(b)   use the same narrative as in the CA85 format

(c)   leave some space between various parts and allow for the later insertion of figures that you may have forgotten to include.

In addition a separate statement of reserves either at the foot of the profit and loss account for the year or in a note to the accounts is the clearest way to compute the year end reserves for the balance sheet and also to comply with the CA85 disclosure requirements (the CA85 requires an analysis of each reserve).

A suggested layout is

Statement of reserves

	Profit and loss account £	*Revaluation reserve* £	*Share premium* £	*Plant replacement* £
As at 1 Jan 19X1	90,000	20,000	Nil	Nil
Profit for the year	89,000			
Revaluation		30,000		
Issue of shares			40,000	
Transfers	(15,000)			15,000
As at 31 Dec 19X1	164,000	50,000	40,000	15,000

A further advantage of the layout is that further reserves can be added as you progress through the question.

8.2   The profit and loss account - format 2

The layout of format 2 needs to be known and occasionally there may be a requirement to use this method. Most cost headings are easily understood, the exceptions being item 5(b), other external charges and item 8, other operating charges. Neither term is defined but a sensible split would be to include factory costs under 5(b) and administrative costs under 8.

Item 2, Change in stocks of finished goods requires some explanation

(a)   an increase in stocks of finished goods and work-in-progress is added to turnover. The presentation implies the increase is 'quasi-income'. The presentation may be most appropriate for an organisation offering professional services. Work-in-progress at the year end represents costs which will be billed (ie, produce income) in the next year.

(b)   a decrease in stocks of finished goods and work-in-progress reduces turnover.

Note that stocks of raw materials are not included in this line - they are instead added to or deducted from raw material expenditure for the year. As no production had been started on this type of stock, it is not appropriate to treat it as 'quasi-income'.

8.3   Example

An extract from the trial balance of Production Ltd as at 30 September 19X3 is given below

	£	£
Turnover		900,000
Stocks:		
Raw materials	40,000	
Work-in-progress	70,000	
Finished goods	60,000	
Raw materials	300,000	
Wages	200,000	
Production overheads	80,000	
Administration salaries	100,000	
Office rent and rates	20,000	
Closing stocks are:		
Raw materials	30,000	
Work-in-progress	62,000	
Finished goods	80,000	

Format 1

Profit and loss account for the year ended 30 September 19X3

	£
Sales	900,000
Cost of sales (working)	578,000
Gross profit	322,000
Administrative expenses (working)	120,000
	202,000

WORKING

Allocation of costs	Cost of sales £	Administrative £
Opening stocks:		
Raw materials	40,000	
Work-in-progress	70,000	
Finished goods	60,000	
Raw materials	300,000	
Wages	200,000	
Production overheads	80,000	
Administrative salaries		100,000
Office rent and rates		20,000
Closing stocks:		
Raw materials	(30,000)	
Work-in-progress	(62,000)	
Finished goods	(80,000)	
	578,000	120,000

Format 2

Profit and loss account for the year ended 30 September 19X3

	£	£
Sales		900,000
Change in stock of finished goods and work-in-progress (W1)		12,000
Raw materials and consumables (W2)	310,000	
Other external charges	80,000	
Staff costs (200 + 100)	300,000	
Other operating charges	20,000	
		(710,000)
		202,000

WORKINGS

		£
(W1)	Closing stock	
	Finished goods	80,000
	Work-in-progress	62,000
	Opening stock	
	Finished goods	(70,000)
	Work-in-progress	(60,000)
	Increase	12,000
(W2)	Raw materials	
	Opening stock	40,000
	Purchases	300,000
	Closing stock	(30,000)
		310,000

9 THE DIRECTORS' REPORT

9.1 Introduction

The company's annual report and accounts must include a Directors' Report. The information to be disclosed is set out in Sch 7 CA85. A checklist of the requirements is given here.

9.2 Checklist of requirements

(1) *Principal activities* Give the principal activities of the company or group together with any changes in those activities during the financial year.

(2) *Business review* A fair review of the activities of the company or group during the year and the position at the end of it.

(3) *Post balance sheet events* Important events affecting the company or group which have occurred since the end of the year.

(4) *Future developments* An indication of likely future developments in the business.

(5) *Research and development* An indication of the activities of the company or group in the field of research and development.

(6) *Dividend* The amount which the directors recommend to be paid as dividends.

(7)   *Asset values* Significant differences between the balance sheet value and market value of freehold or leasehold interests in land.

(8)   *Directors* The names of those who were directors of the company at any time during the financial year.

(9)   *Interests of directors* For each director who holds office at the end of the year disclose the following:

    (a)   Number of shares held.

    (b)   Amount of debentures held.

    (c)   Options for shares or debentures.

(Nil figures should be given if no interest exists.)

The information should be given for the following dates:

    (i)   At the beginning of the financial year or on the date of appointment if appointed during the year; and

    (ii)   At the end of the financial year.

(10)   *Purchase of own shares* Where a company purchases its own shares, or acquires its own shares by forfeiture or in any other manner, there must be disclosure of:

    (a)   number and nominal value of shares purchased;

    (b)   amount paid;

    (c)   reasons for purchases;

    (d)   percentage of called-up share capital which they represent.

(11)   *Disabled employees* If the average number of the company's UK employees exceeds 250, a statement of its policy:

    (a)   for giving full and fair consideration to applications for employment by the company made by disabled persons, having regard to their particular aptitudes and abilities;

    (b)   for continuing the employment of, and for arranging appropriate training for, employees of the company who have become disabled persons during the period when they were employed by the company; and

    (c)   otherwise for the training, career development and promotion of disabled persons employed by the company.

(12)   *Employee involvement* If the average number of the company's UK employees exceeds 250, a statement of its policy for:

    (a)   providing employees systematically with information on matters of concern to them as employees;

    (b)   consulting employees or their representatives on a regular basis so that the views of employees can be taken into account in making decisions which are likely to affect their interests;

    (c)   encouraging the involvement of employees in the company's performance through an employees' share scheme or by some other means;

    (d)   achieving a common awareness on the part of all employees of the financial and economic factors affecting the performance of the company.

(13)   *Donations*   Disclose the total of political and charitable donations if the total is in excess of £200. The total must be split between those for charitable purposes and those for political purposes.

In respect of political donations only, disclose for each donation of more than £200:

(a)   the name of the party or organisation concerned; and

(b)   the amount given.

(14)   *Creditor payment policy* Plcs and large private companies whose parent is a plc, must disclose their payment policy for their suppliers. The directors must state, for the financial year *following* that covered by the annual report, whether it is the company's policy to follow any code or standard on payment practice. If so, the name of the code/standard must be given, together with information on how a copy can be obtained. If not, it must state its policy.

The directors must also state whether it is the company's policy to:

(a)   settle the terms of payment with suppliers when agreeing the terms of each transaction;

(b)   ensure that suppliers are made aware of the terms of payment;

(c)   abide by the terms of payment.

The directors must also state the following figure, expressed in days:

$$\frac{\text{Amount owed to trade creditors at the year end}}{\text{Amount invoiced by suppliers during the year}} \times 365$$

(15)   *Approval*   The board of directors must approve the directors' report and authorise either a director or the company secretary to sign the directors' report on behalf of the board.

Conclusion   (a)   The items listed above are the minimum required to meet the requirements of CA85. It is common practice for other matters to be disclosed in the directors' report although not required by law (eg, the reappointment of auditors at the next annual general meeting). There is no particular order of these matters which must be followed to meet legal requirements.

(b)   There are further disclosure requirements which apply to special category companies such as banks and insurance companies. There are further disclosure requirements under Stock Exchange regulations.

9.3   Activity

Do the following items require disclosure in the directors' report, and if so, how? Jot down notes to explain your answers.

(a)   Overseas plc exported half of its turnover of £400,000.

(b)   Charitable donations of £500 were made, of which £400 was to Oxfam.

9.4   Activity solution

(a)   No. CA85 requires no information with regard to exports.

(b)   Charitable donations   £500

(detail not required).

10   SMALL AND MEDIUM SIZED COMPANIES

10.1   Introduction

CA85 introduced into law a distinction between the requirements in relation to the accounts prepared by a small or medium company for circulation to its members and those which it files with the Registrar of Companies. Small and medium companies (as defined below) may file 'abbreviated' accounts with the Registrar of Companies. They are, however, still required to send a full set of accounts to their members.

The *CA89* removed the term 'modified' accounts from the legislation, and made some amendments to the requirements. In addition, small or medium companies are not required to state in their full accounts whether the accounts have been prepared in accordance with applicable accounting standards.

In 1992 a statutory instrument was issued which:

(a)   amended the small and medium sized company limits;

(b)   reduced the extent of disclosure of small companies in their 'full' financial statements.

10.2   Criteria

A company qualifies as small or medium if, for the financial year in question and the immediately preceding financial year, it is within the limits of at least two of the following three criteria:

Size criteria	Small	Medium
Balance sheet total (ie, total assets)	£1,400,000	£5,600,000
Turnover*	£2,800,000	£11,200,000
Average number of employees	50	250

* adjust pro rata where period more or less than twelve months.

Having once qualified as small or medium, a company does not cease to qualify unless it fails to satisfy the conditions for two consecutive years, in which case it ceases to qualify in the second such year. For example, a company which satisfies the criteria for a small company in, say, 19X2 and 19X3, but not in 19X4, may still file small company accounts in 19X4. If in 19X5 it still does not satisfy the criteria for a small company (but does for a medium company) it may file medium company accounts (but not small company accounts) in 19X5.

10.3   Exemptions and abbreviations permitted for small companies

(a)   A directors' report is not required.

(b)   A profit and loss account is not required.

(c)   An 'abbreviated balance sheet' is allowed. This need contain only the items preceded by capital letters or roman numerals in the formats in *Sch 4 CA85*. This means that the sub-headings preceded by arabic numerals need not be shown.

(d)   Only a limited number of the notes to the accounts.

(e)   Comparative figures are required for (c) and (d) above.

10.4   Exemptions and abbreviations permitted for medium-sized companies

(a)   A full directors' report is required.

(b)   An abbreviated profit and loss account is allowed which begins with the item 'gross profit or loss'. This is done by combining the following items:

   (i)   Using Format 1 combine items 1, 2, 3 and 6.
   (ii)   Using Format 2 combine items 1, 2, 3, 4 and 5.

(c)   A full balance sheet is required.

(d)   A full set of notes is required except that the particulars of turnover attributable to different classes of business and geographical markets need not be disclosed.

(e)   A company is not entitled to file abbreviated accounts if it is:

   (i)   a public company; or
   (ii)   a banking or insurance company; or
   (iii)   an authorised person under the *Financial Services Act 1986*; or
   (iv)   a member of a group containing any such company.

10.5   Responsibility of directors and auditors

When abbreviated individual accounts are filed with the Registrar of Companies, they must be signed by directors of the company and include a statement by the directors, above their signatures, that they have relied on the exemptions for individual accounts on the ground that the company is entitled to be treated as a small or medium company, as the case may be. Where abbreviated group accounts are filed, the directors' statement must also include a reference to this fact.

Where abbreviated accounts are filed, the auditors must provide a special report, stating that the company is entitled to deliver abbreviated accounts and that the accounts have been properly prepared. Where the full accounts have been qualified, the auditors' report on the full accounts must also be attached.

10.6   Small company statutory accounts

Classification as a small company entitles a company to reduce the extent of disclosure in its annual reports for **members**. This new basis considerably reduces the amount of disclosure required, both in the financial statements and in the directors' report.

Details are given below. There is no need to learn the reduced disclosures, but you need to have an appreciation of their extent.

In the balance sheet the items preceded by letters and roman numerals are unchanged and continue to have to be disclosed. However many of the sub-items preceded by arabic numerals can be aggregated together and renamed as appropriate. In the profit and loss account there are no changes to the standard formats. What has changed is the level of disclosure in the notes to the accounts.

10.7   Modifications to the notes to the accounts

The notes relating to the following may be omitted:

(a)   debentures;

(b)   split of freehold, long leasehold and short leasehold within land and buildings;

(c)   provision for taxation and other particulars of tax;

(d)   particulars of long-term debts (terms of repayment, rate of interest, security etc);

(e)   proposed and paid dividends;

(f)   separate statement of certain items of income and expenditure, ie:

   (i)   interest payable;
   (ii)   auditors' remuneration;

(g)   particulars of staff (numbers, emoluments etc);

(h)   breakdown of aggregate amount of directors' emoluments;

(i)   turnover and geographical analysis.

10.8   Modification to the directors' report

The following information need not be given:

(a)   fair review of business and amount to be paid as dividend;
(b)   employee involvement;
(c)   post balance sheet events;
(d)   likely future developments;
(e)   research and development activities;
(f)   asset values.

10.9   Delivery and publication of additional accounts in ECUs

The *Companies Act 1985* includes an optional facility for all companies to prepare and file at Companies House an additional set of statutory accounts translated into ECUs (European Currency Units).

This additional copy is treated as the statutory accounts of the company and therefore must include the auditors' report as it appears in the sterling statutory accounts.

The translation rate used must be the rate at the balance sheet date, and that rate must be disclosed.

10.10   Activity

State whether a company with the following results could file small or medium-sized accounts in the years 19X6 to 19X9.

	Balance sheet total £'000	Turnover £'000	Average number of employees
19X5	1,300	2,500	45
19X6	1,350	2,750	48
19X7 (15 months)	1,700	3,450	49
19X8	1,800	2,950	52
19X9	1,950	3,100	52

10.11   Activity solution

19X6 - Small

19X7 - Small (Turnover should be pro-rated to 12 months).

19X8 - Meets medium-sized criteria.   However only change if the company fails to satisfy small company criteria for two consecutive years.   Therefore can file small company accounts.

19X9 - Medium.

10.12   Other criteria that may be used to identify a small business enterprise

The current definition of a 'small company' is based on size.   However, many people would argue that it is not size alone that makes a small company different from a large company.

Large companies are often listed companies, owned by a large number of outside investors.   They are managed by directors who may not even own shares and who are accountable to the shareholders.   The overriding objective of a large company is to maximise the return to the investors by maximising profit.

Small companies are almost always private companies. They are often owned and managed by the same people. The objective of a small company is usually to make sufficient profit to support the owners and their dependants. Beyond that it may seek to maximise profit, but may equally well have an interest in minimising profits above a certain level, for tax reasons.

The requirements of financial reporting standards are mainly designed to satisfy the information needs of the owners of large companies, that is, external investors. Many recent accounting standards have had the objective of protecting external investors from the consequences of 'creative accounting' by the directors.

The main users of small company financial statements are not normally external investors, but the Inland Revenue, lenders and potential lenders (often high street banks) and the owner/managers themselves. Increasingly it is being argued that the extensive disclosures required by accounting standards are irrelevant to small companies. The recognition and measurement criteria used by large companies may not be appropriate and may even be positively unhelpful to owner/managers of small companies, who often have little specialist accounting knowledge.

10.13 Financial reporting standard for smaller entities (FRSSE)

In addition to the various exemptions now available under the Companies Acts, small companies are exempt from the requirements of FRS 1 *Cash flow statements* and from some of the requirements of SSAP 13 *Accounting for research and development* and SSAP 25 *Segmental reporting.*

The ASB has now acknowledged that many of the provisions of existing accounting standards are not relevant to smaller entities. In 1997 it made a further and more important concession to small companies by issuing the Financial Reporting Standard for Smaller Entities (FRSSE). A revised and updated version of the FRSSE was issued in December 1998.

The FRSSE is a comprehensive standard containing the measurement and disclosure requirements in existing accounting standards and UITF Abstracts that are relevant to most smaller entities, in a simplified form.

Scope

The FRSSE applies to:

(a)   companies incorporated under companies legislation and entitled to the exemptions available for small companies when filing accounts with the Registrar of Companies; or

(b)   entities that would have come into category (a) above had they been companies incorporated under companies legislation.

Compliance with the FRSSE is optional. An entity that chooses to comply with the FRSSE is exempt from all other accounting standards and UITF Abstracts.

True and fair view

The FRSSE requires that financial statements should present a true and fair view of the results for the period and of the state of affairs at the end of the period. To achieve such a view, regard should be had to the substance of any arrangement or transaction into which the entity has entered. To determine the substance of a transaction it is necessary to identify whether the transaction has given rise to new assets or liabilities for the reporting entity and whether it has changed the entity's existing assets or liabilities.

Therefore the requirement to present a true and fair view is explicitly linked with the requirement to have regard to the substance of transactions.

The FRSSE includes paragraphs on consignment stock and debt factoring, but most of the detailed requirements of FRS 5 do not apply. This is because small entities do not normally enter into complex transactions.

Measurement

The measurement bases required are the same as those in existing standards, but they have been simplified. For example:

- for a finance lease, an asset and liability should normally be stated at fair value (SSAP 21 requires them to be stated at the present value of the minimum lease payments)

- finance charges on finance leases may be charged on a straight line basis (SSAP 21 normally requires the actuarial method or the sum of the digits method).

Disclosure

The financial statements should state that they have been prepared in accordance with the FRSSE.

Many disclosures currently required under existing accounting standards are not required by the FRSSE. Examples of disclosures not required include the following:

- analysis of turnover, costs and results into continuing operations, acquisitions and discontinued operations (FRS 3)

- note of historical cost profits and losses and reconciliation of movements in shareholders' funds (FRS 3)

- analysis of stocks into raw materials, work in progress and finished goods (SSAP 9)

- amounts of research and development expenditure charged to the profit and loss account and movements on deferred development expenditure (SSAP 13).

In addition, entities complying with the FRSSE do not have to make most of the disclosures required under SSAP 15 *Accounting for deferred tax*, SSAP 21 *Accounting for leases and hire purchase contracts*, and SSAP 24 *Accounting for pension costs*.

Groups

The FRSSE applies to small groups (as defined by the Companies Acts). Under the Companies Acts, small groups are not required to prepare consolidated accounts, but may choose to do so. The FRSSE does not cover consolidated accounts and small groups preparing consolidated financial statements are required to comply with the accounting practices and disclosure requirements in FRSs 2, 6, 7, 9 and 10 in their present form.

Cash flow statements

The FRSSE encourages, but does not require small entities to prepare a cash flow statement. It has been argued that a cash flow statement is of limited value for small companies because:

- if transactions are normally straightforward, a cash flow statement adds little to the picture already given by the profit and loss account and the balance sheet;

- the gap between the period-end and the date on which the financial statements are finalised may be so long that the usefulness of cash flow information is limited;

- managers in small businesses are well aware of the need to manage cash effectively.

The argument for requiring small companies to prepare a cash flow statement is that management of cash is crucial in small, as well as large businesses. Potential lenders and other users of the financial statements believe that a cash flow statement provides a useful focus for discussion with management as well as a reference point for subsequent more detailed analysis that they might require.

Related party disclosures

The FRSSE requires the disclosure of related party transactions and includes most of the requirements of FRS 8 *Related party disclosures*. The definition of a related party is the same as that in FRS 8. Small entities need only disclose related party transactions that are material to the reporting entity. (FRS 8 also requires disclosure of transactions that are material to the related party.)

Some commentators have argued that the requirements of the Companies Acts provide adequate protection for users of the financial statements of a small entity. However, the ASB believes that related party transactions are often more common and more material in smaller entities than in larger. For example, directors often give personal guarantees in respect of borrowings of the reporting entity.

11   THE AUDIT PROBLEMS OF SMALL BUSINESSES

11.1   Introduction

Many small businesses are not incorporated and so there has never been a statutory audit required of them. In 1994 the DTI introduced regulations freeing small companies from the requirement to be audited, on the debatable argument that the costs of a small company audit exceeded the benefits gained.

Shareholders who own more than 10% of a small company's shares can insist on an audit, and it is of course possible for any small business, incorporated or unincorporated, to choose to be audited. The regulations governing the relaxation of the statutory audit requirement are summarised at the end of this section; here we set out the problems involved in the audit of a small business where an audit is required by law or has been requested by the management of the business.

11.2   Internal control

Two major constraints on effective internal control of small businesses are as follows

(a)   The restricted scope for division of responsibilities owing to the small number of employees.

(b)   The domination of the accounting function by one person.

A further factor is the nature of the internal controls. The extent of management supervision in day-to-day operations is critical. Management supervision is itself an important element of internal control, but the difficulty from the auditor's viewpoint is that little evidence of its effective operation is available at a subsequent date.

Although the auditor can obtain representations from management the basic difficulty still remains. A further point is that while day-to-day supervision is an important check by management on employees, there is little check on management itself. This is not usually so in the case of large companies because of the existence of effective internal audit functions and sophisticated reporting systems.

Finally, the most difficult situation of all from the auditor's viewpoint comes about in the case of a small but rapidly expanding business. So much of the proprietor's time is taken up with steering the business along an expansion path that the extent and effectiveness of day-to-day supervision is very much reduced.

11.3   Auditing aspects

These may be summarised as follows

(a)   **Letter of engagement**

This is of particular importance for two reasons. Firstly, in a situation where the relationship with the client is likely to be less formal than for larger businesses, it removes any misunderstandings the client may have as to the auditor's responsibilities. Secondly, in circumstances where accounting work is often undertaken it makes clear the distinction between audit and accountancy.

(b)   **Substantive procedures**

In the audit of small companies, the emphasis of audit testing will be aimed towards substantive testing as opposed to tests of control. In particular, tests on debtors and stock verification will be very much intensified.

However, if internal control is very poor, no amount of substantive testing will offer the auditor the necessary assurance. For example, if a business receives a large proportion of its income in the form of cash and internal control over the area is poor, no amount of audit testing will satisfy the auditor that the accounting records are complete and accurate and reflect all the transactions. He may then be unable to express an opinion as to truth and fairness.

(c)   **Management representations**

Letters of representation will be relied on to a far greater extent for small businesses than for large businesses. The auditor will have to decide to what extent the representations of management are backed up by supporting evidence, such as the auditor's knowledge of the business and its records, as well as significant ratios.

(d)   **Overall review**

An overall review is not of itself a sufficient basis for expressing an audit opinion on the financial statements. However, the review does provide valuable support for conclusions reached from other audit work.

There is a limit on the extent to which analytical review techniques may be applied to the financial statements of small businesses. Accounting records may be fairly simple and management information such as monthly accounts budgets non-existent. Weaknesses in internal control may cast severe doubts on the completeness and accuracy of the financial statements.

11.4   The application of auditing standards to small companies

Auditors are required to comply with the essential procedures of SASs in the conduct of any audit, so in principle auditing standards apply to the audit of a small company as much as a large company.

11.5   Auditor independence and small companies

Two factors work against auditor independence in small companies

(a)   Involvement of auditor with management. Inevitably, the small company is likely to look to its auditors for professional advice and guidance. It is also likely that the accounting firm may be involved in the preparation of the accounts, and taxation matters.

(b)   Cost pressures. The audit fee is likely to be relatively larger for a small client than a large client. The auditor will be under pressure to restrict costs, and hence audit time. It is, however, the auditor's professional duty to overcome these problems and maintain his independence.

11.6   Should small companies be audited?

There have been a number of attempts over the last decade to relax the statutory audit requirement for small companies. Regulations in this area finally came into force in 1994 and were revised in 1997; these can be summarised as follows:

(a)   A company (other than a charitable company) is totally exempt if:

   (i)   it qualifies as a small company under CA 85;
   (ii) its turnover is not more than £350,000; and
   (iii) its balance sheet total is not more than £1.4m.

(b)   A charitable company is exempt from the audit requirement but must have an accountant's report if:

   (i)   it qualifies as a small company under CA 85;
   (ii) its turnover is more than £90,000 but not more than £350,000; and
   (iii) its balance sheet total is not more than £1.4m.

(c)   The above exemptions do not apply to public companies, banks, insurers, those authorised under the Financial Services Act, parent companies or subsidiaries.

(d)   A company is not exempt if members holding 10% or more of its shares demand an audit at least one month before the end of the financial year.

(e)   Where a company takes advantage of the exemption its directors must make a statement on the balance sheet acknowledging their responsibility for keeping proper accounting records and for preparing accounts that give a true and fair view and comply with the Companies Act.

11.7   The accountant's report

Where a report is required (for charitable companies with turnovers between £90,000 and £350,000), or otherwise prepared voluntarily, it must be prepared by a reporting accountant who must be a member of one of the recognised supervisory bodies for auditors.

The report must state whether, in the reporting accountant's opinion:

(a)   the accounts agree with the accounting records;
(b)   the accounts have been drawn up in accordance with the Act; and
(c)   the company satisfies the requirements for exemption.

11.8   APB guidance

The Auditing Practices Board issued a Statement of Standards for reporting accountants **Audit Exemption Reports** in October 1994 to give guidance to reporting accountants on their report. Note that this guidance is not a SAS because it is not dealing with the topic of auditing. The Statement of Standards describes the procedures to be followed in carrying out the examination work before a report is written and gives an illustrative example of a report. Note that such reports were originally referred to as compilation reports, though this terminology is now not officially encouraged. You may still come across references to compilation reports, though.

11.9   Example of an accountant's report

ACCOUNTANT'S REPORT TO THE SHAREHOLDERS ON THE UNAUDITED ACCOUNTS OF XYZ LIMITED

We report on the accounts for the year ended . . . set out on pages . . . to . . .

Respective responsibilities of directors and reporting accountants

As described on page . . . the company's directors are responsible for the preparation of the accounts, and they consider that the company is exempt from an audit. It is our responsibility to carry out procedures designed to enable us to report our opinion.

Basis of opinion

Our work was conducted in accordance with the Statement of Standards for reporting accountants, and so our procedures consisted of comparing the accounts with the accounting records kept by the company, and making such limited enquiries of the officers of the company as we considered necessary for the purposes of this report. These procedures provide only the assurance expressed in our opinion.

Opinion

In our opinion:

(a)   the accounts are in agreement with the accounting records kept by the company under section 221 of the Companies Act 1985;

(b)   having regard only to, and on the basis of, the information contained in those accounting records:

   (i)   the accounts have been drawn up in a manner consistent with the accounting requirements specified in section 249C(6) of the Act; and

   (ii)   the company satisfied the conditions for exemption from an audit of the accounts for the year specified in section 249A(4) of the Act and did not, at any time within that year, fall within any of the categories of companies not entitled to the exemption specified in section 249B(1).

[Signature]
Reporting accountants   **Address**
Date

11.10   Arguments against abolition

The ACCA have in the past expressed concern over small companies' exemption from audit.

The arguments that have been given against abolition include:

(a)   most auditors consider that it is possible to audit a small company and produce a satisfactory audit report at a reasonable cost;

(b)   if banks and other creditors required their own independent audit, the result might be to increase, not reduce, the costs of a small company;

(c)   the audit is necessary to protect creditors which is important in view of the limited liability of the shareholders; and

(d)   shareholders, particularly minority shareholders, are entitled to full and reliable information about the position of their company.

12   STATEMENTS OF INVESTMENT CIRCULAR REPORTING STANDARDS

The APB has started issuing Statements of Investment Circular Reporting Standards (SIRs) to establish a framework to assist reporting accountants in such engagements. As at 1 December 1998 the APB has issued SIR 100 'Investment circulars and reporting accountants' and SIR 200 'Accountants' reports on historical information in investment circulars'. A further SIR is expected during 1999 dealing with the reporting on prospective financial information.

An **investment circular** is a generic term defined as any document issued by an entity pursuant to statutory or regulatory requirements relating to listed or unlisted securities on which it is intended that a third party should make an investment decision, including a prospectus, listing particulars, circular to shareholders or similar document.

With effect from 1 April 1998 the old Auditing Guideline' Prospectuses and the reporting accountant' was withdrawn, to be replaced by the guidance given in SIRs.

13   OPERATING AND FINANCIAL REVIEW

13.1   Introduction

The ASB issued a Statement in July 1993 recommending that an Operating and Financial Review (OFR) should be included in the annual reports of large companies.

The purpose of an OFR is to give the directors of a company the opportunity to discuss and explain, in a structured and comprehensive way, some of the main factors underlying the company's financial statements, and thus to help users to understand more fully the business and environment in which the company operates.

The ASB recognises that many listed companies' annual reports already include detailed discussion of operations and financing, often in the Chairman's Report. The OFR provides general guidelines to indicate what should be covered in such a review to ensure that it is balanced and complete.

13.2   Characteristics and content

The main characteristics of the OFR are that it should

(a)   be fair, in the sense of being a balanced and objective statement of both good and bad news

(b)   focus on matters of significance

(c)   be presented in the way most likely to be helpful to the user of the annual report in gaining an understanding of the financial circumstances of the business.

The OFR covers two main areas

(a)   The *operating* section of the review would normally include a discussion of the results for the period, indicating the main factors and influences that may have an impact on the future, and a discussion of the ways in which the business is investing to meet future needs and challenges.

(b)   The *financial* review would cover such aspects as the capital structure of the business; the treasury policies adopted; cash flow and current liquidity; borrowing requirements and future needs; and any restrictions on the transfer of funds held overseas.

It is for boards of directors to decide how best the information should be presented within a company's annual report; it is not part of the Statement that a particular format should be followed. The ASB believes however that it is important that the OFR should clearly be seen to be the responsibility of the board of directors as a whole.

The ASB takes the view that much of the material to be included in the OFR is not suitable for inclusion in notes to accounts, and should therefore not be made a requirement of an accounting standard. The Statement on Operating and Financial Review is therefore not mandatory but sets out a generally accepted view on what should be regarded as best practice in this area.

14   THE AUDITORS' STATEMENT ON THE SUMMARY FINANCIAL STATEMENT

14.1   Introduction

The CA89 introduced S251 CA85 which allows a public company whose shares are listed to send shareholders a summary financial statement rather than a copy of the annual accounts, directors' report and audit report.

The summary financial statement must be derived from the annual accounts and directors' report and must follow the detailed requirements concerning its form and content which are set out in the Companies (Summary Financial Statement) Regulations 1990. S251(4) specifies that the summary financial statement shall:

(a)   state that it is only a summary of information in the company's annual accounts and the directors' report;

(b)   contain a statement by the company's auditors of their opinion as to whether the summary financial statement is consistent with those accounts and that report and complies with the requirements of this section and regulations made under it.

(c)   state whether the auditor's report on the annual accounts was unqualified or qualified and, if it was qualified, set out the report in full together with any further material needed to understand the qualification;

(d)   state whether the auditors' report on the annual accounts contained a statement under:

(i)   S237(2) (accounting records or returns inadequate or accounts not agreeing with the records and returns); or

(ii)   S237(3) (failure to obtain necessary information and explanations) and, if so, set out the statement in full.

14.2   The auditors' procedures

Auditing Guideline 506 **The auditors' statement on the summary financial statement** was issued in 1991. There are two main areas of work:

(a)   determine whether the statement is consistent with the annual accounts and the directors' report; and

(b)   determine whether it complies with the requirements of S251(4)(b) CA85 and the Regulations

(a)   Consistency with annual accounts

The auditors are required to state whether, in their opinion, the summary financial statement is consistent with the annual accounts and the directors' report. The auditors are not required to form an opinion on whether the summary financial statement gives a true and fair view.

It is, in any event, most unlikely that the summary financial statement could give a true and fair view in any practical situation, as much of the detailed information given in the annual accounts and directors' report is not presented.

However, they should consider whether, within the inherent limitations of a summary financial statement, the overall impression presented is compatible with that given by the annual accounts and directors' report.

There may be situations where the summary financial statement is not consistent with the full financial statements. Matters causing an inconsistency could include incorrect classification of assets or liabilities, non-disclosures of information relating to an exceptional item, or unduly selective summaries from the directors' report. In this situation the auditor should take legal advice and consider qualifying his report on the summary financial statement.

(b)   Compliance with S251(4)(b) CA85 and the Regulations

(i)   S251(3) states that the summary financial statement shall be derived from the annual accounts and directors' report. The auditors will therefore need to consider whether the summary financial statement contains any material which, although it is not inconsistent with the annual accounts and directors' report, is nevertheless not properly derived from them in the manner specified by the Regulations.

(ii)   If the auditors' report on the annual accounts was qualified, or if it included a statement under S237(2) or (3), then the audit report and/or this statement must be set out in full in the summary financial statement.

(iii)   The auditors should satisfy themselves that the other items required by S251 and the Regulations are also included in the summary financial statement.

(iv)   An inconsistency between the summary financial statement and the annual accounts and directors' report will also mean that the summary financial statement is not properly derived from them, and will therefore lead to a qualification of the auditors' statement.

14.3   The auditors' statement

The auditors' statement on the summary financial statement will incorporate the following elements:

(a)   Addressee

(b)   Introductory paragraph

(c)   Respective responsibilities of directors and auditors

(d)   Basis of opinion

(e)   Opinion

(f)   Other information required by CA 85 eg, if the audit report on the full accounts was qualified

(g)   Date

Example

AUDITOR'S STATEMENT TO THE SHAREHOLDERS OF XYZ PLC

We have examined the summary financial statement set out on page X.

Respective responsibilities of directors and auditors

The summary financial statement is the responsibility of the directors. Our responsibility is to report to you our opinion on its preparation and consistency with the full financial statements and directors' report.

Basis of opinion

We conducted our work in accordance with Auditing Guideline 'The auditors' statement on the summary financial statement' adopted by the Auditing Practices Board.

Opinion

In our opinion the summary financial statement is consistent with the full financial statements and directors' report of XYZ plc for the year ended .... and complies with the requirements of the Companies Act 1985, and regulations made thereunder, applicable to summary financial statements.

Registered auditors   Address

Date

15   CHAPTER SUMMARY

The statutory layouts of the balance sheet and profit and loss account have been shown together with the detailed requirements in the notes.

The directors' report is part of the annual report presented to shareholders.

Small companies are allowed to disclose less in their published accounts to shareholders than other companies. Small and medium companies may file less detailed accounts with the Registrar.

16   SELF TEST QUESTIONS

16.1   What is the difference between items preceded by letters, roman numerals and arabic numerals in the statutory balance sheets? (2.2)

16.2   What is the minimum number of directors who must sign a company's individual balance sheet? (2.4)

16.3   State the wordings of the first five lines in a Format 1 statutory profit and loss account. (6.1)

16.4   Would you expect often to see extraordinary items featuring in companies' published profit and loss accounts in the future? (6.2)

16.5   Must the total paid to the auditors for work not associated with the audit be disclosed in the notes to a set of accounts? (7.2)

16.6   What three aspects of a company's employment policy towards disabled persons must be disclosed in the directors' report? (9.2)

16.7   Define a small company for the purposes of deciding whether a company can file an abbreviated balance sheet with the Registrar. (10.2)

17   EXAMINATION TYPE QUESTION

17.1   Slamometer Ltd

Slamometer Ltd, which has traded for many years, has an authorised and issued capital of 60,000 5.6% preference shares of £1 and 140,000 ordinary shares of £1, all of which are fully paid. The company also has in issue £20,000 9% debenture stock redeemable on 31 December 19X9.

The following draft profit and loss account for the year ended 31 March 19X4 has been prepared:

		£	£
Profit on trading			71,570
Interest received (Gross)			
Imperial Chemical Industries plc			630
Latches Ltd (a private company)			280
			72,480
Less:	Debenture interest	1,800	
	Preference dividend	3,360	
	Corporation tax under-provided for previous year	870	
			6,030
			66,450

The following further information is relevant:

(1)   Total sales for the year were £1,013,000.

(2)   Profit on trading is calculated after charging:

	£
Distribution costs	152,571
Raw materials	366,238
Manufacturing overheads	159,302
Wages of production employees	98,789
Salaries of sales staff	56,400
Depreciation of factory	4,000
Depreciation on plant and machinery	7,300
Office rent	2,300
Management remuneration	91,100
Auditors' remuneration	1,500
Legal and accounting charges	620
Interest on bank overdraft	1,310

(3)   Management remuneration comprises the general manager's salary of £11,000 and the following directors' remuneration:

	Salary £	Fee £
A – Chairman	-	11,500
B – Managing Director	23,000	500
C	17,000	500
D – Sales Director	14,800	500
E – Production Director	12,000	300

(4)   The debenture interest and preference dividend were both paid on 31 March 19X4.

(5)   Corporation tax on the profits of the year ended 31 March 19X4 is estimated at £32,000, based on a rate of 25%.

(6)   The balances on the company's reserves on 31 March 19X3 were:

	£
Share premium account	6,100
Plant replacement reserve	40,000
Retained profits	51,700

(7)   The ordinary share capital of £140,000 includes 15,000 shares issued in June 19X3 at a premium of 30p each.

(8)   The directors decide to propose an ordinary dividend of 12% for the year and to transfer £10,000 to plant replacement reserve.

You are required to prepare the profit and loss account of Slamometer Ltd for the year ended 31 March 19X4 in a form which complies with the Companies Act, together with a schedule showing the movements in reserves during the year. Ignore the requirement to show accounting policies.**(20 marks)**

18 ANSWER TO EXAMINATION TYPE QUESTION

18.1 Slamometer Ltd

**Profit and loss account for the year
ended 31 March 19X4**

Notes		£	£
	Turnover		1,013,000
	Cost of sales		647,929
	Gross profit		365,071
	Distribution costs	224,271	
	Administrative expenses	67,920	
			292,191
			72,880
	Interest receivable	910	
(1)	Interest payable	(3,110)	
			(2,200)
(2)	Profit on ordinary activities before taxation		70,680
(5)	Tax on profit on ordinary activities		32,870
	Profit on ordinary activities after taxation		37,810
(6)	Dividends paid and proposed		20,160
	Transfer to plant replacement reserve		10,000
(7)	Profit for the financial year		7,650

Notes to the accounts

		£
(1)	**Interest payable**	
	Interest on bank overdraft	1,310
	Interest on debenture loan	1,800
		3,110

		£
(2)	The profit on ordinary activities is after charging:	
	Depreciation	11,300
	Staff costs	246,289
	Auditors' remuneration	1,500

		£
(3)	**Staff costs**	
	Wages and salaries	246,289

		£
(4)	**Directors' remuneration**	
	Aggregate emoluments	80,100

(5)   **Taxation**

	£
Corporation tax at 25%	32,000
Taxation under-provided in previous year	870
	32,870

(6)   **Dividends**

	£
Preference dividend	3,360
Proposed ordinary dividend	16,800
	20,160

(7)   **Movements in reserves**

	Share premium account £	Plant replacement reserve £	Retained profits £	Total £
Balance at 1 April 19X3	6,100	40,000	51,700	97,800
Retained profit before transfer	-	-	17,650	17,650
Transfer	-	10,000	(10,000)	-
Premium on shares issued in year	4,500	-	-	4,500
Balance at 31 March 19X4	10,600	50,000	59,350	119,950

WORKING

Classification of expenditure

	Cost of sales £	Distribution costs £	Administrative expenses £
Expenses per note 2			
Distribution costs		152,571	
Raw materials	366,238		
Manufacturing overheads	159,302		
Staff costs	98,789	56,400	
Directors	12,300	15,300	63,500
Depreciation	11,300		
Office rent			2,300
Audit			1,500
Legal and accountancy			620
	647,929	224,271	67,920

(Tutorial note: as the aggregate directors' emoluments are less than £200,000, there is no requirement to disclose the highest paid director's emoluments.*)*

9 ACCOUNTING STANDARDS

INTRODUCTION & LEARNING OBJECTIVES

This chapter covers the revision of accounting standards met at earlier stages in the examinations except for SSAP 2 which has already been dealt with in chapter 1 of this text.

It also introduces several new topics. One of these is long-term contracts, which are covered in SSAP 9. Accounting for long-term contracts may appear complicated at first, but if you concentrate on the bookkeeping entries you will find that many of the items that need to be disclosed fall out quite naturally from the bookkeeping system.

Another new topic is accounting for provisions, which is covered in FRS 12 *Provisions, contingent liabilities and contingent assets*. This was issued in September 1998 and replaces SSAP 18.

You should already be familiar with accounting for depreciation. SSAP 12 has been replaced by FRS 15 *Tangible fixed assets*, which was issued in February 1999. The main principles of accounting for depreciation remain the same. However, FRS 15 also addresses several other important topics that were not previously covered by accounting standards: initial measurement of fixed assets; capitalisation of borrowing costs; and revaluation of fixed assets.

When you have studied this chapter you should be able to do the following:

- State and understand the requirements of SSAPs 9, 13 and 17 and FRSs 12 and 15.
- Calculate amounts to be shown in the financial statements for long-term contracts.

1 SSAP 9

1.1 Introduction

Long-term contracts are covered later in the chapter as this is new material. The key points on the other parts of the standard are as follows.

1.2 Lower of cost and net realisable value

(a) **Cost**

 (1) Bringing stock to present location and condition (cost of purchase and costs of conversion)

 (2) Cost of purchase comprises purchase price including import duties, transport and handling costs and any other directly attributable costs, less trade discounts, rebates and subsidies.

 (3) Cost of conversion comprises

  (A) costs which are specifically attributable to units of production eg, direct labour, direct expenses and sub-contracted work.

  (B) production overheads.

  (C) other overheads, if any, attributable in the particular circumstances of the business to bringing the product or service to its present location and condition.

 (4) Production overhead based on normal level of activity.

(b)   **NRV**

Actual or estimated selling price less all costs to complete (ie, all costs to be incurred in marketing, selling and distribution).

1.3   Valuation methods

(a)   **Acceptable under SSAP 9**

(1)   FIFO
(2)   Unit cost
(3)   Average cost

In certain circumstances

(4)   Standard cost
(5)   Adjusted selling price

(b)   **Unacceptable under SSAP 9**

(1)   LIFO
(2)   Replacement cost
(3)   Base cost

1.4   Disclosure

(a)   Lower of cost/NRV of the separate items of stock or of groups of similar items

(b)   Classify according to CA85 headings

(1)   Raw materials
(2)   Work in progress
(3)   Finished goods and goods for resale
(4)   Payments on account

1.5   Activity

Value the following items of stock:

(a)   Materials costing £12,000 bought for processing and assembly for a profitable special order. Since buying these items, the cost price has fallen to £10,000.

(b)   Equipment constructed for a customer for an agreed price of £18,000. This has recently been completed at a cost of £16,800. It has now been discovered that, in order to meet certain regulations, conversion with an extra cost of £4,200 will be required. The customer has accepted partial responsibility and agreed to meet half the extra cost.

1.6   Activity solution

(a)   Value at £12,000. £10,000 is irrelevant. The rule is lower of cost or net realisable value, not lower of cost or replacement cost. Since the materials will be processed before sale there is no reason to believe that net realisable value will be below cost.

(b)   Value at net realisable value ie, £15,900, as this is below cost (NRV = Contract price, £18,000 – Company's share of modification cost, £2,100).

> **Conclusion**   The basic rule is that stocks are valued at the lower of cost and net realisable value.

2   SSAP 13

2.1   Introduction

SSAP 13 was first issued in 1977 and revised in January 1989.

The term **research and development** can be used to cover a wide range of activity. SSAP 13 follows the OECD classification in defining three broad areas of activity:

(a)   **Pure (or basic) research**: experimental or theoretical work undertaken primarily to acquire new scientific or technical knowledge for its own sake rather than directed towards any specific aim or application.

(b)   **Applied research:** original or critical investigation undertaken in order to gain new scientific or technical knowledge and directed towards a specific practical aim or objective.

(c)   **Development:** use of scientific or technical knowledge in order to produce new or substantially improved materials, devices, products or services, to install new processes or systems prior to the commencement of commercial production or commercial applications, or to improving substantially those already produced or installed.

Development is therefore concerned with using **existing** knowledge to introduce new products or processes.

2.2   Classification of costs

Expenditure on research and development does not consist only of the salaries of scientists or the cost of test tubes. Many costs can properly be regarded as being incurred for research and development purposes. These include:

(a)   Costs of materials.
(b)   Salaries, wages, and other employment costs of workers involved in research and development.
(c)   Depreciation of scientific and other equipment and land and buildings.
(d)   A proportion of overhead costs.
(e)   Related costs, such as patents, licence fees, etc.

2.3   Accounting problems

The problems in accounting for research and development revolve around two of the fundamental accounting concepts: accruals and prudence.

(a)   **Pure and applied research**

Under the accruals concept, income is matched with the costs involved in generating that income. Yet how can expenditure on pure and applied research be matched with any particular period's income? There may be no direct benefit from the expenditure, or it may benefit many periods. Expenditure on pure and applied research can, therefore, be regarded as part of the continuing cost of running the business. Since no one period can be expected to benefit more than another, such expenditure should be written off as incurred. Carrying expenditure forward to future periods would conflict not only with the accruals concept, but with prudent accounting practice.

(b)   **Development expenditure**

In the case of development expenditure, it is likely that future income, or cost reduction, can be directly attributable to a development project. An example of this is a motor car manufacturer who is developing a new model of car. He is incurring costs now in the expectation that they will be recovered from future sales of the car. On the accruals basis, such expenditure should not be written off against the current year's income, but carried forward and set against income from the project in future years.

However, prudence dictates that it is impossible to determine whether future benefits will arise from a development project unless the project and its related expenditure are clearly identifiable. SSAP 13 therefore concludes that development expenditure should normally be written off as incurred, but *may* be carried forward in certain circumstances.

(c)   **SSAP 13 requirements**

The cost of fixed assets acquired or constructed in order to provide facilities for research and development activities over a number of accounting periods should be capitalised and written off over their useful lives through the profit and loss account.

Expenditure on pure and applied research (other than that referred to in the previous paragraph) should be written off in the year of expenditure through the profit and loss account.

Development expenditure should be written off in the year of expenditure except in the following circumstances when it may be deferred to future periods:

(a)   there is a clearly defined project; and

(b)   the related expenditure is separately identifiable; and

(c)   the outcome of such a project has been assessed with reasonable certainty as to:

  (i)   its technical feasibility; and

  (ii)   its ultimate commercial viability considered in the light of factors such as likely market conditions (including competing products), public opinion, consumer and environmental legislation; and

(d)   the aggregate of the deferred development costs, any further development costs, and related production, selling and administration costs is reasonably expected to be exceeded by related future sales or other revenues; and

(e)   adequate resources exist, or are reasonably expected to be available, to enable the project to be completed and to provide any consequential increases in working capital.

In the foregoing circumstances development expenditure may be deferred to the extent that its recovery can reasonably be regarded as assured.

If an accounting policy of deferral of development expenditure is adopted, it should be applied to all development projects that meet the criteria above.

Paras 23-27 SSAP 13

Development expenditure may also be carried forward where companies enter into a firm contract to carry out development work on behalf of third parties on such terms that the related expenditure is to be fully reimbursed (para 17 SSAP 13). Such expenditure should be included in work-in-progress.

2.4   Further problems with development expenditure

If development expenditure is deferred to future periods, three further problems arise:

(a)   How and when should the expenditure be written off?
(b)   What should be done if circumstances surrounding the project change?
(c)   How should development expenditure be shown in the balance sheet?

These problems are considered in turn.

2.5   Writing off deferred development expenditure

The aim in carrying forward such expenditure is to match it against future benefits arising from the developed product. This can be in the form either of revenue from the sale of the product, or of reduced costs from improved production processes.

Deferred development expenditure should be matched against benefits in a sensible and consistent manner. It is not enough to write off the expenditure over an arbitrary number of years: writing off should start when the product begins to be produced commercially.

SSAP 13 states:

If development costs are deferred to future periods, they should be amortised. The amortisation should commence with the commercial production or application of the product, service, process or system and should be allocated on a systematic basis to each accounting period, by reference to either the sale or use of the product, service, process or system or the period over which these are expected to be sold or used.

Para 28 SSAP 13

Example

Improve plc has deferred development expenditure of £600,000 relating to the development of New Miracle Brand X. It is expected that the demand for the product will stay at a high level for the next three years. Annual sales of 400,000, 300,000 and 200,000 units respectively are expected over this period. Brand X sells for £10.

There are two possibilities for writing off the development expenditure:

(a)   in equal instalments over the three year period ie, £200,000 pa; or

(b)   in relation to total sales expected (900,000 units):

				£
Year 1	$\frac{400,000}{900,000}$ × £600,000	=		266,667
Year 2	$\frac{300,000}{900,000}$ × £600,000	=		200,000
Year 3	$\frac{200,000}{900,000}$ × £600,000	=		133,333

2.6   Changing circumstances

Development expenditure should only be carried forward if there is a reasonable chance of setting it against income in the future ie, if the conditions mentioned above are met. If circumstances change, it may be necessary to write off the expenditure at once, on the basis of prudent accounting.

This can occur in a number of situations, including:

(a)   the arrival of possible competing products;
(b)   changes in the general economic climate;
(c)   changes in legislation, such as consumer or environmental changes.

If brought forward development expenditure is written off, it should not be regarded as a charge against prior years' profits.

Deferred development expenditure should be reviewed at the end of each accounting period and where the circumstances which have justified the deferral of the expenditure no longer apply, or are considered doubtful, the expenditure, to the extent to which it is considered to be irrecoverable, should be written off immediately project by project.

Para 29 SSAP 13

2.7   Accounting presentation

The accounting policy on research and development expenditure should be stated and explained.

The total amount of research and development expenditure charged in the profit and loss account should be disclosed, analysed between the current year's expenditure and amounts amortised from deferred expenditure.

Movements on deferred development expenditure and the amount carried forward at the beginning and the end of the period should be disclosed. Deferred development expenditure should be disclosed under intangible fixed assets in the balance sheet.

Paras 30-32 SSAP 13

The requirement to disclose the expenditure charged in the profit and loss account does **not** apply to 'small' unquoted companies. A small company is one which satisfies the criteria (multiplied in each case by ten) for defining a medium-sized company under the CA85 abbreviated accounts provisions.

Thus all quoted companies and large unquoted companies have to disclose the information.

The Companies Act 1985 requires deferred development expenditure to be included as an intangible fixed asset.

An example of an appropriate note to the balance sheet would be as follows:

	£'000	£'000
Deferred development expenditure b/d		320
Expenditure incurred in the period	70	
Expenditure written off in the period	(64)	
		6
Deferred development expenditure c/d		326

The profit and loss account or a note to the profit and loss account would disclose the **total** amount of research and development expenditure. For example:

	£'000
Research and development expenditure:	
Expenditure in year charged	130
Development expenditure amortised	64
	194

The £130,000 does not include the £70,000 appearing in the balance sheet note as it has not been charged in the profit and loss account.

Conclusion   Expenditure on pure and applied research should be written off as it is incurred. Expenditure on development may, if desired, be carried forward provided certain criteria are satisfied.

3   SSAP 17

3.1   Introduction

Suppose the year end of a company is 31 December 19X7 and the directors approve the financial statements at a board meeting held on 22 March 19X8. Certain events occurring during the intervening period will provide information which will help in preparing the financial statements.

These post balance sheet events fall into two categories: adjusting events and non-adjusting events.

> **Definition**   **Post balance sheet events** are those events, both favourable and unfavourable, which occur between the balance sheet date and the date on which the financial statements are approved by the board of directors.

> **Definition**   **The date on which the financial statements are approved by the board of directors** is the date the board of directors formally approves a set of documents as the financial statements. In respect of unincorporated enterprises, the date of approval is the corresponding date. In respect of group accounts, the date of approval is the date when the group accounts are formally approved by the board of directors of the holding company.

> **Definition**   **Adjusting events** are post balance sheet events which provide additional evidence of conditions existing at the balance sheet date. They include events which because of statutory or conventional requirements are reflected in financial statements.

> **Definition**   **Non-adjusting events** are post balance sheet events which concern conditions which did not exist at the balance sheet date.

3.2   Adjusting events

These events provide additional evidence of conditions existing at the balance sheet date. For example, bad debts arising one or two months after the balance sheet date may help to quantify the bad debt provision as at the balance sheet date. Adjusting events may, therefore, affect the amount at which items are stated in the balance sheet.

Examples include:

(a)   Provisions for stock and bad debts.

(b)   Amounts received or receivable in respect of insurance claims which were being negotiated at the balance sheet date.

(c)   Certain special items occurring after the balance sheet date which, for various reasons, are reflected in the current year's financial statements:

   (i)   Proposed dividends.
   (ii)   Appropriations to reserves.
   (iii)   Effects of changes in taxation.
   (iv)   Dividends receivable from subsidiary companies.

3.3   Non-adjusting events

These are events arising after the balance sheet date but which, unlike those events above, do **not** concern conditions existing at the balance sheet date. Such events will not, therefore, have any effect on items in the balance sheet or profit and loss account. However, in order to prevent the financial statements from presenting a misleading position, some form of additional disclosure is required if the events are material, say by way of memorandum note indicating what effect the events would have had on the year end balance sheet.

Examples of non-adjusting events include:

(a)   The issue of new share or loan capital.

(b)   Major changes in the composition of the company (for example, acquisitions of new businesses).

(c)   Financial consequences of losses of fixed assets or stock as a result of fires or floods.

3.4 'Window dressing'

'Window dressing' refers to the practice of entering into certain transactions before the year end and reversing those transactions after the year end. Thus no real transaction has occurred (ie, no substance, only legal form) but the balance sheet reflects the transaction (as it primarily records the legal form of assets and liabilities). The hoped-for effect is to improve the appearance of the balance sheet.

SSAP 17 requires a **disclosure** of such transactions if they are material. They are **not**, however, adjusting events.

Example

UK Finance plc is concerned that it has over-lent to customers in the year to 31 December 19X8 and that its ratio of liquid assets to total assets is too low. It thus arranges a loan of £40 million from another company in December. The loan is repaid in January.

	(a) £m	(b) £m
Liquid assets	10	50
Investments:		
Advances to customers	200	200
Fixed assets	20	20
Less: Creditors: amounts falling due within one year	(10)	(50)
Total assets less current liabilities	220	220

$$\frac{\text{Liquid assets}}{\text{Total assets less current liabilities}} \qquad \frac{10}{220} \times 100 \qquad \frac{50}{220} \times 100$$

$$= 5\% \qquad\qquad = 23\%$$

(a) refers to the balance sheet if the transaction had not been entered into; (b) shows the actual balance sheet at the year end. Clearly (b) looks better if an accepted measure of security/solvency is a 'liquidity' ratio such as calculated above.

3.5 Standard accounting practice – SSAP 17

SSAP 17 *Accounting for post balance sheet events* requires that:

21. Financial statements should be prepared on the basis of conditions existing at the balance sheet date.

22. A material post balance sheet event requires changes in the amounts to be included in financial statements where:

    (a) it is an adjusting event; or

    (b) it indicates that application of the going concern concept to the whole or a material part of the company is not appropriate.

23. A material post balance sheet event should be disclosed where:

    (a) it is a non-adjusting event of such materiality that its non-disclosure would affect the ability of the users of financial statements to reach a proper understanding of the financial position; or

    (b) it is the reversal or maturity after the year-end of a transaction entered into before the year-end, the substance of which was primarily to alter the appearance of the company's balance sheet.

24. In respect of each post balance sheet event which is required to be disclosed under paragraph 23 above, the following information should be stated by way of notes in financial statements:

    (a) the nature of the event; and

    (b) an estimate of the financial effect, or a statement that it is not practicable to make such an estimate.

25. The estimate of the financial effect should be disclosed before taking account of taxation, and the taxation implications should be explained where necessary for a proper understanding of the financial position.

26. The date on which the financial statements are approved by the board of directors should be disclosed in the financial statements.

Paras 21-26 SSAP 17

3.6 Activity

How should the following matters be dealt with?

(a) When drafting the final accounts, a company's accountant includes a figure of £2,000 as the net realisable value of damaged items of stock.

The cost of these items was £3,000, and the normal selling price would be £4,000. Between the balance sheet date and the approval of the accounts the items are sold for £3,100.

(b) A company is engaged in the construction of its own factory. The estimated value on completion is £200,000, costs to date are £80,000 and at the balance sheet date expected further costs to completion were £90,000.

After the balance sheet date serious defects – which must have existed unnoticed for some time – are discovered in the foundations of the building, necessitating partial demolition and rebuilding at an estimated cost of £70,000 (in addition to the estimated further costs to completion of £90,000).

3.7 Activity solution

(a) The valuation in the accounts should be adjusted to £3,000 ie, cost, since net realisable value has, in the event, turned out to be greater than cost. This is an adjusting post balance sheet event.

(b) This is an adjusting post balance sheet event. There is an anticipated loss on the factory of £40,000 (value £200,000 less costs to date £80,000 less estimated further costs £160,000). The asset should, therefore, be valued at £40,000 (costs to date £80,000 less attributable loss £40,000).

3.8 CA85

Para 6 Sch 7 CA85 requires the directors' report to contain:

(a) particulars of any important events affecting the company or any of its subsidiaries which have occurred since the end of that year;

(b) an indication of likely future developments in the business of the company and of its subsidiaries.

Conclusion Adjusting events give rise to changes in the accounts figures. Non-adjusting events are disclosed by way of note.

4   LONG-TERM CONTRACT WORK-IN-PROGRESS

4.1   Definition of a long-term contract

> [Definition]   SSAP 9 defines a long-term contract as 'a contract entered into for the design, manufacture or construction of a single substantial asset or the provision of a service (or of a combination of assets or services which together constitute a single project) where the time taken substantially to complete the contract is such that the contract activity falls into different accounting periods.'

4.2   The key elements in SSAP 9 relating to long-term contracts

Long-term contracts cause special problems due to their length of time relative to accounting periods. As they extend over accounting periods, we need some method of recording turnover, cost of sales and profit over the life of the contract. Otherwise all these items will only be recorded in the profit and loss account of the accounting periods in which the contract ends. This will not be a fair reflection of the activity and profit earned in the earlier accounting period(s).

In addition we need to recognise the nature of the assets and liabilities that arise during the contract period. The assets will change in nature from stocks to debtors (amounts recoverable on contracts). This change results in detailed accounting procedures and disclosure requirements.

The relevant parts of the standard are set out in full below together with some definitions. We will then see how the amounts to be shown in the financial statements are calculated.

4.3   Standard accounting practice

The standard accounting practice for long-term contracts is as follows:

28.   Long-term contracts should be assessed on a contract by contract basis and reflected in the profit and loss account by recording turnover and related costs as contract activity progresses. Turnover is ascertained in a manner appropriate to the stage of completion of the contract, the business and the industry in which it operates.

29.   Where it is considered that the outcome of a long-term contract can be assessed with reasonable certainty before its conclusion, the prudently calculated attributable profit should be recognised in the profit and loss account as the difference between the reported turnover and related costs for that contract.

30.   Long-term contracts should be disclosed in the balance sheet as follows:

   (a)   the amount by which recorded turnover is in excess of payments on account should be classified as 'amounts recoverable on contracts' and separately disclosed within debtors;

   (b)   the balance of payments on account (in excess of amounts (i) matched with turnover; and (ii) offset against long-term contract balances) should be classified as payments on account and separately disclosed within creditors;

   (c)   the amount of long-term contracts, at costs incurred, net of amounts transferred to cost of sales, after deducting foreseeable losses and payments on account not matched with turnover, should be classified as 'long-term contract balances' and separately disclosed within the balance sheet heading 'Stocks'. The balance sheet note should disclose separately the balances of:

      (i)   net cost less foreseeable losses; and
      (ii)   applicable payments on account;

(d)   the amount by which the provision or accrual for foreseeable losses exceeds the costs incurred (after transfers to cost of sales) should be included within either provisions for liabilities and charges or creditors as appropriate.

4.4 Definitions

The following terms are defined in SSAP 9:

Definition   **Attributable profit:** that part of the total profit currently estimated to arise over the duration of the contract, after allowing for estimated remedial and maintenance costs and increases in costs so far as not recoverable under the terms of the contract, that fairly reflects the profit attributable to that part of the work performed at the accounting date. (There can be no attributable profit until the profitable outcome of the contract can be assessed with reasonable certainty.)

Definition   **Foreseeable losses:** losses which are currently estimated to arise over the duration of the contract (after allowing for estimated remedial and maintenance costs and increases in costs so far as not recoverable under the terms of the contract). This estimate is required irrespective of:

(a)   whether or not work has yet commenced on such contracts;

(b)   the proportion of work carried out at the accounting date;

(c)   the amount of profits expected to arise on other contracts.

Definition   **Payments on account:** all amounts received and receivable at the accounting date in respect of contracts in progress.

Turnover is not defined in SSAP 9. However Appendix 1 to SSAP 9 states that turnover (ascertained in a manner appropriate to the industry, the nature of the contracts concerned and the contractual relationship with the customer) and related costs should be recorded in the profit and loss account as contract activity progresses. Turnover may sometimes be ascertained by reference to valuation of the work carried out to date. In other cases, there may be specific points during a contract at which individual elements of work done with separately ascertainable sales values and costs can be identified and appropriately recorded as turnover (eg, because delivery or customer acceptance has taken place).

For examination purposes, turnover is likely normally to represent the value of work done or certified as done.

5 ACCOUNTING FOR LONG-TERM CONTRACTS

5.1 Example

Bloggs Builders undertake a three year contract to build a bridge for £1 million. The following information is extracted from their books and records at the end of years 1, 2 and 3:

		Value of work done £'000	*Costs* £'000	*Payments on account* *Received* £'000	*Invoiced* £'000
Year 1	To date	200	210	150	160
	To complete (estimated)	800	Not known	-	-
Year 2	To date	500	550	535	570
	To complete (estimated)	500	390	-	-
Year 3	To date (completed)	1,000	955	1,000	1,000

You are required to show how this information would be reflected in the accounts for each of the three years.

5.2   Procedure

Step 1 A contract account accumulates the various costs incurred on each contract. By the end of year 1 the account will look as follows:

Contract account

	£		£
Bank/cash for:			
Materials	X		
Labour, etc	X		
	————		
	210,000		
	————		

Because a contract can continue for some time, there is normally provision for the contractor to invoice the customer for parts of the contract (often on a monthly basis). The part invoices are known as **progress payments**. They are credited to a progress payments account (it is thus a type of sales account) and debited to debtors.

By the end of year 1, the account will look as follows:

Progress payments account

	£		£
		Debtors	X
			X
			————
			160,000
			————

Debtors are recorded in the normal way:

Debtors

	£		£
Progress payments account	160,000	Cash	150,000
		Balance c/d	10,000
	————		————
	160,000		160,000
	————		————

Step 2 At the end of year 1 a decision is required as to whether to take a proportion of profit. As the costs to completion are unknown at this stage, the profitable outcome cannot be assessed with reasonable certainty. Thus there can be no attributable profit.

The **value of work done** (given in the example) is recorded in the accounts:

Dr	Progress payments	£200,000	
Cr	Profit and loss account		£200,000

Step 3 The contract account is closed off to the profit and loss account up to the amount of recorded turnover.

Contract account

	£		£
Costs	210,000	Trading account	200,000
		Balance c/d (closing stock)	10,000
	————		————
	210,000		210,000
	————		————

Progress payments account

	£		£
Trading account	200,000	Debtors	160,000
		Balance c/d	40,000
	200,000		200,000

Step 4   Relevant extracts from the accounts at the end of year 1 are as follows.

	£'000	£'000
Profit and loss account		
Turnover		200
Opening stock	-	
Purchases	210	
Closing stock (bal. fig.)	(10)	
Cost of sales		200
Gross profit		-

Balance sheet	£'000
Stock:	
Net cost	10
Applicable payments on account	-
Debtors:	
Amounts recoverable on contracts	40
Progress payments receivable (debtor)	10

Step 5   **Year 2**

Contract account

		£			£
(1)	Balance b/d year 1	10,000	(4)	Trading account	
(2)	Costs in year 2			(see workings)	270,000
	(550 – 210)	340,000		Balance c/d	80,000
		350,000			350,000

Progress payments account

		£			£
(1)	Balance b/d year 1	40,000	(2)	Debtors (570 – 160)	410,000
(3)	Trading account				
	(500 – 200)	300,000			
	Balance c/d	70,000			
		410,000			410,000

Debtors

		£			£
(1)	Balance b/d	10,000	(2)	Cash (535 – 150)	385,000
(2)	Progress payments			Balance c/d	35,000
	account	410,000			
		420,000			420,000

Step 6   Accounts extracts at the end of year 2 are as follows.

	£'000	£'000
Profit and loss account		
Turnover (500 – 200)		300
Opening stock	10	
Purchases (550 – 210)	340	
Closing stock (bal. fig.)	(80)	
Cost of sales		270
Gross profit (see working)		30

Balance sheet

	£'000
Stock:	
Net cost	80
Applicable payments on account	(70)
Debtors:	
Progress payments receivable	35

WORKING

At this stage the profitable outcome of the contract can be foreseen.   The attributable profit is calculated as follows:

	£'000
Contract price	1,000
Costs incurred	(550)
Estimated costs to complete	(390)
Anticipated total profit	60

Based on value of work done the contract is 50% complete (500/1,000).   Therefore, the attributable profit is £30,000 (£60,000 × 50%).

Note **on the sequence of entries**

The numbers in the ledger accounts record the sequence of entries. At the end of the year the turnover figure (given in the example) can be transferred to the trading account from the progress payments account. The transfer of costs from the contract account to the trading account should be computed in **reverse**, ie,

(a)   compute attributable profit (£30,000);
(b)   deduct profit from turnover, giving cost of sales (£270,000).

Step 7   **Year 3**

Contract account

	£		£
Balance b/d	80,000	Trading account	485,000
Costs in year 3 (955 – 550)	405,000		
	485,000		485,000

Progress payments account

	£		£
Trading account	500,000	Balance b/d	70,000
		Debtors (1,000 – 570)	430,000
	500,000		500,000

Profit and loss account

	£'000	£'000
Turnover (1,000 – 500)		500
Opening stock	80	
Purchases (955 – 550)	405	
Closing stock	(-)	
Cost of sales		485
Gross profit		15

(Tutorial note:

	£'000
The total profit on the contract is as follows:	
Contract price	1,000
Costs	955
Total profit	45

This profit is recognised as follows:

Year 1	-
Year 2	30
Year 3	15
	45

)

5.3   Contract accounts – summary of entries

During the accounting period, the following journal entries are required

Expenses incurred:

	Debit	*Credit*	*With*
1	Contract account	Creditors/Cash	Expenses (labour, materials, sub-contractors' charges, site expenses, overheads, depreciation, etc)

Invoices issued to customers:

	Debit	*Credit*	*With*
2	Customer's account	Progress payments invoiced	Invoices issued

Cash received from customers:

	Debit	*Credit*	*With*
3	Cash	Customer's account	Cash received

At the year end: accruals and prepayments:

	Debit	*Credit*	*With*
4A	Contract account	Accruals	Any accruals
4B	Prepayments	Contract account	Any prepayments or stock of unused materials

At the year end: calculate profit to be taken this year:

	Debit	*Credit*	*With*
5	Progress payments invoiced	Profit and loss account	Turnover for the year (probably the work certified for the year)
6	Profit and loss account	Contract account	Costs matched against turnover (probably the balancing figure of turnover less attributable profit).

5.4   Contract accounts – summary of disclosure requirements

SSAP 9 has been criticised by some commentators for scattering entries around the different sections of the balance sheet, rather than concentrating on reporting figures within stocks.   The following balance sheet items are involved:

Stocks - costs incurred, net of transfers to cost of sales.

Debtors - the amount by which the recognised turnover exceeds the payments on account.

Creditors - excess payments on account received.

Provisions for liabilities and charges or creditors - the amount by which the provision for future losses exceeds the costs incurred (after transfers to cost of sales).

SSAP 9 requires that the balance sheet note for stocks should disclose separately:

Net cost less foreseeable losses	X
Applicable payments on account	(X)
Balance of long-term contracts (within stocks)	X

5.5   Contract accounts – example

On 1 July 19X4 Buildem Ltd signed a £300,000 contract to build a new studio for Midlands TV. The following information is relevant to this contract:

		In 19X4 £	*In 19X5* £
(a)	**Expenditure**		
	Labour	24,000	31,000
	Materials	47,300	58,600
	Site expenses	8,450	12,500
	Hire of plant	5,750	1,400
	Plant purchased 1 July 19X4	36,000	-
(b)	**Progress payments invoiced** (based on work certified)	100,000	200,000
(c)	**Cash received from Midlands TV**	90,000	180,000

(1)   Accrued expenses and stocks of unused materials at 31 December 19X4 amounted to £800 and £1,700 respectively:

(i)   Overheads are allocated between contracts at 10% of labour costs.

(ii)   Plant is depreciated at 25% pa straight line on cost.

(iii)   A rectification provision of 4% of the contract price is set aside at the end of each contract.

(2)   The profitable outcome of the contract was apparent on 31 December 19X4. Estimated costs to completion on 31 December 19X4 were £103,500.

(3)   The contract was completed on 31 August 19X5 and Midlands TV paid the 10% retention money on 1 March 19X6. During January 19X6 £10,000 was incurred on maintenance expenditure.

(4)   The progress payments invoiced is to be taken as the value of work performed for the turnover figure in the profit and loss account.

Show the necessary ledger entries in the books of Buildem Ltd and the relevant profit and loss account and balance sheet extracts at 31 December 19X4 and 19X5.

5.6 Solution

19X4 entries are shown separately from 19X5 and 19X6 to emphasise the entries being made for each year.

Studio contract account

19X4		£	19X4		£
	Labour	24,000			
	Materials	47,300			
	Site expenses	8,450			
	Hire of plant	5,750			
	Overheads				
	(10% × £24,000)	2,400			
31 Dec	Depreciation		31 Dec	Trading account (see	
	(6/12 × 25% × £36,000)	4,500		profit and loss account)	65,000
	Accruals c/d	800		Stocks c/d	1,700
				Work in progress c/d	
				(balance)	26,500
		93,200			93,200

Progress payments account

19X4		£	19X4		£
				Midlands TV account	
31 Dec	Trading account	100,000		debtor	100,000

Midlands TV account

19X4		£	19X4		£
	Progress payments			Cash	90,000
	account	100,000		Balance c/d	10,000
		100,000			100,000

Calculation of attributable profit to date at 31 December 19X4

	£	£
Contract price		300,000
Less: Costs to date £(93,200 – 1,700)	91,500	
Estimated costs to complete	103,500	
		195,000
Estimated total profit		105,000

*(**Tutorial note:** there is a case for adding the rectification provision as an additional expected cost ie, reducing estimated total profit by £12,000.)*

$$\frac{\text{Work certified}}{\text{Contract price}} \text{ ie,} \frac{£100,000 \times 105,000}{£300,000} = \qquad 35,000$$

Profit and loss account for the year ended 31 December 19X4

	£
Turnover (given)	100,000
Cost of sales (bal. fig.)	65,000
Profit (calculated)	35,000

Balance sheet as at 31 December 19X4

	£	£	£
Fixed assets:			
Plant	36,000	(4,500)	31,500
Current assets:			
Stock:			
Raw materials		1,700	
Long-term contract balances - net cost	26,500		
Less: Applicable payments on account	Nil		
		26,500	
		28,200	
Debtors:			
Progress payments receivable		10,000	
		38,200	
Creditors: amounts falling due within one year			
Accruals		800	
			37,400
			68,900

Studio contract account (continued)

19X5		£	19X5		£
	Stock b/d	1,700		Accruals b/d	800
	Work in progress b/d	26,500			
	Labour	31,000			
	Materials	58,600			
	Site expenses	12,500			
	Hire of plant	1,400			
	Overheads (10% × £31,000)	3,100			
31 Dec	Depreciation (8/12 × 25% × £36,000)	6,000	31 Dec	Trading account (balance)	152,000
	Rectification (4% × £300,000) provision c/d	12,000			
		152,800			152,800
19X6			19X6		
	Maintenance expenditure	10,000		Provision b/d	12,000
	Profit and loss account (balance)	2,000			
		12,000			12,000

Progress payments account

19X5		£	19X5		£
31 Dec	Trading account	200,000		Midlands TV account debtor	200,000

Midlands TV account

19X5		£	19X5		£
	Balance b/d	10,000		Cash	180,000
	Progress payments account	200,000		Balance c/d	30,000
		210,000			210,000
19X6			19X6		
	Balance b/d	30,000		Cash	30,000

Profit and loss account for the year ended 31 December 19X5

	£
Turnover (given)	200,000
Cost of sales (remaining costs in contract account)	152,000
Profit (bal. fig.)	48,000
Depreciation 4/12 × 25% × 36,000	3,000

(Plant would continue to suffer a depreciation charge on other contracts)

Balance sheet extract as at 31 December 19X5

	£	£
Fixed assets:		
Contract plant, at cost		36,000
Less: Accumulated depreciation (4,500 + 6,000 + 3,000)		13,500
		22,500
Current assets:		
Debtors - progress payments receivable	30,000	
Creditors: amounts falling due within one year		
Rectification provision	12,000	
		18,000
		40,500

6 FRS 15: TANGIBLE FIXED ASSETS

6.1 Introduction

[Definition] **Tangible fixed assets** are assets that have physical substance and are held for use in the production or supply of goods or services, for rental to others, or for administrative purposes on a continuing basis in the reporting entity's activities. (FRS 15).

Fixed assets have the fundamental characteristic that they are held with the object of earning revenue by their use, not by their resale.

6.2 Initial measurement of fixed assets

An entity may acquire fixed assets by purchasing them, or by constructing them for its own use. Occasionally they may be donated to an entity (for example, if the entity is a charity).

FRS 15 states that a tangible fixed asset should initially be measured at its **cost**.

In practice, an asset's cost is:

its purchase price, **less** any trade discounts or rebates, **plus** any further costs directly attributable to bringing it into working condition for its intended use.

Costs that might be incurred by an entity in purchasing a fixed asset include:

- stamp duty and other duties
- legal fees
- delivery and handling costs
- installation costs.

If the entity constructed the fixed asset, rather than buying it, it might incur other costs:

- materials costs
- labour costs
- architects' fees
- direct overheads (eg, power).

Only those costs that are **directly attributable to bringing the asset into working condition for its intended use** should be included in its measurement.

FRS 15 also states that:

(a)   Capitalisation of directly attributable costs should cease when substantially all the activities that are necessary to get the tangible fixed asset ready for use are complete, even if the asset has not yet been brought into use. A tangible fixed asset is ready for use when its physical construction is complete.

(b)   The costs associated with a start up or commissioning period should be included in the cost of the tangible fixed asset only where the asset is available for use but incapable of operating at normal levels without such a start up or commissioning period.

Example

A machine has to be run in and tested before it can be used for producing goods. The costs associated with this are included in the cost of the machine.

After the machine has been run in, there is a further period during which it is operated below its capacity. The machine is capable of operating at full capacity, but demand for the product it makes has not yet built up. Costs associated with this period cannot be included in the cost of the machine.

(c)   The initial carrying amount of tangible fixed assets received as gifts and donations by charities should be the current value of the assets at the date that they are received.

6.3   Example

An entity incurred the following costs in constructing a building for its own use:

	£'000
Purchase price of land	250,000
Stamp duty	5,000
Legal fees	10,000
Site preparation and clearance	18,000
Materials	100,000
Labour (period 1 April 19X7 to 30 September 19X8)	150,000
Architect's fees	20,000
General overheads	30,000
	583,000

The following information is also relevant:

(1)   Material costs were greater than anticipated. On investigation, it was found that material costing £10 million had been spoiled and therefore was wasted and a further £15 million was incurred as a result of faulty design work.

(2)   As a result of these problems, work on the building ceased for a fortnight during October 19X7 and it is estimated that approximately £9 million of the labour costs relate to this period.

(3)   The building was completed on 1 July 19X8 and occupied on 1 September 19X8.

Required

Calculate the cost of the building that will be included in tangible fixed asset additions.

6.4   Solution

Only those costs which are directly attributable to bringing the asset into working condition for its intended use should be included. Therefore, administration and other general overhead costs cannot be included. FRS 15 also states that **abnormal costs should not be included** in the cost of a fixed asset. Abnormal costs include costs caused by design errors, industrial disputes, idle capacity, wasted materials and production delays.

The amount included in tangible fixed assets is computed as follows:

	Total £'000	Exclude £'000	Include £'000
Purchase price of land	250,000		250,000
Stamp duty	5,000		5,000
Legal fees	10,000		10,000
Site preparation and clearance	18,000		18,000
Materials (Note 1)	100,000	25,000	75,000
Labour (150,000 × 3/18 + 9,000) (Note 2)	150,000	34,000	116,000
Architect's fees	20,000		20,000
General overheads	30,000	30,000	–
	583,000	89,000	494,000

Note 1   The costs of spoiled material and faulty design are abnormal costs.

Note 2   Labour costs are only included for the period to 1 July 19X8. The building was available for use on that date, regardless of the fact that it was not actually in use until three months later. The £9 million labour cost incurred during the period of the stoppage is an abnormal cost and is also excluded.

| Conclusion | Fixed assets should initially be measured at cost. Only those costs that are directly attributable to bringing the asset into working condition for its intended use should be included in its measurement.

6.5   Finance costs

Interest on borrowings is often a very significant cost of acquiring or constructing an asset. Opinion is divided on whether or not finance costs should be included in the cost of a tangible fixed asset. Property companies are the most significant advocates of capitalisation - indeed, most of them capitalise interest on loans used to finance the construction of properties. Many supermarket chains have also capitalised finance costs relating to the construction of large 'superstores'.

Arguments for capitalising finance costs

(a)   Finance costs are just as much a cost of constructing a tangible fixed asset as other directly attributable costs.

(b)   Capitalising finance costs results in a tangible fixed asset cost that more closely matches the market price of completed assets. Treating the finance cost as an expense distorts the choice between purchasing and constructing a tangible fixed asset. Capitalisation also means that users of the financial statements can more easily compare companies which construct their fixed assets themselves and those which purchase them from third parties.

(c)   The accounts are more likely to reflect the true success or failure of projects involving the construction of assets.

(d)   Failure to capitalise borrowing costs means that profits may be reduced in periods when fixed assets are acquired. This is misleading as capital investment should increase profits in the long term.

Arguments against capitalising finance costs

(a) Borrowing costs are incurred in support of the whole of the activities of an enterprise. Any attempt to associate borrowing costs with a particular asset is necessarily arbitrary.

(b) Capitalisation of borrowing costs results in the same type of asset having a different carrying amount, depending on the method of financing adopted by the enterprise.

(c) Treating borrowing costs as a charge against income results in financial statements giving more comparable results from period to period. This provides a better indication of the future cash flows of an enterprise. Interest remains a period cost of financing the business and its treatment should not change merely as a result of the completion of a tangible fixed asset.

(d) Capitalisation leads to higher tangible fixed asset costs, which are more likely to exceed the recoverable amount of the asset.

Standard accounting practice

Capitalisation of finance costs is optional. FRS 15 does, however, set out rules that must be followed if interest is capitalised.

(a) Only finance costs that are directly attributable to the construction of a tangible fixed asset should be capitalised as part of the cost of that asset.

(b) The total amount of finance costs capitalised during a period should not exceed the total amount of finance costs incurred during that period.

(c) Capitalisation should begin when:

   (i)   finance costs are being incurred; and
   (ii) expenditures for the asset are being incurred; and
   (iii) activities that are necessary to get the asset ready for use are in progress.

(d) Capitalisation should be suspended during extended periods in which active development is interrupted.

(e) Capitalisation should cease when substantially all the activities that are necessary to get the tangible fixed asset ready for use are complete.

Disclosures

Where finance costs are capitalised, the following disclosures are required:

(a) the accounting policy adopted;
(b) the aggregate amount of finance costs included in the cost of tangible fixed assets;
(c) the amount of finance costs capitalised during the period;
(d) the amount of finance costs recognised in the profit and loss account during the period; and
(e) the capitalisation (interest) rate used to determine the amount of finance costs capitalised during the period.

Given that capitalisation of borrowing costs is optional, FRS 15 provides users of the financial statements with information to help them to compare the financial statements of different entities.

Conclusion   Capitalisation of finance (interest) costs is optional.

6.6   Subsequent expenditure

As well as the initial cost of acquiring a fixed asset, an entity may also incur additional costs in relation to the asset during its life. There are two main categories of subsequent expenditure:

(a)   expenditure to maintain or service the asset (an expense of the period)

(b)   expenditure to improve or upgrade the asset (effectively an addition to fixed assets).

FRS 15 sets out three circumstances in which subsequent expenditure should be capitalised:

(a)   where it provides an enhancement of the economic benefits of the tangible fixed asset in excess of its previously assessed standard of performance

Examples given in FRS 15:

- modification of an item of plant to extend its useful economic life or increase its capacity

- upgrading machine parts to achieve a substantial improvement in the quality of output

(b)   where a component of the tangible fixed asset that has been treated separately for depreciation purposes and depreciated over its individual useful economic life is replaced or restored

(c)   where it relates to a major inspection or overhaul of a tangible fixed asset that restores the economic benefits of the asset that have been consumed by the entity and have already been reflected in depreciation.

All other subsequent expenditure must be recognised in the profit and loss account as it is incurred.

Points (b) and (c) above deal with the situation in which an asset requires substantial expenditure every few years for overhauling and restoring major components. Examples include:

- the replacing of the lining of a blast furnace
- the dry docking of a ship
- the replacing of the roof of a building.

Previously, some entities dealt with this situation by setting up a provision for the expenditure, but FRS 12 *Provisions, contingent liabilities and contingent assets* has now prohibited this treatment (FRS 12 is discussed later in this chapter). Instead, the part of the asset that needs regular replacement should be depreciated separately over its individual useful economic life.

Example

An aircraft is required by law to be overhauled every three years. The cost of the overhaul is estimated at £150,000. How is this expenditure treated in the accounts?

Solution

The overhaul costs of £150,000 are depreciated separately from the rest of the aircraft, so that depreciation of £50,000 is charged each year until the next overhaul. When the expenditure is incurred, at the end of the three year period, it is capitalised and depreciated over the three years until the next major overhaul.

Note the requirement to depreciate major components of the asset separately before the refurbishment/restoration expenditure can be capitalised. Where a fixed asset is not accounted for as several different components, this kind of subsequent expenditure must be treated as normal repairs and maintenance and charged to the profit and loss account as it is incurred.

Conclusion   Subsequent expenditure can only be capitalised if it enhances an asset or if it relates to restoration or replacement of a component of the asset (provided that the component has been separately depreciated).

7   VALUATION OF FIXED ASSETS

7.1   Introduction

The Companies Act 1985 allows tangible fixed assets to be carried either at historic cost or at a valuation. Many entities take advantage of this rule and revalue some of their fixed assets (normally properties). Other entities continue to carry fixed assets at historic cost.

There are strong arguments for carrying assets at current values, which are mainly related to the disadvantages of using historic cost (which will be discussed in Chapter 21). The ASB wishes to encourage the use of current value in financial statements as it believes that this provides relevant information to users. However, until the issue of FRS 15 there was no accounting standard that gave guidance on revaluation. This has led to the following problems:

- valuations are not kept up to date (particularly if property prices are falling);
- entities 'cherry pick', ie, revalue certain assets and not others;
- some entities do not depreciate revalued fixed assets.

7.2   The basic rules

(a)   Revaluation of fixed assets is **optional**.

(b)   If one tangible fixed asset is revalued, all tangible fixed assets of the same class must be revalued. (This means that it is now impossible to 'cherry pick', for example, by revaluing some freehold properties and not others).

(c)   Where an entity adopts a policy of revaluation it need not be applied to all classes of tangible fixed assets held by the entity.

Definition   A **class of tangible fixed assets** is a category of tangible fixed assets having a similar nature, function or use in the business of the entity.

In practice a class of tangible fixed assets might be determined by the Companies Act balance sheet formats, for example: land and buildings; plant and machinery; and fixtures, fittings, tools and equipment. However, narrower classes are allowed, for example: specialised properties; non-specialised properties; and short leasehold properties.

(d)   The carrying amount of a revalued fixed asset should be its **current value** at the balance sheet date.

Definition   The **current value** of a tangible fixed asset to the business is the lower of replacement cost and recoverable amount.

Definition   **Recoverable amount** is the higher of net realisable value and value in use.

This definition of current value is consistent with the value to the business model set out in the draft Statement of Principles (see chapter 7). This is also known as deprival value.

7.3   Frequency and basis of valuation

Frequency

FRS 15 does not insist on annual revaluations, but instead requires the following:

(a)   Non-specialised properties:

- a full valuation every five years with an interim valuation in Year 3 or in other years where there has been a material change in value; *or*

- full valuation on a rolling basis over five year cycles with an interim valuation on the remaining portfolio where there has been a material change in value.

(b)   Specialised properties: valuation at least every five years and in the intervening years where there has been a material change in value.

(c)   Other tangible fixed assets:

- annual valuation where market comparisons or appropriate indices exist; *otherwise*
- valuation at least every five years and in the intervening years where there has been a material change in value.

Five yearly valuations should be carried out by a qualified external or internal valuer. If an internal valuer is used, the valuation should be reviewed by a qualified external valuer.

> **Definition**   An **internal valuer** is a director, officer or employee of the entity. An **external valuer** is not an internal valuer and does not have a significant financial interest in the entity.

Basis

The following valuation bases should be used for revalued properties that are not impaired:

(a)   non specialised properties: existing use value plus directly attributable acquisition costs if material. Disclose open market value where this is materially different

(b)   specialised properties: depreciated replacement cost

(c)   properties surplus to an entity's requirements: open market value less expected direct selling costs where these are material.

Tangible fixed assets other than properties should be valued using market value, where possible. Where market value is not obtainable, depreciated replacement cost should be used.

7.4   Activity

A company revalues its buildings and decides to incorporate the revaluation into its financial statements.

Extract from the balance sheet at 31 December 19X7:

	£'000
Buildings:	
Cost	1,200
Depreciation	144
	1,056

The building is revalued at 1 January 19X8 at £1,400,000. Its useful economic life was 40 years at that date.

You are required to show the relevant extracts from the final accounts at 31 December 19X8.

7.5   Activity solution

	£'000
Profit and loss account (extract)	
Depreciation (1,400 ÷ 40)	35
Notes: Tangible fixed assets: Buildings	
Cost at 1 January 19X8	1,200
Revaluation	200
Valuation at 31 December 19X8	1,400
Accumulated depreciation at 1 January 19X8	144
Revaluation	(144)
Charge for year (1,400,000 ÷ 40)	35
Accumulated depreciation at 31 December 19X8	35
Net book value at 31 December 19X8	1,365
Net book value at 1 January 19X8	1,056
Notes: Reserves	
Revaluation reserve (1,400 − 1,056)	344

Note the presentation of the fixed asset note carefully; it is often examined. The double entry is:

Dr Fixed asset cost	£200,000
Dr Accumulated depreciation	£144,000
Cr Revaluation reserve	£344,000

The accumulated depreciation account is cleared to the revaluation reserve because that depreciation is no longer relevant. After the asset is revalued, depreciation is based on the carrying amount (ie £1,400,000) and the asset is depreciated over its remaining useful economic life from the date of the revaluation.

7.6   Reporting gains and losses on revaluation

Gains

The Companies Act states that the profit and loss account should only include realised gains. A revaluation gain cannot be recognised in the profit and loss account because it is not yet realised (it will only be realised when the asset is sold).

Revaluation gains should normally be recognised in the statement of total recognised gains and losses. The statement of total recognised gains and losses includes all gains and losses incurred by an entity for a period, regardless of whether or not they are realised. You will cover the statement of total recognised gains and losses in a later chapter.

Losses

A revaluation loss may be caused either:

- by a fall in prices (eg, a slump in the property market); or
- by consumption of economic benefits (eg, physical damage or deterioration; this is similar to depreciation).

Unless there is evidence to the contrary, it is assumed that a loss is caused by a fall in prices.

(a)   Revaluation losses that are caused by a clear consumption of economic benefits should be recognised in the profit and loss account.

(b)   Other revaluation losses should normally be recognised in the statement of total recognised gains and losses until the carrying amount reaches its depreciated historical cost. Thereafter they should be recognised in the profit and loss account.

7.7   Activity

A property costing £500,000 was purchased on 1 January 19X4 and is being depreciated over its useful economic life of 10 years. It has no residual value. At 31 December 19X4 the property was valued at £540,000 and at 31 December 19X5 it was valued at £350,000.

How should these revaluations be treated in the accounts for the years ended 31 December 19X4 and 31 December 19X5?

7.8   Activity solution

Year ended 31 December 19X4: a revaluation gain of £90,000 is reported in the statement of total recognised gains and losses.

Year ended 31 December 19X5: a revaluation loss of £130,000 occurs and is dealt with as follows:

	£'000
Statement of total recognised gains and losses (480 – 400)	80
Profit and loss account	50
	130

WORKING	£'000
Cost at 1 January 19X4	500
Less: depreciation (500 ÷ 10)	(50)
	450
Revaluation gain	90
Valuation at 31 December 19X4	540
Less: depreciation (540 ÷ 9)	(60)
	480
Revaluation loss	(130)
Valuation at 31 December 19X5	350
Depreciated historic cost at 31 December 19X5 (500 – 100)	400

7.9   Reporting gains and losses on disposal

The profit or loss on the disposal of a revalued fixed asset should be calculated as the difference between the net sale proceeds and the carrying amount. It should be accounted for in the profit and loss account of the period in which the disposal occurs.

The gain or loss on revaluation has already been included in the accounts (in the statement of total recognised gains and losses) when the asset was revalued. If the profit or loss on disposal were based on the original cost of the asset, the gain or loss on revaluation would be recognised twice.

However, note that if there has been a gain on revaluation it is now realised. FRS 3 requires that when revaluation gains are realised they should be transferred from the revaluation reserve to the profit and loss account reserve. This transfer does not affect the profit for the year. We will be studying FRS 3 in Chapter 12.

7.10   Activity

A property costing £750,000 was purchased on 1 January 19X4 and is being depreciated over its useful economic life of 10 years. It has no residual value.

At 31 December 19X4 the property was valued at £810,000. There was no change to its useful economic life.

On 31 December 19X6 the property was sold for £900,000.

What is the profit or loss on disposal?

7.11   Activity solution

Profit on disposal

	£'000	£'000
Sales proceeds		900
Valuation at 31 December 19X4	810	
Less: depreciation (810 ÷ 9 × 2)	(180)	
Net book value		(630)
		270

7.12   Disclosures where assets have been revalued

For each class of revalued assets, disclose:

(i)   name and qualifications of the valuer(s);

(ii)   bases of valuation;

(iii)   date and amounts of the valuation;

(iv)   depreciated historic cost;

(v)   whether the valuer(s) is (are) internal or external;

(vi)   if the valuation has not been updated because the directors are not aware of any material change, a statement to that effect; and

(vii) date of the last full valuation (if not in the current period).

| Conclusion | Revaluation of fixed assets is optional. Revaluation must be applied to all assets of the same class and must be kept up to date |

8   DEPRECIATION

8.1   Depreciable amount

> [Definition]   **Depreciation** is the measure of the cost or revalued amount of the economic benefits of the tangible fixed asset that have been consumed during the period.

There is a note to the main definition:

Consumption includes the wearing out, using up or other reduction in the useful economic life of a tangible fixed asset whether arising from use, effluxion of time or obsolescence through either changes in technology or demand for the goods and services produced by the asset.

FRS 15 requires that the depreciable amount of a tangible fixed asset should be allocated on a systematic basis over its useful economic life.

> [Definition]   The **depreciable amount** is the cost of a tangible fixed asset (or, where an asset is revalued, the revalued amount) less its residual value.

> [Definition]   **Residual value** is the net realisable value of an asset at the end of its useful economic life.

> [Definition]   The **useful economic life** of a tangible fixed asset is the period over which the entity expects to derive economic benefit from that asset.

The depreciation method used should reflect as fairly as possible the pattern in which the asset's economic benefits are consumed by the entity.

The depreciation charge for each period should be recognised as an expense in the profit and loss account unless it is permitted to be included in the carrying amount of another asset (for example, where it is part of development expenditure that is capitalised).

These definitions and requirements are very similar to those of the old SSAP 12. Depreciation continues to be an application of the accruals concept rather than a means of measuring value. Like SSAP 12, FRS 15 does not prescribe a method of depreciation.

8.2   Change in method

A change from one method of providing depreciation to another is permissible only on the grounds that the new method will give a fairer presentation of the results and of the financial position.

This does not constitute a change in accounting policy. The carrying amount of the tangible fixed asset is depreciated using the revised method over the remaining useful economic life, beginning in the period in which the change is made.

8.3   Subsequent expenditure and impairment reviews

(a)   Where a tangible fixed asset comprises two or more major components with substantially different useful economic lives, each component should be depreciated separately over its individual useful economic life.

(b)   Subsequent expenditure on a tangible fixed asset that maintains or enhances the previously assessed standard of performance of the asset does not negate the need to charge depreciation.

(c)   When either:

    (i)   a tangible fixed asset is not depreciated on the grounds that the charge would be immaterial (either because of the length of the estimated remaining useful economic life or because the estimated residual value of the tangible fixed asset is not materially different from the carrying amount of the asset); or

(ii)   the estimated remaining useful economic life of the tangible fixed asset exceeds 50 years

the asset should be reviewed for impairment, in accordance with FRS 11, at the end of each reporting period. (This does not apply to non-depreciable land.)

These requirements are designed to deal with two particular problems. We have already looked at the first of these, the treatment of subsequent expenditure. FRS 12 has now prevented entities from providing for overhaul and servicing costs. Instead, where a major component of an asset has to be regularly replaced this component is depreciated separately.

The other problem is non-depreciation of revalued assets. In the past, many entities did not charge depreciation on revalued properties on the grounds that the assets were being maintained or refurbished regularly so that the economic life of the property was limitless. This treatment has been common in the hotel, brewing, public house and retail sectors.

It was widely expected that FRS 15 would require that all fixed assets were depreciated, thereby closing what many perceived to be a 'loophole' in SSAP 12. FRS 15 does state that subsequent expenditure does not remove the need to charge depreciation. However, the ASB has recognised that in rare cases, some tangible fixed assets may have very long useful economic lives. Entities can still avoid charging depreciation on the grounds that the charge is immaterial but they must carry out annual impairment reviews (FRS 11 is covered in a later chapter). This is likely to discourage non-depreciation as impairment reviews can be time consuming, complicated and costly and may result in reduced profits (if an impairment loss has to be recognised in the profit and loss account).

8.4   Review of useful economic life and residual value

(a)   Useful economic life should be reviewed at the end of each reporting period and revised if expectations are significantly different from previous estimates. If a useful economic life is revised, the carrying amount of the asset at the date of revision should be depreciated over the revised remaining useful economic life.

(b)   Where the residual value is material it should be reviewed at the end of each reporting period to take account of reasonably expected technological changes based on prices prevailing at the date of acquisition (or revaluation). Any change should be accounted for prospectively over the asset's remaining useful economic life.

8.5   Activity

An asset was purchased for £100,000 on 1 January 19X5 and is being depreciated over 5 years. Residual value was £10,000.

A general review of asset lives was undertaken and at 31 December 19X7 the remaining useful economic life was estimated at 7 years. Residual value was nil.

Calculate the depreciation charge for the year ended 31 December 19X7 and subsequent years.

8.6   Activity solution

	£
Net book value at 31 December 19X6 (100,000 – 36,000)	64,000
Annual depreciation charge (64,000 ÷ 8)	8,000

Note that the estimated remaining life is seven years from 31 December 19X7, but this information is used to compute the current year's charge as well.

8.7   Disclosure

As well as the disclosures required by the Companies Act (see chapter 8) FRS 15 requires the following disclosures for each class of tangible fixed assets:

(a)   the depreciation methods used;

(b)   the useful economic lives or the depreciation rates used;

(c)   total depreciation charged for the period; and

(d)   the effect of a change in useful economic lives or residual value in the period, where material.

Where there has been a change in the depreciation method used in the period, the effect should be disclosed, if material. The reason for the change should also be disclosed.

[Conclusion]   Depreciation should be charged on a systematic basis over the useful economic life of a tangible fixed asset. Tangible fixed assets must be reviewed for impairment annually if they are not depreciated or if their remaining useful economic life is more than 50 years.

9   FRS 12: PROVISIONS, CONTINGENT LIABILITIES AND CONTINGENT ASSETS

9.1   What is a provision?

The Companies Act defines provisions as 'amounts retained as **reasonably necessary** to cover any liability or loss which is either **likely** or certain to be incurred'. Provisions may be made for items such as environmental liabilities, reorganisation costs, litigation and future losses.

Although 'provisions' are often made for items such as depreciation and doubtful debts, strictly speaking these are not provisions, but normal accounting estimates.

The FRS 12 definition is as follows:

[Definition]   A **provision** is a **liability** of **uncertain** timing or amount.

This definition means that provisions are a sub-class of liabilities.

[Definition]   A **liability** is an obligation to transfer economic benefits as a result of past transactions or events. Uncertainty is what distinguishes a provision from another type of liability (such as a trade creditor or an accrued expense).

Note that the FRS 12 definition is narrower than the Companies Act definition. For a provision to be recognised under FRS 12 there must be an **obligation** to incur expenditure.

9.2   The problem

Until the issue of FRS 12, there was no accounting standard covering the general topic of provisions. This led to various problems:

(a)   Provisions were often recognised as a result of an intention to make expenditure, rather than on an obligation to do so.

(b)   Several items were aggregated into one large provision that was reported as an exceptional item (the 'big bath').

(c)   Inadequate disclosure meant that in some cases it was difficult to ascertain the significance of the provisions and any movements in the year.

Example

Shortly before the end of 19X1, the Board of Directors of a company decides to carry out a reorganisation. A provision for reorganisation costs is set up. However, the Board is not committed to the plan and early in 19X2 the decision is reversed.

The directors expect that the company will make losses in the years 19X2 and 19X3. Therefore the provision becomes a provision for future losses and is released to the profit and loss account in 19X2 and 19X3, in each case artificially turning a loss into a small profit.

'Creative accounting' such as this is often justified on grounds of prudence.

FRS 12 has been issued to prevent abuses such as this and to ensure that users of the financial statements are provided with sufficient information to understand the nature, timing and amount of provisions.

9.3   Contingent liabilities and contingent assets

|Definition| A **contingent liability** is:

  (a)   a possible obligation that arises from past events and whose existence will be confirmed only by the occurrence of one or more uncertain future events not wholly within the entity's control; or

  (b)   a present obligation that arises from past events but is not recognised because:

    (i)   it is not probable that a transfer of economic benefits will be required to settle the obligation; or

    (ii)   the amount of the obligation cannot be measured with sufficient reliability.

|Definition| A **contingent asset** is a possible asset that arises from past events and whose existence will be confirmed only by the occurrence of one or more uncertain future events not wholly within the entity's control.

One common example of contingencies arises in connection with legal action. If Company A sues Company B (for example, because it believes that it has incurred losses as a result of Company B's faulty products) then Company B may be liable for damages. Whether or not the damages will actually be paid depends on the outcome of the case. Until this is known, Company B has a contingent liability and Company A has a contingent asset.

Contingencies do not include normal accounting estimates. For example, although the correctness of a provision for doubtful debts will be confirmed (or otherwise) by uncertain future events, it is not a contingent liability.

There are two important changes from SSAP 18:

* The SSAP 18 definition of a contingency included probable gains and losses. Under FRS 12, if a gain or loss is probable it is not a contingency.

* The FRS 12 definition of a contingent liability is narrower than the SSAP 18 definition. For there to be a contingent liability there must be an **obligation**.

9.4 Recognition

Provisions

A provision should only be recognised when:

(a)   an entity has a present obligation (legal or constructive) as a result of a past event; and

(b)   it is probable that a transfer of economic benefits will be required to settle the obligation; and

(c)   a reliable estimate can be made of the amount of the obligation.

[Definition] A **legal obligation** is an obligation that derives from:

   (a)   a contract;
   (b)   legislation; or
   (c)   other operation of law.

[Definition] A **constructive obligation** is an obligation that derives from an entity's actions where:

   (a)   by an established pattern of past practice, published policies or a sufficiently specific current statement, the entity has indicated to other parties that it will accept certain responsibilities; and

   (b)   as a result, the entity has created a valid expectation on the part of those other parties that it will discharge those responsibilities.

FRS 12 explains that:

- A past event gives rise to a present obligation if, taking account of all available evidence, it is **more likely than not** that a present obligation exists at the balance sheet date.

- A transfer of economic benefits is regarded as probable if it is **more likely than not** to occur.

- Only in extremely rare cases will it not be possible to make a reliable estimate of the obligation.

Contingent liabilities

Contingent liabilities should not be recognised. They should be disclosed unless the possibility of a transfer of economic benefits is remote.

Contingent assets

Contingent assets should not be recognised. (Recognition of contingent assets could result in the recognition of profit that may never be realised). If the possibility of an inflow of economic benefits is probable they should be disclosed.

Only if a gain is virtually certain should it be recognised (because it cannot then be a contingency).

9.5 Activity

How should the following items be treated in the financial statements?

(a)   A manufacturer gives warranties at the time of sale to purchasers of its product. Under the terms of the contract for sale the manufacturer undertakes to make good manufacturing defects that become apparent within three years from the date of sale. On past experience it is probable that there will be some claims under the warranties.

(b)   A retail store has a policy of refunding purchases by dissatisfied customers, even though there is no legal obligation to do so. Its policy of making refunds is generally known.

(c)   During 19X9 A gives a guarantee of certain borrowings of B, whose financial condition at that time is sound.

(d)   A furnace has a lining that needs to be replaced every five years for technical reasons. At the balance sheet date, the lining has been in use for three years.

(e)   New laws have been passed that require an entity to fit smoke filters to its factories by 30 June 19Y0. At 31 December 19X9 (the balance sheet date) the entity has not yet fitted the smoke filters.

9.6   Activity solution

These items are taken from the Appendix to FRS 12. For each of the items, ask two questions:

(i)   Is there a present obligation as the result of a past event?

(ii)   Is a transfer of economic benefits in settlement probable?

A provision is recognised if the answer to both questions is yes.

(a)   Present obligation? - Yes. The past (obligating) event is the sale of the product, which gives rise to a legal obligation (under the contract).

Transfer of benefits probable? - Yes. There will probably be claims **for the warranties as a whole.**

Conclusion - Recognise a provision.

(b)   Present obligation? - Yes. The past event is the sale of the product, which gives rise to a constructive obligation (see the definition above).

Transfer of benefits probable? - Yes.

Conclusion - Recognise a provision.

(c)   Present obligation? - Yes. The giving of the guarantee has given rise to a legal obligation.

Transfer of benefits probable? - No.

Conclusion - Do not recognise a provision. Disclose the guarantee as a contingent liability unless the probability of having to honour it is remote.

(d)   Present obligation? - No. No obligation exists independently of the entity's future actions. There is a realistic alternative to incurring the expenditure - the entity could decide not to continue operating the furnace.

Conclusion - Do not recognise a provision. Instead, the cost of the furnace lining should be capitalised and depreciated over five years.

(e)   Present obligation? - No. The obligating event would be either the fitting of the filters (which has not happened) or the illegal operation of the factory without the filters (which has not happened because the filters are not yet legally required).

Conclusion - Do not recognise a provision.

9.7   Measurement

General rules

(a)   The amount recognised as a provision should be the best estimate of the expenditure required to settle the present obligation at the balance sheet date. (This is the amount that an entity would pay to settle the obligation at the balance sheet date or to persuade a third party to assume it).

(b)   In measuring a provision, an entity should take into account:

(i)   the risks and uncertainties surrounding the event (but uncertainty does not justify the creation of excessive provisions or overstatement of liabilities)

(ii)   future events (eg, technological developments) where there is sufficient objective evidence that they will occur.

(c)   Where the effect of the time value of money is material (for example, where a liability will be settled in several years' time), the amount of a provision should be discounted. A risk free rate should be used.

(d)   Provisions should be reviewed at each balance sheet date and adjusted to reflect the current best estimate. They should be reversed if the transfer of economic benefits is no longer probable.

(e)   A provision should only be used for expenditures for which it was originally recognised. (This requirement effectively prevents entities from using 'big bath accounting'.)

Reimbursements

A **reimbursement** is an amount received from a third party to pay part or all of the expenditure required to settle a provision (for example, through an insurance contract).

(a)   A reimbursement should be recognised only when it is virtually certain to be received.

(b)   The reimbursement should be treated as a separate asset (ie, it should not be netted off against the provision to which it relates).

(c)   In the profit and loss account, the expense relating to a provision may be presented net of the income recognised for a reimbursement.

Methods of dealing with uncertainties

These include:

- weighting the cost of all probable outcomes according to their probabilities ('expected value'); and

- considering a range of possible outcomes.

Example - expected value

An entity sells goods with a warranty covering customers for the cost of repairs of any defects that are discovered within the first two months after purchase. Past experience suggests that 90% of the goods sold will have no defects, 5% will have minor defects and 5% will have major defects. If minor defects were detected in all products sold, the cost of repairs would be £10,000; if major defects were detected in all products sold, the cost would be £100,000.

The expected value of the cost of repairs is £5,500 (5% × 10,000 + 5% × 100,000).

Example - possible outcomes

An entity has to rectify a serious fault in an item of plant that it has constructed for a customer.

In this case, the most likely outcome is that the repair will succeed at the first attempt at a cost of £400,000, but a provision for £500,000 is recognised because there is a significant chance that a further attempt will be necessary.

The most likely outcome may be the best estimate of the liability, but other possible outcomes must be considered. Where other possible outcomes are either mostly higher or mostly lower than the most likely outcome, the best estimate will be a higher or lower amount.

9.8   Future operating losses

Provisions should not be recognised for future operating losses.

However, note that FRS 12 only covers provisions which are not covered by another accounting standard. This means that there are still situations in which entities are required to make provisions for future losses (eg, discontinued operations (FRS 3), foreseeable losses on long term contracts (SSAP 9)).

9.9   Onerous contracts

[Definition]   An **onerous contract** is a contract in which the unavoidable costs of meeting the obligation exceed the economic benefits expected to be received under it.

An example: a lease contract for a property that is no longer required and where the lease cannot be cancelled.

If an entity has an onerous contract, a provision should be recognised for the present obligation under the contract (for example, for the best estimate of unavoidable lease payments).

9.10   Restructuring

[Definition]   A **restructuring** is a programme that is planned and controlled by management and materially changes either:
> (a)   the scope of a business undertaken by an entity; or
> (b)   the manner in which that business is conducted.

Examples

(a)   sale or termination of a line of business

(b)   the closure of business locations in a country or region or the relocation of business activities from one country or region to another

(c)   changes in management structure, for example, eliminating a layer of management

(d)   fundamental reorganisations that have a material effect on the nature and focus of the entity's operations.

When does an entity have an obligation to restructure?

Provisions for restructuring costs can only be recognised where an entity has a constructive obligation to carry out the restructuring. A Board decision on its own is **not** sufficient to create an obligation.

This requirement is designed to prevent entities from recognising provisions where there is only an intention to restructure and also from making unnecessary provisions which can then be used to artificially enhance profits in subsequent periods. However, critics of the ASB have argued that in practice most Boards of Directors do not take decisions to restructure lightly.

A constructive obligation to restructure arises only when the entity:

(a)   has a detailed formal plan for the restructuring identifying at least

> (i)   the business or part of the business concerned;

> (ii)   the principal locations affected;

(iii)   the location, function, and approximate number of employees who will be compensated for terminating their services;

(iv)   the expenditures that will be undertaken; and

(v)   when the plan will be implemented; and

(b)   has raised a valid expectation in those affected that it will carry out the restructuring by starting to implement the plan or announcing its main features to those affected by it.

For an entity to have an obligation to sell an operation there must be a binding sale agreement.

Expenses of restructuring

A restructuring provision should include only the direct expenditures arising from the restructuring, which are those that are both:

(a)   necessarily entailed by the restructuring and

(b)   not associated with the ongoing activities of the entity.

The provision should not include costs that relate to the future conduct of the business such as the cost of:

(a)   retraining or relocating staff who will continue with the business;

(b)   marketing; or

(c)   investment in new systems and distribution networks.

9.11   Activity

On 1 December 19X8 the board of an entity decided to close down a division on 31 March 19X9. On 31 January 19X9 a detailed plan for closing down the division was agreed; letters were sent to customers informing them of the decision and redundancy notices were sent to the staff of the division.

Should a provision be recognised in the accounts for the year ended 31 December 19X8?

9.12   Activity solution

No provision should be recognised. There was no present obligation at the balance sheet date. The obligating event is the announcement of the plan, which creates a constructive obligation. This did not take place until after the balance sheet date.

9.13   Disclosure

Provisions

For each class of provision, disclose:

(a)   carrying amount at the beginning and end of the period

(b)   additional provisions made in the period

(c)   amounts used during the period

(d)   unused amounts reversed during the period

(e)   effect of discounting during the period

(f)   a brief description of the nature of the obligation and expected timing of any resulting transfers of economic benefit

(g)   an indication of the uncertainties about the amount or timing of those transfers of economic benefit

(h)   the amount of any expected reimbursement.

Contingent liabilities

For each class of contingent liability (unless remote) disclose:

(a)   an estimate of its financial effect
(b)   an indication of the uncertainties relating to the amount or timing of any outflow
(c)   the possibility of any reimbursement.

Contingent assets

For contingent assets (only where probable) disclose:

(a)   a brief description of their nature
(b)   where practicable, an estimate of their financial effect.

Illustrations

FRS 12 includes examples of disclosures:

Example 1

Warranties

A manufacturer gives warranties at the time of sale to purchasers of its three product lines. Under the terms of the warranty the manufacturer undertakes to repair or replace items that fail to perform satisfactorily for two years from the date of sale. At the balance sheet date a provision of £60,000 has been recognised. The provision has not been discounted as the effect of discounting is not material. The following information is disclosed:

'A provision of £60,000 has been recognised for expected warranty claims on products sold during the last three financial years. It is expected that most of this expenditure will be incurred in the next financial year, and all will be incurred within two years of the balance sheet date.'

Example 2

Decommissioning costs

In 2000 an entity involved in nuclear activities recognises a provision for decommissioning costs of £300 million. The provision is estimated using the assumption that decommissioning will take place in 60–70 years' time. However, there is a possibility that it will not take place until 100–110 years' time, in which case the present alue of the costs will be significantly reduced. The following information is disclosed:

'A provision of £300 million has been recognised for decommissioning costs. These costs are expected to be incurred between 2060 and 2070. However, there is a possibility that decommissioning will not take place until 2100–2110. If the costs were measured based upon the expectation that they would not be incurred until 2100–2110 the provision would be reduced to £136 million. The provision has been estimated using existing technology, at current prices, and discounted using a real discount rate of 2 per cent.'

9.14   FRS 12 in practice

Because there must be an obligation before a provision can be recognised, entities will now not be allowed to recognise provisions in many situations where they would probably have done so in the past. This will prevent the abuses that have taken place in the past, such as 'big bath' accounting.

However, critics of the ASB claim that this will prevent preparers of accounts from being prudent.

Conclusion	A **provision** is a **liability** of **uncertain** timing or amount. A provision should only be recognised when:

        (a)   an entity has a present obligation as a result of a past event; and

        (b)   it is probable that a transfer of economic benefits will be required; and

        (c)   a reliable estimate can be made of the amount of the obligation.

        The amount recognised as a provision should be the best estimate of the expenditure required to settle the present obligation at the balance sheet date.

10   THE AUDIT PROCEDURES REQUIRED TO ENSURE COMPLIANCE WITH THE STANDARDS

10.1   General points

Accounting standards are important to the auditor as compliance with the standards is necessary in order to show a true and fair view. Some of the requirements of the standards can require more work by the auditor than others either because audit evidence is required to ensure compliance or there may be a large degree of judgement involved in the application of the standard.

10.2   Stocks

The main difficulties lie in calculating the costs of conversion. The auditor in particular may be concerned with checking that the inclusion of overheads is only on the basis of the normal level of activity. Costs such as raw materials, labour, transport etc, should be easier to determine.

In the net realisable value calculation the selling price may be purely an estimate, particularly in a volatile market. The auditor will need to be wary of high estimates, particularly in a company which is struggling. Marketing and selling costs may also be difficult to establish.

10.3   Long-term contracts

Even though the final figure on the balance sheet may be small, the auditor needs to confirm the gross costs incurred on each contract to assist him in determining whether profits and losses have been reasonably calculated. The following procedures would apply

(a)   Review the system of charging costs to contracts ie, materials, wages, etc.

(b)   (i)   Test issue and return of materials to each contract with appropriate supporting documentation ie, requisition, issue notes, etc.

          (ii)   Test allocation of wages paid to each contract.

          The extent of testing in each of the above cases will depend on the result of the review carried out in (a).

          In addition, specific tests should be carried out on transactions both before and after the year end to ensure that a proper cut-off has been established.

(c)   (i)   Review nature and method of allocating overheads to each contract.

          (ii)   Test allocations of each contract.

(d)   Test additions on contract ledger cards.

It is also essential that the auditor should take the following matters into consideration in appraising the valuation of the contracts at the year end apart from the requirements of SSAP 9:

(a)   the determination of those contracts which will result in a profit and those which will result in a loss

(b)   the terms of the contracts

   (i)   whether they are fixed prices or contain provisions for adjustment in the event of escalating costs

   (ii)   any penalty provisions, guarantees, etc

   (iii)   planned timetable of the contract

(c)   estimated costs to complete each contract - provision should be made for any expected losses

(d)   architects' valuation of work done to date, and, if available, valuations

(e)   progress payments to date - whether the terms of the contract are being followed

(f)   evidence of technical problems - inspect reports made by the client's officials

(g)   the past record of the company in determining the profit or loss on contracts in progress.

11   CHAPTER SUMMARY

All standards covered in this chapter can be the subject of an examination question in this exam. You need to know the requirements of each standard and be able to apply them to practical situations.

Long-term contracts require the calculation of attributable profit and the transfer of stocks and WIP to cost of sales in the profit and loss account.

Sales are matched with progress payments to determine the balance sheet disclosures.

FRS 15 requires that:

- a tangible fixed asset should initially be measured at its cost;
- where tangible fixed assets are revalued, the valuation is kept up to date;
- tangible fixed assets should be depreciated over their estimated useful economic lives; and
- the useful economic lives and residual values of tangible fixed assets should be reviewed annually and revised where necessary.

FRS 12 requires that provisions should only be recognised when:

- an entity has a present obligation as a result of a past event; and
- it is probable that a transfer of economic benefits will be required; and
- a reliable estimate can be made of the amount of the obligation.

The amount recognised as a provision should be the best estimate of the expenditure required to settle the present obligation at the balance sheet date.

12   SELF TEST QUESTIONS

12.1   What classifications should stocks be disclosed under? (1.4)

12.2   What is the definition of development expenditure? (2.1)

12.3   What is window dressing? (3.4)

12.4   What is a payment on account? (4.4)

12.5   When invoices are issued to a customer on a long-term contract, what is the double entry? (5.3)

12.6   How should a fixed asset be measured initially? (6.2)

12.7   When may subsequent expenditure be capitalised? (6.6)

12.8   What is the double entry for recording a revaluation gain? (7.5)

12.9   What is the definition of depreciation? (8.1)

12.10   When should a provision be recognised? (9.4)

12.11   When is there a constructive obligation to restructure? (9.10)

12.12   What is the main valuation difficulty faced by an auditor of stocks? (10.2)

13   EXAMINATION TYPE QUESTIONS

13.1   SSAP 9: long-term contracts

SSAP 9 *Stocks and long-term contracts* is partly concerned with long-term contract work in progress.

You are required:

(a)   to explain how SSAP 9 justifies the recognition of profits before completion of a long-term contract.   **(4 marks)**

(b)   to explain how SSAP 9 requires the profits and losses on long-term contracts in progress to be calculated.   **(10 marks)**

(c)   Do you consider that the provisions in SSAP 9 concerning long-term contracts are consistent with the requirements of SSAP 2 *Disclosure of accounting policies*, with regard to the fundamental accounting concepts? Justify your view.   **(6 marks)**
                                                                                             (Total: 20 marks)

13.2   Depreciation problems

As the accountant of a small company you have received the following comments or suggestions from other staff regarding depreciation of fixed assets:

(a)   'There is no point in depreciating the freehold buildings because the market value must be considerably in excess of cost.'

(b)   'I estimate that the replacement cost of our machine shop equipment is a good fifty percent more than we paid for it, so should we not increase the depreciation charge from 20% to 30%?'

(c)   'The trading prospects for the next year or two look good – I think we should change the depreciation method for machinery from 20% straight-line to 40% reducing balance so as to get more written off while profits are high.'

You are required to outline how you would respond to each of the above.   **(15 marks)**

14   ANSWERS TO EXAMINATION TYPE QUESTIONS

14.1   SSAP 9: Long-term contracts

(a)   Long-term contracts may last over a period of several years. The SSAP 9 approach permits the recognition of profit each year as work is performed. The alternative - deferring recognition of all profit until the end of the project - would result in profit for the year showing profits on all contracts happening to end in that year, an approach which is subject both to fluctuation and manipulation.

(b)   Calculation involves two elements:

Attributable profits

This is an amount which cannot be computed until the outcome of the contract can be assessed with reasonable certainty. It will be the proportion of the total profit expected to arise over the life of the contract that has been earned at the balance sheet date. Total profit must take into account total costs to completion, estimated future costs of rectification and guarantee work, and likely future cost increases.

Foreseeable losses

Immediate provision should be made for total losses expected to arise over the period of a contract. Such provision should be made as soon as losses are foreseen, even before commencement of contract work. Where a loss-making contract is expected to absorb a major part of the company's capacity for a period, part of related company administration expenses should be included in the computation of the loss.

(c)   SSAP 9 relates to the four fundamental concepts of SSAP 2 as follows:

Accruals Costs of production are matched with the related benefits of the contract as they arise.

Going concern Applies in that the treatment of long-term contracts assumes that the company will continue to exist to perform completion.

Consistency SSAP 9 requires consistency in application of accounting policies on long-term contracts.

Prudence Aspects of SSAP 9's requirements reflect the prudence concept, notably the fact that losses are recognised when anticipated, while income is only recognised in stages as it is earned. Moreover, the whole tone of SSAP 9's guidance on quantifying expected profits and losses is prudent. However, it can be argued that SSAP 9 goes against the prudence concept in requiring recognition of part of long-term contract income before the whole of the related contract work is completed.

14.2   Depreciation problems

(a)   Freehold buildings have a limited life; eventually they will need to be replaced. The buildings are depreciated in order:

(i)   to charge an appropriate amount against distributable profit for each year in order to match the benefits derived from the use of the buildings to the cost associated with their eventual decline in value from original cost; and

(ii)   to retain sufficient funds in the business to provide, at least in part, for their replacement.

The increase in value of the buildings does not extend their useful life, but it indicates that the replacement cost will be higher and, therefore, that the buildings, if included in the accounts at their higher revalued amount, should give rise to a greater depreciation charge.

(b)   The increase in replacement cost of the buildings means that extra sums should be set aside for their replacement. These sums should be appropriated from distributable profit in addition to depreciation. Although depreciation does ensure the retention of funds in the business, it does not provide more funds than the original cost of the asset (or, if based on a revaluation, the revalued amount). Thus, extra funds will need to be set aside. The reason for the shortfall is that the principal aim of the depreciation charge is to match the cost of using an asset to the benefit derived from that asset rather than to retain funds for replacement.

(Tutorial note:

The extra 10% is not depreciation but is an appropriation of profits.

So the bookkeeping should be

Dr   P&L account (reserve)
Cr   Fixed Asset Replacement Reserve

and not

Dr   P&L account
Cr   Accumulated depreciation

The latter entry would merely result in the asset being eliminated from the books more quickly than should be the case.)

(c)   The rate of depreciation should be such as to charge against profits a sum which fairly represents the rate of consumption of the asset through use in the business. The proposed change in the rate of depreciation would only be correct if the asset was to be used more in earlier years in generating the increased profits; otherwise an unfair charge will be made in earlier years and the balance sheet will show figures less representative of the asset's continued usefulness. If it is intended to retain more profits for replacement, then a transfer to a replacement reserve is indicated.

10 ACCOUNTING FOR TAXATION

INTRODUCTION & LEARNING OBJECTIVES

Accounting for taxation is a very frequent element in the large-scale numerical questions set on the preparation of published accounts.

This chapter covers the following topics:

- SSAP 8 *Taxation in the accounts of companies*
- How to approach the taxation aspects of published accounts questions
- SSAP 5 *Accounting for value added tax*

When you have studied this chapter you should be able to do the following:

- Understand how corporation tax is treated in the accounts of companies.
- Understand how to tackle the tax aspects of published accounts questions.
- Understand the accounting treatment of VAT.

1 CORPORATION TAX

1.1 The UK system of corporation tax

Corporation tax is payable by companies on their trading profits, capital gains and their other income.

The taxable profits will not be the same amount as the accounting profits however as:

(a) certain expenditure is not allowed as tax deductible

(b) depreciation is replaced by capital allowances

(c) dividend income from other UK companies is not taxable.

Following the passing of the Finance Act 1998, 'large' companies (defined as those with profits chargeable to corporation tax of more than £1.5 million) must pay their corporation tax in four quarterly instalments based on their anticipated profits for the current year.

Small and medium sized companies continue to pay their corporation tax liability nine months after the end of their accounting period.

1.2 Recording entries relating to corporation tax in the accounting records

The double entry for the corporation tax charge for the year is

		£	£
Dr	Profit and loss account	x	
Cr	Corporation tax account		x

Although the tax payable is only an estimate and often referred to as a corporation tax **provision** it should be included in creditors and not under provisions.

If the estimate is wrong, the under or over provision is dealt with by increasing or decreasing the following year's tax charge.

Although this relates to a prior year, it is not a prior year adjustment as it is simply a revision of an accounting estimate.

The notes to the profit and loss account will disclose the adjustment where it is material.

1.3   Example

	£
Corporation tax provision at 31 May 19X5	316,000
Corporation tax charge for year ended 31 May 19X6	383,500
Corporation tax paid on 28 February 19X6	263,000

Corporation tax account

	£		£	£
Bank (paid)	263,000	Balance b/d		316,000
		P&L a/c		
		Charge for year	383,500	
		Less: Over provision £(316,000 − 263,000)	(53,000)	
Balance c/d	383,500			330,500
	646,500			646,500

Profit and loss account for the year ended 31 May 19X6

Extract

		£
	Profit on ordinary activities before taxation	x
4	Taxation	(330,500)
	Profit on ordinary activities after taxation	x

Notes to the financial statements

4   Taxation

	£
UK corporation tax (at 30%)	383,500
Over provision in previous year	(53,000)
	330,500

1.4   The relationship between taxation and dividends

As dividends are **appropriations** of profit, it follows that they are not deductible as **expenses** in arriving at the corporation tax charge. This is why dividends are shown **after** taxation in the published profit and loss account.

2   THE ACCOUNTING TREATMENT OF UNFRANKED RECEIPTS AND PAYMENTS

2.1   The company as a collecting agent on charges

A company acts as a collecting agent for the Inland Revenue for income tax on certain payments. Payments by companies which are made under deduction of income tax at source are:

(a)   loan stock and debenture interest

(b)   patent and mineral output royalties

(c)   covenants

(d)   annuities.

The income tax is paid over to the Inland Revenue on the fourteenth day after the end of the quarter in which the payment is made.

2.2   Unfranked investment income (UFII)

A company in receipt of debenture interest will receive it net of 20% income tax which the paying company will have deducted at source. This income is known as unfranked investment income.

			£	£
Dr	Cash (net receipt)		x	
	Cr	Debenture interest received		x

It follows that the company (which suffers corporation tax, not income tax) may reclaim the income tax deducted at source from the Inland Revenue. The double entry is to gross up the receipt using an income tax account

			£	£
Dr	Income tax account		x	
	Cr	Debenture interest received		x

The gross debenture interest is therefore credited to profit and loss account.

2.3   Recording transactions involving receipts and payments

Where a company both pays interest and receives unfranked investment income

(i)   Income tax on the excess of interest paid over interest received is paid to the Inland Revenue. If this is unpaid at the year end, it forms part of the tax creditor. Alternatively,

(ii)   Income tax on the excess of interest received over interest paid is repayable to the company. This is done by offset against the corporation tax (CT) liability.

2.4   Example

	£
Loan interest received (gross)	28,000
Loan interest paid (gross)	48,000

Income tax is deducted at 20%.

The income tax account is as follows

Income tax account

	£		£
Interest received account (20% × £28,000)	5,600	Interest paid account (20% × £48,000)	9,600
Balance c/d	4,000		
	9,600		9,600

£4,000 is subsequently paid to the Inland Revenue.

Note that in computational questions in the examination, the question will give the **gross** amount of interest unless there is a specific mention that the sum referred to is a net amount. This is because the information given is normally in the form of a trial balance and the above entries will have already been made.

2.5   Activity

	£
Loan interest received	28,000
Loan interest paid	16,000

Show the income tax account, deducting income tax at 20% from interest amounts.

2.6   Activity solution

Income tax account

	£		£
Interest received account (20% × £28,000)	5,600	Interest paid account (20% × £16,000)	3,200
		Corporation tax account	2,400
	5,600		5,600

The IT recoverable is therefore offset against the CT payable.

3   DISCLOSURE REQUIREMENTS OF COMPANY LAW AND SSAP 8

3.1   Introduction

Although Advance Corporation Tax (ACT) has been abolished, so companies no longer have to pay ACT when a dividend is paid, SSAP 8 has not been withdrawn. This means that the rules of SSAP 8 covering items other than ACT still have to be complied with.

In particular, SSAP 8 requires dividends received to be shown in the profit and loss account at the amount of cash received plus the tax credit. The tax credit is then shown as part of the tax charge for the year in the profit and loss account. This is purely a disclosure requirement and has no effect on the amount of tax actually payable to the Inland Revenue. You should read an exam question carefully to identify the rate to be used for tax credits.

Example

Janeway plc receives a dividend of £9,000 in the year ending 31 December 19X9. Tax credits are available at $^{10}/_{90}$ of the cash amount received. Show extracts from the published profit and loss account for the year ending 31 December 19X9.

Solution

Profit and loss account (extracts) for the year ending 31 December 19X9

	£	£
Income from fixed asset investments ($9,000 \times \frac{100}{90}$)		10,000
Tax on profit on ordinary activities		
UK corporation tax	X	
Tax credits on dividends received ($9,000 \times \frac{10}{90}$)	1,000	
		X

3.2   The profit and loss account

(a)   Taxation charge

The taxation charge in the profit and loss account should include the following items. Where any of the individual items is material, it should be disclosed separately.

(i)   UK corporation tax (remember to give the rate used for the provision);

(ii)   transfers to or from deferred tax;

(iii)   relief for overseas tax;

(iv)   unrelieved overseas tax;

(v)   tax credits on incoming dividends.

(b)   **Investment income**

(i)   Incoming dividends are shown gross ie, cash received plus tax credit.

(ii)   Unfranked investment income is shown gross ie, inclusive of income tax.

(c)   **Annual charges**

These are shown gross.

(d)   **Dividends paid and proposed**

These are appropriated **net** – ie, the actual cash amount paid or payable to shareholders.

3.3   The balance sheet

Proposed dividends should be shown **net** under current liabilities.

3.4   Published accounts questions involving taxation

The treatment of taxation in published accounts often causes considerable difficulties for students. The entries required will vary depending upon the information given but a general approach is given below which should be sufficient for most questions. The main point to remember is to deal with the profit and loss account entries before the computation of the balance sheet liabilities.

3.5   Examples

Example 1

Simple Ltd has estimated its corporation tax liability for the year ended 31 December 19X8 at £180,000, based on taxable profits of £600,000. The corporation tax rate is 30%.

An extract from the trial balance as at 31 December 19X8 shows

	Dr. £	Cr. £
Sales		1,500,000
Cost of sales, distribution and admin. expenses	900,000	
Taxation		3,000

Step 1   Deal with profit and loss account entries

Profit and loss account for the year ended 31 Dec 19X8

	£	£
Sales		1,500,000
Costs		900,000
Profit on ordinary activities before taxation		600,000
Taxation:		
UK corporation tax for the year	180,000	
Over-provision in prior year	(3,000)	
		177,000
Profit on ordinary activities after taxation		423,000

(Tutorial note:

The taxation figure in the trial balance must be the difference between last year's provision and the amount subsequently paid.

The amount is cleared to the profit and loss account.

> Dr. Taxation account
>   Cr. Profit and loss)

Step 2   Deal with balance sheet entries

The only item which affects the balance sheet in this example is the provision for the year (£180,000).

The entry is:

	£	£
Dr. Profit and loss – Tax charge	180,000	
Cr. Balance sheet – Tax creditor		180,000

This will be shown separately under 'Creditors: amounts falling due within one year'.

3.6   Example 2

An extract from the trial balance of More Complex Ltd as at 31 December 19X8 shows:

	Dr. £	Cr. £
Sales		1,500,000
Cost of sales, distribution and admin. expenses	950,000	
Taxation:		
- (last year's provision £20,000; agreed liability £22,500)	2,500	
Interim dividend	22,500	
Dividend received		8,000
Deferred taxation		30,000

Additional information:

(a)   The tax provision for the year on ordinary operations is estimated at £170,000.

(b)   The corporation tax rate is 30% and tax credits are available at $\frac{10}{90}$ of dividends received.

(c)   The transfer to deferred taxation for the year is £15,000.

(d)   The directors are not proposing a final dividend.

Step 1   Completing the profit and loss account:

Profit and loss account for the year ended 31 Dec 19X8

	£	£
Sales		1,500,000
Costs		950,000
		550,000
Investment income $(8,000 \times \times \frac{100}{90})$		8,889
Profit on ordinary activities before taxation		558,889

Taxation:

UK corporation tax for the year at 30%	170,000	
Under-provision in prior year	2,500	
Deferred taxation	15,000	
Tax credits on franked investment income	889	
		188,389
Profit for the financial year		370,500
Dividends		22,500
Profits retained for the year		348,000

Step 2 A working should be set up to record the entries made from the profit and loss account to the balance sheet:

	Current tax liability £	Deferred tax £
Per trial balance	–	30,000
From profit and loss:		
- tax section	170,000	15,000
Year end balance	170,000	45,000

4 SSAP 5 – ACCOUNTING FOR VALUE ADDED TAX

4.1 Introduction

VAT is a form of indirect taxation introduced to the UK on 1 April 1973. It is levied on most goods and services. Although it is eventually borne by the final consumer, VAT is collected at each stage of the production and distribution chain.

4.2 Accounting treatment

The majority of traders act as collection agents (unpaid) for HM Customs and Excise, accounting on a quarterly basis for VAT levied on their sales (or outputs), less VAT suffered on their purchases (or inputs). The simplest way in which this operation can be reflected in the books of account is by opening a VAT account which acts as a personal account with HM Customs and Excise. The VAT account is debited with all VAT suffered on inputs and credited with all VAT charged on outputs. The balance on the account will, therefore, represent the amount due to or from HM Customs and Excise. Entries in the account will be made as follows:

(a)   VAT suffered on inputs:

        Dr Purchases account   with cost excluding VAT
        Dr VAT account   with VAT
           Cr Supplier's account   with cost including VAT

(b)   VAT charged on outputs:

        Dr Customer's account   with sales price including VAT
           Cr Sales account   with sales price excluding VAT
           Cr VAT account   with VAT

(c)   Payments over to Customs and Excise:

        Dr VAT account
           Cr Cash book

(d)   Refunds of excess VAT suffered from Customs and Excise:

> Dr Cash book
> > Cr VAT account

4.3   Illustration

A trader's purchase and sales analysis shows the following information for the last quarter of his financial year:

	£
Taxable inputs	211,500
Taxable outputs	302,143

Both figures include VAT at 17.5%. During this time he paid £17,550 in settlement of the previous quarter's return.

Draft the VAT account to record these transactions (to the nearest £).

Solution

VAT account (a personal account with HM Customs and Excise)

	£		£
VAT on inputs:		VAT on outputs:	
Purchases		Balance b/d	17,550
($17.5/117.5 \times £211,500$)	31,500	Sales	
Cash paid	17,550	($17.5/117.5 \times £302,143$)	45,000
Balance c/d	13,500		
	———		———
	62,550		62,550
	———		———
		Balance b/d	13,500

Note: as the balance on this account represents a normal trade liability, it can be included in creditors on the balance sheet. It would only require separate disclosure in exceptional circumstances.

4.4   Taxable, zero-rated and exempt items

A clear distinction needs to be made between the treatment of traders in taxable items (which may be standard rated or zero-rated), and exempt items:

(a)   **Taxable items: standard-rated**

Because traders in standard-rated items are charged VAT on their purchases and can pass it on to their customers in sales, they do not suffer it as an expense. Consequently, VAT should have no effect on the profit and loss account. The only exceptions to this rule are non-deductible inputs, such as motor cars and certain business entertaining expenses. Because VAT on these items cannot be recovered, it should be included as part of the cost of the items.

(b)   **Taxable items: zero-rated**

These include exports, food, books, newspapers, children's clothes, travel fares and construction. Traders in these items do not charge VAT on outputs, but can recover VAT on their inputs. Therefore, again, VAT should have no effect on the profit and loss account.

(c)   **Exempt (ie, non-taxable) items**

These include land transactions, insurance premiums, postal and health services, betting, education and small businesses. Although such traders do not charge VAT on their outputs, they have no right (unlike zero-rated traders) to recover VAT on their inputs. In such cases the irrecoverable VAT will be added to the trader's costs.

4.5   Standard accounting practice

SSAP 5 requires that:

(a)   Turnover shown in the profit and loss account should exclude VAT on taxable outputs (see also para 95 Sch 4 CA85).

(b)   Irrecoverable VAT on fixed assets and other items disclosed separately in published accounts (eg, capital commitments) should be included in their cost.

4.6   Activity

(a)   A company trading in goods which are subject to VAT at standard rate (17.5%) has a turnover of £2,156,780 including VAT.

What figure for turnover should be disclosed in its published accounts?

(b)   A trader's purchase and sales analysis shows the following information for the last quarter of his financial year:

	£
Taxable inputs	154,006
Taxable outputs	227,493

Both figures include VAT at 17.5%. During the quarter he paid £6,100 in settlement of the previous quarter's return.

Draft the VAT account to record these transactions.

4.7   Activity solution

(a)   The VAT-exclusive figure should be given:

$$\frac{100}{117.5} \times £2,156,780 = £1,835,557$$

(b)

VAT account

	£		£
Purchases		Balance b/d	6,100
(17.5/117.5 × 154,006)	22,937	Sales	
Cash	6,100	(17.5/117.5 × 227,493)	33,882
Balance c/d	10,945		
	———		———
	39,982		39,982
	———		———
		Balance b/d	10,945

Conclusion   For traders whose supplies are taxable (either standard-rated or zero-rated) VAT will have no effect on the profit and loss account, other than in exceptional cases where input VAT is non-recoverable (eg, on the purchase of a car, or expenditure on entertaining).

5   CHAPTER SUMMARY

You need to understand how to deal with taxation figures (VAT, corporation tax and deferred tax) in the accounts of limited companies. You do not need to know - at least for this examination - the detail of how tax liabilities are calculated.

6   SELF TEST QUESTIONS

6.1   What happens to the excess income tax if there is more interest paid than interest received in the accounting period? (2.3)

6.2   Are annual charges shown gross or net in the profit and loss account? (3.2)

6.3   What is the important difference between a trader making zero-rated supplies and a trader making exempt supplies? (4.4)

6.4   Should turnover in a profit and loss account be disclosed net or gross of recoverable VAT? (4.5)

7   EXAMINATION TYPE QUESTION

7.1   Humpledink Ltd

Humpledink Ltd, with an issued share capital of £250,000 in shares of £1 each, makes up its accounts to 31 December of each year, and its corporation tax is normally payable on the following 1 October. On 1 January 19X5 the liabilities for corporation tax are as follows:

Year ended 31 Dec 19X4 £60,000 (estimated on the profits of the year)

During the year ended 31 December 19X5, the liability in respect of the year ended 31 December 19X4 was agreed at £57,500 and paid on 1 July 19X5.

An interim dividend of 5p per share is paid on 30 June 19X5, and the directors propose that a final dividend of 10p per share, making 15p for the year, be paid.

The liability for corporation tax based on the profits of the year ended 31 December 19X5 is estimated to be £75,000.

Assuming that the profit for the year ended 31 December 19X5 before taxation amounted to £150,000, and that the balance of reserves brought forward from the previous year was £120,000, **you are required:**

(a)   to prepare the corporation tax accounts from the information given;

(b)   to prepare the profit and loss account for the year ended 31 December 19X5, as far as the information given permits; and

(c)   to show the treatment of the appropriate items in the balance sheet prepared as at 31 December 19X5.   **(16 marks)**

8   ANSWER TO EXAMINATION TYPE QUESTION

8.1   Humpledink Ltd

(a)

Corporation tax account – Liability year ended 31 December 19X4

	£		£
Profit and loss a/c:		Bal b/f	
Over provision			60,000
£60,000 – £57,500	2,500		
Cash	57,500		
	60,000		60,000

Corporation tax account – Liability year ended 31 December 19X5

	£		£
Bal c/f	75,000	Profit and loss a/c	75,000
	75,000		75,000

(b)   **Profit and loss account for year ended 31 December 19X5**

	£	£
Profit for year before taxation		150,000
Corporation tax based on the profit for year	75,000	
Corporation tax provision for previous year, no longer required	(2,500)	
		72,500
Profit for year available for appropriation		77,500
Less: Appropriations:		
Dividends paid and proposed		(37,500)
Retained profit for financial year		40,000
Retained earnings at 1 January 19X5		120,000
Retained earnings at 31 December 19X5		160,000

(c)   **Balance sheet at 31 December 19X5**

	£
Creditors: amounts falling due within one year	
Corporation tax payable 1 October 19X6	75,000
Proposed dividend	25,000

11 DEFERRED TAXATION

INTRODUCTION & LEARNING OBJECTIVES

SSAP 15 is a difficult standard and can require a lot of study in order to understand its requirements. It may be tested in a discussion question or a computational context. However it is not expected to be a commonly tested topic at this level of accounting and thus you should not spend too much time on this area to the detriment of other areas.

When you have studied this chapter you should be able to do the following:

- Explain the effect of timing differences.
- Outline the requirements of SSAP 15.
- Record entries relating to deferred tax in the accounting records.

1 TIMING DIFFERENCES

1.1 What is deferred taxation?

Deferred taxation is a basis of allocating tax charges to particular accounting periods. The key to deferred taxation lies in the two quite different concepts of profit:

(a) the accounting profit (or the reported profit), which is the figure of profit before tax reported to the shareholders in the published accounts;

(b) the taxable profit, which is the figure of profit on which the Inland Revenue base their corporation tax calculations.

These two figures of profit are unlikely to be the same. The two main areas of difference are:

(a) **Timing differences**

This simply means that certain types of income and expenditure are recognised in different periods for the purposes of financial accounts on the one hand, and taxation on the other.

If the tax charge shown in the published accounts were based purely on the tax payable, then a situation could arise where the tax charge fluctuated over various accounting periods, even though the accounting or reported profit remained the same. Timing differences are the essence of the problem of deferred taxation.

(b) **Permanent differences**

These arise where items taken into account for the purposes of the financial accounts are disallowable or non-taxable.

Permanent differences are quite distinct from timing differences. An example of a permanent difference is disallowable entertaining expenditure. Such expenditure is charged against the accounting profit in the period in which it is incurred, but is never allowed against taxable profit. It is not simply a matter of deciding in which accounting period the item is to be recognised, as is the case with timing differences. Permanent difference items do not *reverse* themselves over a period of time.

An important example of a permanent difference would be depreciation provided on buildings for which an industrial buildings allowance was not available eg, on a shop or office building.

Deferred taxation is **not** concerned with permanent differences.

1.2 Types of timing differences

Timing differences arise from four main sources:

(a) **Short-term timing differences**

These arise from the use of the receipts and payments basis for tax purposes and the accruals basis for the published accounts. Such timing differences are said to **originate** in the accounting period when accrued in the accounts and then **reverse**, normally in the following period when allowed or charged for taxation purposes.

Examples are:

(i) pension costs accrued in the accounts but allowed for tax when paid;

(ii) provisions for repair and maintenance made in the accounts but not allowed for tax purposes until the expenditure is incurred;

(iii) general bad debts provision, allowed for tax purposes only when they become specific.

(b) **Fixed asset timing differences**

A timing difference arises where the capital allowances available in the tax computations are not equal to the related depreciation. Such differences are said to **originate** when this inequality occurs, and to **reverse** at some time in the future. Originating timing differences may give rise to deferred tax liabilities or deferred tax assets. Obviously, timing differences must originate **before** they can reverse.

(c) **Revaluation surpluses on fixed assets**

These arise because the actual taxation liability does not arise until the gain is realised on disposal. The differences **originate** in the year of revaluation and **reverse** in the year of disposal.

SSAP 15 states however that a timing difference does not arise when it is expected that the disposal of the revalued asset and of any subsequent replacement assets would not result in a tax liability after taking into account any expected roll-over relief.

(d) **Losses**

A loss for tax purposes can be available to relieve future profits.

1.3 The purpose of deferred taxation

If the tax charge shown in the profit and loss account were based on the tax actually payable, then the tax charge shown in the published accounts would not bear any relation to the accounting profit, solely because of the way the Inland Revenue allows or requires revenue or expenditure to be allocated to various periods for tax purposes. Full deferred tax accounting eliminates the effect of timing differences in such a way that the tax charge reported to the shareholders is in direct relation to the reported profit.

Remember that deferred taxation does not take account of permanent differences. Permanent differences, if of a material nature, will cause a **distortion** between the tax charge and the accounting or reported profit. This may well require explanation by way of a note to the shareholders.

1.4 The effect of timing differences on accounting and taxable profits

A company makes a profit of £100,000 (after depreciation but before taxation) each year. The company buys an asset in year 1 costing £40,000 and claims a 25% writing down allowance on the reducing balance each year. Depreciation policy is to write off the cost of the asset over five years, on a straight line basis. The rate of corporation tax is 30%.

You are required to calculate the balance on deferred tax at the end of each of the first six years.

1.5   Solution

$\boxed{\text{Step 1}}$ **Calculation for taxation purposes**

	Year 1 £	Year 2 £	Year 3 £	Year 4 £	Year 5 £	Year 6 £
Profit after depreciation before taxation (reported profit)	100,000	100,000	100,000	100,000	100,000	100,000
Add: Depreciation	8,000	8,000	8,000	8,000	8,000	-
	108,000	108,000	108,000	108,000	108,000	100,000
Less: Capital allowances	10,000	7,500	5,625	4,219	3,164	2,373
Taxable profit	98,000	100,500	102,375	103,781	104,836	97,627
Corporation tax payable at 30%	29,400	30,150	30,712	31,134	31,451	29,288

$\boxed{\text{Step 2}}$ **Calculation of deferred taxation**

	£	*Deferred tax account* £	£	*Memorandum re double entry*		£
Year 1						
Capital allowances	10,000					
Depreciation	8,000					
	2,000					
Originating timing difference		2,000				
Charged at 30%			600	Dr Profit and loss account		600
				Cr Deferred taxation account		600
Balance on deferred tax account at year end – Liability			600			
Year 2						
Capital allowances	7,500					
Depreciation	8,000					
	(500)					
Reversing timing difference		(500)				
Credited at 30%			(150)	Dr Deferred taxation account		150
				Cr Profit and loss account		150
Balance on deferred tax account at year end – Liability			450			

Year 3

Capital allowances	5,625			
Depreciation	8,000			
	———			
	(2,375)			

Reversing timing difference	(1,500)			
Credited at 30%		(450)		
Originating timing difference	(875)		}Dr Deferred taxation account	712
Credited at 30%	———	(262)	Cr Profit and loss account	712
	(2,375)	———		

Balance on deferred tax account			
at year end – Asset		(262)	

Year 4

Capital allowances	4,219
Depreciation	8,000
	———
	(3,781)

Originating timing difference	(3,781)			
	———			
Credited at 30%		(1,134)	Dr Deferred taxation account	1,134
		———	Cr Profit and loss account	1,134
Balance on deferred tax account				
at year end – Asset		(1,396)		

Year 5

Capital allowances	3,164
Depreciation	8,000
	———
	(4,836)

Originating timing difference	(4,836)			
	———			
Credited at 30%		(1,451)	Dr Deferred taxation account	1,451
		———	Cr Profit and loss account	1,451
Balance on deferred tax account				
at year end – Asset		(2,847)		

Year 6

Capital allowances	2,373
Depreciation	-
	———
	2,373

Reversing timing difference	2,373			
	———			
Charged at 30%		712	Dr Profit and loss account	712
		———	Cr Deferred taxation account	712
Balance on deferred tax account				
at year end – Asset		(2,135)		

Step 3   **Summary of tax charges reported to the shareholders in the published accounts**

	Year 1 £	Year 2 £	Year 3 £	Year 4 £	Year 5 £	Year 6 £
Reported profit	100,000	100,000	100,000	100,000	100,000	100,000
Corporation tax charge	29,400	30,150	30,712	31,134	31,451	29,288
Deferred tax charge/(credit)	600	(150)	(712)	(1,134)	(1,451)	712
Total tax charge	30,000	30,000	30,000	30,000	30,000	30,000

Conclusion   The total tax charge is 30% of the reported profit each year. If deferred tax were ignored, the tax charge would fluctuate between £29,288 and £31,451 even though the reported profit was constant over the six years.

In this example there are no permanent differences. If there had been, then the tax charge would have been distorted, and would no longer have been 30% of the reported profit.

The entry in year 3 perhaps needs some explanation. In the year depreciation exceeds capital allowances. There is thus a **reversal** of the timing differences which **originated** in year 1. However, the amount by which depreciation exceeds capital allowances in year 3 (£2,375) is greater than the originating timing difference which remains at the beginning of year 3 (£1,500). Therefore, not only has the originated timing difference completely reversed, a new originating timing difference of £875 (£2,375 – £1,500) has arisen. This time, however, it originates due to depreciation exceeding capital allowances. It recognises a future tax **saving** that will arise.

2   ALTERNATIVE METHODS AND BASES OF PROVIDING FOR DEFERRED TAX

2.1   The deferral and liability methods of accounting for deferred taxation

There are two methods of dealing with deferred taxation:

(a)   the **liability** or **accrual** method;

(b)   the **deferral** method (of which there are several variants).

The methods differ as to the treatment of changes in the tax rate, and of reversing timing differences which were created when the rate was different from the current rate.

(a)   The liability method is a method of computing deferred tax whereby it is calculated at the rate of tax that it is estimated will be applicable when the timing differences reverse. Usually the current tax rate is used as the best estimate, unless changes in tax rates are known in advance. As a result, deferred tax provisions are revised to reflect changes in tax rates. Thus, the tax charge or credit for the period may include adjustments of accounting estimates relating to prior periods.

(b)   The deferral method shows deferred tax at the amount of the benefit to the company, in historic cost terms, of being able to defer taxation.

Under this method the deferred taxation account records the originating timing differences at the rates of taxation in operation when those originating timing differences occurred. Unlike the liability method, no adjustment is made to the existing deferred taxation account when changes in taxation rates occur.

Which method is acceptable?

SSAP 11 (issued in August 1975) stated that either method could be used, subject to the accounting policy's disclosure of which method was being adopted. *SSAP 11* came under severe criticism, and its implementation was postponed until December 1976.

The original *SSAP 15* (issued in October 1978) allowed the use of either method.

The revised *SSAP 15* requires the use of the liability method, as it is consistent with the aim of partial provision ie, how much tax is expected to be paid?

2.2 The advantages and disadvantages of the bases used for recording deferred taxation

There are three principal bases for computing deferred tax.

(a) **Nil provision**

The 'nil provision' or 'flow through' method is based on the principle that only the tax payable in respect of a period should be charged in that period. No provision for deferred tax is made.

Nil provision is straightforward and objective. Supporters of nil provision have argued that the taxation liability arises from taxable profits rather than from accounting profits. Whether or not timing differences reverse depends on future transactions and future profits. Some commentators argue that nil provision takes account of tax planning (ie, the extent to which the company can manage the amount and timing of income and expenditure).

However, nil provision can result in large fluctuations in the tax charge (which have already been illustrated in the above example). For this reason, it has been consistently rejected by standard setters.

(b) **Full provision**

The 'full provision' method is based on the principle that financial statements for a period should recognise the tax effects, whether current or deferred, of all transactions occurring in that period.

Advantages of the full provision method:

- It is straightforward to apply and objective.

- It has the effect of smoothing out distortions in the tax charge caused by timing differences. This means that it may provide more useful information for users of the financial statements because it is easier to make inter-temporal comparisons.

- It can be argued that the full provision method matches the tax liability against the revenue to which it relates.

- Some commentators believe that deferred tax is in the nature of a valuation adjustment reflecting the change in value of an entity's assets and liabilities arising from its tax position. For example, claiming accelerated capital allowances on a fixed asset means that the asset is worth less than another asset that is still fully tax-deductible. This change in value should be recognised.

- It is consistent with international practice.

Disadvantages of the full provision method:

- It may lead to the build up of large balances which never crystallise. These may distort key performance measures.

Note: crystallisation refers to the changing of a **provision** (for deferred tax) into a **liability** (for corporation tax).

- It could also be argued that full provision is inconsistent with the ASB's Statement of Principles (because a liability is an **obligation** to transfer benefits).

(c)   **Partial provision**

The 'partial provision' basis requires that deferred tax should be accounted for in respect of the net amount by which it is probable that any payment of tax will be temporarily deferred or accelerated by the operation of timing differences which will reverse in the foreseeable future without being replaced.

SSAP 15 requires the use of the partial provision basis.

Advantages of partial provision:

- It recognises that, if an enterprise is not expected to reduce the scale of its operations significantly, it will sometimes have what amounts to a hard core of timing differences, so that the payment of some tax will be permanently deferred or accelerated.

- It may provide information which has predictive value (because it reflects the amounts that the entity is likely to pay in practice).

Disadvantages of partial provision:

- It takes account of the tax consequences of future transactions, but not the transactions themselves. This has the effect (for example) that credit is taken in the current period for tax relief expected to be available in respect of fixed assets that have not yet been recognised in the financial statements. This contravenes the accruals concept.

- It takes into account future transactions to which the reporting entity is not yet committed. This is inconsistent with the ASB's belief (contained in the Statement of Principles) that items should only be recognised where they arise from past transactions or commitments.

- It relies on forecasts of future expenditure and is therefore time consuming and subjective to apply.

- It is inconsistent with international practice.

3   SSAP 15

3.1   The principles

(a)   **Method of computation**

Deferred tax should be computed under the liability method.

(b)   **Accounting for deferred taxation**

(i)   Tax deferred or accelerated by the effect of timing differences should be accounted for to the extent that it is probable that a liability or asset will crystallise.

(ii)   Tax deferred or accelerated by the effect of timing differences should not be accounted for to the extent that it is probable that a liability or asset will not crystallise.

(c)   **The criteria for deciding the amount of the provision**

(i)   The assessment of whether deferred tax liabilities or assets will or will not crystallise should be based upon reasonable assumptions.

(ii)   The assumptions should take into account all relevant information available up to the date on which the financial statements are approved by the board of directors, and also the intentions of management. Ideally, this information will include financial plans or projections covering a period of years sufficient to enable an assessment to be made of the likely pattern of future tax liabilities. A prudent view should be taken in the assessment of whether a tax liability will crystallise, particularly where the financial plans or projections are susceptible to a high degree of uncertainty or are not fully developed for the appropriate period.

SSAP 15 is deliberately vague as to the time period the projections and financial plans should cover. Each case needs to be looked at on its own merits. The old *SSAP 15* referred to a minimum period of three years. In practice, this was interpreted as a sufficient period to look ahead, rather than merely as a minimum. The appendix to *SSAP 15* does, however, give advice on the period of years to be covered by financial plans. Where the pattern of timing differences is expected to be regular, forecasts for three to five years may be sufficient. However it may need to be longer for an enterprise with an irregular pattern of timing differences.

3.2   Example of calculation of deferred tax charges

ABC plc is a highly profitable company. At 31 December 19X5 the accounts NBV of fixed assets ranking for capital allowances exceeds tax WDV by £750,000, but the company had hitherto not provided for deferred tax.

The company has produced the following forecast resulting from likely capital expenditure over the next few years:

Year	Capital allowances £'000	Depreciation £'000	Timing differences Originating £'000	Reversal £'000
19X6	1,600	1,400	200	
19X7	1,750	1,600	150	
19X8	1,100	1,670		570

19X9 onwards – capital allowances are likely to be well in excess of depreciation

You are required: to show the deferred tax charges for 19X5 to 19X8 following the requirements of *SSAP 15*, and the provisions required in the balance sheet, assuming that there are no other timing differences to be considered. The corporation tax rate is 30%.

3.3   Solution

Step 1   As at 19X5 a reversal of £570,000 can be foreseen in 19X8. This is matched with future originating differences on a LIFO basis as follows:

	£'000			£'000
with 19X7	150	leaving 570 – 150	=	420
with 19X6	200	leaving 420 – 200	=	220
with 19X5	220			

Therefore in 19X5 a provision of £220,000 × 30% must be made.

Step 2   This matching may be calculated using a table of cumulative timing differences:

Year	Timing differences £'000	Forecast cumulative differences 19X5 £'000	19X6 £'000	19X7 £'000
19X6	200	200	-	-
19X7	150	350	150	-
19X8	(570)	(220)	(420)	(570)
19X9 net originating		-	-	-

Step 3   The largest negative figure in each column shows the anticipated reversal of timing differences for each year and so the amount on which the deferred tax balance for the year is based.

Year ended 31 December	Deferred tax balance £'000			Total potential deferred tax £'000		
19X5	$220 \times 30\%$	=	66	$750 \times 30\%$	=	225
19X6	$420 \times 30\%$	=	126	$(750 + 200) \times 30\%$	=	285
19X7	$570 \times 30\%$	=	171	$(750 + 200 + 150) \times 30\%$	=	330
19X8	$0 \times 30\%$	=	–	$(750 + 200 + 150 - 570) \times 30\%$	=	159

Step 4 The profit and loss account charge is found by the movement on the deferred tax account.

Year to 31 December	Profit and loss account charge/(credit) £'000
19X5	66
19X6	60
19X7	45
19X8	(171)

3.4   Example of a tax liability arising

Assume that the pattern of anticipated expenditure had indicated the following position:

Year	Capital allowances £'000	Depreciation £'000	Timing differences £'000
19X6	1,100	1,670	(570)
19X7	1,600	1,400	200
19X8	1,750	1,600	150

19X9 onwards – Capital allowances are likely to be well in excess of depreciation.

Assuming a 30% tax rate, show the effect of applying *SSAP 15* to the financial statements.

3.5   Solution

Year ending 31 December	Profit and loss charge/(credit)		£'000	Balance sheet Provision £'000	Total potential deferred tax £'000
19X5	$30\% \times 570$	=	171	171	225
19X6	$30\% \times (570)$	=	(171)	-	285
19X7			-	-	330
19X8			-	-	159

It is necessary to set up an actual provision of £171,000 because that liability will actually arise (in the 19X6 tax computation, depreciation added back will exceed capital allowances by £570,000, tax effect 30% × £570,000 = £171,000). As at 31 December 19X5, in theory there are timing differences of £750,000 which are capable of reversal. The actual reversal which can be foreseen is £570,000 and this forms the basis of the provision.

3.6   Deferred tax debit balances

(a)   Deferred tax debit balances can arise on most types of timing differences. For example:

A company incurs an accounting loss of £400,000 for the year ended 31 December 19X4. Due to various items of expenditure not being allowed (permanent differences), the taxable loss is £360,000. The relevant tax rate is 30%.

The timing difference here is the amount of loss that can be carried forward to reduce future taxable profits ie, £360,000.

The deferred tax asset is £360,000 × 30% = £108,000.

(b)   **Use of debit balances**

   (i)   The provision for deferred tax liabilities should be reduced by any deferred tax debit balances arising from separate categories of timing differences.

   (ii)   Deferred tax net debit balances should not be carried forward as assets, except to the extent that they are expected to be recoverable without replacement by equivalent debit balances.

3.7   The requirements of SSAP 15 and the Companies Act

(a)   **SSAP 15 profit and loss account**

   (i)   Deferred tax relating to the ordinary activities of the enterprise should be shown separately as a part of the tax on profit or loss on ordinary activities, either on the face of the profit and loss account or in a note.

   (ii)   The amount of any unprovided deferred tax in respect of the period should be disclosed in a note, analysed into its major components.

(b)   **SSAP 15 balance sheet**

   (i)   The deferred tax balance, and its major components, should be disclosed in the balance sheet or notes.

   (ii)   Transfers to and from deferred tax should be disclosed in a note.

   (iii)   Where amounts of deferred tax arise which relate to movements on reserves (eg, resulting from the expected disposal of revalued assets) the amounts transferred to or from deferred tax should be shown separately as part of such movements.

   (iv)   The total amount of any unprovided deferred tax should be disclosed in a note, analysed into its major components.

   (v)   Where the value of an asset is shown in a note because it differs materially from its book amount, the note should also show the tax effects, if any, that would arise if the asset were realised at the balance sheet date at the noted value.

(c)   **Companies Act**

A deferred tax credit balance will be disclosed under the heading 'Provisions for liabilities and charges'. In the notes to the accounts the movements in the account must be shown (this is a requirement for any reserve or provision).

Details of contingent liabilities are required to be disclosed. The unprovided elements of timing differences are in the nature of contingent liabilities. The disclosure is effectively covered by following SSAP 15.

4   THE PROBLEMS OF SSAP 15

4.1   The problems of SSAP 15 and how it might be improved

There are two main practical problems that can be identified in the application of SSAP 15.

(a)   **Subjective nature**

The provision made is dependent on the future. Obviously, estimates have to be made of the future and if the actual results differ from those expected, there will need to be changes to the original entries made. Given the size of potential liabilities that may exist in some companies, the accounting adjustments required may be very large and thus distort future reported profits. From the balance sheet perspective the incorrect estimates may result in unrecorded liabilities.

(b)   **Budgeting**

The estimation of the future is an expensive operation to perform as it requires budgets and calculations derived from those budgets.

SSAP 15 partly addresses its subjective nature by requiring full disclosures of unprovided amounts. The user can thus see the potential amounts which could be accounted for and, if he wishes, he has sufficient information to adjust the accounts to a full provision basis.

The partial provision basis has been heavily criticised in recent years. Most other countries (including the USA) now use full provision.

SSAP 15 was originally issued in response to a tax system and economic conditions very different from those which exist today. The partial provision basis was standardised at a time when 100% first year allowances and high inflation together meant large originating differences each year. Now that 100% allowances have been withdrawn and inflation is low, it is appropriate to debate whether partial provision is still the best basis for providing for deferred tax.

The ASB is currently reviewing SSAP 15. Its most recent proposals are as follows:

(a)   SSAP 15 should be withdrawn and replaced by a new FRS requiring that tax should be provided using the full provision basis.

(b)   In principle, deferred tax should be discounted. This would mitigate the effect of full provision where otherwise large balances would build up without ever crystallising. However, this is likely to cause practical difficulties.

(c)   Disclosures relating to tax should aim to give the reader more insight into the reporting entity's tax affairs and should include a reconciliation between the actual and the expected tax charge.

However, these proposals have been controversial and it may be several years before a new accounting standard is issued.

4.2   The audit problems associated with SSAP 15

The auditor's main duty with regard to deferred tax is to ensure that the company's accounting policy is consistent with SSAP 15.

Three main areas are likely to be of concern to the auditor

- checking the accuracy of the total potential deferred tax charge

- obtaining evidence to confirm that the directors have justified the provision made in the balance sheet

- ensuring that the disclosure in the financial statements is clear and comprehensive, in accordance with the requirements of SSAP 15 and the need to show a true and fair view.

(a)   The total potential deferred tax charge. The auditor should check the calculation category by category, and then prepare an overall reconciliation with the balance sheet position.

(b)   Reviewing management evidence. The types of evidence which management could produce might include

(i)   information regarding the trend of past capital expenditure and depreciation, including their past level of success in forecasting

(ii)   forecasts of future capital expenditure and depreciation

(iii)   cash flow projections and profit forecasts, checking that these tie in with (ii)

(iv)   directors' minutes outlining policy changes, capital expenditure plans, etc

(v)   any special features relating to the industry: for example, availability of supplies

(vi)   letters of representation.

SSAP 15 makes it clear that the position should be reviewed each year since circumstances can always change.

Having reviewed the available audit evidence, the auditor must decide whether or not management have proved their case.

(c)   Checking adequate disclosure. The disclosure requirements of SSAP 15 are extensive and include both the provision made in the accounts and the amount of any unprovided deferred tax.

5   CHAPTER SUMMARY

Deferred taxation arises due to timing differences and the need to apply the accruals concept of matching revenues with the full costs of earning those revenues.

SSAP 15 requires the use of the partial provision basis ie, provide deferred tax to the extent it is expected that additional corporation tax liabilities will arise in the foreseeable future.

6   SELF TEST QUESTIONS

6.1   What are permanent differences? (1.1)

6.2   What are three examples of short-term timing differences? (1.2)

6.3   What is the purpose of deferred tax? (1.3)

6.4   What are the three bases for providing deferred tax? (2.2)

6.5   What does crystallisation mean? (2.2)

6.6   Deferred tax should be accounted for under which method? (3.1)

6.7   What should be disclosed in the profit and loss account in respect of deferred tax? (3.7)

6.8   What are the two main problems with SSAP 15? (4.1)

7   EXAMINATION TYPE QUESTIONS

7.1   Mocots plc

At 30 June 19X10, the following balances were held in the ledger of Mocots plc

	Dr £	Cr £
Deferred taxation		119,540
Value added tax		67,281
Patent royalties payable (net)	36,600	
Income tax		9,876
Debenture interest receivable (net)		16,000
Provision for mainstream corporation tax on 19X9 profits		108,143
Dividends received (in May 19X10) from UK companies (net)		36,000
Ordinary interim dividend (paid in February 19X10)	40,000	

The balance on deferred taxation account consists of	£
Accelerated capital allowances	108,780
Other short-term timing differences	10,760
	119,540

The matters listed below had not been taken into account in arriving at these balances

(1)   In July 19X10, whilst the 19X10 final accounts were in course of preparation, the company received the agreed assessment on the 19X9 profits from the Inland Revenue. The sum due for payment one month later, in August 19X10, was £105,806.

(2)   Income tax due in respect of the March quarter 19X10 (£9,876) had been paid.

(3)   Value added tax due in respect of the March quarter 19X10 (£67,281) had been paid.

(4)   For the June quarter 19X10 VAT input tax (including £19,204 on non-deductible inputs) totalled £342,659 and VAT output tax totalled £291,047.

(5)   A final ordinary dividend was proposed of £120,000.

(6)   Deferred tax differences due to capital allowances (before application of corporation tax rate)

-    originating differences, £46,000
-    reversing differences, £161,000.

(7)   Estimated corporation tax on 19X10 profits was £132,000.

(8)   The transfers to the profit and loss account of figures resulting from all the foregoing information were to be calculated and effected.

Assume that the company's rate of corporation tax is 30%, tax credits are $\frac{10}{90}$ of net dividends received, and that income tax is deducted from debenture interest and patent royalties at 20%.

You are required:

(a)   to open all the accounts listed above and others as necessary, post the transactions for the year to 30 June 19X10 and balance the accounts at that date.   **(18 marks)**

(b)   to prepare extracts from the company's profit and loss account for the year ended 30 June 19X10 and the balance sheet as at that date. You should include any notes on the taxation items required by SSAP 15, so far as the information is available.   **(14 marks)**
(Total: 32 marks)

7.2   SSAP 15

In connection with SSAP 15 *Accounting for deferred tax*:

(a)   Write a description of accounting for deferred taxation which includes all of the main items in the Standard. The description should be appropriate for inclusion in the statement of accounting policies in a company's annual financial report, in accordance with SSAP 2 *Disclosure of accounting policies*.   **(6 marks)**

(b)   Prepare an example of a note on deferred taxation which includes all of the main items in the Standard. The note should be appropriate for inclusion in a company's financial statements and you should use your own figures to illustrate your answer. (You need not show comparative figures and you may assume that the company is not part of a group of companies.)   **(8 marks)**

(c)   Do you consider that the liability method adopts a balance sheet rather than a profit and loss account perspective? Contrast this with the deferral method. State your reasons.   **(6 marks)**

(Total: 20 marks)

8   ANSWERS TO EXAMINATION TYPE QUESTIONS

8.1   Mocots plc

(***Tutorial notes:***

(i)   Concentrate on each aspect of tax - VAT, income tax and corporation tax - separately, where possible.

(ii)   Remember to provide only the relevant P & L account and balance sheet extracts for part (b).)

(a)

Provision for corporation tax account

	£		£
		Balance b/d (re 19X9)	108,143
Balance c/d		Profit and loss account:	
(CT 19X9	105,806	Overprovision for 19X9	
CT 19X10)	132,000	(108,143 − 105,806)	(2,337)
		Provision for 19X10	132,000
	237,806		237,806

Income tax account

	£		£
Bank account	9,876	Balance b/d	9,876
Debenture interest received		Patent royalties	9,150
a/c ($16,000 \times \frac{20}{80}$)	4,000		
Balance c/d	5,150		
	19,026		19,026

Value Added Tax account

	£		£
Bank account	67,281	Balance b/d	67,281
Creditors/bank accounts	323,455	Debtors/bank accounts	291,047
(342,659 − 19,204)		Balance c/d	32,408
	390,736		390,736

Deferred tax account

	£		£
Profit and loss account	34,500	Balance b/d	119,540
($161,000 \times 30\%$) −			
($46,000 \times 30\%$)			
Balance c/d	85,040		
	119,540		119,540

Patent royalties payable account

	£		£
Balance b/d	36,600	Profit and loss a/c (gross)	45,750
Income tax account	9,150		
$(36,600 \times \frac{20}{80})$			
	———		———
	45,750		45,750
	———		———

(b)   **Profit and loss account (extracts) for year ended 30 June 19X10**

	£
Patent royalties (part of cost of sales)	45,750
Income from other fixed asset investments	
Franked Investment Income (Dividend) $(36,000 \times \frac{100}{90})$	40,000
Unfranked Investment Income (Debenture interest)	20,000
Taxation:	
UK corporation tax for the year at 30%	132,000
Overprovision in previous year	(2,337)
Tax credits on dividends received	4,000
Deferred tax transfer	(34,500)
Dividends - Paid	40,000
Proposed	120,000

Balance sheet (extracts) as at 30 June 19X10

	£
Current assets	
Debtor - HM Customs and Excise (VAT)	32,408
Creditors: amounts falling due within one year:	
Inland Revenue (income tax)	5,150
Inland Revenue (corporation tax)	237,806
Proposed ordinary dividend	120,000
Provisions for liabilities and charges	
Deferred taxation (Notes 1 and 2)	85,040

Note 1

	£	£
Deferred taxation		
Accelerated capital allowances	74,280	
Other differences	10,760	
	———	
		85,040
		———

Note 2

Movement in deferred taxation

	£
Balance at 1 July 19X9	119,540
Profit and loss account transfer	(34,500)
	———
Balance at 30 June 19X10	85,040
	———

8.2   SSAP 15

(*Tutorial note:*

Read the requirements to parts (a) and (b) fully. Be careful not to 'rush' into an answer after only a casual initial read. Be specific in your answer; too generalised an answer will not gain a good mark.)

(a)   Deferred taxation is provided on the liability method on all timing differences to the extent that they are expected to reverse in the future, calculated at the rate at which it is estimated that tax will be payable. No deferred taxation is provided on permanent differences or on timing differences which are not expected to reverse.

(b)   Deferred taxation provided in the accounts and the amounts not provided are as follows.

	Provided 19X5 £'000	Not provided 19X5 £'000
Capital allowances in advance of depreciation	35	254
Other differences in recognising revenue and expense items in other periods for taxation purposes	-	16
	35	270
Taxation on valuation surplus	-	200
	35	470

Movement on the deferred taxation account

	£'000
Balance, 1 January 19X5	26
Transfer from profit and loss account	9
Balance, 31 December 19X5	35

(c)   The liability method emphasises the amount of future tax that is likely to become payable. Adjustments are made to the outstanding balance for changes in the taxation rates that will be used in determining the amount of liability. It is thus a balance sheet rather than a profit and loss account perspective. The charge to the profit and loss account results from the calculation of this outstanding liability.

However, with the deferral method, the deferred taxation account records the originating timing differences at the rate of taxation in operation when they occurred. No adjustment is made when changes in taxation rates occur and no effort is made to reflect the expected liability in the balance sheet.

12 FINANCIAL PERFORMANCE

INTRODUCTION & LEARNING OBJECTIVES

Two important accounting standards are covered in this chapter.

FRS 3 *Reporting financial performance* introduced a major change in the presentation of the performance statement: the profit and loss account. It also requires other statements which show either other income or gains and losses or certain items of income and expense in more detail. It is an important standard but in a computational context it is most likely to be tested within a group accounts question.

SSAP 25 *Segmental reporting* requires large companies to present segmental information. Like FRS 3, it is intended to provide users of the financial statements with useful information about the components of an entity's performance.

When you have studied this chapter you should be able to do the following:

- Understand the requirements of FRS 3
- Lay out a profit and loss account following a suggested format in FRS 3
- Define the major terms used in FRS 3
- Outline and apply the requirements of SSAP 25.

1 THE REQUIREMENTS OF FRS 3

1.1 Introduction

FRS 3, issued in October 1992, radically reformed the presentation of the profit and loss account and added a new primary statement to the annual financial statements, the **Statement of total recognised gains and losses**. In addition it virtually eradicated extraordinary items and changed the earnings per share calculation.

To understand *FRS 3* some consideration needs to be given to its predecessor, *SSAP 6*.

1.2 SSAP 6

SSAP 6 *Extraordinary items and prior year adjustments* was issued in April 1974, with the main objective of standardising the treatment of 'unusual' items of income and expenditure and to put a stop to 'reserve accounting'. Reserve accounting meant that unusual items (particularly losses) were commonly dealt with through reserves and thus had no effect on the reported profit of the year.

SSAP 6 was thus based on the 'all inclusive' concept which requires all items of income and expenditure to pass through the profit and loss account.

However, *SSAP 6* saw the profit on ordinary activities as giving important information to the users of accounts which would be distorted by the inclusion of extraordinary items. Hence, these items were included 'below the line' ie, after profit on ordinary activities after taxation.

The importance of profit on ordinary activities as the most important measure of company performance was reinforced because at that time earnings per share was calculated on profits excluding extraordinary items. Furthermore, the stock market's PE ratio is based on EPS.

The end result was that companies could improve the user's view of their performance by treating large items of expense as extraordinary and, although there was a supposedly restrictive definition of 'extraordinary', many companies seemed to be able to fit their 'unusual' expenses within the definition.

Rather than launch an attempt to redefine what should be included as extraordinary, the ASB resolved to try a radically different approach.

1.3 Objective of FRS 3

The objective of the FRS is to require companies to highlight a range of important components of financial performance to aid users in understanding the performance achieved by a reporting entity in a period and to assist them in forming a basis for their assessment of future results and cash flows.

It attempts to achieve the objective by requiring all gains and losses recognised in the financial statements for the period be included in the profit and loss account or the statement of total recognised gains and losses.

Gains and losses may be excluded from the profit and loss account only if they are specifically permitted or required to be taken directly to reserves by an accounting standard or by law.

1.4 Format of the profit and loss account

A layered format is to be used for the profit and loss account to highlight a number of important components of financial performance:

(a)   results of continuing operations (including the results of acquisitions);

(b)   results of discontinued operations;

(c)   profits or losses on the sale or termination of an operation, costs of a fundamental reorganisation or restructuring and profits or losses on the disposal of fixed assets; and

(d)   extraordinary items.

The thrust of this approach can be illustrated diagrammatically as follows:

CONTINUING	DISCONTINUED
Normal operations	Normal operations
The items listed in (c) above	The items listed in (c) above

Extraordinary items - being unusual items outside ordinary activities

Note that exceptional items will comprise the items listed in (c) above, which are disclosed separately on the face of the profit and loss account, and other items which are disclosed separately by way of note only (and are thus within the normal operations boxes).

A sample format is shown below:

Profit and loss account for the year ended 30 June 19X3

	Continuing operations 19X3	Acquisitions 19X3	Discontinued operations 19X3	Total 19X3	Total 19X2 as restated
	£m	£m	£m	£m	£m
Turnover	550	50	175	775	690
Cost of sales	(415)	(40)	(165)	(620)	(555)
Gross profit	135	10	10	155	135

Net operating expenses	(85)	(4)	(25)	(114)	(83)
Less: 19X2 provision			10	10	
Operating profit	50	6	(5)	51	52
Profit on sale of properties	9			9	6
Provision for loss on operations to be discontinued					(30)
Loss on disposal of discontinued operations			(17)	(17)	
Less: 19X2 provision			20	20	
Profit on ordinary activities before interest	59	6	(2)	63	28

Interest payable	(18)	(15)
Profit on ordinary activities before taxation	45	13
Tax on profit on ordinary activities	(14)	(4)
Profit on ordinary activities after taxation	31	9
Minority interests	(2)	(2)
Extraordinary items (included only to show positioning)	-	-
Profit for the financial year	29	7
Dividends	(8)	(1)
Retained profit for the financial year	21	6
Earnings per share	39p	10p

1.5   Continuing and discontinued operations

The analysis between continuing operations, acquisitions (as a component of continuing operations) and discontinued operations should be disclosed to the level of operating profit. The analysis of turnover and operating profit is the **minimum** disclosure required in this respect on the **face** of the profit and loss account.

The example above thus provides more than the minimum disclosure. The minimum disclosures could be shown as follows:

	19X3	19X3	19X2 as restated
	£m	£m	£m
Turnover			
Continuing operations	550		500
Acquisitions	50		
	600		
Discontinued operations	175		190
		775	690
Cost of sales		(620)	(555)
Gross profit		155	135
Net operating expenses		(104)	(83)

Operating profit

Continuing operations	50	40
Acquisitions	6	
	——	
	56	
Discontinued operations	(15)	12
Less: 19X2 provision	10	
	——	
	51	52
	——	——

Note the following points

(a)   In either example, as the full statutory headings have not been shown, a note to the accounts needs to show an analysis of the statutory cost headings between continuing operations, acquisitions (as a component of continuing operations) and discontinued operations.

(b)   The analysis in respect of continuing operations, acquisitions and discontinued operations is required only to the profit before interest level because interest payable is usually a reflection of a company's overall financing policy, involving both equity and debt funding considerations on a group wide basis, rather than an aggregation of the particular types of finance allocated to individual segments of the reporting entity's operations. Any allocation of interest would involve a considerable degree of subjectivity that could leave the user uncertain as to the relevance and reliability of the information.

(c)   The comparative figures should be based on the status of an operation in the financial statements of the period under review and should, therefore, include in the continuing category only the results of those operations included in the current period's continuing operations. The comparative figures appearing under the heading 'continuing operations' may include figures which were shown under the heading of acquisitions in that previous period. No reference needs to be made to the results of those acquisitions, since they are not required to be presented separately in the current year.

The comparative figures for discontinued operations will include both amounts relating to operations discontinued in the previous period and amounts relating to operations discontinued in the period under review, which in the previous period would have been included as part of continuing operations.

The analysis of comparative figures between continuing and discontinued operations is not required on the face of the profit and loss account.

1.6   Definition of discontinued operations

The separate analysis of discontinued operations is one of the routes by which the ASB is attempting to restrict the ambit of extraordinary items. The definition of discontinued operations is however quite strict so as to encourage preparers of financial statements to leave the results of parts of the business being reorganised under the heading of continuing operations.

Definition   Discontinued operations are those that are sold or terminated and that satisfy all of the following conditions

(a)   The sale or termination is completed either in the period or before the earlier of three months after the commencement of the subsequent period and the date on which the financial statements are approved.

(b)   If a termination, the former activities have ceased permanently.

(c)   The sale or termination has a material effect on the nature and focus of the reporting entity's operations and represents a material reduction in its operating facilities resulting either from its withdrawal from a particular market (whether class of business or geographical) or from a material reduction in turnover in the reporting entity's continuing markets.

(d)   The assets, liabilities, results of operations and activities are clearly distinguishable, physically, operationally and for financial reporting purposes.

Operations not satisfying all these conditions are classified as continuing.

Note the timing restriction. If the termination is not completed within the time stated, the turnover and costs of the operations remain in continuing operations.

This does **not** mean, however, that an exceptional item should not be shown in respect of the actual profit/loss or anticipated loss on disposal. This point is discussed below after the definition of exceptional items has been considered.

Note also part (c) of the definition. The nature and focus of a reporting entity's operations refers to the positioning of its products or services in their markets including the aspects of both quality and location. For example, if a hotel company which had traditionally served the lower end of the hotel market sold its existing chain and bought luxury hotels then, while remaining in the business of managing hotels, the group would be changing the nature and focus of its operations. A similar situation would arise if the same company were to sell its hotels in (say) the United States of America and buy hotels in Europe.

The regular sales and replacements of material assets which are undertaken by a company as part of the routine maintenance of its portfolio of assets should not be classified as discontinuances and acquisitions. In the example the sale of hotels and the purchase of others within the same market sector and similar locations would be treated as wholly within continuing operations.

2   CLASSIFICATION OF ITEMS

2.1   Exceptional items

Definition   Material items which derive from events or transactions that fall within the ordinary activities of the reporting entity and which individually or, if of a similar type, in aggregate, need to be disclosed by virtue of their size or incidence if the financial statements are to give a true and fair view.

All exceptional items, other than those stated below, should be included under the statutory format headings to which they relate. They should be separately disclosed by way of note or, where it is necessary in order that the financial statements give a true and fair view, on the face of the profit and loss account.

There are in effect two types of exceptional items; those that are exceptional but are still included in the statutory format headings and those which are separately identified.

The view of the ASB is that exceptional items should not be transferred to a single heading of 'exceptional', because profit before exceptional items could then become the focus of financial statement presentations, with the implication that no exceptional items are expected in the future.

2.2   Items to be shown separately

The following items, including provisions in respect of such items, should be shown separately on the face of the profit and loss account after operating profit and before interest:

(a)   profits or losses on the sale or termination of an operation;
(b)   costs of a fundamental reorganisation or restructuring; and
(c)   profits or losses on the disposal of fixed assets.

Each of the three specific items will be examined in turn.

2.3   Profit or losses on the sale or termination of an operation

The 'sale or termination of an operation' is not defined in *FRS 3*. It encompasses but is not restricted to the term 'discontinued operation'. Thus the item may be part of continuing operations or discontinued operations and therefore needs to be disclosed under its correct heading. It is likely to be an exceptional item as well.

Often the sale or termination straddles two accounting periods. In the first period a provision may be required for losses expected to arise in the following period (under the prudence concept). However, there has been much criticism in recent years on the 'excessive' use of provisions by companies and thus *FRS 3* imposes the following restrictions:

(a)   a provision should not be made unless the company is demonstrably committed to the sale or termination eg, public announcement of specific plans or a binding contract for sale has been entered into after the balance sheet date;

(b)   The provision should cover only:

(i)   the direct costs of the sale or termination;

(ii)   operating losses up to the sale date;

(iii)   less anticipated trading profits (if any).

2.4   Example of the termination of an operation

X plc has a calendar year end. On 30 October 19X7 the board of directors decide to withdraw from a market which is a significant part of the company's existing business. Plans are disclosed to the workforce on 30 November with a termination set at 31 March 19X8.

Actual and projected results of the operation are:

	Actual to 31 December 19X7	*Projected to 31 March 19X8*
	£'000	*£'000*
Sales	45,000	8,000
Operating costs	44,000	12,000
Redundancy and other costs		3,000

The accounts for the year ended 31 December 19X7 are expected to be approved by 18 March 19X8.

Therefore in the accounts for the year ended 31 December 19X7 the operation is not classified as a discontinued operation (due to the timing of the date on which the accounts are approved). A provision should however be disclosed (as an exceptional item) totalling:

	£'000
Projected loss	4,000
Redundancy	3,000
	7,000

If in the 19X8 accounting period actual results of the operation are:

	£'000
Sales	9,400
Operating costs	11,600
Redundancy	3,000

the profit and loss account for the year ended 31 December 19X8 would show:

	Continuing operations 19X8 £'000	Discontinued operations 19X8 £'000	Continuing operations 19X7 £'000	Discontinued operations 19X7 £'000
Turnover	X	9,400	X	45,000
Operating costs:	X	(11,600)		44,000
Less: 19X7 provision		4,000		
Operating profit	X	1,800		1,000
Provision for loss on operations to be discontinued				(7,000)
Loss on termination of discontinued operation		(3,000)		
Less: 19X7 provision		3,000		
Profit (loss) on ordinary activities before taxation	X	1,800		(6,000)

2.5 Costs of a fundamental reorganisation

As the title of this item implies it is only a reorganisation or restructuring having a material effect on the nature and focus of the company's operation that qualifies for separate disclosure. This item will therefore be classified as exceptional as well.

2.6 Disposals of fixed assets

This heading is not intended to include profits and losses that are no more than marginal adjustments to depreciation previously charged.

If an asset has previously been revalued, *FRS 3* standardises the method of computation of the profit or loss.

FRS 3 requires two adjustments to be made where a fixed asset which had previously been revalued is sold. These are:

(a)   difference between proceeds of sale and book value at date of sale - dealt with through the profit and loss account (this is also required by FRS 15);

(b)   amount previously included under revaluation surplus - this now becomes a realised profit but should not be dealt with as part of the reported profit for the year.

2.7 Extraordinary items

[Definition]   Material items possessing a high degree of abnormality which arise from events or transactions that fall outside the ordinary activities of the reporting entity and which are not expected to recur. They do not include exceptional items nor do they include prior period items merely because they relate to a prior period.

The *FRS 3* definition is similar to the *SSAP 6* definition. However, as discontinued activities are shown as ordinary activities and exceptional items include profit/loss on disposals of operations, extraordinary items should become extremely rare. Indeed the ASB contemplated removing extraordinary items completely but did not do so because company law includes extraordinary items in its formats.

To emphasise the change Sir David Tweedie, Chairman of the ASB has stated:

'Martians walking down the street will be extraordinary, everything else is exceptional.'

2.8 Earnings per share

Another route by which the ASB has reduced the importance of extraordinary items is by changing the definition of EPS.

Earnings are now to be calculated after extraordinary items.

2.9 Prior period adjustments

Definition | Material adjustments applicable to prior periods arising from changes in accounting policies or from the correction of fundamental errors. They do not include normal recurring adjustments or corrections of accounting estimates made in prior periods.

Prior period adjustments are defined as in *SSAP 6* except that 'period' rather than 'year' is used.

The cumulative effect of the adjustments has to be noted at the foot of the statement of total recognised gains and losses (see below).

2.10 Audit problems that may arise under FRS 3

Under SSAP 6, there were considerable problems with the interpretation of the definition of extraordinary items, so much so that FRS 3 effectively banned any items from being classified under this heading. The problems associated with extraordinary items have therefore been 'solved' providing that companies do take the hint from the ASB and do not classify any items as extraordinary. It would appear that companies are following the line encouraged by the ASB.

New problems may arise however due to the separate analysis of discontinued activities. Companies may often wish to use this analysis to improve the appearance of continuing operations. A discontinued operation is likely to be loss making or poorly performing relative to the rest of the company's operations; it therefore is better for companies if they can remove the poorly performing sector from the rest of the results.

Auditors will therefore need to consider carefully any suggested split of operations into the discontinued category. They will need evidence that all the FRS 3 conditions for classification as discontinued do apply. Of the conditions, it is the third condition which is the most subjective.

If the definition is satisfied, the auditor needs to check two main areas:

(a) Sales and costs of the discontinued activity have been correctly identified. The auditor needs to be aware that there may be management bias to include too many costs. Overheads for example may be overallocated to the discontinued activity.

(b) Provision for profit/loss on discontinuance. Provisions are, by their nature, subjective.

2.11 Activity

Do the following situations meet the definition of discontinued operations as defined by *FRS 3*?

(a) X plc, an office furniture and equipment manufacturer runs separate divisions of approximately equal size for the two activities. It has now decided to sell the less profitable equipment division and use the funds received to expand the furniture division by growth and acquisition. The decision to sell was made in October 19X5 and the sale completed on 21 March 19X6. The accounts for the year 19X5 were approved on 15 March 19X6.

(b) Y plc as a result of the recession has suffered a downturn in demand and now has productive overcapacity. In order to reduce costs Y plc has decided to transfer production into one of its two factories and to 'moth-ball' the other factory. This decision was made in April 19X3 and the transfer completed in August 19X3. The company has a September year end.

(c)   Z plc a printing company also carries out specialised book binding. This part of the business is carried out in a separate workshop and comprises approximately 0.5% of the total assets of the company and contributes approximately the same proportion of profits.

During 19X4 Z plc sold the bookbinding business to a consortium of the workforce and sold the workshop to the local council. The profit arising from this transaction amounted to £100,000 on profits of £2,400,000 for 19X4.

2.12   Activity solution

(a)   This situation meets three of the four criteria laid down by *FRS 3* but fails to meet the timing restriction. *FRS 3* states that the sale should be completed before the earlier of three months after commencement of the subsequent period and the date on which the financial statements are approved.

(b)   This would not be treated as a discontinued operation as the activities have not ceased permanently. The purpose of this decision is to reduce productive capacity temporarily until there is an upturn in the market.

(c)   This situation appears to meet the *FRS 3* criteria for discontinued operations except that the loss of this part of the business will have no material effect on the operations of Z plc. Therefore it will not be treated as a discontinued operation.

(The size of the profit arising on the sale is not taken into account in the *FRS 3* criteria.)

3   OTHER STATEMENTS REQUIRED

3.1   Statement of total recognised gains and losses

The statement of total recognised gains and losses is a **primary statement** ie, it is required for a true and fair view.

The statement shows items taken straight to reserves as well as to the profit and loss account. This primary income statement has been designed to further discourage users of the financial statements from focusing only on the profit and loss account whilst ignoring reserve movements which could hide a multitude of sins.

The statement is not intended to reflect the realisation of gains recognised in previous periods nor does it deal with transfers between reserves.

Thus, when for example an asset is sold which has previously been revalued, the revaluation gain merely changes from an unrealised reserve to a realised reserve. It is not therefore accounted for in the current year's statement of total recognised gains and losses.

An illustrative statement is shown below:

Statement of total recognised gains and losses for the year ended 30 June 19X3

	19X3	19X2 as restated
	£'000	£'000
Profit for the financial year	29	7
Unrealised surplus on revaluation of properties	4	6
Unrealised (loss)/gain on trade investment	(3)	7
	30	20

Currency translation differences on foreign currency net investments	(2)	5
Total recognised gains and losses relating to the year	28	25
Prior year adjustment (as explained in note X)	(10)	
Total gains and losses recognised since last annual report	18	

3.2   Other statements

FRS 3 requires two other statements to be shown as **notes** to the accounts. The second of these notes, 'Historical cost profits and losses' must however be presented immediately following the profit and loss account or the statement of total recognised gains and losses.

3.3   Reconciliation of movements in shareholders' funds

The reconciliation of movements in shareholders' funds brings together the performance of the period, as shown in the statement of total recognised gains and losses, with all the other changes in shareholders' funds in the period, including capital contributed by or repaid to shareholders.

FRS 3 requires this statement since the change in financial position of an entity can only be fully understood when all changes in shareholders' funds are reported, not just those shown in the statement of total recognised gains and losses.

Illustration

Reconciliation of movements in shareholders' funds for the year ended 30 June 19X3

	19X3	*19X2 as restated*
	£m	*£m*
Profit for the financial year	29	7
Dividends	(8)	(1)
	21	6
Other recognised gains and losses relating to the year (net)	(1)	18
New share capital subscribed	20	1
Net addition to shareholders' funds	40	25
Opening shareholders' funds (originally £375m before deducting prior year adjustment of £10m)	365	340
Closing shareholders' funds	405	365

3.4   Note of historical cost profits and losses

The note of historical cost profits and losses is a memorandum item, the primary purpose of which is to present the profits or losses of companies that have revalued assets on a more comparable basis with those of entities that have not. It is an abbreviated restatement of the profit and loss account which adjusts the reported profit or loss, if necessary, so as to show it as if no asset revaluation had been made. FRS 3 requires this statement to help users of accounts to compare the results of different companies, som of which revalue their assets and some of which do not.

Note of historical cost profits and losses for the year ended 30 June 19X3

	19X3 £m	19X2 as restated £m
Reported profit on ordinary activities before taxation	45	13
Realisation of property revaluation gains of previous years	9	10
Difference between a historical cost depreciation charge and the actual depreciation charge of the year calculated on the revalued amount	5	4
Historical cost profit on ordinary activities before taxation	59	27
Historical cost profit for the year retained after taxation, minority interests, extraordinary items and dividends	35	20

Conclusion   FRS 3 has changed the emphasis in reporting financial performance from ordinary and extraordinary operations to continued and discontinued operations. By doing this it has effectively eliminated the use of extraordinary items.

3.5   Activity

The following figures have been calculated for Phibbs plc for the year ended 31 December 19X9, together with comparatives for the previous year.

	19X9 £m	19X8 £m
Profit before tax	50	35
Tax	(12)	(7)
Profit for the financial year	38	28
Dividends	(18)	(15)
Retained profit	20	13
Unrealised surplus on revaluation of property	2	1
Exchange differences taken to reserves	3	(2)
Opening shareholders' funds	220	204
Share capital issued during the year		
Par value	10	3
Premium	2	1
Additional depreciation charged on property revaluations (ie, over and above what would have been charged on their historical cost)	3	2

You are required to draft the following statements for Phibbs plc for inclusion in the 19X9 accounts:

(a)   statement of total recognised gains and losses;
(b)   reconciliation of movements in shareholders' funds;
(c)   note of historical cost profits and losses.

3.6   Activity solution

(a)

Phibbs plc
Statement of total recognised gains and losses
for the year ended 31 December 19X9

	19X9 £m	19X8 £m
Profit for the financial year	38	28
Unrealised surplus on revaluation of property	2	1
Exchange differences on foreign currency net investments	3	(2)
Total recognised gains and losses relating to the year	43	27

(b)

Reconciliation of movements in shareholders' funds
for the year ended 31 December 19X9

	19X9 £m	19X8 £m
Profit for the financial year	38	28
Dividends	(18)	(15)
	20	13
Other recognised gains and losses relating to the year (net)	5	(1)
New share capital subscribed	12	4
Net addition to shareholders' funds	37	16
Opening shareholders' funds	220	204
Closing shareholders' funds	257	220

(c)

Note of historical cost profits and losses
for the year ended 31 December 19X9

	19X9 £m	19X8 £m
Reported profit before taxation	50	35
Difference between a historical cost depreciation charge and the actual depreciation charge for the year calculated on the revalued amount	3	2
Historical cost profit before taxation	53	37
Historical cost profit for the year retained after taxation and dividends	23	15

4   SSAP 25: SEGMENTAL REPORTING

4.1   Introduction

Many enterprises carry on several classes of business or operate in several geographical areas, with different rates of profitability, different opportunities for growth and different degrees of risk. It is usually not possible for the reader of the financial statements of such enterprises to make judgements about the nature of different activities carried on by the enterprise or of their contribution to the overall financial results of the enterprise unless some segmental analysis of the financial statements is given.

The purpose of segmental information is, therefore, to provide information to assist the readers of financial statements:

(a)   to appreciate more thoroughly the results and financial position of the enterprise by permitting a better understanding of the enterprise's past performance and thus a better assessment of its future prospects; and

(b)   to be aware of the impact that changes in significant components of a business may have on the business as a whole.

4.2   Determining reportable segments

The directors identify the **reportable segments** having regard to differences in:

(a)   return on capital employed;
(b)   risk;
(c)   rate of growth;
(d)   potential for future development for both classes of business and geographical areas.

All **significant** segments should be identified as reportable segments.

Definition   A segment is significant if:

(a)   third party turnover is 10% or more of the total third party turnover;

(b)   its segment result is 10% or more of the combined result of all segments in profit, or in loss (whichever is greater ie, do not net off profits and losses to a net profit figure of say £20,000 and use £2,000 as a significance test when total profits might be £5.02m and losses total £5.00m);

(c)   its net assets are 10% or more of the total net assets.

The directors should review the definitions annually and redefine when appropriate.

4.3   Classes of business

Definition   A **class of business** is defined as a distinguishable component of an entity that provides a separate product or service or a separate group of related products or services.

To identify reportable classes of business, directors should consider the following factors:

(a)   nature of products or services;
(b)   nature of production processes;
(c)   markets in which products or services are sold;
(d)   the distribution channels for the products (eg, are the items sold by retail or mail order?);
(e)   the manner in which the entity's activities are organised;
(f)   any separate legislative framework relating to part of the business (eg, a bank or insurance company).

4.4   Geographical segments

Definition   A **geographical segment** is a geographical area comprising an individual country or group of countries in which an entity operates or to which it supplies products or services.

The analysis should help the users to assess the extent to which the operations are subject to factors such as:

(a)   expansionist or restrictive economic climates;

(b)   stable or unstable political regimes;

(c)   exchange control regulations;

(d)   exchange rate fluctuations.

4.5   Standard disclosures

If an entity has two or more classes of business or operates in two or more geographical segments it should:

(a)   define its classes of business and geographical segments in its financial statements; and

(b)   for each class of business and geographical segment, disclose:

   (i)   turnover, distinguishing

           turnover derived from external customers; and
           turnover derived from other segments;

   (ii)   result before tax, minority interests and extraordinary items;

   (iii)   net assets.

The standard distinguishes:

(a)   **origin** of turnover – the geographical segment from which products or services are supplied;

(b)   **destination** of turnover – the geographical segment to which products or services are supplied.

The geographical segmentation of turnover should be done by origin and also by destination where the latter is different.

Results should normally be given before interest unless the interest income or expense is central to the business when the result should be given after interest.

The net assets should normally be non-interest bearing unless the results are after interest in which case the interest bearing assets and liabilities should be included.

Segmental information should be presented on the basis of the consolidated financial statements.

4.6   Reconciliation

The total of the amounts disclosed by segment should agree with the total in the financial statements. If it does not, the reporting entity should provide a reconciliation between the two figures. Reconciling items should be properly identified and explained.

4.7   Comparatives

Comparatives should be provided. If a change is made to the definitions of the segments or to the accounting policies that are adopted for reporting segmental information, the nature of the change should be disclosed.

4.8   Scope

The standard applies to any entity that:

(a)   is a plc or has a plc subsidiary; or

(b)   is a banking or insurance company; or

(c)   exceeds the criteria multiplied by 10 for defining a medium-sized company.

All other entities are encouraged to apply the provisions of the accounting standard.

If the directors consider that disclosure of any information required by the standard would be seriously prejudicial to the interests of the reporting entity, the information need not be disclosed.

4.9   Pro-forma

The appendix to SSAP 25 provides an illustrative example for guidance only. Part of this is shown below

Class of business	Industry A		Industry B		Other		Group	
	19X1	*19X0*	*19X1*	*19X0*	*19X1*	*19X0*	*19X1*	*19X0*
	£'000	*£'000*	*£'000*	*£'000*	*£'000*	*£'000*	*£'000*	*£'000*
Turnover								
Total sales	33,000	30,000	42,000	38,000	26,000	23,000	101,000	91,000
Inter-segment sales	(4,000)	-	-	-	(12,000)	(14,000)	(16,000)	(14,000)
Sales to third parties	29,000	30,000	42,000	38,000	14,000	9,000	85,000	77,000
Profit before taxation								
Segment profit	3,000	2,500	4,500	4,000	1,800	1,500	9,300	8,000
Common costs							300	300
Operating profit							9,000	7,700
Net interest							(400)	(500)
							8,600	7,200
Group share of the profits before taxation of associated undertakings	1,000	1,000	1,400	1,200	-	-	2,400	2,200
Group profit before taxation							11,000	9,400
Net assets								
Segment net assets	17,600	15,000	24,000	25,000	19,400	19,000	61,000	59,000
Unallocated assets							3,000	3,000
							64,000	62,000
Group share of net assets of associated undertakings	10,200	8,000	8,800	9,000	-	-	19,000	17,000
Total net assets							83,000	79,000

Common costs refer to costs where allocation between segments could mislead. Likewise, the segmental disclosure of net assets might include unallocated assets.

Geographical segments	United Kingdom		North America		Far East		Other		Group	
	19X1	*19X0*	*19X1*	*19X0*	*19X1*	*19X0*	*19X1*	*19X0*	*19X1*	*19X0*
	£'000	*£'000*	*£'000*	*£'000*	*£'000*	*£'000*	*£'000*	*£'000*	*£'000*	*£'000*
Turnover										
Turnover by destination										
Sales to third parties	34,000	31,000	16,000	14,500	25,000	23,000	10,000	8,500	85,000	77,000
Turnover by origin										
Total sales	38,000	34,000	29,000	27,500	23,000	23,000	12,000	10,500	102,000	95,000
Inter-segment sales	-	-	(8,000)	(9,000)	(9,000)	(9,000)	-	-	(17,000)	(18,000)
Sales to third parties	38,000	34,000	21,000	18,500	14,000	14,000	12,000	10,500	85,000	77,000

4.10   Are the current disclosure requirements for segmental reporting sufficient?

SSAP 25 is a key accounting standard in assisting in the interpretation of the accounts of a large enterprise and amplifies the disclosure provisions of the CA85. The ASC took a long time to issue a standard despite the clear need for further disclosures by investment analysts and other users, because of concerns by companies affected by the standard that they would be put at a competitive disadvantage by revealing such information.

Criticisms of the standard can be made as follows.

(a)   The class and geographical segment split is decided by the directors. This, it is argued provides too much flexibility.

However it is difficult to envisage the incorporation of hard and fast rules in a standard. Each company is different and judgements have to be made under any system. Also the standard does give guidance regarding what constitutes a significant segment.

(b)   The computation of return on capital employed (ROCE) is a key indicator of business performance as it measures how efficiently the company is managing to generate profits from the assets in the business. However ROCE may not be able to be validly computed for each segment under SSAP 25 as:

- common costs may or may not be included in the segment result (this is a decision of the directors)
- net assets may have an element of commonality across segments.

4.11   Implications of SSAP 25 for auditors

There is a significant amount of discretion allowed to the directors in applying SSAP 25. The auditor will need to establish the basis for the analysis provided by the directors and check whether they have followed the guidance given in SSAP 25 regarding significant segments. The segments need to be consistent with previous periods but there can be valid reasons for changes as the relative importance of different sectors changes.

Test checks will need to be made of the analyses supplied which must to be reconciled to the aggregate figures in the profit and loss account.

5   CHAPTER SUMMARY

FRS 3 *Reporting financial performance* is concerned with the presentation of the performance statement: the profit and loss account. Results from operations may need to be analysed between continuing (acquisitions separately) and discontinued.

Other statements are required including a statement of total recognised gains and losses.

SSAP 25 *Segmental reporting* requires large companies to prepare and present segmental information in addition to what is required by the Companies Acts. Turnover, results and net assets must be analysed by class of business and geographically.

6   SELF TEST QUESTIONS

6.1   What components of financial performance should be highlighted in the layered format for the profit and loss account required by *FRS 3*? (1.4)

6.2   In order to qualify as a discontinued operation, *FRS 3* has introduced a timing restriction for the sale or termination to be completed. What is this restriction? (1.6)

6.3   What is an exceptional item? (2.1)

6.4   What three items does *FRS 3* require to be shown separately on the face of the profit and loss account? (2.2)

6.5   What change did *FRS 3* make to the definition of EPS? (2.8)

6.6   Is the statement of total recognised gains and losses a primary statement? (3.1)

6.7   What is the definition of a class of business? (4.3)

6.8   What is the definition of a geographical segment? (4.4)

7   EXAMINATION TYPE QUESTIONS

7.1   Performance indicators

The Accounting Standards Board has issued Financial Reporting Standard 3 which has 'the aim of moving the emphasis from concentrating on a single performance indicator to highlighting a range of important components of financial importance'.

You are required to discuss how users of financial statements may be presented with information which is designed to present clearly the key components of performance.   **(15 marks)**

7.2   Innovations plc

Innovations plc is preparing a segmental report to include with its financial accounts prepared for the year ended 30 June 19X9.

The relevant information given below is based on the consolidated figures of Innovations plc and its subsidiaries. Associate company information is not shown.

	19X9 £'000	*19X8* £'000
Sales to customers outside the group by the Fruit Growing division	12,150	13,500
Sales to customers outside the group by the UK companies	27,000	24,300
Sales not derived from Fruit Growing, Canning or Bureau activities	2,700	1,350
Sales made to customers outside the group by the Canning Division	17,550	13,095
Assets used by the US companies	32,400	24,300
Assets not able to be allocated to Fruit Growing, Canning or Bureau activities	13,500	11,003
Assets used by Fruit Growing Division	33,750	32,400
Sales by the Canning Division to other group members	2,970	3,105
Assets used by the Bureau Service	18,765	17,563
Assets used by the UK Companies	43,200	40,500
Sales by the Fruit Growing Division to other group members	1,485	1,688
Sales not allocated to the UK, US or other areas	2,700	1,350
Sales made by group to other areas of the world	1,350	1,215
Expenses not allocated to UK, US or other areas	4,590	3,834
Sales to customers outside the group by US Companies	6,750	5,130
Expenses not allocated to Fruit Growing, Canning or Bureau Service	5,130	4,104
Sales by US Companies to group members	2,160	1,215
Sales to customers outside the group for Bureau Service	5,400	4,050
Sales made by UK companies to other group members	2,700	1,890
Assets used by Canning Division	40,500	33,750
Assets used by Group in other areas	18,360	19,683
Assets not allocated to UK, US or other areas	12,555	10,233

Segmental net operating profit by industry

Fruit Growing	2,565	3,375
Canning	4,725	3,600
Bureau	412	540
Consolidated segmental net operating profit	7,695	6,750

Segmental net operating profit by geographical area

UK	5,130	4,590
US	2,430	1,890
Other areas	270	405
Consolidated segmental net operating profit by geographical area	7,155	6,480

You are required:

(a)   to briefly state;

    (i)   the case for segmental reporting;

    (ii)   the case against segmental reporting.   **(4 marks)**

(b)   to draft an industry and geographical segmental report for inclusion in the annual report to give the maximum information to the shareholders.   **(16 marks)**

(Total: 20 marks)

8   ANSWERS TO EXAMINATION TYPE QUESTIONS

8.1   Performance indicators

Before the publication of Financial Reporting Standard 3 *Reporting financial performance*, companies produced profit and loss accounts which emphasised the 'bottom' line profit achieved from all the operations and activities of the enterprise. This conglomeration concealed important aspects of the periodic financial performance of distinctive components of the enterprise. *FRS 3* has been issued to help remedy this problem, the objective of the standard being to require entities within its scope to highlight a **range** of important components of financial performance, to aid users in understanding the performance achieved by a reporting entity in a period and to assist them in forming a basis for their assessment of future results and cashflows.

The standard requires a changed format to the profit and loss account to help achieve this objective. A 'layered' format is required showing

(i)   results of continuing operations (including the results of acquisitions),

(ii)   results of discontinued operations,

(iii)   profits or losses on the sale or termination of an operation, costs of a fundamental reorganisation or restructuring and profits or losses on the disposal of fixed assets, and

(iv)   extraordinary items.

Items (i) and (iii) result in all cases in a split of turnover and operating profit on the face of the profit and loss account, and an analysis of cost of sales and net operating expenses in the notes (although these items may be split on the face of the profit and loss account). In an effort to solve the problems of extraordinary items, the standard restricts such items to those being (very) unusual items outside ordinary activities. In addition the earnings per share figure is to be calculated after extraordinary items thus removing the anomaly of comparative EPS figures caused by extraordinary items.

Also as an aid to measuring periodic performance, entities are now to provide a statement of total recognised gains and losses (including any unrealised surplus on revaluation of properties) and a reconciliation of movements in shareholders' funds. This last statement should make reserve movements easier to appreciate.

Overall *FRS 3* has been helpful to readers of published accounts, making interpretations of the financial performance of an enterprise more meaningful.

8.2   Innovations plc

(a)   (i)   The objectives of segmental reporting are to provide users with a greater level of information about the results and resources of a group than is available from the profit and loss account and balance sheet.

In addition, disclosure of this information by classes of business and geographical segments allows greater comparability between companies in the same industry.

The disclosure of inter segment sales and profits also gives greater information on the total activities of the group as the consolidated accounts only disclose transactions outside the group.

(ii)   There are the following arguments against segmental reporting:

The additional information provided by groups may put them at a competitive disadvantage especially with overseas companies which may not have to disclose this information.

The requirements of SSAP25 allow the directors considerable flexibility in defining segments. This will reduce comparability.

The costs of providing this information. Although management usually prepares this type of information for its own purposes, it may not be in a form suitable for publication in the financial statements.

(b)   Segmental report for Innovations plc for year ended 30 June 19X9

Classes of business	Fruit growing		Canning		Bureau		Group	
	19X9 £'000	19X8 £'000	19X9 £'000	19X8 £'000	19X9 £'000	19X8 £'000	19X9 £'000	19X8 £'000
Turnover								
Total sales	13,635	15,188	20,520	16,200	5,400	4,050	39,555	35,438
Inter-segment sales	1,485	1,688	2,970	3,105	-	-	4,455	4,793
Sales to 3rd parties	12,150	13,500	17,550	13,095	5,400	4,050	35,100	30,645
Unallocated sales							2,700	1,350
							37,800	31,995
Profit before taxation								
Segment profit	2,565	3,375	4,725	3,600	412	540	7,702	7,515
Inter-segment loss							(7)	(765)
							7,695	6,750
Common costs							(5,130)	(4,104)
Group operating profit							2,565	2,646
Net assets								
Segment net assets	33,750	32,400	40,500	33,750	18,765	17,563	93,015	83,713
Unallocated assets							13,500	11,003
Group net assets							106,515	94,716

Official ACCA *Textbook, published by AT Foulks Lynch*

Geographical segments

	UK		US		Other		Group	
	19X9 £'000	19X8 £'000	19X9 £'000	19X8 £'000	19X9 £'000	19X8 £'000	19X9 £'000	19X8 £'000
Turnover by destination								
Total sales	29,700	26,190	8,910	6,345	1,350	1,215	39,960	33,750
Inter-segment sales	2,700	1,890	2,160	1,215	-	-	4,860	3,105
Sales to 3rd parties	27,000	24,300	6,750	5,130	1,350	1,215	35,100	30,645
Unallocated sales							2,700	1,350
							37,800	31,995
Profit before taxation								
Segment profit	5,130	4,590	2,430	1,890	270	405	7,830	6,885
Inter-segment loss							(680)	(405)
							7,155	6,480
Common costs							(4,590)	(3,834)
Group operating profit							2,565	2,646
Net assets								
Segment net assets	43,200	40,500	32,400	24,300	18,360	19,683	93,960	84,483
Unallocated assets							12,555	10,233
Group net assets							106,515	94,716

13 EARNINGS PER SHARE

INTRODUCTION & LEARNING OBJECTIVES

Earnings per share is an important figure to the users of listed company accounts. Its calculation is stipulated in detail by FRS 14. Due to various complexities of computation, the standard can constitute a full question on its own in the exam. The calculations must therefore be thoroughly understood.

When you have studied this chapter you should be able to do the following:

- Understand the importance of EPS.
- Calculate basic EPS.
- Calculate diluted EPS.

1 EARNINGS PER SHARE

1.1 The need for a standard for earnings per share

The figure 'Earnings per share' (EPS) is used to compute the major stock market indicator of performance, the Price Earnings ratio (PE ratio). The calculation is:

$$\text{PE ratio} = \frac{\text{Market value of share}}{\text{EPS}}$$

Rightly or wrongly, the stock market places great emphasis on a company's PE ratio and therefore a standard form of measurement of EPS is required.

The problems in determining the earnings of a company arise because only one earnings figure can be used in an EPS calculation. As we saw in the previous chapter the issue of FRS 3 to replace SSAP 6 is an attempt by the ASB to overcome the problems of the users of accounts relying excessively on one earnings figure. Whether the approach used by the ASB will prove successful in the long run remains to be seen. There appears to be little evidence so far that the stock market is less reliant on the PE ratio than formerly.

1.2 The requirements of FRS 3 regarding the computation of EPS

FRS 3 amended the calculation of EPS by defining earnings as the profit figure after extraordinary items.

It also encourages companies to publish more than one EPS ie, to show EPS at different levels of profit. Additional EPS can be shown provided that a reconciliation to normal EPS is shown and the additional EPS are shown consistently in successive accounting periods.

1.3 The implications of FRS 3 for the disclosure of EPS

As FRS 3 requires EPS to be computed after all items of income and expense appearing in the profit and loss account, the figure will fluctuate much more than previously due to one off reorganisations or sales of property for example.

The reaction of some companies to this fluctuation is to disclose more than one EPS and to choose for the other EPS, an earnings figure based on 'normal' trading profit.

Investment analysts have reacted to the issue of FRS 3 by issuing their own recommended earnings figure which is based on defining 'normal operations'.

2   THE REQUIREMENTS OF FRS 14 REGARDING EPS

2.1   Computation

$$\text{Earnings per share (in pence)} = \frac{\text{net profit or loss for the period attributable to ordinary shareholders}}{\text{weighted average number of ordinary shares outstanding in the period}}$$

The net profit or loss attributable to ordinary shareholders is the net profit or loss after deducting dividends and other appropriations in respect of non-equity shares (normally preference shares).

2.2   Scope of FRS 14

FRS 14 applies to public companies. Private companies that voluntarily disclose earnings per share must also comply with FRS 14.

2.3   Shares in issue

Where several classes of shares are in issue, then earnings should be apportioned according to dividend rights.

2.4   When to include shares in the calculation

Where there has been an issue of shares during the period, shares are normally included in the weighted average number of shares from the date consideration is receivable, which is generally the date of their issue. For example:

- ordinary shares issued in exchange for cash are issued when cash is receivable;

- ordinary shares issued as a result of the conversion of a debt instrument are included as of the date that interest ceases accruing;

- ordinary shares issued as part of the purchase consideration for an acquisition are included as of the date of the acquisition;

- ordinary shares issued as part of the purchase consideration for a business combination accounted for as a merger are included for all periods presented.

Ordinary shares that are issuable upon the satisfaction of certain conditions (contingently issuable shares) are not included in the computation until all the necessary conditions have been satisfied.

2.5   Issue of shares at full market price during the period

Earnings should be apportioned over the weighted average equity share capital (ie, taking account of when shares are issued during the year).

Example

A company issued 200,000 shares at full market price (£3.00) on 1 July 19X8.

Relevant information

	19X8	*19X7*
Ordinary profit attributable to the ordinary shareholders for the year ending 31 Dec.	£550,000	£460,000
Number of ordinary shares in issue at 31 Dec.	1,000,000	800,000

Calculation of earnings per share

$$19X7 \quad = \quad \frac{£460,000}{800,000} = 57.5p$$

$$19X8 \quad = \quad \frac{£550,000}{800,000 + (\frac{1}{2} \times 200,000)} = 61.11p$$

Conclusion Since the 200,000 shares have only contributed finance for half a year, the number of shares is adjusted accordingly. Note that the solution is to use the earnings figure for the period without adjustment, but divide by the average number of shares weighted on a time basis.

2.6 Bonus issues

When there has been an event that has changed the number of ordinary shares outstanding without a corresponding change in resources (inflow or outflow of cash), the comparative earnings per share figure should also be adjusted.

Example

A company makes a bonus issue of one new share for every five existing shares held on 1 July 19X8.

Relevant information

	19X8	19X7
Ordinary profit attributable to the ordinary shareholders for the year ending 31 Dec.	£550,000	£460,000
Number of ordinary shares in issue at 31 Dec.	1,200,000	1,000,000

Calculation of earnings per share in 19X8 accounts

$$19X7 \quad = \quad \frac{£460,000}{1,200,000} = 38.33p$$

$$19X8 \quad = \quad \frac{£550,000}{1,200,000} = 45.83p$$

In the 19X7 accounts, the EPS for the year would have appeared as 46p (£460,000 ÷ 1,000,000). In the example above, the computation has been reworked from scratch. However, to make the changes required it would be simpler to adjust directly the EPS figures themselves.

Since the old calculation was based on dividing by 1,000,000 while the new is determined by using 1,200,000, it would be necessary to multiply the EPS by the first and divide by the second. The fraction to apply is, therefore,

$$\frac{1,000,000}{1,200,000} \text{ or } \frac{5}{6}$$

Consequently $46p \times \frac{5}{6} = 38.33p$.

Given that the scrip issue has not increased the assets in the company, similarly the market value of each share would be expected to be only 5/6 of the former price, since for every five shares previously held, the shareholder now has six.

Assuming a pre-issue market price of £3.00, five shares would have a market value of £15.00. After the issue six shares would, other things being equal, have the same value. Therefore, one share would have a theoretical post-issue price of £15.00 ÷ 6 = £2.50. The new EPS could in consequence equally well have been calculated by multiplying the old EPS by the theoretical new share price divided by the actual old price

$$(\frac{£2.50}{£3.00} = \frac{5}{6})$$

Since there are now six shares in issue for every five previously held, the number of shares after the issue is similarly

$$1,000,000 \times \frac{6}{5} = 1,200,000$$

or alternatively

$$1,000,000 \times \frac{3.00}{2.50} = 1,200,000$$

These interrelationships are important when considering a rights issue.

2.7   Rights issues

Rights issues present special problems, because they are normally below full market price and therefore combine the characteristics of issues at full market price and bonus issues as above. Determining the weighted average capital, therefore, involves two steps:

Step 1   Adjust for bonus element in rights issue, by multiplying capital in issue before the rights issue by:

$$\frac{\text{Actual cum rights price}}{\text{Theoretical ex rights price}}$$

Step 2   Calculate the weighted average capital in issue as in paragraph 2.5 above.

Example

A company issued one new share for every two existing shares held by way of rights at £1.50 per share on 1 July 19X8. Pre-issue market price was £3.00 per share.

Relevant information

	19X8	*19X7*
Ordinary profit attributable to the ordinary shareholders for the year ending 31 Dec.	£550,000	£460,000
Number of ordinary shares in issue at 31 Dec.	1,200,000	800,000

Calculation of earnings per share

19X7   Original per 19X7 accounts:

$$\frac{£460,000}{800,000} = 57.5p$$

Adjusted for rights issue:

$$57.5p \times \frac{2.50}{3.00} = 47.92p$$

19X8   Based on weighted average number of shares:

1st half-year   –   actual in issue 800,000

                        –   adjusted for bonus element $800,000 \times \frac{3.00}{2.50}$

                              = 960,000

2nd half-year   –   actual in issue, including bonus element, 1,200,000

                              Therefore, EPS $= \dfrac{£550,000}{(960,000 + 1,200,000) \div 2}$

                              = 50.92p

Notes on solution

(1)   19X7

Pre-rights, two shares would be worth £6.00. Ex-rights, three shares would theoretically be worth £6.00 + £1.50 = £7.50, or £2.50 each. The appropriate fraction for the adjustment of comparatives is, therefore, £2.50 divided by £3.00.

The revised EPS figure could have been obtained by dividing the earnings figure of £460,000 by a share number adjusted for the bonus element, ie:

$$800,000 \times \frac{3.00}{2.50} = 960,000$$

$$(\frac{£460,000}{960,000} = 47.92p)$$

(2)   19X8

The calculation must take account of the quasi-capitalisation. The share number used must, therefore, reflect the bonus element for the whole year and the increase in the fund of capital from the half year.

(3)   Relationship of rights issue to issue at full market price and capitalisation

Each of the examples used a pre-issue share price of £3.00. Both the rights issue and the issue at full market price raised £600,000 from shareholders. However, after the rights issue there were 1,200,000 shares in issue, whereas following the issue at full market value there were only 1,000,000.

If the latter had been followed immediately by a capitalisation to bring the number of shares issued up to 1,200,000, the EPS figures would have become:

19X7 $57.5p \times \frac{2.50}{3.00} = 47.92p$

19X8 $61.11p \times \frac{2.50}{3.00} = 50.92p$

These are, as would be expected, the same as those calculated for the rights issue.

2.8   Activity

On 31 December 19X1 the issued share capital consisted of 4,000,000 ordinary shares of 25p each, and the shares were quoted at 100p. On 1 January 19X2 the company made a rights issue in the proportion of 1 for 4 at 50p per share. Its trading results for the last two years were as follows:

	Year ended 30 June	
	19X1	*19X2*
	£	*£*
Net profit after taxation	400,000	425,000

Show the calculation of EPS to be presented in the final accounts in 19X2 (including the comparative figure).

2.9   Activity solution

(a)   **Past earnings per share (comparative figure)**

Because the rights issue contains a bonus element, the past earnings per share figures should be adjusted by the factor:

$$\frac{\text{Theoretical ex rights price}}{\text{Actual cum rights price}}$$

Consider a holder of 100 shares: £

			£
Prior to rights issue	100 shares	worth $100 \times 100p =$	100.00
Taking up rights	25 shares	cost $25 \times 50p =$	12.50
	125		112.50

ie, theoretical ex rights price of each share is $\dfrac{£112.50}{125} = 90p$

Last year, reported earnings per share were $\dfrac{£400,000}{4,000,000} = 10p$

Applying correction factor to calculate adjusted comparative figure of earnings per share:

$$10p \times \frac{\text{Theoretical ex rights price}}{\text{Actual cum rights price}} = 10p \times \frac{90p}{100p} = 9p$$

(b)   **Current earnings per share**

Number of shares 1 July 19X1 to 31 December 19X1 (as adjusted):

$$4,000,000 \times \frac{\text{Actual cum rights price}}{\text{Theoretical ex rights price}} \times \frac{6 \text{ months}}{12 \text{ months}}$$

ie, $4,000,000 \times \dfrac{100}{90} \times \dfrac{6}{12} =$ 2,222,222 shares

Number of shares 1 January 19X2 to 30 June 19X2 (actual):

$$\frac{6 \text{ months}}{12 \text{ months}} = \frac{6}{12} \times 5,000,000 =$$ 2,500,000 shares

Total adjusted shares for year   4,722,222 shares

$\therefore$ Earnings per share $= \dfrac{£425,000}{4,722,222} = 9p$ per share

(Tutorial note: because the rights issue occurred during the current financial year, it is necessary to calculate the weighted average share capital during the year. However, since the rights issue is effectively a combination of an issue at full price and a bonus issue, it is necessary to adjust the number of shares for the six months prior to the rights issue for the bonus element.

For an issue at full price it would be necessary to calculate a weighted average number of shares as indicated by the 6/12 factor. The 100/90 factor in the first six months is used to adjust for the bonus element in the rights issue.*)*

3   DILUTED EARNINGS PER SHARE

3.1   Introduction

As well as basic earnings per share, FRS 14 requires entities to disclose diluted earnings per share. To calculate diluted earnings per share, the net profit attributable to ordinary shareholders and the weighted average number of shares outstanding are adjusted for the effect of all dilutive potential ordinary shares.

> **Definition**   A **potential ordinary share** is a financial instrument or a right that may entitle its holders to ordinary shares.

Examples of potential ordinary shares:

- convertible loan stock
- convertible preference shares
- share warrants and options
- rights granted under employee share schemes
- rights to ordinary shares that are conditional upon the satisfaction of conditions.

Use is often made of potential share issues at a future date as an inducement to purchase fixed interest stock or to reward management.

Diluted earnings per share shows to what extent the amount available for ordinary dividends per share would have been affected if all the potential ordinary shares had been issued.

To calculate diluted earnings per share:

- the net profit or loss for the period attributable to ordinary shareholders is adjusted for:

    - dividends on potential shares (eg, on convertible preference shares)
    - interest (eg, on convertible loan stock)
    - any other changes in income and expense that would result from the conversion

- the weighted average number of ordinary shares that would be issued if all the potential ordinary shares were converted is added to the weighted number of ordinary shares. (Potential ordinary shares should be assumed to have been converted at the beginning of the period, or, if they were not in existence at the beginning of the period, the date of issue.)

Convertible loan stock, convertible preference shares, options and warrants are the types of potential ordinary share that you are most likely to meet in the exam.

3.2   Convertibles

The principles of convertible loan stock and convertible preference shares are similar and will be dealt with together.

Example

On 1 April 19X1, the company issued by way of rights or otherwise £1,250,000 8% convertible unsecured loan stock for cash at par. Each £100 nominal of the stock will be convertible in 19X6/19X9 into the number of ordinary shares set out below:

On 31 December 19X6	124 shares
On 31 December 19X7	120 shares
On 31 December 19X8	115 shares
On 31 December 19X9	110 shares

Relevant information

Issued share capital:

£500,000 in 10% cumulative preference shares of £1;
£1,000,000 in ordinary shares of 25p = 4,000,000 shares.

Corporation tax is 45%.

Trading results for the year ended 31 December

	19X2 £	*19X1* £
Profit before interest and tax	1,100,000	991,818
Interest on 8% convertible unsecured loan stock	100,000	75,000
Profit before tax	1,000,000	916,818
Corporation tax	450,000	412,568
Profit after tax	550,000	504,250

Calculation of earnings per share

		19X2 £	*19X1* £
(1)	**Basic earnings per share**		
	Profit after tax	550,000	504,250
	Less: Preference dividend	50,000	50,000
	Earnings	500,000	454,250
	Earnings per share based on 4,000,000 shares	12.5p	11.4p

(2)	**Diluted earnings per share**				
	Earnings as above		500,000		454,250
	Add: Interest on the convertible unsecured loan stock	100,000		75,000	
	Less: Corporation tax	45,000		33,750	
			55,000		41,250
	Adjusted earnings		555,000		495,500
	Earnings per share based on 5,550,000 shares (19X1 – 5,162,500)		10p		9.6p

Notes:

(A)   Up to 19X5 the **maximum** number of shares issuable after the end of the financial year will be at the rate of 124 shares per £100, viz: 1,550,000 shares, making a total of 5,550,000.

(B)   The weighted average number of shares issued and issuable for 19X1 would have been one-quarter of 4,000,000 plus three-quarters of 5,550,000 ie, 5,162,500.

3.3   Options and warrants

The total number of shares issued on the exercise of the option or warrant is split into two:

(i)   the number of shares that would have been issued if the cash received had been used to buy shares at fair value (using the average price of the shares during the period); and

(ii)   the remainder, which are treated like a bonus issue (ie, as having been issued for no consideration).

The number of shares issued for no consideration is added to the number of shares when calculating the diluted earnings per share.

Example

On 1 January 19X7 a company issues 1,000,000 shares under option. The net profit for the year is £500,000 and the company already has 4,000,000 ordinary shares in issue at that date.

During the year to 31 December 19X7 the average fair value of one ordinary share was £3 and the exercise price for the shares under option was £2.

Solution

$$\text{Basic earnings per share:} \quad \frac{£500,000}{4,000,000} = 12.5p$$

Diluted earnings per share:

Number of ordinary shares in issue	4,000,000
Number of shares under option	1,000,000
Number of shares that would have been issued at fair value:	
(1,000,000 × 2/3)	(666,667)
	4,333,333

$$\text{Earnings per share:} \quad \frac{£500,000}{4,333,333} = 11.5p$$

3.4   The order in which to include dilutive securities in the calculation

Only potential ordinary shares that would dilute basic earnings per share should be taken into account when computing the diluted figure.

Where there is more than one issue of dilutive share the calculation is in two stages:

1.   For each issue, calculate earnings per incremental share.
2.   Adjust basic earnings per share for each issue from the most dilutive to the least dilutive.

4   PRESENTATION AND DISCLOSURE OF EARNINGS PER SHARE

4.1   Presentation

(a)   Basic and diluted earnings per share should be presented on the face of the profit and loss account for each class of ordinary share.

(b)   Basic and diluted earnings per share must be presented with equal prominence.

(c)   Basic and diluted earnings per share should be presented even if the amounts are negative (ie, a loss per share).

4.2   Additional disclosures

The following information should be disclosed for both basic and diluted earnings per share:

(a)   the amounts used as numerators and a reconciliation of those amounts to the net profit or loss for the period; and

(b)   the weighted average number of ordinary shares used as the denominator and a reconciliation of the denominators to each other.

If an alternative measure of earnings per share is disclosed (as permitted by FRS 3) this should be:

(a)   calculated using the weighted average number of ordinary shares determined in accordance with FRS 14;

(b)   presented consistently over time;

(c)   reconciled to the amount required by FRS 14;

(d)   not presented more prominently than the version required by FRS 14; and

(e)   the reason for calculating the additional version should be explained.

The reconcilation and explanation should appear adjacent to the earnings per share disclosure, or a reference should be given to where they can be found.

5   THE SIGNIFICANCE OF THE DIFFERENT FIGURES FOR EARNINGS PER SHARE THAT A COMPANY MAY DISCLOSE

5.1   Basic EPS

(a)   **Standard calculation per FRS 14**

The standard calculation reflects the earnings performance of the company taking into account all costs and revenues that have occurred during the year.

(c)   **Other measures**

FRS 3 and FRS 14 permit alternative EPS figures to be calculated at different levels of profit. Possible alternatives to the FRS 14/FRS 3 calculation include:

(i)   IIMR headline earnings
(ii)   excluding exceptional items
(iii)   excluding discontinued operations.

IIMR headline earnings is basic earnings adjusted for profits and losses on sales and terminations, profits and losses on the sale of fixed assets, amortisation of goodwill and other unusual items. It includes exceptional items that are not required to be disclosed separately.

5.2   Diluted EPS

Diluted EPS shows what the current year's EPS would be if all the dilutive potential ordinary shares in issue had been converted. Because it always has to be disclosed it can be used to assess trends in past performance.

In theory, diluted EPS serves as a warning to equity shareholders that the return on their investment may fall in future periods. However, diluted EPS as currently required by FRS 14 is not intended to be forward looking but an additional past performance measure. For example, when calculating diluted EPS where there are warrants or options, fair value is based on the average price of an ordinary share for the period, rather than the market price at the period end. Therefore diluted EPS is only of limited use as a prediction of future EPS.

5.3 Limitations of EPS as a performance measure

Although EPS is believed to have a real influence on the market price of shares, it has several important limitations as a performance measure:

(a) It does not take account of inflation. Apparent growth in earnings may not be real growth.

(b) It is based on historic information and therefore it does not necessarily provide predictive value. High earnings and growth in earnings may be achieved at the expense of investment which may generate increased earnings in the future.

(c) An entity's earnings are affected by the choice of its accounting policies. Therefore it may not always be appropriate to compare the EPS of different companies.

6 CHAPTER SUMMARY

Basic EPS is calculated and disclosed for all listed companies. Complications arise if there has been a change in the amount of ordinary share capital in the period.

Entities are also required to calculate and disclose diluted EPS.

6 SELF TEST QUESTIONS

6.1 What is the denominator of the basic EPS calculation? (2.1)

6.2 When is the weighted average method used to determine the number of shares to use in an EPS calculation? (2.5)

6.3 Does a bonus issue reduce or increase EPS? (2.6)

6.4 What is the ratio used in a rights issue to adjust for the bonus element of the rights? (2.7)

6.5 Give three examples of potential dilutions in an EPS calculation. (3.1)

7 EXAMINATION TYPE QUESTION

7.1 R plc

You are given the following information relating to R plc:

	Year to 31 December 19X7 £'000	19X8 £'000
Trading profit before taxation	1,300 CR	1,800 CR
Taxation	700 DR	1,000 DR
Preference dividends	100 DR	100 DR
Ordinary dividends	250 DR	300 DR
Prior year adjustment (note 1)	-	200 DR

Notes:

(1) The prior year adjustment relates to an accounting policy change affecting the trading profit of R plc. The 19X7 information given above does not reflect this change.

(2) On 30 June 19X8, a fully subscribed 1-for-4 rights issue at £1.50 per share was made by R plc. The market price before the rights issue was £2.00.

(3) The issued ordinary share capital of R plc at 1 January 19X7 was 2 million shares of 10 pence each. No changes, other than the above rights issue, were made to R plc's ordinary share capital in 19X7 and 19X8.

You are required

(a)   to calculate for R plc, in accordance with the requirements of Financial Reporting Standard 14:

    (i)   the earnings per share for the year ended 31 December 19X7;

    (ii)   the earnings per share for the year ended 31 December 19X8;

    (iii)   the adjusted earnings per share for the year ended 31 December 19X7 to be included as a comparative figure in the 19X8 financial statements.   **(10 marks)**

(b)   to list the limitations of earnings per share as a measure of corporate performance.

(5 marks)
(Total: 15 marks)

8   ANSWER TO EXAMINATION TYPE QUESTION

8.1   R plc

(a)   (i) $\dfrac{600-100(\text{W}1)}{2,000} = 25\text{p}$

    (ii) $\dfrac{800-100(\text{W}1)}{2,302.632(\text{W}3)} = 30.4\text{p}$

    (iii) $\dfrac{600-100-200}{2,000} \times \dfrac{190}{200} = 14.25\text{p}$

*(**Tutorial note:** We have assumed that the prior year charge of £200,000 only affects the 19X7 profits and not those of earlier years as well. Since we are not given any further information such an assumption is acceptable.)*

(b)   The limitations of earnings per share as a measure of corporate performance can be summarised as follows:

    (i)   They are based on the level of earnings, which may be manipulated by management to show continued growth.

    (ii)   FRS 3 and FRS 14 now require that earnings are calculated after both exceptional and extraordinary items, but prior period adjustments are still excluded. There is a temptation for companies to boost EPS by classifying one-off charges as fundamental errors and charging them against opening profits.

    (iii)   Comparability of performance between companies on the basis of EPS is reduced where accounting policies differ.

WORKINGS

(W1)

	19X7 £'000	19X8 £'000
Trading profit	1,300	1,800
Tax	(700)	(1,000)
Profit after tax	600	800
Dividends - Ordinary	(250)	(300)
- Prefs	(100)	(100)
	250	400

(W2)   Theoretical ex-rights price

$$£2 - £(2 - 1.50) \times \frac{1}{4+1} = £1.90$$

(W3)   Weighted average no of shares

	In issue		Weighted average
To 30.6.X8	2,000,000	$\times \frac{6}{12} \times \frac{2.00}{1.90(W2)}$	1,052,632
Rights issue	500,000		
	2,500,000	$\times \frac{6}{12}$	1,250,000
			2,302,632

14 FRS 4, FRS 13 AND FRS 5

INTRODUCTION & LEARNING OBJECTIVES

This chapter covers three recent accounting standards: FRS 4 **Capital instruments,** FRS 13 **Derivatives and other financial instruments: disclosures** and FRS 5 **Reporting the substance of transactions**. FRS 4 and FRS 5 are likely to be frequently examined, particularly FRS 5. A whole question on FRS 13 is less likely, though it may be examined as part of a larger question on capital instruments or other topics.

All three standards were issued in response to problems caused by complex transactions (including 'creative accounting' abuses). FRS 4 requires reporting entities to classify and present capital instruments in the financial statements in a way which reflects the obligations of the issuer. FRS 13 requires entities to disclose information about the way in which they use derivatives and other financial instruments to manage risk. FRS 5 requires reporting entities to reflect the substance of transactions in their financial statements, rather than their strict legal form.

The requirements of both FRS 4 and FRS 5 are based on the definitions of assets and liabilities in the ASB's draft Statement of Principles. The best way to approach these accounting standards is to concentrate on the principles underpinning them.

When you have studied this chapter you should be able to do the following:

- Understand why it was necessary to introduce FRS 4, FRS 13 and FRS 5.
- Understand and be able to apply the requirements of FRS 4.
- Understand and be able to apply the requirements of FRS 13.
- Understand the requirements of FRS 5.
- Determine the substance of a transaction according to the principles in FRS 5.

1 FRS 4: CAPITAL INSTRUMENTS

1.1 Introduction

Definition A capital instrument is any type of share or loan stock issued as a means of raising finance.

Examples of capital instruments are shares, debentures and loans. In recent years the number and variety of capital instruments has increased enormously with issues of convertible debt, deep discount bonds, participating preference shares, etc and a number of different bases of accounting have been proposed.

The new types of instrument were often designed to allow companies to show an issue as equity rather than debt (to reduce the balance sheet gearing ratio) and also to avoid charging the profit and loss account with interest until the accounting period in which the issue was redeemed (to improve reported profits in the meantime).

The ASB recognised the problems that were arising in this area and issued FRS 4 in December 1993.

1.2 Objectives of standard

FRS 4 considers the following areas:

(a) the circumstances in which capital instruments should be reported as debt - that is, amongst liabilities - and as shares

(b)   the methods by which the amounts representing such instruments and transactions in respect of them, such as payments of interest and the costs of issuing them, should be stated in the accounts

(c)   disclosure requirements.

1.3   The classification of capital instruments

It is sometimes suggested that examples of instruments which seem not to be easy to classify as liabilities or as shares require either the abandonment of the distinction or the introduction of a new category into the balance sheet. The FRS does not propose this course should be taken. It requires instead that the distinction between shares and debt be maintained, and that guidance is given for accounting for capital instruments within these categories. In the case of group accounts, minority interests represent a third category.

> **Conclusion**   All capital instruments should be accounted for on the balance sheet within one of the following categories:
>
> (a)   liabilities;
> (b)   shareholders' funds;
> (c)   minority interests (in the case of consolidated accounts).

Extract from FRS 4 (para 24)

Capital instruments should be classified as liabilities if they contain an obligation to transfer economic benefits (including a contingent obligation to transfer economic benefits). Capital instruments that do not contain an obligation to transfer economic benefits should be reported within shareholders' funds.

The FRS is thus following the definition of a liability in the Statement of Principles.

1.4   Effect of legal status of shares

The above classification is not used to determine the accounting for a company's shares. Shares have a distinct legal status reflected in the limitations imposed by companies legislation on the circumstances in which payments may be made in respect of them. It is also impossible to classify shares as liabilities within the constraints of the statutory formats for the balance sheet.

Although there are practical and legal difficulties in classifying shares as liabilities, another distinction - that between equity and non-equity shares - is practicable.

> **Definition**   Equity shares are any shares other than non-equity shares.

> **Definition**   Non-equity shares possess any of the following characteristics:
>
> (a)   the rights of the shares to receive payments (in dividends, on redemption, or otherwise) are limited to an amount that is not calculated by reference to the company's assets or profits or equity dividends;
>
> (b)   the rights of the shares to participate in a surplus on a winding up are limited to an amount that is not calculated by reference to the company's assets or profits; and/or
>
> (c)   they are redeemable shares.

For example, preference shares are an example of non-equity shares.

1.5   Summary of classification

The principal disclosures required by the FRS may be summarised as follows

Item	*Analysed between*	
Shareholders' funds	Equity interests	Non-equity interests
Minority interests in subsidiaries	Equity interests in subsidiaries	Non-equity interests in subsidiaries
Liabilities	Convertible liabilities	Non-convertible liabilities

Points to note

(a)   The law requires that shares are reported separately from liabilities, but some kinds of shares have features which resemble debt in some respects. FRS 4 therefore requires that

Shareholders' funds should be analysed between amounts attributable to equity and non-equity interests.

(b)   Outside interests in shares in subsidiaries are normally reported as minority interests in subsidiaries. Since such shares, like those issued by the company itself, may either be equity or non-equity, FRS 4 also requires that

Minority interests in subsidiaries should also be analysed between equity and non-equity interests.

(c)   Although convertible debt may be settled by the issue of shares, the company remains liable to repay it until such time as the holder elects to convert. FRS 4 therefore requires that

Convertible debt should be reported as a liability, but in order that the reader can assess the prospective cash flows relating to the instrument, it should be separately disclosed.

1.6   Accounting for capital instruments

There are two main topics:

(a)   the amount at which the instrument is recorded in the balance sheet (the carrying amount)

(b)   the calculation of the finance costs and their allocation between accounting periods.

(a) and (b) are to a large extent interdependent. The first step is to calculate the initial carrying amount. This will be the fair value of the consideration less issue costs. Fair value is not defined and thus general principles should be used.

1.7   Accounting for issue costs

The previous practice for the costs of issuing capital instruments was diverse. FRS 4 requires that

Costs incurred directly in connection with the issue of capital instruments should be accounted for as deductions from the proceeds of issue.

The effect of this requirement is that, where material costs are incurred in the issue of debt, the amount at which the debt is initially stated will be less than it would otherwise be. The issue costs will be reflected in a higher finance cost over the life of the issue.

In the case of an issue of equity shares, the proposal is consistent with the provisions of the *Companies Act* that the costs of issue be taken to the share premium account. Where there is no share premium account, the cost of issuing shares should be taken directly to reserves. The issue costs will be reported in the statement of total recognised gains and losses.

1.8   Accounting for finance costs

Once the initial carrying amount has been determined it will be stated at that amount on the balance sheet. If the instrument is *equity* shares this amount will not change in subsequent accounting periods. For other instruments the carrying amount may well change because of the allocation of finance costs.

The finance cost is defined as the difference between the amount of the fair value of consideration less issue costs and the payments required to be made by the issuer of the instrument.

The finance cost should be allocated to periods over the term of the debt at a constant rate on the carrying amount (ie, the same requirement as in SSAP 21 for lessees accounting for their obligations under finance leases).

The carrying amount of instruments (other than equity shares) thus becomes

the net proceeds plus finance charges recognised in the accounts less payments made.

1.9   Example

Debt is issued for £1,000. The debt is redeemable at £1,250. The term of debt is five years and carries interest of 5.9 pa.

The debt would initially be recognised at £1,000. The finance cost of the debt is the difference between the payments required by the debt which total £1,545 ((5 × £59) + £1,250) and the proceeds of £1,000, that is £545. In order to allocate these costs over the term of the debt at a constant rate on the carrying amount they must be allocated at the rate of 10%. The movements on the carrying amount of the debt over its term would be as follows:

Year	Balance at beginning of year £	Finance cost for year (10%) £	Cost paid during year £	Balance at end of year £
1	1,000	100	(59)	1,041
2	1,041	104	(59)	1,086
3	1,086	109	(59)	1,136
4	1,136	113	(59)	1,190
5	1,190	119	(1,250 + 59)	-

1.10   Audit implications of FRS 4

The auditor needs to be satisfied on two counts:

(a)   that capital instruments are disclosed correctly in the accounts, for example as debt, non-equity shares or equity shares; and

(b)   that the costs associated with capital instruments are accounted for correctly, for example are spread on a fair basis over redeemable debt's period to redemption.

FRS 4 contains a set of application notes giving helpful guidance on how specific complex types of capital instruments should be dealt with; these may give the auditor some help in ensuring that the instruments he is dealing with are being accounted for correctly.

2   FRS 13: DERIVATIVES AND OTHER FINANCIAL INSTRUMENTS: DISCLOSURES

2.1   The problem

Large companies are making increasing use of a wide range of complex financial instruments. These include:

- primary financial instruments (eg, shares and bonds)
- derivative financial instruments (eg, futures, options and swaps).

(Definition)   A **financial instrument** is any contract that gives rise to both a financial asset of one entity and a financial liability or equity instrument of another entity.

(Definition)   A **derivative financial instrument** is a financial instrument that derives its value from the price or rate of some underlying item, such as interest rates, exchange rates and stock market and other indices.

Derivative financial instruments include futures, options, forward contracts, interest rate and currency swaps, interest rate caps, collars and floors, forward interest rate agreements, and commitments to purchase shares or bonds.

Underlying items include equities, bonds, interest rates, exchange rates and stock market and other indices.

Because the value of derivatives depends on movements in underlying items, if an entity uses derivatives, it is exposed to risk.

(Definition)   **Risk** is uncertainty as to the amount of benefits. The term includes both potential for gain and exposure to loss (FRS 5).

Entities may use derivatives in order to manage risk. However, in recent years there have been several cases in which companies have failed as a result of using derivatives.

The use of derivatives poses several problems for users of financial statements:

- Because many derivatives have no cost, they might not appear in the balance sheet, even if they represent substantial assets or liabilities of the company.

- Gains and losses are normally not recorded until cash is exchanged.

- The value of a derivative can change very rapidly, thus exposing an entity to the risk of large profits or losses.

2.2   Risks associated with financial instruments

An appendix to FRS 13 describes the types of risks associated with financial instruments. The two most familiar of these are credit risk and liquidity risk.

(Definition)   **Credit risk** is the possibility that a loss may occur from the failure of another party to perform according to the terms of a contract.

Credit risk can often be assessed from the nature of an entity's business and the numerical disclosures of gross debtors and provisions.

(Definition)   **Liquidity risk** (or funding risk) is the risk that an entity will encounter difficulty in realising assets or otherwise raising funds to meet commitments associated with financial instruments.

Liquidity risk can often be deduced from the current and quick ratios and from the disclosure of the terms and conditions of borrowing.

Two other important types of risk are associated with financial instruments - cash flow risk and market price risk.

Definition **Cash flow risk** is the risk that future cash flows generated by a monetary financial instrument will fluctuate in amount.

Definition **Market price risk** is the possibility that future changes in market prices may change the value, or the burden, of a financial instrument.

The main components of market price risk likely to affect most entities are:

(a)   Interest rate risk - the risk that the value of a financial instrument will fluctuate because of changes in market interest rates.

(b)   Currency risk - the risk that the value of a financial instrument will fluctuate because of changes in foreign exchange rates.

(c)   Other market price risk - the risk that the value of a financial instrument will fluctuate as a result of changes in market prices caused by factors other than interest rates or currencies. This category includes risks stemming from commodity prices and share prices.

The relationship between cash flow risk and market price risk can have a significant effect on the risk profile of the entity. Transactions to reduce one of these risks may have the effect of increasing the other risk.

2.3   Activity

An entity has two interest bearing investments. One of the investments earns interest at a fixed rate of 8% per annum. The rate of interest earned on the other is 1% above base rate.

The base rate rises to 10%. What happens to:

(a)   the market price of the two investments
(b)   the cash flow of the entity?

2.4   Activity solution

Fixed rate investment: the market price will probably fall, so that the entity may make a loss when it sells the investment, but the amount of interest and therefore cash received stays the same. In other words, there is market price risk, but no immediate cash flow risk.

Floating rate investment: the market price is likely to stay about the same, but the interest and cash receivable increases. This investment exposes the entity to cash flow risk, but not to significant market price risk.

From this example we can see that the choice of which risk the management seeks to reduce will have an important bearing on the entity's financial position, financial results and cash flows. However, users of the financial statements have traditionally had very little information about an entity's exposure to these risks.

The ASB believed that there was an urgent need to improve the disclosure of financial instruments. FRS 13 was issued in order to ensure that reporting entities disclose information that enables users to assess:

(a)   the risk profile of the entity for each of the main financial risks arising in connection with financial instruments; and

(b)   the significance of such instruments and contracts to the entity's financial position, performance and cash flows.

2.5   Scope of FRS 13

(a)   **Entities**

FRS 13 applies to public and listed companies.

(b)   **Instruments to be dealt with in the disclosures**

FRS 13 applies to **all financial instruments** (except those specifically excluded), not just to derivatives. Financial instruments give rise to both a financial asset of one entity and a financial liability or equity instrument of another entity.

[Definition]   A **financial asset** is any asset that is:

(a)   cash;

(b)   a contractual right to receive cash or another financial asset from another entity;

(c)   a contractual right to exchange financial instruments with another entity under conditions that are potentially favourable; or

(d)   an equity instrument of another entity.

[Definition]   A **financial liability** is any liability that is a contractual obligation:

(a)   to deliver cash or another financial asset to another entity; or

(b)   to exchange financial instruments with another entity under conditions that are potentially unfavourable.

The following items are **excluded** from the disclosures:

(a)   interests in subsidiary, quasi-subsidiary and associated undertakings, partnerships and joint ventures (unless held exclusively with a view to subsequent resale)

(b)   employers' obligations to employees under employee share option and employee share schemes

(c)   pension and similar assets and liabilities

(d)   rights and obligations under operating leases

(e)   equity shares and options and warrants relating to equity shares issued by the reporting entity.

(c)   **Short term debtors and creditors**

Either all or none of short term debtors and creditors should be excluded from the disclosures.

(d)   **Non-equity shares**

Non-equity shares should be dealt with in the disclosures in the same way as financial liabilities, but should be disclosed separately.

2.6 Activity

Which of the following items are financial instruments?

(a) debentures to be settled in cash
(b) plant and equipment
(c) goodwill
(d) warrants or options to subscribe for shares of the reporting entity
(e) a forward contract that will be settled in another financial instrument
(f) prepayments for goods or services
(g) stocks
(h) a forward contract that will be settled by the delivery of goods

2.7 Activity solution

Items (a), (d) and (e) are financial instruments.

2.8 Narrative disclosures

(a) An explanation should be provided of the role that financial instruments have had during the period in creating or changing the risks the entity faces in its activities. This should include:

- an explanation of the objectives and policies for holding or issuing financial instruments and similar contracts; and

- the strategies for achieving those objectives (in both cases as agreed by the directors) that have been followed during the period

(b) If these disclosures reflect a significant change from the explanations provided for the previous accounting period, this should be disclosed and the reasons for the change explained.

(c) If the directors agreed, before the date of approval of the financial statements, to make a significant change to the role that financial instruments will have in creating or changing the risks of the entity, that change should be explained.

(d) An explanation should be provided of how the period end numerical disclosures shown in the financial statements reflect the objectives, policies and strategies disclosed.

These disclosures should be given in the financial statements or in some other statement available with the financial statements, eg, the operating and financial review.

2.9 Numerical disclosures

(a) **Interest rate risk**

Analyse the aggregate carrying amount of financial liabilities, by principal currency, between liabilities:

- at fixed interest rates
- at floating interest rates
- on which no interest is paid.

(b) **Currency risk**

Provide an analysis of the net amount of monetary assets and liabilities at the balance sheet date, showing the amount denominated in each currency, analysed by reference to the functional currencies of the operations involved.

(c)   **Liquidity**

Present a maturity profile of the carrying amount of financial liabilities, showing amounts falling due:

- in one year or less, or on demand
- in more than one year but not more than two years
- in more than two years but not more than five years
- in more than five years.

Determine the maturity profile by reference to the earliest date on which payment can be required or on which the liability falls due.

(d)   **Fair values**

Group the financial assets and financial liabilities (whether recognised or unrecognised) into appropriate categories and for each category disclose either:

- the aggregate fair value at the balance sheet date together with the aggregate carrying amount; or

- the aggregate fair value of items with a positive fair value and, separately, the aggregate fair value of items with a negative fair value, in both cases as at the balance sheet date and in each case accompanied by the relevant aggregate carrying amount.

Disclose the methods and any significant assumptions used in determining fair value.

Fair values need not be disclosed if it is not practicable to estimate them with sufficient reliability. The following should be provided instead:

- a description of the item and its carrying amount

- the reasons why it is not practicable to estimate fair value with sufficient reliability

- information about the principal characteristics of the underlying financial asset or liability that is pertinent to estimating its fair value.

2.10   Measurement of financial instruments

FRS 13 represents the first stage of the ASB's financial instruments project and the ASB is now turning its attention to the measurement of financial instruments. The ASB's Discussion Paper *Derivatives and other financial instruments* proposed that all financial instruments should be measured at **current value**. The ASB believes that historic cost is no longer suitable for financial instruments because:

- many derivatives have no cost and therefore do not appear in the balance sheet;

- gains and losses are not recorded until cash is exchanged, which means that management is able to choose when to report gains and losses for their accounts;

- many companies already use current rates for internal reporting purposes.

The ASB is expected to issue a FRED in the year 2000.

| Conclusion | FRS 13 requires public and listed companies to make narrative and numerical disclosures of information about their financial instruments. They must provide an explanation of the ways in which financial instruments have created or changed the risks the company faces during the period. |

3   FRS 5: REPORTING THE SUBSTANCE OF TRANSACTIONS

3.1   Introduction

FRS 5 was issued in April 1994. Its main thrust is to ensure that financial statements report the substance of transactions and not merely their legal form. The view held by the ASB is that, before the issue of the FRS, users could be left unaware of the total assets employed in a business and of its overall financing. Detailed disclosures in the notes is no substitute for inclusion in the accounts.

3.2   The ways in which companies have tried to keep items off the balance sheet

'Reporting the substance of transactions' is a reaction to the practice of 'off balance sheet financing' which became popular in the 1980s. As the term indicates, the most widely recognised effect is the omission of liabilities from the balance sheet. However the assets being financed are also excluded with the result that the resources of the company and its financing are understated.

Ways in which companies have tried to keep items off the balance sheet in the past include the following.

(a)   **Leasing of assets**

Prior to the issue of SSAP 21 leases were not capitalised ie, the asset and its related financial commitment were not shown on the lessee's balance sheet.

(b)   **Controlled non-subsidiaries**

Prior to the CA89 and FRS 2 under the old, looser definition of a subsidiary, companies could control other companies but, as they were not technically subsidiaries, they were not consolidated in the group accounts. We have yet to cover consolidated accounts in this text, but the effect of non-consolidation is that the assets and liabilities of the subsidiary are not included within the total assets and liabilities of the group.

Since the CA89 companies have become more ingenious in arranging their affairs so that off balance sheet arrangements continued to occur in entities which were not classified as subsidiaries under the new legislation. FRS 5 tackles these issues.

(c)   **Window dressing**

Companies may enter into transactions shortly before the year end to 'improve' the look of the balance sheet. These transactions reverse shortly after the year end. Such transactions are covered by SSAP 17 but this only requires disclosure in the notes, not changes in the financial statements.

(d)   **Innovations in the financial markets**

A number of (often complex) arrangements were developed for which the accounting entries were not immediately obvious. It was the growth in these arrangements which resulted in the determination of the ASB to issue an accounting standard on the substance of transactions. We refer to some of these innovations in our coverage of the standard below.

3.3   FRS 5: General principles

FRS 5 sets out general principles covering the following

(a)   what is excluded from the scope of the standard
(b)   how to determine the substance of a transaction
(c)   whether any resulting assets and liabilities should be included in the balance sheet
(d)   at what point there should be changes in previously recognised assets
(e)   what disclosures are necessary

(f)   whether any 'vehicle' companies incorporated into a transaction should be consolidated.

(g)   under what circumstances a 'linked' presentation is appropriate.

The FRS also contains application notes showing how its proposals are to be applied to six specific transaction types - consignment stock, sale and repurchase agreements, factoring, securitised assets, loan transfers and Private Finance Initiative contracts.

3.4   Scope of the standard

Certain transactions are excluded from the standard because of the special nature of the transactions and further thought is required by the ASB before it tackles them.   The main exclusions relate to financing arrangements such as forward contracts, futures, foreign exchange and interest rate swaps.

Where the general principles of the standard seem to apply to an asset or liability which is subject to the requirements of a more specific standard (eg, SSAP 9 covers stocks), the specific requirements of the other standard apply.

3.5   Determining the substance of a transaction

Common features of transactions whose substance is not readily apparent are

(a)   the separation of the legal title to an item from the ability to enjoy the principal benefits and exposure to the principal risks associated with it

(b)   the linking of a transaction with one or more others in such a way that the commercial effect cannot be understood without reference to the series as a whole, and

(c)   the inclusion in a transaction of one or more options whose terms make it highly likely that the option will be exercised.

A key step in determining the substance of a transaction is to identify its effect on the assets and liabilities of the entity.

Assets are, broadly, rights or other access to future economic benefits controlled by an entity. Liabilities are, broadly, an entity's obligations to transfer economic benefits.

Risk often indicates which party has an asset.   Risk is important, as the party which has access to benefits (and hence an asset) will usually also be the one to suffer or gain if the benefits ultimately differ from those expected.

These points are considered in detail in the ASB's Statement of Principles.

3.6   Inclusion of assets and liabilities in the balance sheet

Assets and liabilities should be included in the balance sheet where there is both

(a)   sufficient evidence that an asset or liability exists, and

(b)   the asset or liability can be measured at a monetary amount with sufficient reliability.

3.7   Transactions in previously recognised assets

An asset should cease to be recognised only where two conditions are both fulfilled - that the entity retains no significant access to material benefits, and any risk it retains is immaterial in relation to the variation in benefits likely to occur in practice.

3.8   Disclosures

Disclosure of a transaction should be sufficiently detailed to enable the user of the financial statements to understand its commercial effect.

A transaction may need to be disclosed whether or not it results in additional assets and liabilities being recognised. Where assets or liabilities are recognised but their nature differs from that of items usually found under the relevant balance sheet heading, the differences should be explained. For example certain assets may not be available for use as security for liabilities.

To the extent that a transaction has not resulted in the recognition of assets or liabilities it is still necessary to consider whether disclosure of its nature and effect is required in order to give a true and fair view. For example the transaction may give rise to guarantees or other obligations.

3.9   Quasi-subsidiaries

Some off balance sheet financing arrangements include the use of another entity (a 'vehicle') to house certain assets and liabilities. Normally, the arrangement will be structured so that the vehicle does not meet the legal definition of a subsidiary. Where the commercial effect is no different from that which would result were the vehicle a subsidiary, the vehicle will meet FRS 5's definition of a 'quasi subsidiary'.

> *Definition*   A **quasi-subsidiary** of a reporting entity is a company, trust, partnership or other vehicle that, though not fulfilling the definition of a subsidiary, is directly or indirectly controlled by the reporting entity and gives rise to benefits for that entity that are in substance no different from those that would arise were the vehicle a subsidiary.

In identifying quasi-subsidiaries, regard should be had to the benefits arising from the net assets of the 'vehicle'. Evidence of which party gains these benefits is given by which party is exposed to the risks inherent in them.

Where an entity has a quasi-subsidiary, the quasi-subsidiary should be included in consolidated accounts in the same way as if it were a subsidiary.

Where one or more quasi-subsidiaries are included in consolidated financial statements, this fact should be disclosed. A summary of the financial statements of each quasi-subsidiary should be disclosed in the notes to the financial statements.

3.10   Linked presentation and offset

Elements of FRS 5 are responding to comments requesting certain assets and liabilities to be linked together (ie, the gross amount of assets and liabilities are shown but are also netted off) or offset (ie, only the net amount shown).

3.11   Linked presentation

The linked presentation is available for certain non-recourse finance arrangements. Non-recourse finance involves selling an asset such as a debtor to a third party. If the seller does not have to make any payments to the purchaser if the debtor does not eventually pay the debt, the seller no longer has an asset (ie, the debtor) as it does not meet the recognition criteria in the FRS (all significant benefits and risks have been transferred).

In some non-recourse finance arrangements however, an entity retains significant benefits and risks associated with a specific item, but the maximum loss it can suffer is limited to a fixed monetary amount. In such circumstances a 'linked' presentation is required to present the nature of such an arrangement.

Example

Extract from balance sheet

	£	£
Debtor	80,000	
Less: Non-returnable amounts received on sale of debtor	80,000	
		-

Pressure for the above approach came from certain financial institutions (eg, banks) which wanted to show their gross 'assets' (eg, mortgages advanced) even though they had passed on the assets, in this particular form, to another entity.

3.12   Offset

Offsetting of an asset and liability is generally not allowed, but here also the FRS is attempting to respond to special cases. It allows offset when the items do not constitute 'separate assets and liabilities'. Its main area of use would be certain types of bank balances and overdrafts.

Example

X plc has a bank overdraft of £50,000 at the Anytown branch of Northbank and a credit balance of £10,000 on another account at the same branch. The bank has a legal right of set-off between the two balances.

Extract from balance sheet

	£
Bank overdraft	40,000

4   APPLICATION NOTES

4.1   Introduction

Detailed application notes are included on

(a)   consignment stock
(b)   sale and repurchase agreements
(c)   factoring of debts
(d)   securitised mortgages
(e)   loan transfers
(f)   private finance initiative (PFI) and similar contracts.

The notes are meant to clarify, rather than to override, the general principles of the FRS but they are mandatory.

4.2   Consignment stock

Consignment stock is stock held by one party but legally owned by another, on terms which give the holder the right to sell the stock in the normal course of his business, or at his option to return it unsold to the legal owner. Legal title may pass when one of a number of events has occurred, for example, when the dealer has held the stock for a specified period such as six months, or when the dealer has sold the goods. The sales price may be determined at the date of supply, or it may vary with the length of the period between supply and purchase, or it may be the manufacturer's factory price at sale.

Other terms of such arrangements include a requirement for the dealer to pay a deposit, and responsibility for insurance. The arrangement should be analysed to determine whether the dealer has in substance acquired the stock before the date of transfer of legal title.

FRS 5 states that the key factor will be who bears the risk of slow moving stock. The risk involved is the cost of financing the stock for the period it is held. In a simple arrangement where stock is supplied for a fixed price that will be charged whenever the title is transferred and there is no deposit, the manufacturer bears the slow movement risk. If, however, the price to be paid increases by a factor that varies with interest rates and the time the stock is held, then the dealer bears the risk. If the price charged to the dealer is the manufacturer's list price at the date of sale, then again the risks associated with the stock fall on the manufacturer. Whoever bears the slow movement risk should recognise the stock on the balance sheet.

Consignment stock arrangements are most common in the motor trade.

Example

On 1 January 19X6 Gillingham plc, a manufacturer, entered into an agreement to provide Canterbury plc, a retailer, with machines for resale. Under the terms of the agreement Canterbury plc pays a fixed rental per month for each machine that it holds and also pays the cost of insuring and maintaining the machines. The company can display the machines in its showrooms and use them as demonstration models.

When a machine is sold to a customer, Canterbury plc pays Gillingham plc the factory price at the time the machine was originally delivered. All machines remaining unsold six months after their original delivery must be purchased by Canterbury plc at the factory price at the time of delivery.

Gillingham plc can require Canterbury plc to return the machines at any time within the six month period. In practice, this right has never been exercised. Canterbury plc can return unsold machines to Gillingham plc at any time during the six month period, without penalty. In practice, this has never happened.

At 31 December 19X6 the agreement is still in force and Canterbury plc holds several machines which were delivered less than six months earlier. How should these machines be treated in the accounts for the year ended 31 December 19X6?

Solution

The key issue is whether Canterbury plc has purchased the machines from Gillingham plc or whether they are merely on loan.

It is necessary to determine whether Canterbury plc has the benefits of holding the machines and is exposed to the risks inherent in those benefits.

Gillingham plc can demand the return of the machines and Canterbury plc is able to return them without paying a penalty. This suggests that Canterbury plc does not have the automatic right to retain or to use them.

Canterbury plc pays a rental charge for the machines, despite the fact that it may eventually purchase them outright. This suggests a financing arrangement as the rental could be seen as loan interest on the purchase price. Canterbury plc also incurs the costs normally associated with holding stocks.

The purchase price is the price at the date the machines were first delivered. This suggests that the sale actually takes place at the delivery date. Canterbury plc has to purchase any stocks still held six months after delivery. Therefore the company is exposed to slow payment and obsolescence risks. Because Canterbury plc can return the stocks before that time, this exposure is limited.

It appears that both parties experience the risks and benefits. However, although the agreement provides for the return of the machines, in practice this has never happened.

Conclusion: the machines are assets of Canterbury plc and should be included in the balance sheet.

4.3 Sale and re-purchase of stock

Sale and re-purchase agreements are arrangements under which assets are sold by one party to another on terms that provide for the seller to re-purchase the assets in certain circumstances. The sale may be at market value or at some agreed percentage of market value. The re-purchase arrangement may take a number of forms, for example, a commitment on the part of the seller, an option granted to the seller to require resale (a call option) or an option granted to the buyer to require re-purchase (a put option). The arrangements often contain provisions to enable the seller to make use of the asset during its ownership by the buyer.

The re-purchase price may be variable (depending on the original price and the period during which the asset has been held by the purchaser), agreed at the time of re-purchase or subject to market price movements. The re-purchase price may also be designed to permit the purchaser to recover incidental holding costs if these do not continue to be met by the seller.

FRS 5 states that the key question is whether the commercial effect is that of a sale or of a secured loan. A secured loan transaction will usually have the following features

(a)   the seller will secure access to all future benefits inherent in the asset, often through call options

(b)   the buyer will secure adequate return on the purchase (interest on the loan, often through adjustment of the re-purchase price) and appropriate protection against loss in value of the asset bought (often through put options).

The analysis should look at all features of the agreement that are likely to have a commercial effect in practice.

Sale and re-purchase arrangements are common in property development and in maturing whisky stocks.

Example

X plc has sold a building to Z Ltd, an investment company, for £1m when the current market value was £2m. X can repurchase the property at any time within the next three years for the original selling price (£1m) plus a sum, added quarterly, based on the bank base lending rate plus 2%. How should X plc account for this transaction?

Solution

The substance of this deal is a secured loan from Z to X, with the expectation being that X will exercise its option to repurchase the building. No sale should therefore be recognised; the £1m is a loan received from Z Ltd.

4.4 Debt factoring

Factoring of debts is a well established method of obtaining finance. In most forms of factoring, debts are sold to the factor, but the latter's degree of control over, and responsibility for those debts will vary from one arrangement to another. A significant accounting question is only likely to arise where the factoring arrangement leads to the receipt of cash earlier than would have been the case had the debts been unfactored. If this is so, the question to be answered is whether the seller has in substance received either a loan on the security of his debtors or receipts that are appropriately credited to reduce a debtor.

If the seller is in essence a borrower, and the factor a lender, then the arrangements will be such as to provide that the seller pays the equivalent of interest to the factor on the timing difference between amounts received by him from the factor and those collected by the factor from the debtor. Such payment would be in addition to any other charges.

FRS 5 states that the key factor in the analysis will be who bears the risk (of slow payment) and the benefit (of early payment) by the debtors. If the finance cost reflects events subsequent to transfer, then the transfer is likely to be equivalent to obtaining finance because the seller is bearing the risks and rewards of the debtors. If the cost is determined when the transfer is made, with no other variable costs, then it is likely to be a straightforward sale.

The risk of bad debts is unlikely to be relevant to the analysis, as the exposure to such risk is agreed between the seller and the factor and charges will reflect this, just as in a normal credit insurance contract.

Example

On 1 January 19X6 Lewis plc entered into an agreement with Factoring plc whereby it transferred title to its debtors to Factoring plc subject to a reduction in bad debts based on past experience. Lewis plc received a payment of 90% of the total of net debtors. Under the terms of the agreement, the company had the right to a future sum the amount of which depended on whether and when the debtors paid. Factoring plc had the right of recourse against Lewis plc for any additional losses up to an agreed maximum amount.

At 31 December 19X6, title had been transferred to debtors with an invoice value of £10 million less a bad debt provision of £300,000 and Lewis plc was subject under the agreement to a maximum potential debit of £100,000 to cover losses.

What is the appropriate accounting treatment for this transaction in the balance sheet of Lewis plc at 31 December 19X6?

Solution

As Lewis plc retains the risk of slow payment and bad debts the substance of the transaction is that of a financing arrangement and the company has not disposed of the debtors.

Under the terms of the factoring agreement, finance will be repaid only from the proceeds generated by the debtors. There appears to be no possibility of any claim against Lewis plc being made other than against proceeds generated from the debtors. The finance appears to be non-returnable. There is only recourse for losses up to a fixed amount. These are indications that linked presentation is appropriate.

Balance sheet (extract)

	£m	£m
Current assets		
Gross debts (after providing for bad debts)	9.7	
Less: non returnable proceeds ((90% × 9.7) - 0.1)	(8.63)	
	——	1.07
Cash		8.73
Creditors: amounts falling due within one year		
Recourse under factored debts		0.1

4.5   Securitised assets

Securitisation involves the transfer of assets to a special purpose 'vehicle' which finances their purchase by the issue of debt, for example loan notes. The assets act as security for the loan notes, although the note holders are not exposed to any risks associated with the assets.

The assets transferred may be property, or stock or receivables such as trade debts. However this type of arrangement is most common in the UK for mortgages.

Suppose Company A issues mortgages to home buyers. It is responsible for setting the mortgage rate and term and for credit control. A is known as the 'originator' as it originates the mortgages.

A packages together a group of mortgages and 'sells' them to Company B. B issues loan notes offering the mortgages as security. Then B uses the proceeds from issuing the loan notes, to settle with A. B is known as the 'issuer'.

B usually has negligible equity, and the shares that it has are usually owned by a charitable trust or by a 'friend' of A. A does not control the friendly party and thus B is not a legal subsidiary of A.

A will usually continue to service the mortgages and will extract profit from B by a servicing fee.

Where the originator retains significant benefits or risks then the mortgages remain as an asset and the money it received is shown as a liability.

The amounts may be shown under a linked presentation (see above) if the necessary conditions are satisfied.

Derecognition of the asset is only appropriate where the originator has not retained any significant benefits.

4.6 Loan transfers

Loan transfers involve transferring the benefits and risks of a loan to a third party. Effectively the loan is 'sold' like a tangible asset.

The same principles apply here as for securitised assets.

4.7 Private Finance Initiative and similar contracts

Under a typical Private Finance Initiative (PFI) contract, a private sector 'operator' constructs a capital asset (eg, a hospital, a road, a school) and uses that asset to provide services to a public sector 'purchaser'. The key accounting issue is which party holds the asset, the purchaser or the operator?

A PFI contract should be analysed in two stages:

(i)   Exclude any separable elements of the contract that relate only to services (these are not relevant to deciding which party has the asset);

(ii)   Assess the remainder of the contract.

If the contract can be 'split' into property and service elements the property element is treated as a lease under SSAP 21. This means that where the purchaser has substantially all of the risks and rewards of ownership of the property, the purchaser has an asset and a liability to pay for it.

If the contract cannot be 'split' FRS 5 should be applied. This means that the asset is recorded by the party that bears the profits or losses (risks and rewards) relating to the asset.

Government departments are not legally obliged to comply with accounting standards, but the fact that the ASB has set out 'best practice' will put pressure on them to do so.

5 CHAPTER SUMMARY

FRS 4 *Capital instruments* requires capital instruments to be analysed between debt, non-equity shares and equity shares.

FRS 13 *Derivatives and other financial instruments: disclosures* requires entities to make narrative and numerical disclosures about their financial instruments.

FRS 5 *Reporting the substance of transactions* is a complex standard. The principle is that the substance of any transaction should be reported in the financial statements. This may mean that an asset or liability is recorded which otherwise would not be recorded, or an asset or liability may be removed from the financial statements. A special linked presentation is allowed in certain circumstances.

6   SELF TEST QUESTIONS

6.1   What is a capital instrument? (1.1)

6.2   What are the three categories within which capital instruments may be reported in the balance sheet? (1.3)

6.3   When should a capital instrument be classified as a liability? (1.3)

6.4   How should finance costs be accounted for? (1.8)

6.5   What is a financial instrument? (2.1)

6.6   What are the main narrative disclosures required by FRS 13? (2.8)

6.7   Where is 'window dressing' covered in an accounting standard? (3.2)

6.8   What is the general definition of an asset? (3.5)

6.9   What is a quasi-subsidiary? (3.9)

6.10   What is the difference between 'linking' and 'offset'? (3.10)

7   EXAMINATION TYPE QUESTION

7.1   D Ltd

FRS 5 - Reporting the Substance of Transactions - requires that a reporting entity's financial statements should report the substance of the transactions into which it has entered. FRS 5 states that in order to determine the substance of a transaction it is necessary to identify whether the transaction has given rise to new assets or liabilities for the reporting entity and whether it has changed the entity's existing assets or liabilities.

You are the management accountant of D Ltd which has three principal activities. These are the sale of motor vehicles (both new and second-hand), the provision of spare parts for motor vehicles, and the servicing of motor vehicles.

During the financial year ended 31 August 19X6, the company has entered into a type of business transaction not previously undertaken. With effect from 1 January 19X6, D Ltd entered into an agreement whereby it received motor vehicles on a consignment basis from E plc, a large manufacturer. The terms of the arrangement were as follows:

(a)   On delivery, the stock of vehicles remains the legal property of E plc.

(b)   Legal title to a vehicle passes to D Ltd either when D Ltd enters into a binding arrangement to sell the vehicle to a third party or six months after the date of delivery by E plc to D Ltd.

(c)   At the date legal title passes, E plc invoices D Ltd for the sale of the vehicles. The price payable by D Ltd is the normal selling price of E plc at the date of delivery, increased by 1% for every complete month the vehicles are held on consignment by D Ltd. Any change in E plc's normal selling price between the date of delivery and the date legal title to the goods passes to D Ltd does not change the amount payable by D Ltd to E plc.

(d)   At any time between the date of delivery and the date legal title passes to D Ltd, the company (D Ltd) has the right to return the vehicles to E plc provided they are not damaged or obsolete. D Ltd does not have the right to return damaged or obsolete vehicles. If D Ltd exercises this right of return then a return penalty is payable by D Ltd as follows:

Time since date of delivery	*Penalty as a percentage of invoiced price* *
Three months or less	50%
Three to four months	75%
More than four months	100%

* ie, the price that would otherwise be payable by D Ltd if legal title to the vehicles had passed at the date of return.

(e)   E plc has no right to demand return of vehicles on consignment to D Ltd unless D Ltd becomes insolvent.

The managing director suggests that the vehicles should be shown as an asset of D Ltd only when title passes, and the purchase price becomes legally payable.

You are required to write a report to the managing director which

(a)   explains how (under the principles established in FRS 5) an asset or liability is identified, and when an asset or liability should be recognised and should cease to be recognised, in the financial statements of a business. **(12 marks)**

(b)   evaluates, in the light of the principles you have explained in (a), the correctness, or otherwise of the managing director's suggested accounting treatment for the new transaction. **(8 marks)**
(Total: 20 marks)

8   ANSWER TO EXAMINATION TYPE QUESTION

8.1   D Ltd

Answer plan

Report format.

(a)   Definition of an asset; benefits and risks; definition of a liability; recognition tests; subsequent transactions; ceasing to recognise an asset.

(b)   Need to account for substance over form; outline key issue; consider benefits and risks; analyse terms of agreement; conclusion; required treatment.

Tutorial note: A straightforward question on FRS 5. The problem in part (b) is reasonably easy, but note the analysis. Following these steps should concentrate your mind and ensure some marks, even when the transaction is more complex than this.

REPORT

To: Managing Director of D Ltd

From: Management accountant

Subject: Comments on the treatment of assets and liabilities   **Date: XX XX XX**

(a)   **Recognising assets and liabilities**

The central requirement of FRS 5 *Reporting the substance of transactions* is that entities should report the commercial substance of transactions in their financial statements, rather than their strict legal form. A key step in determining the substance of a transaction is to identify its effect on the assets and liabilities of the entity.

FRS 5 defines an asset as 'rights or other access to future economic benefits controlled by an entity as a result of past transactions or events'. Control is the ability to obtain the future economic benefits relating to an asset and to restrict the access of others to those benefits. This means that it is more than the management of an asset. In practice, an entity which has access to benefits usually suffers or gains if those benefits turn out to be different from those expected. The ability to obtain benefits also implies exposure to risks. Evidence of whether an entity has benefits (and therefore has an asset) is given by whether it is exposed to the risks inherent in those benefits.

A liability is defined as 'an obligation to transfer economic benefits as a result of past transactions or events'. If an entity cannot avoid an outflow of resources, it has a liability. The reason for the obligation may be legal or commercial (for example, an entity may have no realistic alternative to refunding the price of defective goods, even though there is no legal obligation to do so).

An asset or a liability should be recognised if there is sufficient evidence of its existence. Evidence of the existence of an asset or liability may include evidence that a future inflow or outflow of benefit will occur.

Assets and liabilities cannot be recognised unless they can be measured at a monetary amount with sufficient reliability. The fundamental concept of prudence is relevant here. A liability should be recognised where a reasonable estimate of the amount can be made. A greater level of reliability is necessary before an asset can be recognised.

Where a liability is contingent upon the outcome of uncertain future events, it is not recognised unless a present benefit exists as a result of a past event and the transfer of economic benefits is probable (in accordance with the requirements of FRS 12).

Subsequent transactions may affect assets that have previously been recognised in the financial statements. For example, an asset may be financed by means of a sale and repurchase agreement. Provided that this does not result in any significant changes to the entity's rights to benefits and exposure to risks inherent in those benefits, it should continue to recognise the asset in its financial statements. (The entity may also need to recognise a liability for the finance.)

Where a transaction transfers to others all significant rights to benefits associated with an asset and significant exposure to the risks inherent in those benefits, the entire asset should cease to be recognised.

(b)   **Accounting treatment for the new transaction**

You have suggested that we only recognise the vehicles when title passes to us, which is to account for the strict legal form of the transaction. FRS 5 requires us to account for the commercial substance of the transaction, which may not be the same.

The key issue is whether D Ltd has the benefits and is exposed to the risks associated with the vehicles. If the company has the benefits and risks then it should recognise the vehicles in its financial statements.

The benefits normally associated with holding stock are:

- the right to sell the stock and obtain future cash flows;
- insulation from increases in price charged by the manufacturer; and
- the right to use the stock.

The risks normally associated with holding stock are:

- the risk of making a loss on the sale;
- slow movement (possibly with increased holding and financing costs); and
- obsolescence.

D Ltd has the right to sell the vehicles, as E plc cannot normally demand their return (a benefit). The price at which it buys the vehicles depends on the date of delivery, not the date on which legal title passes (insulation from price rises – a benefit). D Ltd has the right to use the vehicles (a benefit).

E plc can demand the return of the vehicles if D Ltd becomes insolvent, but in practice, this is unlikely to happen.

D Ltd pays a penalty if it returns the vehicles to E plc. The size of the penalty means that D plc stands to lose a significant sum if it returns the vehicles (a risk). Although the transfer price rises by 1% for every complete month that the vehicles are held, this additional charge is effectively an interest charge (increased stock holding costs – a risk). D plc cannot return damaged or obsolete stock (a risk).

In this case, it is fairly clear that D Ltd has the benefits and is exposed to the risks associated with holding the vehicles as stock, even before legal title passes. In order to comply with the requirements of FRS 5, all vehicles held by the company at 31 August 19X6 must be included in the balance sheet as stock. This also means that there will be a corresponding liability to E plc included in current liabilities, representing the amount that will be paid for the stock plus any accrued finance charges.

15 CASH FLOW STATEMENTS

INTRODUCTION & LEARNING OBJECTIVES

Cash flow statements are likely to be examined by means of computational questions. Their importance and topicality suggest that they will occur frequently.

The balance sheet and profit and loss account of a business give a good indication of how healthy it is financially and how successfully it is performing. But neither statement gives direct information about a crucial aspect in the stability and success of any business: namely, its ability to generate cash.

FRS 1 requires companies to publish a cash flow statement showing how cash inflows have been generated and how the cash has been spent. The preparation of cash flow statements will be illustrated by a number of examples.

A revised version of FRS 1 was issued in October 1996. The mechanics of preparing a cash flow statement remained exactly the same, but there were changes to the format of the cash flow statement and the standard headings under which cash flows are reported. The revised FRS also incorporated new definitions, of which the most important is the amended definition of cash.

When you have studied this chapter you should be able to do the following:

- Understand the requirements of FRS 1 (revised) in relation to the preparation of cash flow statements for individual companies.
- Apply your knowledge to the preparation of such statements in examination questions.

1 FRS 1 – CASH FLOW STATEMENTS

1.1 Introduction

FRS 1 *Cash flow statements* was issued in September 1991 and replaced SSAP 10 *Statements of source and application of funds*. It requires 'large' reporting entities to include a cash flow statement in their annual accounts. A revised version of FRS 1 was issued in 1996.

1.2 Objective of cash flow statements

The objective of FRS 1 is to ensure that reporting entities falling within its scope:

(a) report their cash generation and cash absorption for a period by highlighting the significant components of cash flow in a way that facilitates comparison of the cash flow performance of different businesses; and

(b) provide information that assists in the assessment of their liquidity, solvency and financial adaptability.

Users of financial statements need information on the liquidity, viability and financial adaptability of entities. Deriving this information involves the user in making assessments of the future cash flows of the entity. Future cash flows are regarded (in financial management theory and increasingly in practice in large companies) as the prime determinant of the worth of a business.

To help to achieve the objective of cash flow reporting, the FRS requires that individual cash flows should be classified under certain standard headings according to the activity that gave rise to them. The standard headings required in a cash flow statement are:

(a)   operating activities
(b)   dividends from joint ventures and associates (relevant for group cash flow statements only)
(c)   returns on investments and servicing of finance
(d)   taxation
(e)   capital expenditure and financial investment
(f)   acquisitions and disposals
(g)   equity dividends paid
(h)   management of liquid resources
(i)   financing.

The objective of the standard headings is to ensure that cash flows are reported in a form that highlights the significant components of cash flow and facilitates comparison of the cash flow performance of different businesses.

Cash flows relating to the management of liquid resources and financing can be combined under a single heading provided that the cash flows relating to each are shown separately and separate subtotals are given.

Each cash flow should be classified according to the substance of the transaction giving rise to it. The substance of a transaction determines the most appropriate standard heading under which to report cash flows that are not specified in the standard categories.

1.3   Definitions

The definition of cash is central to the preparation and interpretation of cash flow statements.

> [Definition]   **Cash** is cash in hand and deposits repayable on demand with any qualifying financial institution, less overdrafts from any qualifying financial institution repayable on demand. Deposits are repayable on demand if they can be withdrawn at any time without notice and without penalty or if a maturity or period of notice of not more than 24 hours or one working day has been agreed. Cash includes cash in hand and deposits denominated in foreign currencies.

> [Definition]   An **overdraft** is a borrowing facility repayable on demand that is used by drawing on a current account with a qualifying financial institution.

> [Definition]   A **qualifying financial institution** is an entity that as part of its business receives deposits or other repayable funds and grants credits for its own account.

> [Definition]   **Cash flow** is an increase or decrease in an amount of cash.

The bottom line in the cash flow statement is the **total cash flow** for the period, in other words, the total increase or decrease in the amount of cash.

The practical effect of these definitions is that the cash flow statement reports inflows and outflows of 'pure' cash. Short term deposits and loans are not included within the definitions.

1.4   Illustration

The following illustration is included in FRS 1. It shows a cash flow statement for a single company. It illustrates the standard headings and examples of items within the standard headings.

The illustration includes the reconciliations and notes required by FRS 1. The reconciliations may be shown adjoining the cash flow statement or in the notes. If they adjoin the cash flow statement they should be clearly labelled and kept separate.

Note 1 gives the components of the net cash flows reported under each heading. These can be shown on the face of the cash flow statement or in the notes.

XYZ LTD

CASH FLOW STATEMENT FOR YEAR ENDED 31 DECEMBER 19X6

Reconciliation of operating profit to net cash inflow from operating activities

	£'000
Operating profit	6,022
Depreciation charges	899
Increase in stocks	(194)
Increase in debtors	(72)
Increase in creditors	234
Net cash inflow from operating activities	6,889

CASH FLOW STATEMENT

	£'000
Net cash inflow from operating activities	6,889
Returns on investments and servicing of finance (note 1)	2,999
Taxation	(2,922)
Capital expenditure (note 1)	(1,525)
	5,441
Equity dividends paid	(2,417)
	3,024
Management of liquid resources (note 1)	(450)
Financing (note 1)	57
Increase in cash	2,631

Reconciliation of net cash flow to movement in net debt (note 2)

	£'000
Increase in cash in the period	2,631
Cash to repurchase debenture	149
Cash used to increase liquid resources	450
Change in net debt	3,230
Net debt at 1 Jan 19X6	(2,903)
Net funds at 31 Dec 19X6	327

Notes to Cash Flow Statement

(1)   **Gross cash flows**

	£'000	£'000
Returns on investments and servicing of finance		
Interest received	3,011	
Interest paid	(12)	
		2,999
Capital expenditure		
Payments to acquire intangible fixed assets	(71)	
Payments to acquire tangible fixed assets	(1,496)	
Receipts from sales of tangible fixed assets	42	
		(1,525)
Management of liquid resources		
Purchase of treasury bills	(650)	
Sale of treasury bills	200	
		(450)
Financing		
Issue of ordinary share capital		211
Repurchase of debenture loan		(149)
Expenses paid in connection with share issues		(5)
		57

(2)   **Analysis of changes in net debt**

	At 1 Jan 19X6 £'000	Cash flows £'000	Other changes £'000	At 31 Dec 19X6 £'000
Cash in hand, at bank	42	847		889
Overdrafts	(1,784)	1,784		
		2,631		
Debts due within 1 year	(149)	149	(230)	(230)
Debts due after 1 year	(1,262)		230	(1,032)
Current asset investments	250	450		700
Total	(2,903)	3,230	–	327

2   CLASSIFICATION OF CASH FLOWS

2.1   Operating activities

Standard accounting practice

Cash flows from operating activities are in general the cash effects of transactions and other events relating to operating or trading activities. Net cash flow from operating activities represents the net increase or decrease in cash resulting from the operations shown in the profit and loss account in arriving at operating profit.

Operating cash flows may be reported in the cash flow statement on a net or gross basis.

A reconciliation between the operating profit (for non-financial companies normally profit before interest) reported in the profit and loss account and the net cash flow from operating activities should be given.   This reconciliation should disclose separately the movements in stocks, debtors and creditors related to operating activities and other differences between cash flows and profits.

There are two main methods for reporting net cash flow from operating activities.

The **direct method** shows operating cash receipts and payments (including, in particular, cash receipts from customers, cash payments to suppliers and cash payments to and on behalf of employees), aggregating to the net cash flow from operating activities.

The **indirect method** starts with operating profit and adjusts it for non-cash charges and credits to reconcile it to the net cash flow from operating activities.

A comparison of the two methods is shown below.   The methods differ only as regards the derivation of the item 'Net cash inflow from operating activities'. Subsequent inflows and outflows are the same.

Direct method		Indirect method	
	£'000		£'000
Cash received from customers	15,424	Operating profit	6,022
Cash payments to suppliers	(5,824)	Depreciation charges	899
Cash paid to and on behalf of employees	(2,200)	Increase in stocks	(194)
		Increase in debtors	(72)
Other cash payments	(511)	Increase in creditors	234

Net cash inflow from operating activities	6,889		6,889

The principal advantage of the direct method is that it shows operating cash receipts and payments. Knowledge of the specific sources of cash receipts and the purposes for which cash payments were made in past periods may be useful in assessing future cash flows.   However, the ASB does not believe at present that in all cases the benefits to users of this information outweigh the costs to the reporting entity of providing it and, therefore, has not required the information to be given.

The principal advantage of the indirect method is that it highlights the differences between operating profit and net cash flow from operating activities.   Many users of financial statements believe that such a reconciliation is essential to give an indication of the quality of the reporting entity's earnings.   Some investors and creditors assess future cash flows by estimating future income and then allowing for accruals adjustments;   thus information about past accruals adjustments may be useful to help estimate future adjustments.

Accordingly, the FRS requires the cash flow statement to show the net cash flow from operating activities, supplemented by a reconciliation of operating profit for the period to the net cash flow from operating activities.   The result is that reporting entities **must** give the information required by the indirect method and that they **may** also give the information required by the direct method.

2.2   Calculation of net cash flow from operating activities

Operating profit is computed using the accruals concept; net cash flow from operating activities only records the cash inflows and outflows arising out of trading.   Net cash inflow can be derived:

(a)   from the accounting records of the entity by totalling the cash receipts and payments directly; or

(b)   operating profit can be adjusted by the relevant amounts in the profit and loss account and the opening and closing balance sheets which represent the differences between cash flows and amounts accrued.

In most situations the latter approach is quicker and easier. It also results in the production of the reconciliation statement which is required.

The main categories of items in the profit and loss account and on a balance sheet which form part of the reconciliation between operating profit and net cash flow from operating activities are:

(a)   **Depreciation**

Depreciation is a book write off of capital expenditure. Capital expenditure will be recorded under 'capital expenditure' at the time of the cash outflow. Depreciation therefore represents an **addition** to operating profit in deriving cash inflow.

(b)   **Profit/loss on disposal of fixed asset**

The cash inflow from a sale needs to be recorded under 'capital expenditure'. Following the issue of FRS 3, most profits and losses on disposal are no longer included in operating profit, but occasionally it may be necessary to adjust operating profit. A loss on disposal is added to operating profit; a profit on disposal is deducted from operating profit.

(c)   **Balance sheet change in debtors**

A sale once made creates income irrespective of the date of cash receipt. If the cash has not been received by the balance sheet date however there is no cash inflow from operating activities for the current accounting period. Similarly opening debtors represent sales of a previous accounting period most of which will be cash receipts in the current period.

The **change** between opening and closing debtors will thus represent the adjustment required to move from operating profit to net cash inflow.

- An increase in debtors is a deduction from operating profit. More sales are not being received in cash in the current period than are being brought forward from the previous period.

- A decrease in debtors is an addition to operating profit.

(d)   **Balance sheet change in stocks**

Stock at the balance sheet date represents a purchase which has not actually been charged against current operating profits. As however cash was spent on its purchase or a creditor incurred, it does represent an actual or potential cash outflow. Strictly, the amount of stock paid for in cash should be calculated and operating profit adjusted by the movement in such stocks between the two balance sheet dates. A corresponding adjustment would be made to creditors (see below) to the extent that the expense relating to such creditors will not have been charged in the profit and loss account.

In practice the overall movement in stock would be taken due to:

- the practical difficulties of determining how much stock has not been paid for at the balance sheet date; and

- the advantages of showing an adjustment to profit which corresponds to movements in stock as shown on the balance sheet.

(e)   **Balance sheet change in creditors**

A purchase represents the incurring of expenditure and a charge or potential charge to the profit and loss account. It does not represent a cash outflow until paid. To the extent that a purchase results in a charge to the profit and loss account:

- An increase in creditors between two balance sheet dates is an addition to operating profit.

- A decrease in creditors is a deduction from operating profit.

If the purchase does not result in a charge to the profit and loss account in the current year, the corresponding creditor is not included in the reconciliation of operating profit to net cash inflow. For example a fixed asset creditor is not included. As has already been stated in (d) above a creditor for purchases which form part of stock at the balance sheet date, should also not be included but in practice will be.

2.3   Activity

A new business made operating profits of £300,000 in its first year. Extracts from the closing balance sheet are given below. Calculate the net cash inflow from operating activities.

	£
Debtors	125,000
Stocks	118,000
Creditors	135,000

	£
An analysis of creditors showed:	
For raw materials	102,700
For fixed asset	12,000
For various expenses	13,500
Accruals	6,800

2.4   Activity solution

	£
Operating profit	300,000
Increase in stocks	(118,000)
Increase in debtors	(125,000)
Increase in creditors (135 – 12)	123,000
Net cash inflow from operating activities	180,000

The calculation also forms the reconciliation of operating profit to net cash inflow.

To show the real adjustments from operating profit to net cash inflow relating to stocks and creditors a calculation would be required of the amount of stocks which have not been paid for. If this information has been obtained in the above example, say £50,000, the reconciliation statement becomes:

	£
Operating profit	300,000
Increase in stocks (118 – 50)	(68,000)
Increase in debtors	(125,000)
Increase in creditors (135 – 12 – 50)	73,000
Net cash inflow from operating activities	180,000

2.5   Calculation of gross cash flows from operating activities (the direct method)

As previously stated, reporting entities may use the direct method for reporting net cash flow from operating activities. The relevant cash flows can be derived:

(a)   from the accounting records of the entity by totalling the cash receipts and payments directly; or

(b)   from the opening and closing balance sheets and profit and loss account for the year by constructing summary control accounts for:

- sales (to derive cash received from customers)
- purchases (to derive cash payments to suppliers)
- wages (to derive cash paid to and on behalf of employees)

The methods are illustrated later as VAT needs to be considered; see 2.10 below.

2.6   Returns on investments and servicing of finance

'Returns on investments and servicing of finance' are receipts resulting from the ownership of an investment and payments to providers of finance; non-equity shareholders (eg, the holders of preference shares) and minority interests, excluding those items required to be classified under another heading.

Cash inflows from returns on investments and servicing of finance include:

(a)   interest received, including any related tax recovered;

(b)   dividends received net of any tax credits.

Cash outflows from returns on investments and servicing of finance include:

(a)   interest paid (even if capitalised), including any tax deducted and paid to the relevant tax authority;

(b)   cash flows that are treated as finance costs under FRS 4;

(c)   the interest element of finance lease rental payments;

(d)   dividends paid on non-equity shares of the entity.

The ASB believes that the presentation of net cash flow from operating activities should not be affected by the capital structure of the reporting entity. Thus payments resulting from the servicing of finance ie, interest and non-equity dividends paid should be shown together.

Interest and dividend receipts for a trading company may arise from long term investing activities, temporary investment of surplus funds or perhaps operating activities. The different categories would often be difficult to analyse and so the receipts are grouped together.

It follows from the above classification that cash flow from operating activities shown in the reconciliation of operating profit to net cash inflow is stated before interest receipts and payments.

2.7   Taxation

Standard accounting practice

The cash flows included under the heading taxation are cash flows to or from taxation authorities in respect of the reporting entity's revenue and capital profits. Cash flows in respect of value added tax are dealt with separately (see below).

Taxation is given a separate category in the cash flow statement as the taxation cash flows of a reporting entity in relation to revenue and capital profits may result from complex computations that are affected by the operating, investing and financing activities of an entity. The ASB believes that it is not useful to divide taxation cash flows into constituent parts relating to the activities that gave rise to them because the apportionment will, in many cases, have to be made on an arbitrary basis.

Computation of tax paid

In many statements there will only be one figure shown; the UK corporation tax paid in the year. Some companies may have overseas tax paid which it may be appropriate to disclose separately.

The creation of a taxation account recording all opening and closing tax balances relating to corporation tax is often the easiest way to derive the tax paid for the year.

2.8   Activity

Extracts from X Ltd's profit and loss account for the year ended 31 December 19X8 show:

	£	£
Turnover		X
Costs		X
Dividends received		125,000
Profit on ordinary activities before taxation		X
Taxation:		
Corporation tax	300,000	
Deferred tax	50,000	
Tax credits on dividends received	25,000	
		375,000
Dividends:		
Interim	96,000	
Final	240,000	
		336,000

Extracts from X Ltd's balance sheets are:

	31 December 19X7 £	19X8 £
Creditors: amounts falling due within one year:		
Corporation tax	170,000	331,000
Provisions for liabilities and charges:		
Deferred tax	110,000	130,000

Calculate the amount of tax paid by X Ltd in the year.

2.9   Activity solution

Taxation account

	£		£
Tax paid (bal fig)	169,000	Balances b/d	
Balances c/d		Corporation tax	170,000
Corporation tax	331,000	Deferred tax	110,000
Deferred tax	130,000	Profit and loss:	
		Corporation tax	300,000
		Deferred tax	50,000
	630,000		630,000

There is sufficient information to compute the tax paid in the year directly, but it is often easier to compute tax as a balancing figure rather than directly. All tax items are inserted into a tax account except tax credits on dividend income as the tax credits are merely a debit and credit on the face of the profit and loss account.

2.10   VAT

The existence of VAT raises the question of whether the relevant cash flows should be reported gross or net of the tax element and how the balance of tax paid to, or repaid by, the taxing authorities should be reported.

The cash flows of an entity include VAT where appropriate and thus strictly the various elements of the cash flow statement should include VAT. However, this treatment does not take into account the fact that normally VAT is a short-term timing difference as far as the entity's overall cash flows are concerned and the inclusion of VAT in the cash flows may distort the allocation of cash flows to standard headings.

In order to avoid this distortion and to show cash flows attributable to the reporting entity's activities, FRS 1 requires amounts to be shown net of sales taxes and the net movement on the amount payable to, or receivable from, the taxing authority should be allocated to cash flows from operating activities unless a different treatment is more appropriate in the particular circumstances concerned. The following example illustrates a method that can be adopted.

2.11   Example

The balance sheets of a business are:

	Last year £	This year £
Fixed assets	153,364	149,364
Stocks	-	-
Debtors	265,840	346,000
Cash	-	165,166
Creditors	(219,204)	(318,890)
	200,000	341,640
Share capital	200,000	200,000
Reserves	-	141,640
	200,000	341,640

Creditors consist of:

(a)   creditors from purchases ledger;

(b)   VAT creditor;

(c)   PAYE/NI creditor.

The summarised control accounts of the business are shown below. All sales and purchases are at a 17.5% VAT rate.

Sales ledger control

	£		£
Balance b/d – Debtors	265,840	Cash receipts	1,787,440
Sales	1,867,600	Balance c/d – Debtors	346,000
	2,133,440		2,133,440

Purchases ledger control

	£		£
Cash paid	1,336,300	Balance b/d – Creditors	198,400
		Purchases	
Balance c/d		– cost of sales	1,200,650
– fixed asset creditor	46,000	– administration	112,890
– other	223,640	– fixed assets	94,000
	1,605,940		1,605,940

VAT

	£		£
VAT on purchases	209,633	Balance b/d	
Cash paid	46,084	– VAT owing	12,164
Balance c/d		VAT on sales	278,153
– VAT owing	34,600		
	290,317		290,317

Wages control

	£		£
Net wages paid	175,390	Balance b/d	
PAYE and NI	64,500	PAYE and NI	8,640
Balance c/d		Cost of sales	145,900
PAYE and NI	14,650	Administration	100,000
	254,540		254,540

Extracts from the profit and loss account for the year are:

	£	£
Sales		1,589,447
Cost of sales		
Purchases (no stocks)	1,021,830	
Wages and salaries	145,900	
Depreciation	84,000	
		(1,251,730)
Administration		
Purchases	96,077	
Salaries	100,000	
		(196,077)
Operating profit and retained profit for the year		141,640

Prepare the cash flow statement using the direct method and a note reconciling operating profit to net cash inflow from operating activities.

2.12   Solution

 Step 1   **Calculate the cash received from customers**

The sales ledger control account shows cash receipts at £1,787,440. This sum includes VAT at 17.5%. Excluding VAT gives:

$$\frac{100}{117.5} \times 1{,}787{,}440 = £1{,}521{,}226$$

However this figure does not reflect that VAT is accounted for on sales when invoiced. Thus VAT on sales is removed (ie, as per the VAT account) rather than VAT on sales receipts.

	£
Cash receipts	1,787,440
Less: VAT on sales	278,153
(which as all sales are standard rated can be computed from	
the profit and loss account: 1,589,447 × 17.5%)	
	1,509,287

An alternative approach, which is easier to adopt if control accounts have not been provided is to reconstruct a control account from the balance sheets and the profit and loss account with the effect that the balancing figure of cash received will be the correct figure to use without any further calculation.

Thus in the example, a sales ledger control constructed from the final accounts would show:

Sales ledger control

	£		£
Balance b/d	265,840		
(Debtors include VAT)		Cash receipts (bal fig)	1,509,287
Sales from profit and			
loss account	1,589,447	Balance c/d	346,000
(therefore excluding VAT)			
	1,855,287		1,855,287

The balancing figure has effectively been calculated as gross cash receipts less VAT on sales invoiced.

[Step 2]   **Calculate cash payments to suppliers**

Similar principles apply to the calculation of cash received from customers. In addition however care needs to be taken to exclude capital expenditure purchases as they are not a cash outflow from operating activities.

		£	£
Cash payments per control account			1,336,300
Less: Payments for fixed asset (94,000 – 46,000)			(48,000)
			1,288,300
Less:	VAT on purchases per VAT account	209,633	
Less:	VAT on capital purchases		
	$\frac{17.5}{117.5} \times 94{,}000$	(14,000)	
			(195,633)
			1,092,667

[Step 3]   **Now deal with 'other items'**

'Other items' is the movement in the VAT creditor (34,600 – 12,164) £22,436. This could be netted off against cash payments to suppliers.

The adjustment is required because receipts and payments are being shown net of VAT (see the extract from FRS 1).

Step 4   **Calculate the change in creditors**

The change in creditors included in the reconciliation statement includes trade creditors (excluding fixed asset creditors) and any accruals relating to wages and salaries.

The change in VAT creditor is also included. Although cash receipts from customers and cash paid to suppliers are required by FRS 1 to be shown on a VAT exclusive basis the VAT movement also has to be allocated to operating activities.

	Last year £	This year £
Trade creditors	198,400	223,640
PAYE/NI	8,640	14,650
VAT	12,164	34,600
	219,204	272,890
Increase		53,686

Step 5   **Calculate the expenditure on fixed assets**

Fixed assets purchased per the purchases ledger control account are £94,000. This sum includes VAT. The VAT exclusive price is £80,000. This amount agrees with the movement in fixed assets per the balance sheets:

Fixed assets (NBV)

	£		£
Balance b/d – Debtors	153,364	Depreciation charge	84,000
Addition (bal fig)	80,000	Balance c/d	149,364
	233,364		233,364

There is a creditor at the year end. Cash expenditure is thus (80,000 – 46,000) £34,000. This does not represent the genuine cash payment as the £80,000 excludes VAT but the £46,000 includes VAT. It is however the same method by which cash payments to suppliers has been derived in gross operating cash flows ie, cash paid equals:

	£
Purchases net of VAT	80,000
Movement in purchases creditor	46,000
	34,000

Step 6   **The cash flow statement can now be prepared**

Extract from cash flow statement

	£
Operating activities	
Cash received from customers	1,509,287
Cash payments to suppliers	(1,092,667)
Cash paid to and on behalf of employees	
(175,390 + 64,500)	(239,890)
Other items	22,436
	————
Net cash inflow from operating activities	199,166
Capital expenditure	
Purchase of fixed assets	(34,000)
	————
Increase in cash	165,166
	————

Reconciliation of operating profit to net cash inflow from operating activities

	£
Operating profit	141,640
Depreciation charges	84,000
Increase in stock	-
Increase in debtors	(80,160)
Increase in creditors	53,686
	————
	199,166
	————

2.13   Capital expenditure and financial investment

The cash flows included in 'capital expenditure and financial investment' are those related to the acquisition or disposal of any fixed asset other than one required to be classified under 'acquisitions and disposals' and any current asset investment not included in liquid resources. (Acquisitions and disposals and liquid resources are explained below.)

If no cash flows relating to financial investment fall to be included under this heading the caption may be reduced to 'capital expenditure'.

Cash inflows from capital expenditure and financial investment include:

(a)   receipts from sales or disposals of property, plant or equipment; and

(b)   receipts from the repayment of the reporting entity's loans to other entities or sales of debt instruments of other entities other than receipts forming part of an acquisition or disposal or a movement in liquid resources.

Cash outflows from capital expenditure and financial investment include:

(a)   payments to acquire property, plant or equipment; and

(b)   loans made by the reporting entity and payments to acquire debt instruments of other entities other than payments forming part of an acquisition or disposal or a movement in liquid resources.

2.14   Acquisitions and disposals

The cash flows included in 'acquisitions and disposals' are those related to the acquisition or disposal of any trade or business, or of an investment in an entity that is, or, as a result of the transaction, becomes or ceases to be either an associate, a joint venture, or a subsidiary undertaking.

Cash inflows from acquisitions and disposals include:

(a)   receipts from sales of investments in subsidiary undertakings, showing separately any balances of cash and overdrafts transferred as part of the sale;

(b)   receipts from sales of investments in associates or joint ventures; and

(c)   receipts from sales of trades or businesses.

Cash outflows from acquisitions and disposals include:

(a)   payments to acquire investments in subsidiary undertakings, showing separately any balances of cash and overdrafts acquired;

(b)   payments to acquire investments in associates and joint ventures; and

(c)   payments to acquire trades or businesses.

It follows that this caption does not normally appear in the cash flow statement of a single company. The exception would be if a company had acquired or disposed of an unincorporated business during the period.

Under the previous version of FRS 1, capital expenditure and acquisitions and disposals were reported together under the same caption, 'investing activities'.

Entities undertake investing activities in order to maintain the current level of operations and sometimes to expand the current level of operations. The cash flow statement does not distinguish between different types of investing activity, on the grounds that this is not feasible.

However, when the ASB revised FRS 1, it recognised that useful information would be provided by analysing investing activities into capital expenditure and acquisitions and disposals of investments. The notes to the FRS state that 'this distinction should not be interpreted as reflecting on the one hand maintenance expenditure and on the other expenditure for expansion because, depending on the circumstances, these may be included under either heading'.

2.15   Equity dividends paid

The cash outflows included in 'equity dividends paid' are dividends paid on the reporting entity's, or, in a group, the parent's equity shares.

This is another change introduced by the revised FRS. Previously, all dividends paid or received were reported under 'returns on investments and servicing of finance'.

Equity dividends paid are now reported separately from interest and other dividends paid to highlight the fact that payment of equity dividends is discretionary. In contrast, an entity has no discretion over the amount or the timing of interest payable and no discretion over the amount of non-equity dividends.

Equity and non-equity shares are defined in accordance with FRS 4 *Capital instruments.*

2.16   Management of liquid resources

The 'management of liquid resources' section should include cash flows in respect of liquid resources as defined below.

Definition   **Liquid resources** are current asset investments held in readily disposable stores of value. A readily disposable investment is one that:

(a)   is disposable by the reporting entity without curtailing or disrupting its business;

and is either:

(b)(i)   readily convertible into known amounts of cash at or close to its carrying amount; or

(b)(ii)   traded in an active market.

This definition does not specify the type of investment that would be classed as a liquid resource. Instead it has been drafted in general terms, in order to emphasise the liquidity of the investment and its function as a readily disposable store of value. In practice, term deposits, government securities, loan stock, equities and derivatives might form part of an entity's liquid resources. Short term deposits would also fall within the definition. Because of the requirement that they should be readily convertible into known amounts of cash at or close to their carrying amount, deposits that are more than one year from maturity on acquisition would not normally be classed as liquid resources.

Each entity should explain what it includes as liquid resources and any changes in its policy.

Cash inflows in management of liquid resources include:

(a)   withdrawals from short term deposits not qualifying as cash in so far as not netted (see below); and

(b)   inflows from disposal or redemption of any other investments held as liquid resources.

Cash outflows in management of liquid resources include:

(a)   payments into short term deposits not qualifying as cash in so far as not netted; and

(b)   outflows to acquire any other investments held as liquid resources.

Cash inflows and outflows within the management of liquid resources may be netted against each other if they are due to short maturities and high turnover occurring from rollover or reissue (for example, short term deposits).

This section of the cash flow statement has been introduced by the revised version of FRS 1. It is designed to provide information about the way that entities manage their cash and similar assets. It distinguishes cash flows in relation to cash management from cash flows arising from other investment decisions (for example, the acquisition and disposal of fixed asset investments).

Liquid resources include many of the items which would have been classified as 'cash equivalents' under the 'old' version of FRS 1.

2.17   Financing

Financing cash flows comprise receipts or repayments of principal from or to external providers of finance.

Financing cash inflows include:

(a)   receipts from issuing shares or other equity instruments; and

(b)   receipts from issuing debentures, loans, notes and bonds and from other long term and short term borrowings (other than overdrafts).

Financing cash outflows include:

(a)   repayments of amounts borrowed (other than overdrafts);

(b)   the capital element of finance lease rental payments;

(c)   payments to reacquire or redeem the entity's shares; and

(d)   payments of expenses or commissions on any issue of equity shares.

2.18   Example

Extracts from the opening and closing balance sheets of a company show:

	31.12.19X8	31.12.19X9
	£'000	£'000
Creditors: amounts falling due after more than one year		
10% convertible unsecured loan stock	434	280
12% Debenture	-	158
Share capital and reserves:		
Ordinary shares of £1 each	150	296
8% convertible preference shares	30	30
Share premium	78	130

During the year the following events occurred:

(a)   £48,000 of 10% convertible unsecured loan stock was converted into 16,000 ordinary shares; the remaining reduction represents the purchase and cancellation of the loan stock by the company for total consideration of £90,000.

(b)   A bonus issue of one for five ordinary shares (in issue at beginning of the year) was made from share premium.

(c)   A fresh issue of ordinary shares was made to provide further funds.

Prepare the financing section of the cash flow statement.

2.19   Solution

The financing section of the cash flow statement would appear as follows:

	£'000	£'000
Financing:		
Issue of debentures	158	
Issue of shares	150	
Purchase of loan stock	(90)	
Net cash inflow from financing		218

WORKING

Changes in financing during the year

	Ordinary share capital	Pref. share capital	Share premium	Loans
	£'000	£'000	£'000	£'000
Balance at 1 Jan 19X9	150	30	78	434
Conversion of loan stock	16		32	(48)
Issue of debentures				158
Bonus issue	30		(30)	
Purchase of loan stock				
− consideration				(90)
− par value (434 − 48 − 280) = 106				
− profit on repurchase (106 − 90)				(16)
Share issue (bal fig)	100		50	
Balance at 31 Dec 19X9	296	30	130	438

(Tutorial note: the conversion of £48,000 nominal value of loan stock into £16,000 nominal value of shares means that the premium on issue of the shares is the difference between the two nominal values.*)*

3   NET DEBT, EXCEPTIONAL ITEMS AND NON-CASH TRANSACTIONS

3.1   Reconciliation of movements in net debt

FRS 1 requires a note reconciling the movement of cash in the period with the movement in net debt. (An example of this reconciliation was illustrated earlier in the chapter.) This reconciliation can be given either adjoining the cash flow statement or in a note. If the reconciliation adjoins the cash flow statement, it should be clearly labelled and kept separate.

The objective of the reconciliation is to provide information that assists in the assessment of liquidity, solvency and financial adaptability.

Definition	**Net debt** is the borrowings of the reporting entity (comprising debt as defined in FRS 4, together with related derivatives and obligations under finance leases) less cash and liquid resources. Where cash and liquid resources exceed the borrowings of the entity reference should be made to 'net funds' rather than to 'net debt'.

Non-equity shares of the entity are excluded from net debt because, although these have features that may be similar to those of borrowings, they are not actually liabilities of the entity. (This distinction between liabilities and non-equity shares is consistent with the requirements of FRS 4.)

The definition also excludes debtors and creditors because, while these are short term claims on and sources of finance to the entity, their main role is as part of the entity's trading activities. (Movements in debtors and creditors are dealt with as part of operating activities.)

The changes in net debt should be analysed from the opening to the closing component amounts showing separately, where material, changes resulting from:

(a)   the cash flows of the entity;
(b)   the acquisition or disposal of subsidiary undertakings;
(c)   other non-cash changes; and
(d)   the recognition of changes in market value and exchange rate movements.

Where several balance sheet amounts or parts thereof have to be combined to form the components of opening and closing net debt, sufficient detail should be shown to enable the cash and other components of net debt to be traced back to amounts shown under the equivalent captions in the balance sheet. This is done by means of a note analysing net debt.

3.2   Example

Extracts from the opening and closing balance sheets of a company show:

	31 Dec 19X8	31 Dec 19X9
	£'000	£'000
Current assets		
Investments - Government stock	118	74
Cash at bank	40	5
Creditors: amounts falling due within one year		
Loan	120	100
Overdraft	-	47
Creditors: amounts falling due after more than one year		
Loan	100	-

(a)   The government stock consists of a number of holdings all of which were made with a view to disposal by the company within two months of acquisition.

(b)   The loan was originally made in December 19X8 with repayments required of £20,000 every two months.

(c)   The overdraft is repayable on demand.

Show the cash flow for the year ended 31 December 19X9, the reconciliation of net cash flow to movement in net debt and the note analysing movements in net debt.

3.3   Solution

	£'000
Decrease in cash for the year (40 − 5 + 47)	82

Reconciliation of net cash flow to movement in net debt (note)

Decrease in cash in the period	(82)
Cash outflow from decrease in debt	120
Cash inflow from sale of liquid resources (118 − 74)	(44)
Change in net debt	(6)
Net debt at 1 January 19X9	(62)
Net debt at 31 December 19X9	(68)

Analysis of changes in net debt

	At 1 Jan 19X9 £'000	Cash flows £'000	Other changes £'000	At 31 Dec 19X9 £'000
Cash at bank	40	(35)		5
Overdrafts	-	(47)		(47)
		(82)		
Debts due within 1 year	(120)	120	(100)	(100)
Debts due after 1 year	(100)		100	-
Current asset investments	118	(44)		74
Total	(62)	(6)	-	(68)

3.4   Exceptional items

Exceptional items in the profit and loss account

Where cash flows relate to items that are classified as exceptional or extraordinary in the profit and loss account they should be shown under the appropriate standard headings, according to the nature of each item. The cash flows relating to exceptional or extraordinary items should be identified in the cash flow statement or a note to it and the relationship between the cash flows and the originating exceptional or extraordinary item should be explained.

Discontinued operations and provisions

Re-organisation charges that are exceptional must be disclosed separately and explained.

Cash flows in respect of operating items relating to provisions are included in operating activities, even if the provision was not included in operating profit. Examples of such cash flows are redundancy payments falling under a provision for the termination of an operation or for a fundamental reorganisation or restructuring, also operating item cash flows provided for on an acquisition.

Exceptional cash flows

Where cash flows are exceptional because of their size or incidence but are not related to items that are treated as exceptional or extraordinary in the profit and loss account, sufficient disclosure should be given to explain their cause and nature.

For a cash flow to be exceptional on the grounds of its size alone, it must be exceptional in relation to cash flows of a similar nature.

3.5   Major non-cash transactions

Standard accounting practice

'Material transactions not resulting in movements of cash of the reporting entity should be disclosed in the notes to the cash flow statement if disclosure is necessary for an understanding of the underlying transactions.'

Consideration for transactions may be in a form other than cash. The purpose of a cash flow statement is to report cash flows and non-cash transactions should, therefore, not be reported in a cash flow statement.   However, to obtain a full picture of the alterations in financial position caused by the transactions for the period, separate disclosure of material non-cash transactions is also necessary.

Examples of non cash transactions are:

(a)   certain acquisitions and disposals of subsidiaries by a group;

(b)   finance leases;

(c)   certain changes in debt and equity.

3.6   HP and finance leases

Hire purchase and finance leases are accounted for by the lessee/purchaser capitalising the present value of the minimum lease payments. A liability and a corresponding asset are produced which do not reflect cash flows in the accounting period.

The cash flow statement records the cash flow, ie, the rentals paid. As each rental represents a payment of interest and capital FRS 1 requires a split between the two elements:

(a)   the interest element shown under servicing of finance;

(b)   the capital element shown under financing.

The interest element will already be computed as it is charged (and disclosed in the financial statements) in arriving at profit before taxation.   Deducting the interest charge from rentals paid provides the capital paid in the year.

Note that the above paragraph assumes that rentals are paid frequently eg, monthly, and there is thus effectively no/little difference between interest charged against profits for a twelve month period and interest within the rentals **paid** over a twelve month period. If the rental payment dates do not closely coincide with the end of an accounting period, it may be necessary to compute the interest element relating to rentals actually paid.

The non-cash flow elements of a finance lease may need to be disclosed:

(a)   if the finance lease is of such significance that it is classified as a major non-cash transaction; and/or

(b)   in the note reconciling the net cash flow to the movement in net debt (as the finance lease liability may have been aggregated with eg, bank loans on the balance sheet).

3.7   Example

A company entered into a number of finance leases during the current year. There were no such leases in the previous year.

Extracts from the accounts show:

Extracts from balance sheets

	31 Dec 19X2	31 Dec 19X1
	£'000	£'000
Fixed assets:		
Leased property under finance lease	5,710	4,000
Less: Accumulated depreciation	1,714	1,000
	3,996	3,000
Liabilities:		
Non-current obligations under finance leases	3,251	2,645
Current obligations under finance leases	1,315	1,150
	4,566	3,795

Notes to the accounts - Profit and loss account

Profit is stated after charging:

	£'000
Depreciation of owned assets	2,300
Depreciation of assets held under finance leases	714
Finance charges payable:	
Finance leases	856
Interest	1,325
Hire of plant and machinery - operating leases	360
Hire of other assets - operating leases	190

Produce extracts from the cash flow statement as far as information is available.

3.8   Solution

Extract from cash flow statement for year ended 31 December 19X2

	£'000
Returns on investments and servicing of finance:	
Interest element of finance lease rentals	(856)
Interest paid	(1,325)
Financing:	
Capital element of finance lease rentals (working)	(939)

WORKING

(Note: grouping the current and non-current obligations together and deriving new finance leases from the increase in fixed asset cost allows the capital element of the rentals to be computed as a balancing figure.

Operating leases are treated like any other expense.*)*

Obligations under finance leases

	£'000		£'000
Capital element of rentals		Balance b/d	
paid in year	939	Current and non current	3,795
Balance b/d		New finance leases	
Current and non current	4,566	(from fixed asset increase)	1,710
	5,505		5,505

4   SCOPE OF FRS 1

FRS 1 applies to all financial statements intended to give a true and fair view of the financial position and profit or loss (or income and expenditure) except those of:

(a)   subsidiary undertakings where 90 per cent or more of the voting rights are controlled within the group, provided that consolidated financial statements in which the subsidiary undertakings are included are publicly available.

(b)   companies incorporated under companies legislation and entitled to the exemptions available in the legislation for small companies when filing accounts with the Registrar of Companies.

(c)   entities that would have been in category (b) above if they were companies incorporated under companies legislation.

(d)   mutual life assurance companies, pension funds, some open-ended investment funds and some building societies.

FRS 1 exempts subsidiary undertakings where 90% or more of the voting rights in the subsidiary are controlled within its group. In this situation, it is likely that the liquidity, solvency and financial adaptability of the subsidiary will depend upon the group, rather than its own cash flows. Groups often have centralised cash management operations and cash balances can be moved around a group rapidly. For this reason, historical cash flow information of individual group companies does not always contribute to an assessment of future cash flows.

5   USEFULNESS OF THE CASH FLOW STATEMENT

5.1   Advantages of the cash flow statement

A cash flow statement can provide information which is not available from balance sheets and profit and loss accounts.

(a)   It may assist users of financial statements in making judgements on the amount, timing and degree of certainty of future cash flows.

(b)   It gives an indication of the relationship between profitability and cash generating ability, and thus of the quality of the profit earned.

(c)   Analysts and other users of financial information often, formally or informally, develop models to assess and compare the present value of the future cash flow of entities. Historical cash flow information could be useful to check the accuracy of past assessments.

(d)   A cash flow statement in conjunction with a balance sheet provides information on liquidity, viability and adaptability. The balance sheet is often used to obtain information on liquidity, but the information is incomplete for this purpose as the balance sheet is drawn up at a particular point in time.

(e)   Cash flow cannot easily be manipulated and is not affected by judgement or by accounting policies.

5.2   Limitations of the cash flow statement

Cash flow statements should normally be used in conjunction with profit and loss accounts and balance sheets when making an assessment of future cash flows.

(a)   Cash flow statements are based on historical information and therefore do not provide complete information for assessing future cash flows.

(b)   There is some scope for manipulation of cash flows. For example, a business may delay paying creditors until after the year-end, or it may structure transactions so that the cash balance is favourably affected. It can be argued that cash management is an important aspect of stewardship and therefore desirable. However, more deliberate manipulation is possible (eg, assets may be sold and then immediately repurchased). Following the issue of FRS 5 *Reporting the substance of transactions* users of the financial statements will be alerted to the true nature of such arrangements.

(c)   Cash flow is necessary for survival in the short term, but in order to survive in the long term a business must be profitable. It is often necessary to sacrifice cash flow in the short term in order to generate profits in the long term (eg, by investment in fixed assets). A huge cash balance is not a sign of good management if the cash could be invested elsewhere to generate profit.

Neither cash flow nor profit provide a complete picture of a company's performance when looked at in isolation.

5.3   The strict cash approach

Cash is very narrowly defined in FRS 1 (revised). It does not include investments or short term deposits, however liquid or near maturity. The effect of this definition is that the bottom line of the cash flow statement shows the increase or decrease in 'pure' cash for the period.

Under the original version of FRS 1, the cash flow statement showed the movement in cash and cash equivalents. Cash equivalents were defined as 'short term, highly liquid investments which are readily convertible into known amounts of cash without notice and which were within three months of maturity when acquired'.

This definition was widely criticised by commentators and by preparers of financial statements. In particular, the three-month limit was regarded as arbitrary. Deposits which in practice were used as part of treasury management had to be classified as investments, thus presenting a potentially misleading picture to users of the financial statements.

In revising FRS 1, the ASB decided to use pure cash as the basis of the cash flows reported in the cash flow statement. However, it has also introduced a section for cash flows relating to the management of liquid resources. It believes that this approach has the following advantages:

(a)   it avoids an arbitrary cut-off point in the definition of cash equivalents;

(b)   it distinguishes cash flows arising from accumulating or using liquid resources from those for other investing activities; and

(c)   it provides information about an entity's treasury activities that was not previously available to the extent that the instruments dealt in fell within the definition of cash equivalents.

5.4   The advantages and disadvantages of the direct and indirect methods

The two methods which can be used to prepare the cash flow statement are the direct (gross) and indirect (net) methods as we have seen.

The advantages of the direct method are as follows.

(a)   Information is shown which is not shown elsewhere in the financial statements.   This is therefore of advantage to the user of the information.

(b)   The method does show the true cash flows involved in the trading operations of the entity.

The disadvantage is the significant cost that there may be in preparing the information.   Given that the information is not revealed elsewhere in the financial statements, it follows that there must be some cost in obtaining the information.

The advantages of the indirect method are as follows.

(a)   Used in conjunction with the note which reconciles operating profit to net cash flow from operating activities, the user can easily relate trading profits to cash flow and thus understand the 'quality' of the earnings made by the entity in the accounting period.   Earnings are of a good quality if they are represented by real cash flows now or in the near future.

(b)   There is a low cost in preparing the information.

The disadvantage is the lack of information on the significant elements of trading cash flows.

6   INTERPRETATION OF CASH FLOW DATA

6.1   Introduction

The estimation of the future cash flows is very important in determining the solvency or otherwise of a business.

The financial accounts are, of course, historical records, but they can provide some evidence of solvency.   This section summarises the areas to consider.

6.2   Interpretation of the cash flow statement

The cash flow statement should be the initial data to review.   Points to watch for within the various headings in the cash flow statement include

(a)   **Cash generation from trading operations**

The figure should be compared to the operating profit.   The reconciliation note to the cash flow statement is useful in this regard.   Overtrading may be indicated by

(i)   high profits and low cash generation
(ii)   large increases in stock, debtors and creditors

(b)   **Dividend and interest payouts**

These can be compared to cash generated from trading operations to see whether the normal operations can sustain such payments.   In most years they should.

(c)   **Capital expenditure and financial investment**

The nature and scale of a company's investment in fixed assets is clearly shown.

(d)   **Management of liquid resources and financing**

The subtotal 'cash inflow/outflow before use of liquid resources and financing' indicates the financing required unless existing cash is available.   The changes in financing (in pure cash terms) are clearly shown.   There may be a note to the cash flow statement provided which links the inflows/outflows with the balance sheet movement.   There may be significant non-cash flow changes in the capital structure of the business.

Gearing can be considered at this point.

(e)   **Cash flow**

The statement clearly shows the end result in cash terms of the company's operations in the year. Do not overstate the importance of this figure alone however. A decrease in cash in the year may be for very sound reasons (eg, there was surplus cash last year) or may be mainly the result of timing (eg, a new loan was raised just after the end of the accounting period).

To help in determining the future cash position other areas of the published accounts should be considered as illustrated below.

6.3   Cash requirements

There are four areas to consider when identifying whether or not the company has sufficient cash.

(a)   **Repayment of existing loans**

All loans to be repaid in the next couple of years should be considered including any convertible loans if the conversion rights are unlikely to be exercised.

(b)   **Increase in working capital**

If the business is expanding (making more sales) working capital will also need to increase. The extra cash needed to finance the expansion can easily be calculated by comparing working capital to sales.

$$\frac{\text{Stocks} + \text{debtors} - \text{creditors}}{\text{Turnover}} \times 100\%$$

Suppose this is 20% and turnover is currently £5m, a 10% increase in turnover requires finance of £0.1m (£5m × 10% × 20%) to increase the working capital.

(c)   **Capital expenditure requirements**

The notes to the financial statements should disclose capital expenditure contracted for.

It is necessary to consider if the company will have sufficient cash to meet this capital expenditure.

(d)   **Other commitments**

(i)   **Contingent liabilities**

Most contingent liabilities do not crystallise, but if the liabilities are very high their crystallisation can cause real problems for the company. Some analysts compare the contingent liabilities with ordinary shareholders' funds to assess the materiality of those commitments. In particular any sharp increases in the amounts involved should act as a warning.

(ii)   **Leasing commitments**

If these are material, they should be carefully monitored in relation to the cash available. The accounts should disclose both finance lease commitments (for new leases where repayments have not commenced) and also operating lease commitments.

6.4   Cash shortfall

If there appears to be a cash shortfall, the company may have to take one or more of the following steps

(a)   increase its overdraft (if it is not already at the limit)

(b)   increase its longer term borrowings. Remember that the articles often restrict the borrowings by reference to shareholders' funds, which may need to be artificially increased, for example by revaluing assets.

Alternatively the company may ask the shareholders to pass a resolution changing the borrowing restriction

(c)   raising money through a share issue (the company must have a good record of profitability and of dividend growth, and the share price must be high)

(d)   tightening credit and stock control, paying creditors later

(e)   limiting capital expenditure

(f)   entering into sale and leaseback arrangements (it will need some assets which are not already charged)

(g)   selling some assets (for example investments, or parts of the business which are less related to the main trade), and

(h)   purchasing a cash-rich company by issuing shares in consideration.

The company should consider most measures in preference to

(a)   reducing dividends, or
(b)   reducing its level of activity.

7   CHAPTER SUMMARY

FRS 1 attempts to address a deficiency previously perceived in published accounts, namely that the profit and loss account and balance sheet do not provide sufficient information about a company's ability to generate cash. The standard applies to the accounts of large companies only.

8   SELF TEST QUESTIONS

8.1   What are the nine headings in an FRS 1 cash flow statement? (1.2)

8.2   What is the definition of cash in FRS 1? (1.3)

8.3   Distinguish between the direct method and the indirect method of reporting net cash flow from operating activities. (2.1)

8.4   To adjust operating profit when calculating the net cash inflow from operating activities, is depreciation added or subtracted? (2.2)

8.5   State four items which would be shown under 'returns on investments and servicing of finance' in a cash flow statement. (2.6)

8.6   In a cash flow statement, are cash flows normally shown inclusive or exclusive of recoverable VAT? (2.10)

8.7   State two items which would be shown under 'management of liquid resources' in a cash flow statement. (2.16)

8.8   What companies fall within the scope of FRS 1? (4)

9   EXAMINATION TYPE QUESTIONS

9.1   Forthright plc

The draft profit and loss account for the year ended 31 December 19X9 with comparatives is as follows.

19X8		19X9	19X8		19X9
£'000		£'000	£'000		£'000
9,722	Overheads	15,134	12,532	Sales	19,080
360	Depreciation	384	3,654	Balance b/d	4,238
1,274	Corporation tax	1,852			
	Dividends (ordinary)				
72	Interim	224			
520	Final	820			
4,238	Balance c/d	4,904			
16,186		23,318	16,186		23,318

Draft balance sheets at 31 December are as follows:

19X8		19X9	19X8		19X9
£'000		£'000	£'000		£'000
	Land and buildings			Share capital (in 25p	
1,600	(cost)	2,000		ordinary shares fully	
2,914	Plant	4,176	2,400	paid)	2,600
-	Patents	380	-	Share premium	560
984	Stock at cost	2,256	4,238	Retained earnings	4,904
4,582	Debtors	7,368	1,580	Creditors	2,730
718	Bank balance	-	-	Overdraft	804
			2,060	Corporation tax	3,762
			520	Proposed dividends	820
10,798		16,180	10,798		16,180

The following information is available:

(a)   Plant with a net book value of £260,000 was disposed of on 1 December 19X9 for £184,000.

(b)   A rights issue at 95p per share was made during the year ended 31 December 19X9.

You are required to prepare for Forthright plc a cash flow statement for the year ended 31 December 19X9, in a form suitable for publication.   **(15 marks)**

9.2   Solid plc

The summarised balance sheets of Solid plc at 31 December 19X7 and 19X8 are as follows:

	19X8 £	19X7 £
Issued share capital (ordinary shares)	150,000	100,000
Share premium	35,000	15,000
Profit and loss account	36,000	11,500
Debentures	30,000	70,000
Deferred taxation	18,000	11,000
Creditors	48,000	34,000
Bank overdraft	-	14,000
Corporation tax payable	15,000	10,500
Proposed dividends	20,000	10,000
Depreciation on plant and machinery	54,000	45,000
Depreciation on fixtures and fittings	15,000	13,000
	421,000	334,000
Freehold property at cost	130,000	110,000
Plant and machinery at cost	151,000	120,000
Fixtures and fittings at cost	29,000	24,000
Stock	51,000	37,000
Debtors	44,000	42,800
Government stock	4,600	-
Cash at bank	11,400	200
	421,000	334,000

The following information is relevant:

(a)   There had been no disposal of freehold property in the year.

(b)   A machine tool which had cost £8,000 (in respect of which £6,000 depreciation had been provided) was sold for £3,000, and fixtures which had cost £5,000 (in respect of which depreciation of £2,000 had been provided) were sold for £1,000. Profits and losses on those transactions had been dealt with through the profit and loss account.

(c)   The corporation tax liability in respect of the year ended 31 December 19X7, amounting to £10,500, had been paid during the year.

The profit and loss account charges in respect of tax were: corporation tax £12,500; deferred tax £9,500.

(d)   The premium paid on redemption of debentures was £2,000, which has been written off to profit and loss account.

(e)   The proposed dividend for 19X7 had been paid during the year.

(f)   Interest received during the year was £450. Interest charged in the profit and loss account for the year was £6,400. Accrued interest of £440 is included in creditors at 31 December 19X7 (nil at 31 December 19X8).

You are required to prepare a cash flow statement for the year ended 31 December 19X8, together with notes as required by FRS 1.   **(20 marks)**

10   ANSWERS TO EXAMINATION TYPE QUESTIONS

10.1   Forthright plc

Cash flow statement for the year ended 31 December 19X9

Reconciliation of operating profit to net cash inflow from operating activities

	£'000
Operating profit (W5)	3,562
Depreciation	384
Increase in stocks	(1,272)
Increase in debtors	(2,786)
Increase in creditors	1,150
Net cash inflow from operating activities	1,038

Cash flow statement

	£'000	£'000
Net cash inflow from operating activities		1,038
Taxation		
Corporation tax paid (W4)		(150)
Capital expenditure		
Receipts from the sale of plant	184	
Payments to acquire land & buildings	(400)	
Payments to acquire plant (W1)	(1,830)	
Payments to acquire patents	(380)	
Net cash outflow from capital expenditure		(2,426)
Equity dividends paid (W3)		(744)
Net cash outflow before financing		(2,282)
Financing		
Rights issue (2,600 – 2,400 + 560)	760	
Net cash inflow from financing		760
Decrease in cash		(1,522)

Reconciliation of net cash flow to movement in net debt (Note)

	£'000
Decrease in cash in the period	(1,522)
Net funds at 1 January 19X9	718
Net debt at 31 December 19X9	(804)

Note: Analysis of changes in net debt

	At 1 January 19X9 £'000	Cash flows £'000	At 31 December 19X9 £'000
Cash at bank	718	(718)	-
Bank overdraft	-	(804)	(804)
Total	718	(1,522)	(804)

WORKINGS

(W1)

Plant

	£'000		£'000
B/d	2,914		
		Disposals	260
Additions (to balance)	1,830	Depreciation (W2)	308
		C/d	4,176
	4,744		4,744

(W2) **Depreciation**

	£'000
Total per Q	384
Loss on sale of plant (260 – 184)	(76)
On plant	308

(W3)

Dividends

	£'000			£'000
Cash (to balance)	744	B/d		520
		P&L a/c	– interim	224
C/d	820		– final	820
	1,564			1,564

(W4)

Corporation tax

	£'000		£'000
Cash (to balance)	150	B/d	2,060
C/d	3,762		
		P&L a/c	1,852
	3,912		3,912

(W5)

	£'000
Sales	19,080
Overheads	(15,134)
Depreciation	(384)
Operating profit	3,562

10.2   Solid plc

Cash flow statement for the year ended 31 December 19X8

	£	£
Reconciliation of operating profit to net cash inflow from operating activities		
Operating profit (W7)		75,450
Depreciation charges (W5)		19,000
Increase in stocks (51,000 – 37,000)		(14,000)
Increase in debtors (44,000 – 42,800)		(1,200)
Increase in creditors [48,000 – (34,000 – 440)]		14,440
Net cash inflow from operating activities		93,690

Cash flow statement

	£	£
Net cash inflow from operating activities		93,690
Returns on investments and servicing of finance:		
Interest received	450	
Interest paid (6,400 + 440)	(6,840)	
		(6,390)
Taxation:		
Corporation tax paid (W6)		(10,500)
Capital expenditure:		
Purchases of tangible fixed assets (W2)	(69,000)	
Receipts from sales of tangible fixed assets	4,000	
		(65,000)
Equity dividends paid		(10,000)
Net cash outflow before use of liquid resources and financing		1,800
Management of liquid resources:		
Purchase of government stock		(4,600)
Financing:		
Issue of share capital (50,000 + 20,000)	70,000	
Redemption of debentures	(42,000)	
		28,000
Increase in cash in the period		25,200

Reconciliation of net cash flow to movement in net debt (Note)

	£
Increase in cash in the period	25,200
Cash outflow from redemption of debentures	42,000
Cash outflow from purchase of current asset investments	4,600
Change in net debt resulting from cash flows	71,800
Premium on redemption of debentures	(2,000)
Change in net debt for the period	69,800
Net debt at 1 January 19X8	(83,800)
Net debt at 31 December 19X8	(14,000)

Note: Analysis of changes in net debt

	At 1 January 19X8 £	Cash flows £	Other changes £	At 31 December 19X8 £
Cash at bank	200	11,200	-	11,400
Bank overdraft	(14,000)	14,000	-	-
Debentures	(70,000)	42,000	(2,000)	(30,000)
Current asset investments	-	4,600	-	4,600
Total	(83,800)	71,800	(2,000)	(14,000)

WORKINGS

(W1)

Plant and machinery account – At cost

	£		£
Balance b/d	120,000	Disposals a/c	8,000
Additions	39,000	Balance c/d	151,000
	159,000		159,000

(W2)

Fixtures and fittings account – At cost

	£		£
Balance b/d	24,000	Disposals a/c	5,000
Additions	10,000	Balance c/d	29,000
	34,000		34,000

Fixed assets – additions summary:

	£
Freehold property	20,000
Plant and machinery	39,000
Fixtures and fittings	10,000
	69,000

(W3)

Plant and machinery account – Depreciation

	£		£
Disposal a/c	6,000	Balance b/d	45,000
Balance c/d	54,000	Charge for year	15,000
	60,000		60,000

(W4)

Fixtures and fittings account – Depreciation

	£		£
Disposal a/c	2,000	Balance b/d	13,000
Balance c/d	15,000	Charge for year	4,000
	17,000		17,000

(W5)

Fixed assets disposals account

	£		£
Plant cost	8,000	Plant depreciation	6,000
Fittings cost	5,000	Fittings depreciation	2,000
		Cash proceeds:	
		Plant	3,000
		Fittings	1,000
		Depreciation under-	
		provided (bal fig)	1,000
	13,000		13,000

Depreciation – summary:

	£
Plant	15,000
Fixtures	4,000
Disposals	1,000
	20,000

(W6)   **Taxation**

The only figure relating to tax that requires computation for the cash flow statement is the total tax paid in the accounting period.

To determine the tax paid it is only necessary to insert all opening and closing balances relating to tax and the profit and loss account tax charge into a 'tax account'.

Tax account

	£		£
Cash paid (bal fig)	10,500	Balance b/d	
Balance c/d:		Deferred tax	11,000
Deferred tax	18,000	Corporation tax	10,500
Corporation tax	15,000	Profit and loss a/c	
		Deferred tax	9,500
		Corporation tax	12,500
	43,500		43,500

(W7)   **Profit and loss account**

As operating profit is required, reconstruct the profit and loss account up to this figure:

Profit and loss account

	£	£
Operating profit (bal fig)		75,450
Loss on disposal of fixed assets		(1,000)
Interest received		450
Interest paid		(6,400)
Premium on redemption of debentures		(2,000)
		66,500
Taxation		
Corporation tax	12,500	
Deferred tax	9,500	
		(22,000)
		44,500
Dividends		(20,000)
Retained profit for year		24,500
Balance b/d		11,500
Balance c/d		36,000

16 FURTHER FIXED ASSET ACCOUNTING

INTRODUCTION & LEARNING OBJECTIVES

There is no single accounting standard on fixed assets but rather a number of standards on particular types of fixed assets.

This chapter brings together the topics which are new to this level of accounting. Tangible fixed assets (FRS 15) and research and development (SSAP 13) have been covered in an earlier chapter.

Goodwill and its relation, intangible assets, is a major area of controversy. You will appreciate the problems in this area better after you have studied group accounts and you should therefore return to this area later in your studies.

When you have studied this chapter you should be able to do the following:

- Explain and apply the provisions of SSAP 4.
- Explain and apply the provisions of SSAP 19.
- Explain and apply the provisions of FRS 10.
- Discuss the goodwill/intangible assets controversy.
- Explain and apply the provisions of FRS 11.

1 SSAP 4 – ACCOUNTING FOR GOVERNMENT GRANTS

1.1 The provisions of SSAP 4

SSAP 4 was originally introduced following the advent of regional development grants under the *Industry Act 1972*. These grants were often related to capital expenditure and thus a standard was necessary to state how the grant should be accounted for.

Since the issue of *SSAP 4* the variety of forms of government assistance available to industry has greatly increased: many are discretionary in nature both as to whether they are given at all and as to the amount given. Frequently the terms on which grants are given do not make clear precisely the expenditure to which they are related. The problem facing accountants today is thus how to relate grants to specific expenditure.

The ASC considered *SSAP 4* and concluded that there was a need for a substantial revision to the standard. Accordingly an exposure draft, *ED 43*, was issued in 1988.

A revised *SSAP* was issued in July 1990.

[Definition] **Government** is widely defined to include national government and all tiers of local and regional government. It also includes EC bodies.

[Definition] **Grants** include cash or transfers of assets.

1.2 General principles

Grants should not be recognised in the profit and loss account until the conditions for receipt have been complied with and there is reasonable assurance that the grant will be received. (This is prudent.)

Subject to this condition, grants should be recognised in the profit and loss account so as to match them with the expenditure towards which they are intended to contribute. (Application of the accruals concept.)

1.3   Revenue grants

In the absence of evidence to the contrary, grants should be assumed to contribute towards the expenditure that is the basis for their payment. The explanatory foreword illustrates this principle by stating that if the grant is paid when evidence is produced that certain expenditure has been incurred, the grant should be matched with that expenditure.

However, if the grant is paid on a different basis, for example achievement of a non-financial objective, such as the creation of a specified number of new jobs, the grant should be matched with the identifiable costs of achieving that objective.

1.4   Alternative feasible ways of treating capital based government grants received

Grants for fixed asset purchases should be recognised over the expected useful lives of the related assets.

SSAP 4 permits two treatments. The explanatory foreword states that both treatments are acceptable and capable of giving a true and fair view:

(a)   write off the grant against the cost of the fixed asset and depreciate the reduced cost; or

(b)   treat the grant as a deferred credit and transfer a portion to revenue each year, so offsetting the higher depreciation charge on the original cost.

Method (a) is obviously far simpler to operate. Method (b), however, has the advantage of ensuring that assets acquired at different times and in different locations are recorded on a uniform basis, regardless of changes in government policy.

However, the *CA85* requires that fixed assets should be stated at purchase price and this is defined as actual price paid plus any additional expenses. Legal opinion on this matter is that companies should not deduct grants from cost. Thus method (a) may only be adopted by unincorporated bodies.

In practice, it remains to be seen whether companies will stop using method (a). The law was actually implemented in the *CA81*, but a large number of companies continue to use the method which contravenes the legislation.

ED 43 sought to remove the alternative in *SSAP 4* for capital-based grants to be dealt with either by deduction from the related asset or by setting up a deferred credit. It was considered that there are compelling arguments in favour of the deferred credit approach, not least being that it is difficult to reconcile the deduction from asset approach with the specific requirements of *Sch 4 CA85*. However, opinion swung back to giving a choice when the new *SSAP* was issued.

The two ways of dealing with capital grants are shown in the following example.

1.5   Example of accounting for capital grants

A company opens a new factory in a development area and receives a government grant of £15,000 in respect of capital equipment costing £100,000. It depreciates all plant and machinery at 20% pa straight-line.

Show the balance sheet extracts to record the grant in the first year under methods (a) and (b) above.

1.6   Solution

(a)   **Write off against asset**

Balance sheet extract

	£
Fixed assets:	
Plant and machinery at cost (100 – 15)	85,000
Less: Depreciation (20% × 85)	17,000
	68,000

(b)   **Deferred credit**

Government grant deferred credit account

	£		£
Profit and loss a/c transfer for		Cash grant	15,000
year: 20% × £15,000	3,000		
Balance c/d	12,000		
	15,000		15,000
		Balance b/d	12,000

Balance sheet extract

	£
Fixed assets:	
Plant and machinery at cost	100,000
Less: Depreciation	20,000
	80,000
Deferred income:	
Government grant	12,000

1.7   Other grants

Purpose of grant	*Recognise in profit and loss account*
To give immediate financial support	When receivable
To reimburse previously incurred costs	When receivable
To finance general activities over a period	In relevant period
To compensate for a loss of income	In relevant period

1.8   Provisions and contingent liabilities

The explanatory foreword states that enterprises should consider regularly whether there is a likelihood of a breach of conditions on which the grant was made. If such a breach has occurred or appears likely to occur, the likelihood of having to make a repayment should be considered.

If there is an obligaton to repay the grant and the repayment is probable then it should be provided for in accordance with the requirements of FRS 12. It should be accounted for by being set off against any unamortised deferred income relating to the grant. Any excess should be immediately charged to profit and loss account.

1.9   Activity

A Ltd has been awarded government assistance in the form of a training grant. Suggest three ways in which the grant could be accounted for.

1.10   Activity solution

SSAP 4 requires that grants should be matched with expenditure to which it is intended to contribute.

Hence A Ltd could account for the training grant as follows:

(a)   Match it against direct training costs.

(b)   Match it against employee salary costs over the period of time training takes place.

(c)   Take it to profit and loss account over the estimated period during which A Ltd or the employees are expected to benefit from the training.

1.11   Disclosure

The following information should be disclosed:

(a)   accounting policy

(b)   effects of government grants

- amount credited to profit and loss account
- balance on deferred income account

(c)   if other forms of government assistance have had a material effect on the results

- the nature, and
- an estimate of those effects.

(d)   potential liabilities to repay grants should if necessary be disclosed in accordance with *FRS 12*.

2   SSAP 19 – ACCOUNTING FOR INVESTMENT PROPERTIES

2.1   Introduction

Under the general requirements of *FRS 15* all fixed assets having a finite useful life should be subject to a depreciation charge. Investment property companies objected to this requirement and as the ASC conceded they had reasonable grounds for objecting, *SSAP 19* was issued. *SSAP 19*: **Accounting for investment properties** provides a solution to the problem of investment property accounting, and should be looked at as an addition to *FRS 15*.

2.2   Why investment properties need a different accounting treatment

SSAP 19 justifies the different accounting treatment for investment properties on the following grounds. It concludes that such assets are not held for consumption within the operations of the business but are held as investments. Therefore to the user of the financial statements, the most important information about such assets relates to their current value. Calculation of depreciation in such circumstances does not benefit the user from a balance sheet perspective nor a profit and loss account perspective as the asset is not consumed in the business operations.

Another way of justifying the special treatment is that the disposal of such an asset would not materially affect the trading operations of the business; it therefore cannot be relevant to depreciate such items.

2.3   Standard accounting practice (as amended by the ASB in 1994)

(a)   Investment properties should not be subject to periodic charges for depreciation on the basis set out in *FRS 15*, except for properties held on lease which should be depreciated on the basis set out in *FRS 15* at least over the period when the unexpired term is 20 years or less.

(b)   Investment properties should be included in the balance sheet at their open market value.

(c)   The names of the persons making the valuation, or particulars of their qualifications, should be disclosed together with the bases of valuation used by them. If a person making a valuation is an employee or officer of the company or group which owns the property, this fact should be disclosed.

(d)   Changes in the value of investment properties should not be taken to the profit and loss account but should be disclosed taken to the statement of total recognised gains and losses (being a movement on an investment revaluation reserve), unless a deficit on an individual investment property is expected to be permanent, in which case it should be charged in the profit and loss account of the period.

Definition   An investment property is an interest in land and/or buildings:

(a)   in respect of which construction work and development have been completed; and

(b)   which is held for its investment potential, any rental income being negotiated at arm's length.

The following are exceptions from the definition:

(a)   A property which is owned and occupied by a company for its own purposes is not an investment property.

(b)   A property let to and occupied by another group company is not an investment property for the purposes of its own accounts or the group accounts.

2.4   Example

Industrial Ltd produces accounts to 31 December. On 1 January 19X8 it moved from its factory in Bolton to a new purpose-built factory in Rochdale (expected life of fifty years). The old premises were available for letting from 1 January 19X8 and a lease was granted on 30 September 19X8 to B Ltd at an annual rental of £8,000. A valuation of the old premises at 31 December 19X8 was £160,000.

Extracts from the balance sheet as at 31 December 19X7 were:

Fixed assets

	Cost £	Depreciation £	NBV £
Land and buildings:			
Old premises	200,000	80,000	120,000
New premises	450,000		450,000

2.5   Solution

Extracts from the balance sheet as at 31 December 19X8 are:

Fixed assets

	Cost £	Depreciation £	NBV £
Land and buildings	450,000	9,000	441,000
Investment property at valuation			160,000

Reserves

Investment revaluation reserve	40,000

2.6   Treatment of annual valuations

SSAP 19 regards the total investment property revaluation reserve as being available to cover temporary deficits.

2.7   Example

Newline Investment Co Ltd purchased three investment properties on 31 December 19X1, and the following valuations have been made during the period to 31 December 19X4:

	31 Dec 19X1 £'000	31 Dec 19X2 £'000	31 Dec 19X3 £'000	31 Dec 19X4 £'000
Property A	200	180*	120*	120
Property B	300	330	340	310**
Property C	400	440	450	450
Total	900	950	910	880

*   deficit expected to be temporary
**   deficit expected to be permanent

Show the balance on the investment revaluation reserve for each balance sheet date.

2.8   Solution

The investment revaluation reserve would be disclosed for the various years as follows:

	Year ended 31 December		
	19X2 £'000	19X3 £'000	19X4 £'000
Balance b/d	Nil	50	10
Net revaluation	50	(40)	–
Balance c/d	50	10	10

The permanent deficit of £30,000 arising on property B in the year ended 31 December 19X4 will be charged through the profit and loss account.

2.9   Activity

State whether the following are investment properties and if so whether they should be depreciated.

(a)   A freehold property bought for its investment potential and leased to an associated company at an arm's length rental.

(b)   A leasehold property let to a third party. The leasehold has 18 years to run.

(c)   An office building owned and occupied by a company.

(d)   A leasehold property with 24 years left to run which is let to a subsidiary at an arm's length rental.

2.10   Activity solution

(a)   This is an investment property. An associated company is not a group company. The property should not be depreciated under *SSAP 19*.

(b)   This is an investment property. As the lease has less than 20 years to run it should be depreciated.

(c)   This is not an investment property as it is used by the company for the purposes of its own business.

(d)   This is not an investment property as it is occupied by a group company.

2.11   The validity and legality of SSAP 19

The legality of SSAP 19 is questioned as the requirement not to depreciate is in conflict with the requirement of the CA85 to depreciate assets with a finite useful life.

SSAP 19 states however that the treatment is necessary in order to show a true and fair view and thus use is made of the overriding provisions of the CA85 to show such a true and fair view.

The justification of the different treatment of investment properties was explained earlier. Some commentators argue however that despite such arguments, SSAP 19 does not represent a valid treatment and is merely an example of the ASC giving way to the demands of pressure groups (ie, the property investment companies). A property investment company has a very high value of assets relative to its profits. This is mainly due to the fact that an investment is made in property in order to make not only returns of income (ie, rent) but also capital (when the property is eventually sold). The annual changes in the value of the properties are not reflected in the profit and loss account (as they are unrealised) and therefore to charge depreciation against the 'income' part of the overall profit anticipated is unreasonable.

3   PROBLEMS OF ACCOUNTING FOR GOODWILL

3.1   Nature of goodwill

FRS 10 contains the following definitions:

> **Definition**   **Purchased goodwill** is the difference between the cost of an acquired entity and the aggregate of the fair values of that entity's identifiable assets and liabilities.

> **Definition**   **Identifiable assets and liabilities** are the assets and liabilities of an entity that are capable of being disposed of or settled separately, without disposing of a business of the entity.

FRS 10 does not include a definition of fair value, but FRS 7 defines it as follows:

> **Definition**   **Fair value** is the amount at which an asset or liability could be exchanged in an arm's length transaction between informed and willing parties, other than in a forced or liquidation sale.

There is an important distinction between purchased and non-purchased goodwill (sometimes called inherent goodwill or internally generated goodwill).

Purchased goodwill arises when one business acquires another as a going concern. The term therefore includes goodwill arising on the inclusion of a subsidiary or associated company in the consolidated accounts.

Purchased goodwill will be recognised within the accounts because at a specific point in time the fact of purchase has established a figure of value for the business as a whole which can be compared with the fair value of the individual net assets acquired. The difference will be incorporated in the accounts of the acquiring company as the cost of the acquisition.

Purchased goodwill has a limited life: as time passes the reputation, for instance, of the business under its former owners ceases to have any value because potential customers begin to form a view of its performance under the present ownership. Purchased goodwill ought, therefore to be depreciated.

The question of what life to use is considered below.

Goodwill exists in any successful business. However, if the business has never changed hands this goodwill will not be recognised in the accounts because no event has occurred to identify its value. It can only be subjectively estimated. This is inherent goodwill.

Of course, a business which has acquired another and thus purchased goodwill, may then build up inherent goodwill of its own, but only the former will be reflected in the accounts.

There is no universally accepted method of accounting for goodwill. The ASB itself summed up the problem in a Discussion Paper:

> 'Purchased goodwill is..an accounting anomaly. Every method of accounting for it results in inconsistencies with other aspects of financial reporting.'

Despite these problems, purchased goodwill arises from a distinct transaction that must be accounted for.

3.2   The advantages and disadvantages of each of the methods of accounting for goodwill

In this section the principal ways of accounting for purchased goodwill in the past are listed, with the major arguments for and against each of them:

(a)   **Carry as an asset, amortised over useful life through the profit and loss account**

Arguments for:

(i)   Goodwill is an asset on which capital has been expended in exchange for benefits which will materialise in future periods. Although different in quality and character from other assets, it does exist and can be purchased or sold, and as such it should be treated as an asset.

(ii)   The expense of acquiring purchased goodwill should be matched against the extra earnings generated from its acquisition.

(iii)   Amortisation reflects the replacement of purchased goodwill with inherent goodwill over a period of time.

Arguments against:

(i)   Comparability is lost when one type of goodwill ('purchased') is treated as an asset while another ('non-purchased') is not recognised as such.

(ii)   The life of goodwill is indeterminate in the extreme, and even if determined, a single event may drastically alter that life. Any amortisation period is therefore too arbitrary to be realistic.

(b)   **Eliminate against reserves on acquisition**

Arguments for:

(i)   Goodwill is not an asset in the normal sense of the word; it is not independently realisable and many of the factors contributing to it are beyond the control of management. Thus, it is not prudent to carry goodwill as an asset in the balance sheet and, as a once-and-for-all expense of acquisition, it should be written-off as it arises.

(ii)   Goodwill will usually be worthless in a forced liquidation.

Arguments against:

(i)   Since consideration has been given, then clearly an asset existed. If so, then it would seem excessively prudent to write it off immediately.

(ii)   It is assumed that the accounts are prepared on a going concern basis, which renders point (ii) above irrelevant.

(iii)   Elimination is inconsistent with the treatment of other fixed assets, which must be capitalised and depreciated or amortised.

(c)   **Carry as a permanent asset unless permanent diminution (impairment) in value becomes evident**

Arguments for:

(i)   Purchased goodwill does not lose value with the passage of time as it should be maintained in the normal course of business.

(ii)   Following the principles of FRS 15, that depreciation should be provided on the cost less the net realisable value of an asset, if the goodwill is maintained then net realisable value will be equal to or exceed cost so that no write-off will be appropriate.

(iii)   The expenditure incurred in the normal course of business to generate inherent goodwill is charged to profit and loss. If purchased goodwill is also depreciated, there will be a double charge.

Arguments against:

(i)   Purchased goodwill is not maintained, but over a period of time is consumed and replaced by newly generated inherent goodwill which is not accounted for.

(ii)   The residual value of purchased goodwill is nil; it is the inherent goodwill by which it has been replaced which is subsequently valued.

(iii)   The expense of maintaining inherent goodwill is a normal trading charge falling on any business; the depreciation of purchased goodwill is the consequence of a business acquisition.

This method is also contrary to the CA85, which requires purchased goodwill of an individual company to be treated as an asset subject to depreciation.

(d)   **The dangling debit**

Under this approach, goodwill is shown as a deduction from the subtotal of share capital and reserves.

Advocates of the 'dangling debit' approach argue that goodwill is not an asset in the normal sense of the word, having no objective value. Goodwill arises only because of the accounting conventions of double entry bookkeeping, and should be presented in such a way as to balance the accounts without creating any accounting entries. The dangling debit gives the fullest possible disclosure and allows the user of accounts to treat it in any way considered appropriate. Investment analysts normally disregard goodwill, and the dangling debit presenting goodwill outside the normal framework of results is in line with this approach.

This method has been rejected on the grounds of ambiguity; it is writing-off goodwill against reserves while implying that the goodwill remains available as a form of asset. In addition, it is contrary to the CA85, which does not permit the setting-off of an asset with a liability.

(e)   **The separate write off reserve**

This is a development of the dangling debit approach and is designed to overcome the legal problems associated with the dangling debit.

A reserve is created and named as a 'goodwill write-off reserve' or something similar. The goodwill is then charged against this reserve leaving a negative balance equivalent in amount to the goodwill. It is thus effectively the same as the dangling debit approach and thus the same advantages and disadvantages apply. However as it is a reserve there are no CA85 problems as an asset is not being offset against a liability.

3.3   Negative goodwill

Most purchased goodwill is positive goodwill, that is, the price paid for the entity is more than the total fair values of the net assets acquired. Negative goodwill arises where an entity is purchased for less than the total fair values of its identifiable net assets. This may occur for a number of reasons, for example, a business may be sold at a bargain price because the vendor needs to achieve a quick sale. Alternatively, the purchase price of a business may be reduced to take account of future reorganisation costs or probable future losses.

The possible methods of accounting for negative goodwill are as follows:

(a)   **Recognise immediately as a gain in the profit and loss account or the statement of total recognised gains and losses**

The rationale for this treatment is that negative goodwill arises from a bargain purchase. The value of the business acquired is not less than the fair values of its net assets and therefore the purchaser has made a gain.

Arguments against:

(i)   Recognition in the profit and loss account contravenes the Companies Acts as the gain is not realised until the assets acquired are depreciated or sold.

(ii)   Recognition in the statement of total recognised gains and losses treats the negative goodwill as a revaluation gain, but recognition of a gain on non-monetary assets before they are realised is inconsistent with the requirements of other accounting standards.

(iii)   Not all negative goodwill arises from bargain purchases; some is attributable to expected future losses and therefore should not be treated as an immediate 'gain'.

(b)   **Take to a capital reserve**

The main argument for this treatment is that negative goodwill is not a liability or deferred income in the normal sense of the word and therefore it should not be treated as such.

The main argument against this treatment is that it artificially inflates reserves and shareholders' funds. Negative goodwill does not represent an actual reserve, and therefore should not be treated as one.

(c)   **Eliminate against the fair value of assets acquired**

Arguments for:

(i)   It is consistent with the principle that assets should initially be recognised at cost.

(ii)   It helps to prevent unrealistically high fair values being assigned to assets whose values are very subjective. True bargain purchases are uncommon and cost may represent a realistic estimate of fair value.

(iii)   This method is consistent with much international practice (eg, in the US).

Arguments against:

(i)   Fair values can be different from cost and stating assets acquired at lower than their fair values would be inconsistent with FRS 7.

(ii)   This method cannot be used where negative goodwill is attributable to future losses.

(d)   **Include on the balance sheet and release to the profit and loss account over the periods expected to benefit**

The rationale for this treatment is that it matches negative goodwill with the costs that gave rise to it. It can be used for all negative goodwill, including that attributable to future losses.

The main argument against this method is that any 'amortisation' of negative goodwill is bound to be subjective.

3.4   Goodwill from the viewpoint of management and users of the financial statements

The previous two sections have set out the conceptual arguments for and against each of the main methods of accounting for goodwill.

The three main methods of accounting for positive purchased goodwill also have practical advantages and disadvantages for management and for users of the financial statements.

(a)   **The viewpoint of management**

Preparers of accounts have tended to resist capitalisation and amortisation of goodwill, because amortisation results in reduced profits. Opponents of amortisation have also argued that, where large sums are spent on maintaining and developing the value of an acquired business, a requirement to amortise a significant part of the investment over an arbitrary period has no economic meaning.

The main alternative, elimination against reserves, also has disadvantages. Immediate elimination of goodwill gives the impression that the acquirer's net worth has been depleted or even eliminated. A 'weak' balance sheet may result in the company being perceived as a 'target' in take-over bids and may make it difficult for the company to raise finance.

Carrying goodwill in the balance sheet indefinitely unless there is an impairment in value recognises that purchased goodwill is neither an identifiable asset like other assets, nor an immediate loss in value. It also avoids the reduction of profits through an amortisation charge and the elimination of reserves. However, to establish whether there has been an impairment in value it is necessary to carry out an impairment review. This relies on forecasts of future cash flows and may be subjective. Impairment reviews may also be time consuming and costly.

(b)   **The viewpoint of users of the financial statements**

Immediate elimination against reserves has many disadvantages for users of the financial statements:

(i)   If goodwill is not included in the assets on which a return must be earned, management is not held accountable for the amount that it has invested in goodwill.

(ii)   Costs attributed to building up internally generated goodwill are offset against profits in the profit and loss account. The costs of purchased goodwill are not charged in the profit and loss account. This means that companies that grow by acquisition may appear to be more profitable than those that grow organically.

If goodwill is carried as an asset in the balance sheet, users are better able to judge the performance of management. Although purchased goodwill is not in itself an asset, it is part of a larger asset, the investment in another business. Including goodwill as an asset reflects management's success (or otherwise) in maintaining its value and generating a return from its investment.

However, if goodwill is carried in the balance sheet it must either be amortised or reviewed for impairment in value. Both these approaches rely on the judgement of management and can only be subjective.

4 THE ISSUES RAISED IN RECENT YEARS BY THE BRAND (AND OTHER SIMILAR ASSETS) VALUATION CONTROVERSY

4.1 Introduction

> **Definition** Intangible assets are non-financial fixed assets that do not have physical substance but are identifiable and are controlled by the entity through custody or legal rights.

The accounting treatment of intangible assets has been the subject of controversy in recent years. Most of the controversy has centred on brands, but intangible assets may comprise patents, licences, publishing titles, franchises, quotas and other types of asset.

The term 'brand' is difficult to define precisely. The constituents of a brand include a recognised name, a product or range of products, an established operation and market position, marketing and other specialist know-how, and trading connections.

It is a wider term than 'trade name' as if a brand is purchased, the acquisition often involves the acquisition of many of the supporting functions which make the brands produce profits.

Thus a brand is a combination of factors expected to produce enhanced earnings just like goodwill. This analysis is further supported by the fact that brands and goodwill are commonly valued using earnings multiples.

4.2 The problem

To understand the problem it is necessary to consider the context which gave rise to it.

(a) Some companies, following an acquisition, have assigned fair values to intangible assets of various types rather than to goodwill.

Companies who make such a classification avoid having to apply the treatment required for accounting for goodwill to the assets thus identified ie, the intangible asset could be carried forward in the balance sheet indefinitely without mandatory review.

(b) There is the possibility that it will become widespread practice to incorporate similar assets in the balance sheet by revaluation rather than by acquisition.

The balance sheet would thus include 'home-grown' intangibles as well as those which had been acquired at a known cost or an assigned fair value.

No one would deny that intangible assets are of real economic value to businesses, and in certain industry sectors, they are of overwhelming importance to the success of the enterprise. The debate is not on that issue; it is on whether it is within the compass of the present accounting model to capture and convey useful information about such assets. By their nature many intangible assets have characteristics which cause accounting difficulty.

4.3   Arguments for and against including brands and similar intangible assets in the balance sheet

Arguments for inclusion

(a)   Including intangible assets in the balance sheet reflects the 'real' value of the business.

(b)   Since goodwill and development costs may be capitalised, capitalising other intangibles results in consistency of accounting treatment.

(c)   It would result in increased earnings per share, increased net asset value per share and reduced gearing.

(d)   It would provide useful information to users of the accounts.

(e)   Realistic asset values are believed to discourage potential take-over bids.

Arguments against inclusion

(a)   The balance sheet cannot possibly reflect the 'real' (or market) value of a business, as this depends on the market's perception of its future performance, not on the current value of its assets.

(b)   Many intangibles cannot be measured at a monetary value with sufficient reliability. According to the draft Statement of Principles, they should therefore not be recognised as assets.

(c)   Even if it were possible to arrive at a valuation, this would be time consuming, costly and inherently subjective.

5   FRS 10: GOODWILL AND INTANGIBLE ASSETS

5.1   Why a new accounting standard was necessary

FRS 10 was issued in December 1997 and replaced SSAP 22 *Accounting for goodwill*. Most commentators regarded SSAP 22 as unsatisfactory because it permitted a choice between two different accounting treatments. Entities chose the accounting treatment which gave the most favourable view of earnings and net assets. The preferred alternative, immediate elimination against reserves, was criticised for two main reasons:

(a)   it gave the impression that the acquirer's net worth had been depleted or eliminated; and

(b)   the financial statements overstated the rate of return on acquired investments.

In addition, there was clearly a need for an accounting standard which dealt with other intangible fixed assets. The similarities between goodwill and certain intangible assets such as brand names made it appropriate to consider the two together.

5.2   Objective

The objective of FRS 10 is to ensure that:

(a)   capitalised goodwill and intangible assets are charged in the profit and loss account in the periods in which they are depleted; and

(b)   sufficient information is disclosed in the financial statements to enable users to determine the impact of goodwill and intangible assets on the financial position and performance of the reporting entity.

Note that the FRS applies to all intangible assets with the exception of:

(a)   oil and gas exploration and development costs;

(b)   research and development costs (already covered by SSAP 13); and

(c)   any other intangible assets that are specifically addressed by another accounting standard.

5.3   Goodwill

(a)   Positive purchased goodwill should be capitalised and classified as an intangible fixed asset on the balance sheet.

(b)   Internally generated goodwill should not be capitalised.

5.4   Other intangible assets

FRS 10 recognises that there are many types of intangible asset. Although some intangible assets are very similar to goodwill, some can be readily identified and reliably valued.

(a)   An intangible asset purchased separately from a business should be capitalised at its cost.

Examples of assets which might be purchased separately from a business include copyrights, patents and licences.

(b)   An intangible asset acquired as part of the acquisition of a business should be capitalised separately from goodwill if its value can be measured reliably on initial recognition. It should initially be recorded at its fair value.

(c)   If its value cannot be measured reliably, an intangible asset purchased as part of the acquisition of a business should be subsumed within the amount of the purchase price attributable to goodwill.

Most purchased brand names are likely to be subsumed within goodwill, but the ASB has not specifically prohibited their recognition.

(d)   An internally developed intangible asset may be capitalised only if it has a readily ascertainable market value.

In practice, very few internally generated intangibles have a readily ascertainable market value. The ASB does not believe that it is possible to determine a market value for unique intangible assets such as brands and publishing titles and so the recognition of internally generated brand names is effectively prohibited.

This treatment of internally generated intangible assets is consistent with the treatment of internally generated goodwill. If it is accepted that internally generated goodwill is never recognised because it cannot be valued objectively, it follows that internally generated brand names should not be recognised either.

| Conclusion | Positive purchased goodwill should be included in the balance sheet as an intangible fixed asset. Other intangible assets may be recognised if they can be reliably valued.

5.5   Amortisation

Once they have been recognised, FRS 10 requires that intangible assets are treated in exactly the same way as goodwill. There are two reasons for this:

(a)   Even if assets such as brand names are not part of goodwill, they are so similar to goodwill that they should be accounted for in the same way.

(b)   If intangibles must be treated in the same way as goodwill, there is no longer any advantage in separately recognising brand names and similar assets.

Standard accounting practice

(a)   Where goodwill and intangible assets are regarded as having limited useful economic lives, they should be amortised on a systematic basis over those lives.

(b)   There is a rebuttable presumption that the useful economic lives of purchased goodwill and intangible assets are limited to 20 years or less.

(c)   A residual value may be assigned to an intangible asset only if the residual value can be measured reliably. No residual value may be assigned to goodwill.

(d)   The straight line method of amortisation should normally be used unless another method can be demonstrated to be more appropriate.

(e)   The useful economic lives of goodwill and intangible assets should be reviewed at the end of each reporting period and revised if necessary.

5.6   Where useful economic life is longer than 20 years

In most cases, goodwill and intangible assets will probably be amortised over a period of less than 20 years. However, FRS 10 does recognise that they may occasionally have longer useful economic lives or that their lives may even be indefinite.

A useful economic life may be regarded as longer than 20 years or indefinite if:

(a)   the durability of the acquired business or intangible asset can be demonstrated and justifies estimating the useful economic life to exceed 20 years; and

(b)   the goodwill or intangible asset is capable of continued measurement (so that annual impairment reviews will be feasible).

Where goodwill and intangible assets are regarded as having indefinite useful economic lives, they should not be amortised.

Note that the Companies Acts do not allow purchased goodwill or intangible assets to be carried indefinitely as assets in the balance sheet. If goodwill and intangible assets are not amortised it will be necessary to make the additional disclosures required by UITF Abstract 7, as the 'true and fair view override' will be invoked.

5.7   Impairment reviews

Impairment reviews are required as follows:

(a)   **Where goodwill and intangible assets are amortised over 20 years or less**

   (i)   At the end of the first full financial year following the acquisition; and

   (ii)   in other periods if events or changes in circumstances indicate that the carrying value may not be recoverable.

(b)   **Where goodwill and intangible assets are amortised over more than 20 years**

   Impairment reviews are required at the end of each reporting period.

If the review indicates that there has been a diminution in value, the goodwill and intangible assets must be written down accordingly. The revised carrying value should be amortised over the current estimate of the remaining useful economic life (unless the asset is not being amortised because it has an indefinite life). This is similar to the treatment of tangible fixed assets where there has been a diminution in value.

The ASB has now issued FRS 11 *Impairment of fixed assets and goodwill.* Impairment reviews should be carried out in accordance with the requirements of this new accounting standard.

5.8   Negative goodwill

(a)   Negative goodwill should be recognised and separately disclosed on the face of the balance sheet, immediately below the goodwill heading and followed by a subtotal showing the net amount of the positive and negative goodwill.

(b)   Negative goodwill up to the fair values of the non-monetary assets (eg, fixed assets) acquired should be recognised in the profit and loss account in the periods in which the non-monetary assets are recovered, whether through depreciation or sale.

(c)   Any negative goodwill in excess of the fair values of the non-monetary assets acquired should be recognised in the profit and loss account in the periods expected to be benefited.

> **Conclusion**   Goodwill and intangible assets should normally be amortised over a period of 20 years or less, but may be amortised over a longer period or maintained in the balance sheet indefinitely provided that certain conditions are met.

5.9   Disclosures

Recognition and measurement

Main disclosures:

(a)   Describe the method used to value intangible assets.

(b)   Disclose the following information separately for positive goodwill, negative goodwill and each class of intangible asset included on the balance sheet:

    (i)   cost or revalued amount at the beginning of the financial period and at the balance sheet date;

    (ii)   the cumulative amount of provisions for amortisation and impairment at the beginning of the financial period and at the balance sheet date;

    (iii)   a reconciliation of the movements; and

    (iv)   the net carrying amount at the balance sheet date.

(c)   The profit or loss on each material disposal of a previously acquired business or business segment.

Amortisation

Disclose the following:

(a)   Methods and periods of amortisation of goodwill and intangible assets and the reasons for choosing those periods.

(b)   Details of changes in amortisation period or method.

(c)   Grounds for amortising goodwill or intangible assets over a period that exceeds 20 years (if applicable).

Negative goodwill

(a)   Disclose the periods in which negative goodwill is being written back in the profit and loss account.

(b)   Where negative goodwill exceeds the fair values of the non-monetary assets, the amount and source of the 'excess' negative goodwill and the periods in which it is being written back should be explained.

6   FRS 11: IMPAIRMENT OF FIXED ASSETS AND GOODWILL

6.1   Why a new accounting standard was needed

> **[Definition]**   **Impairment** is a reduction in the recoverable amount of a fixed asset or goodwill below its carrying amount.

It is accepted practice that a fixed asset should not be carried in financial statements at more than its recoverable amount, but there has been very little guidance as to how recoverable amount should be identified or measured.

The Companies Act requires provision to be made for permanent diminutions in the value of fixed assets, but does not include guidance as to:

(a)   what constitutes a permanent (as opposed to a temporary) diminution; and

(b)   the way in which diminutions should be presented in the financial statements.

SSAP 12 required that where there was a permanent diminution in value, the asset should be immediately written down to its recoverable amount and then depreciated over its remaining useful economic life. This meant that in most cases the diminution was charged immediately to the profit and loss account and was effectively treated as additional depreciation. However, the issue is more complicated where a fixed asset has been revalued.

Example

An asset costing £100,000 was purchased on 1 January 19X1 and has a useful economic life of 10 years. On 1 January 19X3 it was revalued to £150,000. On 1 January 19X5 it was estimated that the recoverable amount of the asset was only £100,000.

How could this impairment be treated in the financial statements for the year ended 31 December 19X5?

Solution

There are several possibilities. In theory (provided that the asset is not an investment property), the preparers of the financial statements could decide not to recognise the impairment on the grounds that it is temporary, but this would be unlikely to give a true and fair view.

In practice, there are two options:

(a)   Treat the impairment as a fall in value:

> Dr   Revaluation reserve   £12,500
> Cr   Fixed assets   £12,500

The impairment is recorded in the statement of total recognised gains and losses, but does not affect the results for the year. This is similar to the treatment of a temporary diminution required by SSAP 19.

(b)   Treat the impairment as additional depreciation:

> Dr   Depreciation expense   £12,500
> Cr   Fixed assets   £12,500

This is similar to the treatment of a permanent diminution required by SSAP 19 and results in a charge to the profit and loss account for the year.

From this we can see that this lack of guidance has reduced the comparability of financial statements. In addition, impairment losses would not always be recognised as soon as they occurred.

The need for guidance on how to calculate and recognise impairment has become more urgent with the issue of recent accounting standards:

- FRS 10 *Goodwill and intangible assets* requires annual impairment reviews where goodwill and intangible assets have a useful life exceeding twenty years.

- FRS 15 *Tangible fixed assets* requires annual impairment reviews where:
    - no depreciation charge is made on the grounds that it would be immaterial; or
    - the estimated remaining useful economic life of an asset is more than 50 years.

6.2   Scope

FRS 11 applies to purchased goodwill that is recognised in the balance sheet and all fixed assets except:

(a)   investment properties as defined by SSAP 19
(b)   fixed assets falling within the scope of FRS 13 (eg, investments).

Note that FRS 11 applies to investments in subsidiaries, associates and joint ventures because these are outside the scope of FRS 13.

6.3   The basic principle

Impairment is measured by comparing the carrying value of the asset with its recoverable amount. If the carrying amount exceeds the recoverable amount, the asset is impaired and should be written down. (Note that this effectively abolishes the distinction between temporary and permanent diminutions in value by treating all diminutions as permanent).

> **Definition**   **Recoverable amount** is the higher of the amounts that can be obtained from selling the asset (net realisable value) or using the asset (value in use).

> **Definition**   **Net realisable value** is the amount at which an asset could be disposed of, less any direct selling costs.

> **Definition**   **Value in use** is the present value of the future cash flows obtainable as a result of an asset's continued use, including those resulting from its ultimate disposal.

This is the same principle as **deprival value** and the definitions are based on the value to the business model in the ASB's draft Statement of Principles. The reasoning behind it is that, when a fixed asset becomes impaired, the decision must be made whether to continue to use it or to sell it. This decision is based on the cash flows that can be generated by following each course of action, so that an entity will not continue to use the asset if it can realise more cash by selling it and vice versa. This means that when an asset is stated at the higher of net realisable value or value in use it is recorded at its greatest value to the entity.

6.4   Activity

The following information relates to three assets:

	A £'000	B £'000	C £'000
Net book value	100	150	120
Net realisable value	110	125	100
Value in use	120	130	90

(a)   What is the recoverable amount of each asset?

(b)   Calculate the impairment provision for each of the three assets.

6.5   Activity solution

(a)   A: £120,000, B: £130,000, C: £100,000

(b)   A: Nil, B: £20,000, C: £20,000

6.6   When to carry out an impairment review

Impairment reviews should be carried out if:

(a)   events or changes in circumstances indicate that the carrying amount of an asset may not be recoverable; or

(b)   when required by FRS 10 or by FRS 15.

They are **not** required otherwise.

Indications that assets may have become impaired include:

(a)   a current period operating loss in the business in which the fixed asset or goodwill is involved or a net cash outflow from the operating activities of the business, combined with either past or expected future operating losses or net cash outflows from operating activities

(b)   a significant decline in a fixed asset's market value during the period

(c)   evidence of obsolescence or physical damage to the fixed asset

(d)   a significant adverse change in the business or the market in which the fixed asset or goodwill is involved (eg, the entrance of a major competitor)

(e)   a commitment by management to undertake a significant re-organisation

(f)   a major loss of key employees

(g)   a significant increase in market interest rates or other market rates of return that are likely to affect materially the fixed asset's recoverable amount.

6.7   Net realisable value

The net realisable value of an asset that is traded on an active market should be based on market value.

Net realisable value is the amount at which an asset could be disposed of, less any direct selling costs. Direct selling costs might include:

- legal costs
- stamp duty
- costs relating to the removal of a sitting tenant (in the case of a building).

Redundancy and reorganisation costs (eg, following the sale of a business) are **not** direct selling costs.

6.8   Value in use

Value in use is the present value of the future cash flows obtainable as a result of an asset's continued use.

Therefore there are two steps to the calculation:

1   estimate future cash flows
2   discount them to arrive at their present value.

(a)   Where possible, value in use should be estimated for individual assets. However, it may not always be possible to identify cash flows arising from individual fixed assets. If this is the case, value in use is calculated for income generating units (groups of assets that produce independent income streams).

(b)   Income generating units are identified by dividing the total income of the entity into as many largely independent income streams as is reasonably practicable.

(c)   Estimates of future cash flows should be:

    (i)   based on reasonable and supportable assumptions;

    (ii)   consistent with the most up to date budgets and plans that have been formally approved by management; and

    (iii)   should assume a steady or declining growth rate for the period beyond that covered by formal budgets and plans.

(d)   The discount rate used to arrive at the present value of the expected future cash flows should be the rate of return that the market would expect from an equally risky investment.

Conclusion   Impairment is measured by comparing the carrying amount of an asset with its recoverable amount. Recoverable amount is the higher of net realisable value and value in use.

6.9   Allocating impairment losses

Impairment losses may arise in relation to income generating units, rather than individual assets. Sometimes it may be obvious that specific assets are impaired (for example, they may be known to be damaged or obsolete). Otherwise, the loss is allocated to the assets in the income generating unit in the following order:

1.   goodwill;
2.   other intangible assets;
3.   tangible assets (on a pro-rata or more appropriate basis).

This means that the loss is allocated to assets with the most subjective valuations first.

No intangible asset with a readily ascertainable market value should be written down below its net realisable value.

No tangible asset with a net realisable value that can be measured reliably should be written down below its net realisable value.

6.10   Activity

An impairment loss of £60,000 arises in connection with an income generating unit. The carrying amount of the assets in the income generating unit, before the impairment, is as follows:

	£'000
Goodwill	20
Patent (with no market value)	10
Tangible fixed assets	40
	70

How is the impairment loss allocated?

6.11   Activity solution

The impairment loss is allocated as follows:

	Before impairment £'000	Loss £'000	After impairment £'000
Goodwill	20	(20)	–
Patent (with no market value)	10	(10)	–
Tangible fixed assets	40	(30)	10
	70	(60)	10

6.12   Recognising impairment losses in the financial statements

(a)   **Assets carried at historic cost**

Impairment losses are recognised in the profit and loss account. The impairment is effectively treated as additional depreciation.

(b)   **Assets which have been revalued**

Impairment losses are normally recognised in the statement of total recognised gains and losses until the carrying value of the asset falls below depreciated historical cost. Impairments below depreciated historical cost are recognised in the profit and loss account. The impairment is treated as a downward revaluation.

Where a fixed asset has been revalued but the impairment is caused by a clear consumption of economic benefits (e.g. because it is damaged) the loss is recognised in the profit and loss account. This type of impairment is treated as additional depreciation, rather than as a loss in value.

(c)   **Revision of useful economic life**

The remaining useful economic life and residual value of the asset should be reviewed and revised if necessary. The revised carrying amount should be depreciated over the revised estimate of the remaining useful economic life.

Notice that these rules are the same as the rules for recognising revaluation gains and losses (FRS 15).

6.13   Activity

At 1 January 19X7 a fixed asset had a carrying value of £20,000, based on its revalued amount, and a depreciated historical cost of £10,000. An impairment loss of £12,000 arose in the year ended 31 December 19X7.

How should this loss be reported in the financial statements for the year ended 31 December 19X7?

6.14   Activity solution

Assuming that the loss is not a reduction in the service potential of the asset, a loss of £10,000 will be recognised in the statement of total recognised gains and losses and the remaining loss of £2,000 will be recognised in the profit and loss account.

6.15   Restoration of past impairment losses

After an impairment loss has been recognised, it may reverse. The reversal can only be recognised under certain conditions.

(a)   **Tangible fixed assets and investments in subsidiaries, associates and joint ventures**

The restoration of past impairment losses should be recognised only when the recoverable amount of a tangible fixed asset has increased because of a change in economic conditions or in the expected use of the asset.

The reversal should be recognised in the current period's profit and loss account, unless it arises on a previously revalued fixed asset, in which case the reversal should be credited to the revaluation reserve and shown in the statement of total recognised gains and losses.

(b)   **Goodwill and intangible assets**

The reversal of an impairment loss should be recognised in the current period, if and only if:

(a)   the original loss was caused by an external event and subsequent external events clearly and demonstrably reverse the effects of that event in a way that was not foreseen in the original impairment calculations; or

(b)   the loss related to an intangible asset with a readily ascertainable market value and this has increased to above the intangible asset's impaired carrying amount.

In all cases, the reversal of the loss should be recognised to the extent that it increases the carrying amount of the asset up to the amount that it would have been had the original impairment not occurred.

6.16   Presentation and disclosure

(a)   Impairment losses recognised in the profit and loss account should be included within operating profit under the appropriate statutory heading. They should be disclosed as an exceptional item if appropriate.

(b)   Impairment losses recognised in the statement of total recognised gains and losses should be disclosed separately on the face of that statement.

(c)   In the notes to the financial statements in the accounting periods after the impairment, the impairment loss should be treated as follows:

(i)   for assets held on a historical cost basis, the impairment loss should be included within cumulative depreciation: the cost of the asset should not be reduced

(ii)   for revalued assets held at a market value, the impairment loss should be included within the revalued carrying amount.

(iii)   for revalued assets held at depreciated replacement cost, an impairment loss charged to the profit and loss account should be included within cumulative depreciation: the carrying amount of the asset should not be reduced; an impairment loss charged to the statement of total recognised gains and losses should be deducted from the carrying amount of the asset.

(d)   Other required disclosures include:

(i)   the discount rate applied (where the impairment loss is based on value in use)

(ii)   the reason for any reversal of an impairment loss recognised in a previous period, including any changes in the assumptions upon which the calculation of recoverable amount is based.

Conclusion   Impairment losses are normally recognised in the statement of total recognised gains and losses if the asset has been revalued and the impairment is not due to a consumption of economic benefits. Otherwise impairment losses are recognised in the profit and loss account.

7   THE WAY THE AUDITOR ENSURES COMPLIANCE WITH THE STANDARDS

7.1   SSAP 4

The auditor needs to check into the availability of grants related to both income and capital expenditure in the accounting period. In particular, he should refer to the conditions set by the government to the grants; they may be repayable under certain circumstances. A contingent liability note may be required as a result.

Only the deferred credit method is allowed for those entities falling within the provisions of the CA85. Therefore, the auditor should check that this method is followed by companies and that the correct transfers are made to the profit and loss account each period.

7.2   SSAP 19

The auditor needs to establish whether any assets of the company fall within the definition in SSAP 19. If so, the main practical problem relates to the audit of the valuation and the changes made to that valuation.

The auditor will need to obtain similar evidence as to the reasonableness of the valuation as he would for any other valuation undertaken by the directors. A particularly relevant standard will be SAS 520 *Using the work of an expert* (see later in the text).

Where the investment property(ies) represent a **substantial** proportion of the total assets of a listed company, SSAP 19 suggests that the valuation is undertaken annually by a person holding a recognised professional qualification and at least every five years by an external valuer.

7.3   FRS 10

The main points the auditor needs to verify for any goodwill arising in the accounting period are as follows.

(a)   Examine the methods used to determine the fair value of the consideration given to purchase the shares of the subsidiary and the fair value of the net assets in the subsidiary at the date of acquisition. This area raises significant accounting problems which are the subject of FRS 7 (see later in the text).

(b)   The accounting treatment of the goodwill once it has been quantified needs to be checked to ensure it is being accounted for in compliance with the decision of the board of directors.

(c)   A check is required that the detailed disclosure requirements of FRS 10 are complied with.

8   CHAPTER SUMMARY

There are two feasible approaches to the accounting treatment of capital grants but companies have to use the deferred credit method.

An investment property is precisely defined and that definition needs to be carefully learned.

FRS 10 requires that positive purchased goodwill is included in the balance sheet as an intangible fixed asset. Other intangible assets may be included in the balance sheet if they can be reliably valued. Goodwill and intangible assets should normally be amortised over a period of 20 years or less, but may be amortised over a longer period or maintained in the balance sheet indefinitely provided that certain conditions are met.

FRS 11 requires that fixed assets and goodwill are not carried at a value above their recoverable amount. Recoverable amount is the higher of net realisable value and value in use.

9   SELF TEST QUESTIONS

9.1   How does the prudence principle affect the treatment of grants? (1.2)

9.2   Why should companies account for grants using the deferred credit method? (1.4)

9.3   Investment properties should be included on the balance sheet at what value? (2.3)

9.4   Changes in value of an investment property should go where? (2.3)

9.5   What is the definition of identifiable net assets? (3.1)

9.6   What is the 'dangling debit'? (3.2)

9.7   What is a brand? (4.1)

9.8   How should non-purchased goodwill be accounted for? (5.3)

9.9   What is value in use? (6.3)

9.10   When should an impairment review be carried out? (6.6)

10   EXAMINATION TYPE QUESTION

10.1   Maxichip Ltd

Maxichip, a manufacturing company, commenced trading on 1 March 19X1. Extracts from the draft accounts for the year ended 28 February 19X4 show:

Profit and loss account

	£'000		£'000
Cost of sales	37,270	Sales	43,000
Administrative expenses	494	Grant received	300
Debenture interest	190		

Balance sheet as at 28 February 19X4

	£'000		£'000
Ordinary share capital	3,000	Leasehold buildings	
Debenture stock	1,500	- cost	2,500
		- depreciation	200
		Plant - cost	2,000
Profit and loss account at		- depreciation	400
1 March 19X3	1,300		
Suspense account			
- grant	280		

You also obtain the following information

(1)   Grants received consisted of £100,000 on plant and £200,000 for buildings. Plant expenditure was £500,000 and buildings £900,000.

(2)   Depreciation is charged on the straight line method at the following rates.

> Buildings 6%
> Plant 20%

with a full year's charge in the year assets are acquired.

No depreciation has been charged for the current year.

(3)   The appropriate amount of the opening balance on the grants suspense account to be transferred to profit and loss account is £30,000. This is in addition to any amounts required to be transferred in respect of grants received in the year ended 28 February 19X4.

You are required to prepare the company's financial statements for the year ended 28 February 19X4 insofar as you are able from the available information. Notes should include an analysis of fixed assets and deferred credits.   **(15 marks)**

11   ANSWER TO EXAMINATION TYPE QUESTION

11.1   Maxichip Ltd

Profit and loss account extracts for the year ended 28 February 19X4

	£'000
Sales	43,000
Cost of sales (37,270 + 550 − 62)	37,758
Gross profit	5,242
Administrative expenses	494
Interest paid	190
Profit on ordinary activities before taxation	4,558

Balance sheet extracts as at 28 February 19X4

	£'000
Tangible fixed assets (note 1)	
Land and buildings	2,150
Plant	1,200
	3,350

Creditors: amounts falling due after more than one year
    Debenture stock   1,500
Accruals and deferred income (note 2)   518

Capital and reserves
    Called up share capital
    Ordinary shares   3,000

Notes to the accounts

(1)   **Fixed assets**

	Leasehold buildings £'000	Plant £'000
Cost		
At 1 March 19X3 (bal. fig.)	1,600	1,500
Additions	900	500
At 28 February 19X4	2,500	2,000
Depreciation		
At 1 March 19X3	200	400
Charge for the year		
6% × 2,500	150	
20% × 2,000		400
At 28 February 19X4	350	800
NBV at 28 February 19X4	2,150	1,200
NBV at 28 February 19X3	1,400	1,100

(2)   **Deferred credit – analysis**

	£'000
At 1 March 19X3	280
Received during year	300
Transferred to Profit and loss account (Working)	(62)
At 28 Feb 19X4	518

WORKING

	£'000
Deferred credit transfer	
Per question	30
Re additions	
Buildings	
6% × 200,000	12
Plant	
20% × 100,000	20
	62

17 GROUP ACCOUNTING - 1

INTRODUCTION & LEARNING OBJECTIVES

This is a core area of the syllabus which you should expect to be examined frequently, invariably in the form of a computational question requiring the actual preparation of consolidated accounts.

So far we have been looking at the accounts of individual companies. In this chapter we begin to consider what happens when the activities of a business are conducted not through the medium of a single company, but through a number of companies. Although each company remains a separate entity in law, the economic reality is that they form a combined group. A set of accounts showing the combined results and financial position is called a set of consolidated accounts. In this chapter we look at the preparation of a consolidated balance sheet; in the next chapter we tackle the consolidated profit and loss account.

When you have studied this chapter you should be able to do the following:

- Prepare a consolidated balance sheet for a group of companies with a simple group structure.
- Make appropriate adjustments in respect of goodwill and minority interests.

1 INTRODUCTION TO CONSOLIDATED ACCOUNTS

1.1 What is a 'group'?

Although every company is a separate entity from the legal point of view, from the economic point of view several companies may not be separate at all. In particular, when one company owns enough shares in another company to have a majority of votes at that company's annual general meeting, the first company may appoint all the directors of, and decide what dividends should be paid by, the second company. This degree of control enables the first company to manage the trading activities and future plans of the second company as if it were merely a department of the first company.

The first company referred to above is called a 'holding company' or 'parent undertaking', and the second is called a 'subsidiary'. These terms are defined in the Companies Act, discussed later. For the moment it is sufficient to note that the essential feature of a group is that one company controls all the others **absolutely**.

Company law recognises that this state of affairs often arises, and requires further items to be included in the accounts of companies related in this way. The further items include those enacted with the intention of enabling a reader of one company's accounts to identify all the other companies in the group.

They also include a requirement that the holding company must produce 'group accounts', showing the results of the whole group, in addition to its usual accounts: s229 CA85.

1.2 Normal form of group accounts

Group accounts could consist of a variety of things, but in normal circumstances much the best way of showing the results of a group is to imagine that all the transactions of the group had been carried out by a single equivalent company and to prepare a balance sheet, a profit and loss account, and (if required) a cash flow statement for that company. These accounts are called 'consolidated accounts'.

Two different methods of accounting have been developed to deal with the preparation of consolidated accounts. These are 'acquisition accounting' and 'merger accounting'.

There are five Accounting Standards which are relevant to the preparation of consolidated accounts:

FRS 2   *Accounting for subsidiary undertakings*
FRS 6   *Acquisitions and mergers*
FRS 7   *Fair values in acquisition accounting*
FRS 9   *Associates and joint ventures*
FRS 10   *Goodwill and intangible assets*

A further accounting standard FRS 8 *Related party disclosures* may affect the presentation of group accounts. As FRS 8 also has important implications for auditors, it is dealt with in the auditing chapters of this textbook.

1.3   General procedure

Each company in a group prepares its accounting records and annual financial statements in the usual way. From the individual companies' balance sheets, the holding company prepares a consolidated balance sheet for the group, and likewise a consolidated profit and loss account from the individual companies' profit and loss accounts.

2   THE BASIC BALANCE SHEET CONSOLIDATION

2.1   The model – Example

Balance sheets at 31 December 19X4

	H Ltd £'000	H Ltd £'000	S Ltd £'000	S Ltd £'000
Fixed assets		60		40
Investment in S Ltd at cost		50		
Current assets	40		40	
Less: Current liabilities	20		30	
Net current assets		20		10
		130		50
Ordinary share capital (£1 shares)		100		50
Profit and loss account		30		-
		130		50

H Ltd acquired all the shares in S Ltd on 31 December 19X4 for a cost of £50,000.

The consolidated balance sheet will differ from that of H Ltd's (the holding company's) balance sheet, in that the balance on 'investment in subsidiary account' will be replaced by the underlying net assets which the investment represents. (This is similar to the preparation of the combined balance sheet for a branch and head office, where the asset 'branch account' is replaced by the net assets of the branch.)

The cost of the investment in the subsidiary is effectively cancelled with the ordinary share capital and reserves of the subsidiary in calculations known as **consolidation schedules** which are discussed in more detail below. However, in this simple case, it can be seen that the relevant figures are equal and opposite, and therefore cancel directly.

This leaves a balance sheet showing:

(i)   the net assets of the whole group **(H + S)**;

(ii)   the share capital of the group which is always solely the share capital of the holding company **(H only)**; and

(iii)   the profit and loss account comprising profits made by the group: in this case we have profits made by the holding company but none made by the subsidiary to bring in to the calculations.

So, by cross casting the net assets of each company, and taking care of the investment in S Ltd and the share capital of S Ltd we arrive at the consolidated balance sheet given in the solution below.

Solution

H Ltd
Consolidated balance sheet at 31 December 19X4

	£'000	£'000
Fixed assets £(60 + 40)		100
Current assets £(40 + 40)	80	
Creditors: amounts falling due within one year £(20 + 30)	50	
Net current assets		30
Total assets less current liabilities		130
Called up share capital (£1 ordinary shares)		100
Profit and loss account		30
		130

Note: Under no circumstances will any share capital of any subsidiary company ever be included in the figure of share capital on the consolidated balance sheet.

The vertical presentation should be used in the examination and the headings and format should be in keeping with the requirements of CA 85 and accounting standards in so far as the information given allows.

2.3   **Goodwill on consolidation**

When the investment in the subsidiary costs more or less than the net assets acquired in the subsidiary, there will be a difference between the cost of the investment in the subsidiary and the share capital of the subsidiary.

By modifying the previous example we can tackle this problem:

Balance sheets at 31 December 19X4

	H Ltd		*S Ltd*	
	£'000	£'000	£'000	£'000
Fixed assets		60		40
Investment in S Ltd at cost		60		
Current assets	30		40	
Less: Current liabilities	20		30	
Net current assets		10		10
		130		50
Ordinary share capital (£1 shares)		100		50
Profit and loss account		30		-
		130		50

H Ltd acquired all the shares in S Ltd on 31 December 19X4 for a cost of £60,000.

In this case the cost of the shares in S Ltd exceeds S Ltd's share capital by £10,000. This is the goodwill on consolidation or premium on acquisition. It represents the excess of the purchase consideration over the fair value of the net assets acquired. The calculation may be set out as a consolidation schedule as follows:

	£'000	£'000	Notes
Cost of investment		60	1
Less: Share of net assets acquired (at fair value)			
Ordinary share capital	50		2
Profit and loss account	-		3
	50		
Group share	× 100%	(50)	4
		10	5

Notes to the calculation.

1   The cost of the investment will appear in the balance sheet of H Ltd. If there is more than one investment details will be given of the cost of individual investments in the question.

2   We are actually comparing the cost of the investment with the net assets of the subsidiary acquired, as represented by the share capital and reserves of the subsidiary at the date of acquisition. Remember **Net assets = Capital + Reserves.**

3   In this case there are no reserves of the subsidiary to consider. However, it is important to note here that the reserves which are taken into consideration in the calculation of goodwill are those at the **date of acquisition** of the subsidiary. Whilst the share capital of the subsidiary is unlikely to have altered since that date, the profit and loss account will have changed.

4   As 100% of the shares in S Ltd were acquired, we compare the cost of the shares with 100% of the net assets of S Ltd. If only a proportion of the shares are acquired, say 90%, we compare the cost of those shares with the appropriate share (90%) of the net assets acquired. This is further illustrated later on in the chapter.

5   The resulting goodwill is dealt with in accordance with FRS 10 *Goodwill and intangible assets*.

FRS 10 requires that purchased goodwill is normally included in the balance sheet as an intangible asset and amortised (depreciated) over its estimated useful life.

Having first calculated goodwill, the net assets of the holding company and the subsidiary can be cross cast and the consolidated balance sheet completed.

H Ltd
Consolidated balance sheet at 31 December 19X4

	£'000	£'000
Intangible assets		10
Tangible assets £(60 + 40)		100
Current assets £(30 + 40)	70	
Creditors: amounts falling due within one year £(20 + 30)	50	
Net current assets		20
Total assets less current liabilities		130

Called up share capital (£1 ordinary shares)			100
Profit and loss account			30
			——
			130
			——

Where the cost of the investment is less than the net assets purchased, a credit balance appears on the adjustment account ie, a profit. This is known as **negative goodwill** or **discount on acquisition**. It is shown separately on the face of the balance sheet immediately beneath the goodwill heading and written back to the profit and loss account over the periods expected to benefit.

Conclusion Goodwill represents the difference between the amount paid to acquire the net assets of a subsidiary and the fair value of those net assets.

2.4   Determining the fair values of net assets

The ASB published FRS 7 in September 1994 to help preparers of accounts to determine the fair values of assets and liabilities at the date of an acquisition, so that the purchased goodwill arising can be correctly calculated. The general idea is that the fair value is 'the amount at which an asset or liability could be exchanged in an arm's length transaction between informed and willing parties, other than in a forced or liquidation sale'. The application of this principle is studied in detail later in this text.

Where an exam question gives the fair values of net assets at the date of acquisition which differ from book values, the calculation of goodwill and the consolidation must be carried out by reference to the fair values given.

2.5   Reserves

In the examples above, the unrealistic case of a company (S Ltd), where the shareholders' interest consisted solely of ordinary share capital, was considered. Usually, of course, shareholders' interest includes also the profit and loss account reserve. An additional point is that H Ltd may have acquired the controlling interest in S Ltd part way through the year. When looking at the revenue reserves of S Ltd at the year end, a distinction must be made between:

(a)   those reserves of S Ltd which existed at the date of acquisition by H Ltd (**pre-acquisition reserves**); and

(b)   the increase in the reserves of S Ltd which arose after acquisition by H Ltd (**post-acquisition reserves**).

Example

Balance sheets at 31 December 19X4

	H Ltd		S Ltd	
	£'000	£'000	£'000	£'000
Fixed assets		50		40
Investment in S Ltd at cost		70		-
Current assets	30		40	
Less: Current liabilities	20		10	
	——		——	
		10		30
		——		——
		130		70
		——		——
Ordinary share capital (£1 shares)		100		50
Profit and loss account		30		20
		——		——
		130		70
		——		——

You are further informed that H Ltd acquired **all** the shares in S Ltd at 30 June 19X4 when the profit and loss account reserves of S Ltd amounted to £15,000. Goodwill is to be amortised over 5 years from the date of acquisition, with a full year's charge in the year of acquisition.

Step 1 First, deal with the goodwill which is effectively computed at the date of take-over. The cost of the investment (£70,000) is compared with the net assets of S Ltd at 30 June 19X4 as represented by ordinary share capital (£50,000) and profit and loss account reserves (£15,000). Note that what are concerned are the reserves at the date of acquisition (£15,000) as opposed to reserves at the date of consolidation (£20,000). The calculation becomes:

Goodwill on consolidation

	£'000	£'000
Cost of investment		70
Less: Share of net assets acquired		
Ordinary share capital	50	
Profit and loss account	15	
	$65 \times 100\%$ 65	
		5
Amortisation charge		(1)
NBV of goodwill		4

Step 2 In addition, a new consolidation schedule, a **consolidated profit and loss account reserve**, is required. The object of this account is to show the distributable profit of the group at the balance sheet date. Profits made by S Ltd prior to acquisition by H Ltd (pre-acquisition profits) are not regarded as those of the group whereas profits of S Ltd arising **after** acquisition (post-acquisition profits) **are** regarded as group profits. Allocate the reserves of S Ltd at the balance sheet date (31 December 19X4) between pre-acquisition and post-acquisition. Pre-acquisition reserves are effectively capitalised, being dealt with in the goodwill consolidation schedule (shown above), whereas post-acquisition reserves, together with the present balance on H Ltd reserves, are transferred to consolidated profit and loss account reserves.

The consolidated revenue reserves or profit and loss account reserves schedule is set out as follows:

	£'000
H Ltd: (all)	30
S Ltd: (only post acquisition i.e., now − on acquisition)	
(20 − 15)	5
Less: Goodwill amortised	(1)
	34

Step 3   The consolidated balance sheet now appears as follows:

H Ltd
Group balance sheet at 31 December 19X4

	£'000	£'000
Fixed assets:		
Intangible assets		4
Tangible assets £(50 + 40)		90
Current assets £(30 + 40)	70	
Creditors: amounts falling due within one year £(20 + 10)	30	
		40
Total assets less current liabilities		134
Called up share capital (£1 ordinary shares)		100
Consolidated profit and loss account		34
		134

2.6   Minority interests

What happens if H Ltd owns only 80% of the ordinary shares of S Ltd? In this case there is said to be minority interests of 20%. What problems does this present?

The main decision to make on accounting principles is whether to consolidate all the net assets of S Ltd, or merely to consolidate the proportion of the net assets represented by the shares held and the proportion of the reserves which apply to those shares ie, consolidate only 80% of the net assets of S Ltd.

The dominant principle is that the directors are preparing accounts of their custody of all the assets under their control, even though there are owners other than the holding company.

Therefore, the generally accepted solution is to consolidate all the subsidiary's net assets and then bring in a counterbalancing liability on the consolidated balance sheet to represent that part of the assets controlled but not owned.

This liability is presented quite separately in the consolidated balance sheet. It is **not** part of the shareholders' funds. For the purposes of balance sheet presentation, this is referred to as **minority interests** in the CA85. It must be shown as a separate main heading on the balance sheet either:

(a)   after item J on the Balance sheet format 1 (Accruals and deferred income); or
(b)   after item K (Capital and reserves).

Acceptable presentations are therefore:

		£
(a)	Total assets less current liabilities, say	2,000
	Less: Minority interests	160
		1,840
	Called up share capital	1,500
	Profit and loss account	340
		1,840

(b)   Total assets less current liabilities   2,000

      Called up share capital   1,500
      Profit and loss account   340
      Minority interests   160

                                                                          2,000

The presentation which is not allowed is:

	£
Total assets less current liabilities	2,000
Called up share capital	1,500
Minority interests	160
Profit and loss account	340
	2,000

The last presentation implies that minority interests are part of shareholders' funds.

Example

Balance sheets at 31 December 19X4

	H Ltd £'000	H Ltd £'000	S Ltd £'000	S Ltd £'000
Fixed assets		50		40
Investment in S Ltd at cost		70		-
Current assets	30		40	
Less: Current liabilities	20		10	
		10		30
		130		70
Ordinary share capital (£1 shares)		100		50
Profit and loss account		30		20
		130		70

H Ltd acquired 40,000 £1 shares in S Ltd on 30 June 19X4 for £70,000, when the profit and loss account reserves of S Ltd amounted to £15,000. Goodwill is amortised over 6 years from the date of acquisition, with a full year's charge in the year of acquisition.

Solution

A third consolidation schedule is required to calculate the minority interest in the net assets of the subsidiary.

Minority interest

Net assets of S at the balance sheet date

	£'000
Share capital	50
Profit and loss account	20
	70

Minority %		× 20%
		14

The other two consolidation schedules will appear as shown below. Each is affected by the fact that the holding company now owns only 80% of the shares in the subsidiary.

Goodwill

	£'000	£'000
Cost of investment		70
Less: Share of net assets acquired		
Share capital	50	
Profit and loss account	15	
	65	
Group share	× 80%	
		(52)
		18
Amortisation charge		(3)
		15

Profit and loss account

	£'000
H Ltd: all	30
S Ltd: H Ltd's share of S Ltd's post acquisition profits	
80% (20 − 15)	4
Less: Goodwill amortised	(3)
	31

Note how the reserves of S Ltd are allocated during the consolidation process:

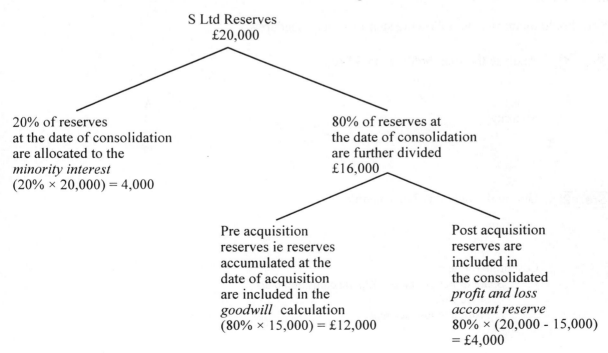

S Ltd Reserves
£20,000

20% of reserves at the date of consolidation are allocated to the *minority interest* (20% × 20,000) = 4,000

80% of reserves at the date of consolidation are further divided £16,000

Pre acquisition reserves ie reserves accumulated at the date of acquisition are included in the *goodwill* calculation (80% × 15,000) = £12,000

Post acquisition reserves are included in the consolidated *profit and loss account reserve* 80% × (20,000 - 15,000) = £4,000

Similarly, the share capital of S Ltd is allocated to the goodwill calculation (the group's share, 80%) and to the minority interest calculation (the minority's share, 20%).

Taking the balances from the consolidation schedules and then adding the other balance sheet items together, the consolidated balance sheet can be constructed:

	£'000	£'000
Fixed assets:		
Intangible assets		15
Tangible assets £(50 + 40)		90
Current assets £(30 + 40)	70	
Creditors: amounts falling due within one year £(20 + 10)	30	
		40
Total assets less current liabilities		145
Called up share capital (£1 ordinary shares)		100
Profit and loss account		31
Minority interests		14
		145

Conclusion This last example includes all the three basic elements of a balance sheet consolidation:

(a)   reserves in subsidiary company;

(b)   acquisition of less than 100% of S Ltd's shares;

(c)   acquisition earlier than balance sheet date.

The example should be reworked.

3   STEP-BY-STEP PROCEDURE FOR BALANCE SHEET CONSOLIDATION

3.1   Introduction

You should memorise the following step-by-step procedure.

Step 1   Analyse the shareholdings in S Ltd

	%
Group	A
Minority	B
	100

Step 2   Goodwill consolidation schedule

Goodwill

	£	£
Cost of investment		X
Less: Share of net assets of S Ltd at acquisition date		
Share capital	X	
Profit and loss account	X	
	X	

Group share	× A%	(X)
		—
Goodwill		X
Amortised to date		(X)
		—
		X
		—

Step 3   Reserves consolidation schedule

Profit and loss account reserve

		£
H Ltd:		X
S Ltd:	Group share of S's post acquisition profits	
	A% (S now − S at acquisition)	X
Less:	Goodwill amortised (from step 2)	(X)
		—
		X
		—

Step 4   Minority interest consolidation schedule

Minority interest

	£
Net assets of S Ltd at the balance sheet date	
Share capital	X
Profit and loss account	X
	—
	X
Minority share	× B%
	—
	X
	—

Step 5   Prepare the consolidated balance sheet, comprising:

(i)   balances on consolidation schedules (steps 2 to 4 above); **plus**

(ii)   items in original balance sheets not transferred to consolidation schedules.

3.2   Activity

The summarised draft balance sheets of a group at 31 December 19X4 were:

	H Ltd	S Ltd		H Ltd	S Ltd
	£	£		£	£
Sundry assets	106,000	34,500	Share capital (£1 ord.)	100,000	20,000
Investment in S Ltd			Profit and loss account	22,000	6,500
(shares at cost)	27,000	–	Creditors	11,000	8,000
	———	———		———	———
	133,000	34,500		133,000	34,500

Prepare the consolidated balance sheet for each of the following alternatives:

(a)   H Ltd acquired all the shares in S Ltd on 1 January 19X4, when S Ltd had profit and loss account reserves of £6,000.

(b)   Facts as in (a) above, except that only 16,000 ordinary shares in S Ltd were purchased for £27,000.

(c)   Facts as in (a) above, except that only 16,000 ordinary shares in S Ltd were purchased for £27,000 on 1 January 19X4. Freehold property which was not depreciated was estimated by the directors of H Ltd to be under-valued by £5,000 on 1 January 19X4. No adjustment has been made in the books of S Ltd.

(Hint: Adjust for the revaluation in S Ltd's books before consolidating. The revaluation reserve becomes part of the subsidiary's shareholders' interest and is treated in exactly the same way as the other reserves.)

Goodwill is amortised over 10 years from the date of acquisition.

3.3   Activity solution

Note: your balance sheets should be prepared in vertical format. The examiner will occasionally give you 'draft' horizontal balance sheets as above, but your solution should always accord with best practice.

(a)

Step 1   Shareholdings in S Ltd

	%
Group	100
Minority	-
	100

Step 2   Goodwill

	£	£
Cost of investment		27,000
Less: Share of net assets of S Ltd at the acquisition date		
Share capital	20,000	
Profit and loss account	6,000	
	26,000	
Group share	× 100%	
		26,000
Goodwill		1,000
Amortisation charge		(100)
		900

Step 3   Reserves

Consolidated profit and loss account reserve

	£
H Ltd:	22,000
S Ltd: 100% (6,500 – 6,000)	500
Less: Goodwill amortised	(100)
	22,400

Step 4   Minority interest

There is no minority interest at the balance sheet date as H Ltd owns 100% of the shares of S Ltd.

Step 5   H Ltd Group

Consolidated balance sheet at 31 December 19X4

	£
Goodwill	900
Sundry assets	140,500
Creditors	(19,000)
Total assets less current liabilities	122,400
Called up share capital	100,000
Profit and loss account	22,400
	122,400

(b)

Step 1   Shareholdings in S Ltd

	%
Group	80
Minority	20
	100

Step 2   Goodwill

	£	£
Cost of investment		27,000
Less: Share of net assets of S Ltd at the acquisition date		
Share capital	20,000	
Profit and loss account	6,000	
	26,000	
Group share	× 80%	
		(20,800)
Goodwill		6,200
Amortisation charge		(620)
		5,580

Step 3   Reserves

Consolidated profit and loss account reserve

	£
H Ltd:	22,000
S Ltd: 80% (6,500 – 6,000)	400
Less: Goodwill amortised	(620)
	21,780

Step 4   Minority interest

Net assets of S Ltd at the balance sheet date

	£
Share capital	20,000
Profit and loss account	6,500
	26,500
Minority share	× 20%
	5,300

Step 5   H Ltd Group

Consolidated balance sheet at 31 December 19X4

	£
Goodwill	5,580
Sundry assets	140,500
Creditors	(19,000)
Total assets less current liabilities	127,080
Called up share capital	100,000
Profit and loss account	21,780
Minority interest	5,300
	127,080

(c)

Step 1   Shareholdings in S Ltd

	%
Group	80
Minority	20
	100

Step 2   Goodwill

	£	£
Cost of investment		27,000
Less: Share of net assets of S Ltd at the acquisition date		
Share capital	20,000	
Profit and loss account	6,000	
* Revaluation reserve	5,000	
	31,000	
Group share	× 80%	
		(24,800)
Goodwill		2,200
Amortisation charge		(220)
		1,980

* As the asset was revalued to fair value at the acquisition date, the revaluation surplus arose prior to the acquisition and is therefore included in the goodwill calculation as a pre-acquisition reserve.

Step 3   Reserves

Consolidated profit and loss account reserve

	£
H Ltd:	22,000
S Ltd: 80% (6,500 – 6,000)	400
Less: Goodwill amortised	(220)
	22,180

Revaluation reserve

This is an entirely pre-acquisition reserve and therefore none will be included in group reserves.

Step 4   Minority interest

Net assets of S Ltd at the balance sheet date

	£
Share capital	20,000
Profit and loss account	6,500
Revaluation reserve	5,000
	31,500
Minority share	× 20%
	6,300

Step 5   H Ltd

Consolidated balance sheet at 31 December 19X4

	£
Goodwill	1,980
Sundry assets (106,000 + 34,500 + 5,000)	145,500
Creditors (11,000 + 8,000)	(19,000)
	128,480
Called up share capital	100,000
Profit and loss account	22,180
Minority interest	6,300
	128,480

4   INTER-COMPANY ITEMS

4.1   Introduction

The individual balance sheets of the holding company and subsidiary companies are likely to include inter-company items ie, amounts owing between the group companies. These inter-company items must be eliminated when the consolidated balance sheet is prepared, in order to show the proper position of the economic unit, the group.

4.2   Current accounts

At the year end current accounts may not agree, owing to the existence of in-transit items such as goods or cash. The usual rules are:

(a)   If the goods or cash are in transit between the holding company and the subsidiary, make the adjusting entry to the balance sheet of the holding company, irrespective of the direction of transfer ie,

Dr   Cash in transit
Cr   Current account with subsidiary

Note that this is for the purpose of consolidation only.

(b)   If the goods or cash are in transit between subsidiaries, then adjust in the books of the ultimate recipient.

(c)   Once in agreement, the current accounts may be contra'd and cancelled as part of the process of cross casting the upper half of the balance sheet. This can be achieved, along with any other adjustments, as a working paper which would show:

(i)   the upper half of the balance sheets of each company;

(ii)   all adjustments to these figures along with cancelled inter-company items; and

(iii)   the final figures which will appear in the upper half of the consolidated balance sheet, resulting from the cross casting of items in (i) and (ii) above.

However, as this working paper would take time to generate in an exam, it is useful to use the balance sheets given in the exam paper itself to form this working paper.

Example

Balance sheets at 31 December 19X4

	H Ltd £	S Ltd £
Investment in S Ltd (at cost)	19,000	
S Ltd current account	10,000	
H Ltd current account		(9,000)
Cash at bank	10,000	23,000
Sundry net assets	41,000	16,000
	80,000	30,000
Share capital (£1 ord)	50,000	10,000
Profit and loss account	30,000	20,000
	80,000	30,000

H Ltd bought 7,500 shares in S Ltd on 1 January 19X4 when the balance on the profit and loss account reserve of S Ltd was £12,000. The current account difference has arisen as a cheque sent by S Ltd to H Ltd on 30 December 19X4 was not received by H Ltd until 3 January 19X5.

Goodwill is amortised over 5 years from the date of acquisition, with a full year's charge in the year of acquisition.

Solution

An adjustment for cash in transit has to be made before the consolidation can be completed. An extra step is therefore required in the consolidation procedure; it is a good idea to make this sort of adjustment early on so that it is not forgotten.

Step 1   Shareholdings in S Ltd

	%
Group	75
Minority	25
	100

Step 2   Adjustments

Cash in transit

Dr:	Cash in transit	£1,000	
Cr:	S Ltd current account		
	(H's balance sheet)		£1,000

Cancel the current accounts which are now in agreement. (Note that at this stage the top half of the consolidated balance sheet can nearly all be completed - a useful tip for the exam room when time is of the essence).

	H Ltd £	S Ltd £	Group £
Investment in S Ltd (at cost)	19,000		
S Ltd current account	(1,000)̶ 10,000̶		
H Ltd current account		(2,000)̶	
Cash at bank	10,000	23,000	**33,000**
Cash in transit	**1,000**	-	**1,000**
Sundry net assets	41,000	16,000	**57,000**
	80,000	30,000	

Step 3   Goodwill

	£	£
Cost of investment		19,000
Less: Share of net assets of S Ltd at the acquisition date		
Share capital	10,000	
Profit and loss account	12,000	
	22,000	
Group share	× 75%	
		16,500
Goodwill		2,500
Amortisation charge		(500)
		2,000

Step 4   Reserves

Consolidated profit and loss account

	£
H Ltd:	30,000
S Ltd: 75% (20,000 – 12,000)	6,000
Less: Goodwill amortised	(500)
	35,500

Step 5   Minority interest

Net assets of S Ltd at the balance sheet date

	£
Share capital	10,000
Profit and loss account	20,000
	30,000
Minority share	× 25%
	7,500

Step 6   H Ltd

Consolidated balance sheet at 31 December 19X4

	£
Goodwill	2,000
Cash at bank (10,000 + 23,000)	33,000
Cash in transit	1,000
Sundry net assets	57,000
	93,000
Called up share capital	50,000
Profit and loss account	35,500
Minority interest	7,500
	93,000

Conclusion   When current accounts between members of a group disagree as a result of cash in transit, the balance sheets show the correct position from each individual company's point of view, but adjustment is required before the consolidation can be performed. The two current accounts will then cancel as the balance sheets are cross-cast.

4.3   Profits

Where goods have been sold by one group company to another at a profit and some of these goods are still in the purchaser's stock at the year end, then the profit loading on these goods is **unrealised** from the viewpoint of the group as a whole.

This is because we are treating the group as if it is a single entity. No-one can make a profit by trading with himself.

(a)   **Wholly-owned subsidiary**

Where goods are sold by S Ltd (a wholly-owned subsidiary) to H Ltd (its holding company), or by H Ltd to S Ltd, and some of the goods are in stock at the year end, there are two steps:

(i)   calculate the unrealised profit in closing stock; and

(ii)   make the consolidation adjustment for the unrealised profit, either as a double entry prior to drawing up the consolidated balance sheet:

Dr   Consolidated profit and loss account reserve
Cr   Consolidated stock

or by making the adjustment to H Ltd's balance sheet in the consolidation working papers, as was done with cash in transit:

Dr: Profit and loss account reserve
Cr: Stock

(in H Ltd's balance sheet)

Either method reduces stock to cost and removes unrealised profit from the group reserves. The second option is the most efficient in an exam as it is less likely to be forgotten.

(b)   **Partly-owned subsidiary**

Suppose H Ltd owns 90% of S Ltd. During the year S Ltd sells goods to H Ltd at cost plus 25%. At the year end the closing stock of H Ltd includes £8,000 of goods, at invoice value, acquired originally from S Ltd. What adjustments are required in the consolidation working papers?

In the past this was an area in which opinions differed. The CA89 requires intra-group profits to be eliminated but where a subsidiary is partly owned it allows the elimination to be either of the whole of the profit or in proportion to the group's shareholding in the subsidiary.

FRS 2 removes the choice as to whom should suffer the deduction of intra-group profit.

Profit or losses on any intra-group transactions should be eliminated in full. The elimination should be set against the interests held by the group and the minority interest in proportion to their holdings in the undertaking whose individual financial statements recorded the eliminated profits or losses.

Thus, sales from the holding company to the subsidiary produce profits in the holding company. Any unrealised profits should be charged against the group. Sales from the subsidiary to the holding company produce profits in the subsidiary company. The unrealised profits should be split between the group and the minority.

Returning to the example, the **total** unrealised profit is:

$$\frac{25}{125} \times £8,000 \;=\; £1,600$$

Note: the denominator in the fraction. The £8,000 is at **selling** price to S Ltd ie, 100 + 25.

Consolidated stock must be reduced (credited) by £1,600, the minority interest will be reduced by its share of this (10% × 1,600), £160, and the remaining 90%, £1,440, will be borne by the group as a reduction in revenue reserves.

Again, this may be achieved by means of a consolidation adjustment put through prior to drawing up the balance sheet.

		£	£
Dr	Consolidated revenue reserves		
	90% × 1,600	1,440	
Dr	Minority interests		
	10% × 1,600	160	
Cr	Consolidated stock		1,600

Alternatively, if an adjustment is made to S Ltd's balance sheet in the consolidation working papers, this will automatically be achieved as the consolidation schedules are prepared. The adjustment is:

Dr:	Profit and loss account reserve	£1,600	
Cr:	Stock		£1,600

(in S Ltd's balance sheet)

A note to the accounts would show 'Provision has been made for the whole of the unrealised profit in stock.' This note should appear in the statement on accounting policies.

If H Ltd had sold the goods to S Ltd the journal entry required would be the same as in (a) above.

Conclusion   Profits made by members of a group on transactions with other group members are quite properly recognised in the accounts of the individual companies concerned. But in terms of the group as a whole, such profits are **unrealised** and must be eliminated from the consolidated accounts as a consolidation adjustment.

Example

Balance sheets at 31 December 19X4

	H Ltd £	S Ltd £
Investment in S Ltd (at cost)	75,000	
Stock	12,000	5,000
Other net assets	83,000	95,000
	170,000	100,000
Share capital (£1 ord)	50,000	40,000
Profit and loss account	120,000	60,000
	170,000	100,000

H Ltd acquired 32,000 shares in S Ltd on 1 January 19X4 when the balance on the profit and loss account of S Ltd was £50,000. During the year S Ltd sold goods to H Ltd for £80,000 making a standard mark up of 25%. At 31 December 19X4, H Ltd included in its stock value £5,000, being the price paid for goods purchased from S Ltd.

Goodwill is amortised over 3 years from the date of acquisition, with a full year's charge in the year of acquisition.

Solution

Step 1   Shareholdings in S Ltd

	%
Group	80
Minority	20
	100

Step 2   Adjustments

Unrealised profit on stock

$$5,000 \times \frac{25}{125} = £1,000$$

S Ltd sold the goods and made the profit, therefore make a consolidation adjustment to the balance sheet of S, so that both the group and the minority will bear their share of the provision for unrealised profit.

	H Ltd £	S Ltd £			Group £
Investment in S Ltd (at cost)	75,000				
Stock	12,000	5,000	–	1,000	**16,000**
Other net assets	83,000	95,000			**178,000**
	170,000	~~100,000~~	99,000		
Share capital (£1 ord)	50,000	40,000			
Profit and loss account	120,000	60,000	–	1,000	
	170,000	~~100,000~~	99,000		

Step 3   Goodwill

	£	£
Cost of investment		75,000
Less: Share of net assets of S Ltd at the acquisition date		
Share capital	40,000	
Profit and loss account	50,000	
	90,000	
Group share	× 80%	
		72,000
Goodwill		3,000
Amortisation charge		(1,000)
		2,000

Note: this calculation is unaffected by the provision for unrealised profit as the net assets of S Ltd at the date of acquisition are sold.

Step 4	Reserves	
	Consolidated profit and loss account	£
	H Ltd:	120,000
	S Ltd: 80% [(60,000 − 1,000)* − 50,000]	7,200
	Less: Goodwill amortised	(1,000)
		126,200

Step 5	Minority interest	
	Net assets of S Ltd at the balance sheet date	
		£
	Share capital	40,000
	Profit and loss account (60,000 − 1,000)*	59,000
		99,000
	Minority share	× 20%
		19,800

* the revised reserves figure from step 2, as reduced by the provision for unrealised profit.

Step 6	H Ltd	
	Consolidated balance sheet at 31 December 19X4	£
	Goodwill	2,000
	Stock (12 + 5 − 1)	16,000
	Other net assets (83 + 95)	178,000
		196,000
	Called up share capital	50,000
	Profit and loss account	126,200
	Minority interest	19,800
		196,000

Statement of accounting policies

Stock

Provision has been made for the whole of the unrealised profit on stock.

5 PREFERENCE SHARES AND DEBENTURES IN SUBSIDIARIES

5.1 Preference shares in a subsidiary company

As a **general** rule, preference shares held by one company in another are irrelevant in determining whether the holding company/subsidiary company relationship exists. (There are exceptions to this eg, **participating** preference shares: these are not important from a computational viewpoint.)

The treatment of holdings in preference shares reflects the entitlement of preference shareholders to participate in profits on the winding up of a company. Generally, preference shareholders are only entitled to repayment of their share capital, whereas ordinary shareholders are entitled to their share capital and their share of any profits. This affects the calculations and the consolidation schedules as detailed below.

(a)   Shareholdings in S Ltd

	Ordinary shares %	Preference shares %
Group	A	C
Minority	B	D
	100	100

The % holdings of each type of share is calculated.

(b)   Goodwill on consolidation

	£	£
Cost of investment (ordinary + preference shares)		X
Less: Share of net assets acquired		
Ordinary share capital	X	
Profit and loss account	X	
	X	
Group share	× A%	
		(X)
Preference share capital	X	
Group share	× C%	
		(X)
		X

The group shareholding percentage in ordinary shares is applied to the ordinary share capital and reserves, whilst the group shareholding percentage in preference shares is applied to the preference share capital.

(c)   Reserves

The calculation is performed as usual, taking the ordinary shareholding percentage (A%) of the subsidiary's post acquisition profits.

(d)   Minority interest

	£	£
Net assets of S Ltd attributable to ordinary shareholdings:		
Ordinary share capital	X	
Profit and loss account	X	
	X	
Minority share	× B%	
		X
Attributable to preference shareholdings:		
Preference share capital	X	
Minority share	× D%	
		X
		X

Official ACCA *Textbook, published by AT Foulks Lynch*

Again, share capital and reserves are split between those attributable to ordinary shareholdings and those attributable to preference shareholdings. The minority interest in each is then found separately.

Example

The draft balance sheet of S Ltd at 31 January 19X5 is as follows:

	£		£
Net assets	180,000	Ordinary share capital	100,000
		Profit and loss account	30,000
		Preference share capital	50,000
	180,000		180,000

At 31 January 19X5 H Ltd has reserves of £150,000 on the profit and loss account. H Ltd acquired 70% of the ordinary share capital of S Ltd at a cost of £90,000 when the reserves of S Ltd amounted to £10,000 and 40% of the preference share capital at a cost of £22,000 when the reserves of S Ltd amounted to £15,000. Goodwill has been fully amortised.

Show the consolidation schedules and shareholdings in S Ltd workings.

Solution

Shareholdings in S Ltd

	Ordinary shares %	Preference shares %
Group	70	40
Minority	30	60
	100	100

Goodwill

	£	£
Cost of investment (90 + 22)		112,000
Less: Share of net assets of S Ltd at the acquisition date		
Ordinary share capital	100,000	
Profit and loss account	10,000	
	110,000	
Group share	× 70%	
		(77,000)
Preference share capital	50,000	
Group share	× 40%	
		(20,000)
Goodwill - fully amortised		15,000

Reserves - consolidated profit and loss account

		£
H:		150,000
S:	70% (30,000 – 10,000)	14,000
Less:	Goodwill amortised	(15,000)
		149,000

Minority interest

	£	£
Net assets of S Ltd		
Attributable to ordinary shareholdings		
Ordinary share capital	100,000	
Profit and loss account	30,000	
	130,000	
Minority share	× 30%	
		39,000
Attributable to preference shareholdings:		
Preference share capital	50,000	
Minority share	× 60%	
		30,000
		69,000

(Tutorial notes:

(1)   The revenue reserves of S Ltd at the date of the purchase of the preference shares by H Ltd are irrelevant.

(2)   What would happen if H Ltd owned 70% of the ordinary share capital of S Ltd, but none of the preference share capital? In this case all the nominal value of the preference capital would be dealt with in the minority interests account. Hence, it is quite possible to have the apparent contradiction of crediting the minority interests account with the majority of preference share capital.*)

5.2   Debentures in a subsidiary company

Debentures are also irrelevant for the purpose of determining the holding company/subsidiary relationship.

Procedure

(a)   The nominal value of debentures held by the holding company is cancelled with that same value of debentures of the subsidiary as the balance sheets are cross cast. This leaves the debentures of the subsidiary, held by outsiders, in the balance sheet.

(b)   Preference shares of the subsidiary company **not** held by the holding company are included in the minority interest on the consolidated balance sheet. Debentures held by outsiders are shown separately on the consolidated balance sheet – they are **not** part of the minority interest.

5.3   Activity

Maximus Ltd acquired 90,000 £1 ordinary shares, 50,000 £1 preference shares and £10,000 debentures in Minimus Ltd on 30 June 19X1.

The balances in the books of Maximus Ltd and Minimus Ltd as at 31 December 19X4 were as follows:

	Maximus Ltd £	*Minimus Ltd* £
Ordinary shares of £1	500,000	120,000
8% non-cumulative preference shares of £1	-	80,000
7% debentures	-	40,000
Capital reserve	50,000	30,000
Profit and loss account	150,000	66,000
Provision for depreciation	70,000	55,000
Creditors	130,000	32,500
	900,000	423,500
Fixed assets, at cost	450,000	280,000
90,000 ordinary shares in Minimus Ltd, at cost	185,000	-
50,000 preference shares in Minimus Ltd, at cost	55,000	-
£10,000 debentures in Minimus Ltd	10,000	-
Current assets	200,000	143,500
	900,000	423,500

You are also given the following information:

(a)   The capital reserve and profit and loss account reserves of Minimus Ltd as at 30 June 19X1 were £12,000 and £30,500 respectively.

(b)   The stock of Minimus Ltd at 31 December 19X4 includes £22,800 in respect of goods purchased from Maximus Ltd. Maximus invoices Minimus at cost plus 20%.

(c)   Goodwill is amortised over 5 years from the date of acquisition with a full year's charge in the year of acquisition.

You are required to prepare the consolidated balance sheet of Maximus Ltd and its subsidiary Minimus Ltd as at 31 December 19X4. Workings should be shown.

Follow the step-by-step procedure outlined earlier to tackle this question.

5.4   Activity solution

Step 1   Shareholdings in Minimus Ltd

	Ordinary shares	*Preference shares*
Group	3/4 (75%)	5/8 (62.5%)
Minority	1/4 (25%)	3/8 (37.5%)

Step 2   Adjustments

1   Unrealised profit on stock $= \dfrac{20}{120} \times £22,800$

     $= £3,800$

The profit was made by Maximus Ltd, therefore put though a consolidation adjustment on the balance sheet working paper of Maximus Ltd.

2   Cancel debentures

Working paper:

The balance sheets given in the question, as adjusted and cross cast to give the upper half of the consolidated balance sheet are as follows at this stage:

		Maximus Ltd £		*Minimus Ltd* £	*Group* £
Ordinary shares of £1		500,000		120,000	
8% non-cumulative preference shares of £1		-		80,000	
7% debentures		-	30,000	~~40,000~~	**30,000**
Capital reserve		50,000		30,000	
Profit and loss account	(3,800)	150,000		66,000	
Provision for depreciation		70,000		55,000	**125,000**
Creditors		130,000		32,500	**162,500**
		900,000		423,500	
Fixed assets, at cost		450,000		280,000	**730,000**
90,000 ordinary shares in Minimus Ltd		185,000			
50,000 preference shares in Minimus Ltd, at cost		55,000			
£10,000 debentures in Minimus Ltd	-	~~10,000~~			
Current assets	(3,800)	200,000		143,500	**339,700**
		900,000		423,500	

Step 3 Goodwill

	£	£
Cost of investment (185 + 55)		240,000
Less: Share of net assets at acquisition		
Ordinary share capital	120,000	
Capital reserve	12,000	
Profit and loss account	30,500	
	162,500	
Group share	× 75%	
		(121,875)
Preference share capital	80,000	
	× 62.5%	
		(50,000)
Goodwill		68,125
Amortisation charge (68,125 ÷ 5 × 4)		(54,500)
		13,625

Step 4   Reserves

		£
1	Consolidated profit and loss account	
	Maximus Ltd: per question	150,000
	Unrealised profit on stock	(3,800)
	75% (66,000 – 30,500)	26,625
	Less: Goodwill amortised	(54,500)
		118,325

		£
2	Capital reserve	
	Maximus Ltd	50,000
	Minimus Ltd 75% (30,000 – 12,000)	13,500
		63,500

(Tutorial note: All reserves are dealt with in the same way. The only difference is that goodwill is amortised through the profit and loss account rather than any other reserve.)

Step 5   Minority interest

	£	£
Net assets of Minimus Ltd		
Attributable to ordinary shareholdings		
Ordinary share capital	120,000	
Capital reserve	30,000	
Profit and loss account	66,000	
	216,000	
Minority share	× 25%	
		54,000
Attributable to preference shareholdings		
Preference share capital	80,000	
Minority share	× 37.5%	
		30,000
		84,000

Step 6   Prepare the consolidated balance sheet.

Consolidated balance sheet of Maximus Ltd and its subsidiary, Minimus Ltd at 31 December 19X4

	£	£
Fixed assets:		
Intangible assets:		
Cost	68,125	
Amortisation	54,500	
		13,625
Tangible assets:		
Cost	730,000	
Depreciation	125,000	
		605,000
		618,625

Current assets	339,700	
Creditors (amounts falling due within one year)	162,500	
Net current assets		177,200
Total assets less current liabilities		795,825
Creditors (amounts falling due after more than one year)		
7% debentures		(30,000)
Minority interests		(84,000)
		681,825
Capital and reserves:		
Called up ordinary share capital, allotted and fully paid		500,000
Capital reserves		63,500
Profit and loss account		118,325
		681,825

6 DIVIDENDS AND DEBENTURE INTEREST OF SUBSIDIARIES

6.1 Introduction

In dealing with consolidations which involve one group company paying a dividend or interest instalment to another group company, it is easy to get confused, especially if the information given includes one or more dividends incorrectly or incompletely treated. We need to determine, for each dividend or interest instalment:

(a)   what entries should have been made by each company involved;

(b)   what entries have actually been made;

(c)   the entries to correct or complete the treatment;

and then continue with the consolidation.

6.2 Dividends – The correct treatment

If the dividend is paid by the year-end:

Paying company:	Dr	Profit and loss account ('Dividend paid')
	Cr	Cash
Receiving company:	Dr	Cash
	Cr	Profit and loss account ('Dividend received')

On consolidating the balance sheet, no adjustment will be required.

If the dividend is outstanding at the year-end:

Paying company:	Dr	Profit and loss account ('Dividend payable/proposed')
	Cr	Proposed dividend/Declared dividend (a creditor)
Receiving company:	Dr	Dividend receivable (a debtor)
	Cr	Profit and loss account ('Dividend receivable')

On consolidating the balance sheet, a cancellation must be made between the current asset, 'dividend receivable' as shown in the receiving company's books and the 'proposed dividend' shown in the paying company's books. If only part of the dividend is payable to the other group company, then that part payable to outsiders must be shown as a current liability in the consolidated balance sheet with the heading 'dividend payable to minority shareholders'.

6.3   Dividends not accrued

Where the correct entries have not been made in the books of the company the general procedure is to make entries in the balance sheet working papers to give effect to the missing entries and, if necessary, to reverse any wrong entries.

Example

Upminster Ltd acquired 80% of the ordinary share capital of Barking Ltd several years ago when the balance on the profit and loss account of Barking Ltd was £12,000. Their respective draft balance sheets at 31 December 19X4 are as follows:

	Upminster Ltd £	Barking Ltd £
Fixed assets	100,000	92,000
Investment in Barking Ltd	55,000	-
Current assets	45,000	31,000
	200,000	123,000
Ordinary share capital	100,000	50,000
Preference share capital	-	10,000
Profit and loss account	80,000	42,000
Proposed dividend	-	10,000
Sundry creditors	20,000	11,000
	200,000	123,000

Upminster has not made any entry for the dividend receivable from Barking for the year. A proposed preference dividend of £2,000 by Barking Ltd has not been accounted for by either company. Upminster Ltd purchased 30% of the preference shares for £3,500 some years ago.

Goodwill has been fully amortised.

Prepare the consolidated balance sheet for Upminster Ltd and its subsidiary company at 31 December 19X4.

Solution

Step 1   Shareholdings in Barking Ltd

	Ordinary shares %	Preference shares %
Group	80	30
Minority	20	70
	100	100

Step 2   Adjustments

1   Proposed preference dividend by Barking Ltd

Dr: Profit and loss account	£2,000	
Cr: Proposed dividend		£2,000

2   Dividends receivable by Upminster

  Dr: Dividends receivable
        (ordinary: 80% × 10,000)   £8,000
  Dr: Dividends receivable
        (preference: 30% × 2,000)   £600

  Cr: Profit and loss account   £8,600

3   Cancel dividends receivable/payable when the upper half of the balance sheet is cross cast.

Working paper:

	Upminster Ltd £	Barking Ltd £	Group £
Fixed assets	100,000	92,000	**192,000**
Investment in Barking Ltd	55,000	-	
Current assets	45,000	31,000	**76,000**
Dividends receivable (2) ~~8,000~~ (2) ~~600~~	200,000	123,000	
Ordinary share capital	100,000	50,000	
Preference share capital	-	10,000	
Profit and loss account (2) + **8,600**	80,000	42,000 (2,000) (1)	
(Proposed dividend) becomes:			
Dividend payable to minority shareholders	- 2,000	10,000 + 2,000 (1) 1,400	**3,400**
Sundry creditors	20,000	11,000	**31,000**
	200,000	123,000	

Tutorial note: these amendments may be made to the balance sheets given in the question as this ensures they are not forgotten. However, it is also important that your **answer** also shows these amendments, hence the figures bracketed in the schedules and balance sheet following.

Step 3   Goodwill

	£	£
Cost of investment		55,000
Less: Share of net assets at acquisition		
Ordinary share capital	50,000	
Profit and loss account	12,000	
	62,000	
Group share	× 80%	
		(49,600)
Preference share capital	10,000	
Group share	× 30%	
		(3,000)
Goodwill - fully amortised		2,400

Step 4   Reserves

Consolidated profit and loss account

	£
Upminster Ltd: (80,000 + 8,600)	88,600
Barking Ltd: 80% (42,000 − 2,000 − 12,000)	22,400
Less: Goodwill amortised	(2,400)
	108,600

Step 5   Minority interest

Net assets

	£	£
Attributable to ordinary shareholdings		
Ordinary share capital	50,000	
Profit and loss account (42,000 − 2,000)	40,000	
	90,000	
Minority share	× 20%	
		18,000
Attributable to preference shareholdings		
Preference share capital	10,000	
	× 70%	
		7,000
		25,000

Consolidated balance sheet of Upminster Ltd and its subsidiary, Barking Ltd as at 31 December 19X4

	£	£
Fixed assets:		
Tangible assets (100 + 92)		192,000
Current assets (45 + 31)	76,000	
Creditors (amounts falling due within one year):		
Sundry creditors (20 + 11)	31,000	
Dividend payable to minority shareholders	3,400	
	34,400	
Net current assets		41,600
Total assets less current liabilities		233,600
Capital and reserves:		
Called up ordinary share capital allotted and fully paid	100,000	
Reserves – profit and loss account	108,600	
		208,600
Minority interests		25,000
		233,600

6.4   Debenture interest payable by a subsidiary

The procedure for dealing with debenture interest payable is exactly the same as for ordinary or preference dividends payable by a subsidiary. The **only** difference is in the description of the group liability to pay debenture interest. This liability has nothing to do with minority shareholders – it is simply a creditor like any other.

7   CHAPTER SUMMARY

When the activities of a business are conducted through a number of different companies, it is normal to prepare group accounts **in addition to** the individual accounts prepared by each company.

The usual form of group accounts is 'consolidated accounts'. Under this method, the activities of all the group companies are represented as being, in effect, those of a single entity (the group).

The basic procedure for preparing a consolidated balance sheet is to add together the assets and liabilities shown in the accounts of each individual company. However, adjustments are necessary to deal with:

- cancelling items
- goodwill on acquisition
- minority interests
- inter-company transactions.

A step-by-step approach to the task was described and exemplified.

8   SELF TEST QUESTIONS

8.1   What is the normal form of group accounts? (1.2)

8.2   What is represented by the excess of the price paid over the fair value of the separable net assets acquired? (2.3)

8.3   What is the required accounting treatment in FRS 10 for positive purchased goodwill? (2.3)

8.4   Why must a distinction be drawn between a subsidiary's pre-acquisition and post-acquisition reserves? (2.5)

8.5   How are current account balances between the holding company and the subsidiary accounted for in drawing up a consolidated balance sheet? (4.2)

8.6   How does FRS 2 require that unrealised profits in year-end stocks should be accounted for? (4.3)

8.7   If H holds 100% of S's ordinary shares but only 10% of S's preference shares, is S still a subsidiary of H? (5.1)

8.8   What is the correct accounting treatment for intra-group dividends during an accounting period? (6.2)

9   EXAMINATION TYPE QUESTIONS

9.1   Hanson Ltd

Several years ago, Hanson Ltd acquired the following shares in Pickford Ltd:

		£
75,000	Ordinary shares of £1 – cost	93,100
15,000	6% Preference shares of £1 – cost	16,050
		109,150

At the date of acquisition, the accumulated profits of Pickford Ltd amounted to £11,000. The summarised balance sheets of the two companies at 31.12.X8 were as follows:

	Hanson Ltd £	Pickford Ltd £
Ordinary shares of £1	350,000	100,000
6% preference shares of £1	-	60,000
Profit and loss account	348,420	132,700
Sundry creditors	93,400	51,150
	791,820	343,850

	£	£
Fixed assets	431,100	219,350
Investments	109,150	-
Stock	143,070	71,120
Debtors	89,200	36,230
Cash at bank	19,300	17,150
	791,820	343,850

During the year, Hanson Ltd sold goods whose invoice value was £24,000 to Pickford Ltd. These goods were invoiced at cost plus 25%, and one-quarter were still in Pickford's stock at the year end.

Goodwill has been fully amortised.

You are required to prepare the consolidated balance sheet of Hanson Ltd as at 31 December 19X8.

(20 marks)

9.2   Pixie and Dixie

On 1 January 19X7, Pixie Ltd acquired the following shareholdings in Dixie Ltd. At the date of both acquisitions, the accumulated profits of Dixie Ltd amounted to £20,000.

	Number of shares	Cost of investment £
£1 Ordinary shares	37,500	58,000
£1 Preference shares	16,000	15,000
		73,000

The balance sheets of the two companies at 31 December 19X9 were as follows:

	Pixie Ltd £	Dixie Ltd £
Ordinary share capital	200,000	50,000
7% Preference share capital	-	40,000
Profit and loss account	120,000	38,000
Sundry creditors	56,100	22,100
Proposed dividends:		
Ordinary	20,000	2,500
Preference	-	1,400
	396,100	154,000

Fixed assets	210,000	110,600
Current assets	113,100	43,400
Investment in Dixie Ltd	73,000	-
	396,100	154,000

You further ascertain that:

Current assets of Pixie Ltd includes £42,000 of goods acquired originally from Dixie Ltd. Dixie Ltd invoiced these goods at cost plus 20%.

Pixie Ltd has not accounted for dividends receivable from Dixie Ltd.

Goodwill is amortised over 4 years from the date of acquisition, with a full year's charge in the year of acquisition.

You are required to prepare the consolidated balance sheet of Pixie Ltd and its subsidiary as at 31 December 19X9.

(20 marks)

11   ANSWERS TO EXAMINATION TYPE QUESTIONS

11.1   Hanson Ltd

Hanson Ltd and its subsidiary
Group balance sheet as at 31 December 19X8

	£	£
Fixed assets		650,450
Current assets		
Stock (W5)	212,990	
Debtors	125,430	
Cash at bank	36,450	
	374,870	
Creditors: amounts falling due within one year	144,550	
Net current assets		230,320
Total assets less current liabilities		880,770
Minority interests (W4)		(103,175)
		777,595
Capital and reserves		
Called up share capital		350,000
Profit and loss account (W3)		427,595
		777,595

WORKINGS

(W1)   Shareholdings in Pickford Ltd

	Ordinary %	Preference %
Group	75	25
Minority	25	75
	100	100

(W2)   Goodwill

	£	£
Cost of investment		109,150
Less: Share of net assets at acquisition		
Ordinary share capital	100,000	
Profit and loss account	11,000	
	111,000	
	× 75%	
		(83,250)
Preference share capital	60,000	
	× 25%	
		(15,000)
Goodwill - fully amortised		10,900

(W3)   Consolidated reserves

	£
Hanson Ltd:	348,420
Less: Provision for unrealised profit on stock	
(25/125 × 1/4 × 24,000)	(1,200)
Pickford Ltd: 75% (132,700 − 11,000)	91,275
Less: Goodwill amortised	(10,900)
	427,595

(W4)   Minority interest

Net assets of Pickford Ltd

	£	£
Ordinary share capital	100,000	
Profit and loss account	132,700	
	232,700	
	× 25%	
		58,175
Preference share capital	60,000	
	× 75%	
		45,000
		103,175

(W5)   Consolidated stock

	£
Hanson Ltd	143,070
Provision for unrealised profit	(1,200)
Pickford Ltd	71,120
	212,990

11.2   Pixie and Dixie

Pixie Ltd and its subsidiary
Group balance sheet as at 31 December 19X9

	£	£
Fixed assets (320,600 + 1,125)		321,725
Current assets (W2)	149,500	
Creditors: amounts falling due within one year		
Sundry	78,200	
Proposed dividends	20,000	
Minority dividends payable (W3)	1,465	
	99,665	
Net current assets		49,835
Total assets less current liabilities		371,560
Minority interests (W7)		(44,250)
		327,310
Capital and reserves		
Called up share capital		200,000
Profit and loss account (W6)		127,310
		327,310

WORKINGS

(W1)   Shareholdings in Dixie Ltd

	Ordinary	*Preference*
Group	75%	40%
Minority	25%	60%
	100%	100%

(W2)   Consolidated current assets

	£
Pixie Ltd:	113,100
Dixie Ltd:	43,400
Less: Provision for unrealised profit on stock (W3)	(7,000)
	149,500

(W3)   Stock - unrealised profit

	£
Stock held by Pixie purchased from Dixie	42,000
Unrealised profit $\frac{20}{120} \times 42{,}000$	7,000
Group share 75%	5,250
Minority interest 25%	1,750

(Tutorial note: as the subsidiary recorded the original profit, the elimination must be shared between the group and the minority. This may be achieved if the unrealised profit is deducted from Dixie Ltd stock and reserves on the balance sheet working papers.)

Official ACCA *Textbook, published by AT Foulks Lynch*

(W4)   Treatment of proposed dividends of Dixie Ltd

	Ordinary £	Preference £	Total £
Proposed dividends	2,500	1,400	3,900
Less: Cancelled with dividends receivable by Pixie Ltd	(1,875)	(560)	(2,435)
Dividend payable to minority shareholders	625	840	1,465

(W5)   Goodwill

	£	£
Cost of investment		73,000
Less: Share of net assets at acquisition		
Ordinary share capital	50,000	
Profit and loss account	20,000	
	70,000	
	× 75%	
		(52,500)
Preference share capital	40,000	
	× 40%	
		(16,000)
		4,500
Amortisation charge (4,500 ÷ 4 × 3)		(3,375)
		1,125

(W6)   Consolidated reserves

	£	£
Pixie Ltd: Per question	120,000	
Add: dividends receivable (W4)	2,435	
		122,435
Dixie Ltd: 75% (38,000 – 7,000 (W3) – 20,000)		8,250
Less: Goodwill amortised		(3,375)
		127,310

(W7)   Minority interest

Net assets of Dixie Ltd

	£	£
Ordinary share capital	50,000	
Profit and loss account (38,000 – 7,000)	31,000	
	81,000	
	× 25%	
		20,250
Preference share capital	40,000	
	× 60%	
		24,000
		44,250

18 GROUP ACCOUNTING - 2

INTRODUCTION & LEARNING OBJECTIVES

This chapter covers the consolidated profit and loss account. The preparation of a consolidated profit and loss account is just as popular in exam questions as a consolidated balance sheet. In some exam questions both statements are required.

Students generally find the profit and loss account more difficult than the balance sheet. Use of a consolidation schedule can help to make the task more manageable.

Associated companies are often included within computational group accounts questions. The techniques for dealing with associates and subsidiaries are different and therefore associates are best handled by producing separate workings to the consolidation schedule.

When you have studied this chapter you should be able to do the following:

- Prepare a consolidated profit and loss account for a group.
- Account for associated undertakings.

---

1 CONSOLIDATED PROFIT AND LOSS ACCOUNT

1.1 Introduction

Just as the profit and loss account of a single company shows the results of the year's trading of that company, so does the consolidated profit and loss account show the results of trading in the year by the holding company together with its subsidiaries.

Consolidated profit and loss accounts are prepared by combining the information given in the profit and loss accounts of the individual companies, after making any adjustments that may be necessary to eliminate inter-company items, unrealised profits and so on.

1.2 Basic form of consolidated profit and loss accounts

Consolidated profit and loss accounts have an underlying form as follows:

Section   *Purpose*

A   To show the results achieved with the assets under the directors' control.

B   To show how much of the net gains shown in Section A accrue to holding company shareholders, and how much to others.

C   To show how the directors intend to dispose of the gains accruing to holding company shareholders.

At Section A will be shown the whole of turnover, cost of sales, gross profit, ... taxation, and profit or loss on ordinary activities after taxation (or equivalent Format 2 items).

At Section B will be shown an item included in the CA89 statutory formats, namely a deduction for minority interests' share of the profits of subsidiaries not wholly owned by the group.

At Section C will be shown dividends, capitalised profits (if any), retained profits or transfers to reserves.

Extraordinary items, if any, are shown net of any minority share between Sections B and C.

The usual layout will be illustrated in examples later in this chapter; for the moment the main point to appreciate is that at Section A all the figures are for the whole of the operations controlled by the holding company directors, and the share of the minority shareholders is deducted later. It is conventional to do this, because then the ratio of gross profit to capital employed, using figures from the consolidated profit and loss account and consolidated balance sheet, will be the whole profits of the business divided by the whole capital employed of the business, and will depend only on the performance of the business: it will not be affected by whether the holding company owns all or only a part of the subsidiary companies.

1.3   Composition of group unchanged in current year

In this section it is assumed that no new subsidiaries are acquired during the year, nor are any existing subsidiaries disposed of.

Consider the following simple example:

Example

H Ltd acquired, several years ago, the entire ordinary share capital of S Ltd. Their results for the year ended 30 November 19X4 were as follows:

	H Ltd £	*S Ltd* £
Turnover	8,500,000	2,200,000
Total costs	7,650,000	1,980,000
Trading profit before taxation	850,000	220,000
Taxation	400,000	100,000
	450,000	120,000

Solution

The consolidated profit and loss account is arrived at by a simple 'combining exercise'.

Consolidated profit and loss account for year ended 30 November 19X4

	£
Turnover	10,700,000
Total costs	9,630,000
Group profit on ordinary activities before taxation	1,070,000
Tax on profit on ordinary activities	500,000
Profit for the year retained	570,000

1.4   The effect of a minority interest

What happens if, in the previous example, H Ltd acquired only 75% of the share capital of S Ltd?

This does **not** affect turnover and cost of sales. They remain the same, as we wish to show total income under the control of the holding company. The minority shareholders' interest in the profit is shown after the group tax charge. The calculation is $25\% \times £120,000 = £30,000$.

1.5   Activity

Now prepare the consolidated profit and loss account assuming a 25% minority interest.

1.6   Activity solution

Consolidated profit and loss account for year ended 30 November 19X4

	£
Turnover	10,700,000
Total costs	9,630,000
Group profit on ordinary activities before taxation	1,070,000
Tax on profit on ordinary activities	500,000
Profit on ordinary activities after taxation	570,000
Minority interests	30,000
Profit for the year retained	540,000

(Tutorial note:

	£
Profit retained by H Ltd	450,000
H Ltd share of retained profit of S Ltd 75% × £120,000	90,000
	540,000

)

1.7   Revenue reserves brought forward

So far we have carefully avoided the problem of revenue reserves brought forward from the previous year. As far as the **consolidated** profit and loss account is concerned, the balance brought forward consists of:

(a)   H Ltd's **own** profit and loss account balance brought forward; and

(b)   H Ltd's share of the **post-acquisition** retained profits of S Ltd.

1.8   Activity

Facts as in the previous example, but you are provided with additional information:

(a)   Profit and loss account balances brought forward at the beginning of the year amounted to £2,300,000 for H Ltd and £400,000 for S Ltd.

(b)   H Ltd acquired the shares in S Ltd when the revenue reserves of S Ltd amounted to £100,000.

Calculate the brought forward and carried forward figure for the consolidated profit and loss account. Ignore goodwill.

1.9   Activity solution

	£
Brought forward	
H Ltd	2,300,000
S Ltd 75% × £(400,000 − 100,000)	225,000
	2,525,000
Retained for the year	540,000
Carried forward	3,065,000

It is important to note that the calculation of retained profits brought forward is of the same form as the calculation of group reserves in the balance sheet. To demonstrate that this is so, here are extracts from the working papers for the balance sheet consolidations at 30 November 19X3 and 30 November 19X4:

Consolidated profit and loss account reserves,

at 30 November 19X3:

		£'000
H Ltd		2,300
S Ltd 75% (400 – 100)		225
		2,525

at 30 November 19X4:

		£'000
H Ltd**		2,750
S Ltd 75% (520 – 100)**		315
		3,065

**   Reserves of the two companies at the end of the year are:

	H Ltd £	S Ltd £
Retained profit brought forward	2,300,000	400,000
Retained profit for the year	450,000	120,000
Retained profit carried forward	2,750,000	520,000

1.10   Inter-company dividends – Ordinary shares

Most complications in preparing consolidated profit and loss accounts arise because of dividends paid from one company to another.

Investment income of the holding company may, for example, include:

(a)   ordinary dividends received (or receivable) from subsidiaries; and

(b)   income from trade investments.

Only (b) is shown separately as income in the consolidated profit and loss account, inter-company dividends being eliminated on consolidation.

The subsidiaries in a group will often pay dividends in order to transfer surplus cash to the holding company. No net profit or loss accrues to the group in the process. For example, if Leg Ltd owns 80% of the ordinary shares of Foot Ltd, and Foot Ltd pays an ordinary dividend of £10,000, then £2,000 will be paid to the outside shareholders in Foot Ltd and £8,000 will be paid to Leg Ltd. Suppose the balance sheets of Foot Ltd before and after the dividend were:

	Before £	After £
Sundry net assets	13,000	3,000
Share capital	1,000	1,000
Reserves	12,000	2,000
	13,000	3,000

and that the reserves of Foot Ltd at acquisition were £2,000. We can then summarise the effects of the dividend on the group as follows:

(a)   **Goodwill on acquisition**

The amount to be deducted from the cost of investment is 80% of the net assets acquired, 80% × £(1,000 + 2,000) = £2,400, which is obviously unaffected by dividends paid some years later.

(b)   **Minority interests**

			£
Before	20% ×	£13,000	2,600
After	20% ×	£3,000	600
Reduction in group liability			2,000
Compare: Reduction in group cash			2,000

We see that the group neither gains nor loses overall on account of the minority's portion of the dividend.

(c)   **Consolidated profit and loss account reserve**

		£
Before	80% × £(12,000 – 2,000)	8,000
After	80% × £(2,000 – 2,000)	Nil
Reduction in consolidated reserves arising from Foot Ltd		8,000

There is, however, a compensating effect, in that the reserves of Leg Ltd increased by £8,000 on receipt of the dividend from Foot Ltd. Since all of Leg Ltd's reserves are incorporated into the consolidated reserves, there will be no net effect on consolidated reserves.

However, while there is no net effect on the total amount of consolidated reserves, there is a change in their composition: there is an increase in the amount of consolidated reserves which are reserves of the holding company, and a reduction in the amount of consolidated reserves which are part of the reserves of the subsidiary companies; and thus there will be an effect on the consolidated statement of reserves.

1.11   Activity

The profit and loss accounts for H Ltd and S Ltd for the year ended 31 August 19X4 are shown below. H Ltd acquired 75% of the ordinary share capital of S Ltd several years ago.

	H Ltd		S Ltd	
	£	£	£	£
Turnover		2,400,000		800,000
Total costs		2,160,000		720,000
Trading profit		240,000		80,000
Investment income:				
Dividend received from S Ltd	1,500			
Dividend receivable from S Ltd	6,000			
		7,500		-
		247,500		80,000

Taxation		115,000		38,000
		132,500		42,000
Dividends:				
Paid	-		2,000	
Proposed	60,000		8,000	
		60,000		10,000
Retained profit for year		72,500		32,000

Prepare the consolidated profit and loss account. Ignore goodwill.

1.12   Activity solution

The main point to remember is that inter-company dividends must be eliminated. Furthermore, as far as the minority's share of the subsidiary's current year profits is concerned, the object of the consolidated profit and loss account is to show the minority's share of the profit after taxation, and **not** how this figure is split between dividends and retained profit.

Minority interests in profit of subsidiary are 25% × £42,000 = £10,500.

Consolidated profit and loss account for year ended 30 November 19X4

	£
Turnover (2,400 + 800)	3,200,000
Total costs (2,160 + 720)	2,880,000
Group profit on ordinary activities before taxation	320,000
Tax on profit on ordinary activities (115 + 38)	153,000
Profit on ordinary activities after taxation	167,000
Minority interests	10,500
Profit after taxation attributable to H Ltd	156,500
Dividend proposed by H Ltd	60,000
Profit for the year retained	96,500

1.13   Inter-company dividends – preference shares

The main complication here is the calculation of the minority interests in the profits of the subsidiary. It is essential to keep quite clear:

(a)   the minority interests in the ordinary shares; and
(b)   the minority interests in the preference shares.

Example

H Ltd acquired 80% of the ordinary share capital and 40% of the preference share capital of S Ltd many years ago. The profit and loss account of S Ltd for the current year was:

	£	£
Sales		2,700,000
Total costs		2,300,000
		400,000

Taxation		140,000
		260,000
Dividends:		
Preference	10,000	
Ordinary	80,000	
		90,000
Retained		170,000

Compute the minority interests.

Solution

Procedure

	Total £		Minority interests £
Profit after taxation (S Ltd)	260,000		
Less: Preference dividend	10,000	(60%)	6,000
Available for ordinary shareholders	250,000	(20%)	50,000
Total			56,000

The minority interests' share of the profits of S Ltd amounts to £56,000.

The preference dividend normally represents the full entitlement to profits of the shareholders. The ordinary dividend, however, represents how much of the remaining profits will be paid to the ordinary shareholders or retained (for their ultimate benefit) within the company. Therefore, the deduction of the preference dividend from the total profits available to shareholders in S Ltd merely represents the total profits accruing to one class of shareholder. The ordinary dividend does not represent this and, therefore, is not relevant to the calculation.

1.14   Additions to the group during the current year

The main problem here is how to deal with the pre-acquisition profits of the new subsidiary. The approach is to exclude the pre-acquisition items of the subsidiary from the relevant group figures.

1.15   Activity

The trading results of H Ltd and S Ltd for the year ended 31 July 19X4 were as follows:

	H Ltd £	S Ltd £
Turnover	1,430,000	600,000
Total costs	1,160,000	504,000
Trading profit	270,000	96,000
Less: Taxation	135,000	48,000
Retained profit	135,000	48,000
Reserves brought forward	900,000	200,000
	1,035,000	248,000

H Ltd acquired 75% of the ordinary share capital of S Ltd on 28 February 19X4. Assume that profits are earned evenly over the year. Ignore goodwill.

1.16   Activity solution

Consolidated profit and loss account for year ended 31 July 19X4

	£
Turnover £(1,430,000 + 5/12 × 600,000)	1,680,000
Total costs £(1,160,000 + 5/12 × 504,000)	1,370,000
Profit on ordinary activities before taxation £(270,000 + 5/12 × 96,000)	310,000
Tax on profit on ordinary activities £(135,000 + 5/12 × 48,000)	155,000
Profit on ordinary activities after taxation	155,000
Minority interests £(25% × 5/12 × (96,000 – 48,000))	5,000
Profit for the financial year	150,000
Reserves brought forward	900,000
Reserves carried forward	1,050,000

Note: that the reserves brought forward can only consist of H Ltd's reserves, as S Ltd was not a subsidiary at that date.

1.17   Pre-acquisition dividends

A pre-acquisition dividend is a dividend paid to a holding (parent) company by a subsidiary out of pre-acquisition profits. There are two possible ways of accounting for pre-acquisition dividends in the accounts of the parent and in the consolidated accounts:

(a)   Treat the dividend as a return to the parent company of part of the cost of its investment (ie, a reduction in the carrying value of the parent's investment in the subsidiary). This is the traditional view of pre-acquisition dividends. The reasoning for it is that only post-acquisition profits can be treated as profits of the group and therefore only dividends paid out of post-acquisition profits can be treated as income. A further argument for this treatment is that a dividend paid out of pre-acquisition profits reduces the value of the parent's investment in the subsidiary to less than cost.

(b)   Treat the dividend as a realised profit in the hands of the parent (ie, as investment income). The rationale for this treatment is that the payment of a pre-acquisition dividend does not cause a permanent diminution in the value of the parent's investment in the subsidiary. Therefore no write-down is necessary.

The Companies Acts are silent on this matter. Appendix 1 of FRS 6 *Acquisitions and mergers* states that a pre-combination dividend should be applied to reduce the carrying value of the investment in the subsidiary to the extent that its payment represents a diminution in the investment's value. To the extent that this is not necessary, the dividend will be a realised profit in the hands of the parent company.

Although this note relates to the treatment in the accounts of the parent company only, some commentators have interpreted it as effectively applying to the consolidated accounts as well. Others argue that pre-acquisition dividends cannot be treated as part of consolidated reserves because a company cannot 'buy' another company's past profits for its own use, nor can it trade with itself. It has also been suggested that this treatment would be contrary to FRS 5 as it does not reflect the substance of the transaction.

The examiner has said that examination questions will specify the company's policy in respect of pre-acquisition dividends.

1.18   Example

The facts are the same as in the Activity above, except that on 1 March 19X4 S Ltd pays a dividend of £12,000 and goodwill of £50,000 arises on the acquisition. Show the journal entry for recording the dividend received in the books of H Ltd and calculate consolidated reserves at 31 July 19X4 assuming that:

(a)   the dividend is treated as investment income; and

(b)   the dividend is treated as a return of the cost of the investment.

1.19   Solution

(Tutorial note: In the consolidated profit and loss account, investment income received by H Ltd is cancelled against the dividend paid by S Ltd.*)*

(a)   **Investment income**

Journal entry

Dr   Cash (75% × 12,000)   £9,000
        Cr   Investment income   £9,000

Consolidated reserves

	£	£
H Ltd (1,035,000 + 9,000)		1,044,000
S Ltd: at the year-end (248,000 – 12,000)	236,000	
at acquisition (200,000 + 28,000)	(228,000)	
	8,000	
Group share (75%)		6,000
		1,050,000

The dividend is treated as occurring post-acquisition, although it is paid out of pre-acquisition profits.

(b)   **Return of cost of investment**

Journal entry

Dr   Cash (75% × 12,000)   £9,000
        Cr   Cost of investment   £9,000

Consolidated reserves

	£	£
H Ltd		1,035,000
S Ltd: at the year-end (248,000 – 12,000)	236,000	
at acquisition (200,000 + 16,000)	(216,000)	
	20,000	
Group share (75%)		15,000
		1,050,000

1.20   Calculating the pre-acquisition dividend

In the example above, it was clear that the whole of the dividend was paid out of pre-acquisition profits. However, in some cases, the dividend has to be apportioned between the pre and post acquisition period. There are two ways of doing this:

(a)   time apportionment

(b)   take the pre-acquisition dividend to be the portion of the dividend which cannot have been paid out of post-acquisition reserves.

Example

The facts are as in the previous example, except that S Ltd proposed a final dividend of £24,000 on 31 July 19X4.

Method (a)

	Total	Pre-acq (7/12)	Post-acq (5/12)
	£	£	£
Profit for the year	48,000	28,000	20,000
Dividends proposed	(24,000)	(14,000)	(10,000)
	24,000	14,000	10,000

Method (b)

	Total	Pre-acq	Post-acq
	£	£	£
Profit for the year	48,000	28,000	20,000
Dividends proposed	(24,000)	(4,000)	(20,000)
	24,000	24,000	-

Method (a) is the traditional method and probably the most theoretically correct. Method (b) has the advantage of minimising pre-acquisition dividends and is normally favoured by those who argue for the 'modern' treatment of pre-acquisition dividends. Again, the examiner should give some indication of which method he requires.

1.21   Legal requirements – holding company's profit and loss account

Legal requirements are dealt with in more detail in a later section, but there is one dispensation offered by the Companies Act of which advantage is widely taken – the ability of a company not to publish its own profit and loss account.

Ordinarily, a holding company (not being a wholly owned subsidiary) must publish:

(a)   its own balance sheet; and
(b)   a consolidated balance sheet; and
(c)   its own profit and loss account; and
(d)   a consolidated profit and loss account.

A holding company may dispense with the need to publish its own profit and loss account (s.228 CA85), provided that:

(a)   the company has prepared group accounts in accordance with CA85; and

(b)   the notes to the holding company's **individual** balance sheet show the amount of the holding company profit or loss for the financial year; and

(c)   the company discloses that it is taking advantage of this exemption.

The profit or loss for the financial year is the profit or loss after all income, expenses, taxation and extraordinary items but before appropriations for dividends or transfers to reserves.

2   CONSOLIDATION WORKING PAPERS

2.1   Introduction

The following examples bring together the principles explained in the previous sections and illustrate an approach that can be taken to show sufficient detail to support the figures computed for the published consolidated profit and loss account. For many of the required figures the consolidated figure is no more than the addition of the holding and subsidiary companies' figures, and thus a 'master' schedule is used to show the additions made.

2.2   Example of approach

The draft profit and loss accounts for the year ended 31 March 19X7 of the companies in a group are as follows:

	Tyndale Ltd £	Wycliffe Ltd £	Luther Ltd £
Turnover	216,300	24,400	126,000
Cost of sales	136,269	15,372	79,380
Gross profit	80,031	9,028	46,620
Administrative expenses	(21,630)	(2,440)	(12,600)
Income from shares in group companies	7,512	-	-
Net profit before taxation	65,913	6,588	34,020
Taxation	28,119	3,172	16,380
Net profit after taxation	37,794	3,416	17,640
Dividends	20,000	1,952	10,080
Transfer to reserves	17,794	1,464	7,560
Reserves brought forward	36,728	7,076	23,940
Reserves carried forward	54,522	8,540	31,500

The history of the group is as follows:

(a)   Tyndale bought 75% of the ordinary shares (the only type) in Wycliffe Ltd seven years ago when that company's reserves amounted to £5,124. Goodwill of £5,000 arose on the acquisition.

(b)   Luther Ltd has an issued share capital of 100,000 ordinary shares of £1 each. Tyndale purchased 60,000 of these two years ago when the balance on Luther Ltd's reserves was £16,380. Goodwill of £10,000 arose on the acquisition.

Goodwill is amortised over 5 years from the date of acquisition with a full year's charge in the year of acquisition.

Prepare the consolidated profit and loss account for the year ended 31 March 19X7.

Solution

Step 1   Reconcile the intra-group dividends.

Reconciliation of intra-group dividends

	£
Per Tyndale, received	7,512
Should agree with:	
Wycliffe, paid £1,952 × 75%	1,464
Luther, paid £10,080 × 60%	6,048
	7,512

Therefore, no adjustments are required.

Step 2   Set out the master schedule.

Master schedule

	Tyndale Ltd	Wycliffe Ltd	Luther Ltd	Adjustments	Consolidated
Group details	H	75% 12 months	60% 12 months		
	£	£	£	£	£
Turnover	216,300	24,400	126,000		366,700
Cost of sales	(136,269)	(15,372)	(79,380)		(231,021)
Administrative expenses	(21,630)	(2,440)	(12,600)	(2,000)	(38,670)
Investment income	-	-	-		-
Taxation	(28,119)	(3,172)	(16,380)		(47,671)
Net profit after taxation	30,282	3,416	17,640	(2,000)	49,338
Minority interests (25%; 40%)	-	(854)	(7,056)		(7,910)

Note: The consolidation adjustment represents the amortisation of goodwill (10,000 ÷ 5).

Step 3   Calculate the reserves brought forward

	£
Tyndale	36,728
Wycliffe 75% × £(7,076 − 5,124)	1,464
Luther 60% × £(23,940 − 16,380)	4,536
Less goodwill amortised: Wycliffe	(5,000)
Luther (10,000 ÷ 5)	(2,000)
	35,728

Step 4   The consolidated profit and loss account can now be prepared

Tyndale Ltd and its subsidiaries
Consolidated profit and loss account for the year ended 31 March 19X7

	£
Turnover	366,700
Cost of sales	231,021
Gross profit	135,679
Administrative expenses	(38,670)
Profit on ordinary activities before taxation	97,009

Tax on profit on ordinary activities	47,671
Profit on ordinary activities after taxation	49,338
Minority interests	7,910
Net profit after taxation attributable to shareholders of Tyndale Ltd (Note 1)	41,428
Dividends	20,000
	21,428

Statement of reserves

	£
At 31 March 19X6	35,728
Retained profits	21,428
At 31 March 19X7	57,156

Note

1   Net profit after taxation attributable to shareholders of Tyndale Ltd.

Tyndale Ltd has taken advantage of the legal dispensation not to publish its own profit and loss account. Its net profit after taxation is £37,794.

Explanatory notes

(a)   The master schedule is drafted with a column for each company and a 'consolidated' column. The group structure is summarised at the head of each column.

The meaning of the notes is that Tyndale is the holding company; Wycliffe is a 75% owned subsidiary and has been for the present year; Luther is 60% owned for the present year.

(b)   In any example with intra-group dividends, begin by reconciling the amounts receivable by the holding company with the amounts payable by the subsidiaries. This may reveal errors or omissions in accounting for the dividends and, if so, they should be corrected before beginning the consolidation.

Under no circumstances whatever do dividends of subsidiaries ever appear in the consolidated profit and loss account. As discussed previously, their only effect on consolidated reserves is to alter their composition and thus alter the figures in the consolidated statement of reserves of the group.

(c)   For items from 'turnover' to 'net profit after tax' (from ordinary activities), we enter:

For holding company	the full amount
For subsidiary owned throughout the year	the full amount
For subsidiaries acquired during the year	the amount representing post-acquisition transactions

(d)   The figure of £49,338 net profit on ordinary activities after tax completes Section A of the consolidated profit and loss account, and it represents the total profit from ordinary activities that the directors have obtained by using the assets that they control.

However, not all of this will accrue to the shareholders of Tyndale Ltd and now, in Section B of the account, the amount that accrues to the minority shareholders in the subsidiaries will be deducted.

In this case, because all the companies have only ordinary shares, it is easy to calculate the minority share. It is simply the minority shareholders' fraction of the ordinary shares, multiplied by the last figure, net profit after tax, in the column for the relevant subsidiary.

The resulting sub-total is the amount of profit from ordinary activities that accrues to the holding company shareholders, and it completes Section B of the account.

(e)   Group reserves brought forward consist of:

   (i)   all the holding company's profit;
   (ii)   the group share of the subsidiaries' post acquisition profits;
   (iii)   less goodwill amortised up to the beginning of the current accounting period.

(f)   Once the master schedule has been filled in, the actual consolidated profit and loss account can be written out, using the figures from the 'consolidated' column. The account should follow the statutory formats. Minority interests are required, under the group accounting provisions of the CA85, to be shown immediately after profit on ordinary activities after taxation.

(g)   The note to the accounts gives the information required by S228 CA85 when a holding company does not publish its own profit and loss account. The figure is the holding company's own net profit before dividends taken from its own profit and loss account. Beware, though, as the holding company's own profit should include any dividends receivable from subsidiaries; if these have not been included in the profit and loss account given, you must add them in for the purpose of this note. Strictly speaking, this would be a note to the holding company's individual balance sheet, rather than to the consolidated profit and loss account. In practice, the disclosure is often shown in this way, but the point is unlikely to be tested in the exam.

3   CANCELLATION OF INTRA-GROUP TRANSACTIONS

3.1   Introduction

In the previous chapter on group accounts we dealt with the treatment of unrealised profits on stock arising from intra-group trading. In consolidating the profit and loss accounts a rather more involved adjustment is required.

If in a certain year:

(a)   A Ltd buys a stock item for £60;
(b)   A Ltd sells it to B Ltd for £80, B Ltd being a member of the same group as A Ltd;
(c)   B Ltd still holds the item at the balance sheet date; then

the profit and loss accounts of the two companies will include, in respect of these events:

	A Ltd £	B Ltd £
Turnover	80	-
Cost of sales	60	-
Gross profit, and hence every other profit and loss account sub-total	20	-

This £20 is the unrealised profit whose cancellation in the balance sheet was discussed before. In the profit and loss account we must also eliminate the £80 and £60 as the profit and loss account of a single company that had carried out the same transactions as A Ltd and B Ltd would contain no entries at all in respect of it.

What if B Ltd had sold the item for £95 by the balance sheet date? The profit and loss accounts of the two companies would then have shown:

	A Ltd £	B Ltd £
Turnover	80	95
Cost of sales	60	80
Gross profit (and other sub-totals)	20	15

Both companies have realised their profits and so these should not be adjusted. However, a single equivalent company would show in its profit and loss account:

	£
Turnover	95
Cost of sales	60
Gross profit (and other sub-totals)	35

In this case we need eliminate only the £80 from turnover and the £80 from cost of sales in order to establish the correct turnover and cost of sales figures.

In either case the adjustment is conveniently carried out by means of an extra column in the master schedule.

Effect on minority interests

If the unrealised profit originally arose in the subsidiary, the minority interests must be adjusted for their share in the unrealised profit. However this is an adjustment made in calculating their share of post tax profits; in the first instance all the unrealised profit must be eliminated to determine the correct amount of gross profit earned by the group trading as if it were a single entity.

3.2   Example

The profit and loss accounts of Entry Ltd and Exit Ltd for the year ended 31 July 19X7 are as follows:

	Entry Ltd £	Exit Ltd £
Turnover	6,956	3,290
Cost of sales	3,108	1,470
Gross profit	3,848	1,820
Administrative expenses	(1,184)	(560)
Income from shares in group companies	140	
Net profit on ordinary activities before taxation	2,804	1,260
Tax on profit on ordinary activities	1,258	595
Net profit after taxation	1,546	665
Dividends	800	350
Profit transferred to reserves	746	315

Statement of reserves

	Entry Ltd £	Exit Ltd £
As at 31 July 19X6	797	3,955
Retained profit	746	315
As at 31 July 19X7	1,543	4,270

Further information

(a)   On 1 August 19X5 Entry Ltd acquired 6,000 of the issued 10,000 ordinary shares and 2,000 of the issued 5,000 7% net preference shares of £1 each in Exit Ltd. At that date the reserves of Exit Ltd were £980. Goodwill of £2,000 arose on the acquisition.

(b)   In the year ended 31 July 19X7 Entry Ltd sold to Exit Ltd goods costing £500 for £625 (20% profit margin).

(c)   At 31 July 19X7 Exit Ltd had sold 40% of these goods for £300.

(d)   Goodwill is amortised over 5 years from the date of acquisition.

Prepare the consolidated profit and loss account of Entry Ltd and its subsidiary for the year ended 31 July 19X7.

3.3   Solution

Step 1   Reconciliation of dividends

| Expected preference dividends of Exit | = | £5,000 × 7% |
| | = | £350 |

Therefore, no ordinary dividend paid or proposed by Exit.

| Entry's share | = | £2,000 × 7% |
| | = | £140 |

Therefore, no adjustment required.

Step 2   Rules for dealing with inter-company trading

(a)   Eliminate from sales **all** inter-company sales at the selling price.

Therefore deduct £625.

(b)   Compute unrealised profit in goods not sold ie, the same calculation as for the consolidated balance sheet.

Closing stock re goods sold from Entry to Exit

60% × £625 = £375

Unrealised profit

20% × £375 = £75

(c)   The reduction in cost of sales is a **balancing figure** (£625 – £75) = £550.

Thus if there are no unrealised profits, cost of sales is reduced by the same amount as sales.

The figures shown/computed in (a) to (c) can now be transferred to the consolidation schedule.

As the sale was made by the holding company there is no adjustment to minority interests required (see Tutorial note below minority interests).

Step 3

Master schedule

	Entry Ltd	Exit Ltd	Adjustments	Consolidated
Group details	H	60% 12 months		
	£	£	£	£
Turnover	6,956	3,290	(625)	9,621
Cost of sales	(3,108)	(1,470)	550	(4,028)
Gross profit	3,848	1,820	(75)	5,593
Administrative expenses	(1,184)	(560)	(400)	(2,144)
Taxation	(1,258)	(595)	-	(1,853)
Profit after taxation	1,406	665	-	1,596

Step 4   **Minority interests**

		Minority interest %	Minority interest £
	£		
Minority interest:			
Profit after tax	665	100	
Preference dividend	(350)	60	210
To ordinary shareholders	315	40	126
			336

(Tutorial note: if the unrealised profit on inter-company trading originally arose in the subsidiary the minority interests' share in profits would be reduced by:

40% × £75 = £30

£306 would thus be shown in the consolidated profit and loss account. Note in particular that the unrealised profit of £75 would still have to be deducted to arrive at consolidated gross profit.*)*

Step 5   **Reserves b/f**

	£
Entry Ltd	797
Exit Ltd (60% × (3,955 − 980))	1,785
Goodwill amortised (2,000 ÷ 5)	(400)
	2,182

Step 6

Entry Ltd and its subsidiary
Consolidated profit and loss account for year ended 31 July 19X7

	£
Turnover	9,621
Cost of sales	4,028
Gross profit	5,593
Administrative expenses	2,144
Profit on ordinary activities before taxation	3,449

Tax on profit on ordinary activities	1,853
Profit on ordinary activities after taxation	1,596
Minority interests	336
Profit attributable to shareholders in Entry Ltd	1,260
Dividends	800
Profit transferred to reserves	460

Statement of reserves

	£
As at 31 July 19X6	2,182
Retained profit	460
As at 31 July 19X7	2,642

3.4   Intra-group interest

Where a holding company makes a loan to a subsidiary company, the resulting interest represents an expense in the subsidiary shown under the heading 'interest payable and similar charges'. The holding company will include the interest under the heading 'income from other fixed asset investments' (where the loan is long term).

On consolidation both these amounts must be eliminated by making an appropriate entry in the adjustments column in the consolidation schedule.

4   THE ACCOUNTING TREATMENT OF ASSOCIATED UNDERTAKINGS

4.1   Introduction

Where a company owns more than 50% of the share capital of another company, the *CA85* requires group accounts. The law in effect recognises the influence which a parent company may exert over a subsidiary company and the existence of an economic unit, the **group**. If a parent company's accounts were to show only dividends received or receivable from subsidiaries, the shareholders of the parent company would not be given sufficient information regarding the underlying profitability of the unit, the group. Consequently, group accounts normally include the parent company's share of the post-acquisition profits of subsidiaries.

However, if a company, H Ltd, which has subsidiaries, owns (say) 40% of the ordinary share capital of another company, A Ltd, then A Ltd does not come within the legal definition of subsidiary company. H Ltd **may** nevertheless be able to exert considerable influence over A Ltd. It would thus seem sensible to allow H Ltd to show information in its accounts about its share of the profits of A Ltd.

FRS 9 provides rules for accounting for associated companies ie, companies which fall into the position described above.

The *CA89* introduced into law the requirement for associated **undertakings** to be included in group accounts under the **equity** method. The equity method is the method detailed by *FRS 9*.

The term **undertakings** includes companies and unincorporated businesses. As the *CA89* requires the word 'undertaking' to be used in the published accounts, the rest of this section will follow the *CA89* terminology, where it is sensible to do so.

4.2   What is an 'associated undertaking'?

(a)   **Company law**

An associated undertaking will come within the definition of a **participating interest** in the investing company's **individual** accounts.

> **Definition**   A participating interest is an interest held in the shares of another undertaking, held for the long term, with a view to exercising control or influence to secure a benefit to the investor's own activities.   Where an investor holds 20% or more of the shares there is a presumption that this is a participating interest.

In the group accounts participating interests are split into **interests in associated undertakings** and **other participating interests**.

> **Definition**   An associated undertaking means an undertaking in which an undertaking included in the consolidation has a **participating interest** and over whose operating and financial policy it exercises a significant influence, and which is not –
>
> (i)   a subsidiary undertaking, or
>
> (ii)   a joint venture dealt with in the group accounts by proportional consolidation *(Note:* only **unincorporated** undertakings can be dealt with using proportional consolidation*)*.

Where an undertaking holds 20 per cent or more of the voting rights in another undertaking, it shall be presumed to exercise such an influence over it unless the contrary is shown.

To summarise, most participating interests are associated undertakings.   The difference between the two terms mainly relates to the type of share capital held.   A participating interest arises when 20% of **any** type of share capital is held.   An associated undertaking requires a 20% or more **equity** voting shareholding.

(b)   **FRS 9**

The FRS 9 definition is quite complex, but is essentially similar to the company law definition.

> **Definition**   An **associate** is an entity (other than a subsidiary) in which another entity (the investor) has a **participating interest** and over whose operating and financial policies the investor exercises a **significant influence**.

> **Definition**   A **participating interest** is an interest held in the shares of another entity on a long term basis for the purpose of securing a contribution to the investor's activities by the exercise of control or influence arising from or related to that interest.

> **Definition**   The exercise of **significant influence** means that the investor is actively involved and is influential in the direction of its investee through its participation in policy decisions covering aspects of policy relevant to the investor, including decisions on strategic issues such as:
>
> (a)   the expansion or contraction of the business, participation in other entities or changes in products, markets and activities of its investee; and
>
> (b)   determining the balance between dividend and reinvestment.

The main thing to note is that the emphasis of the FRS 9 definition is different to that in the Companies Act. Under the Companies Act, a holding of 20% or more is presumed to be an associate unless it can clearly be demonstrated otherwise. SSAP 1 (which preceded FRS 9) used a similar definition. In practice, this meant that the 20% threshold was normally the only factor taken into account, so that many investments were treated as associates when the investee did not actually exercise significant influence.

The FRS 9 definition centres on the actual substance of the relationship between the parties (ie, whether significant influence is exercised in practice) rather than its strict legal form (the size of the shareholding).

An investing company's ability to exercise significant influence may depend on the other shareholdings as well as its own. For example, if A Ltd holds 30% of the shares in B Ltd, but the remaining 70% of the shares in B Ltd are held by C plc, then A Ltd is extremely unlikely to be able to exercise significant influence over B Ltd.

However, in questions you should assume that a shareholding of between 20% and 50% is an associate unless you are given information which suggests otherwise.

Conclusion | A company is an associated undertaking if the investing company exercises significant influence over it. A shareholding of between 20% and 50% normally gives significant influence.

4.3 Types of associated undertaking situations

The accounting treatment varies depending upon whether the investing company:

(a)   has subsidiaries and is thus obliged to prepare group accounts anyway; or

(b)   has no subsidiary.

In most cases the investing company has subsidiaries and thus prepares group accounts. This situation is covered here.

4.4 Activity

What are the headings in the *CA85* group account formats for the balance sheet and the profit and loss account which are used for associated undertakings?

4.5 Activity solution

In the balance sheet under Fixed Asset Investments:

'Interests in associated undertakings'

In the profit and loss account after arriving at operating profit:

'Income from interests in associated undertakings'.

5   THE EQUITY METHOD OF ACCOUNTING

5.1 Equity accounting in the consolidated balance sheet

Definition | **Equity accounting** is a method of accounting that brings an investment into its investor's financial statements initially at its cost, identifying any goodwill arising. The carrying amount of the investment is adjusted in each period by the investor's share of the results of its investee less any amortisation or write-off for goodwill, the investor's share of any relevant gains or losses, and any other changes in the investee's net assets including distributions to its owners, for example, by dividend.

The investment in the associate is therefore stated at

	(i)	cost
plus	(ii)	group share of retained post-acquisition profits
less	(iii)	amounts written off (eg, goodwill amortised).

Assuming goodwill has been fully amortised, this will be equal to the investing company's share of net assets in the associate.

5.2   Example

H plc acquired 25% of the ordinary share capital of A plc for £640,000 some years ago when the profit and loss reserves of A plc stood at £720,000. Goodwill arising on the acquisition has been fully amortised. H plc appointed two directors to the board of A plc and the investment is regarded as long term. Both companies prepare accounts to 31 December each year. The summarised balance sheet of A plc on 31 December 19X4 is as follows

	£'000
Sundry net assets	2,390
Capital and reserves	
Called up share capital	800
Share premium	450
Profit and loss account	1,140
	2,390

A plc has made no new issues of shares nor has there been any movement in the share premium account since H plc acquired its holding.

Show at what amount the investment in A plc will be shown in the consolidated balance sheet of H plc as on 31 December 19X4.

5.3   Solution

Investment in associated undertakings

$25\% \times £2,390,000 = £597,500$

This figure could also be calculated as:

	£
Cost	640,000
Share of post-acquisition profits (25% × (1,140 - 720))	105,000
Less: Goodwill amortised (W1)	(147,500)
	597,500

WORKINGS

(W1)   Goodwill

	£	£
Cost		640,000
Less: Share of net assets at acquisition		
Share capital	800,000	
Share premium	450,000	
Reserves	720,000	
25% ×	£1,970,000	(492,500)
Goodwill - fully amortised		£147,500

5.4 Effect on total reserves

Total reserves in the published accounts will be changed in two main ways due to the equity accounting of the associate.

(i) Reserves will be increased by the group share of post acquisition reserves.

(ii) Reserves will be decreased by any goodwill amortised.

The consolidation schedule for group reserves will include these two items in respect of associated undertakings as shown below:

Consolidated profit and loss account reserve

	£'000
H:	X
S: S% (now - acquisition)	X
A: 25% (now - acquisition) (1,140 – 720)	105
Less: Goodwill amortised	
S	(X)
A	(147.5)
	X

5.5 Equity accounting in the consolidated profit and loss account

The **group share** of the following are brought in

(i) operating profit

(ii) exceptional items

(iii) interest receivable

(iv) interest payable

(v) taxation.

Amortisation of goodwill arising on acquisition of an associate should be deducted from the group share of operating profit and should be separately disclosed.

5.6 Example

Following on from the facts in para 5.2 above, the consolidated profit and loss account of H plc (before including any amounts for A plc) and the profit and loss account of A plc for the year ended 31 December 19X4 are as follows

	H plc £'000	A plc £'000
Turnover	11,000	4,000
Cost of sales	(6,500)	(3,000)
Gross profit	4,500	1,000
Distribution costs	(1,000)	(500)
Administrative expenses	(700)	(300)
Operating profit	2,800	200
Interest receivable	300	200
Interest payable	(100)	(100)
Profit on ordinary activities before taxation	3,000	300
Taxation	(1,200)	(60)
Profit on ordinary activities after taxation	1,800	240
Minority interests	(300)	–
Profit attributable to the group	1,500	240

Dividends proposed	(300)	(50)
Retained profit for the year	1,200	190
Retained profit b/f	6,300	950
Retained profit c/f	7,500	1,140

Prepare the consolidated profit and loss account for H plc for the year ended 31 December 19X4.

5.7   Solution

	£'000	£'000
Turnover		11,000
Cost of sales		(6,500)
Gross profit		4,500
Distribution costs		(1,000)
Administrative expenses		(700)
Group operating profit		2,800
Share of operating profit in associates (25% × 200)		50
Interest receivable		
Group	300	
Associates (25% × 200)	50	
		350
Interest payable		
Group	100	
Associates (25% × 100)	25	
		(125)
Profit on ordinary activities before taxation		3,075
Taxation		
Group	1,200	
Associates (25% × 60)	15	
		(1,215)
Profit on ordinary activities after taxation		1,860
Minority interests		(300)
Profit attributable to the group		1,560
Dividends		(300)
Retained profit for the year		1,260
Retained at 1 January 19X4 (W1)		6,210
Retained at 31 December 19X4		7,470

WORKINGS

(W1)   **Retained profit b/d**

	£'000
H plc	6,300
A plc 25%(950 – 720)	58
Less: Goodwill amortised (per previous example)	(148)
	6,210

5.8   Transactions between the group and the associate

Trading transactions and/or loans may be made between member companies of the group (ie, holding company and subsidiaries) and the associate. As the associate is not consolidated it follows that these transactions are not cancelled out. For example a loan made by the holding company to an associate will remain as a loan on the consolidated balance sheet (as an asset). The liability recorded in the associate's balance sheet will merely reduce the net assets (which are recorded as one figure - share of net assets - on the consolidated balance sheet).

An adjustment will only be required if there is unrealised profit at the balance sheet date ie, stocks exist as a result of the trading. FRS 9 requires an adjustment for the group's share of the unrealised profit. The elimination should be taken in the consolidated profit and loss against either the group or the associate according to which of them recorded the profit on the transaction. The adjustment in the balance sheet should be made against

(a)   consolidated stock (if the unrealised profit is in respect of part of this stock)

or

(b)   investment in associate (if the stock is in the associate).

5.9   Applying the equity method - further points

Statement of total recognised gains and losses

The investor's share of the total recognised gains of its associates should be included in the statement of total recognised gains and losses. If the amounts are material, they should be shown separately under each heading either in the statement or in a note to the statement.

General principles

(a)   The consideration paid for the acquisition and the goodwill arising should be calculated using fair values.

(b)   Investor and associate should apply the same accounting policies.

(c)   The accounts of the associate should have the same financial year-end as those of the investor. If this is impracticable, earlier financial statements of the associate may be used, provided they are prepared for a financial year that ended not more than three months earlier.

(d)   The date on which an investment becomes an associate is the date on which the investor begins to hold a participating interest and to exercise significant influence.

(e)   The date on which an investment ceases to be an associate is the date on which the investor ceases to hold a participating interest and to exercise significant influence.

6   JOINT VENTURES

6.1   Introduction

In Chapter 4 you studied the accounting treatment of joint ventures in the accounts of the individual venturers and the preparation of separate accounts for joint ventures. FRS 9 sets out the accounting treatment for joint ventures in the consolidated financial statements.

The term 'joint venture' is used very widely in practice to cover all types of jointly controlled activity. Jointly controlled operations, assets and entities may all be described as joint ventures. FRS 9 defines 'joint venture' in a much narrower sense.

> **Definition** A **joint venture** is an entity in which the reporting entity holds an interest on a long-term basis and is **jointly controlled** by the reporting entity and by one or more other venturers under a contractual arrangement.

> **Definition** A reporting entity **jointly controls** a venture with one or more other entities if none of the entities alone can control that entity but all together can do so and decisions on financial and operating policy essential to the activities, economic performance and financial position of that venture require each venturer's consent.

A joint arrangement to carry out a single project is unlikely to meet the definition of a joint venture.

> **Definition** A **joint arrangement that is not an entity** is a contractual arrangement under which the participants engage in joint activities that do not create an entity because it would not be carrying on a trade or business of its own.

> **Conclusion** A joint venture is an **entity** which is jointly controlled by the reporting entity and by one or more other venturers.

6.2   Accounting treatment

(a)   **Joint arrangements that are not entities**

Participants in a joint arrangement that is not an entity should account for their own assets, liabilities and cash flows, measured according to the terms of the agreement governing the arrangement.

(b)   **Joint ventures**

In the investor's **individual financial statements**, investments in joint ventures should be treated as fixed asset investments and shown either at cost, less any amounts written off, or at valuation.

In the **consolidated financial statements** joint ventures should be included using the gross equity method.

> **Definition** The **gross equity method** is a form of equity method under which the investor's share of the aggregate gross assets and liabilities underlying the net amount included for the investment is shown on the face of the balance sheet and, in the profit and loss account, the investor's share of the investee's turnover is noted.

This means that the treatment is the same as for associates, but with additional disclosure:

–   the investor's share of turnover is shown in the consolidated profit and loss account (but not as part of group turnover);

–   the investor's share of the gross assets and liabilities are shown in the consolidated balance sheet (instead of the investor's share of the net assets).

Conclusion   Joint ventures are included in the consolidated financial statements using the gross equity method.

6.3   Illustration

FRS 9 includes illustrative examples of ways of disclosing information about joint ventures. Example 1 from FRS 9 is shown below. Note that the example also includes associates.

CONSOLIDATED PROFIT AND LOSS ACCOUNT

The format is illustrative only. The amounts shown for 'Associates' and 'Joint ventures' are subdivisions of the item for which the statutory prescribed heading is 'Income from interests in associated undertakings'. The subdivisions may be shown in a note rather than on the face of the profit and loss account.

	£m	£m
Turnover: group and share of joint ventures	320	
Less: share of joint ventures' turnover	(120)	
Group turnover		200
Cost of sales		(120)
Gross profit		80
Administrative expenses		(40)
Group operating profit		40
Share of operating profit in		
Joint ventures	30	
Associates	24	
		54
		94
Interest receivable (group)		6
Interest payable		
Group	(26)	
Joint ventures	(10)	
Associates	(12)	
		(48)
Profit on ordinary activities before tax		52
Tax on profit on ordinary activities*		(12)
Profit on ordinary activities after tax		40
Minority interests		(6)
Profit on ordinary activities after taxation and minority interest		34
Equity dividends		(10)
Retained profit for group and its share of associates and joint ventures		24

* Tax relates to the following: Parent and subsidiaries (5)

Joint ventures (5)

Associates (2)

CONSOLIDATED BALANCE SHEET

	£m	£m	£m
Fixed assets			
Tangible assets		480	
Investments			
Investments in joint ventures:			
Share of gross assets	130		
Share of gross liabilities	(80)		
		50	
Investments in associates		20	
			550
Current assets			
Stock		15	
Debtors		75	
Cash at bank and in hand		10	
		100	
Creditors (due within one year)		(50)	
Net current assets			50
Total assets less current liabilities			600
Creditors (due after more than one year)			(250)
Provisions for liabilities and charges			(10)
Equity minority interest			(40)
			300
Capital and reserves			
Called up share capital			50
Share premium account			150
Profit and loss account			100
Shareholders' funds (all equity)			300

7   DISCLOSURE REQUIREMENTS FOR ASSOCIATES AND JOINT VENTURES

7.1   All associates and joint ventures

(a)   For each associate or joint venture included in the financial statements of the investing group, disclose the following:

   (i)   name;

   (ii)   proportion of the issued shares in each class held by the investing group;

   (iii)   accounting period or date of the financial statements used if different from those of the investing group;

   (iv)   an indication of the nature of its business.

(b)   Disclose any notes relating to the financial statements of associates that are material to understanding the effect on the investor of its investments.

(c)   Indicate the extent of any statutory, contractual or exchange control restrictions on the ability of an associate to distribute its reserves.

(d)   Disclose the amounts owing and owed between the investor and its associates or joint ventures, analysed into amounts relating to loans and amounts relating to trading balances.

(e)   Where an investor holding 20% or more of the voting rights of another entity does not treat it as an associate, a note should explain the reasons for this.

7.2   Detailed disclosures where associates and joint ventures are material to the investing group

One of the disadvantages of the equity method is that it only provides limited information about associates and joint ventures.   In particular, only one figure is included in the balance sheet, representing the group share of the associates' net assets.   It is possible for material liabilities to be hidden in this figure, enabling investors to use equity accounted entities as a form of off balance sheet finance.

For this reason, FRS 9 requires additional disclosures where size thresholds are exceeded.   The thresholds are applied by comparing the investor's share for its associates or joint ventures of **any** of the following:

- gross assets
- gross liabilities
- turnover
- operating results (on a three year average)

with the corresponding amounts for the investor group (excluding associates and joint ventures).

(a)   Where the **aggregate** of the investor's share in its associates or its joint ventures exceeds a **15% threshold** with respect to the investor group, a note should give the aggregate of the investor's share in its associates of the following:

- turnover (associates only; for joint ventures it must always be disclosed)
- fixed assets
- current assets
- liabilities due within one year
- liabilities due after one year or more.

(b)   Where the investor's share in any **individual** associate or joint venture exceeds a **25% threshold** with respect to the investor group, a note should name that associate or joint venture and give its share of each of the following:

- turnover
- profit before tax
- taxation
- profit after tax
- fixed assets
- current assets
- liabilities due within one year
- liabilities due after one year or more.

7.3   Activity

You are provided with the following information about H plc and its associated undertaking, A Ltd for the year ended 30 June 19X8:

	H plc £'000	A Ltd £'000
Turnover	110,000	60,000
Operating profit	30,000	16,000
Profit before tax	25,000	12,000
Taxation	10,000	4,000
Profit after tax	15,000	8,000
Fixed assets	250,000	160,000
Current assets	40,000	24,000
Creditors due within one year	45,000	24,000
Creditors due after more than one year	110,000	40,000

H plc holds 25% of the equity share capital of A Ltd.

Show the additional disclosures required in respect of A Ltd in the consolidated financial statements of the H plc group for the year ended 30 June 19X8.

7.4   Activity solution

Additional disclosures for associates

	£'000	£'000
Share of turnover of associates (25% × 60,000)		15,000
Share of assets		
Share of fixed assets (25% × 160,000)	40,000	
Share of current assets (25% × 24,000)	6,000	
		46,000
Share of liabilities		
Liabilities due within one year or less (25% × 24,000)	6,000	
Liabilities due after more than one year (25% × 40,000)	10,000	
		(16,000)
Share of net assets		30,000

WORKING

H plc's share of the total assets of the associate exceeds 15%. (Note that the disclosures have to be made if **any** of the thresholds are exceeded.)

Turnover $\dfrac{25\% \times 60,000}{110,000} =$ 14%

Operating profit $\dfrac{25\% \times 16,000}{30,000} =$ 13%

Total assets $\dfrac{25\% \times 184,000}{290,000} =$ 16%

Total liabilities $\dfrac{25\% \times 64,000}{155,000} =$ 10%

8   CHAPTER SUMMARY

As with a consolidated balance sheet, the basic procedure for preparing a consolidated profit and loss account is simply to add together the profit and loss accounts for the individual companies within the group.

A convenient way to do this is by means of the master schedule illustrated in this chapter. On this schedule you can proceed to enter adjustments for:

- inter-company transactions (including trading transactions, disposal of assets and payment of dividends and interest by subsidiaries to the holding company)

- minority interests.

Associates are included in the group accounts under the equity method ie, a share of the respective items is included in the profit and loss account and the share of net assets is recorded in the consolidated balance sheet. Joint ventures are included in the group accounts under the gross equity method.

9   SELF TEST QUESTIONS

9.1   What comprises a group's consolidated reserves balance brought forward at the start of a year? (1.7)

9.2   What conditions must a company satisfy before it is relieved of the need to publish its own holding company profit and loss account? (1.20)

9.3   If a holding company and a 75% subsidiary both have turnover of £10,000 for a year, will consolidated turnover be £20,000 or £17,500? (2.2)

9.4   How is intra-group interest dealt with in the consolidated profit and loss account? (3.4)

9.5   How does *CA85* define an associated undertaking? (4.2a)

9.6   How does FRS 9 define significant influence? (4.2b)

9.7   At what amount is the investment in an associated undertaking shown in the consolidated balance sheet? (5.1)

10   EXAMINATION TYPE QUESTIONS

10.1   N and S

N plc acquired 60% of the ordinary shares of S Ltd several years ago when the reserves of S Ltd were £80,000. N plc also acquired 20% of the preference shares of S Ltd on the same date.

The summarised profit and loss accounts of the two companies for the year ended 30 September 19X7 are as follows:

| | N plc | | S Ltd | |
	£'000	£'000	£'000	£'000
Sales		4,500		1,100
Cost of sales		2,320		620
Gross profit		2,180		480
Expenses		1,400		220
Trading profit		780		260
Investment income		52		
Profit before taxation		832		

Taxation	200		80
Profit after taxation	632		180
Dividends paid:			
Ordinary	140		20
Preference	15		10
Dividends proposed:			
Ordinary	280		60
Preference	15		10
	450		100
Profit retained	182		80
Reserves brought forward	600		250
Reserves carried forward	782		330

N plc sold goods to S Ltd during the year at an invoice price of £250,000. The goods were invoiced at cost + 25%. Of these goods, one half were still in S Ltd's stock at the end of the year.

You are required to prepare the consolidated profit and loss account for the year ended 30 September 19X7. Ignore goodwill.   **(14 marks)**

10.2   H, S and A

You are given the following abbreviated profit and loss accounts of three companies, H Ltd, S Ltd and A Ltd. H Ltd acquired an 80% holding in S Ltd paying £6,000 for goodwill when the reserves of S Ltd amounted to £40,000. H Ltd acquired a 25% holding in A Ltd at a cost of £81,200, when the reserves of A Ltd amounted to £32,000. A Ltd is an associated company with a share capital of £250,000 (ordinary shares).

Profit and loss accounts for the year ended 31.12.X5

	H Ltd £	S Ltd £	A Ltd £
Trading profit	800,000	100,000	140,000
Investment income	5,000	-	-
UK Corporation tax	(400,000)	(50,000)	(70,000)
	405,000	50,000	70,000
Dividend paid	103,000	-	8,000
	302,000	50,000	62,000
Balance b/d	2,000,000	130,000	100,000
Balance c/d	2,302,000	180,000	162,000

	£
Investment income of H Ltd comprises:	
Dividend from A Ltd	2,000
Dividend from trade investment	3,000
	5,000

You are required:

(a)   to prepare a consolidated profit and loss account for the year ended 31.12.X5 which complies with standard accounting practice.

(b)   to show the extracts in the consolidated balance sheets as at 31.12.X4 and 31.12.X5 relating to the investment in the associated company.

All goodwill has been fully amortised at 1.1.X5. Ignore the grossing up of dividends received on the face of the profit and loss account. **(20 marks)**

11 ANSWERS TO EXAMINATION TYPE QUESTIONS

11.1 N and S

Consolidated profit and loss account for the year ended 30 September 19X7

	£'000
Sales	5,350
Cost of sales	2,715
Gross profit	2,635
Expenses	1,620
Profit on ordinary activities before taxation	1,015
Taxation	280
Profit on ordinary activities after taxation	735
Minority interests (W3)	80
Profit attributable to N plc	655
Dividends paid and proposed	450
Retained profit for the year	205
Reserves brought forward (W4)	702
Reserves carried forward (W5)	907

WORKINGS

Consolidation schedule

	N £'000	S £'000	Adjusted £'000	Consolidated £'000
Sales	4,500	1,100	(250)	5,350
Cost of sales	2,320	620	(225)	2,715
Gross profit (W1)	2,180	480	(25)	2,635
Expenses	1,400	220		1,620
Taxation	200	80		280

(1) **Unrealised profit in stock**

$$\frac{25}{125} \times 250,000 \times \tfrac{1}{2} = £25,000$$

(Tutorial note:

The unrealised profit is eliminated in full against the group as it is the holding company which originally recorded the profit.*)*

(2) **Dividends received by N from S**

	£'000
Preference 20% × 20	4
Ordinary 60% × 80	48
All investment income is intra-group	52

(3)   **Minority interest**

	£'000		Minority interest £'000
Profit after taxation of S	180		
Preference dividend	20	80%	16
For ordinary shareholders	160	40%	64
			80

(4)   **Reserves brought forward**

	£'000
N	600
S 60% × (250 – 80)	102
	702

(5)   **Reserves carried forward**

	£'000
N	782
S 60% × (330 – 80)	150
Unrealised profit in stock provision carried forward	(25)
	907

11.2   H, S and A

(a)   **H Ltd and its subsidiary – Group profit and loss account for the year ended 31 December 19X5**

	£
Group operating profit	900,000
Share of operating profit of associated undertakings	35,000
Investment income	3,000
Profit on ordinary activities before taxation	938,000
Tax on profit on ordinary activities	467,500
Profit on ordinary activities after taxation	470,500
Minority interests	10,000
Profit attributable to members of the parent undertaking	460,500
Dividends	103,000
Amount added to group reserves brought forward	357,500

Notes to profit and loss account:

1   **Statement of retained reserves**

	Total
	£
Retained reserves at 1 January 19X5	2,072,300
Retained profit for the year	357,500
Retained reserves at 31 December 19X5	2,429,800

2   **Tax on profit on ordinary activities**

	£
Corporation tax at x%	450,000
Associated undertaking	17,500
	467,500

(b)   **Balance sheet extracts**

	31.12.X4	31.12.X5
	£	£
Interest in associated undertaking		
Group share of net assets (other than goodwill)	87,500	103,000

(*Tutorial note:*

Journal entry required in consolidated working papers is: Dr Investment in associate, Cr accumulated reserves £15,500.)

Consolidation schedule

Details	H £	S 80% £	Consolidation adjustments £	Total £	A 25% £
Trading profit	800,000	100,000		900,000	
Share of profit				35,000	35,000
Investment income	3,000			3,000	
	803,000	100,000		938,000	
Tax	400,000	50,000		(450,000)	
Share of tax				(17,500)	(17,500)
	403,000	50,000		470,500	17,500
Minority interest 20% × 50,000		10,000		(10,000)	
		40,000		460,500	
Inter co dividend 25% × 8,000	2,000				(2,000)
Profit before dividend	405,000				
Dividend	103,000			103,000	
Retained for year	302,000	40,000		357,500	15,500

WORKINGS

(1)   **Investment in associate**

	Acquisition £	31.12.X4 £	31.12.X5 £
Shares	250,000	250,000	250,000
Reserves	32,000	100,000	162,000
Net assets	282,000	350,000	412,000
Group share 25%	70,500	87,500	103,000
Cost of investment	81,200		
Goodwill - fully amortised	10,700		

(2)   **Reserves brought forward**

	£
Associate	
25% × (100,000 − 32,000)	17,000

	£
Group	
H	2,000,000
S 80% × (130,000 − 40,000)	72,000
Goodwill amortised - S	(6,000)
A (W1)	(10,700)
	2,055,300

19 GROUP ACCOUNTING - 3

INTRODUCTION & LEARNING OBJECTIVES

This chapter starts by considering the alternative means by which group accounts could be prepared. This could be tested by the examiner providing relatively simple data for you to compute alternatives and then to comment on the results.

Acquisition and merger accounting are the two main methods of consolidation. There is continuing controversy as to the appropriateness of merger accounting and thus a question requiring a comparison of merger and acquisition accounting is likely to prove popular to the examiner.

You should find the computations for mergers quite straightforward. In fact they are easier than acquisition accounting.

The chapter concludes by considering the regulatory environment of groups. There is a fair amount of learning of definitions to do.

When you have studied this chapter you should be able to do the following:

- Explain the different methods under which group accounts could be presented.
- Compute accounts under the merger method.
- State the legal and professional requirements relating to group accounts.

1 THE DIFFERENT METHODS WHICH COULD BE USED TO PREPARE GROUP ACCOUNTS

1.1 Meaning of group accounts

The *CA85* (as amended by the *CA89*), *FRS 2* and *FRS 6* require a holding company to prepare **group** accounts, which must normally be **consolidated** accounts comprising a consolidated balance sheet and a consolidated profit and loss account. The group accounts shall give a true and fair view of the companies included in the consolidation as a whole.

The use of the two terms above – group accounts and consolidated accounts – implies the terms are not the same. Group accounts can be defined as any set of information which gives information about the financial affairs of the group. Consolidated accounts are thus one form of group accounts.

In most circumstances consolidation presents group accounts in the most informative way. There are circumstances where consolidation may not be appropriate and the *CA85* and *FRS 2* allow/require non-consolidation. These situations are dealt with later in this chapter.

At this point we briefly consider the alternative forms in which group accounts could, **theoretically**, be prepared.

1.2 Form of group accounts

The major ways in which group accounts are or could be presented are:

(a) **Consolidated financial statements under the entity concept**

This is by far the most common form of group accounts. Consolidated financial statements are prepared by replacing the cost of investments with the individual assets and liabilities underlying that investment. If the subsidiary is only partly owned this does not affect the amount of assets and liabilities of the subsidiary which are consolidated, but results in the need to show the minority shareholders' interest in those net assets.

Definition   The entity concept focuses on the existence of the group as an **economic** unit rather than looking at it only through the eyes of the dominant shareholder group. It concentrates on the resources controlled by the entity.

The two forms of consolidation under this concept are **acquisition** accounting (the usual method you have seen in the previous chapters) and **merger** accounting (suitable in rare circumstances as explained later in this chapter).

(b)   Accounting for subsidiaries under the equity method

Under the equity method group accounts record the share of profits attributable to the parent company from the subsidiary and the parent company's **share** in the net assets of the subsidiary. Thus, minority shareholders' interest in the net assets are not shown.

The equity method is required to be used in certain circumstances by *FRS 2* where consolidation would give a misleading view. The equity method is **not** a method of consolidation but a different form of presenting group accounts.

(c)   Consolidated financial statements under the proprietary concept

This is different from the entity concept only where there are minority interests.

The proprietary concept emphasises ownership through the controlling shareholding and produces accounts primarily for the shareholders of the parent company.

There are two main variants:

(i)   the **parent company** concept which in terms of the mechanics of consolidation is similar to the entity concept except that minority interests are shown as quasi-liabilities;

(ii)   the **proportional consolidation** method in which only the group share of individual assets and liabilities are included in the relevant group totals. Thus minority shareholders' interest in the net assets is not shown.

(d)   Show separate accounts for the parent company and its subsidiary/ies

It has been argued that in complex groups consolidated accounts are too all-embracing to be of any value and can, by setting off and consolidating unlike items, produce a misleading impression of the group's activities. In such a situation, the disclosure of the separate accounts of the companies within the group may give a more meaningful picture of the group.

Chart of possible alternative methods of presenting group accounts

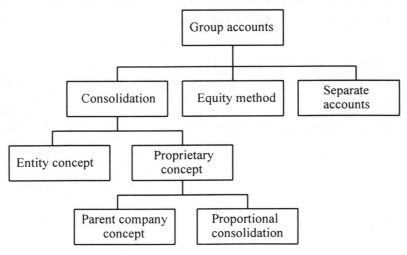

1.3   Example - Comparison of consolidation and equity methods

The separate summarised accounts for the year to 31 December 19X2 of H and S are:

Balance sheets as at 31 December 19X2

	H £	S £
Share capital	2,000	1,000
Reserves	3,000	2,000
Long-term debt	-	8,000
	5,000	11,000
Fixed assets	2,200	10,000
Cost of investment	1,800	-
Net current assets	1,000	1,000
	5,000	11,000

Profit and loss accounts for year ended 31 December 19X2

	H £	S £
Sales	4,000	20,000
Cost of sales	3,500	18,900
Operating profit	500	1,100
Interest payable	-	800
	500	300
Tax	270	160
Retained profit for year	230	140

H acquired an 80% interest in S four years ago when the reserves of S were £500.

Show the group balance sheets and profit and loss accounts under the consolidation method, the equity method, and the proportional consolidation methods. Assume that goodwill is written off in equal instalments over six years.

Step 1   Goodwill - This will be the same under each method.

	£
Share capital and reserves of S at acquisition	1,500
H Ltd share 80% × £1,500	1,200
Cost of investment	1,800
Goodwill	600
Less: Written off after four years	400
	200

Step 2   **Minority interest at 31 December 19X2** - only included under the consolidation method.

	£
Net assets of S Ltd at 31 December 19X2	3,000
Minority share	20%
	600

Step 3   **Group reserves** - The same amount of profit is dealt with under any of the methods.

	£
H Ltd	3,000
S Ltd 80% £(2,000 – 500)	1,200
	4,200
Less: Goodwill written-off	400
	3,800

Group balance sheet of H Ltd and subsidiary as at 31 December 19X2

	Consolidation	Equity	Proportional consolidation
	£	£	£
Net assets			
Fixed assets	12,200	2,200	10,200
Goodwill arising on acquisition of investment in subsidiary	200	200	200
Share of net assets in subsidiary (80% × £3,000)	-	2,400	-
Net current assets	2,000	1,000	1,800
	14,400	5,800	12,200
Capital employed			
Share capital	2,000	2,000	2,000
Reserves	3,800	3,800	3,800
	5,800	5,800	5,800
Minority interests	600	-	-
Long-term debt	8,000	-	6,400
	14,400	5,800	12,200

Group profit and loss accounts of H Ltd for the year ended 31 December 19X2

	Consolidation	Equity	Proportional consolidation
	£	£	£
Sales	24,000	4,000	20,000
Cost of sales	22,400	3,500	18,620
Operating profit	1,600	500	1,380

Share of profit of subsidiary
 (80% × £300)

Share of profit of subsidiary (80% × £300)		240	
Interest payable	800		640
Goodwill written off	100	100	100
	700	640	640
Tax £(270 + 160)	430		
£(270 + (80% × 160))		398	398
	270	242	242
Minority interest 20% × £140	28		
Profit attributable to H Ltd Group	242	242	242

1.4   Evaluating the alternative group accounting methods

(a)   The group balance sheets are completely different in form, and give contrasting images of the financial stability of the group. The equity group balance sheet appears to show a safe state of affairs. The consolidated balance sheets, however, reveal the considerable long-term debt incurred by the subsidiary.

It is because the equity method fails to reveal the underlying assets and liabilities that its use is not regarded as a valid method of showing group accounts in the majority of situations, and it is therefore only used when, for some reason, consolidation is regarded as inappropriate. The equity method is, however, used in accounting for **associates**.

(b)   The proportional method of consolidation has not found favour in the UK as, although it does reveal the underlying assets and liabilities of the subsidiary, it implies that all the assets of the subsidiary are not under the control of the parent company.

The *CA85* does, however, recognise the proportional consolidation method.

A **joint venture** may be included in the group accounts by proportional consolidation. It must be an **unincorporated** body and must be managed jointly with one or more undertakings which are not part of the group. It is unlikely that proportional consolidation will be extensively used in the UK because FRS 9 requires joint ventures to be consolidated using the gross equity method.

2   THE MERGER METHOD OF ACCOUNTING

2.1   Introduction

Business combinations arise when one or more companies become subsidiaries of another company. Two different methods have been developed to account for business combinations - acquisition accounting and merger accounting. The ASB issued FRS 6 in September 1994 to standardise the situations in which each method should be applied.

The main criterion employed to determine the appropriate method or methods of accounting is whether or not the combination is based principally on a share for share exchange. Merger accounting is considered to be an appropriate method of accounting when two groups of shareholders continue, or are in a position to continue, their shareholdings as before but on a combined basis. Acquisition accounting is, therefore, required when there is a transfer of the ownership of at least one of the combining companies, and substantial resources leave the group as consideration for that transfer. Conversely, when only limited resources leave the group, merger accounting may be used.

FRS 6 defines mergers and acquisitions as follows:

Definition   A **merger** is a business combination that results in the creation of a new reporting entity formed from the combining parties, in which the shareholders of the combining entities come together in a partnership for the mutual sharing of the risks and benefits of the combined entity and in which no party to the combination in substance obtains control over any other, or is otherwise seen to be dominant, whether by virtue of the proportion of the shareholders' rights in the combined entity, the influence of its directors or otherwise.

Definition   An **acquisition** is a business combination that is not a merger.

The two different methods of consolidation are designed to reflect the substance of the two different types of business combination. Acquisition accounting primarily reflects the **purchase** of one company by another and the fact that the purchaser **controls** the net assets of the subsidiary. The net assets acquired are included at their fair values and only post-acquisition profits of the subsidiary are included in consolidated reserves. Merger accounting reflects the **pooling of interests** of two more or less equal partners. The two sets of accounts are effectively added together.

FRS 6 Acquisitions and mergers deals only with accounting in the consolidated accounts and not with accounting in the individual company accounts (although some guidance is provided in an appendix to the standard). However, the entries at the individual company stage can affect the entries at the consolidated accounts stage and thus the accounts of the holding company are dealt with first.

2.2   Accounts of the holding company – basic situation

The investment in a new subsidiary will be shown as a fixed asset investment in the parent company's own accounts. The amount at which this investment will be stated will depend upon which method of accounting is to be used on consolidation:

(a)   If acquisition accounting is to be used, then the investment will be recorded at cost, which will normally be the fair value of the consideration given.

(b)   If merger accounting is to be used, then the investment will be recorded at the nominal value of the shares issued as purchase consideration plus the fair value of any additional consideration.

2.3   Example

A plc makes an offer to all the shareholders of B plc to acquire their shares on the basis of one new £1 share (market value £3) plus 25p for every two £1 shares (market value £1.10 each) in B plc. The holders of 95,000 shares in B plc (representing 95% of the total shares) accept this offer.

2.4   Solution

The investment in B plc will be recorded in the books of A plc as follows:

(a)   If acquisition accounting is to be used on consolidation:

	£	£
Dr Investment in B plc	154,375	
Cr £1 ordinary shares		47,500
Cr Share premium		95,000
Cr Cash		11,875
	154,375	154,375

(b)   If merger accounting is to be used on consolidation:

	£	£
Dr Investment in B plc	59,375	
Cr £1 ordinary shares		47,500
Cr Cash		11,875
	59,375	59,375

2.5   Accounts of the holding company – the effect of merger relief

S130 CA85 states that if a company issues shares at a premium, whether for cash or otherwise, a sum equal to the aggregate amount or value of the premium on those shares shall be transferred to a share premium account.

S131 CA85 provides that where a company has, by an arrangement including the exchange of shares, secured at least a 90% equity holding in another company then *S130 CA85* shall not apply to the premium on any shares which are included in the purchase consideration. This provision is known as the 'merger relief' provision.

In the example above A plc did, by an arrangement including the exchange of shares, secure at least a 90% equity holding in another company and hence would not transfer £95,000 to the share premium account, and would then record the investment in B plc at £59,375 – exactly the same figure as arrived at if merger accounting were to be used on consolidation. In the situation where acquisition accounting is to be used on consolidation, the holding company would credit the share premium to a merger reserve, thus:

	£	£
Dr Investment in B plc	154,375	
Cr £1 ordinary shares		47,500
Cr Merger reserve		95,000
Cr Cash		11,875
	154,375	154,375

Such a setting up of a merger reserve in the accounts of the parent company is **not** obligatory. However, if acquisition accounting is to be used on consolidation, then the investment must, for consolidation purposes, be stated at its fair value. If a merger reserve has been set up then the investment will be stated at its fair value. If a merger reserve has not been set up in the accounts of the parent company, then a consolidation adjustment must be made so as to introduce this reserve and so as to uplift the investment to its fair value.

In the above example the consolidation adjustment would be:

	£	£
Dr Investment in B plc	95,000	
Cr Merger reserve		95,000

2.6   The requirements of FRS 6 and the Companies Acts regarding merger accounting

We have established that there are two main methods of consolidation, the acquisition method (the normal method) and the merger method (used in the rare cases where two equal partners are uniting together with no party having an acquisitive intent). The purpose of the rules in CA 89 and FRS 6 is to identify precisely the circumstances that must exist before a combination is classified as a merger (so that merger accounting must be used). If these circumstances do not exist then the combination is classified as an acquisition, and acquisition accounting must be used.

The conditions laid down in CA 89 and FRS 6 to identify a merger are as follows:

CA89 conditions

1.   The subsidiary was acquired by an arrangement providing for the issue of equity shares by the parent company or its subsidiaries.

2.   The group has obtained at least 90% of the 'relevant shares' (being shares with unrestricted rights to participate in distributions).

3.   The fair value of consideration given other than equity shares does not exceed 10% of the nominal value of the equity shares issued.

4.   The adoption of merger accounting complies with generally accepted accounting principles or practice.

Condition number 4 effectively gives statutory backing to the FRS 6 conditions that must be satisfied for a merger to exist.

FRS 6 conditions

(a)   The use of merger accounting for the combination must be permitted by CA89.

(b)   Specific criteria must be met:

    1.   No party to the combination is portrayed as either acquirer or acquired, either by its own board or management or by that of another party to the combination.

    2.   All parties to the combination participate in establishing the management structure for the combined entity. Such decisions are made on the basis of a consensus between the parties to the combination.

    3.   The relative sizes of the combining entities are not so disparate that one party dominates the combined entity by virtue of its relative size.

    4.   The consideration received by equity shareholders comprises primarily equity shares in the combined entity. Any non-equity consideration represents an immaterial proportion of the fair value of the consideration received by the equity shareholders.

    5.   No equity shareholders of any of the combining entities retain any material interest in the future performance of only part of the combined entity.

Where all the CA 89 and FRS 6 conditions are met, then the combination is a merger and merger accounting must be used. FRS 6 recognises that the great majority of business combinations will not satisfy all the conditions, so that acquisition accounting will remain the normal method of consolidation in the majority of cases.

2.7   Activity

P is a parent company about to make an offer to acquire another company S.

The initial proposal is to issue 1,000 ordinary shares of £1 each worth £3 per share together with £200 cash.

Demonstrate whether these proposals meet the *CA89* requirements for merger accounting

2.8   Activity solution

The scheme would not meet the requirements of *CA89* as the cash element is more than 10% of the nominal value of the equity shares.

	Nominal value	
	£	%
Equity shares 1,000 @ £1	1,000	100
Cash	200	20

This problem could be overcome by P making a bonus issue of 1 for 1 held and then offering to issue 2,000 equity shares worth £1.50 each to the shareholders of S.

	Nominal value	
	£	%
Equity shares 2,000 @ £1	2,000	100
Cash	200	10

2.9   Consolidated accounts – the mechanics of merger accounting

In merger accounting it is not necessary to adjust the carrying values of the assets and liabilities of the subsidiary to fair value either in its own books or on consolidation. However, appropriate adjustments should be made to achieve uniformity of accounting policies between the combining companies.

In the group accounts for the period in which the merger takes place, the profits or losses of subsidiaries brought in for the first time should be included for the entire period without any adjustment in respect of that part of the period prior to the merger. Corresponding amounts should be presented as if the companies had been combined throughout the previous period and at the previous balance sheet date.

A difference may arise on consolidation between the carrying value of the investment in the subsidiary (which will normally be the nominal value of the shares issued as consideration plus the fair value of any additional consideration) and the nominal value of the shares transferred to the issuing company.

(a)   Where the carrying value of the investment is less than the nominal value of the shares transferred, the difference should be treated as a reserve arising on consolidation.

(b)   Where the carrying value of the investment is greater than the nominal value of the shares transferred, the difference is the extent to which reserves have been in effect capitalised as a result of the merger and it should therefore be treated on consolidation as a reduction of reserves.

2.10   Contrast with the equity and acquisition method

On 31 December 19X6 F plc purchased 29,000 shares in B Ltd by issuing 58,000 shares as consideration. The market value of F plc's shares on that date were £2.50 each.

The balance sheets of the two companies immediately before the share exchange were as follows:

	F plc £'000	B Ltd £'000
£1 ordinary shares	100	30
Profit and loss account	120	90
	220	120
Sundry net assets	220	120

As at 31 December 19X6, the fair value of B Ltd's sundry net assets was £15,000 in excess of their book value.

You are required to prepare consolidated balance sheets as at 31 December 19X6 reflecting the above information, on the basis of:

(a)   acquisition accounting; and

(b)   merger accounting.

2.11   Solution

(a)   **Acquisition accounting**

Step 1   For consolidation purposes the investment in B Ltd must be recorded at its fair value:

	£	£
Dr Cost of investment	145,000	
Cr £1 ordinary shares (58,000 @ £1)		58,000
Cr Merger reserve (58,000 @ £1.50)		87,000
	145,000	145,000

Alternatively the merger reserve would be established as a consolidation adjustment only.

Step 2   If acquisition accounting is to be used, assets must be recorded at their fair value:

	£	£
Dr Sundry net assets	15,000	
Cr Revaluation reserve		15,000

This may be done in the subsidiary's books or as a consolidation adjustment.

Step 3   Consolidation schedules:

Goodwill

	£'000	£'000
Cost of investment		145
Less: Share of net assets at acquisition		
Share capital	30	
Revaluation reserve	15	
Profit and loss account	90	
	$135 \times 29/30$	130.5
Goodwill		14.5

Consolidated reserves

Profit and loss account

	£'000
F:	120
B: 29/30 (90 – 90)	-
	120

Revaluation reserve

All pre-acquisition, therefore none will appear in the consolidated balance sheet.

Merger reserve

	£'000
F:	87

Minority interest

Net assets of B

	£'000	£'000
Share capital	30	
Revaluation reserve	15	
Profit and loss account	90	
	135 × 1/30	4.5

Step 4

Consolidated balance sheet as at 31 December 19X6

	£'000
Goodwill	14.5
Sundry net assets (220 + 120 + 15)	355.0
	369.5
£1 ordinary shares (100 + 58)	158.0
Merger reserve	87.0
Profit and loss account	120.0
Minority interests	4.5
	369.5

(b)   **Merger accounting**

Step 1   The investment in B Ltd is recorded as the nominal value of shares issued by F plc:

	£	£
Dr Cost of investment	58,000	
Cr £1 ordinary shares		58,000

Assets are not restated to their fair value.

Step 2   Consolidation schedules:

'Difference' on consolidation

	£'000
Cost of investment - nominal value of shares issued (+ any other consideration at fair value)	58
Less: Nominal value of shares acquired	(29)
Difference - write off to consolidated profit and loss account reserve	29

Consolidated reserves

Profit and loss account

	£'000
F:	120
B: 29/30 × 90	87
Less: Difference on consolidation	(29)
	——
	178

Minority interest

Net assets of B

	£'000	£'000
Share capital	30	
Profit and loss account	90	
	——	
	120 × 1/30	4

Step 3   **Consolidated balance sheet as at 31 December 19X6**

	£'000
Sundry net assets (220 + 120)	340
	——
£1 ordinary shares (100 + 58)	158
Profit and loss account	178
Minority interests	4
	——
	340
	——

2.12   Notes on comparison

Although consolidated revenue reserves have been recorded as £178,000 under merger accounting and £120,000 under acquisition accounting, this does not mean that distributable reserves are greater. Distributions are made from the profits of individual companies, not by groups.

Differences which are sometimes described as goodwill can arise in merger accounting, but these differences are not goodwill as they are not based on the fair values of the consideration given and the separable net assets acquired. Such differences should always be adjusted against consolidated reserves.

The equity method has not been shown in figures in the example because, in contrast to the merger method, the equity and acquisition methods have the same features. In summary the contrasts relate to three matters:

(a)   **Pre-acquisition profits**

There is no concept of pre-acquisition profits under merger accounting as there is under the equity and acquisition methods. The holding company and the subsidiary are deemed to have been together since incorporation and therefore, conceptually, there can be no profits earned before acquisition.

(b)   **Fair value of assets**

Under the equity and acquisition methods, the net assets of the subsidiary need to be revalued to fair value at acquisition so that goodwill/premium on acquisition is correctly computed and that the true cost of the purchase of the stake by the holding company is recorded.

Conceptually, there is no acquisition under merger accounting and therefore fair values are irrelevant.

(c)   **Corresponding amounts**

Under merger accounting the comparative figures disclosed in the financial statements in the year of the merger will be restated to include the relevant amounts from the subsidiary. Once again, there is conceptually no date of acquisition and therefore all historical data should reflect the assumption that the two entities have always been combined.

3   FAIR VALUES IN ACQUISITION ACCOUNTING

3.1   Introduction

In order to account for an acquisition, the acquiring company must measure the cost of what it is accounting for, which will normally represent:

(a)   the cost of the investment in its own balance sheet; and

(b)   the amount to be allocated between the identifiable net assets of the subsidiary and goodwill in the consolidated financial statements.

For acquisition accounting, the CA 1989, FRS 2 and FRS 6 require the cost of investment to be based on the fair value of the consideration given, but they do not elaborate on how this is to be determined. FRS 7 *Fair values in acquisition accounting* was issued by the ASB in September 1994 to deal with this and other related problems.

3.2   Objective of FRS 7

The objective of FRS 7 is two-fold:

(a)   to ensure that when a business entity is acquired by another, all the assets and liabilities that existed in the acquired entity at the date of acquisition are recorded at fair values reflecting their condition at that date; and

(b)   to ensure that all changes to the acquired assets and liabilities and the resulting gains and losses, that arise after control of the acquired entity has passed to the acquirer are reported as part of the post-acquisition financial performance of the acquiring group.

3.3   Reasons why the FRS was needed

Both the objectives stated above should solve accounting problems which have arisen in the past.

First, how should the fair value of acquired assets and liabilities be measured? For example, should a long-term debtor be recorded at its monetary amount or should a discounting calculation be carried out? Should a non-monetary fixed asset be recorded at its replacement cost or its net realisable value? FRS 7 discusses the correct approach to take in order to identify such fair values.

Second, should an acquiring company be permitted to include a provision for future operating losses among the liabilities at the date of acquisition? Such a practice became common in the 1980s in UK takeovers. An acquiring company would set up a large provision for future reorganisation costs/operating losses among the net assets acquired. Setting up the provision had no effect on profits; it increased the purchased goodwill figure, so increased the amount debited directly to reserves on acquisition. (Before the issue of FRS 10, immediate elimination against reserves was the preferred method of accounting for goodwill.) However, after acquisition, losses or costs that would have been charged against profits could then be charged directly against the provision, thus increasing the reported profit figure. The larger the provision, the higher the reported profits figure could be; many UK companies appeared to be abusing this principle in the 1980s and setting up large contingent provisions for expenses that were not known at the date of the acquisition. *FRS 7* acts to ban such behaviour.

3.4   Requirements of FRS 7

The FRS's main requirements are that

(a)   The assets and liabilities recognised in the allocation of fair values should be those of the acquired entity that existed at the date of acquisition. They should be measured at fair values that reflect the conditions at the date of acquisition.

(b)   The liabilities of the acquired entity should not include provisions for future operating losses. Changes in the assets and liabilities resulting from the acquirer's intentions or from events after the acquisition should be dealt with as post-acquisition items. Similarly, costs of reorganisation and integrating the business acquired should be dealt with as post-acquisition costs and do not affect the fair values at the date of acquisition.

(c)   Fair values should be based on the value at which an asset or liability could be exchanged in an arm's length transaction. The fair value of monetary items should take into account the amounts expected to be received or paid and their timing.

(d)   Unless they can be measured at market value, the fair values of non-monetary assets will normally be based on replacement cost, but should not exceed their recoverable amount as at the date of acquisition.

The FRS also describes the application of the required principles to determine fair values for particular categories of assets and liabilities, including fixed assets, stocks, pension schemes, deferred taxation and long-term receivables and liabilities. A period of investigation of an acquired company for the purpose of fixing adjustments to fair values and purchased goodwill is proposed which ends on the date on which the first post-acquisition financial statements of the acquirer are approved by the directors.

3.5   Significance of requirements re provisions

As stated earlier, previous practice had been to make a provision for reorganisation costs/losses following the acquisition. This had two main effects

(a)   As the provision was a reduction from the net asset value of the acquired business, goodwill (the balancing figure) was increased. As goodwill was then normally written off to reserves, the provision had not been set up through the profit and loss account of the year.

(b)   As costs were incurred in reorganising the business in the post acquisition period, they were set off against the provision. They therefore bypassed the profit and loss account.

Sir David Tweedie's (Chairman of the ASB) response to this was, "The contention that reorganisation expenses or losses to be incurred following an acquisition should be deemed to be existing liabilities of the acquired company is perverse; the amount of goodwill arising on the acquisition actually goes up, and usually nothing gets charged to the profit and loss account. Accounting in this way for a gleam in the acquirer's eye is simply not rational."

FRS 7 "is wholly consistent with the information set approach underlying FRS 3. The accounts should disclose what actually happens after new acquisitions enter the group. The costs of digesting acquisitions should, like future losses, be charged through the profit and loss account when they occur and be separately disclosed if necessary. Post-acquisition performance should not be masked by the creation and release of provisions that were not liabilities of the acquired company before it was purchased."

Although FRS 10 has now effectively prohibited elimination of goodwill against reserves, these requirements of FRS 7 are still very necessary. If goodwill is amortised over a long period, the effect of the charge on each year's results may be relatively small. Without FRS 7 it would still be possible for preparers of financial statements to use provisions in order to artificially enhance post acquisition results in the short term.

3.6   Example

Excel plc acquired a 100% interest in Redundant Ltd on 30 November 19X5. Redundant has been making losses which the directors of Excel hope to turn around into profits. The net assets of Redundant were

	Book values £	Fair values £
Fixed assets	300,000	360,000
Net current liabilities	(40,000)	(40,000)
	260,000	320,000

Excel paid £200,000 for Redundant.

FRS 7 emphasises that the goodwill/negative goodwill arising is

	£
Cost of investment	200,000
Less Fair value of net assets acquired	320,000
Negative goodwill	120,000

A provision for future reorganisation costs/losses should not be established in the group accounts. If future losses of £150,000 are anticipated before Redundant is back in a profit-making position and a provision is created, the goodwill/negative goodwill would be

	£	£
Cost of investment		200,000
Less Fair value of assets	320,000	
Provision	150,000	
		170,000
Goodwill		30,000

The balance sheet would show (if prepared at 30 November 19X5)

Consolidated accounts (re Redundant)

	£
Fixed assets	360,000
Net current liabilities	(40,000)
Provisions for liabilities and charges	(150,000)
	170,000

The goodwill of £30,000 is included in the consolidated balance sheet and amortised over its useful economic life.

The provision would be released to the group profit and loss account over the period during which the losses were anticipated to occur, ie the post acquisition losses have bypassed the profit and loss account. Such an accounting treatment is now unacceptable following FRS 7.

3.7   Allocation of fair values to assets and liabilities

(a)   **Tangible fixed assets**

The fair value of a tangible fixed asset should be based on:

(i)   market value, if assets similar in type and condition are bought and sold on an open market; or

(ii)   depreciated replacement cost.

The fair value should not exceed the recoverable amount of the asset.

(b)   **Intangible assets**

The fair value should be based on the asset's replacement cost, which is normally its estimated market value.

(c)   **Stocks and work-in-progress**

Stocks that the acquired company trades on a market in which it participates as both a buyer and a seller should be valued at current market prices. Other stocks should be valued at the lower of replacement cost and net realisable value.

(d)   **Quoted investments**

Quoted investments should be valued at market price.

(e)   **Monetary assets and liabilities**

The fair value should take into account the amounts expected to be received or paid and their timing. Fair value should be determined by reference to market prices, where available, by reference to the current price at which the business could acquire similar assets or enter into similar obligations, or by discounting to present value.

3.8   Activity

X plc acquired 80% of the ordinary share capital of Y Ltd on 30 September 19X4 for £320,000.

The net assets of Y Ltd at that date had a book value of £350,000.

The following information is relevant:

(a)   Y Ltd's freehold factory is included in the accounts at £100,000 and no adjustment has been made to recognise the valuation of £120,000 put on the property when it was professionally revalued on 15 September 19X4.

(b)   The fair value of Y Ltd's stock at 30 September 19X4 is estimated to be £4,000 less than its book value at that date.

(c)   In August 19X4 Y Ltd made a decision to close down a small workshop with the loss of some jobs. The net costs of closure are estimated at £10,000. No provision has been made at 30 September 19X4.

What is the goodwill arising on the acquisition of Y Ltd?

3.9   Activity solution

Step 1   Adjust the value of Y Ltd's net assets at 30 September 19X4 to fair value.

	£
Net assets per question	350,000
Revaluation of property	20,000
Write-off of stock	(4,000)
Provision for reorganisation costs	(10,000)
	356,000

Step 2   Calculate goodwill.

	£
Fair value of consideration	320,000
Net assets acquired 80% × £356,000	284,800
Goodwill arising	35,200

4   THE REQUIREMENTS OF CA 85 AND FRS 2 REGARDING GROUPS OF COMPANIES

4.1   Introduction

In this section the statutory and professional requirements for the preparation of group accounts are covered. Some of these provisions have already been dealt with in the computational examples.

4.2   Purpose of consolidated accounts

The CA85 requires group accounts to be in the form of consolidated accounts which give a 'true and fair' view.

FRS 2 *Accounting for subsidiary undertakings* states that the purpose of consolidated accounts is to

> present financial information about a parent undertaking and its subsidiary undertakings as a single economic entity to show the economic resources controlled by the group, the obligations of the group and the results the group achieves with its resources.

The first step, however, is to decide what constitutes a group.

4.3   Definition of subsidiary undertaking

The CA89 extended the definition of a subsidiary beyond the previous (CA85) definition to implement the EC Seventh Directive. FRS 2 assists in interpreting the legal definition.

The definitions of a subsidiary under CA85 applied when either

(a)   more than 50% of the equity shares were held, or
(b)   there was control over the composition of the board of directors.

These definitions caused difficulties mainly due to the possibilities of creating a dependent company which was not legally a subsidiary and which could then be used for various 'off balance sheet' activities.

The CA89 fundamentally changed the definitions and brought more of these dependent companies into the group accounts. It is important to note that the new definitions for accounting purposes refer to a subsidiary undertaking rather than a subsidiary company. A subsidiary undertaking may include a partnership or an unincorporated business.

There are five alternative definitions of a subsidiary

Definition   the parent holds a majority of the rights to vote at general meetings of the undertaking/company on all or substantially all matters; or

the parent is a member and has a right to appoint or remove directors having a majority of the rights to vote at board meetings of the undertaking/company on all or substantially all matters; or

the parent is a member and has the right to control alone a majority of the rights to vote at general meetings of the undertaking/company pursuant to an agreement with other shareholders; or

the parent has a right to exercise a dominant influence over the undertaking by virtue of provisions in the memorandum or articles or by a lawful contract; or

the parent has a participating interest and actually exercises a dominant influence or the parent and subsidiary undertaking are managed on a unified basis.

For the fourth definition above the existence of a dominant influence is only deemed to apply if the parent has a right to give directions on operating or financial policies and the subsidiary directors are obliged to comply with those directions whether or not they are for the benefit of the subsidiary.

For the fifth definition above a participating interest means an interest in shares, held for the long term to secure a contribution to its activities by the exercise of control or influence. A holding of 20% or more is presumed to be a participating interest unless the contrary can be shown.

4.4   Exemptions from consolidation

Exemptions from consolidation are allowed/required in various circumstances by CA89 and FRS 2. These are dealt with in the next section.

4.5   Date of acquisition of subsidiary

The date for accounting for an undertaking becoming a subsidiary undertaking is the date on which control passes to its new parent. This ties in with the control concept being the dominant factor in defining a subsidiary.

4.6   The formats of group accounts

The CA89 states that the formats for an individual company apply and are adapted to groups and included within Sch 4A CA85. The following amendments are made to the individual company formats (based upon Format 1)

(a)   'Minority interests' appears as a major heading in the balance sheet either immediately after item J 'Accruals and deferred income' or after item K 'Capital and reserves'.

(b)   'Minority interests' in the profit and loss account appears as an Arabic numeral item between items 14 (profit after tax) and 15 and items 18 (tax on extraordinary items) and 19.

The first minority interest shows the minority shareholders' share of post tax profits. The second minority interest shows the minority shareholders' share of extraordinary items.

FRS 2 confirms the above disclosures in respect of minority interests.

4.7   Consolidation techniques

The CA89 introduced into the law various rules on consolidation accounting. FRS 2 confirms the rules or reduces the choice in some instances.

There are three main areas

(a)   **Accounting policies**

Uniform group accounting policies should be used for determining the amounts to be included in the consolidated financial statements. In exceptional cases different policies may be used with disclosure.

Clearly if the aggregate figures are to make sense they should have been derived using common policies.

(b)   **Accounting periods and dates**

The accounts of all subsidiaries to be used in preparing consolidated financial statements should have the same financial year-end and be for the same accounting period as those of the parent company. Where the financial year of a subsidiary differs from that of the parent company, interim financial statements for that subsidiary prepared to the parent company's accounting date should be used. If this is impracticable, earlier financial statements of the subsidiary undertaking may be used, provided they are prepared for a financial year that ended not more than three months earlier.

(c)   **Intra-group transactions**

In the past there has been a variety of methods adjusting for the effect of intra-group transactions. Such transactions may result in profits or losses being included in the book value of assets in the consolidation.

The rules have been extensively covered in the computations in earlier chapters.

5   EXEMPTIONS AND EXCLUSIONS

5.1   Introduction

The CA89 and FRS 2 recognise certain situations in which either

(a)   a holding company is exempted from preparing group accounts, or

(b)   a subsidiary should or may be excluded from consolidation with the rest of the group.

5.2   Exemptions for intermediate holding companies

An intermediate holding company is a company which has a subsidiary but is also itself a subsidiary of another company.

For example

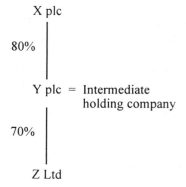

An intermediate holding company is exempt from the requirement to prepare group accounts if

(a)   none of its securities is listed anywhere in the EC, and

(b)   its immediate holding company is incorporated in the EC.

Provided that

(a)   it is wholly owned by that immediate parent, or

(b)   its immediate parent holds more than 50% and notice for the preparation of group accounts has not been served from shareholders owning either more than one half of the remaining shares or 5% of the total shares.

Various detailed conditions apply for this exemption including the need for the intermediate holding company to be included in the group accounts of an EC parent. A copy of these accounts must be filed with the Registrar of Companies together with an English translation.

5.3   Exemptions for small and medium-sized groups

A parent company need not prepare group accounts if the group headed by that parent has less than at least two of the following conditions

Annual turnover	£13.44m gross or £11.2m net
Balance sheet assets	£6.72m gross or £5.6m net
Average employees	250

The 'gross' figures are those calculated prior to any consolidation adjustments whereas the 'net' figures are those after the consolidation adjustments, such as the elimination of intra-group balances, have been made. A company may satisfy the relevant limits on either a net or a gross basis or by a mixture of the two.

The purpose of allowing the calculations to be made using the higher gross figures is to prevent a parent company from having to prepare group accounts in order to discover that it does not need to prepare group accounts.

Surprisingly, if the accounting period is more or less than one year the turnover limit specified is not adjusted on a pro-rata basis as it is for individual company abbreviated accounts limits.

The right to the exemption from preparing group accounts does not apply if any company in the group is

(a)   a public company, or
(b)   a banking or insurance company, or
(c)   a company authorised under the Financial Services Act.

5.4   Excluded subsidiaries

Under the Companies Act 1985 there are cases where subsidiary undertakings need not or must not be included in the consolidation. Where all of the subsidiaries fall within the exclusions, group accounts are not required.

FRS 2 is based on the premise that the value of the information provided by the consolidated accounts depends on the extent to which the information about the group is complete ie, all undertakings are consolidated. Thus a subsidiary should only be excluded in exceptional circumstances. Where such exceptional circumstances are identified FRS 2 makes exclusions mandatory rather than optional.

(a)   **Different activities**

Subsidiaries must be excluded from consolidation where their activities are so different from other undertakings in the consolidation that their inclusion would be incompatible with the obligation to give a true and fair view. The exclusion does not apply merely because some of the undertakings are industrial, some commercial and some provide services or because they carry on industrial or commercial activities involving different products or providing different services.

This is the only mandatory exclusion under the Companies Act.

Where a subsidiary is excluded because of dissimilar activities, the group accounts should include separate financial statements for that subsidiary. They may be combined with the financial statements of other subsidiaries with similar operations if appropriate.

In the group accounts the investment in the subsidiary should be stated using the equity method of accounting.

(b)   **Materiality**

The Companies Act states that a subsidiary undertaking may be excluded from the consolidation where its inclusion is not material for the purpose of giving a true and fair view.

Two or more undertakings may be excluded on these grounds only if they are not material when taken together.

FRS 2 (like any Accounting Standard) does not deal with immaterial items and therefore does not cover this exclusion.

(c)   **Severe long-term restrictions**

A subsidiary should be excluded from the consolidation where severe long-term restrictions substantially hinder the exercise of the rights of the parent company over the assets or management of that undertaking.

Subsidiaries excluded from consolidation are to be treated as fixed asset investments. They are to be included at their carrying amount when the restrictions came into force, subject to any write down for impairment in value, and no further accruals are to be made for profits or losses of those subsidiary undertakings, unless the parent undertaking still exercises significant influence. In the latter case they are to be treated as associates.

(d)   **Disproportionate expense or undue delay**

In the CA85 a subsidiary may be excluded from the consolidation where the information necessary for the preparation of group accounts cannot be obtained without disproportionate expense or undue delay. Whether the expense is disproportionate or the delay undue should be judged in the context of that information to the group accounts.

FRS 2, however, states that neither reason can justify excluding a subsidiary.

(e)   **Temporary investment**

A subsidiary should be excluded from the consolidation where the interest of the parent company is held exclusively with a view to subsequent resale and the undertaking has not previously been included in consolidated group accounts prepared by the parent company.

The investment in the subsidiary will be shown as a current asset at the lower of cost and net realisable value.

Summary

Reason	CA89	FRS 2	Treatment
Different activities	Mandatory	Mandatory (in exceptional circumstances only)	Equity accounting
Severe long-term restrictions	Optional	Mandatory	If restrictions in force at date of acquisition carry initially at cost. If restrictions came into force at a later date equity account at date when restrictions came into force. Consider need for provision for impairment in value.
Immaterial	Optional	Not applicable	-
Disproportionate expense or undue delay	Optional	Not permissible	-
Temporary investment	Optional	Mandatory	Current asset at the lower of cost and NRV

6   CHAPTER SUMMARY

Group accounts could be presented under a variety of methods but the most common form is acquisition accounting.

Merger accounting is only allowed by FRS 6 providing certain conditions are fulfilled. It is necessary to record the issue of shares at nominal value in the accounts of the holding company in order for merger accounting to work effectively at the consolidated accounts stage.

7   SELF TEST QUESTIONS

7.1   What form will group accounts normally take? (1.1)

7.2   What are the features of consolidation under the entity concept? (1.2)

7.3   When does *CA85* allow the proportional consolidation method to be used? (1.4)

7.4   What are the two methods of accounting for business combinations? (2.1)

7.5   In the parent company accounts how will an investment in a new subsidiary be shown if acquisition accounting is to be used? (2.2)

7.6   What are the requirements of *S130 CA85*? (2.5)

7.7   What are the requirements exempting intermediate holding companies from preparing group accounts? (5.2)

7.8   What are the size criteria for small/medium-sized group exemptions? (5.3)

7.9   For what reasons **may** a subsidiary be excluded from consolidation under *CA85*? (5.4)

7.10   Where a subsidiary is a temporary investment how should it be shown in the consolidated accounts? (5.4(e))

8   **EXAMINATION TYPE QUESTIONS**

8.1   **Laurel & Hardy**

On 1 September 19X5 when the balance on Laurel plc's profit and loss reserves was £390,000 an offer by Hardy plc for all of the shares of Laurel plc was accepted by the holders of 95% of the shares.

The purchase price was to be satisfied by a one-for-one share exchange plus ten pence per share payable by Hardy plc.

The market values of the shares on 1 September 19X5 were

Hardy plc	£0.75 ordinary shares	£1.30
Laurel plc	£0.50 ordinary shares	£1.10

At 31 December 19X5 the draft balance sheets of each company were as follows

	Hardy plc £'000	*Laurel plc* £'000
Fixed assets - tangible assets	7,360	897
Current assets	3,380	1,018
Suspense account -		
Cash paid to shareholders of Laurel plc	57	-
Creditors - amounts falling due within one year	(1,809)	(1,036)
Total assets less current liabilities	8,988	879
Creditors - amounts falling due after		
more than one year	(900)	(60)
Provisions for liabilities and charges - deferred tax	(230)	(89)
	7,858	730
Capital and reserves		
Called up share capital	4,125	300
Profit and loss account	3,733	430
	7,858	730

Notes: the share exchange has not been reflected in the above balance sheets. The market value of Laurel plc's freehold land is considered to be £103,000 above the NBV shown in the accounts, throughout 19X5.

Goodwill is amortised over 5 years from the date of acquisition, with a full year's charge in the year of acquisition.

You are required to prepare company and consolidated balance sheets for Hardy plc as at 31 December 19X5 using both acquisition accounting and merger accounting.   **(20 marks)**

8.2   **Subsidiary company**

The CA85 before amendment by the CA89 defined a subsidiary company as follows

S Ltd is a subsidiary of H Ltd if

(i)   H Ltd is a member of S Ltd (or a subsidiary of H Ltd is a member of S Ltd) and H Ltd controls the composition of the board of directors of S Ltd.

or   (ii)   H Ltd holds more than half the equity share capital (by nominal value).

or   (iii)   S Ltd is a subsidiary of a subsidiary of H Ltd.

The equity share capital is that capital which has more than a fixed interest in distributions (by dividend or on winding up).

You are required:

(a)   to define a subsidiary company for the purposes of preparing group accounts under the Companies Act 1989.

(b)   to state what you consider to be the faults in the old CA85 definition.   **(10 marks)**

9   ANSWERS TO EXAMINATION TYPE QUESTIONS

9.1   Laurel & Hardy

Merger accounting

Hardy plc
Consolidated balance sheet as at 31 December 19X5

	Group £'000	Company £'000
Fixed assets:		
Tangible assets	8,257.0	7,360.0
Investments	-	484.5
Current assets	4,398.0	3,380.0
Creditors - amounts falling due within one year	(2,845.0)	(1,809.0)
Total assets less current liabilities	9,810.0	9,415.5
Creditors - amounts falling due after more than one year	(960.0)	(900.0)
Provisions for liabilities and charges - deferred tax	(319.0)	(230.0)
	8,531.0	8,285.5
Capital and reserves		
Called up share capital	4,552.5	4,552.5
Profit and loss account	3,942.0	3,733.0
Minority interests	36.5	-
	8,531.0	8,285.5

Notes to the accounts

(a)   570,000 £0.50 ordinary shares of Laurel plc were acquired on 1 September 19X5 in exchange for 570,000 new £0.75 ordinary shares in Hardy plc and a cash payment amounting to £57,000.

(b)   The combination of the businesses of Laurel plc and Hardy plc has been accounted for as a merger.

(c)   The fair value of the consideration given by Hardy plc to the shareholders of Laurel plc amounted to £798,000.

Acquisition accounting

Hardy plc
Consolidated balance sheet as at 31 December 19X5

	Group £'000	Company £'000
Fixed assets:		
Intangible assets	35.72	
Tangible assets	8,360.00	7,360.00
Investments	-	798.00
Current assets	4,398.00	3,380.00
Creditors - amounts falling due within one year	(2,845.00)	(1,809.00)
Total assets less current liabilities	9,948.72	9,729.00
Creditors - amounts falling due after more than one year	(960.00)	(900.00)
Provisions for liabilities and charges - deferred tax	(319.00)	(230.00)
	8,669.72	8,599.00

	Group £'000	Company £'000
Capital and reserves		
Called up share capital	4,552.50	4,552.50
Merger reserve	313.50	313.50
Profit and loss account	3,762.07	3,733.00
Minority interests	41.65	-
	8,669.72	8,599.00

Notes to the accounts

(a)   570,000 £0.50 ordinary shares of Laurel plc were acquired on 1 September 19X5 in exchange for 570,000 new £0.75 ordinary shares in Hardy plc and a cash payment amounting to £57,000.

(b)   The combination of the businesses of Laurel plc and Hardy plc has been accounted for as an acquisition.

WORKINGS

(a)   **Minority interests**

	£
5% × shares of £300,000	15,000
5% × profit and loss reserves of £430,000	21,500
	36,500 M
5% × revaluation reserves of £103,000	5,150
	41,650 A

(b)   **Difference on consolidation**

	£	£
Merger		
Cash		57,000
NV shares issued (570,000 × £0.75)		427,500
		484,500
Less: NV shares received (570,000 × £0.50)		285,000
Write off to consolidated P & L account		199,500

Acquisition

Cash		57,000
MV shares issued (570,000 × £1.30)		741,000
		798,000

Less:	Shares 95% × £300,000	285,000	
	P & L Reserves 95% × £390,000	370,500	
	Revaluation reserves 95% × £103,000	97,850	
			753,350
			44,650
Amortisation charge (44,650 ÷ 5)			(8,930)
			35,720

(c)   **Profit and loss reserves**

Merger

Hardy	3,733,000
Laurel (95% × 430,000)	408,500
Less: Difference on consolidation	(199,500)
	3,942,000

Acquisition

Hardy	3,733,000
Laurel (95% × 40,000)	38,000
Less: goodwill amortised	(8,930)
	3,762,070

9.2   **Subsidiary company**

(a)   S Ltd is a subsidiary of H Ltd if any of the following conditions apply

   (i)   The parent holds a majority of the rights to vote at general meetings of the undertaking/company on all or substantially all matters.

   (ii)   The parent is a member and has a right to appoint or remove directors having a majority of the rights to vote at board meetings of the undertaking/company on all or substantially all matters.

   (iii)   The parent is a member and has the right to control alone a majority of the rights to vote at general meetings of the undertaking/company pursuant to an agreement with other shareholders.

   (iv)   The parent has a right to exercise a dominant influence over the undertaking by virtue of provisions in the memorandum or articles or by a lawful contract.

   (v)   The parent has a **participating interest** and actually exercises a dominant influence or the parent and subsidiary undertaking are managed on a unified basis.

For definition (v) above a **participating interest** means an interest in shares, held for the long term, to secure a contribution to its activities by the exercise of control or influence. A holding of 20% or more is presumed to be a participating interest unless the contrary can be shown.

(b)   There were two main problems in the old definition

    (i)   A situation may have arisen in which none of the conditions was fully satisfied and yet H had substantial influence over S. If a holding was not above 50% but was significant, the company may have been an associated company and the equity method of accounting would have been used. However, a holding of 50% or just below may have effectively given H control over S.

    (ii)   H may have held more than one half of the equity shares but was unable to exercise fully control due to the lack of voting rights. Equity shares could, for example, comprise ordinary shares and participating preference shares. H may have held more than half of the combined set but not half of the ordinary shares (where the voting power normally lies).

    In the new definition situation (i) is likely to be covered (definition (v)) and in situation (ii) the company is not a subsidiary as no control exists.

20 SUNDRY ACCOUNTING STANDARDS

INTRODUCTION & LEARNING OBJECTIVES

This chapter covers the remaining accounting standards in the syllabus. Both SSAP 20 and 24 are complex standards but parts of SSAP 20 are reserved for later examinations. Note that FRS 8 *Related party disclosures* is dealt with later in this text together with the auditing implications of related party transactions.

You may find SSAP 24 a difficult area mainly because of the technical terms that are used.

When you have studied this chapter you should be able to do the following:

- State the requirements of SSAP 20 regarding the individual company.
- Outline and apply the requirements of SSAP 24.

1   SSAP 20: FOREIGN CURRENCY TRANSLATION

1.1   Foreign currency conversion and translation

Definition   Foreign currency conversion is the process of physically exchanging one currency for another currency.

An individual converts currency when he buys, say, Spanish pesetas for sterling at the start of a holiday. If he has any money left at the end of the holiday, he reconverts the pesetas to sterling. If the exchange rate has changed in the meantime he will make a gain or loss on the transaction less the costs of commission and the buy/sell price spread.

A business will also convert currencies when it has to pay for an item which it has purchased which is denominated in another currency. For example a UK business may purchase goods from a French supplier and agree to pay a certain number of francs. When it comes to pay for the goods, it is likely to have to convert sterling into francs to pay for the goods.

From a business viewpoint however, the need to **translate** items denominated in a foreign currency is more important.

Definition   Foreign currency translation is the statement of an item denominated in a foreign currency in terms of the domestic reporting currency.

SSAP 20 identifies two sets of circumstances in which a business must consider how to deal with foreign currency amounts within its accounts

(a)   direct business transactions
(b)   operations conducted through a foreign entity.

1.2   Direct business transactions

Whenever a UK business enters into a contract where the consideration is expressed in a foreign currency, it will be necessary to translate that foreign currency amount at some stage into sterling for inclusion into its own accounts. Examples include

(i)   imports of raw materials
(ii)   exports of finished goods
(iii)   importation of foreign-manufactured fixed assets
(iv)   investments in foreign securities
(v)   raising an overseas loan.

Translation may be necessary at more than one time. For example, the import of raw materials creates a foreign currency liability when the goods are supplied and for which a sterling value must be incorporated in the books. Where settlement is delayed due to normal credit terms, the actual sterling cost of settlement may differ from the liability initially recorded.

Similarly, the sterling value of a long-term loan is likely to fluctuate from one period to another.

1.3   Operations conducted through a foreign entity

Companies frequently establish local subsidiaries in foreign countries through which to conduct their operations. These subsidiaries will maintain full accounts in the local currency and these accounts must clearly be translated into the currency of the parent before they can be consolidated.

This aspect is not examinable at this level.

1.4   Methods of translation

There are two exchange rates which can generally be used to translate any foreign currency balance. These are

(a)   **The historic rate**

This is simply the exchange rate which applied at the date of the transaction.

(b)   **The closing rate**

This is the rate of exchange ruling at the balance sheet date.

Thus, a fixed asset acquired for Fr 100,000 when the exchange rate was Fr 12 = £1 and now translated for inclusion in a balance sheet when the exchange rate has moved to Fr 10 = £1 could either be shown at

(a)   Historic rate – £8,333 or
(b)   Closing rate – £10,000

It should be clear that selection of an appropriate translation rate will have a significant impact on balance sheet values and on reported profits. Where the historic rate is employed, the value of the asset is unchanging. However, if the closing rate is applied, the book value is increased by £1,667 and this must be reflected either in reported profits or as a movement in reserves.

1.5   The requirements of SSAP 20

We need only examine the effects of transactions in an individual company.

It is quite likely that during an accounting period, a company (whether situated in the UK or abroad) will enter into transactions in a currency other than its own domestic (ie, functional) currency. The results of these transactions should be translated and recorded in the company's accounting records

(a)   at the date the transaction occurred

(b)   using the rate of exchange in operation on that date (or where appropriate, at the rate of exchange at which it is contracted to settle the transaction in the future).

No further translation will be required for non-monetary assets (eg, fixed assets, stock or investments) carried at historic costs. However, monetary items at the balance sheet date are retranslated at the closing rate of exchange with differences taken to profit and loss account. This would include debtors, creditors, bank balances and loans, where any of these amounts are expressed in a foreign currency.

1.6   Fixed assets

Once these assets have been translated at the historic rate and recorded they are carried in terms of the currency of the individual company.

Thus where a UK company purchases plant and machinery, for its own use in the UK, from an American supplier on 30 June 19X7 for $90,000 when the rate of exchange was £1 = $1.80, it will record the asset at £50,000 ($90,000 @ 1.80). No further translation will occur. All depreciation charged on this asset will be based on £50,000.

1.7   Debtors

Where goods are sold to overseas customers and payment is to be received in a currency other than the functional currency, the following transactions must be recorded

(a)   the sale – at the rate of exchange applicable at the time of sale
(b)   the receipt of cash – the actual proceeds.

Any exchange difference (the balance on the debtors' account) will be reported as part of the profit for the period from normal operations.

Example

If on 7 May 19X6 a UK company sells goods to a German company for DM 48,000 when the rate of exchange was £1 = DM 3.2, the sale will be recorded:

	£	£
Dr Customer DM 48,000 @ 3.2	15,000	
Cr Sales		15,000

Assuming on 20 July 19X6 the customer remits a draft for DM 48,000 which realises £15,150

	£	£
Dr Bank	15,150	
Cr Customer		15,150

The credit balance of £150 on the debtor's account will represent a profit on exchange to be taken to profit and loss account as part of the operating profit for the year.

1.8   Activity

Facts are as above except that the company prepares accounts to 30 June annually. At the balance sheet date the rate of exchange was £1 = DM 3.15. What will be the movements on the debtors account?

1.9   Activity solution

Debtor's account

19X6		DM	£	19X6		DM	£
May 7	Sales a/c	48,000	15,000	Jun 30	Balance c/d (at 3.15)	48,000	15,238
June 30	P&L a/c- (profit on exchange)		238				
		48,000	15,238			48,000	15,238
Jul 1	Balance b/d	48,000	15,238	Jul 10	Bank a/c (proceeds)	48,000	15,150
				Jun 30	P&L a/c (loss on exchange)		88
						48,000	15,238
		48,000	15,238				

Note:

In practice

(a)   as a monetary item, debtors are retranslated at the balance sheet date with the exchange difference taken to the profit and loss account

(b)   average rates of exchange (say on a monthly basis) might be used for translating the sales into the functional currency

(c)   exchange differences would be transferred (as they were recognised) to a separate account, the balance on which would be transferred to profit and loss account at the end of the accounting period.

1.10   Creditors

The same principles as those set out for debtors apply to creditors.

1.11   Activity

A British company buys goods from a Swiss supplier for Sw Fr 8,700 when the rate of exchange was £1 = Sw Fr 3. The British company settled the amount due with a bankers draft for Sw Fr 8,700 when the rate of exchange was £1 = Sw Fr 2.8. Prepare the supplier's account.

1.12   Activity solution

The supplier's account would appear as follows

	SwFr	£		SwFr	£
Bank account (remittance (2.8))	8,700	3,107	Purchases account (3)	8,700	2,900
			P&L a/c (loss on exchange)		207
	8,700	3,107		8,700	3,107

1.13   Loans

Where a company raises a loan abroad, denominated in a currency other than its own currency, the amount outstanding must be retranslated at the closing rate at each year end. Again, this is because a loan is a monetary item. Any difference on exchange must form part of the profit from normal operations.

Example

A UK company takes out a 5 year loan of $1m from an American bank. The sterling proceeds amounted to £555,556 (when rate of exchange was £1 = $1.80). At the balance sheet date the rate had moved to £1 = $1.70.

The loan must be translated at this rate to £588,235. The loss on exchange of £(588,235 – 555,556) = £32,679 will be reported as part of profit from normal operations. Retranslation will occur at each balance sheet date.

	$	£		$	£
Bal c/d @ 1.7	1,000,000	588,235	Bank @ 1.8	1,000,000	555,556
			P&L a/c (loss on exchange)		32,679
	$1,000,000	£588,235		$1,000,000	£588,235

1.14   Contracted rate of exchange

Where a transaction is to be settled at a contracted rate of exchange, that rate **should** be used.

Example

A UK company purchased an item of plant from a German manufacturer for DM 100,000, when the rate was £1 = DM 3.18 but the contract specified settlement in three months at an exchange rate of £1 = DM 3.2. At the time of settlement, the actual exchange rate was £1 = DM 3.19.

The effect of the specified rate is to **freeze** the sterling cost of the plant from the start. Accordingly, it will be debited in the accounts at the certain sterling cost of

DM 100,000 ÷ 3.2 = £31,250

1.15   Use of forward contracts

Where a trading transaction is covered by a related or matching forward contract, the rate of exchange specified in that contract **may** be used.

Example

A UK company sells goods to a US corporation on 30 June for $200,000. The contract provides for settlement on 30 September. The UK company sells $200,000 forward three months on 30 June.

Rates of exchange are

	Spot	*3 months forward*
30 June	1.75	1.78
30 September	1.72	

By selling dollars forward, the UK company guarantees the ultimate sterling receipt, irrespective of exchange rate movements. Accordingly, these ultimate proceeds may be reflected immediately as a sale and as a debtor

$200,000 ÷ 1.78 = £112,360

In this case, no exchange differences will arise.

1.16 Summary

(a) **Transactions during accounting period**

These should be translated and recorded at the rate of exchange ruling at the date of the transaction. In practice, an average rate might be used.

(b) **Monetary items at balance sheet date**

Where these items (debtors, creditors, bank balances, loans) are denominated in a foreign currency they should be translated and recorded at the closing rate (or, if appropriate, at the rate at which the transaction is contracted to be settled).

(c) **Exchange differences**

Except to the extent that they relate to extraordinary items, all exchange differences should be reported as part of normal operating profit.

1.17 Classification of exchange differences

(a) Gains or losses from trading transactions should normally be included under 'other operating income or expense'.

(b) Gains or losses arising from financing arrangements should be disclosed separately as part of 'other interest receivable (payable) and similar income (expense)'.

1.18 The validity of the effect of exchange differences on reported earnings

All the exchange differences that we have calculated in this section are included in the profit and loss account and thus affect reported earnings. Consideration needs to be given to whether this effect is valid ie, are they 'proper' gains and losses which should be included in the profit and loss account? The general principle for inclusion of items in the profit and loss account is that gains should be realised (as in the SSAP 2 concept of realisation).

For transactions which have been **settled** in the accounting period, the inclusion of exchange gains and losses is valid as the gains/losses are already reflected in local currency cash flows. A settled transaction means the debtor, for example, has paid his debt or the business has paid a creditor.

Where a transaction has not been settled by the end of the accounting period we need to distinguish between short-term and long-term monetary items.

(a) A short-term trade debtor or creditor will be received or paid in cash shortly after the year end. The amount received or paid may be different from the rate of exchange ruling at the balance sheet date but, in most cases, not materially so. As the exchange difference is likely to be reflected in cash flows, the exchange gain/loss is validly reported as part of earnings.

(b) A long-term item, for example a foreign currency loan, is retranslated to closing rate at the end of each accounting period. This may result in reported gains in one period followed by a compensatory loss in the following accounting period as the exchange rates fluctuate. It is therefore uncertain as to whether a calculated gain or loss will eventually be reflected in cash flows.

SSAP 20 agrees that there is uncertainty but argues that exchange differences on long-term monetary items need to be reflected in the profit and loss account in accordance with the accruals concept. However in cases where there is doubt about the convertibility of the currency in question, exchange gains on long-term monetary items should be restricted ie, prudence overtakes the accruals concept.

2   SSAP 24: ACCOUNTING FOR PENSION COSTS

2.1   The current regulatory position on pensions outlined in SSAP 24

The publication of *SSAP 24* in 1988 represented the culmination of a major project on pension costs undertaken by the ASC that included two EDs.

The provision of a pension is part of the remuneration package of many employees. Pension costs form a significant proportion of total payroll costs and they give rise to special problems of estimation and of allocation between accounting periods.

2.2   Types of pension schemes

Pension schemes to which this Statement applies may be divided into **defined contribution** schemes and **defined benefit** schemes.

In a defined contribution scheme the employer will normally discharge his obligation by making agreed contributions to a pension scheme and the benefits paid will depend upon the funds available from these contributions and investment earnings thereon. The cost to the employer can, therefore, be measured with reasonable certainty. A number of pension schemes in the United Kingdom and Ireland, including many smaller ones, are defined contribution schemes.

In a defined benefit scheme, however, the benefits to be paid will usually depend upon either the average pay of the employee during his or her career, or more typically, the final pay of the employee. In these circumstances, it is impossible to be certain in advance that the contributions to the pension scheme, together with the investment return thereon, will equal the benefits to be paid. The employer may have a legal obligation to provide any unforeseen shortfalls in funds or, if not, may find it necessary to meet the shortfall in the interests of maintaining good employee relations. Conversely, if a surplus arises the employer may be entitled to a refund of, or reduction in, contributions paid into the pension scheme. Thus, in this type of scheme the employer's commitment is generally more open than with defined contribution schemes and the final cost is subject to considerable uncertainty. The larger UK schemes are generally of the defined benefit kind and these cover the great majority of members of schemes.

2.3   Actuarial considerations

In view of the very long-term nature of the pensions commitment it is necessary to make use of actuarial calculations in determining the pension cost charge in respect of defined benefit schemes. In the case of defined contribution schemes there is no need for actuarial advice in order to establish the pension cost although such advice may be required for other purposes in connection with the operation of the scheme.

In defined benefit schemes the choice of assumptions and the choice of valuation method can each have a major effect on the contribution rate calculated at each valuation. The choice of assumptions can be as significant as the choice of method.

The assumptions which the actuary must make in carrying out his valuation will be about matters such as future rates of inflation and pay increases, increases to pensions in payment, earnings on investments, the number of employees joining the scheme, the age profile of employees and the probability that employees will die or leave the company's employment before they reach retiring age. The actuary will view the assumptions as a whole; he will make assumptions which are mutually compatible, in the knowledge that, if experience departs from the assumptions made, the effects of such departures may well be offsetting, notably in the case of investment yields and increases in prices and earnings.

2.4   The accounting objective and how it is achieved

The accounting objective of *SSAP 24* is that the employer should recognise the expected cost of providing pensions on a systematic and rational basis over the period during which he derives benefit from the employee's services.

For defined contribution schemes this objective is achieved by charging against profits the amount of contributions payable to the pension scheme in respect of the accounting period.

For defined benefit schemes this objective is achieved by the actuary calculating a 'regular' pension cost which is a substantially level percentage of the current and expected future pensionable payroll (on the basis of the current actuarial assumptions).

2.5   Surpluses and deficits in defined benefit schemes

As a result of actual events not coinciding with actuarial assumptions, 'experience' surpluses and deficits will inevitably arise in defined benefit schemes between actuarial valuations (which are normally carried out every three years).

The standard requires that these surpluses and deficits are normally eliminated over the expected remaining service lives of current employees in the pension scheme, using the matching concept. The pension cost charge in the profit and loss account is then said to comprise a regular cost and a variation from regular cost.

2.6   Standard accounting practice

Para

80.   Subject to the provisions of paragraphs 81 to 83, variations from the regular cost should be allocated over the expected remaining service lives of current employees in the scheme. A period representing the average remaining service lives may be used if desired.

81.   The provisions of paragraph 80 should not be applied where, and to the extent that, a significant change in the normal level of contributions occurs because contributions are adjusted to eliminate a surplus or deficiency resulting from a significant reduction in the number of employees covered by the enterprise's pension arrangements. Where the significant reduction in the number of employees is related to the sale or termination of an operation, the associated pension cost or credit should be recognised immediately to the extent necessary to comply with FRS 3. In all other cases where there is a reduction in contributions arising from a significant reduction in employees the reduction of contributions should be recognised as it occurs. Amounts receivable may not be anticipated; for example, the full effect of a contribution holiday should not be recognised at the outset of the holiday, but rather spread over its duration.

82.   In strictly limited circumstances prudence may require that a material deficit be recognised over a period shorter than the expected remaining service lives of current employees in the scheme. Such circumstances are limited to those where a major event or transaction has occurred which has not been allowed for in the actuarial assumptions, is outside the normal scope of those assumptions and has necessitated the payment of significant additional contributions to the pension scheme.

83.   Where a refund that is subject to deduction of tax in accordance with the provisions of the UK Finance Act 1986, or equivalent legislation, is made to the employer, the enterprise may depart from the requirements of paragraph 80 and account for the surplus or deficiency in the period in which the refund occurs.

84.   Where ex gratia pensions are granted the capital cost, to the extent not covered by a surplus, should be recognised in the profit and loss account in the accounting period in which they are granted.

85.   Where allowance for discretionary or ex gratia increases in pensions is not made in the actuarial assumptions, the capital cost of such increases should, to the extent not covered by a surplus, be recognised in the profit and loss account in the accounting period in which they are initially granted.

Paras 80-85 SSAP 24

2.7   Example

The actuarial valuation as at 31 December 19X1 of the defined benefit pension scheme of a company showed a deficit of £30 million. The actuary recommended that the deficit be eliminated by lump sum payments of £15 million per annum for two years, in addition to the regular cost of £5 million per annum. The average remaining service life of employees in the scheme was estimated as eight years.

2.8   Solution

The pension cost charge for the next eight years should be:

$$\text{£5 million} + \frac{\text{£30 million}}{8} = \text{£8.75 million}$$

The funding and accounting policies will therefore be as follows:

	Funding £m	Accounting £m	Prepayment £m
19X2	20	8.75	11.25
19X3	20	8.75	22.50
19X4	5	8.75	18.75
19X5	5	8.75	15.00
19X6	5	8.75	11.25
19X7	5	8.75	7.50
19X8	5	8.75	3.75
19X9	5	8.75	-
	70	70.00	

The prepayment will be disclosed on the balance sheet.

If the deficit of £30 million were deemed to fall under the 'strictly limited circumstances' mentioned above in *SSAP 24 (para 82)* then the deficit should be recognised over the two years during which it is made up. The funding policy and the accounting policy would then be the same.

2.9   Activity

The actuarial valuation as at 30 June 19X0 of the defined benefit pension scheme of a company showed a surplus of £20 million. The actuary recommended that the surplus be eliminated by the company taking a contribution holiday for two years, followed by two years of reduced contributions of £6 million per annum, before reverting to the regular cost of £8 million. The average remaining service life of employees in the scheme was estimated as ten years.

Show the funding and accounting policies.

2.10   Activity solution

The pension cost charge for the next ten years should be:

$$\text{£8 million} - \frac{\text{£20 million}}{10} = \text{£6 million}$$

	Funding £m	Accounting £m	Accrual £m
19X0	-	6	6
19X1	-	6	12
19X2	6	6	12
19X3	6	6	12
19X4	8	6	10
19X5	8	6	8
19X6	8	6	6
19X7	8	6	4
19X8	8	6	2
19X9	8	6	
	60	60	

Note: the accrual effectively represents a timing difference which originates in years 19X0 and 19X1 to form a deferred tax asset and which reverses over years 19X2 to 19X9. *SSAP 15* requires that any provision for deferred tax liabilities be reduced by any deferred tax assets arising from separate categories of timing differences.

2.11   Refunds of contributions

The *Finance Act 1986* introduced rules stating that any surplus in a defined benefit scheme had to be reduced to 5% of the scheme assets within a period of five years (by means of contribution holidays, periods of reduced contributions and increases in benefits) or else a refund would have to be made to the employer which would be taxed at 40%. The refund may be taken directly to the profit and loss account as income or it may be treated as deferred income and released to the profit and loss account over the estimated remaining service lives of employees in the scheme.

2.12   Disclosure requirements

The following disclosures should be made in respect of a **defined contribution** scheme:

(a)   the nature of the scheme (ie, defined contribution);

(b)   the accounting policy;

(c)   the pension cost charge for the period;

(d)   any outstanding or prepaid contributions at the balance sheet date.

The following disclosures should be made in respect of a **defined benefit** scheme:

(a)   the nature of the scheme (ie, defined benefit);

(b)   whether it is funded or unfunded (ie, assets held outside or inside the employer's business);

(c)   the accounting policy and, if different, the funding policy;

(d)   whether the pension cost and provision (or asset) are assessed in accordance with the advice of a professionally qualified actuary and, if so, the date of the most recent formal actuarial valuation or later formal review used for this purpose. If the actuary is an employee or officer of the reporting company, or the group of which it is a member, this fact should be disclosed;

(e)   the pension cost charge for the period together with explanations of significant changes in the charge compared to that in the previous accounting period;

(f)   any provisions or prepayments in the balance sheet resulting from a difference between the amounts recognised as cost and the amounts funded or paid directly;

(g)   the amount of any deficiency on a current funding level basis, indicating the action, if any, being taken to deal with it in the current and future accounting periods;

(h)   an outline of the results of the most recent formal actuarial valuation or later formal review of the scheme on an ongoing basis.

This should include disclosure of:

(i)   the actuarial method used and a brief description of the main actuarial assumptions;
(ii)   the market value of scheme assets at the date of their valuation or review;
(iii)   the level of funding expressed in percentage terms;
(iv)   comments on any material actuarial surplus or deficiency indicated by (iii) above;

(i)   any commitment to make additional payments over a limited number of years;

(j)   the accounting treatment adopted in respect of a refund made in accordance with the provisions of paragraph 83 where a credit appears in the financial statements in relation to it;

(k)   details of the expected effects on future costs of any material changes in the group's and/or company's pension arrangements.

Where a company or group has more than one pension scheme, disclosure should be made on a combined basis, unless disclosure of information about individual schemes is necessary for a proper understanding of the accounts. For the purposes of (g) above, however, a current funding level basis deficiency in one scheme should not be set off against a surplus in another.

2.13   Definition of terms

(Definition)   A **current funding level actuarial valuation** considers whether the assets would have been sufficient at the valuation date to cover liabilities arising in respect of pensions in payment, preserved benefits for members whose pensionable service has ceased and accrued benefits for members in pensionable service, based on pensionable service to and pensionable earnings at, the date of valuation including revaluation on the statutory basis or such higher basis as has been promised.

The 'accrued benefits' method is the prime example of a current funding level actuarial valuation.

(Definition)   An **ongoing actuarial valuation** is a valuation in which it is assumed that the pension scheme will continue in existence and (where appropriate) that new members will be admitted. The liabilities allow for expected increases in earnings.

The 'prospective benefits' method is the prime example of an ongoing actuarial valuation.

(Definition)   An **ex gratia pension** or **discretionary or ex gratia increase** in a pension is one which the employer has no legal, contractual or implied commitment to provide.

3   THE AUDIT IMPLICATIONS OF THE ABOVE STANDARDS

3.1   SSAP 20

The auditor needs to design tests to identify items denominated in a foreign currency. Care needs to be taken here. For example, the purchase of goods from a French supplier does not necessarily mean that the purchase is denominated in a foreign currency. The invoice from the supplier may be expressed in sterling ie, the French business is taking on the exchange risk (perhaps because it considered it to be necessary in order to outbid competitors).

Once items have been identified, a sample of transactions needs to be checked for the correct application of exchange rates and the correct reporting of exchange differences.

Particular care is required with regard to long-term foreign currency liabilities. If a gain is to be reported, this may need to be restricted if there are doubts as to the convertibility of the currency in which the loan has been taken out.

3.2   SSAP 24

A defined contribution scheme presents no special audit problems. The liability of the company is limited to the percentage of salary it has agreed to pay into the scheme. For a defined benefit scheme, the legal and moral obligations of the company to provide pensions to its employees need to be considered. Legally the company may have no commitment to make good an expected shortfall in the pension fund but, if it is morally obliged to do so, a liability exists for accounting purposes.

It is sensible to liaise with the auditors of the pension fund as a means of obtaining sufficient evidence.

The actuary is the expert on the scheme as to whether there are sufficient funds within it to meet expected liabilities. The auditing standard *Using the work of an expert* is relevant here. The auditor must still come to a judgement as to whether the scheme is sufficiently funded.

If there is under/overfunding the accounting implications may be a requirement to show an accrual or prepayment on the balance sheet.

For any type of scheme there will be normal substantive procedures to check payments have been correctly made to the providers of the pension scheme and that amounts deducted from employees have been correctly passed on to the pension scheme.

4   CHAPTER SUMMARY

SSAP 20 requires items denominated in a foreign currency to be, generally, translated at the rate of exchange ruling at the date of the transaction. Exchange differences arise when the transaction is settled or retranslation is required at the balance sheet date.

The accounting objective of SSAP 24 is to recognise the expected cost of providing pensions on a systematic and rational basis over the employees' working lives.

5   SELF TEST QUESTIONS

5.1   What are examples of direct business transactions which may need translating into sterling? (1.2)

5.2   What are the two methods of translation? (1.4)

5.3   Are fixed assets retranslated at each balance sheet date? (1.6)

5.4   If a transaction is to be settled at a contracted rate, what translation rate should be used? (1.14)

5.5   What is a monetary item? (1.16)

5.6   What are the two types of pension schemes? (2.2)

6   EXAMINATION TYPE QUESTION

6.1   Tour Operators Ltd

Tour Operators Ltd had the following transactions in the year ended 30 October 19X8

(1)   Stage payments for construction of hotel in Spain

Invoices dated	Amount (Pesetas 000)
31 May 19X8	18,000
31 July 19X8	18,500
30 September 19X8	21,000

The invoices were all paid on the invoice date with the exception of the invoice dated 30 September 19X8 which was being disputed. The payment date was 30 November 19X8.

(2)   Purchase of aircraft seats on flights throughout the summer of 19X8 on Español airlines. A contract to take at least 4,000 seats (at 15,000 pesetas per seat) per month for June, July and August was signed on 31 March 19X8.

Invoice amount (Pesetas 000)	Date of invoice	Date paid
64,000	8 July	31 July
68,200	9 August	30 August
72,000	9 September	30 September

(3)   Payments of wages:

(a)   To Miss X a courier who had a contract of employment giving a salary of £680 a month plus free accommodation

Dates paid	Pesetas
31 July	140,360
30 August	145,000
30 September	132,000

(b)   To Miss Y another courier, who had a salary of 180,000 Pesetas a month paid at the end of July, August and September.

(4)   Sold a block booking of holidays in Spain to a Swiss travel agent on 16 April 19X8 for 1,980,000 swiss franks. An invoice was raised for this amount with sums payable by the travel agent to be

| 30 August | SF 980,000 |
| 30 September | SF 1,000,000 |

The amounts were paid on the due dates. Tour Operators took out a forward cover contract to sell SF 980,000 on 30 August and SF 1,000,000 on 30 September.

Exchange rates to £1	Pesetas	Swiss Francs
31 March 19X8	196.54	
16 April 19X8		3.12
31 May 19X8	200.00	
8 July 19X8	211.11	
31 July 19X8	206.41	
9 August 19X8	208.60	
30 August 19X8	213.24	2.96
9 September 19X8	198.89	
30 September 19X8	194.12	3.24
30 October 19X8	189.56	
30 November 19X8	194.89	

At 16 April 19X8 forward cover rates were	
30 August 19X8	3.16
30 September 19X8	3.17

You are required to write up the relevant ledger accounts (except the cash book and the profit and loss account) to record these transactions for the year ended 30 October 19X8.

Make entries to the nearest £.   **(15 marks)**

7   ANSWER TO EXAMINATION TYPE QUESTION

7.1   Tour Operators Ltd

Fixed asset hotel

			£		£
31.5.X8	$\dfrac{18,000,000}{200}$	Cash	90,000		
31.7.X8	$\dfrac{18,500,000}{206.41}$	Cash	89,627		
30.9.X8	$\dfrac{21,000,000}{194.12}$	Creditor	108,181		

Creditor

		£			£
30.10.X8	$\dfrac{21,000,000}{189.56}$		30.9.X8	Fixed asset	108,181
	Bal c/d	110,783	30.10.X8	Profit and loss	2,602
		110,783			110,783

Purchases

			£		£
8.7.X8	$\dfrac{64,000,000}{211.11}$	Creditor	303,159		
9.8.X8	$\dfrac{68,200,000}{208.60}$	Creditor	326,942		
9.9.X8	$\dfrac{72,000,000}{198.89}$	Creditor	362,009		

Creditor - Español airlines

			£			£
31.7.X8	$\dfrac{64,000,000}{206.41}$	Cash	310,063	8.7.X8	Purchases	303,159
30.8.X8	$\dfrac{68,200,000}{213.24}$	Cash	319,827	9.8.X8	Purchases	326,942
30.9.X8	$\dfrac{72,000,000}{194.12}$	Cash	370,905	9.9.X8	Purchases	362,009
				30.10.X8	Profit and loss - Loss on exchange	8,685
			1,000,795			1,000,795

(Tutorial note: The contract to purchase a certain number of seats would not be recorded in the books of account except at the balance sheet date when a decision would be required as to whether to accrue for the commitment. In the question the commitment relates to purchases made in the current financial year.*)*

Wages

			£		£
31.7.X8	$\dfrac{140,360}{206.41}$	Cash - Miss X	680		
	$\dfrac{180,000}{206.41}$	Cash - Miss Y	872		
30.8.X8	$\dfrac{145,000}{213.24}$	Cash - Miss X	680		
	$\dfrac{180,000}{213.24}$	Cash - Miss Y	844		
30.9.X8	$\dfrac{132,000}{194.12}$	Cash - Miss X	680		
	$\dfrac{180,000}{194.12}$	Cash - Miss Y	927		

Sales

		£				£
			16.4.X8	$\dfrac{980,000}{3.16}$	Debtor	310,127
				$\dfrac{1,000,000}{3.17}$	Debtor	315,457

Debtor

		£			£
16.4.X8	Sales	310,127	30.8.X8	$\dfrac{980,000}{3.16}$	310,127
		315,457	30.9.X8	$\dfrac{1,000,000}{3.17}$	315,457
		625,584			625,584

(Tutorial note:

A sale was made of holidays in April 19X8. Therefore at that date

> Dr   Debtors
> Cr   Sales

with SF1,980,000 at forward exchange rates.

As Tour Operators knows it can sell the Swiss francs at the forward rates, there is thus no exchange difference when the francs are received on the respective dates. Tour Operators sells the francs it receives to the bank at the agreed forward rates.

SSAP 20 does not stipulate that the forward exchange rate must be used. As an alternative the sale could be translated at the 'spot' rate of exchange ruling at 16 April 19X8, ie,

$$\dfrac{1,980,000}{3.12} = £634,615$$

The debtor could either

(i)   be recorded at the same amount with exchange differences arising on 30 August 19X8 and 30 September 19X8 totalling £9,031 (£634,615 – £625,584).

(ii)   be recorded at the forward exchange rates, ie, £625,584 with £9,031 recorded at the same date as the premium cost for forward exchange cover. The £9,031 would be charged to profit and loss account over the period covered by the forward contract (in this case all in 19X7/X8).*

21 THEORETICAL MATTERS

INTRODUCTION & LEARNING OBJECTIVES

This chapter deals with the complex issues involved in the measurement of income in a period of changing price levels. You will find it takes time to become acquainted with the terminology and the issues involved. There is currently no accounting standard in issue which deals with the topic of changing price levels. Instead, before its demise, the ASC published a *Handbook: Accounting for the effects of changing prices* to stimulate debate in this area. The Handbook discusses all aspects of the topic but contains no mandatory guidance for preparers of accounts.

The most important parts of this chapter to understand are the alternative definitions of capital maintenance, and the calculation of deprival value.

When you have studied this chapter you should be able to do the following:

- Outline concepts related to economic income.
- Understand the principles of alternative capital maintenance concepts.
- Be aware of various theoretical concepts.

1 TRADITIONAL HISTORICAL COST ACCOUNTING

1.1 The traditional approach

The traditional approach to accounting has the following features

(a)   accounting transactions are recorded at their original historical monetary cost

(b)   items and events for which no monetary transaction has occurred are usually ignored altogether

(c)   the income for each period is normally taken into account only when the revenue is realised in the form of cash or in some form which will soon be converted into cash

(d)   the profit for the period is found by matching the income against the cost of items consumed in generating the revenue for the period (such items include fixed assets which depreciate through use, obsolescence or the passage of time) and

(e)   in every case a prudent view is taken of the value of assets, income and expenses.

These features of accounting have served users well over many years in accounting for the stewardship of the directors. However, in periods in which prices change significantly, historical cost accounts have grave deficiencies.

1.2 The deficiencies of historical cost accounts

(a)   The net book value of fixed assets is often substantially below their current value.

(b)   The balance sheet figure for stock reflects prices ruling at the date of purchase or manufacture rather than those current at the year end.

(c)   Charges made in arriving at the profit do not reflect the current value of assets consumed. The effect is to exaggerate the profit in real terms.

If the profit determined in this way were distributed in full, the level of operations would have to be curtailed.

(d)   No account is taken of the effect of increasing prices on monetary items. For example, the cash tied up in debtors increases even where the volume of operations remains the same.

(e)   The overstatement of profits and the understatement of assets prevents a meaningful calculation of return on capital employed.

As a result of the above, users of accounts find it extremely difficult to assess a company's progress from year to year or to compare the results of different operations.

1.3   Example

Company A acquires a new machine in 19X4. This machine costs £50,000 and has an estimated useful life of ten years.

Company B acquires an identical machine in 19X5, except that it buys a machine exactly one year old, with an estimated useful life of nine years. The cost of the machine is £48,000.

Depreciation charges (straight-line basis) in 19X5 are as follows

Company A	$\frac{1}{10} \times £50,000$	=	£5,000
Company B	$\frac{1}{9} \times £48,000$	=	£5,333

Net book values at the end of 19X5 are

Company A	£50,000 – (2 × £5,000)	=	£40,000
Company B	£48,000 – £5,333	=	£42,667

Both companies are using identical machines during 19X5, but the profit and loss accounts will show quite different profit figures because of adherence to historical cost. Ask yourself the question whether the comparison of balance sheets and profit and loss accounts for the two companies in 19X5 is meaningful.

1.4   Advantages of the historical cost approach

One of the principal advantages claimed for this approach is that it reduces subjectivity to a minimum. Subjectivity refers to the extent to which the accounts can be affected by personal opinion as opposed to verifiable factual information.

In spite of this claim, subjective opinions are extremely important in conventional accounting. The following are examples

(a)   Revaluation of fixed assets where the revaluation is actually incorporated into the accounts as opposed to merely being referred to in a note to the accounts.

(b)   Depreciation charges require subjective estimates of useful life and estimated scrap value at the end of this useful life.

(c)   Stock may be stated at net realisable value where this is estimated to be less than cost.

(d)   Provision for doubtful debts and obsolete and slow-moving stocks requires subjective opinions, even if these opinions are backed up by reference to factual data.

(e)   Treatment of long-term contracts requires subjective estimations of (eg) expected cost to complete the contract.

Although the use of the historical cost principle has been the chief problem in recent years, the debate may be widened to cover various aspects of the traditional approach.

1.5   Deficiencies of the traditional approach

(a)   As noted above, adherence to original historical costs leads inevitably to the misstatement of asset values and profitability. Balance sheets no longer represent a meaningful representation of the economic state of affairs of a business.

(b)   Disregarding items and events for which no monetary transaction has occurred may mean that accounts do not portray the actual economic factors determining the success or failure of the business.

(c)   By recognising only revenue which is realised, changes in wealth that are of benefit to shareholders will be indefinitely disregarded.

(d)   The process of matching expenses with revenue is inevitably subjective and possibly pointless, as it is the level and timing of cash flows which determine economic values.

(e)   By taking a biased view of the uncertainty associated with a business, its strength and performance are deliberately misrepresented (albeit prudently).

These criticisms have done much to undermine the confidence of both the preparers and users of financial statements. Academic accountants have produced a panoply of proposals for the reform of traditional accounting. Many of these ideas, which are reviewed below, have dealt with the need for accounts to reflect current price levels in a period of changing prices. In the light of the seriousness of the situation the practitioners have shown some interest in these ideas, but no practical solution has been arrived at.

2   THE MEASUREMENT OF INCOME

2.1   Economic and accounting approaches to income measurement

The historical cost convention helps to facilitate verification of the figures reported to shareholders and other users of accounts. However, figures derived from historical costs have a number of weaknesses when used in economic decision-making. Consequently, a number of writers have turned to economic concepts in the search for alternative approaches to measuring business income.

2.2   Economic income - the contribution of Irving Fisher

The fundamental concept of income found in economic theory is derived from the work of the American economist Irving Fisher. He suggested that economic income should be viewed as a series of perceived events of psychic experiences called 'enjoyment'. In the rational, utilitarian world of economic analysis enjoyment is derived from the consumption of goods and services. Fisher therefore regards income as equivalent to the consumption of goods and services. He regards capital as the store of value which produces the flow of goods and services.

His approach is not without its weaknesses. It is generally accepted that before income can be measured it is necessary to consider the impact of consumption upon the store of capital. If capital is lost or consumed, there will be a reduction in the future supply of goods and services, and thus a reduction in income. Fisher does not take account of this aspect of the relationship between income and capital. Later economists have drawn a distinction between consumption of goods and services in a period and the consumption which is possible only after capital has been maintained, for which the term 'income' is reserved.

The contribution of Fisher was to highlight the role played by the consumption of goods and services in determining a person's income, and the role played by capital in acting as a stock of future income.

2.3   Economic income - the contribution of Sir John Hicks

It was a British economist, Sir John Hicks, who developed and extended the Fisher Theory of Income. Modern thinking is based upon the ideas of Fisher and Hicks, usually referred to as the Hicksian or Fisher-Hicks Income Theory.

Fisher identified the importance of maintaining capital in determining the income of each period. His theory deals with individuals rather than corporations, but can easily be adapted to deal with the latter. Hicks argued that the income of a person in a defined period is the maximum amount which a person can consume without impairing his 'well-offness'. His wealth or 'well-offness' is determined by the value of his fund of capital.

Thus, in order to determine the income of a specific period, it is necessary to measure the value of a person's capital, both at the beginning and at the end of the period. If the capital has not changed in value the person will have had no income, if it has increased in value then income will have been earned. The increase may be withdrawn and consumed. In practice, the fund of capital may have given rise to goods, services or cash during the period and this must be taken into account in ascertaining the income of the period. If the value of the capital stock was identical at the beginning and at the end of the period, then the value consumed would equate to the income of the period.

However, it will often be the case that the value of the fund of capital will have changed. Where it has risen the person will have added to his capital stock, or saved. His income will thus be the amount consumed plus the amount saved. Where the value of capital has fallen, the amount 'dis-saved' must be restored from the amount consumed. Unless the value of capital is maintained the future flow of income will diminish and the person will be less 'well off' than he was. Maintaining 'well-offness' is a precondition in determining the periodic income under the Hicksian approach.

2.4   The Hicks model of income

Following the economic principles outlined above, the Hicks income model, often referred to as 'economic income', may be summarised as

$$Y \quad = \quad C + S$$

where

$Y \quad = \quad$ income
$C \quad = \quad$ consumption
$S \quad = \quad$ savings (which may be positive or negative)

'Savings' refers to the increase or decrease in the capital stock of the firm, so that savings will be computed as

$$S \quad = \quad K_t - K_{t-1}$$

where

$K_t \quad = \quad$ Capital at end of period
$K_{t-1} \quad = \quad$ Capital at beginning of period

so that income is found by the formula

$$Y \quad = \quad C + (K_t - K_{t-1})$$

In order to determine the value of capital, it is necessary to discount all future cash flows to their present value.

2.5   Economic income and accounting income

Both economic income and accounting income can be defined as the difference between opening and closing capital, adjusted for amounts put in or taken out by the investor. The difference between the two arises because capital is measured in different ways. Accounting capital measures the total of the individual identifiable assets and liabilities of the business, while economic capital measures the present value of the future cash flows. The difference between the two is termed 'subjective goodwill', being regarded as subjective because of the reliance on estimates of future cash flows in its computation.

2.6   Significance of economic income

Economic income does not form a practical basis for accounting measurement, because it fails to meet the accountant's basic requirements for reliability and objectivity. Problems include

(a)   The need to predict future cash flows. Clearly this is highly subjective.

(b)   When predictions as to cash flows are revised there is no objective solution to the problem of allocating windfall gains between income and capital.

(c)   Similarly, there may well be variations over time in estimates of the appropriate discount rate, leading to major revisions of the present value of predicted cash flows.

(d)   Economic income is subject to fluctuations in the timing as well as in the amounts of predicted cash flows.

(e)   The ability to maintain the potential income stream requires the opportunity to reinvest surplus cash receipts, or to disinvest any shortfall of cash receipts, at the prescribed interest rate.

Thus, 'economic income' can never, in itself, be a practical basis for accounting measurement. Nevertheless, an awareness of economic income principles is valuable to the accountant because

(a)   it helps to explain why any form of accounting income measurement falls short of a full portrayal of economic reality and

(b)   it gives an ideal picture of income measurement against which the utility of practical accounting systems can be assessed.

3   VALUATION OF ASSETS AND LIABILITIES

3.1   The case for current value accounting

A widely-quoted definition of accounting is that suggested by the American Accounting Association: the process of identifying, measuring and communicating economic information to permit informed judgements and decisions by the users of information.

If we consider the traditional historical cost basis of measurement used by accountants, we can see that it fails to relate directly to any of the three decisions that might reasonably be made about an asset.

(a)   Another, similar asset might be purchased. In this case management will need to know the current replacement cost, which might have changed substantially since the present asset was purchased.

(b)   The asset might be sold. In this case management will need to know the amount which would be realised from sale, less any costs involved in disposal ie, the net realisable value. Again this bears no relationship to historical cost.

(c)   The asset might be used in the business. In this case management will need to estimate the future cash flows arising from the asset and discount these to their present value ie, their 'economic value'. Clearly, there is no relationship with historical cost in this case.

Historical cost does have the merit of being easily ascertained and objective, but as we have seen it does not relate directly to any decision that might be taken in relation to an asset. Historical cost might be regarded as giving some indication as to replacement cost, but in times of major fluctuations in price levels this relationship becomes remote. Thus, the experience of high levels of inflation has stimulated interest in finding a more useful basis of measurement than historical cost accounting, but the case for finding an alternative does not depend simply on the problems of inflation.

3.2 Entry values

Current entry value, often referred to as replacement cost, has been widely considered as a possible basis of measurement to value assets and to determine the cost of items consumed. Support for replacement cost has been particularly strong in the Netherlands, having been advocated by Limperg and used by a number of major companies, particularly the Phillips group. In the English-speaking world the American writers Edwards and Bell have argued the case for replacement cost, with an analysis of the annual surplus, termed 'business income', into a number of parts.

3.3 Current exit value accounting

Another value-based approach has been current exit value accounting, based on the use of net realisable values. Such a system of accounting has not been adopted in practice in any country in the world. However, a number of academic writers, particularly Professor Chambers of Sydney University, have argued the case for current exit values. Professor Chambers has gone so far as to formulate a complete accounting system called 'continuously contemporary accounting', commonly abbreviated to 'CoCoA'.

3.4 Deprival value

In the 1930s JC Bonbright, in a book on the problems of valuation for insurance purposes, put forward the notion of measurement of 'deprival value', being the loss a business would suffer if deprived of an asset. Professor Baxter of the London School of Economics realised that deprival value could be relevant for accounting purposes, and in SSAP 16 deprival value, there termed 'value to the business' was adopted as a basis of valuation.

The ASB has made use of the value to the business model in its draft Statement of Principles and in FRSs 11 and 15.

To identify deprival value we need to identify all three of the measures of value discussed above. Then we can identify two important relationships between values

> Recoverable amount = The higher of net realisable value and economic value

This is because if management own an asset, they have control over the choice between use and disposal, and if it is economically rational they will choose the option having the highest value.

> Deprival value = The lower of replacement cost and recoverable amount

This is because if deprived of an asset, management have a choice as to whether or not to replace it. If they are economically rational they will replace the asset only if they can generate a surplus either by resale or by use.

The three measures of value to be considered in order to compute deprival value can relate to each other in six different ways

						Deprival value
(a)	EV >		RC >		NRV	RC
(b)	NRV >		RC >		EV	RC
(c)	EV >		NRV >		RC	RC

(d)	NRV >	EV >	RC	RC
(e)	RC >	NRV >	EV	NRV
(f)	RC >	EV >	NRV	EV

Where

RC	=	Replacement cost
NRV	=	Net realisable value
EV	=	Economic value

If we consider each situation in turn

(a)   This is a common situation for a fixed asset, which presumably would not have been acquired unless economic value exceeded cost.

(b)   This is a common case for stock, which presumably would not have been acquired except in the expectation of a profitable sale.

In practice, if a business is trading profitably, we would expect either this or (a) to apply. Thus, for such a business, replacement cost will be the normal measure of deprival value.

(c)&(d) May be considered together, both relating to the situation in which replacement cost is lower than both economic value and net realisable value. Where such a situation arises, the business may profitably either use or deal in the asset concerned. For example, a motor trader may both hire out and deal in motor cars.)

We would expect the business to use the asset in situation (c) and sell it in situation (d); but in either case replacement cost is the appropriate measure of deprival value.

(e)   Where net realisable value exceeds economic value, then if management have identified this position we would expect the asset to be earmarked for disposal. Thus, such a situation is easily identified.

(f)   Where economic value exceeds net realisable value, then we would expect management to retain the asset in use, so that there is no easy way to identify this situation.

'Deprival value' avoids the implicit assumptions that assets will be replaced (as with replacement cost) or liquidated (as critics argue in the case of CoCoA). However, a number of arguments have been put forward against deprival value, including the following

(a)   The balance sheet may include the total of a number of different valuation bases (RC, NRV, EV), so that the significance of the total equity figure is unclear.

(b)   The basis of this approach is a hypothetical deprival which has not taken place, and there is some debate as to whether this is a satisfactory basis for measuring actual past events.

(c)   In the situation where economic value emerges as a measure of deprival value (case (f) above), then this measure is subject to all the practical difficulties involved in the measurement of economic income.

3.5   Activity

(a)   **Normal business**

A company owns a machine with a five year useful life and no residual value. At 31 December 19X2 the machine is two years old. The replacement cost at that date of a brand new machine of the same type is £100,000.

If the machine were sold it would fetch about £30,000 but there would be dismantling costs of about £5,000.

It is estimated that the machine could generate cash flows of £40,000 per annum if it were used in the business for the next three years. Assume that the cash flows arise at the end of the year and that a factor of 10% per annum is appropriate for discounting purposes.

Calculate the deprival value of the asset.

(b)   Company anticipating closure

Assume that the facts are as in (a) above but that the business is in such a poor state that there are no positive cash flows to be obtained from continuing to use the asset.

Calculate the deprival value of the asset.

(c)   Company with low NPV

Assume that the facts are as in (a) above but that the cash flows associated with the continued use of the asset are £22,000 per annum.

Calculate the deprival value of the asset.

3.6   Activity solution

			£
(a)	NRC =	Gross replacement cost	100,000
		Less: Accumulated depreciation $\frac{2}{5}$	40,000
			60,000
	NRV =	Sale proceeds	30,000
		Less: Costs to sell	5,000
			25,000

NPV = discounted value of future cash flows

		£
Year 1	$\dfrac{40,000}{1.1} =$	36,363
Year 2	$\dfrac{40,000}{1.21} =$	33,057
Year 3	$\dfrac{40,000}{1.331} =$	30,052
Total		99,472

DV =   lower of £60,000 and (higher of £25,000 and £99,472)

Deprival value is the replacement cost of £60,000

(b)	RC as before	60,000
	NRV as before	25,000
	NPV when there are no cash flows =	Nil

DV = lower of £60,000 and (higher of £25,000 and nil)

Deprival value is the net realisable value of £25,000

(c)	RC as before	60,000
	NRV as before	25,000
	NPV = discounted value of future cash flows	

$$\text{Year 1} \quad \frac{22,000}{1.1} = \qquad 20,000$$

$$\text{Year 2} \quad \frac{22,000}{1.21} = \qquad 18,181$$

$$\text{Year 3} \quad \frac{22,000}{1.331} = \qquad 16,529$$

Total   54,710

DV =   lower of £60,000 and (higher of £25,000 and £54,710)

Deprival value is the net present value of £54,710

3.7   The concept of Current cost accounting

Current cost accounting (CCA) is based on the deprival method of valuation of assets. In order to reflect deprival values the balance sheet assets of stock and fixed assets require revaluation. All other assets and all liabilities are monetary in nature (ie, they are already stated at current value in HC accounts) and therefore do not need to be adjusted.

The reflection of deprival values on the balance sheet results in additional charges in the profit and loss account to reflect the true cost of using stocks and fixed assets in the production of goods. This aspect of CCA is examined later after we have considered various capital maintenance concepts.

4   CONSTANT PURCHASING POWER ACCOUNTING

4.1   Concept

Under constant purchasing power (CPP) accounting the accounts are adjusted so that all figures are shown in terms of money with the same purchasing power. It is thus necessary to adjust items by means of a general price index. In the UK the index used for these purposes is the Retail Price Index (RPI) and items are generally restated in terms of the purchasing power at the end of the financial period. This approach formed the basis of PSSAP 7, which was proposed by the ASC in 1974, but withdrawn following government support for current cost accounting.

4.2   Key features

In converting the figures in the basic historical cost accounts into those in the supplementary current purchasing power statement a distinction is drawn between

(a)   monetary items and
(b)   non-monetary items.

[Definition]   Monetary items are those whose amounts are fixed by contract or otherwise in terms of numbers of pounds, regardless of changes in general price levels. Examples of monetary items are cash, debtors, creditors and loan capital.

Holders of monetary assets lose general purchasing power during a period of inflation to the extent that any income from the assets does not adequately compensate for the loss; the converse applies to those having monetary liabilities.

Definition Non-monetary items include such assets as stock, plant and buildings. The retention of the historical cost concept requires that holders of non-monetary assets are assumed neither to gain nor to lose purchasing power by reason only of changes in the purchasing power of the pound.

The owners of a company's equity capital have the residual claim on its net monetary and non-monetary assets. The equity interest is therefore neither a monetary nor a non-monetary item.

5   CAPITAL MAINTENANCE CONCEPTS

5.1   Principles of accounting for price level changes

The above discussion of CCA and CPP accounting has concentrated on the balance sheet and the valuation of assets. We now need to consider the effect of this approach on the profits that are recognised.

Total gains and losses accruing to the owners in a period must equal the difference between the net assets at the beginning and end of the accounting period. The valuation method for recording the net assets therefore determines total gains and losses. However it is important to distinguish 'profit' from other gains and losses as users need information about the quality of particular gains and losses eg, whether they are realised or relate to assets essential to the entity's operations which are likely to be sold.

The determination of profit is determined by the capital maintenance concept which is adopted.

Capital maintenance concepts can be classified as

(a)   Physical capital maintenance (PCM) alternatively known as operating capital maintenance (OCM). PCM is associated with CCA.

(b)   Financial capital maintenance (FCM).

FCM can be further divided into 'Money' FCM and CPP FCM. CPP FCM is CPP accounting.

5.2   Example of capital maintenance concepts

A company begins with share capital of £100 and cash of £100. At the beginning of the year one item of stock is bought for £100. The item of stock is sold at the end of the year for £150. Its replacement cost at that time is £120 and general inflation throughout the year is 10%. Any 'profit' is distributed to shareholders at the end of the year.

	Financial capital maintenance		Physical capital maintenance
	'Money' £	CPP £	£
Sales	150	150	150
Less: Cost of sales	100	100	120
Operating profit	50	50	30
Less: Inflation adjustment (alternatively shown by increasing cost of sales to £110)	-	10	-
Profit for year	50	40	30
Dividend	50	40	30
	-	-	-
Capital and non-distributable reserves at year end	100	110	120

The increase in capital and reserves of £10 for CPP is the credit entry for the £10 inflation adjustment. The £20 for PCM is the credit entry for the increased cost of sales. The £20 is known as a 'realised holding gain'. It is a gain (the stock was worth more in money terms when it was used in the business compared to when it was purchased), it arose purely from holding onto the stock in a period of rising prices and it is realised as the product has been sold by the firm.

Under 'money' FCM there is no attempt to adjust for inflation ie, the accounts are historic cost accounts.

Under CPP FCM the emphasis is on maintaining the purchasing power of the opening capital. The shareholders require funds of £110 in order to maintain their purchasing power. (£110 buys the same quantity of goods at the year end as £100 at the beginning of the year).

Note:

(a)   The OCM adjustment is based on the specific price changes affecting stocks. This can be calculated by reference to an index for the industry but strictly the company should calculate its own index based on stock purchases during the year. Thus the calculations are very complex and time consuming (and hence expensive) to perform.

(b)   The OCM balance sheet total figure is sufficient to replace the stock which is the whole objective.

5.3   Providing equivalent information in a supplementary form

Where the profit and loss account is not inflation adjusted, supplementary information can be provided in the notes by way of 'adjusted earnings statements'.

Using the numbers in the example above

Adjusted earnings statement under

	CPP financial capital maintenance £	*Physical capital maintenance* £
Historical cost operating profit (ie, before dividend)	50	50
Less: Current cost operating adjustments	-	(20)
Less: Inflation adjustment to opening shareholders' funds	(10)	-
Profit/current cost profit	£40	£30

5.4   Real terms accounting

Real terms accounting is a further capital maintenance concept based on combining CPP FCM and PCM.

It is a method which the ASB currently favours and appears in the draft Chapter 6 of the Statement of Principles. There are in fact several variations of real terms accounting but the basic idea is to show in the operating profit statement, the figures as in the PCM statement and to show the inflation adjustment to shareholders' funds in the statement of Total Recognised Gains and Losses.

Thus the figures would be

Profit and loss account

	£
Sales	150
Less: Cost of sales	120
Current cost operating profit	30
Dividend	30

Statement of total recognised gains and losses

	£
Current cost operating profit	30
Gain from holding stock (ie, credit entry for the increased cost of sales)	20
Nominal money profit	50
Less: Amount to maintain purchasing power of shareholders' investment	10
Current purchasing power profit	40

As with the CPP FCM concept above, it does not follow that the real terms gain (£40) could be fully distributed if the company wishes to continue in business at the same level of activity. This is because the maintenance of a company's real financial capital does not guarantee the maintenance of its operating capital.

5.5 Choice of capital maintenance concept

There are two main factors to consider when choosing a capital maintenance concept. These are the needs of the user and the nature of the company's business.

(a) **Users**

Shareholders will generally be interested in maximising the purchasing power of their investment. Thus a financial capital maintenance view may seem the most appropriate choice. (This could be CPP capital maintenance or a real terms approach.)

Managers and employees may consider that the company's major objective is perpetuating its existence by maintaining its ability to produce similar quantities of goods and services as those produced at the present time. This viewpoint is compatible with PCM. It must be stressed that if the company does not maintain its operating capacity, there will be a reduction in the scale of its activities which may mean that employees are made redundant.

(b) **Nature of business**

CPP FCM or real terms accounting is more suitable for companies in which asset value increases are viewed as an alternative to trading as a means of generating profits. The true measure of the performance of such companies is their ability to produce 'real' profits above the profits which arise from general inflation. The best measure of the success of such companies is based on real terms ie, opening capital is adjusted by a general index and the change in specific values of assets is assessed.

5.6 Example

A company begins with share capital of £1,000 which is represented by a freehold building costing £900 and cash of £100. At the beginning of the year stock is bought for £100. The item of stock is sold at the year end for £150. Its replacement cost at that time is £120 and general inflation throughout the year is 10%. The freehold property is worth £1,200 at the year end. (Ignore depreciation).

Statement of total recognised gains and losses

	£
Current cost operating profit	30
Add: Realised holding gain from stock	20
Unrealised holding gain from property (1,200 – 900)	300
	350
Less: Inflation adjustment (£1,000 at 10%)	(100)
Real terms profit	£250

By adding in the unrealised gain on the freehold property the bottom line profit figure shows clearly the overall change in shareholders' wealth during the period.

Companies which experience large fluctuations in the price of their inputs, such as oil companies, find that results on an historical cost basis are difficult to interpret and prefer a PCM basis for reporting profits. Similarly, a manufacturing company which needs to maintain its present operating capital would use PCM.

6   REFLECTING THE CPP METHODOLOGY IN THE FINANCIAL STATEMENTS

6.1   Introduction

In this and the next section, examples of the methods used to prepare CPP and CCA accounts are shown. You will not be required to compute the figures for the exam but a study of these methods may help you to understand the underlying concepts.

6.2   The preparation of CPP accounts

CPP accounts are prepared by adjusting all the amounts in the accounts to reflect the value of money at one point in time. Thus, the unit of measurement is the 'CPP unit' rather than the monetary unit. In principle the CPP unit can be based on the value of money at any point in time. In practice the value of money at the balance sheet date is used, in which case CPP can be termed **current** purchasing power accounting.

CPP accounts are prepared by updating all items in the profit and loss account, and all non-monetary items in the balance sheet, by the CPP factor:

$$\frac{\text{Index at the balance sheet date}}{\text{Index at date of entry in accounts}}$$

Depreciation is adjusted by reference to the date of acquisition of the related fixed asset item.

Monetary items in the balance sheet are not adjusted, because their value in CPP units is their monetary amount.

In the CPP accounts it is necessary to compute a gain or loss from holding monetary items in times of inflation. In principle this can be found by adjusting all entries in the accounts for each monetary item by the CPP factor, so that the difference between the 'CPP balance' and the actual monetary balance represents the gain or loss on holding that item.

6.3   Example of the preparation of CPP accounts

W Ltd was formed on 1 January 19X8, with a fully-subscribed share capital of £200,000. On the same date a loan of £100,000 was raised.

On 31 March 19X8, storage facilities with a twenty-year life and no residual value were purchased for £150,000. On the same date 1,000 widgets were purchased for £100,000. On 30 June 19X8, 600 widgets were sold for £90,000. Expenses of £10,000 were paid on 30 June 19X8. All transactions were for cash.

The company provides a full year's depreciation in the year of acquisition of an asset.

A general price index moved:

1	January	19X8	660
31	March	19X8	715
30	June	19X8	780
31	December	19X8	858

Assuming straight-line depreciation, you are required to:

(a)   prepare historical cost accounts for the year to 31 December 19X8; and

(b)   prepare CPP accounts for the year to 31 December 19X8.

6.4   Solution

Step 1   Remember you need to update **all** of the items in the profit and loss account by the CPP factor:

$$\frac{\text{Index at the balance sheet date}}{\text{Index at date of entry in accounts}}$$

You also need to calculate the loss or gain on monetary items. These calculations are shown in detail in Workings 1 and 2.

W Ltd
Profit and loss account for the year ended 31 December 19X8

	HC £	£	CPP factor	CPP £	CPP £
Sales		90,000	$\frac{858}{780}$		99,000
Purchases	100,000		$\frac{858}{715}$	120,000	
Less: Closing stock	40,000		$\frac{858}{715}$	48,000	
Cost of sales		60,000			72,000
Gross profit		30,000			27,000
Depreciation	7,500		$\frac{858}{715}$	9,000	
Expenses	10,000		$\frac{858}{780}$	11,000	
		17,500			20,000
					7,000
Loss on monetary items (48,000(W1) – 30,000(W2))					(18,000)
Net profit/(loss)		12,500			(11,000)

Step 2 In the balance sheet it is only the non-monetary items which are adjusted.

Balance sheet as at 31 December 19X8

	£	£		CPP £	CPP £
Plant:					
Cost		150,000	$\frac{858}{715}$		180,000
Depreciation		7,500	$\frac{858}{715}$		9,000
		142,500			171,000
Current assets:					
Stock	40,000		$\frac{858}{715}$	48,000	
Bank	130,000		-	130,000	
		170,000			178,000
		312,500			349,000
Loan		(100,000)			(100,000)
		212,500			249,000
Share capital		200,000	$\frac{858}{660}$		260,000
Retained profit/(loss)		12,500			(11,000)
		212,500			249,000

WORKINGS

			HC £	CPP factor	CPP CPP £
(1)	**Bank movements**				
	1 January 19X8	Shares issued	200,000	$\frac{858}{660}$	260,000
	1 January 19X8	Loan raised	100,000	$\frac{858}{660}$	130,000
	31 March 19X8	Storage	(150,000)	$\frac{858}{715}$	(180,000)
	31 March 19X8	Purchases	(100,000)	$\frac{858}{715}$	(120,000)
	30 June 19X8	Sales	90,000	$\frac{858}{780}$	99,000
	30 June 19X8	Expenses	(10,000)	$\frac{858}{780}$	(11,000)
	Loss on monetary items (Bal fig)				48,000
	31 December 19X8	Balance	130,000		130,000
(2)	**Loan movement**				
	1 January 19X8	Loan raised	100,000	$\frac{858}{660}$	130,000
	Gain on monetary item (Bal fig)				(30,000)
	31 December 19X8	Balance	100,000		100,000

Note that this is a simple example designed to illustrate the principles of CPP. In practice, with more complex examples, less detailed translation methods are used, particularly to avoid the amount of analysis of monetary items that would be necessary with the example above.

7   REFLECTING THE CCA METHODOLOGY IN THE FINANCIAL STATEMENTS

7.1   A family of techniques

Current cost (or replacement cost) accounting is not a single system of accounting - there are several variants. We will concentrate on general principles, in particular those relating to stock and fixed assets.

(a)   The current cost profit and loss account is charged with the value to the business of assets consumed during the period. In particular, the charges for consuming stocks (cost of sales) and fixed assets (depreciation) are based on current rather than historical values.

(b)   The current cost balance sheet reflects the current value of stock and fixed assets.

7.2   Fixed assets and depreciation

(a)   **Balance sheet**

The general rule is that fixed assets should be included in the balance sheet at their value to the business ie, the amount of compensation a company would require if it were deprived of the asset.

Thus, in most cases, the value to the business of property is its market value on an existing use basis, while for plant and machinery it is net current replacement cost.

Considering plant and machinery, how is net current replacement cost calculated? There are three basic stages:

(i)   Calculate the gross replacement cost (GRC) of a new but otherwise identical asset at the balance sheet date.

(ii)   Allowing for the age of the asset, calculate a depreciation provision based on GRC.

(iii)   Net current replacement cost equals (i) less (ii), and is shown in the current cost balance sheet.

If GRC cannot be calculated by reference to suppliers' price lists, an alternative is to use specific price indices. These are produced by the Office for National Statistics (ONS).

Example

A company bought an item of plant on 30 June 19X3 at a cost of £4,000. Its expected useful life was ten years, with a nil value at the end. An identical model of plant is no longer available, but you have obtained the following specific price indices which you consider are suitable for the purpose:

30 June 19X3	Index = 132
31 December 19X8	Index = 195

You are required to calculate net current replacement cost at 31 December 19X8, assuming the estimated useful life of the asset has not been revised.

Solution

		£
Gross replacement cost at 31 Dec 19X8 £4,000 × $\frac{195}{132}$		5,909
Accumulated depreciation $\frac{5.5}{10}$ × £5,909		3,250
Net current replacement cost		2,659

(b)   **Profit and loss account**

It is now necessary to consider the calculation of the depreciation charge for the current cost profit and loss account. For simplicity, the depreciation charge will be based on the year-end replacement cost of the fixed asset. Current cost depreciation can be based on the average replacement cost during the year, but the arithmetic is a little more complex.

Example

A company acquired a fixed asset on 1 January 19X4 at a cost of £800. Its estimated useful life was five years, with a nil terminal value. A new, but otherwise identical, asset would cost £800 and £960 on 31 December 19X4 and 19X5 respectively.

You are required:

(i)   to prepare the current cost (CCA) and historical cost (HCA) balance sheet extracts at each year end in respect of fixed assets;

(ii)   to prepare the relevant depreciation charges;

(iii)   to prepare the relevant fixed asset ledger accounts for 19X5.

Solution

(i)   **Balance sheets at 31 December**

	19X4		*19X5*	
	HCA £	*CCA* £	*HCA* £	*CCA* £
Cost	800	800	800	960
Accumulated depreciation	160	160	320	384
	640	640	480	576

(ii)   **Profit and loss accounts**

	19X4		*19X5*	
	HCA £	*CCA* £	*HCA* £	*CCA* £
Depreciation charge	160	160	160	192

(iii)

Fixed asset - gross replacement cost (GRC)

19X5		£	19X5		£
1 Jan	Replacement cost b/d	800	31 Dec	GRC c/d	960
31 Dec	Revaluation reserve				
	(bal fig)	160			
		960			960

Fixed asset - accumulated replacement cost depreciation

19X5		£	19X5		£
31 Dec	CCA provision c/d		1 Jan	Provision b/d	160
	(2/5 × £960)	384	31 Dec	Depreciation (CCA)	192
			31 Dec	Revaluation reserve	
				(bal fig)	32
		384			384

Notes:

(1)   The net amount credited direct to revaluation reserve is £(160 − 32) ie, £128.

(2)   The value to the business of the fixed asset is its net current replacement cost of £576: £(960 − 384).

7.3   Stock and the cost of sales

The essence of current cost accounting is that, when an item of stock is sold, the proceeds of sale must be matched against the current cost of the stock at the date of sale (representing the value to the business of stock consumed).

Example

A company purchased some goods on 31 January 19X2 at a cost of £250. These goods were sold on 31 March 19X2 for proceeds of £320 when the cost of replacing the goods was £272.

(a)   **Historical cost accounting**

Under HCA, proceeds of sale (£320) would be compared with historical cost (£250) to show profit on sale of £70.

(b)   **Current cost accounting**

	£
Proceeds of sale	320
Current cost of sales	272
Current cost (or operating) profit	48
Current cost of sales	272
Historical cost of sales	250
Realised 'holding gain'	22

Of the original (HCA) profit of £70, £48 would be credited to the CCA profit and loss account, while £22 would be taken direct to revaluation reserve. Although the £22 is part of proprietor's funds, it would be regarded as non-distributable, being required to maintain the capital of the business intact in real terms.

How is current cost of sales calculated? In theory, it is calculated separately for each asset item. In practice, certain short-cut methods may be acceptable.

8   OTHER THEORETICAL MATTERS

8.1   Agency theory

Modern organisational theory views an organisation as being comprised of various interest groups or stakeholders. The relationships between the various interested parties in the firm are often described in terms of agency theory. Agency relationships occur when one party, the principal, employs another party, the agent, to perform a task on their behalf. The agent will be employed since he may have special skills, or the principal might not have the time to carry out the task himself.

For example, directors can be seen as the agents of shareholders, employees as the agents of directors and auditors as agents of shareholders.

Each principal needs to recognise that although he is employing the agent, the agent will have interests of his own to protect and thus may not carry out fully the requirements of the principal. For example

(a)   directors have a duty of stewardship of the company's assets. However they are also interested in their level of remuneration and if this increases, the assets of the company go down. The decision to award directors pay increases is effectively in the hands of the directors themselves.

(b)   auditors report to shareholders. However auditors know the decision to reappoint them is effectively in the hands of the directors. They therefore have a potential conflict of interest in carrying out their function and also remaining on good terms with the directors.

The principal will therefore try to construct the agency relationship so that actions that are in the agent's self-interest are also in the best interests of the principal. Directors might for example be paid a part of their remuneration in the form of a profit-related bonus, to encourage them to earn high profits for the company, which would benefit the shareholders.

The principal may incur 'monitoring costs' to check that the agent is acting in the principal's interests. The setting up of an internal audit department would be an example of monitoring costs.

Agency theory helps to explain why directors of companies take part in creative accounting practices to try to report artificially high profits for their companies to trigger bonus payments to themselves. Directors could take a more detached view of the financial results of their companies if their pay was totally independent of the reported results.

8.2   Efficient markets hypothesis (EMH)

You may have come across this idea in financial management. The EMH is a theory regarding the degree of efficiency with which stock markets are able to reflect the 'true' financial position of a company into its share price.

EMH is usually broken down into three categories

(a)   **The weak form**

Share prices fully reflect knowledge of historic share price movements and patterns.

It follows that the current share price is the best estimate of the share's value. Thus it makes no sense to talk about a share being 'below' its normal value just because its present price is less than the former. There is no evidence to suggest that the price will climb to its so called 'normal' level rather than fall still further.

(b)   The semi-strong form

Current share prices reflect not only historic share price information but also current publicly available information about the company.

(c)   The strong form

Current share prices reflect not only historic share price patterns and current public knowledge, but also all possible (ie, inside) information about the company.

If the hypothesis is correct then the mere publication of the information should have no impact on the share price, consequently it should not be possible to make profits by dealing in response to 'inside' information.

The evidence suggests that either the weak form or the semi-strong form is the most appropriate description of the efficiency of stock markets.

The main impact of EMH is on auditing and relates to

(a)   the need or otherwise to keep information about a company confidential. If the strong form of EMH is correct then there can be no insider dealing

(b)   the need to be concerned with 'creative accounting' by the directors attempting to improve reported results. If the semi-strong form of EMH is correct then the stock market will see through such practices.

8.3   Positive and normative accounting concepts

The terms 'positive' and 'normative' are used in social sciences to distinguish two approaches to the developing of theory and the construction of practical solutions.

A normative approach considers that theories can be developed without reference to current practice. A theory, once proved as 'true', can then be used to develop accounting practice. The emphasis therefore is on developing a statement of what should occur in a good accounting system ignoring what is currently happening in practice.

A positive approach is based on observing actual accounting practice. Rules are based on observed common patterns of practice. Another name which is used for this approach is 'descriptive' accounting. Over time a generally agreed method of accounting is found.

The positive approach is similar to the approach taken by the ASC while the ASB is attempting more of a normative approach.

The positive approach has the merit of pragmatically arrived at solutions which have the general support of the preparers of accounting information provided that the rate of change in the business community is not so fast that it constantly changes the current attitude of what is or is not acceptable accounting practice. This was the problem besetting the ASC when companies were expanding by take-over and merger in the 1980s and 'creative' accounting solutions were developed to show the acquisitions in the best possible light to the shareholders.

Positive accounting theory predicts management's attitudes to different accounting practices by analysing the costs and benefits associated with each practice. For example, the managers of newly privatised utilities such as British Gas will want to report low profit levels to avoid adverse reactions from the government, the public and the regulator. However, high profits might earn bonuses for senior managers. Positive theory can thus be used to appraise proposed new accounting standards by looking at their effects in the real world.

It remains to be seen whether the more normative approach taken by the ASB will be better. A major problem in a social science in developing theories is to state assumptions which are specific enough to arrive at practical solutions but still obtain agreement over the theory. Often, the theoretical principles are so generally drawn that they are of little help in a practical way.

9   CHAPTER SUMMARY

The debate as to the measurement of income, assets and liabilities is made important by the deficiencies of HC accounting in an era of changing prices.

CPP and CCA are two possible solutions or partial solutions with the ASB favouring a real terms approach.

10   SELF TEST QUESTIONS

10.1   What are five deficiencies of HC accounting in a period of changing prices? (1.2)

10.2   What is the Hicksian definition of wealth? (2.3)

10.3   What is the difference between economic income and accounting income? (2.5)

10.4   What is another name for entry value accounting? (3.2)

10.5   In the definition of deprival value what is the recoverable amount? (3.4)

10.6   How is deprival value arrived at? (3.4)

10.7   What happens when a business owns monetary assets in a period of inflation? (4.2)

10.8   What is PCM? (5.1)

10.9   Is FCM associated with CCA? (5.1)

11   EXAMINATION TYPE QUESTION

11.1   Barty plc

The following relates to the accounts of Barty plc, a property investment company.

The accounts contain

Balance sheet as at 31 December 19X7

	19X7 £'000	19X6 £'000
Investment properties at market value	14,125	12,579
Other assets	140	421
	14,265	13,000
Called-up share capital	2,000	2,000
Profit and loss account	4,720	4,597
Investment property revaluation reserve	7,545	6,403
	14,265	13,000

Profit and loss account for the year ended 31 December 19X7

	£'000
Rental income	1,526
Administrative expenses	(160)
Profit before tax	1,306
Taxation	(793)
Profit after tax	573
Dividends paid and proposed	(450)
Retained profit	123

Adjusted earnings statement for the year ended 31 December 19X7

	£'000	£'000
Net profit after tax for the year		573
Unrealised gains for the year on		
revaluations of investment properties	925	
Less: Inflation adjustment to shareholders' funds	(520)	
Real holding gains		405
Total real gains		978
Dividends paid and proposed		(450)
Amount retained		528

Further information

(1)   Investment properties are revalued annually at each year end.
(2)   Investment properties were acquired for £621,000 during 19X7.
(3)   The Retail Price Index has risen by 4% during 19X7.

You are required to comment on the adjusted earnings statement prepared by the company.

(10 marks)

12   ANSWER TO EXAMINATION TYPE QUESTION

12.1   Barty plc

Barty is a company which invests in property. As such it is a value-based company which is attempting to maximise the return to shareholders primarily by long term capital growth in the value of the investments.

The traditional profit and loss account concentrates on current revenue and matches the immediate return of the shareholders (ie, dividends) with the rental income.

The adjusted earnings statement recognises that the shareholders are interested in both revenue and capital gains. As can be seen, the unrealised gains exceed the revenue profit which is to be expected from such a company.

The shareholders are also interested in the protection from general inflation of their investment in the company. The inflation adjustment of £520,000 is the amount needed to maintain the purchasing power of the shareholders' investment during the year. Their equity investment at the beginning of the year was £13m, and applying 4% inflation gives £520,000. The unrealised gains are comfortably protecting the shareholders' investment.

22 INTERPRETATION OF FINANCIAL STATEMENTS

INTRODUCTION & LEARNING OBJECTIVES

This chapter considers the exam question or part of an exam question requiring an analysis of financial information. Many of the ratios may already be known to you.

The production of reports is often required in the context of the financial analysis of a business and the syllabus specifically refers to the writing of such reports. There is, in fact, little that can be written to advise you on the production of reports other than to stress the importance of presenting an answer in the format required by the examiner.

When you have studied this chapter you should be able to do the following:

- Calculate useful financial ratios.
- Produce reports analysing results over time or between entities.

---

1 INTERPRETATION OF FINANCIAL INFORMATION

1.1 Horizontal analysis

The most straightforward method of analysing financial statements is simply to compare the current year with the previous year and to note and rationalise any significant changes. This is often performed in analytical review procedures before proceeding to any detailed audit work. It is known as 'horizontal analysis', but its formal title is hardly important as it amounts to the application of basic common sense. It is a form of 'inter temporal' analysis ie, a comparison between accounting periods.

The line by line comparison must be performed whilst also considering

(a)   the change in turnover, and

(b)   the relevance of anything else you may know about the company.

In practice an analyst will find any other information in the directors' report, in the chairman's report or in press cuttings about the company or the industry in which it operates.

In an examination question, this other information is usually found in the opening lines of the question, where you will be told

(a)   what the company does, and

(b)   why you are being asked to interpret the accounts.

Further information is then usually provided in the notes following on from the numerical information.

You must ensure that your answer makes best use of this additional information. In a good answer all of the points will be referred to and used to rationalise the observed trends.

The change in turnover underpins the analysis. Assuming a 30% increase in turnover, we might predict a 30% increase in everything else in the profit and loss account. Balance sheet changes, for example in stocks and debtors, may be rationalised in the same way. The following sections are intended to prompt some ideas for the profit and loss account.

1.2   Gross profit

If gross profit has not increased in line with turnover, you need to establish why not.   Is the discrepancy due to

(a)   increased 'purchase' costs; if so are the costs under the company's control (ie, does the company manufacture the goods sold)?

(b)   stock write offs (likely where the company operates in a volatile market place, such as fashion retail), or

(c)   other costs being allocated to cost of sales - for example, research and development expenditure.

The other information in the question should provide some clues.

1.3   Operating profit

By the time you have reached operating profit there are many more factors to consider.   If you are provided with a breakdown of expenses you can use this for further line by line comparisons.   Bear in mind that

(a)   some costs are fixed or semi-fixed (for example property costs) and therefore not expected to change in line with turnover

(b)   other costs are variable (for example, packing and distribution, and commission).

1.4   Activity

In arriving at operating profit various significant items which may affect the analysis may have been included. List some examples

1.5   Activity solution

(a)   Exceptional items
(b)   depreciation of tangible fixed assets
(c)   research and development (if not already dealt with)
(d)   advertising expenditure
(e)   staff costs which may have risen in line with inflation
(f)   pension costs including any surpluses or deficiencies (dealt with according to SSAP 24)
(g)   amortisation of intangibles (including goodwill)
(h)   directors' emoluments, and
(i)   government grants received.

The list above is not intended to be comprehensive, but it may serve as a source of ideas and it should prompt your own thoughts.

1.6   Profit before tax

In moving from operating profit to profit before tax, two items appear

(a)   investment income, and
(b)   interest payable.

It is unlikely that either of these will move in line with turnover.   However, a simple year on year comparison may highlight other changes, such as

(a)   changes in holdings of investments
(b)   leasing charges, and

(c)   increased borrowings.

These figures may tie in with the balance sheet. Check them against

(a)   the investments held (both fixed and current), and
(b)   the level of borrowings (particularly the bank overdraft).

1.7   Profit after tax

It is useful to compute the 'rate' of tax by comparing the tax charge to the profits before tax. The rate should be fairly constant from year to year. The company's policy for providing deferred tax may also be relevant.

1.8   Extraordinary items

There should be sufficient information in the notes to explain the nature of any extraordinary item. It is worth considering whether the item is really extraordinary in nature. Analysts very often treat extraordinary items as exceptional to overcome the subjectivity involved in the classification. Given that FRS 3 has virtually outlawed extraordinary items the need for this should become very rare indeed.

1.9   Dividends

Dividends should be compared to the previous year. Even when profit for the year has declined, a fall in dividends for a plc is an extremely worrying sign. Major companies usually try to avoid this where at all possible.

2   CALCULATION OF USEFUL RATIOS FROM COMPANY OR GROUP FINANCIAL STATEMENTS

2.1   Introduction

Ratio analysis is a more sophisticated technique for analysing financial statements. It is the next step after the so-called horizontal analysis.

In general, ratio analysis should only be used in answering exam questions where the question specifically calls for use of ratios.

For example the question might state "using the principal analytical ratios". In this case the following should be calculated

(a)   return on capital employed
(b)   profit margin (usually net profit to sales)
(c)   current or quick ratio, and
(d)   gearing ratio.

Very often the question gives no indication of which ratios to calculate, in which case you must make a choice.

2.2   Choice of ratios

The variety of ratios that could be calculated is vast; so it is important to restrict the calculations by being selective. The ratios chosen should be the key ones relevant to the requirements of the question. These may be further limited by the available information (ie, there may be some you are simply unable to calculate). This point is considered further below.

Ratios can be classified into three main groups, these are summarised in the table below.

Type	Reflect	Examples
Profitability	Performance of company and its managers including the efficiency of asset usage	ROCE GP% Stock turnover Debtors and creditors days
Financial	Financial structure and stability of the company	Gearing Current and liquidity ratios
Investment	Relationship of the number of ordinary shares and their price to the profits, dividends and assets of the company	EPS P/E ratio Dividend yield Dividend cover Net assets per share

The managers of the company are likely to be concerned about all aspects of the company and therefore may want to know about all of the key ratios in each category.

Shareholders or potential investors are concerned primarily with the investment ratios though certain financial stability and profitability measures are also likely to be of interest (for example gearing and ROCE).

Creditors are most likely to be concerned about financial stability, though a bank, acting as a major source of finance, will usually also look at profitability.

2.3   Commenting on the ratio

Ratios are meaningless on their own, thus most of the marks in an exam question will be available for sensible, well explained and accurate comments on the key ratios.

If you doubt that you have anything to say the following points should serve as a useful checklist

(a)   what does the ratio literally mean?
(b)   what does a change in the ratio mean?
(c)   what is the norm?
(d)   what are the limitations of the ratio?

2.4   Further information required

Any analyst in practice will be limited in the analysis he can perform by the amount of information available. He is unlikely to have access to all the facts which are available to a company's management.

Similarly, an auditor carrying out analytical review perhaps at the planning stage of the audit is likely to come up with a long list of further information he needs, or questions he would like to ask.

In the examination the information which can be provided about a company in any one question will be limited. Part (a) of such a question could well ask you to interpret the available information, perhaps in the context of an auditor planning the audit. Part (b) could easily ask you to state what further information you require.

3   PROFITABILITY RATIOS

3.1   Return on capital employed (ROCE)

The absolute figure of profit earned is not, in itself, significant since the size of the business earning that profit may vary enormously. It is significant to consider the size of the profit figure relevant to the size of the business, size being expressed in terms of the quantity of capital employed by that business.

The return on capital employed is the ratio which measures this relationship. It is a key *business objective,* and is thus the key ratio in assessing financial achievement. It reflects the *earning power* of the business operations.

The ratio in simple form is

Definition $$\frac{\text{Profit}}{\text{Capital employed}} \times 100\%$$

ROCE is also known as the **primary ratio** because it is often the most important measure of profitability.

The ratio shows how efficiently a business is using its resources. If the return is very low, the business may be better off realising its assets and investing the proceeds in a high interest bank account! (This may sound extreme, but should be considered particularly for a small, unprofitable business with valuable assets such as freehold property). Furthermore a low return can easily become a loss if the business suffers as a downturn.

Once calculated, ROCE should be compared with

(a)   *previous years' figures* - provided there have been no changes in accounting policies, or suitable adjustments have been made to facilitate comparison (note, however that the effect of not replacing fixed assets is that their value will decrease and ROCE will increase)

(b)   *company's target ROCE* - where the company's management has determined a target return as part of its budget procedure, consistent failure by a part of the business to meet the target may make it a target for disposal

(c)   *the cost of borrowings* - if the cost of borrowing is say 10% and ROCE 7%, then further borrowings will reduce EPS unless the extra money can be used in areas where the ROCE is higher than the cost of borrowings

(d)   *other companies in same industry* - care is required in interpretation, since there may be

(i)   different accounting policies eg, research and development expenditure, stock valuation and depreciation

(ii)   different ages of plant - where assets are written down to low book values the ROCE will appear high

(iii)   leased assets which may not appear in the balance sheet at all. (SSAP 21 requires assets held under finance leases to be on the balance sheet but not those held under operating leases).

3.2   Activity

A company has revalued its fixed assets during the most recent accounting period. How will this affect the calculation of ROCE?

3.3   Activity solution

Any upward revaluation of fixed assets causes a reduction in ROCE by

(a)   increasing the capital employed, and

(b)   decreasing profits, by a higher depreciation charge.

3.4   Alternative calculations

Return on capital employed can be calculated in a number of different ways.

One version is the return on shareholders' equity which is more relevant for existing or prospective shareholders than management.

$$\text{Return on equity} = \frac{\text{Profit after interest and after preference dividends}}{\text{Ordinary share capital + reserves}}$$

Profit may be before or after tax. After tax is a more accurate reflection of profits (management should seek to minimise tax) however you will know that deferred tax provisions are likely to be subjective so profit before tax may be more objective.

The other commonly used ROCE is

$$\text{Overall return} = \frac{\text{Operating profit}}{\text{Share capital + reserves + all borrowings}}$$

This is used by managers assessing performance.

3.5   Further points

(a)   Treatment of associates and investments

Where the profit excludes investment income, the balance sheet carrying amounts for associates and investments should be deducted from the capital employed.

This gives an accurate measure of trading performance. If associates and investments are not deducted, the overall profit figure should include income from investments and associates.

(b)   Purchased goodwill may be being amortised over an unrealistically long period. Some analysts are suspicious of any goodwill and eliminate it before carrying out their detailed analysis.

(c)   Large cash balances are not contributing to profits and some analysts therefore deduct them from capital employed (to compare operating profits with operating assets). However it is usually acceptable not to make this adjustment as ROCE is a performance measure and management have decided to operate with that large balance.

3.6   Gross profit percentage

Definition $\dfrac{\text{Gross profit}}{\text{Turnover}} \times 100\%$

This is the margin that the company makes on its sales.

It is expected to remain reasonably constant. Since the ratio consists of a small number of components, a change may be traced to a change in

(a)   selling prices - normally deliberate though sometimes unavoidable, for example because of increased competition

(b)   sales mix - often deliberate

(c)   purchase cost - including carriage or discounts

(d)   production cost - materials, labour or production overheads

(e)   stock - errors in counting, valuing or cut-off; stock shortages.

Inter-company comparison of margins can be very useful but it is especially important to look at businesses within the same sector. For example food retailing is able to support low margins because of the high volume of sales. A manufacturing industry would usually have higher margins.

Low margins usually suggest poor performance but may be due to expansion costs (launching a new product) or trying to increase market share. Lower margins than usual suggest scope for improvement.

Above average margins are usually a sign of good management although unusually high margins may make the competition keen to join in and enjoy the 'rich pickings'.

A trading profit margin is

Definition $\dfrac{\text{Trading profit}}{\text{Turnover}}$ (before interest, investment income and tax)

This is affected by more factors than the gross profit margin but it is equally useful and if the company does not disclose a cost of sales (perhaps using format 2) it may be used on its own in lieu of the GP%.

One of the many factors affecting the trading profit margin is depreciation, which is open to considerable subjective judgement. Inter-company comparisons should be made after suitable adjustments to align accounting policies.

3.7   Stock turnover

Definition $\dfrac{\text{Cost of sales}}{\text{Stocks}} = $ times pa

This yields a multiple expressed as, say, 10 times per annum. If format 2 is used, then simply compare turnover and stocks, though bear in mind that this is also affected by the margin achieved by the company.

An alternative is to express this as so many days stock

$$\frac{\text{Stocks}}{\text{Cost of sales}} \times 365 \text{ days}$$

Sometimes an average (based on the average stock) is calculated which has a smoothing effect but may dampen the effect of a major change in the period.

An increasing number of days (or a diminishing multiple) implies that stock is turning over less quickly. This is usually regarded as a bad sign

(a)   it may reflect lack of demand for the goods
(b)   it may reflect poor stock control, with its associated costs such as storage and insurance
(c)   it may ultimately lead to stock obsolescence and related write offs.

However, it may not necessarily be bad where

(a)   management are buying stock in larger quantities to take advantage of trade discounts

(b)   management have increased stock levels to avoid stockouts, and

(c)   the increase is slight and due to distortion of the ratio caused by comparing a year end stock figure with cost of sales for the year and that year has been one of increasing growth.

Stock turnover ratios vary enormously with the nature of the business. For example, a fishmonger would have a stock turnover period of 1-2 days, whereas a building contractor may have a stock turnover period of 200 days. Manufacturing companies may have a stock turnover ratio of 60-100 days; this period is likely to increase as the goods made become larger and more complex.

For large and complex items (for example rolling stock or aircraft) there may be sharp fluctuations in stock turnover according to whether delivery took place just before or just after the year end.

A manufacturer should take into consideration

(a)   reliability of suppliers; if the supplier is unreliable it is prudent to hold more raw materials, and

(b)   demand; if demand is erratic it is prudent to hold more finished goods.

3.8   Debtors turnover

Definition $\dfrac{\text{Trade debtors}}{\text{Turnover}} \times 100\%$

This can be expressed as a percentage as above or as a number of days

$$\dfrac{\text{Trade debtors}}{\text{Turnover}} \times 365 \text{ days}$$

The trade debtors used may be a year end figure or the average for the year. Where an average is used to calculate a number of days the ratio is the average number of days' credit taken by customers.

For cash based businesses like supermarkets, debtors days is unlikely to exceed 1 as there are no true credit sales.

For other businesses the result should be compared with the stated credit policy. A period of 30 days or 'at the end of the month following delivery' are common credit terms.

Increasing debtors days is usually a bad sign as it suggests lack of proper credit control. However, it may be due to

(a)   a deliberate policy to extend the stated credit period to attract more trade, and

(b)   one major new customer being allowed different terms.

Falling debtors days is usually a good sign, though it could indicate that the company is suffering a cash shortage.

The debtors days ratio can be distorted by

(a)   using year end figures which do not represent average debtors

(b)   debt factoring which results in very low debtors, and

(c)   other credit finance agreements such as hire purchase, where there is insufficient analysis of turnover (HP debtors should be shown separately) to calculate proper ratios.

3.9   Creditors days

This is usually expressed as

Definition $\dfrac{\text{Trade creditors}}{\text{Purchases}} \times 365 \text{ days}$

and represents the credit period taken by the company from its suppliers. An average of trade creditors may also be used.

Where purchases are not known, cost of sales is used, or failing that, sales.

The ratio is always compared to previous years. Once again there are two main contrasting points

(a)   a long credit period may be good as it represents a source of free finance, or

(b)   a long credit period may indicate that the company is unable to pay more quickly because of liquidity problems.

Note that if the credit period is long

(a)   the company may develop a poor reputation as a slow payer and may not be able to find new suppliers

(b)   existing suppliers may decide to discontinue supplies, and

(c)   the company may be losing out on worthwhile cash discounts.

4   SHORT-TERM FINANCIAL STABILITY

4.1   Introduction

Two ratios are used to measure a business's ability to meet its own short-term liabilities. These are

(a)   current or working capital ratio

> **Definition** $\dfrac{\text{Current assets}}{\text{Current liabilities}}$

(b)   liquidity, acid test or quick assets ratio

> **Definition** $\dfrac{\text{Current assets - stock}}{\text{Current liabilities}}$

It is not usually appropriate to calculate both ratios when answering a time pressured exam question as trends in the ratios are likely to be similar.

As a general rule calculate only the current ratio unless the company has slow moving stocks (for example in the construction industry) in which case calculate the quick ratio instead.

4.2   Current ratio

The current ratio measures the adequacy of current assets to meet its short term liabilities. It reflects whether the company is in a position to meet its liabilities as they fall due.

Traditionally a current ratio of 2 or higher was regarded as appropriate for most businesses to maintain creditworthiness, however more recently a figure of 1.5 is regarded as the norm.

A higher figure should be regarded with suspicion as it may be due to

(a)   high levels of stocks and debtors (check working capital management ratios), or

(b)   high cash levels which could be put to better use (for example by investing in fixed assets).

The current ratio should be looked at in the light of what is normal for the business. For example, supermarkets tend to have low current ratios because

(a)   there are no trade debtors, and

(b)   there is usually very tight cash control as there will be considerable investment in developing new sites and improving sites.

It is also worth considering

(a)   availability of further finance, for example is the overdraft at the limit? - very often this information is highly relevant but not disclosed in the accounts

(b)   seasonal nature of the business - one way of doing this is to compare the interest charges in the profit and loss account with the overdraft and other loans in the balance sheet; if the interest rate appears abnormally high this is probably because the company has had higher levels of borrowings during the year

(c)   long term liabilities and when they fall due and how will they be financed, and

(d)   nature of the stocks - as stated above where stocks are slow moving, the quick ratio probably provides a better indicator of short term liquidity.

4.3   Quick ratio

This is also known as the acid test ratio because by eliminating stocks from current assets it provides the acid test of whether the company has sufficient resources (debtors and cash) to settle its liabilities. Norms for the quick ratio range from 1 to 0.7.

Like the current ratio it is relevant to consider the nature of the business (again supermarkets have very low quick ratios).

Sometimes the quick ratio is calculated on the basis of a six week time frame (ie, the quick assets are those which will turn into cash in six weeks; quick liabilities are those which fall due for payment within six weeks). This basis would usually include the following in quick assets

(a)   bank, cash and short term investments, and
(b)   trade debtors

thus excluding prepayments and stocks.

Quick liabilities would usually include

(a)   bank overdraft which is usually repayable on demand
(b)   trade creditors, tax and social security, and
(c)   proposed dividends.

Corporation tax may be excluded.

When interpreting the quick ratio, care should be taken over the status of the bank overdraft. A company with a low quick ratio may actually have no problem in paying its creditors if sufficient overall overdraft facilities are available.

Both the current and quick ratio may be distorted by **window dressing;** for example, if the current ratio is 1.4 and trade creditors are paid just before the year end out of positive cash balances, the ratios improve as shown below

	Before	*Repayment of £400 trade creditors*	*After*
Current assets	£1,400	-£400	£1,000
Current liabilities	£1,000	-£400	£600
Current ratio	1.4		1.7

5   LONG-TERM FINANCIAL STABILITY

5.1   Introduction

The main points to consider when assessing the longer-term financial position are as follows

(a)   gearing
(b)   financial balance
(c)   overtrading.

5.2 Gearing

'Gearing' is the relationship between a company's equity capital (known as residual return capital) and reserves and its fixed return capital.

A company is *highly geared* if it has a substantial proportion of its capital in the form of preference shares or debentures or loan stock.

A company is said to have *low gearing* if only a small proportion of its capital is in the form of preference shares, debentures or loan stock.

A company financed entirely by equity shares has *no gearing.*

The importance of gearing can be illustrated by an example as follows

5.3 Activity

Two companies, A plc and B plc, both have capital of £10,000. A plc has it all in the form of equity shares of £1 each, B plc has 5,000 £1 equity shares and £5,000 of 10% debentures.

Both companies earn profits of £5,000 in year 1 and £2,000 in year 2. Tax is assumed at 35% and the dividend paid is 10p per share.

The capital position is therefore as follows:

	A plc £	B plc £
Shares	10,000	5,000
Debentures	-	5,000
	£10,000	£10,000

What is the EPS in each year?

5.4 Activity solution

	A plc Year 1 £	A plc Year 2 £	B plc Year 1 £	B plc Year 2 £
Profit before tax and debenture interest	5,000	2,000	5,000	2,000
Debenture interest	-	-	500	500
			4,500	1,500
Taxation (35%)	1,750	700	1,575	525
Earnings	3,250	1,300	2,925	975
Dividend (10%)	1,000	1,000	500	500
Retained profits	£2,250	300	£2,425	475
Earnings per share	32.5p	13p	58.5p	19.5p

5.5 Effects of gearing

The effects of gearing can be seen to be as follows

(a)   debenture interest is an allowable deduction *before taxation,* whereas dividends are paid out of profits *after taxation;* company B has consistently higher retained profits than Company A.

(b)   earnings of a highly geared company are more sensitive to profit changes; this is shown by the following table

Company	A plc	B plc
Change in profit before interest and taxation	-60%	-60%
Change in earnings	-60%	$-66\frac{2}{3}\%$

The reason for the fluctuation is obviously the element of debenture interest which must be paid regardless of profit level.

This more than proportionate change in earnings is important in relation to the share price of the companies. Many investors value their shares by applying a multiple (known as the P/E ratio) to the earnings per share. Applying a multiple of *say* 10 to the EPS disclosed above would indicate share valuations as follows

Company	A plc		B plc	
Year	*1*	*2*	*1*	*2*
Share price	£3.25	£1.30	£5.85	£1.95

Thus the share price of a highly geared company will often be more volatile than a company with only a small amount of gearing.

Not all companies are suitable for a highly geared structure. A company must have two fundamental characteristics if it is to use gearing successfully. These are as follows

(a)   **Relatively stable profits**

Debenture interest must be paid whether or not profits are earned. A company with erratic profits may have insufficient funds in a bad year with which to pay debenture interest. This would result in the appointment of a receiver and possibly the liquidation of the company.

(b)   **Suitable assets for security**

Most issues of loan capital are secured on some or all of the company's assets which must be suitable for the purpose. A company with most of its capital invested in fast depreciating assets or stocks subject to rapid changes in demand and price would not be suitable for high gearing.

The classic examples of companies which are suited to high gearing are those in property investment and the hotel/leisure services industry. These companies generally enjoy relatively stable profits and have assets which are highly suitable for charging. Note that nonetheless these are industries that could be described as cyclical.

Companies not suited to high gearing would include those in the extractive industries and high-tech industries where constant changes occur. These companies could experience erratic profits and would generally have inadequate assets to pledge as security.

There are two methods commonly used for expressing gearing

(a)   the debt/equity ratio, calculated by taking

$$\frac{\text{Loans} + \text{redeemable preference share capital}}{\text{Ordinary share capital} + \text{reserves} + \text{minority interest}}$$

This is more sensitive than (b)

(b)   the percentage of capital employed represented by borrowings

$$\frac{\text{Loans} + \text{redeemable preference share capital}}{\text{Total capital}}$$

where total capital is loans, redeemable preference share capital, ordinary share capital, reserves and minority interests.

5.6   Financial balance

'Financial balance' is the balance between the various forms of available finance relative to the requirements of the business.

A business must have a *sufficient level of long-term capital* to finance its long-term investment in fixed assets. Part of the investment in current assets would also be financed by relatively permanent capital with the balance being provided by trade credit and other short-term borrowings. Any expansion in activity will normally require a broadening of the long-term capital base, without which 'overtrading' may develop (see below).

Suitability of finance is also a key factor. A permanent expansion of a company's activities should not be financed by temporary, short-term borrowings. A short-term increase in activity such as the 'January sales' in a retail trading company could ideally be financed by overdraft.

A major addition to fixed assets such as the construction of a new factory would not normally be financed on a long-term basis by overdraft. It might be found, however, that the expenditure was temporarily financed by short-term loans until construction was completed, when the overdraft would be 'funded' by a long-term borrowing secured on the completed building.

5.7   Overtrading

Overtrading arises where a company expands its turnover fairly rapidly without securing additional long-term capital adequate for its needs. The symptoms of overtrading are

(i)   stocks increasing, possibly more than proportionately to sales
(ii)   debtors increasing, possibly more than proportionately to sales
(iii)   cash and liquid assets declining at a fairly alarming rate, and
(iv)   creditors increasing rapidly.

The above symptoms simply imply that the company has expanded without giving proper thought to the necessity to expand its capital base. It has consequently continued to rely on its creditors and probably its bank overdraft to provide the additional finance required. It will reach a stage where creditors will withhold further supplies and bankers will refuse to honour further cheques until borrowings are reduced. The problem is that borrowings cannot be reduced until sales revenue is earned, which in turn cannot be achieved until production is completed, which in turn is dependent upon materials being available and wages paid. Overall result - deadlock and rapid financial collapse!

This is a particularly difficult stage for any small to medium company. They have reached a stage in their life when conventional creditor and overdraft facilities are being stretched to the maximum, but they are probably too small to manage a flotation. In many cases, by proper planning, the company can arrange fixed term loan funding from the bank rather than relying exclusively on overdraft finance.

6   INVESTORS' RATIOS

6.1   Earnings per share (EPS)

The calculation of EPS was covered earlier.

The EPS is used primarily as a measure of profitability thus an increasing EPS is seen as a good sign. The EPS is also used to calculate the price earnings ratio which is dealt with below.

The limitations of EPS may be listed as follows

(a)   In times of rising prices EPS will increase as profits increase. Thus any improvement in EPS should be viewed in the context of the effect of price level changes on the company's profits.

(b)   Where there is a new share issue, the shares are included for, say, half of the year on the grounds that earnings will also increase for half of the year. However, in practice a new project does not begin generating normal returns immediately, so a new share issue is often accompanied by a decrease in EPS.

(c)   EPS is dependent on an earnings figure which is a subjective measure. Some elements of that earnings figure are particularly subjective, such as the movements on provisions.

(d)   FRS 3 emphasises that one earnings figure should not be used as a key performance measure. This is to take a far too simplistic approach to the analysis of performance.

(e)   EPS cannot be used as a basis of comparison between companies as the number of shares in issue in any particular company is not related to the amount of capital employed. For example, two companies may have the same amount of capital employed but one company has 100,000 £1 shares in issue and reserves of £4,900,000. Another company may have 5 million 50p shares in issue and reserves of £2,500,000. If earnings are the same, EPS is different.

(f)   EPS is an historical figure based on historic accounts. This is a disadvantage where it is used for a forward looking figure such as the price earnings ratio. This is considered below.

(g)   The diluted EPS (DEPS) is a theoretical measure of the effect of dilution on the basic EPS. There is no evidence to suggest that even the most sophisticated analysts use the DEPS. This is because of its hypothetical nature. In the past the DEPS has served as a warning to equity shareholders that their future earnings will be affected by diluting factors. Following the introduction of FRS 14 the DEPS will have less predictive value as it has become an additional measure of past performance. Thus notes in the accounts relating to convertible loan stock, convertible preference shares and share options should all be analysed carefully.

6.2   Price/Earnings ratio

This is the most widely referred to stock market ratio, also commonly described as an earnings multiple. It is calculated as the 'purchase of a number of years' earnings' but it represents the market's consensus of the future prospects of that share. The higher the P/E ratio, the faster the growth the market is expecting in the company's future EPS. Correspondingly, the lower the P/E ratio the lower the expected future growth.

Another aspect of interpreting it, is that a published EPS exists for a year and therefore the P/E ratio given in a newspaper is generally based on an increasingly out of date EPS. To give an extreme but simple example

X plc

For the year ended 31 December 19X6   EPS = 10p

- Overall market P/E ratio = 10

- P/E ratio for X plc = 20 (because market expects above average growth)

- Market price at 30 April 19X7 (date of publication of previous year's accounts) = £2

- During the year X plc does even better than expected and by 29 April 19X8 the share price is up to £3, therefore giving a P/E ratio of 30 (based on EPS for year ended 31 December 19X6)

- Year ended 31 December 19X7 EPS = 15p, announced on 30 April 19X8. This is in line with expectations so share price is unchanged and P/E ratio drops again to 20 (£3/15p).

6.3   Dividend yield gross

This is the (gross) percentage of the dividend to the market price. The dividends are grossed up to show the amount including tax credit (at the rate of 10% ie, $\frac{10}{90}$ of the net amount) .

6.4   Dividend cover

This is the relationship between available profits and the dividends payable out of the profits, the dividends being calculated on a maximum distribution basis. The *Financial Times* adjusts profits to exclude non-trading profits and losses.

7   ASSESSING INFORMATION WEAKNESSES IN THE FINANCIAL STATEMENTS

7.1   Ratio analysis for specific purposes

The main point to emerge from a study of ratios is that there is no single group of ratios suitable for all purposes; specific ratios are required for specific purposes, and the analysis must be developed accordingly.

Furthermore, even within a specific area there is no comprehensive list of applicable ratios. There are certain crucial ratios, and they are developed and built according to the pointers provided by the key ratios and the information available.

7.2   Problems of ratios

The chief limitations of the usefulness of ratio analysis are as follows

(a)   Unless ratios are calculated in a uniform manner, from uniform data, comparisons can be very misleading.

        The consistency concept in SSAP 2 provides some uniformity within the same organisation over time but does not, in itself narrow the differences between organisations.

(b)   The accounting periods covered by the financial statements may not reflect representative financial positions.

        Many businesses produce accounts to a date on which there is relatively low amounts of trading activity. Retail organisations often have an end of February accounting date (after the peak pre-Christmas trading and the January sales). As a result the items on a balance sheet are not representative of the items throughout the accounting period.

        Consider stock levels in a retail organisation. They may vary as shown in the graph below

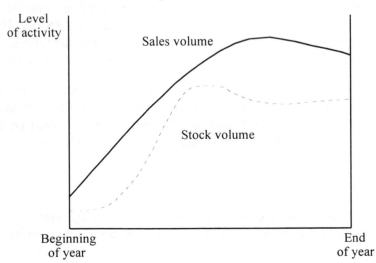

Adding opening and closing stock and dividing by two, will not produce a fair average.

(c)   Financial statements themselves have limitations eg, they contain arbitrary estimates and figures which are based on personal decisions.

(d)   The application of accounting policies in the preparation of financial statements must be understood when attempting to interpret financial ratios.

In the section below you will see a number of accounting standards discussed. Most of these problems relate to subjectivity in applying accounting standards.

(e)   The earning power of a business may well be affected by factors which are not reflected in the financial statements. Thus, these do not necessarily represent a complete picture of a business, but only a collection of those parts which can be translated into money terms eg, the size of the order book is normally ignored in financial statements.

(f)   Ratios must not be used as the sole test of efficiency. Concentration on ratios may inhibit the incentive to grow and expand, to the detriment of the long-term interests of the company.

(g)   A few simple ratios do not provide an automatic means of running a company. Business problems usually involve complex patterns which cannot be solved solely by the use of ratios.

(h)   The effect of inflation.

The problem of interpreting data in a period of changing prices is covered below.

7.3   Management discretion in the choice of accounting policies

If a company changes an accounting policy, it must, under SSAP 2 have good reasons to make a change. It must also restate comparative figures in the published accounts and summarised five or ten year data for the new policy. Therefore the user of the accounts has some assurance in using the financial data. However, the user must be aware of the extent to which policies are changed as it is relatively easy for the directors to come up with 'good' reasons for making a change. It is likely that the real reason for the change in policy is that the new policy puts the current results of the company in a more favourable light.

Set out below are some accounting standards for which management has discretion as to the application of the requirements of the standard. You will also find it useful to review the comments made in the previous chapters regarding the auditing problems of various standards. Many of the auditing problems are related to the discretion available to directors in implementing a standard.

7.4   FRS 14

The main problem with the original earnings per share calculation and the effect of the extraordinary/exceptional classification has been removed by FRS 3. However EPS can still be manipulated by changes in capital structure during the year and the time lag between the actual effect on earnings of such changes and the point at which they are dealt with in the EPS calculation.

For example a purchase of own shares during the year will reduce pro rata the weighted average number of shares. This is done because the outflow of cash will lead to reduced earnings. However, there is likely to be a delay in the reduction of earnings (perhaps until next year) and the short term EPS may appear to increase. Obviously a share issue at full market price during the year would have the opposite effect.

7.5   SSAP 4

Only the deferred credit method is allowable under the *Companies Act 1985*. Since this method releases the grant to profit and loss account in line with depreciation on the asset concerned it suffers from the same limitations as FRS 15 (see below).

7.6   FRS 15

The choice of depreciation method is left with the directors of a company provided it achieves the objectives of FRS 15. This involves an assessment of the useful economic life and the pattern of wearing out over that life (ie, whether a straight line or reducing balance charge would be most appropriate). Because of this choice there is scope for manipulation.

Many companies do not charge depreciation on freehold properties on the grounds that high on-going maintenance and refurbishment costs mean that estimated residual value is always kept at greater than cost and that the asset's life effectively becomes infinite. Although FRS 15 discourages this practice by requiring impairment reviews, it has not actually prohibited it.

In addition a change of method or useful economic life, neither of which are dealt with as a prior period adjustment, can be used to adjust profits. For a change of method the effect on *current period* profits has to be disclosed where material, but such a change can increase profits for many years to come.

7.7   FRS 12

Although FRS 12 is less subjective than SSAP 18, entities are still required to decide whether or not a transfer of economic benefits is 'probable'. FRS 12 gives some guidance, but there is still scope for creative interpretation of the term.

7.8   SSAP 21

The main scope for manipulation here is with the misuse of the so-called '90% test'. Companies have used this to keep leased assets and their corresponding liabilities off the balance sheet and so improve ratios such as gearing.

7.9   SSAP 24

Although the detail of an actuary's work is beyond this syllabus you are aware that there are different valuation methods. So two different actuaries at identical companies may value the pension fund differently. One company may end up with a surplus to account for, another perhaps a deficit.

There are also different means of spreading, for example, a surplus. We consider primarily the straight line method. This divides the surplus by the average remaining service lives (an estimate in itself) to give a level capital amount per annum. Interest could be added to the unamortised balance each year to give a total charge. The total amount spread will be greater than the original surplus because of this interest element. There are other methods which could lead to very different figures in the profit and loss account.

7.10   SSAP 25

Applying only to listed and large companies, SSAP 25 increases significantly the amount of information that has to be disclosed. The more information is disaggregated, the more useful it is for interpretation or analytical review purposes.

However, there is scope for manipulation. The 'common costs' and 'unallocated assets' can hide a multitude of sins. It is up to the directors to decide what constitutes a reportable segment, and they may decide that a particular loss making division does not, until it is combined with one that makes greater profits.

8   PRODUCTION OF WRITTEN REPORTS ON THE POSITION AND PROGRESS OF COMPANIES

8.1   Introduction

The syllabus requires the preparation and presentation of reports for a variety of users and purposes. This section summarises the general principles to follow.

The particular problems of producing written reports in the context of inter firm and inter temporal comparisons are detailed in the following sections.

8.2   Layout of the report

In practice, there are several possible ways of setting out a report. Usually a report contains two basic sections

(a)   main body, including conclusions arrived at

(b)   statistical appendices and supplementary statements which back up the comments or conclusions in (a) above.

In an exam answer it may not be practical to maintain this split in which case it is helpful to state by a particular section that it would normally go into an appendix.

The following is a suitable approach to setting out a report

(a)   Index to report

(b)   Addressee, Date and Title

(c)   Introduction

       Introduce the reader to the aim or purpose of the report, for example 'Analysis of the accounts of X Ltd for the two years ended 31 December 19X8'.

(d)   Assumptions

       State key assumptions.

(e)   Information used

       State the source of the financial information included in the report. Mention the extent to which the report has been limited by specific instructions.

(f)   Conclusions

       State as clearly as possible.

       Note: some reports state the conclusions at the beginning of the report. This is a perfectly acceptable alternative to the above approach.

(g)   Appendices

       Containing detailed figures.

9   INTER TEMPORAL COMPARISONS

9.1   Introduction

A significant weakness of HC accounting is the misleading impression of the trend of a company's performance over a period of time as no account is taken of changes in the real value of money. Current cost valuations do not remedy this defect as the valuations reflect prices ruling at a balance sheet date and previous years' accounts only reflect valuations at previous years' prices.

Published accounts give comparative information in two main areas

(a)   The corresponding amounts for items shown in the balance sheet, profit and loss account and notes. Such amounts are required by the *Companies Act 1985* for virtually all items disclosed in the accounts.

(b)   Any historical summary provided. Such summaries, which often taken the form of five or ten year summaries, are not required by law, but have nevertheless become a common feature in the annual reports of listed companies. Historical summaries will usually be disclosed as information supplemental to the financial statements.

9.2   How comparability may be improved

(a)   **The use of ratios**

The following ratios are comparable from one year to another

(i)   current cost operating profit/net operating assets
(ii)   current cost earnings/equity interest
(iii)   total gains/total assets
(iv)   total gains/equity interest
(v)   operating assets/equity interest
(vi)   net borrowings/equity interest.

These ratios can provide useful information, but such information is inevitably limited.

(b)   **Restatement of comparative information in terms of a constant unit of measurement**

Amounts expressed in pounds sterling of different dates can be restated in units of constant purchasing power by using a general price index. The form of the calculation is thus similar to the adjustment made to shareholders funds in 'real terms accounting'.

9.3   The ASC Handbook

In the mid 1980's the ASC issued *Accounting for the effects of changing prices: a Handbook* which gave advice to businesses if they wished to voluntarily provide price adjusted information in their accounts. The Handbook recommends that *historical* summaries of *current cost* information should be restated in units of constant purchasing power.

The Handbook does not recommend that *historical* cost information is restated in units of current purchasing power.

The objective of restating amounts in units of constant purchasing power is to eliminate the distortion of inter-year comparisons caused by the effects of changing prices. As this restatement will not reflect the effect of changing prices on the company's performance during the period or on its position at the end of the period, it is not a complete system of accounting for the effects of changing prices.

Nevertheless, historical cost information restated in units of constant purchasing power is sometimes mistakenly thought or taken to be a proper system of accounting for the effects of changing prices. In order to prevent such misunderstanding occurring it will usually be appropriate to restate only historical cost figures which will be the same under the current cost convention, such as turnover and dividends per ordinary share.

9.4   Calculating the restated figures

Current cost balance sheet information is based on current costs at the balance sheet date. Consequently only prior year balance sheets will need to be restated.

Current cost profit and loss account information is based on average current costs during the accounting period. This means that to be strictly comparable it should be adjusted to the balance sheet date. Whether it is worthwhile restating the profit and loss account information (including the latest information) into year-end pounds rather than average pounds will depend upon the comparisons to be made and the rate of general inflation involved.

The restated figures can be calculated in two ways; by reference to the movement in the average RPI for each year (the average method) or by reference to the movement in the RPI from one year-end to the next (the year-end method). The average method is the more appropriate method for restating profit and loss account information. The year-end method is more appropriate for the restatement of balance sheet information and is consistent with the objective of restating previously reported figures in pounds of the balance sheet date. Either method is acceptable as long as it is applied consistently.

In the following illustration the average RPI for each year has been used. Thus the 19X2 turnover figure has been calculated as

$$\frac{\text{Index for current year}}{\text{Index for year data taken from}} \times \text{Data}$$

$$\frac{373.1}{320.4} \times £29,314 = £34,136\left(19\text{X}5 \text{ } £m\right)$$

9.5   Illustration

PLC historical summary

As reported   **£ million**

	19X1	19X2	19X3	19X4	19X5
Turnover	25,737	29,314	32,381	37,933	**40,986**
Current cost operating profit	2,460	2,930	3,289	3,901	**4,438**
Earnings per ordinary share	63.9p	39.4p	47.5p	76.8p	**87.4p**
Dividends per ordinary share	20.25p	20.25p	24.0p	30.0p	**34.0p**
Net assets at current cost	32,564	38,799	47,021	52,564	**56,163**
Adjusted for the average UK retail price index of	295.0	320.4	335.1	351.8	**373.1**

£ million

	19X1	19X2	19X3	19X4	19X5
Turnover	32,551	34,136	36,053	40,230	**40,986**
Current cost operating profit	3,111	3,412	3,662	4,137	**4,438**
Earnings per ordinary share	80.8p	45.9p	52.9p	81.4p	**87.4p**
Dividends per ordinary share	25.61p	23.58p	26.72p	31.82p	**34.0p**
Net assets at current cost	41,185	45,181	52,353	55,747	**56,163**

10   INTER FIRM COMPARISONS

10.1   How comparability can be improved

Comparisons may usefully be made between different organisations providing similar outputs.

There are however problems of obtaining information about competitor firms. This can be resolved if use is made of an *inter-firm comparison* scheme. In the public sector, some of the problems have been resolved by government public sector organisations presenting performance indicators in their annual report.

10.2   Inter-firm comparison schemes

In order to provide the basis of comparison referred to above, schemes of inter-firm comparisons have been set up in a number of industries. The general principle of such schemes is that particular firms supply data to an independent collator. In order to ensure comparability, data must be presented on a uniform basis.

Data on other companies is collated and made available to participants in an anonymous form (firms are identifiable by a number only). This last point is important, since companies do not normally wish their close rivals to be provided with detailed financial information about their operations. Individual companies may then compare their ratios with those typical of the industry, so as to establish which areas of operations appear to be operating below par and may be improved - since firms are identified by a number, the results can be represented so that Firm No 1 has the highest return on capital, Firm No 2 the next highest, and so on. Management will know their own firm and its position and will study the report to see the detailed reasons for its high or low placing.

Companies taking part in an IFC scheme do so under the auspices and guidance of a Trade Association, or of the Centre for Inter-Firm Comparisons (CIFC) which was set up by the British Institute of Management and the British Productivity Council in 1959.

For an IFC scheme to be successful

(a)   Participants must be assured that the information they supply will be treated confidentially.

(b)   The participants must all belong to a similar industry.

(c)   Uniform costing and accounting methods must be used.

Uniform costing may be defined as 'the use by several undertakings of the same costing systems' ie, the same basic costing methods and superimposed principles and techniques. The main factors requiring a uniform approach are

(a)   bases for overhead apportionment and absorption methods

(b)   depreciation treatment

(c)   classification of costs

(d)   accounting periods.

10.3   Advantages and disadvantages of inter-firm comparison schemes

Advantages of IFC schemes are

(a)   Areas of inefficiency in relation to competitors are revealed.

(b)   The ratios are so selected by the trade association that management's attention is focused on the vital areas of the business.

(c)   The expertise of the trade association is available to participators.

(d)   Management is motivated by the competition with other companies.

(e)   Cost of subscription is low.

Disadvantages of IFC schemes are

(a)   There is no guarantee that truly uniform information has been submitted.

(b)   Participants are anonymous.

(c)   A company has to submit its own figures.

10.4   Example of Inter-firm comparison

Some ratios for a company, AB Ltd, which is a light engineering company are shown below.

	Management ratios		*Unit*	*Industry*	*AB Ltd*
		1st quartile		15.1	
(a)	Operating profit / Operating capital	median	%	27.0	14.1
		3rd quartile		37.2	
		1st quartile		6.0	

(b)	$\dfrac{\text{Operating profit}}{\text{Sales}}$	median	%		9.3	5.2
		3rd quartile			41.6	
		1st quartile			6.2	
(c)	$\dfrac{\text{Marketing cost}}{\text{Sales}}$	median	%		8.6	9.4
		3rd quartile			10.9	
		1st quartile			15.2	
(d)	$\dfrac{\text{Sales}}{\text{Finished goods stock}}$	median	times		20.7	54.6
		3rd quartile			35.9	
		1st quartile			30.2	
(e)	$\dfrac{\text{Debtors}}{\text{Average daily sales}}$	median	days		33.5	42.8
		3rd quartile			35.4	
		1st quartile		£	170,000	
(f)	$\dfrac{\text{Sales}}{\text{Number of salesmen}}$	median	£	195,000		152,000
		3rd quartile		£	215,000	

11 THE INTERPRETATION OF CURRENT COST AND CURRENT PURCHASING POWER ACCOUNTS

11.1 Current cost accounts

In many ways, ratios based on current cost accounts (CCA) may provide more useful information than ratios based on historic cost accounts (HCA).

(a) CCA accounts reflect current asset values. This means that ROCE is not distorted by out of date asset values and the 'real' return can be seen. Inter-company comparisons based on CCA accounts are likely to be more accurate because they circumvent the problems caused by the use of the modified historical cost convention (ie, where some entities revalue fixed assets and others do not).

(b) CCA profits are stated after the operating capacity of the business has been maintained. This means that ratios based on CCA accounts normally give a more realistic picture of the 'true' performance of a company.

However, CCA accounts have some limitations and these should be borne in mind when interpreting ratios based on them.

(a) Valuation of assets is always subjective. In addition, it may be difficult to arrive at a current value for an asset which is unique or which is not traded in an active market. This subjectivity limits the usefulness of inter-company comparisons, especially comparisons between companies that do not operate in the same industry sector.

(b) CCA accounts show the effect of specific price changes, but not the effect of general inflation. Depreciation and cost of sales are restated, but general expenses, tax and interest are not. This should be taken into account when interpreting trends.

(c) The CCA profit and loss account is adjusted to reflect the effect of changes in monetary working capital and the effect of gearing. These adjustments have been criticised as being arbitrary and some experts believe that the gearing adjustment is not theoretically sound. This raises the question as to whether CCA earnings can be interpreted as 'real' earnings.

(d)   CCA profit is profit after maintaining the operating capacity of the business. This is not necessarily the 'real' return on shareholders' funds as this will also be affected by general inflation.

11.2   Current purchasing power accounts

Ratios based on current purchasing power accounts (CPP) may also provide useful information.

(a)   CPP accounts are adjusted for the general effect of inflation. This means that inter-temporal comparisons are more meaningful than those based on HCA information.

(b)   CPP takes account of both realised and unrealised holding gains and therefore earnings and ROCE can be said to represent the 'real' return on shareholders' funds.

(c)   CPP is more objective than CCA and therefore it can be argued that inter-company comparisons based on CPP accounts are more meaningful than those based on CCA and HCA information.

The main limitation of CPP is that it does not take account of specific price changes. This affects the interpretation of CPP accounts.

(a)   CPP earnings and the information in the CPP profit and loss account are not necessarily relevant to a manufacturing business. It is possible for a business to make a profit under CPP and yet not have maintained its physical operating capacity.

(b)   Asset values under CPP do not necessarily represent their current values or their value to the business. This means that ROCE and gearing may be distorted.

12   CHAPTER SUMMARY

Ratios are one means of analysing financial statements. Ratios can be grouped into categories: profitability, short-term financial stability and long-term financial stability, and investor ratios.

Ratios are only as good as the underlying information and this must therefore be considered as to its reliability and the degree to which it may have been manipulated.

13   SELF TEST QUESTIONS

13.1   What is horizontal analysis? (1.1)

13.2   What are the principal analytical ratios? (2.1)

13.3   How is the stock turnover ratio computed? (3.7)

13.4   What is the difference between the current ratio and the quick ratio? (4.1)

13.5   What is overtrading? (5.7)

13.6   What are the limitations of EPS as a measure of performance? (6.1)

13.7   What problems may ensue with the choice of a particular year end for a company? (7.2)

13.8   What ratios are comparable despite changing prices? (9.2)

13.9   What conditions are necessary for the implementation of an IFC scheme? (10.2)

14   EXAMINATION TYPE QUESTION

14.1   Wandafood Products

The following five year summary relates to Wandafood Products plc, and is based on financial statements prepared under the historic cost convention.

	19X9	*19X8*	*19X7*	*19X6*	*19X5*
Financial ratios					
Profitability					
Margin $\dfrac{\text{Trading profit}}{\text{Sales}}$ %	7.8	7.5	7.0	7.2	7.3
Return on assets $\dfrac{\text{Trading profit}}{\text{Net operating assets}}$ %	16.3	17.6	16.2	18.2	18.3
Interest and dividend cover					
Interest cover $\dfrac{\text{Trading profit}}{\text{Net finance charges}}$ times	2.9	4.8	5.1	6.5	3.6
Dividend cover					
$\dfrac{\text{Earnings per ordinary share}}{\text{Dividend per ordinary share}}$ times	2.7	2.6	2.1	2.5	3.1
Debt to equity ratios					
$\dfrac{\text{Net borrowings}}{\text{Shareholders funds}}$ %	65.9	61.3	48.3	10.8	36.5
$\dfrac{\text{Net borrowings}}{\text{Shareholders funds plus minority interests}}$	59.3	55.5	44.0	10.1	33.9
Liquidity ratios					
Quick $\dfrac{\text{Current assets less stock}}{\text{Current liabilities}}$ %	65.9	61.3	48.3	10.8	36.5
Current $\dfrac{\text{Current assets}}{\text{Current liabilities}}$ %	133.6	130.3	142.2	178.9	174.7
Asset ratios					
$\dfrac{\text{Sales}}{\text{Net operating assets}}$ times	2.1	2.4	2.3	2.5	2.5
$\dfrac{\text{Sales}}{\text{Working capital}}$ times	8.6	8.0	7.0	7.4	6.2
Per share					
Earnings per share ....p	15.65	13.60	10.98	11.32	12.18
Dividends per share ....p	5.90	5.40	4.90	4.60	4.10
Net assets per share ....p	102.10	89.22	85.95	85.79	78.11

Net operating assets include tangible fixed assets, stock, debtors and creditors. They exclude borrowings, taxation and dividends.

You are required to prepare a report on the company, clearly interpreting and evaluating the information given. Include comments on possible effects of price changes which may limit the quality of the report.

(30 marks)

(ACCA Advanced Accounting Practice June 1990)

15   ANSWER TO EXAMINATION TYPE QUESTION

15.1   Wandafood Products

(*Tutorial notes:*

(i)   A typical interpretation question with the 'chore' of calculating the ratios removed.

(ii)   Use the grouping of the ratios as a guide to the format of your report.

(iii)   Remember to avoid repeating the data given in the question and make sensible suggestions, including the need for more information.

(iv)   Make sure your answer includes comments on the effect of changing price levels on a 'trend analysis' of this type.)

REPORT

To: Directors - Wandafood Products plc

From: AN Alyst - Certified Accountant

Date: X-X-19XX

Subject: **Interpretation and evaluation of five year summary**

The following comments are based on a financial ratio analysis of the financial statements of Wandafood Products plc for the five year period 19X5 to 19X9. The ratios and their method of computation are contained in the appendix to this report.

(*Tutorial note:*

The appendix would contain the information given in the question.

The ratios have been 'grouped' to aid interpretation - this report follows the same structure.)

Profitability

The level of trading profit in relation to both sales and operating assets has remained relatively stable over the five year period. The profit margin percentage declined in the early years of this period but has improved steadily since 19X7, reaching its peak in 19X9. Management should attempt to discover the reason for this trend, eg cost savings or increased selling price, and endeavour to maintain it. However, the level of profitability is now requiring the highest relative level of net operating assets. Management should be encouraged to make the optimum use of the assets available, but it is possible that the significant drop (over 7%) from 19X8 to 19X9 is the result of the acquisition of new assets which have yet to generate a return.

Interest and dividend cover

The interest cover has been very variable over the five year period but does not appear to indicate any specific problem for the company. However, there is a constant downward trend from 19X6 and if this trend were to continue the company may find it difficult to raise finance from lenders who use such a ratio as an indicator of a company's ability to meet its interest payments. Probably of more interest to such a group is the level of cash available to make such payments, making the liquidity ratios of more relevance.

The dividend cover indicates that in recent years the amount of earnings retained in the business for capital maintenance and expansion has increased. This may be as a result of prudent management but the level of dividends must be maintained to give the owners (shareholders) a 'fair' return on their investment. This would be of particular interest to shareholders investing for periodic income not capital growth.

Debt to equity ratios

These ratios will be of interest to the lenders and shareholders considered in the previous section. The two ratios, one with and one without minority interests as part of equity, both follow the same pattern and the level of minority interests within the group has therefore probably been fairly constant.

These ratios, often referred to as 'gearing ratios' indicate that the relative amount of long term finance provided by borrowings is increasing. This would account for the declining trend in interest cover discussed earlier. The level of gearing has become higher such that 40% of long term finance was provided by borrowings in 19X9 compared with only 10% in 19X6. This may be as a result of taking advantage of 'cheaper' long finance but management should take care; the higher the gearing the riskier any investment in the company, particularly in periods of volatile profitability where fixed interest payments cannot be 'flexed' in line with the variable profit levels.

Liquidity ratios

These ratios are important indicators of the short term viability of the company. It is important to remember that companies often go into receivership because of cash problems rather than a lack of profitability.

At present the company has insufficient liquid or near liquid assets to meet its current liabilities. This may initially be considered to show a sign of weakness in the company but this position has existed since 19X6 and is therefore likely to currently be at an acceptable level. However, management must ensure that the position does not deteriorate. If it did the company may find itself unable to continue to operate.

Asset ratios

The ratio of sales to net operating assets shows a slight decline. As mentioned earlier this could be a result of increased investment in fixed assets but could also indicate falling relative sales. Management should ensure that any downtrend in 'real' sales levels is not allowed to continue.

The sales to working capital indicates a fall in the relative value of working capital. This is linked to the liquidity problem but indicates that there may be a more efficient use of the net current assets.

Per share

The three ratios indicate an improving earnings, dividends and net assets per share position. This may prove to be very useful if future long term funds are to be requested from equity investors, either new shareholders or from current shareholders by way of a rights issue. The ratio relating to net assets indicates that the company is perhaps financing additional assets by way of retained profits. The dividends per share have increased steadily which is a good management policy and the earnings per share have increased likewise.

Overall the position for shareholders looks favourable but it is necessary to consider these ratios in the light of the market prices of the shares during the five year period. This would enable the calculation of the Price/Earnings (P/E) ratio, considered to be a very useful market indicator. The use of the share price would put these 'per share' ratios into a proper perspective.

Concluding remarks

In relation to some of the points made in this report it is important that management consider the company's ratios in the light of those of other similar organisations. The company could consider participating in an inter-firm comparison scheme, which, while maintaining non-identification of participants, enables the comparison of the company's financial ratios with other similar companies and averages for that business sector.

Finally, the ratios used to compile this report have been calculated using information contained in financial statements prepared under the historic cost convention. It may be necessary to adjust some of the figures to reflect price level changes, particularly where one figure in the ratio is affected by inflation at a different rate to the other figure in the ratio. For example some assets may require adjustment by reference to a specific index of price level changes while another would be adjusted using a general price index. This could materially affect the trend indicated by a ratio. It is generally advisable to attempt to express all the figures in the financial statements for the five years in pounds at the same date, perhaps based on the retail price index.

23 REVISION OF AUDITING

INTRODUCTION & LEARNING OBJECTIVES

This chapter revises the basic aspects of auditing which you have covered at an earlier stage in your examinations. Some of the statements of auditing standards (SASs) introduced by the APB might however be new to you. They are covered at various stages in the remaining chapters.

When you have studied this chapter you should be able to do the following:

- Explain the basic principles involved in auditing.
- Outline the audit process, the regulatory framework of auditing, and the significance of audit evidence.

1 THE NATURE, PURPOSE AND SCOPE OF AN AUDIT

1.1 What is an audit?

An audit is the independent examination of evidence from which the financial statements of an enterprise are derived in order to give the reader of those statements confidence as to the truth and fairness of the state of affairs which they disclose.

The APB Glossary of terms defines an audit as:

Definition An exercise whose objective is to enable auditors to express an opinion whether the financial statements give a true and fair view of the entity's affairs at the period end and of its profit or loss for the period then ended and have been properly prepared in accordance with the applicable reporting framework.

The above definition is of necessity very broad because it encompasses the audit of any enterprise, not just that of a limited company. Unless specified in this text, the term audit is employed where it refers to an independent examination of the financial statements of an enterprise where such an examination is conducted with a view to expressing an opinion as to whether those statements give a true and fair view. The term true and fair view is a standard one used by auditors and which is derived from legislation. Section 236, Companies Act 1985 requires an auditor to state whether in his opinion the balance sheet and profit and loss account show a true and fair view without at any point explaining what is meant by true and fair view. As will be seen later, the accountancy profession has derived its own interpretation. Note for the moment that the auditor does not certify the financial statements but reports whether in his opinion they give a true and fair view.

1.2 The development of the modern audit

It was recognised many years ago that whenever a fiduciary relationship with financial implications existed there was a need for an outsider with sufficient independence and objectivity to review the accounts of stewardship and to express an opinion as to their honesty or otherwise. Modern auditing has developed since the concept of a company as a separate legal entity came into existence. This led to the separation of ownership from management and a consequent need to safeguard the interests of the owners (the shareholders), who in all but the smallest of businesses (where shareholders and directors were one and the same) were not involved in the day-to-day decisions made by the management. Directors must therefore be accountable for their actions to the shareholders on a regular basis. This accountability mainly occurs at the Annual General Meeting of a company in which the financial statements are formally presented to shareholders.

Increasingly the services of professional accountants were being sought and employed in the latter part of the nineteenth century and it was then that several professional accountancy bodies were formed. The Companies Act 1900 re-introduced the compulsory audit requirement, although the auditor was only expected to express an opinion on the balance sheet. However in the years preceding the Companies Act 1948, there were a number of cases which indicated the importance of the profit and loss account.

The Companies Act 1948 represented a major stepping stone in the development of the modern audit. For the first time, the auditor was required to express an opinion on the profit and loss account and the balance sheet, both of which should be presented to the shareholders at the annual general meeting. In addition, the Act required that auditors should possess a recognised professional qualification and detailed provisions were laid down regarding their duties, powers and responsibilities. Minimum disclosure levels were also laid down, together with the main objectives of the audit report.

The Companies Act 1948 together with subsequent Acts have been consolidated into the Companies Act 1985. This latter Act itself has been amended by the Companies Act 1989. The provisions of these Acts will be dealt with later in this text in so far as they affect the syllabus.

1.3   The detection of fraud and error

Following a judgement in 1859, stating that it was part of the appointed auditor's duties to discover fraudulent misrepresentations, the detection of fraud and error became the major objective of company audits. However, during the latter part of the nineteenth century, there was a growing school of thought that the prevention of fraud and error as opposed to its detection should be the major objective of the auditor, and that the management of a company should play a greater part and accept a larger degree of responsibility in this respect.

The leading case, which established the fact that the auditor should not be responsible for finding every fraud or error is the Kingston Cotton Mill case of 1896. Here the judgement pronounced that the auditor's role should be likened to that of a watchdog rather than a bloodhound, and that what was required of him was that he should act with such reasonable care and skill as was appropriate in the circumstances. Later cases confirmed this view of the auditor.

Obviously, with the growth of professionalism, the degree of care and skill expected of the auditor increased in the eyes of the public. The various accountancy bodies recognised this fact and sought by various means to improve the standard of auditing, as will be seen later.

There is no statutory duty to seek out fraud. The auditor's duty under statute is confined to expressing an opinion as to whether the financial statements under review show a true and fair view of the company's results and position. To discharge this duty, he must carry out such audit procedures as he thinks necessary in the light of the company's circumstances and of current auditing standards. Material discrepancies should be discovered as a result of normal audit procedures and of course the moral effect of an audit may itself act as a deterrent. The detection of error or fraud is not the main objective of the audit.

1.4   Objectives of the audit

The need for an audit centres around the requirements of the users. The financial statements account annually to the shareholders for the stewardship of the directors and the management. There are also many other outside parties who use the financial statements as a basis for making decisions regarding a company. Bankers, trade and loan creditors as well as potential investors and employees all have an interest in the state of the company's financial affairs. The independent audit requirement fulfils the need to ensure that those financial statements are objective, free from bias and manipulation and relevant to the needs of the users.

Since the late 1940s, the emphasis in approaching an audit has shifted from the detailed checking of individual items towards an overall review of the systems in operation followed by an examination of the records and the financial statements prepared therefrom. Amongst the reasons for the major shift of emphasis are:

(a)   the increasing size and complexity of modern enterprises;

(b)   the development of more accurate and sophisticated computerised systems;

(c)   the requirements that the auditor should also report on the profit and loss account which entails a review of all transactions during the period, not simply of year end balances as before.

1.5   The primary objectives

The primary audit objectives are derived from statute and fall under two main headings:

(a)   To express an expert and independent opinion upon the truth and fairness of the information contained in the financial statements.

Such information needs to be objective in that it should:

(i)   serve the informational needs and financial interests of the users, primarily the shareholders to whom the auditor's report is addressed;

(ii)   be produced on the basis of verifiable and objective evidence;

(iii)   be free from bias which could be detrimental to the prime users' needs and interests.

The information contained in the financial statements should conform to statutory requirements.

The bases and policies employed should be generally acceptable both to the accountancy profession and to the business community. In addition, they should be appropriate to the nature and circumstances of that particular business, and should be applied consistently from year to year.

(b)   To ascertain and evaluate the reliability of the accounting systems as the basis for the preparation of financial statements which give a true and fair view.

The aim of verifying the accuracy and reliability of the underlying records and documents (by examination and testing) is to obtain support for the expression of an opinion on the financial statements. To do this, the auditor must judge the suitability of the systems and the data produced as the basis for evaluating accounting information.

1.6   The secondary objectives

(a)   As an extension of the above primary objectives, the auditor should consider the possibility of fraud, errors and irregularities and their effect on the true and fair view given by the financial statements. This responsibility will be discharged by planning and carrying out the audit so as to have a reasonable expectation of detecting major mis-statements in the financial statements resulting from such irregularities.

(b)   A relatively recent development involves the provision of advice to clients. The auditor uses his knowledge of the client's affairs and his own knowledge based on experience to give recommendations on the system of internal control and on the efficiency of the accounting system, as well as advice on financial areas such as tax planning. The most common method of giving advice is through the Letter of Weakness (or Management Letter) which is concerned with the weaknesses in the system of internal control found during the course of the audit.

While service to the client in this area should be a very important by-product of the primary audit function, it is quite separate from the auditor's basic aim of supporting his opinion on the financial statements. There are no fixed provisions as regards the extent to which the auditor should give advice, although obviously where the situation is sufficiently serious, he has a duty to bring the matter to his client's attention, as well as taking it into account when writing his report to the shareholders.

1.7 The scope of an audit

Audit work can be performed in a variety of broad approaches.

(a) **Complete audits**

The audit work is undertaken and completed in a single period following the end of the company's financial year. This approach is likely to apply to small businesses where most of the audit evidence is obtained by verification of items in the books against documentary evidence.

(b) **Interim and final audits**

For larger clients the audit is often divided into two phases. The interim audit, performed during the financial year of the client, is primarily concerned with reviewing the accounting system of the enterprise. The final (or balance sheet) audit, which occurs after the year end, is mainly concerned with the verification of the financial statements. Many examination questions assume this distinct split in the audit work.

(c) **Continuous audits**

The audit is carried out continuously during the financial year of the client. Such an approach is only likely to apply to the largest of enterprises where the volume and complexity of the work are sufficient for members of the audit staff to be always present.

1.8 Other types of audit

The exam is almost entirely concerned with the external audit of a company. There are however other forms of auditing of which you should be aware.

Two broad divisions can be made:

(a) internal auditing
(b) public sector auditing.

1.9 Internal audit

An internal auditor is employed by the directors of a company to assist them in co-ordinating the performance of an organisation. In some cases the work involved may be similar to the work of an external auditor but it is often not restricted in this way. It may encompass an evaluation of the efficiency and effectiveness of managers for example.

1.10 Public sector auditing

Firms of accountants who spend most of their time carrying out external audits may also be employed in the audit of public sector organisations. If so, they will carry out their functions within the framework laid down by statute other than the Companies Act.

The statutory arrangements for auditing each of the elements of the public sector is shown below:

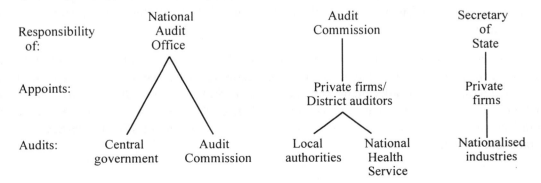

The Comptroller and Auditor General (C and AG) is head of the National Audit Office. As head of that office he has three main responsibilities:

(a)   control of issues and receipts of government funds;

(b)   regulatory audits of government departments; and

(c)   discretionary reviews (including VFM see below).

In carrying out these responsibilities the C and AG will examine, certify and report upon the appropriation accounts, (these being the main accounts of government departments).

The Audit Commission was set up under the Local Government Finance Act 1982 and its main responsibilities are noted below:

(a)   appointing auditors (after consultation with local authorities);

(b)   preparation and review of a code of audit practice;

(c)   direction of extraordinary audits;

(d)   undertaking comparative and other studies of economy, efficiency and effectiveness (see below); and

(e)   publication of an annual report on the discharge of its functions.

One of the many duties of a Minister (Secretary of State) would be to appoint private firms of accountants to undertake the audit of nationalised industries. The audit would be carried out in a similar fashion to that of large public limited companies (plc's) in the private sector, the similarity being that both nationalised industries and plcs are large organisations run on commercial lines.

1.11   Value for money (VFM)

In the public sector, particularly for local authorities, the traditional audit roles have been extended and now incorporate the concern for value for money (VFM). The Audit Commission has saved local authorities, and hence taxpayers, considerable sums of money through VFM audits.

VFM can simply be described as 'getting the best possible combination of services from the least resources' ie, to maximise the benefits available at the lowest cost to the taxpayer. It is generally taken to mean the pursuit of economy, efficiency and effectiveness.

In brief

'Economy' is a measure of inputs to achieve a certain service.
'Effectiveness' is a measure of outputs ie, services and facilities.
'Efficiency' is the optimum of economy and effectiveness ie, the measure of outputs over inputs.

2   THE REGULATORY FRAMEWORK OF AUDITING

2.1   Legislative influences

The auditor carries out his task because of legal obligations imposed upon companies to have an audit. As a consequence of this it is reasonable for 'the law' to frame statutes and regulations within which the auditor must work.

Governments, through various Companies Acts, have required auditors to express opinions on financial statements. They have also required auditors to be 'recognised' ie, government has given official recognition to individuals and members of professional bodies to carry out an audit. The detailed monitoring of the auditing profession by the government has been by the Department of Trade and Industry (DTI). The government minister responsible for the DTI is the Secretary of State for Trade and Industry.

More recently the European Community (EC) issued the Eighth Directive requiring more detailed regulations on the qualifications of auditors throughout the EC.

The Eighth Directive regulations have been included in the Companies Act 1989.

2.2   Qualification

An auditor must be

(a)   a member of a recognised supervisory body (RSB) and

(b)   eligible under the rules of the RSB.

The idea of RSBs was introduced by the Companies Act 1989.   In 1991 the Association was recognised as an RSB by the DTI.

The rules of the RSBs must ensure that the following persons only are eligible for appointment as company auditor

(a)   individuals who hold appropriate qualifications, and

(b)   firms controlled by qualified persons (note that an auditor may be an individual, a firm or a body corporate).

   The CA89 specifies that a firm will be 'controlled by' qualified persons if 51% of the ownership and control is in the hands of qualified persons.

The rules and practices of the RSBs must be such that two main criteria are satisfied:

(a)   only 'fit and proper' persons can be appointed as company auditors.   This takes into account their professional conduct (including their employees) and some of their associates (depending on the legal status of the applicant: body corporate, partnership or individual).   The ACCA application for registration enquires into a firm's financial integrity, disciplinary record and professional standing.

(b)   company audit work is conducted properly and with integrity.   This covers a number of areas:

   (i)   the standards of performing the audit, including compliance with Statements of Auditing Standards and related publications, and quality control procedures

   (ii)   general ethical standards that members will have to abide by covering rules such as professional integrity and independence

   (iii)   procedures to maintain competence (such as adequate recruitment, training and supervision)

   (iv)   procedures to ensure compliance, monitoring and enforcement.

An RSB's rule book must therefore cover:

(a)   monitoring and enforcement of compliance

(b)   admission of members and hence eligibility to audit

(c)   expulsion of members

(d)   disciplinary procedures (with appeals procedure)

(e)   complaints investigation.   This covers complaints against both the members and the RSB itself

(f)   adequacy of professional indemnity insurance cover.

The Association's 'Qualification and Audit Regulations' came into force in 1991, and are effectively the ACCA's rule book as an RSB.

It is possible that in monitoring compliance, the RSB could lay itself open to litigation relating to damages arising in respect of any action or omission following from the exercise of their statutory duties. Provided that such action or omission was not in 'bad faith' the Companies Act 1989 exempts RSBs from such damages.

Membership via qualification with a recognised qualifying body (RQB) is a pre-requisite of membership of an RSB (and hence entitlement to audit).

2.3 Auditing standards and guidelines

April 1980 saw the publication of the first Auditing Standards and Guidelines. Until April 1991 these documents were produced by the Auditing Practices Committee (APC) as a sub-committee of the Consultative Committee of Accountancy Bodies (CCAB).

The APC developed Auditing Standards and Guidelines on behalf of the members of the CCAB.

It was only when the document had been approved separately by each of the bodies that it could be issued. In effect each of the member bodies of the CCAB had an independent right of veto.

In April 1991 the APC was replaced by the Auditing Practices Board (APB), in a similar way to the Accounting Standards Board replacing the old ASC.

2.4 Statements of auditing standards

The APB was established in 1991 by the CCAB, to replace the old APC. In SAS 010 **The scope and authority of APB pronouncements,** issued in May 1993, the APB set out its objectives as being to advance standards of auditing, ensure public confidence in the auditing process and to meet the needs of users of financial statements.

In particular it will take an active role in the development of the regulation of the profession and will publish the principles and procedures with which auditors are required to comply, along with explanatory material to assist in interpretation. The main differences between it and its predecessor are that its non-practitioner members (academics, lawyers and industrialists) have voices on the board and that the board can issue standards in its own right (ie, CCAB members can no longer veto the issue of standards).

Published documents fall into three categories

(a)   **Statements of auditing standards (SASs)**

These contain the basic principles and essential procedures with which auditors are expected to comply, along with explanatory material. Failure to comply with standards may lead to regulatory action by the relevant accountancy body which might ultimately lead to the loss of audit registration (the right to conduct company audits). Standards are also taken into account in legal proceedings.

Standards show the extent to which compliance is achieved with International Standards on Auditing (as with Accounting standards) but UK standards prevail where there is a conflict.

(b)   **Practice notes (PNs)**

PNs give guidance to assist auditors in applying auditing standards in particular circumstances and industries. They are not examinable.

(c)   **Bulletins**

Bulletins provide auditors with timely guidance on new or emerging issues. They are not examinable.

The SASs which are examinable for this paper are listed at the front of this book.

2.5   Independence of auditors

This section of the ACCA Rules of professional conduct deals with independence in an audit context.

The Rules stress that a member's objectivity must be beyond question if he is to report as auditor. That objectivity can only be assured if the member *is*, and *is seen to be* independent.

This basic principle is then followed by discussion and illustration in a number of identified areas of risk. The most important areas of risk are considered in more detail below.

2.6   Integrity, objectivity and independence - areas of risk

(a)   **Undue dependence on an audit client**

It is recognised that a dependence on income from a particular client may impair objectivity. A firm which derives most of its income from one client for instance might find it difficult to make a stand on a particular issue as the loss of that client (either through the auditor's removal or his resignation) would have a disastrous effect on the firm's financial position.

It is therefore recommended that recurring fees paid by one client or group of connected clients should not exceed 15% of the gross practice income (this requirement is relaxed for those years when a practice is being established or wound down).

However, where the public interest is involved (for example in the case of listed and other public interest companies) the appropriate figure should be 10% of the gross practice income.

(b)   **Family and other personal relationships**

Problems may arise where:

(i)   a practice or anyone closely connected with it has a mutual business interest with a client, or with an officer or employee of a client;

(ii)   an officer or employee is closely connected with a partner or member of staff.

The following persons would normally be regarded as being closely connected with a *person:*

(i)   spouse;
(ii)   minor children (including stepchildren);
(iii)   a company in which he has a $\geq 20\%$ interest.

The following persons should normally be regarded as being closely connected with a *practice*:

(i)   a partner or, in the case of a corporate practice, a director or shareholder;
(ii)   a person closely connected with (i) above;
(iii)   an employee of the practice.

These categories are not exhaustive. For example, persons not related in any way by blood or marriage, may nevertheless enjoy a friendship closer than any blood relationship. The auditor must always bear in mind the need to maintain not merely independence but also the manifest appearance of independence.

The threat to independence may be less where a partner or senior member of staff is not personally engaged on the audit in question, where his or her office is distant from the reporting office and where effective safeguards are in place in the internal procedures of the practice. Such safeguards might include rotation of the engagement partner and/or of senior members of staff. Similarly, a connection with a junior member of staff of the practice is less likely to be a threat than a connection with a senior member of staff or partner.

A member should not personally take part in the conduct of the audit of a company if he or she has, during the period upon which the report is to be made, or at any time in the two years prior to the first day thereof been an officer (other than auditor) or employee of that company.

(c) Beneficial interests in shares and other investments

A practice should ensure that it does not have as an audit client a company in which a partner or anyone closely connected with a partner has a beneficial interest, nor should it employ on the audit a member of staff if that member of staff, or a person closely connected with him has a beneficial interest.

(d) Loans

Again, independence may be threatened.

A practice or anyone closely connected with it should not, either directly or indirectly, or by way of a trust or other intermediary:

(i) make a loan to or guarantee borrowings by an audit client;

(ii) accept a loan from such a client; or

(iii) have borrowings or other obligations guaranteed by such a client.

(e) Goods and services: hospitality

Objectivity may be threatened or appear to be threatened by acceptance of goods, services or hospitality from an audit client.

(f) Provision of other services to audit clients

There is no objection in principle to this but care must be taken not to perform management functions or to make management decisions.

Accountancy work, however, should not be performed for a public company except in relation to assistance of a routine clerical nature or in emergency situations. Such assistance might include, for example, work on the finalisation of statutory accounts, including consolidations and tax provisions. The scale and nature of such work should be regularly reviewed.

(g) Actual or threatened litigation

Objectivity may be threatened (or appear to be) where there is actual or threatened litigation between an auditor and his client. The adversarial position would call into question the auditor's ability to report fairly and impartially on the company's accounts. In an action, under the circumstances, management may be unwilling to disclose relevant information to the auditor.

3 FUNDAMENTAL PRINCIPLES AND CONCEPTS WHICH AFFECT AUDITING

3.1 SAS 100: Objective and general principles governing an audit of financial statements

Auditing standards

100.1 The auditor is required to:

(a) obtain sufficient appropriate evidence in accordance with SASs to determine if the financial statements are free of material misstatement and are prepared in accordance with relevant legislation and Accounting Standards;

(b) issue a report containing a clear expression of his opinion.

100.2   Auditors are required to comply with all ethical guidance issued by their relevant professional body.

3.2   Materiality

As can be seen from the above standard, materiality is a fundamental concept.

Materiality is defined in the APB Glossary of terms as follows:

[Definition]   Materiality is an expression of the relative significance or importance of a particular matter in the context of financial statements as a whole. A matter is material if its omission or misstatement would reasonably influence the decisions of an addressee of the auditors' report.

3.3   Audit tests to determine whether an item is material

The problem is which particular tests the auditor should apply in coming to his decision as to whether an item is, or is not, material. The following are the important points that must be taken into consideration:

(a)   An item is material if knowledge of it would be likely to influence the user of the financial statements.

(b)   Materiality is a relative factor and should be considered in relative terms. £1,000 may be absolutely immaterial in the accounts of a large company, whereas in a small undertaking the reverse would probably be true. Further, under this heading the item must be considered in relation to:

(i)   The accounts as a whole.

(ii)   The total of which it would form part.

(iii)   The corresponding amount in previous years.

(c)   The degree of latitude allowable in deciding on the amount attributable to a particular item. Some items, such as directors' fees, are capable of exact definition; others, such as depreciation and provisions for obsolete or damaged stock, are at best an intelligent estimate. The overriding consideration must be whether the accounts disclose a true and fair view.

The following is a list of items likely to affect the auditor's decision as to the material importance or otherwise of an item:

(a)   **Degree of approximation.** The degree of estimation which is unavoidably inherent in arriving at the amount of an item may be a factor in deciding on materiality eg, contingent provisions, stock and work-in-progress, and taxation provisions.

(b)   **Losses or low profits.** The use of the profit figure for comparison tends to be vitiated when the profits are abnormally low or where there is a loss; when judging the materiality of items in the profit and loss account in such cases, the more normal dimensions of the business have to be considered.

(c)   **Critical points.** The view given by accounts may sometimes be affected by the trend of profit or turnover and of various expense items. An inaccuracy which might not otherwise be judged to be material could have the effect of reversing a trend or turning a profit into a loss, or of creating or eliminating the margin of solvency in a balance sheet. When an item affects such a critical point in the accounts, then its materiality has to be viewed in that narrower context.

(d)   **Disproportionate significance.** An item of small amount may nevertheless be of material significance in the context of a company's particular circumstances, especially if the context would lead the reader to expect the item to be of substantial amount.

    (e)   **Offset and aggregation.** It frequently happens that two items, which might each be material taken separately, will be of opposite effect. Care should be taken in offsetting such items. For example, a profit arising as a result of a change in the basis of accounting should not be offset against a non-recurring loss. It may also be necessary where there is a large number of small items for them to be aggregated to ascertain if they are material in total.

Just as materiality should be constantly in mind when carrying out every part of an audit assignment eg, in assessing the possible monetary effect of errors or frauds caused by a weakness in internal control or the need to verify assets held in Fiji owned by an international company, so it is important to bear materiality in mind in answering examination questions on auditing.

3.4   SAS 220: Materiality and the audit

220.1   Auditors are required to consider materiality and its relationship with audit risk when conducting an audit.

The concept of audit risk is explained in the next chapter. What you should appreciate here is that auditors should plan and perform the audit to be able to provide reasonable assurance that the financial statements are free of material misstatement. The assessment of what is material is a matter of professional judgement. The amount (quantity) and nature (quality) of misstatements need to be considered.

The possibility of small errors should be considered cumulatively.

As regards qualitative aspects, these are concerned with inadequate descriptions or information contained within the financial statements.

Materiality should be considered at both the overall financial statements level and in relation to an individual account balance.

Materiality and audit work

220.2   Auditors are required to consider materiality when determining the nature, timing and extent of audit procedures.

If factors are identified which result in the revision of their preliminary materiality assessment the auditors should consider the implications for their audit approach and, if necessary, modify the nature, timing and extent of planned audit procedures.

220.3   In evaluating whether the financial statements give a true and fair view, auditors should assess the materiality of the aggregate of uncorrected misstatements.

3.5   Concept of truth and fairness

In SAS 100 the auditor's 'clear expression' is on whether the accounts are true and fair. The term true and fair was first used in the CA48. However, a number of preceding Acts had used similar phrases.

The original Joint Stock Act 1844 (the first Companies Act) required companies to present a full and fair balance sheet, though the meaning of this phrase was never defined.

In the 1844 Act a company was required to keep full and true accounts. By the 1900 Act the auditor was required to state whether the balance sheet was properly drawn up so as to exhibit a true and correct view. This phrase was retained through the 1929 Act, and only modified to true and fair in the 1948 Act.

At no stage has any statutory definition of the meaning of these terms been provided.

3.6   Meaning of true and fair

Truth in accounting is quite different from scientific truth. Accounting does not deal with that type of truth which has a fixed and unchanging quality. Costs and revenues for any accounting period which is less than the full life of each venture involved cannot be determined with precision. In accounting only cash draws close to the concept of scientific truth, but since the value of cash changes with time, it lacks total correspondence with the precision of scientific truth.

The word fair can have the following meanings: on the one hand clear, distinct and plain, and on the other impartial, just and equitable. All can be considered relevant when fair is used in an accounting context.

The auditor should attempt to ensure that the accounts which are the subject of his audit present clearly and equitably the financial state of affairs of the enterprise. This suggests that in order to achieve the statutory true and fair view it is necessary not only to present certain information impartially but also that this data is shown in such a way that it is clearly understood by the user.

3.7   Attempts at definition of the true and fair view

The following quotations represent authoritative views on the meaning of true and fair view.

A true and fair view implies that all statutory and other information is not only available but is presented in a form in which it can be properly and readily appreciated. (Sir Russell Kettle)

A true and fair view implies appropriate classification and grouping of items... (and) consistent application of generally accepted principles. (The Institute of Chartered Accountants in Australia - Recommendations on Accounting Principles 1964)

...the meaning attached to (the words true and fair) has been built up over the years by standards of presentation specifically required by the Act; established accounting techniques; case law decisions; the natural desire of responsible directors of companies and auditors to ensure that the facts and figures which are presented to the public properly reflect the position; and last but not least common sense. (Sir Henry Benson in 1962)

For an auditor to be able to say that a financial statement is true and fair it must be:

(1)   relevant to the business transactions etc, it purports to describe.

(2)   objective, being free from any bias ... and being based on unprejudiced and verifiable evidence which is capable of supporting it. (Lee)

... true and fair has become a term of art. It is generally understood to mean a presentation of accounts drawn up according to accepted accounting principles using accurate figures as far as possible and reasonable estimates otherwise, and arranging them so as to show within the limits of current accounting practice as objective a picture as possible free from wilful bias, distortion, manipulation or concealment of material facts. (Lee)

It must be concluded that there has been little success in defining true and fair. JG Chastney in his report for the Research Committee of the ICAEW (True and fair view - history, meaning and the impact of the 4th Directive) found similar difficulties and concluded the term is almost impossible to define.

3.8   Activity

Attempt to write down a brief summary of the meaning of true and fair.

3.9   Activity solution

There is no statutory or professional definition of true and fair.

True and fair is a technical term and the phrase must be looked at as an entirety.

To show a true and fair view accounts must be prepared:

(a)   in accordance with generally accepted principles.

(b)   on a consistent basis.

(c)   so as not to be misleading.

4   THE NATURE OF THE AUDIT PROCESS

4.1   Alternative approaches to an audit

In order to achieve the audit objectives, evidence is required. In practice there are two main ways this evidence is acquired.

(a)   **Systems approach**

The evaluation of **internal control** forms the basis of the audit. Detailed testing of items in the financial statements is kept to a minimum.

(b)   **Direct verification approach**

More detailed testing of items in the financial statements is carried out. The opinion is based upon the ability of the auditor to obtain relevant and reliable evidence from a number of sources.

In most situations the systems based approach is used as it is the most efficient method of arriving at an audit opinion.

4.2   Risk-based audit

The risk-based audit is a development of the systems based audit. It is increasingly used by auditors in order to concentrate on high risk clients and on high risk areas of a client's business rather than perform detailed audit tests on all areas of a client's business. It enables a cost effective audit to be achieved.

The auditor aims to ensure that there is no more than a 5% risk that his opinion on the financial statements is incorrect.   Or, in other words, he is ensuring that he is 95% certain that his opinion on the financial statements is correct. (Audit confidence is measured here as 100% minus audit risk). The percentage used (ie, 95%) is one of convention only. It implies (correctly) that we can never be 100% sure of any conclusion.

The elements of audit risk are considered later.

5   THE IMPORTANCE OF AUDIT EVIDENCE

5.1   Introduction

The APB Glossary of terms defines audit evidence as follows:

Definition   Audit evidence is the information auditors obtain in arriving at the conclusions on which their report is based. Audit evidence comprises source documents and accounting records underlying the financial statement assertions and corroborative information from other sources.

Financial statement assertions are looked at in detail later in this text. They are the representations of the directors that are embodied in the financial statements.

The APB has issued SAS 400 to give guidance on the quantity and quality of evidence that auditors must collect before expressing their opinion.

5.2   SAS 400: Audit evidence

Auditing standards

400.1   Auditors should obtain sufficient appropriate audit evidence to be able to draw reasonable conclusions on which to base the audit opinion.

400.2   In seeking to obtain audit evidence from tests of control, auditors should consider the sufficiency and appropriateness of the audit evidence to support the assessed level of control risk.

400.3   In seeking to obtain audit evidence from substantive procedures, auditors should consider the extent to which that evidence together with any evidence from tests of controls supports the relevant financial statement assertions.

5.3   Applying SAS 400 in practice

The audit is an expression of opinion. However, it is the opinion of an expert. As such it should have been formed after gathering and examining appropriate evidence. Unfortunately there is no set way that evidence can be measured, and the auditor needs to use his professional judgement to decide on how much evidence he needs to form an opinion.

The auditor will be influenced by:

(a)   the materiality of the matter being examined. The more material the matter is, the more evidence the auditor will wish to have.

(b)   the relevance and reliability of evidence. The more relevant and reliable the evidence is, the less the auditor will need.

(c)   the cost and time involved in obtaining the evidence. If the auditor has two pieces of evidence to choose from, he will gather the one which takes less time to obtain. Remember the audit should be as efficient and cost effective as possible.

5.4   Sufficiency of evidence

The auditor can rarely be certain of the validity of the financial statements. However, he needs to obtain sufficient relevant and reliable evidence to form a reasonable basis for his opinion thereon. The auditor's judgement as to what constitutes sufficient relevant and reliable audit evidence is influenced by such factors as:

(a)   his knowledge of the business of the enterprise and the industry in which it operates;

(b)   the degree of risk of misstatement through errors or irregularities; this risk may be affected by such factors as:

   (i)   the nature and materiality of the items in the financial statements;

   (ii)   the auditor's experience as to the reliability of the management and staff of the enterprise and of its records;

5.5   Relevance of evidence

The relevance of the audit evidence should be considered in relation to the overall audit objective of forming an opinion and reporting on the financial statements. To achieve this objective the auditor needs to obtain evidence to enable him to draw reasonable conclusions in answer to the following questions.

Balance sheet items

(a)   Have all of the assets and liabilities been recorded?

(b)   Do the recorded assets and liabilities exist?

(c)   Are the assets owned by the enterprise and are the liabilities properly those of the enterprise?

(d)   Have the amounts attributed to the assets and liabilities been arrived at in accordance with the stated accounting policies, on an acceptable and consistent basis?

(e)   Have the assets, liabilities and capital and reserves been properly disclosed?

Profit and loss account items

(f)   Have all income and expenses been recorded?

(g)   Did the recorded income and expense transactions in fact occur?

(h)   Have the income and expenses been measured in accordance with the stated accounting policies, on an acceptable and consistent basis?

(i)   Have income and expenses been properly disclosed where appropriate?

Tests should be relevant to the financial statements. The financial statements consist of the balance sheet, profit and loss account, cash flow statement and statement of total recognised gains and losses, together with notes and other statements and explanatory material, all of which are identified in the auditors' report as being the financial statements.

5.6   Reliability of evidence

Although the reliability of audit evidence is dependent upon the particular circumstances, the following general presumptions may be found helpful:

(a)   documentary evidence is more reliable than oral evidence;

(b)   evidence obtained from independent sources outside the enterprise is more reliable than that secured solely from within the enterprise;

(c)   evidence originated by the auditor by such means as analysis and physical inspection is more reliable than evidence obtained from others.

The auditor should consider whether the conclusions drawn from differing types of evidence are consistent with one another. When audit evidence obtained from one source appears inconsistent with that obtained from another, the reliability of each remains in doubt until further work has been done to resolve the inconsistency. However, when the individual items of evidence relating to a particular matter are all consistent, then the auditor may obtain a cumulative degree of assurance higher than that which he obtains from the individual items.

5.7   Techniques of audit testing

Techniques of audit testing in order to obtain audit evidence fall into the following broad categories:

(a)   **Inspection**

Reviewing or examining records, documents or tangible assets. Inspection of records and documents provides evidence of varying degrees of reliability depending upon their nature and source. Inspection of tangible assets provides the auditor with reliable evidence as to their existence, but not necessarily as to their ownership, cost or value.

(b)   **Observation**

Looking at an operation or procedure being performed by others with a view to determining the manner of its performance. Observation provides reliable evidence as to the manner of the performance at the time of observation, but not at any other time.

(c)   **Enquiry and confirmation**

Seeking relevant information from knowledgeable persons inside or outside the enterprise, whether formally or informally, orally or in writing. The degree of reliability that the auditor attaches to evidence obtained in this manner is dependent on his opinion of the competence, experience, independence and integrity of the respondent.

(d)   **Computation**

Checking the arithmetical accuracy of accounting records or performing independent calculations.

(e)   **Analytical procedures**

The analysis of relationships between items of financial and/or non-financial data to identify predicted patterns or unexpected relationships. Analytical procedures are important enough to warrant their own auditing standard, SAS 410, covered later in this text.

The five techniques may be used for both tests of control and substantive testing. Note carefully the meaning of these techniques and their limitations.

5.8   Activity

Give your opinion as to the nature and reliability of each of the following techniques of providing audit evidence and give an example of each.

(a)   Inspection
(b)   Observation
(c)   Enquiry

5.9   Activity solution

(i)   **Inspection** - this covers the physical review or examination of records, documents and tangible assets. The reliability of this technique depends on the nature of the evidence and additional work may be required to determine ownership, valuation and contractual obligations. An example is examining copy sales invoices for authorisation.

(ii)   **Observation** - this technique involves looking at an operation or procedure being performed by others with a view to determining the manner of its performance. However, this observation may not be typical of the usual conduct of the operation or procedure. An example is the distribution of wage packets to see that internal control procedures are adhered to.

(iii)   **Enquiry** - seeking relevant information from knowledgeable persons inside or outside the enterprise, whether formally or informally, orally or in writing. The reliability of this technique depends on the qualification and integrity of the source. An example is the seeking of formal representations from management on the value of a material subsidiary company in an overseas country. A further example is the circularisation of debtors for independent verification of year-end balances.

6   REVISION OF AUDIT GUIDELINES

6.1   Introduction

Several APC Auditing Guidelines remain examinable because no new mandatory guidance has yet emerged from the APB, and you are expected to know the contents of these Guidelines, namely:

> 401   Bank reports for audit purposes
> 405   Attendance at stocktaking

The above Guidelines are described here. In addition Guidelines 308, 407 and 506 are covered elsewhere in this text.

6.2   Bank reports (Auditing Guideline 401)

The obtaining of the bank certificate is an *essential* part of the audit and is recommended in Auditing Guideline 401 'Bank reports for audit purposes'. In order to assist the banks in the administration of the letters, a standard request letter has been agreed with the clearing banks. The form of the standard letter was revised by Practice Note 16, but this is not examinable at this paper. The procedure for sending out the standard letter is set out below.

Procedure

Auditors should adopt the following procedures in connection with requests to banks for audit purposes:

(a)   The standard letter set out in the Appendix to the guideline should be sent in duplicate on each occasion by the auditor on his own notepaper to the manager of each bank branch with which it is known that the client holds an account or has dealt with since the end of the previous accounting period.

(b)   Auditors should ensure that the bank receives the client's authority to permit disclosure. The clearing banks state that this authority must be evidenced by either:

    (i)   the client's countersignature to the standard letter; or

    (ii)   a specific authority contained in an accompanying letter; or

    (iii)   a reference in the standard letter to the client's specific written authority given on a specified earlier date, which remains in force.

(c)   Wherever possible, the letter should reach the branch manager at least two weeks in advance of the date of the client's financial year end. Special arrangements should be made with the bank if, because of time constraints, a reply is needed within a few days.

(d)   The dates to be entered on the standard letter are normally the closing dates of:

    (i)   the client's accounting period for which the report is requested; and

    (ii)   the client's previous accounting period for which a full bank report was compiled (if, exceptionally, audited accounts are produced other than for an accounting period, alternative dates should be substituted).

(e)   In reviewing the bank's reply it is important for auditors to check that the bank has answered all questions in full.

(f)   Auditors will need to check the authenticity of any letters not received directly from the bank branch concerned. If an auditor receives a bank report without having made a previous request, he should check with the branch concerned that the report has been prepared in compliance with the terms of the standard letter.

6.3   Attendance at stocktaking (Auditing Guideline 405)

The overall purpose of the auditor's attendance is to assess the effectiveness of the client's stocktaking procedures. There are three aspects of the auditor's duties, covering the times before, during and after the stocktaking.

Before the stocktaking

The auditor should carry out the following:

(a)   review prior year's working papers;

(b)   familiarise himself with the nature, volume and location of stocks;

(c)   consider controlling and recording procedures over stock;

(d)   identify problem areas in relation to the system of internal control;

(e)   decide whether reliance can be placed on internal auditors;

(f)   if stock held by third parties is material, or the third party is insufficiently independent or reliable, then arrange a stocktake attendance at the third party's premises;

(g)   otherwise, arrange third party confirmation;

(h)   if the nature of the stocks is specialised then he will need to arrange expert help or to review the client's own arrangements.

(i)   examine the client's stocktaking instructions: if found to be inadequate, the matter should be discussed with the client with a view to improving them prior to the stocktake.

During the stocktaking

The main task is to ensure that the client's staff are carrying out their duties effectively. The auditor should:

(a)   Make two-way test counts from factory floor to stock sheets, and from stock sheets to factory floor.

(b)   Make notes of items counted, damaged stock, instances where the stocktaking procedures are not being followed.

(c)   Examine and test control over the stock sheets. The client should keep a stock sheet register.

(d)   Examine cut-off procedures (see below).

(e)   Pay particular attention to goods held on behalf of third parties (for example, goods on consignment).

(f)   Reach a conclusion as to whether or not the stocktaking was satisfactory, and hence provides reliable evidence supporting the final stock figure.

After the stocktaking

The auditor should check cut-off details, review the final stock sheets and follow up test counts and queries. He should also ensure that any continuous stock records have been adjusted or reconciled to the physical count and all differences investigated.

Cut-off

Whatever the nature of the business the effectiveness of the auditor's work in this connection must depend largely on the system of internal control exercised over the movements of stock, and the recording of the relevant transactions in the books. For this purpose the auditor should examine the link between purchases records and stocks and between sales records and stocks, to ensure that there is complete accord between the physical stock brought into account, the records of the physical movements of the stock and the financial records of purchases and sales, debtors and creditors. This is known as 'cut-off' procedure. Also note that the same term may encompass the recording of cash in the correct accounting period.

Tests the auditor would carry out to ensure correct cut-off include the following.

(a)   During stocktake attendance note the serial numbers of the last sales invoice, despatch note and goods received note generated before the stocktake.

(b)   Check the year-end despatch notes to sales invoices and vice versa to ensure that despatches and the related invoice fall either both before or both after the year end.

(c)   Similarly for purchases, ensure year-end goods receipts notes and related purchase invoices are correctly treated.

(d)   Check documentation giving rise to internal movements of stock and ensure correct classification as raw materials, work in progress and finished goods.

7   CHAPTER SUMMARY

An audit has primary and secondary objectives. The audit is carried on within a largely self-regulatory framework set by the professional accounting bodies. There are various broad approaches that can be taken in the audit process. A system based audit has developed a risk based approach in recent years.

8   SELF TEST QUESTIONS

8.1   What is the definition of an audit? (1.1)

8.2   What case established that the auditor should not be responsible for finding every fraud and error? (1.3)

8.3   What are the two primary objectives of an audit? (1.5)

8.4   What does RSB mean? (2.2)

8.5   What is a PN? (2.4)

8.6   SAS 100 requires what? (3.1)

8.7   What audit tests can be carried out to determine whether an item is material? (3.3)

8.8   State five categories of audit testing techniques. (5.7)

9   EXAMINATION TYPE QUESTION

9.1   Stages of an audit

(a)   Outline the basic stages of an audit.   **(10 marks)**
(b)   What do you understand by the concept of materiality in relation to an audit?   **(10 marks)**
                                                                    (Total: 20 marks)

10   ANSWER TO EXAMINATION TYPE QUESTION

10.1   Stages of an audit

(a)   The planning of the audit:

(i)   ascertain the nature and constitution of the enterprise;

(ii)   send a letter of engagement, stating clearly the duties of the auditor;

(iii)   consider and timetable the work which is seen to be required.

Ascertain and assess the accounting system.

Consider the ways in which sufficient, relevant and reliable audit evidence can be obtained.

Ascertain, evaluate and test the adequacy of controls within the accounting system of the enterprise.

Carry out tests on transactions within the accounting records.

Verify the existence and values of assets, liabilities and capital in the balance sheet.

Confirm that income and expenditure in the profit and loss account accurately reflect the operations of the business.

Examine the financial statements for compliance with relevant statutes and accounting standards.

Review the financial statements as a whole.

Decide the wording and draft the auditors' report.

(b)   It is the auditor's chief duty to express an opinion as to whether or not the accounts which he audits show a true and fair view. By its very nature the true and fair view concept is a general one and the auditor is often faced with deciding if a particular error or omission is so fundamental that the accounts do not show a true and fair view.

The APB Glossary of terms give guidance in this area by stating that a matter is material if its omission or misstatement would reasonably influence the decisions of an addressee of the auditors' report. This definition is amplified in SAS 220 where specific guidance is given in particular circumstances.

Before an auditor qualifies the accounts under his scrutiny he must, therefore, consider whether or not the points on which he is unsatisfied are material or not. To do this, the following points must be considered:

(a)   Is the item so fundamental that the accounts can no longer be said to show a true and fair view?

(b)   Materiality is a relative factor and the item must be considered in relation to the accounts as a whole, the total of which it would form part and the corresponding amount in the previous years.

(c)   Some items are capable of exact calculation. Others such as depreciation are merely estimated and, providing the estimate is reasonable, should be acceptable.

Under the *Companies Act 1985* the disclosure of certain items depends upon whether or not they are material eg, amount of contingent liabilities, capital commitments, transfer to reserves.   Other items, however, are specifically required to be shown eg, directors' emoluments and the audit fee. If these are incorrect, the items must be material since the accounts will not then comply with the *Companies Act.*

In conclusion, therefore, an auditor must take into account the degree of approximation necessary in calculating a particular item, the size of the company and the level of its profits and its significance in relation to the company as a whole. Then the basic question to be answered is 'Does the mis-statement or omission of this item impair the true and fair view principle?'

24 AUDIT RISK AND AUDIT SAMPLING

INTRODUCTION & LEARNING OBJECTIVES

This chapter concentrates on the planning of an audit. A fair amount of the chapter should be revision to you except perhaps for the emphasis on a 'risk' based approach to auditing. It is to be expected that the examiner will stress the risk based approach in his questions.

Planning and administering the audit represent tasks performed by the audit manager and partner and are thus more likely to be examined in this paper which is seeking to test 'advanced auditing'.

The principles and techniques of sampling are also covered.

The ability to draw valid conclusions from testing a sample of business transactions is a vital requirement in order to control the costs of an audit. Clearly if valid assumptions are to be drawn, the auditor will need to plan carefully his sample size and the techniques used to select that sample.

When you have studied this chapter you should be able to do the following:

- Explain the principles of audit risk and its constituent elements.
- Explain the use of audit sampling in the conduct of an audit.

1 ADVANCED ASPECTS OF AUDIT PLANNING

1.1 Managing the audit client

The chart below illustrates the main stages in the planning process of a 'modern' audit ie, one which takes a risk based approach.

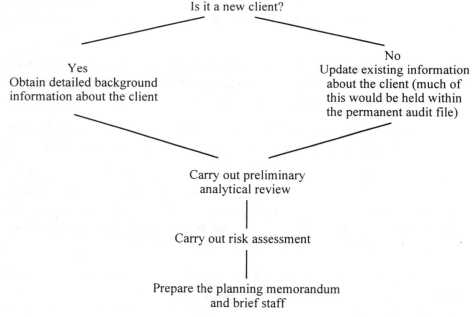

Is it a new client?

Yes
Obtain detailed background
information about the client

No
Update existing information
about the client (much of
this would be held within
the permanent audit file)

Carry out preliminary
analytical review

Carry out risk assessment

Prepare the planning memorandum
and brief staff

1.2 Obtaining information about the client

At the start of the planning process it is vital that the auditor has a detailed understanding of the client's business. Clearly, if it is a new client more time will be spent obtaining this knowledge.

The most important source of this information is obviously the client. As well as arranging a meeting the auditor will also want to obtain copies of management accounts, budgets, forecasts and board minutes.

The requirement to obtain knowledge of the business is contained in SAS 210. The requirements are stated in the next section.

1.3   Preliminary analytical review

Once the information above has been obtained the auditor can carry out the preliminary analytical review. This would involve calculating key ratios and comparing current year results (which may only be available in the form of budgets and/or management accounts) with previous years.

The main purpose of such a review is to identify risk areas of the audit. For example, a significant and unexpected change in a gross profit percentage could indicate a material error in sales or cost of sales (including stock).

Analytical review is covered in detail later in this text.

1.4   Risk assessment

Once the auditor understands the client's business and is familiar with the numbers he can move onto the most important stage - risk assessment.

This is the area within planning that is perhaps most likely to be examined. SAS 300 covers this area; the requirements are stated below.

1.5   The planning memorandum

The preparation of a planning memorandum setting out the outline audit approach is a procedure adopted by most firms. Most practising firms have formalised the planning exercise for all but the very small audit assignment by using a standard planning memorandum. An example is shown in section 4.

2   RELEVANT SASs

2.1   SAS 210: Knowledge of the business

The content of this SAS makes previous good practice mandatory. It deals with the knowledge of the business both prior to accepting appointment and following acceptance.

2.2   Auditing standards

210.1   Auditors should have or obtain a knowledge of the business of the entity to be audited sufficient to enable them to identify and understand the events, transactions and practices that may have a significant effect on the financial statements or the audit thereof.

210.2   The audit engagement partner should ensure that the audit team obtains such knowledge of the business of the entity being audited as may reasonably be expected to be sufficient to enable it to carry out the audit work effectively.

Prior to acceptance of an engagement, the auditors should obtain a preliminary knowledge of the industry and of the ownership, management and operations of the entity to be audited, sufficient to enable them to consider their ability and willingness to undertake the audit.

Following acceptance of an engagement, the auditors should obtain further and more detailed knowledge and information sufficient to enable them to plan the audit and develop an effective audit approach.

In succeeding periods, the auditors should consider the information gathered previously and should perform procedures designed to identify significant changes that have taken place since the last audit.

2.3   SAS 140: Engagement letters

The guidance notes accompanying SAS 140 state that the SAS is intended for audit engagements and notes that auditors often prepare separate letters for services such as tax and accounting. The notes specifically state that an engagement for the provision of 'investment business' advice would ordinarily require a separate letter.

2.4   Auditing standards

140.1   The auditors and the client should agree on the terms of the engagement, which should be recorded in writing.

140.2   Auditors should agree the terms of their engagement with new clients in writing. Thereafter auditors should regularly review the terms of engagement and if appropriate agree any updating in writing.

140.3   Auditors who, before the completion of the audit, are requested to change the engagement to one which provides a different level of assurance, should consider the appropriateness of so doing. If auditors consider that it is appropriate to change the terms of engagement, they should obtain written agreement to the revised terms.

140.4   Auditors should ensure that the engagement letter documents and confirms their acceptance of the appointment, and includes a summary of the responsibilities of the directors and of the auditors, the scope of the engagement and the form of any reports.

2.5   Recurring audits

It is not necessary to agree a new engagement letter each year, although it may be appropriate to remind the client of the original letter. Where there have been any changes or any indication of misunderstanding, it may be appropriate to produce a new letter.

2.6   Audit of components

The guidance notes give points to consider when deciding whether or not to agree a separate engagement letter with a subsidiary, branch or division where they are their auditors as well as being the auditor of the parent entity.

3   AUDIT RISK

3.1   The logic of assessing audit risk

Audit risk could be defined as the risk that the auditor gets it wrong! More technically, it is the risk that either he fails to qualify when there is a material mis-statement in the financial statements or possibly that he qualifies when it was not necessary. Some level of audit risk will have to be accepted. In practice a firm will quantify its acceptable level of audit risk.

Total audit risk is determined by three individual factors:

(a)   Inherent risk (or IR);
(b)   control risk (or CR); and
(c)   detection risk (or DR).

These three risks multiplied together give total audit risk.

Thus: $AR = IR \times CR \times DR$

These risks are explained below. Remember though that it is the auditor's judgement that is always used to determine the value to be placed on these items - there is no hard and fast rule that the auditor can follow.

3.2   How the auditor assesses inherent risk and control risk in establishing the detection risk

(a)   **Inherent risk**

Definition   The risk that a material error may arise from the nature of the business.

This risk will be affected by such items as how much the company is subject to market forces, the cash situation of the company, the trading history of the company, and the nature and incidence of unusual transactions.

(b)   **Control risk**

Definition   The risk that a material error will be neither prevented nor detected by the internal control system of the business.

This risk will be affected by such factors as the internal control system at the company and the integrity of the staff operating the system and the extent of supervisory controls.

(c)   **Detection risk**

Definition   The risk that any remaining material error (ie, material error not detected from the analysis of inherent risk, or material error not identified by the internal control system), is not detected by the auditor's own tests.

The level of detection risk is therefore dependent on the assessment of inherent and control risks and will determine the type and amount of audit testing to be carried out. Detection risk is found by using the equation already given above, but re-arranging it to give:

$$DR = AR \div (IR \times CR)$$

This simply means that the less effective the control system, or the greater the chance that the nature of the business means a higher risk of error, then the greater will be the level of detection risk. The auditor will therefore need to increase his audit testing. This will compensate for the poorer controls of the client and/or the greater risk from the nature of the client's business.

3.3   The detailed assessment of inherent risk

Inherent risk needs to be considered at two levels. In developing the overall audit plan, the auditors should assess inherent risk at the **financial statement** level. In developing the audit programme, the auditors should relate such assessment to **material account balances and classes of transactions**.

In the absence of knowledge or information to enable the auditors to make an assessment of inherent risk for a specific material account balance or class of transactions, the auditors should assume that inherent risk is high.

To assess inherent risk, the auditors use their experience of the entity from previous audits together with professional judgement to evaluate numerous factors, examples of which are:

At the financial statement level

(a)   the integrity of management

(b)   management experience and knowledge and changes in management during the period, for example the inexperience of management may affect the preparation of the financial statements of the entity.

(c)   unusual pressures on management, for example circumstances that might predispose management to misstate the financial statements, such as the industry experiencing a large number of business failures or an entity that lacks sufficient capital to continue operations.

(d)   the nature of the entity's business, for example the potential for technological obsolescence of its products and services, the complexity of its capital structure, the significance of related parties and the number of locations and geographical spread of its production facilities, and

(e)   factors affecting the industry in which the entity operates, for example economic and competitive conditions as indicated by financial trends and ratios, and changes in technology, consumer demand and accounting practices common to the industry.

At the account balance and class of transactions level

(a)   financial statement accounts likely to be susceptible to misstatement, for example accounts which required adjustment in the previous period or which involve a high degree of estimation

(b)   the complexity of underlying transactions and other events which might require the use of the work of an expert

(c)   the degree of judgement involved in determining account balances

(d)   susceptibility of assets to loss or misappropriation, for example assets which are highly desirable and movable such as cash

(e)   the completion of unusual and complex transactions, particularly at or near period end, and

(f)   transactions not subjected to ordinary processing.

3.4   The detailed assessment of control risk

In order to assess control risk, the auditors need to obtain an understanding of the accounting system and the control environment.

An understanding of the accounting system enables the auditors to identify:

(a)   major classes of transactions in the entity's operations

(b)   how such transactions are initiated

(c)   significant accounting records, supporting documents and accounts in the financial statements, and

(d)   the accounting and financial reporting process, from the initiation of significant transactions and other events to their inclusion in the financial statements.

An understanding of the control environment enables the auditors to assess the likely effectiveness of control procedures. A strong control environment, for example one with strong budgetary controls and an effective internal audit function, increases the effectiveness of control procedures.

After obtaining an understanding, the auditors then make a preliminary assessment of control risk.

The preliminary assessment of control risk is the process of evaluating the likely effectiveness of an entity's accounting and internal control systems in preventing and correcting material misstatements. There is always some control risk because of the inherent limitations of any internal control system.

The more effective the entity's accounting and internal control systems are assessed to be, the lower the auditors' assessment of control risk. Where the auditors obtain satisfactory audit evidence from tests of control as to the effectiveness of the accounting and internal control systems, the extent of substantive procedures may be reduced.

The auditors may conclude that the accounting and internal control systems are not effective or that it is likely to be inefficient to adopt an audit approach which relies on tests of control. In these circumstances the auditors plan the audit approach as if they had made an adverse preliminary assessment of control risk, and sufficient appropriate audit evidence needs to be obtained entirely from substantive procedures.

The auditors should then plan tests of control (ie, compliance tests) to support that assessment, carry out those tests and then determine whether the preliminary assessment of control risk is supported.

3.5   SAS 300: Accounting and internal control systems and audit risk assessments

The wording and order of the individual standards within the SAS illustrate very well the procedures for assessing audit risk. They are as follows:

300.1   Auditors should obtain an understanding of the accounting and internal control systems sufficient to plan the audit and develop an effective audit approach. Auditors should use professional judgement to assess the components of audit risk and to design audit procedures to ensure it is reduced to an acceptably low level.

300.2   In developing their audit approach and detailed procedures, auditors should assess inherent risk in relation to financial statement assertions about material account balances and classes of transactions, taking account of factors relevant both to the entity as a whole and to the specific assertions.

300.3   In planning the audit, auditors should obtain and document an understanding of the accounting system and control environment sufficient to determine their audit approach.

300.4   If auditors, after obtaining an understanding of the accounting system and control environment, expect to be able to rely on their assessment of control risk to reduce the extent of their substantive procedures, they should make a preliminary assessment of control risk for material financial statement assertions, and should plan and perform tests of control to support that assessment.

300.5   If intending to rely on tests of control performed in advance of the period end, auditors should obtain sufficient appropriate audit evidence as to the nature and extent of any changes in design or operation of the entity's accounting and internal control systems within the accounting period since such procedures were performed.

300.6   Having undertaken tests of control, auditors should evaluate whether the preliminary assessment of control risk is supported.

300.7   Auditors should consider the assessed levels of inherent and control risk in determining the nature, timing and extent of substantive procedures required to reduce audit risk to an acceptable level.

300.8   Regardless of the assessed levels of inherent and control risks, auditors should perform some substantive procedures for financial statement assertions of material account balances and transaction classes.

3.6   Activity

Two companies: Stephen Ltd and Jenny Ltd are summarised below:

Type of risk	Stephen Ltd	Jenny Ltd
Inherent	Retail supermarket	Insurance brokers
Control	Extensive computer systems and large internal audit department	No formal controls: claims paid with little review by senior staff

Stephen Ltd has a business that provides goods for which demand is steady and with a good internal control system. Jenny Ltd is subject very much to market forces and bad weather etc, with little formal internal controls. Which company will have the greater detection risk and therefore a higher level of audit testing?

3.7   Activity solution

The answer, of course, is Jenny Ltd. It has a potentially volatile business, and a poor internal control system. The risk of error is higher. Detection risk increases the level of audit testing. This will help to ensure that the financial statements do not contain any material errors.

3.8   APB Consultation Draft 'Providing assurance on internal controls'

In March 1998 the APB published draft proposals for a framework of principles to guide auditors and reporting accountants when providing assurance on internal controls. Demands on auditors and accountants to provide such assurance are growing. Some commentators believe that, in the not too distant future, auditors' provision of assurance on internal control may become as important as their traditional role of providing assurance on historical financial statements. The APB hope that responses to its consultation draft will enable it to influence thinking and practice in this area in the future.

4   THE PLANNING MEMORANDUM

4.1   Use in practice

Although the planning memorandum will be prepared before detailed audit work commences, it is important to bear in mind the fact that the planning stage does not end there. There will inevitably be adjustments to the original plan which can only be discovered later. A significant breakdown in internal control may entail more work, a change in the timing of stocktakes may mean rescheduling the audit. The work of planning is therefore a continuous process throughout the audit.

A planning memorandum will provide evidence of initial decisions as to the appropriate procedures relevant to each assignment recorded together with adjustments and additions to those procedures resulting from audit tests and review processes. The following is an example of such a checklist designed to achieve planning and control objectives (taken from Accountants Digest 119 *Audit File Review*). Most of the points covered should act as a revision to you from your earlier auditing studies.

Prepared by:
Date:
Reviewed by:
Date:

PLANNING MEMORANDUM

1   **Job timetable**

Give provisional dates of timing of audit work:	**Planned Date**	**Actual Date**

Planning meeting with client
Commencement of interim audit
Conclusion of interim audit
Management letter (interim)
Debtors/Creditors circularisation
Physical stocktaking
Commencement of final audit
Conclusion of final audit
Typed draft financial statements
to client for discussion and approval
Auditors' report signed
Management letter (final)

2   **Changes since previous audit**   **Detailed comments**

2(a)   In the nature of the client's business (for example, changes in product range, terms of sales etc)

2(b)   In the management structure or key financial/accounting personnel.

2(c)   In the accounting system (including those resulting from previous management letters).

2(d)   In external requirements (for example, SSAPs, statutes, rules etc)

3   Planning decisions

3(a)   The main changes in the audit programme from the previous period are (give both changes in tests and in sample sizes).

3(b)   Indicate on an audit area basis whether it is intended to seek reliance on internal controls:
Sales and debtors
Purchases and creditors
Stock and work in progress
Salaries and wages
Bank and cash
Fixed assets
Other (specify)

3(c)   Indicate those areas in which material errors have been identified in previous periods and audit emphasis to be placed thereon.

3(d)   The following systems areas are to be (re-) flowcharted.

3(e)   The following sections of the permanent file are to be created/ updated.

3(f)   Specialist assistance required (specify).

3(g)   Indicate whether an audit panel meeting is mandatory for this client prior to signing of audit report.

3(h)   Prepare a summary of schedules and other details that client staff will provide for us.

3(i)   Where we provide accountancy services indicate whether:
(i)   our accountancy and audit work has been planned to avoid duplication of work;

(ii)   staff engaged on the accountancy work have been briefed as to the assurance that will be placed on their work and the audit objectives that are relevant.

3(j)   State briefly other services we provide for the client and their impact on nature and timing of audit work.

4   Other auditors (joint, primary, secondary)

4(a)   Identify, as appropriate, primary, secondary or joint auditors.

4(b)   State briefly the proposed liaison with
          other auditors:
          (i)   at the planning stage of the audit;
          (ii)   during the transactions audit;
          (iii) at the final audit.

4(c)   Where we are primary auditors:
          state briefly the methods by which
          the firm will be satisfied about the
          quality and reliability of the work
          of other auditors (for example,
          review of audit plans, working
          paper review, questionnaire). Indicate
          whether we are adopting a rotational
          reviewing approach.

4(d)   State timetable for:
          (i)   review of other auditors' plans;
          (ii)   despatch of questionnaires;
          (iii) receipt of audited financial statements;
          (iv)   receipt of completed questionnaires;
          (v)   agreement of inter-company balances;
          (vi)   review of other auditors' working papers.

4(e)   State briefly:
          (i)   whether we are aware of any
                 reason why we should not rely
                 on the work and report of
                 any secondary auditors, and

          (ii)   our audit approach in such
                 circumstances.

5   Internal audit department

5(a)   Indicate to what extent we are
          able to reduce the level of
          our audit tests by relying on
          relevant internal audit work.

5(b)   State briefly the liaison with
          the internal auditors

          (i)   at the planning stage of the audit;
          (ii)   during the transactions audit;
          (iii) at the final audit.

6   Briefing instructions

6(a)   State any particular sequence
          in which the work is to be
          carried out.

6(b)   State any specific points which
          require particular attention
          or parts to be done by a
          specific person.

6(c)   Insert date when briefing
          meeting with audit team held
          and names and levels of
          staff briefed:

7   Supervision and review

7(a)   State any particular stages
          (or areas of difficulty) at
          which the senior is to refer
          back to the manager.

7(b)   State how, and at what stages,
          it is proposed to supervise
          and review the transactions
          audit.

	Previous year (actual) %	Budget for year %	Management accounts to .... %

8   Financial ratios

8(a)   From the most recent management information, extract the following ratios (if management information not reliable or available include such observations in 8(b) below).

Gross profit: sales
Distribution costs: sales
Administrative costs: sales
Net profit before tax: sales
Net profit before tax: total net assets/liabilities
Rate of stock turnover
Number of weeks debtors
Current assets (excluding stock): current liabilities
Shareholders' funds: total assets

8(b)   State the conclusions drawn and steps to be taken in the light of 8(a).

9   Time budget

State briefly the reasons for significant variances in current year budget with budget and actual time of previous year.

4.2   In the exam

In answering a question in the exam on planning you may have to put together a planning memorandum. The examiner is unlikely to provide you with a standard form and the marks will not allow scope for anything as ambitious as the above!

The examiner will mainly be testing whether you have spotted the potential problems with this client and suggested in outline how they might be dealt with.

5   AUDIT PROGRAMME DESIGN AND TESTING

5.1   Introduction

The audit programme is essentially a record of the audit testing. It specifies the nature and extent of the checking, and the members of staff who have carried out the work. It also contains evidence of review of work.

The audit programme should

(a)   provide a basis for allocation of work and staff

(b)   pinpoint audit responsibility

(c)   ensure continuity among staff: for example, if a member of the audit team is away sick it should be easy for another person to take over

(d)   facilitate audit review by senior, manager and partner.

The audit programme is an important part of the auditor's working papers and records a significant part of the audit evidence required to justify the audit opinion.

Nevertheless, audit programmes should be constructed carefully. They should not stifle initiative, and the work specified should be regarded as a minimum and not a maximum.

You are unlikely to be asked to produce an audit programme, but rather a list of tests. However, an example of an audit programme is reproduced below as this does bring together all the objectives and tests for one area.

5.2   How the audit programme reflects the application of audit objectives

Detailed audit work involves the testing of controls and substantive procedures. The extent and form of testing is decided by reference to overall and detailed objectives. It is important to set out the audit objectives for each area as shown in the example below. The objectives of a test of controls are different from the objectives of a substantive test and the distinction must be kept clear in order that valid conclusions are drawn.

Although tests of controls and substantive tests have different audit objectives, the two types of test may be carried out at the same time on the same sample. This allows a reduction in the volume of work in, for example, extracting a sample. The implicit assumption being made in such an approach is that the tests of controls will not reveal sufficient errors to result in a change in the level of control risk. The substantive sample thus extracted on the basis of the initial assessment of control risk will thus be valid.

If the control risk does need reassessment, a further sample will be required.

5.3   Example

AUDIT PROGRAMME	Prepared by:
AUDIT AREA: Wages and Salaries	Date:
Client:	Reviewed by:
Period:	Date:

(a)   **Tests of controls**

Control objectives

To establish that:

(i)   the computation of wages and salaries is only in respect of the client's employees and at authorised rates of pay.

(ii)   wages and salaries are in accordance with records of work performed eg, time, output, commissions on sales.

(iii)   payrolls are calculated accurately.

(iv)   payments are only made to the correct employees.

(v)   payroll deductions are correctly accounted for and paid to the appropriate third parties.

(vi)   all transactions related to wages and salaries are accurately entered in the accounting records.

Tests of controls	**File reference**	**Comments**
1 Test sample of time records etc for approval by responsible official		
2 Test authority for payment of casual labour		
3 Observe wages distribution for adherence to procedures		
4 Test authorisation for payroll amendments		

5   Test control over payroll amendments

6   Examine evidence of checking of payroll calculations

7   Examine evidence of approval of payrolls
     by a responsible official

8   Examine evidence of independent checks
     on payrolls

9   Inspect payroll reconciliations

10   Examine explanations for payroll expense variance

11   Test authorities for payroll deductions

12   Test controls over unclaimed wages.

(b)   Substantive tests

Audit objectives

To establish the completeness,
accuracy and validity of the wages and
salaries records.

1   Select sample of time records etc, and test
     casts and calculations

2   Test sample of personnel records for:
     (a)   rates of pay

     (b)   authorisation of changes in rates
            of pay

     (c)   leavers' and joiners' personal details

3   Select payrolls and:

     (i)   check to time records etc
     (ii)   test to personnel records
     (iii) test casts and calculations
     (iv)   vouch deductions

4   Vouch sample of payroll reconciliations

5   Test totals of cheques drawn to net pay due

6   Test postings of payrolls to nominal ledger
     accounts

5.4   Activity

Draw up a list of control objectives that would be relevant in the sales cycle of a manufacturing company.

5.5   Activity solution

(a)   Customers' orders should be controlled and recorded in order to execute them promptly and determine any provision required for losses arising from unfulfilled commitments.

(b)   Goods shipped and work completed should be controlled to ensure that invoices are issued and revenue recorded for all sales.

(c)   Goods returned and claims by customers should be controlled in order to determine the liability for goods returned and claims received but not entered in the debtors' records.

(d)   Invoices and credits should be appropriately checked as being valid before being entered in the debtors' records.

(e)   Valid debtors' transactions, and only those transactions, should be accurately entered in the accounting records.

(f)   There should be procedures to ensure that sales invoices are subsequently paid and that doubtful amounts are identified in order to determine any provisions required.

6   SAS 200: PLANNING

6.1   Introduction

The overall plan should describe in broad terms the scope and conduct of the audit, involving such matters as:

*   knowledge of the client;

*   risk and materiality;

*   nature, timing and extent of procedures;

*   co-ordination, direction, supervision and review;

*   other matters including going concern, special conditions, special terms of engagement and the need for reports.

6.2   Auditing standards

200.1   Auditors should plan the audit work so as to perform the audit in an effective manner.

200.2   Auditors should develop and document an overall audit plan describing the expected scope and conduct of the audit.

200.3   Auditors should develop and document the nature, timing and extent of planned audit procedures required to implement the overall audit plan.

200.4   The audit work planned should be reviewed and, if necessary, revised during the course of the audit.

7   THE USE OF AUDIT SAMPLING IN THE CONDUCT OF AN AUDIT

7.1   Definition of sampling

Definition   Audit sampling is defined as the application of audit procedures to less than 100% of the items within an account balance, class of transactions or other population, as representative of that population, to enable the auditor to obtain and evaluate evidence of some characteristic of that population and to assist in forming a conclusion concerning that characteristic.

7.2   The use of sampling

Sampling is normally appropriate for areas in which there are a large number of similar transactions. In such areas eg, credit sales for the period, it is not cost effective to test all transactions. Even if the costs were ignored, full testing would not necessarily achieve the specified audit objectives for that area eg, full testing on sales invoices for example would not verify that all sales are recorded (ie, it may not demonstrate completeness).

The use of sampling allied to properly thought out objectives and properly constructed tests allows more valid conclusions to be reached than the (now outdated) traditional system of testing as 'many transactions as possible' in the time available.

Cases where sampling is not appropriate include the following situations.

- The auditor is 'on enquiry' as a result of previous information.

- Populations are too small for valid conclusions to be drawn and, in any event, it is quicker to test all transactions rather than spend time constructing a sample.

- All the transactions in a particular area are of great monetary significance.

- The data may be 'sensitive' items, such as directors' emoluments which require precise disclosure in the financial statements.

- The audit area does not consist of items of the same kind ie, there is a non-homogeneous population.

7.3   SAS 430: Audit sampling

The APB has issued SAS 430 on the topic of audit sampling; the remainder of this chapter deals with all examinable aspects of sampling using the terminology of the SAS.

7.4   Identifying and applying sampling techniques

The steps involved in sampling can be summarised as follows:

- Sample design
- Selection of the sample
- Evaluation of the sample

8   DESIGNING THE SAMPLE

8.1   Extract from SAS 430

'When designing the size and structure of an audit sample, auditors should consider the specific audit objectives, the nature of the population from which they wish to sample, and the sampling and selection methods.'

8.2   Audit objectives

This could be whether tests of control or substantive testing is to be carried out, and in the case of the latter whether there is a specific direction to the test ie, overstatement or understatement.

8.3   Population

The *population* is any group of items sharing a common characteristic. Examples are all the debtors at a balance sheet date and all the goods and services received in a year. The essential feature of a population is that it must be homogeneous, that is it must be composed of similar or uniform parts. Suppose that the population consists of all wage calculations for a year, but the auditor knows that the wages supervisor changed half way through the year. He may judge that the possibility of error is greater after the change than before. Hence there are really two populations. The sampling plan for each population will be different.

Note that sampling *from* a population does not establish its completeness. This has been considered earlier. To test for understatement (or completeness) the test should go from source documentation (sometimes referred to as the reciprocal population) *to* the financial statements.

8.4   Stratification

In cases where the auditor is concerned with the discovery of overstatement errors and considers that the largest monetary errors are likely to occur in the largest individual items he may wish to stratify the population by value. He can then direct the major part of his audit effort to those items with the highest individual value.

Example:

	Number of items in stratum	*Value of stratum*	*Test size*
Above £1m	10	£36m	10
£250,000 to £1m	150	£95m	50
£50,000 to £250,000	1,000	£93m	50
£10,000 to £50,000	3,000	£60m	35
Less than £10,000	7,000	£15m	15

Selecting the items to be tested

The purpose of audit sampling is to draw a conclusion about the entire population from which the sample was selected. Thus it is necessary that the sample items should be selected in such a way that they can be expected to be representative of the population as a whole. A sample cannot be relied on to be representative unless it is drawn from the whole of the population. The aim is to ensure that within each stratum all sample units should have a quantifiable (often an equal) chance of being selected.

Representative selection methods commonly in use include random, value weighted, systematic or haphazard selection. Sampling one or a few blocks of items in sequence will not generally be representative.

If the sample is not representative of the population as a whole, the idea of sampling becomes invalid.

8.5   Sample size

Extract from SAS

When determining sample sizes, auditors should consider sampling risk, the tolerable error and the expected error.

(a)   **Sampling risk**

  Sampling risk arises from the possibility that the auditors' conclusion, based on a sample, may be different from the conclusion that would be reached if the entire population were subjected to the same audit procedure.

Auditors are faced with sampling risk in both tests of control and substantive procedures as follows:

Tests of control (compliance tests)

(i)   risk of under reliance: the risk that, although the sample result does not support the auditor's assessment of control risk, the actual compliance rate supports such an assessment

(ii)   risk of over reliance: the risk that, although the sample result supports the auditors' assessment of control risk, the actual compliance rate does not support such an assessment, and

Substantive procedures

(i)   risk of incorrect rejection: the risk that, although the sample result supports the conclusion that a recorded account balance or class of transactions is materially misstated, in fact it is not materially misstated, and

(ii)   risk of incorrect acceptance: the risk that, although the sample result supports the conclusion that a recorded account balance or class of transactions is not materially misstated, in fact it is materially misstated.

(b)   **Tolerable error**

> **Definition**   Tolerable error is the maximum error in the population that the auditors are willing to accept and still conclude that the audit objective has been achieved.

Tolerable error is considered during the planning stage and, for substantive procedures, is related to the auditors' judgement about materiality. The smaller the tolerable error, the larger the sample size needs to be.

(c)   **Expected error**

If the auditors expect error to be present in the population, a larger sample than when no error is expected ordinarily needs to be examined to conclude that the actual error in the population is not greater than the planned tolerable error. Smaller sample sizes are justified when the population is expected to be error free.

In determining the expected error in a population, auditors consider such matters as error levels identified in previous audits, changes in the entity's procedures and evidence available from other procedures.

9   SELECTION OF THE SAMPLE

9.1   Extract from SAS

'Auditors should select sample items in such a way that the sample can be expected to be representative of the population in respect of the characteristics being tested.'

As has been seen above for sampling conclusions to be valid a representative sample must be selected. There are many different possible selection techniques that could be adopted; the most common are summarised below.

9.2   Random selection

Simple random sampling is a method of sample selection in which every item in a population has the same statistical probability of being selected as every other item and every combination of items has the same probability of being selected as every other combination of the same number of items. The sample will therefore be representative of the population as a whole. This involves selecting from a source of random numbers, either by the use of computer programs which generate random numbers or of random number tables.

It can be used for both tests of control and substantive tests. This method of selection is also appropriate in non-statistical sampling, but it is often more time-consuming than other sample selection methods.

9.3   Value weighted selection

This involves using the currency unit value rather than the items as the sampling population. Each individual pound in the population is given an equal chance of selection. For example, one pound is selected out of the first two thousand and thereafter each two thousandth pound is selected. Since an individual currency unit cannot be examined, the item which includes that pound is selected for examination. The advantage of value weighted selection is that high-value items have a greater chance of being selected and audit effort is directed to them. Since each currency unit, and thus each item, has a chance of being selected this method achieves a representative sample.

This should not be confused with 100% examination of items above a certain value, in which items below that value stand no chance of being selected and thus the result cannot be representative. The chance of each item being selected is proportional to the value of that item and in effect a perfectly stratified sample is selected. Formal value weighted selection involves totalling cumulatively the currency value of each item in the account balance, which can be time-consuming unless computer-assisted audit techniques are used.

The most common form of value weighted selection used in practice is monetary unit sampling (MUS). Such techniques are useful where the objective of the test is to test for overstatement, but not for understatement. Items materially understated have less chance of being selected using this method.

9.4   Systematic selection

In systematic sample selection the auditor calculates a uniform sampling interval by dividing the population size by the sample size. Having determined a starting point every item corresponding to the sampling interval is selected. For example, if a population to be sampled is 600 items and the sample size is 50 the sampling interval will be 12. One of the first 12 items will be selected as the starting point and thereafter every twelfth item will be selected. In determining the starting point each of the first 12 items (in this example) should have a chance of being selected. The starting point may be selected haphazardly or randomly.

Systematic selection is suitable for both tests of control and substantive tests and particularly useful when sampling from non-monetary populations, for example despatch notes.

One problem with systematic selection is that it may not achieve a representative sample where the population is arranged in a fixed pattern. For example, if every 50th item in a population has a particular characteristic (say it arises from the Bristol branch) then systematic selection may result in a sample containing a greater or smaller proportion of items with that characteristic than exist in the population as a whole.

9.5   Block sampling

Block sampling is not generally an appropriate selection method because populations might be expected to be structured in such a way that items in a sequence have similar characteristics to each other but different characteristics to items elsewhere in the population. Block sampling consists of selecting a number of adjacent transactions or items - for example, all sales invoices in a particular week or all customer receivable balances with a name beginning with particular letters.

There are two main disadvantages of this approach. First the block selected may not be typical of the characteristics of the population as a whole. Although of course this is an inherent problem in any form of sample selection it is more apparent in block sampling where all testing is concentrated in a small part of the population. Secondly, in order to minimise audit costs, it is probable that only relatively few blocks of items may be selected. This is particularly the case where the sampling unit is a period of time rather than individual items. For example, if transactions are being selected for vouching it may seem to be practicable only to select a few days' transactions out of the whole year. A sample with only a few blocks is then unlikely to be adequate to reach a reasonable conclusion. Nevertheless block sampling can result in significant cost savings in audit time, and there are some occasions where practical considerations may require the use of block sampling, for example when visiting a branch.

9.6   Haphazard selection

This is a selection process in which the auditor attempts to give all items in a population a chance of being selected by choosing items haphazardly. You may know this technique as 'judgmental' sampling, which is not an ideal way to describe it. The auditor should avoid conscious bias and predictability in selecting items. For example, a tendency to favour items in a particular location on a page or in a file or never to choose the first or last item in a listing should be avoided. Also bias should not be introduced by only examining items from current periods or by only selecting items that are easily available or by selecting items consciously because of their size or because they appear unusual. Haphazard selection is commonly used in non-statistical sampling for both tests of control and substantive tests but because it is not truly random it is not sufficiently rigorous for statistical sampling.

10   EVALUATION OF TEST RESULTS

10.1   Extract from SAS

Having carried out, on each sample item, those audit procedures which are appropriate to the particular audit objective, auditors should

(a)   analyse any errors detected in the sample; and

(b)   draw inferences for the population as a whole.

10.2   Analysis of errors in the sample

In analysing the errors detected in the sample, the auditors first need to determine that an item in question is in fact an error.

In designing the sample, auditors define those conditions which constitute an error by reference to the audit objectives. For example, in a substantive procedure relating to the recording of accounts receivable, a misposting between customer accounts does not affect the total accounts receivable. Therefore, it may be inappropriate to consider this an error in evaluating the sample results of this particular procedure, even though it may have an effect on other areas of the audit such as the assessment of doubtful accounts.

11   STATISTICAL SAMPLING

11.1   Definitions

> **Definition**   Statistical sampling requires the use of random selection and uses probability theory to determine the sample size, evaluate quantitatively the sample results and measure the sampling risk.

> **Definition**   Non-statistical sampling may use non-random sample selection methods, does not rely on probability theory and requires more subjectivity in making sampling decisions.

11.2   Conditions necessary for the use of statistical sampling

If statistical sampling is to be used, the following conditions need to be present:

(a)   The population to be tested must be homogeneous - that is to say, it must consist of items of the same kind, with the same level of audit risk. (This is necessary if the statistical theory is to be valid.)

(b)   The population must be fairly large, otherwise the benefits of the technique will not be achieved.

(c)   Expectation of error must be low - in other words the systems area to be checked must already have been assessed by the auditor as reliable. (This again is necessary for the statistical theory to be valid.)

(d)   The items in the population must be easily identifiable once selected, so that checking of the items chosen is easily carried out.

11.3   Advantages and disadvantages of statistical sampling

Advantages	Disadvantages
(a) Conclusions can be drawn in quantitative terms	(a) May be difficult to extract samples, especially if documents are not sequentially numbered
(b) Sample selected will be unbiased	(b) Initiative may be stifled and staff become de-motivated
(c) Its use forces clarification of audit objectives in that confidence and precision levels must be pre-determined	(c) Results may be misunderstood if staff are not properly trained in the use of the technique
(d) Time and money may be saved by the avoidance of excessive checking	(d) It is not suitable for all applications
(e) Acceptance of the known risk involved in statistical sampling is preferable to the unknown risk when large number of items are selected judgmentally	(e) Although judgement is reduced at the more detailed selection and testing level, the importance of judgement when deciding the confidence level, precision and meaning of error is greatly increased
(f) More precise information can be given to the client in the letter of weakness	

11.4   Non-statistical sampling

This also has its advantages as follows:

(a)   The 'test check' has been used by auditors for generations, it is well understood and well refined by experience.

(b)   An auditor brings experience and technical expertise into his sample selection. One might even say he has a sixth sense he can use in finding fraud, error or unusual items. This cannot be denied but the sixth sense can more properly be incorporated into a statistical scheme.

(c)   No special knowledge of statistics is required by staff. This disadvantage of the statistical method can, in fact, be overcome fairly easily, but in any case more rational use of scarce resources (audit staff) will negate this advantage of the judgement approach.

(d)   More time is spent on auditing with judgement sampling and less on the mechanics of constructing the sample and computing the mathematical implications of the results found. This is a more valid advantage and is the reason why a number of large firms do not use statistical sampling.

12   SAMPLING METHODS

12.1   Attribute sampling

Definition   Attribute sampling provides results based on two possible values (ie, correct and not correct).

As a consequence it is generally used in tests of control where the objective of a test is non-monetary in nature ie, does a control operate or not.   Each deviation from a prescribed control procedure is therefore given an equal weight in the evaluation of results.

However, in response to demands from audit firms for a statistical method which could measure monetary deviations, an attribute sampling technique was developed by statisticians which could express a conclusion in monetary terms - **monetary unit sampling (MUS)**. This is used in substantive testing and is considered below.

12.2   Illustration of attribute sampling

A sample size is computed by reference to two inter-related factors:

(a)   confidence level
(b)   precision limit.

Confidence has similar qualities to setting a risk level eg, being 95% confident is equivalent to accepting a 5% risk. The lower the level of confidence required the lower the sample size needs to be. Commonly, 95% is used.

Precision is the maximum error rate that is accepted in a sample. The higher the number of errors accepted, the lower the sample required. However, the maximum normally used in practice is 2%. It is asserted that if there are more than 2 errors per 100, it will not be possible to rely on the control at all.

Various tables have been devised by audit firms to make the calculations easier to perform. Sample size is computed by the following fraction and using the table underneath.

$$\text{Sample size} = \frac{\text{Reliability factor (R - Factor)}}{\text{Precision}}$$

Table R-factors and levels of assurance

Confidence level/ assurance required	Risk level	R- Factor No errors	R- Factor One error anticipated
99%	1%	4.6	6.61
95%	5%	3.0	4.75
90%	10%	2.3	3.89
85%	15%	1.9	3.38
80%	20%	1.6	3.0
70%	30%	1.2	2.44

Example

A test of control on the authorisation of purchase invoices is to be performed. The auditor wishes to be 95% confident and is prepared to accept a 2% error rate.

If no errors are anticipated sample size is therefore

$$\frac{3.0}{0.02} = 150 \text{ items}$$

Note that the sample size is unrelated to the size of the population being tested ie, sample size is the same if the total number of purchase invoices is 50,000 or 500,000 in the year. You can now see the time saving opportunities given by sampling.

12.3   Activity

What is the sample size if one error is anticipated in the sample?

12.4   Activity solution

$$\frac{4.75}{0.02} = 237 \text{ items}$$

12.5   Variables sampling

Definition   Variables sampling is concerned with monetary amounts and can test either whether a certain statement is true or false or give an estimate of the true value of a population.

For example the technique can result in a conclusion that the auditor is 95% confident that the true value of the population lies between £59.6m and £60.4m and the best estimate is £60m. It is therefore ideally suited to substantive testing which needs to be expressed in monetary terms.

However the calculations involved are very lengthy and can only be performed easily by computer applications. As a consequence the attribute sampling method MUS has been widely adopted instead by auditing firms.

12.6   Monetary unit sampling

There are various permutations of MUS. The example below uses MUS in conjunction with reliability factors (R factors) as seen above.

An R factor is a translation of the required level of confidence into a number which can be easily used to compute a sampling interval. Instead of a mass of statistical tables there are six required R factors which match six confidence levels:

Required confidence level	*R factor*
39%	0.5
63%	1.0
78%	1.5
86%	2.0
95%	3.0
97%	3.5

An example of cumulative monetary unit sampling and R factors is now shown.

12.7   Example

Stocks are to be tested to determine whether they are overstated. The audit population is thus the stock sheets containing monetary valuations. These total £900,000. The auditor decides:

(a)   **The required confidence level**

Often 95% confidence is looked for.

(b)   **The precision limit**

In the context of monetary sampling the precision limit can be set at a monetary level rather than a percentage of error level. This can be a more satisfactory method of deciding a precision limit, as it can be directly related to the concept of materiality eg, is £50,000 material? If the total of errors below £50,000 is not material then the discovery of many small errors still allows the auditor to draw a conclusion from his work.

With attribute sampling, the number of errors (and not their monetary effect) determines the conclusion to be drawn. If £50,000 is the maximum acceptable amount of error the precision limit will be set at a slightly lower figure so that if a small number of errors are found, the maximum amount of error in statistical terms will be under £50,000. The precision limit is thus, say, £42,000.

The sampling interval is computed by dividing the precision limit by the R factor which is relevant to the confidence level. A 95% confidence level gives an R factor of 3.

$$\frac{42,000}{3} \quad = \quad \text{£14,000 sampling interval}$$

A sample of $\dfrac{900,000}{14,000} = 64$ items will be chosen.

A random number between 1 and 14,000 is needed to start the selection process - say 10,109 is selected.

The sample is thus chosen as follows:

Stock item	Value of each item	Cumulative total	£'s selected
1	6,000	6,000	
2	40	6,040	
3	3,000	9,040	
4	16,500	25,540	10,109
			24,109
5	100	25,640	
6	8,600	34,240	
7	3,680	37,920	
8	800	38,720	38,109
9	13,800	52,520	52,109
say 300	Total 900,000	900,000	

Stock items 4, 8 and 9 have been selected. As every £ has an equal chance of selection, the items with the highest value have the greatest chance of selection. Indeed with a sampling interval of 14,000 every item with a value in excess of £14,000 must be selected.

13   CHAPTER SUMMARY

This chapter has emphasised the importance of planning not only at the initial stage of an audit but also revising the plan, if necessary, throughout the audit. Consideration of audit risk is regarded as a key element in planning the audit.

In this area the examiner is most likely to set 'case-study' style questions. Such questions give you some information on a client. You must show that you have spotted the problems unique to the audit of that client and how you would overcome them. The 'clues' in the question should help you to see what the risks are for that company.

Sampling is a necessary and valid means of forming conclusions on audit evidence. The sampling process involves sample design, selection of the sample and evaluation of the sample.

Sampling may either be by statistical or non-statistical methods.

14   SELF TEST QUESTIONS

14.1   In SAS 210 what is the purpose of obtaining knowledge of the business? (2.2)

14.2   What is the definition of inherent risk? (3.2)

14.3   What is the definition of detection risk? (3.2)

14.4   Inherent risk is considered at what two levels? (3.3)

14.5   What does the planning memorandum provide evidence of? (4.1)

14.6   What is the definition of audit sampling? (7.1)

14.7   What are the three steps in audit sampling? (7.4)

14.8   What is sampling risk? (8.5)

14.9   What is the selection technique of systematic selection? (9.4)

14.10   What is the definition of statistical sampling? (11.1)

15   EXAMINATION TYPE QUESTION

15.1   Gnome Publications Ltd

You are the manager in charge of the audit of Gnome Publications Ltd, a publishing company based in Oxford, with a year end of 31 August.

It is your first year in charge of the audit, although the company has existed and your firm has been its auditors for three years. From discussions with the engagement partner and the new managing director Miss Hughes you have ascertained the following information.

The company is a wholly owned subsidiary of GTI Ltd, a close private holding company.

The company's main business is the writing, production, printing and marketing of technical publications. The company sells these publications both to fellow group companies in the training field and also to external bodies (universities etc).

The company has grown rapidly with a turnover now of approximately £5m. However, the results have been poor, with profits around the £100,000 mark.

Miss Hughes, the new managing director was appointed on 1 January 19X8. Her objective is to produce better results and as part of her motivation she has a remuneration package that is partly profit-related.

The company has recently invested heavily in Desk Top Publishing equipment and is in the process of changeover from more traditional typesetting methods. There are some 'teething problems' but Miss Hughes is convinced these can be sorted out shortly. Old equipment will be scrapped.

Accounting transactions are recorded on a microcomputer (an IBM-clone, the NAFF) using a well-known off the shelf package, Sagg. No management accounts are prepared other than the monthly nominal ledger printout from the Sagg system.

The final financial statements are prepared by the group accountant (based in London) who travels to Oxford for two days during October for this purpose.

You are required to prepare a file memorandum setting out the factors you would consider in assessing the audit for this client and summarising the implications on the audit approach. **(15 marks)**

16   ANSWER TO EXAMINATION TYPE QUESTION

16.1   Gnome Publications Ltd

FILE MEMORANDUM

Client: Gnome Publications Ltd

Date: X-X-19XX

Period   Year end 31 August 19X8

Re: Preliminary audit risk assessment

(a)   **Inherent audit risk consideration in relation to the company as a whole**

    (i)   **Results and management motivation**

        The company has not been producing the results that might be expected given its turnover.

        There will therefore be general pressure on Miss Hughes to produce better results which may increase the risk of overstatement of profits by over-generous stock valuation for example or under-provision for liabilities.

        The profits related remuneration package of Miss Hughes will add to this general motivation to window dress favourably the results.

    (ii)   **Ownership**

        The company is a 100% subsidiary of a privately owned group and final financial statements are produced by the group accountant. In addition the bulk of sales are to other group companies.

        This may increase the risk of profits in the final financial statements being manipulated to suit the purposes of the owners of the group, either by group-recharging adjustments or in the inter-company transfer prices.

    (iii)   **Accounting systems**

        The accounts are maintained on micro by the administrative assistant who has no formal accounts training. As a result the risk of errors in basic preparation of the accounts may be increased.

        Set against this risk will be the additional controls imposed by the system itself. We are familiar with the Sagg software and have found it both reliable and very suitable for this size and type of business.

    (iv)   **Final accounts preparation**

        The accounts are prepared quickly quite soon after the year end. It is likely that many figures may be very approximate estimates (eg, stock valuations, accruals) hence liable to mis-statements.

(b)   **Inherent audit risk in specific account areas**

    (i)   **Stocks**

        Stocks will be particularly liable to overstatement. This is due to

        (1)   the risk of deliberate manipulation as in (i) above, and

        (2)   the high risk of obsolete stock.

Technical publications which have a high unit cost must be updated regularly. Out of date publications are virtually worthless, so stocks even just a few months old may need to be written off.

(ii)   Equipment

The old equipment is being scrapped as new technology is introduced. There is a corresponding risk of understatement of proceeds.

In addition, from discussions with Miss Hughes it appears that the new equipment may turn out to be unsuitable. If so it will have a very low realisable value and there will be significant write offs.

(iii)   Inter company transactions

Because of the lack of independence of the group, there may be a particular risk of misstatement of

(1)   inter-group sales
(2)   group management charges.

(c)   Control risk

(i)   Lack of segregation of duties

It is inevitable in this size of business that there will be a lack of segregation. It does however increase the risk of errors or irregularity.

(ii)   Lack of management control

Although Miss Hughes keeps a close eye on the running of the business, no proper budgets or management accounts are prepared. There is similarly no effective control from the group accountant.

(iii)   Authorisations

On the other hand the transactions of the company are closely controlled, all significant expenditure requiring the authority of Miss Hughes.

(d)   Summary of conclusions

The risks identified above indicate the company is a high inherent risk entity with strong motivations for inflation of profits.

All staff should be aware of the likely direction of any deliberate manipulation of the accounts.

Particular attention should be paid to the audit of key areas identified in section (b) above.

25 SUBSTANTIVE TESTING AND ANALYTICAL REVIEW

INTRODUCTION & LEARNING OBJECTIVES

In the previous chapter we saw, through the use of the audit risk model how the nature and extent of substantive testing could be established. In this chapter we consider the substantive procedures used to obtain audit evidence required to satisfy the audit objectives.

Audit objectives can be categorised by reference to financial statement assertions and tests should be related to assertions so that the results of testing can provide firm conclusions.

Substantive testing may be by tests of details and/or analytical review. Analytical review can provide conclusions on the reasonableness of the data.

When you have studied this chapter you should be able to do the following:

- Discuss the use of substantive testing in the verification of financial statements.
- Relate conclusions on tests to audit risk and materiality.
- Describe the major analytical review techniques.

1 SUBSTANTIVE TESTING

1.1 The nature of substantive testing and substantive analysis

Definition Substantive analysis is the process of determining the extent of substantive evidence required, the objectives to be achieved by particular substantive tests, and the evaluation of the results.

Substantive analysis is developed and laid out by creating and using audit programmes for material account balances and transactions.

Definition Substantive testing refers to the procedures used to obtain audit evidence required to satisfy the audit objectives set out by substantive analysis.

There are two broad categories of substantive testing.

(a)   Tests of details

(b)   Analytical procedures.

Both of these categories are considered in this chapter.

The key link between substantive testing and substantive analysis is the setting of the audit objectives for which tests need to be designed. The objectives can be categorised by reference to **financial statement assertions.** This is a term used in SAS 400: Audit evidence.

The principles of obtaining audit evidence were covered in an earlier chapter but it is relevant here to repeat SAS 400.3.

> In seeking to obtain audit evidence from substantive procedures, auditors should consider the extent to which that evidence . . . supports the relevant financial statement assertions.

Definition Financial statement assertions are the representations of the directors, explicit or implicit, that are embodied in the financial statements.

By approving the financial statements, the directors are making representations about the information therein. In the audit of the financial statements, the auditor performs substantive tests in order to determine whether there are material misstatements in the financial statements. The central objective of the substantive procedures is to consider the extent to which the evidence gained supports the relevant financial statement assertions.

1.2   A classification of financial statement assertions

The classification below is from SAS 400.

(a)   Existence

   Assertion: An asset or liability exists at a given date.

   Auditors spend a great deal of time on this assertion confirming the existence of assets such as tangible fixed assets, stock, debtors and cash. Clearly this is a fundamental assertion; no other assertion is relevant if the asset or liability does not exist.

(b)   Rights and obligations

   Assertion: An asset or liability pertains to an entity at a given date.

   The auditor must ensure that it is the business which owns the asset at the balance sheet date. There are many situations where an asset could be on the business premises but belong to someone else. Stock, for example, may have been sold but not yet delivered. In a small business, some of the assets may belong to the major shareholder.

(c)   Occurrence

   Assertion: A transaction or event took place which pertains to the entity during the relevant period.

   Also relevant to this assertion is **authority** ie, there was proper authority to acquire an asset, or incur a debt, or to pay expenses during the accounting period. This is an assertion which is commonly tested by compliance procedures of part of the accounting system.

(d)   Completeness

   Assertion: There are no unrecorded assets, liabilities, transactions or events, or undisclosed items.

   The auditor needs to design his tests so that the completeness assertion is satisfied. It is fairly easy to perform detailed substantive testing on the 'wrong' documents which fails to address this issue. A test of completeness needs to be initiated with the underlying documents and completed with the entry in the financial statements. Using the terminology of directional testing, tests for understatement are required. Detailed testing starting with items in the financial statements will still be necessary to test that what items are there should be there but using only those tests will not satisfy the completeness assertion.

(e)   Valuation

   Assertion: An asset or liability is recorded at an appropriate carrying value.

   An asset or liability may initially and subsequently be carried at cost and thus this amount needs to be verified as the cost incurred or the liability taken on. In addition, there are many instances, particularly for assets where the item changes in value eg, depreciation for fixed assets and reduction to net realisable value for current assets.

The auditor needs to verify:

- the initial cost and
- the changes in value.

(f)   Measurement

Assertion: A transaction or event is recorded at the proper amount and revenue and expense is allocated to the proper period.

This assertion refers to the profit and loss account. The initial transactions will normally be recorded at original cost (thus corresponding with the asset or liability side of the transactions as under (e) above). Most of these items will then be transferred to the profit and loss account in the same accounting period but year end adjustments such as accruals and prepayments are required to ensure the 'revenue and expense is allocated to the proper period'.

(g)   Presentation and disclosure

Assertion: An item is disclosed, classified and described in accordance with the applicable reporting framework.

This refers to the application of relevant legislation and applicable accounting standards to the location and disclosure of the item in the financial statements. The auditor must, as part of his verification procedures check that the items in the financial statements are correctly disclosed, classified and described. Thus, for example, stocks need to be categorised by its main types in the balance sheet. The auditor needs to check the accuracy of this classification.

1.3   The use of substantive testing in the verification of financial statements

As stated above there are two categories of substantive tests: tests of details and analytical procedures.

Tests of details can be further divided between tests of individual assets and liabilities (normally performed after the balance sheet date) and tests of transactions (normally performed during interim audit). Both types of tests of details seek to obtain corroborating information on accounting data used to prepare the financial statements.

You may be asked to devise appropriate tests for various items appearing in the financial statements. This requirement may be part or all of a question. Rather than learn long lists of tests for specific items it is better to learn the principles of testing and devise tests to suit the particular circumstances given to you. Use of the financial statement assertions allows objectives of the testing to be set out, followed by specific tests.

The practical significance of the classification is that audit evidence is required for **each** assertion. For example, audit evidence obtained for the existence of stock does not compensate for the failure to obtain sufficient audit evidence on the valuation of stock.

This is not to say that more than one assertion cannot be supported through one test. There are tests which may provide audit evidence about more than one assertion. For example a test on the collection of cash from debtors after the end of the accounting period will provide evidence regarding both existence and valuation.

Examples of the type of substantive tests which are related to financial statement assertions are set out below.

(a)   Existence

- This is primarily relevant for tangible assets
- Physical inspection eg, stock count
- Inspection of documents eg, share certificates

(b)   Rights and obligations

- Documentary evidence is the prime source
- Land and buildings - documents of title
- Monetary assets - documentary evidence from debtors, banks

(c)   Occurrence

- Vouch transactions from recorded amounts in accounting records to source documents (preferably external source documents)

- For example, purchases are checked back to suppliers' invoices

(d)   Completeness

- This is a mirror image of occurrence

- If inherent risk is considered, expenses and liabilities are more likely to be incomplete than income and assets. Therefore more substantive tests are needed in these areas

- Vouch transactions from externally sourced documents to accounting records

- For example, suppliers' statements are checked to purchases

- Check numerical sequence of documentation

(e & f) Valuation and measurement

- These two assertions can often be tested with the same substantive procedure

- They often involve accounting estimates by management. SAS 420 **Audit of accounting estimates** is a useful source of reference in this regard (see below)

- Valuation of fixed assets - evidence from third parties

- Physical inspection for existence will also give evidence of condition of assets

(g)   Presentation and disclosure

- This assertion often involves management judgement. Relate amounts to appropriate accounting standards

1.4   Activity

For many companies investments in stocks and shares represent a substantial portion of total assets, for others investments are only temporary assets, or merely reflect incidental aspects of company operations. For the auditor, investments in stocks and shares represent assets with high inherent audit risk.

You are required:

(a)   to list **five** audit objectives sought by the auditor when examining investments in stocks and shares.

(b)   to explain what is meant by 'inherent audit risk' and show why investments in stocks and shares represent assets with a high inherent audit risk.

(c)   to describe the audit procedures which would verify the existence and ownership of investments in stocks and shares.

(d)   to describe how the auditor would determine that all investment income from stocks and shares had been properly recorded in the accounting records.

1.5   Activity solution

(a)   Five audit objectives in the examination of stocks and shares are:

  (i)   ensuring that shares are correctly valued at the end of the year - particularly for any fall in value;

  (ii)   checking that the shares exist by reference to share certificates, which are kept in a safe location;

  (iii)   vouching all dividends received to the profit and loss account;

  (iv)   ensuring that the company actually owns the shares, again by reference to the share certificates;

  (v)   checking the financial statements for correct presentation.

(b)   Inherent risk is the risk of material error arising from the nature of the client and its business. This risk will vary according to the client and even the area being audited within one client.

  Stocks and shares have a high inherent risk factor due to the following factors:

  (i)   Valuation

  Shares are normally valued in the financial statements at cost of purchase. At the end of the year, any permanent fall in value must be accounted for. Assessing whether a fall in value at the end of the year is temporary or permanent can be difficult due to the fact that share prices in the future are uncertain.

  (ii)   Income

  Checking completeness of income can be difficult. Dividends are not paid on set days each year, and can be for varying amounts. There is a need to ensure that the company has received all dividends due to it by reviewing dividend records from companies that the client has invested in and agreeing these to the client's bank account.

  (iii)   Fraud and theft

  Share certificates can be forged and sold by employees for cash. As share certificates are easy to sell, good internal control systems are needed to ensure safe custody of share certificates so that they are not misappropriated by employees.

(c)   Audit procedures to confirm the existence and ownership of stocks and shares would include the following:

  (i)   Vouching of share certificates. The share certificate will be evidence of both existence of the shares, and ownership, because the client company name will be stated on the share certificate to confirm who holds the shares.

  Where the certificates are kept at a third party, then either a confirmation letter should be sent to agree the shares held, or the auditor should attend the third party premises and inspect the certificates there to confirm existence and ownership.

  The auditor should always ensure that a receipt is obtained from the client or third party when certificates are returned after inspection.

  Any shares that do not have the client's name on, should be agreed to a trust or other document to confirm beneficial ownership in the client's name.

(ii)   If the certificate was purchased during the year, then sight of the contract note will also confirm ownership; this will show the shares being sold to the client, with the client name appearing on the contract note.

(iii)   A review of contract notes during the year will also identify shares sold. These sales should be agreed to the record of sales in the ledgers to ensure that they have been correctly recorded. Certificates that the client no longer owns will therefore be no longer held.

(d)   Audit work to ensure that all income had been recorded in the accounts from stocks and shares would include:

(i)   Agree an independent summary of dividends due (eg, Extel cards) to the actual dividends received in the cash book.

(ii)   Check the calculation of the dividend by multiplying the number of shares held by the amount of the dividend, and ensuring this matches the cash receipt figure. Care will be needed here to ensure that any shares sold ex-div still have the dividend received by the client.

(iii)   For any fixed interest securities, agreeing the calculation of the interest due based on the nominal value and the interest rate, to the actual amount received in the cash book.

(iv)   Analytical review of dividends received this year to the last few years to ensure completeness of dividends (taking into account all sales and purchases during this time).

1.6   SAS 420: Audit of accounting estimates

[Definition]   An accounting estimate is an approximation of the amount of an item in the absence of a precise means of measurement.

Examples are depreciation and other provisions, the reduction of stock to NRV and the doubtful debt provisions against debtors.

The risk of a material misstatement in this area is greater than others because of uncertainties regarding the outcome of events.

In addition, evidence supporting accounting estimates is generally more persuasive than conclusive and therefore auditor judgement is important.

Auditing standards

420.1   Auditors should obtain sufficient appropriate audit evidence regarding accounting estimates.

420.2   Auditors should obtain sufficient appropriate audit evidence as to whether an accounting estimate is:

(a)   reasonable in the circumstances; and

(b)   appropriately disclosed (when required).

420.3   Auditors should adopt one or a combination of the following approaches in the audit of an accounting estimate:

(a)   review and test the process used by management or the directors to develop the estimate;

(b)   use an independent estimate for comparison with that prepared by management or the directors;

(c)   review subsequent events.

420.4   Auditors should make a final assessment of the reasonableness of the accounting estimate based on their knowledge of the business and whether the estimate is consistent with other audit evidence obtained during the audit.

1.7   Formulating conclusions on substantive tests

The substantive tests should have been clearly related to the audit objectives for a particular class of transactions or balances. When the results have been obtained and errors are discovered, the errors need to be assessed in terms of which financial statement assertion(s) have not been supported. Remember that the significance of the classification of financial statement assertions is that audit evidence is required for **each** assertion.

A decision is then required as to whether further audit evidence is required to support the assertion.

Errors revealed need to be considered in relation to materiality and audit risk. Materiality and audit risk are related in the following way.

The assessment of materiality during audit planning assists in the determination of an efficient and effective audit approach. In determining an audit approach to areas within the financial statements, the preliminary materiality assessment helps the auditors decide such questions as what items to examine and whether to use sampling techniques. This enables the auditors to select audit procedures that, in combination, reduce to an acceptably low level the risk of the auditors giving an inappropriate opinion on the financial statements (audit risk).

The assessment of materiality during audit planning may differ from that at the time of evaluating the results of audit procedures. This may be because of a change in circumstances or a change in the auditors' knowledge as a result of the audit, for example if the actual results of operations and financial position are different from those anticipated by the auditors when the audit was planned.

The mechanics of relating errors to materiality levels are to list the errors found and, if a sample of transactions has been tested, project those errors to the total population to estimate the total error. The projected total error is then compared to the overall materiality level. If it exceeds the materiality level, the auditors should consider the need for further testing and/or making adjustments to the financial statements.

Some of these points are considered in SAS 220 **Materiality and the audit**.

2   ANALYTICAL REVIEW

2.1   The relationship between substantive analysis and analytical review

As stated at the start of this chapter, analytical review can be used as a source of substantive evidence. It is a type of substantive testing and substantive testing is required to support the process of substantive analysis. The central question it answers is whether the information in accounting records is consistent with the auditor's prior expectations.

The differences between analytical review and tests of details are as follows

(a)   It provides conclusions on reasonableness of data rather than precision.

(b)   It cannot easily be linked to specific assertions (ie, the nature or cause of a difference).

(c)   It is therefore less persuasive than tests of details.

It may still be used to provide substantive evidence as it is cost effective, provides corroboratory evidence and may be necessary due to the unavailability of other evidence.

2.2   Analytical review at the detailed testing stage

In deciding the extent of use of analytical review, the auditor should consider the cost and level of assurance connected with each form of testing. In most cases, analytical review procedures will be used in conjunction with other substantive tests.

The auditor should assess the risk that analytical review procedures may fail to detect material error. The extent of reliance placed on the results of analytical review should be based on the assessment of this risk.

In assessing this risk the auditor will consider the following factors

(a)   the relevance, reliability, comparability and independence of the data being used

(b)   for internally generated data, the adequacy of the controls over the preparation of financial and non-financial information

(c)   the accuracy with which the figures being examined by analytical review procedures can be predicted

(d)   the materiality of the items.

The auditor may rely largely or even entirely on analytical review procedures for validating certain items not individually significant to the financial statements taken as a whole.

2.3   Analytical review

The APB Glossary of terms defines analytical procedures as follows:

[Definition]   Analytical procedures are the analysis of relationships:

(a)   between items of financial data, or between items of financial and non-financial data, deriving from the same period; or

(b)   between comparable financial information deriving from different periods,

to identify consistencies and predicted patterns or significant fluctuations and unexpected relationships, and the results of investigations thereof.

SAS 410 **Analytical procedures** gives examples of comparisons that may usefully be made:

(a)   comparing financial information with:

(i)   comparable information for prior periods;
(ii)   anticipated results of the entity, from budgets or forecasts;
(iii)   predictive estimates prepared by the auditors;
(iv)   similar industry information.

(b)   values of appropriate accounting ratios.

2.4   The major analytical review techniques

What are these trying to achieve? Essentially, they are ensuring that the various items making up the financial statements are consistent with

(a)   each other (for example, the relationship between debtors and sales, or between current assets and current liabilities).

(b)   known trends (for example, the likely effects of government restraints on hire purchase business).

(c)   the auditor's knowledge of the business.

The auditor should ask the following three key questions.

(a)   What data, ratios and statistics exist which are of significance for the business?

(b)   With what should they compare?

(c)   Are there any variations between (a) and (b) which the auditor would expect to occur?

The auditor should allow for the effect of

(i)   General inflation (as measured by the retail price index).

(ii)   Specific price changes (goods and services used by the enterprise).

(iii)   Seasonal factors.

(iv)   Industrial disputes, including those affecting key suppliers.

(v)   Changes in the level of business activity in the economy.

(vi)   Technological changes making products or services obsolete.

(vii)   Changes in management policy eg, expanding or contracting operations (this should be apparent from a review of management or directors' minutes).

(viii) The effect of government action eg, changes in monetary policy, taxation, legislation.

As regards (a) and (b) the position may be summarised as follows

(a) *Types of data, ratios, etc*	*(b)* *Comparisons with*
Financial data (eg, items in annual statements, management accounts, budgets, account balances)	(i) Corresponding period (ii) Budgets and forecasts
Non-financial data (eg, production and employment statistics)	(i) Entries in accounting records (ii) Other financial data
Ratios and percentages (developed from financial and non-financial data eg, stock turnover ratios)	(i) Preceding period (ii) Budgets and forecasts (iii) Industry statistics

Remember that there are two points to look out for

(a)   The changes which do occur but which differ significantly from those expected.
(b)   The changes which would normally be expected to occur but which fail to do so.

The auditor should investigate both categories fully.

2.5   How analytical review procedures can be used in audit planning and risk assessment

The planning of an audit will usually take place before the annual financial statements are available and thus analytical review procedures will be performed on interim financial statements or budgets or management accounts, etc. The purposes of analytical review at the planning stage are

(a)   to improve the auditor's understanding of the enterprise and

(b)   to identify areas where the recorded value varies from the auditor's expectations enabling him to direct audit resources accordingly.

The mechanics of using analytical review at the planning stage would be to maintain a running schedule of key ratios and compare these with the ratios disclosed by the interim/draft accounts. Examples of key ratios include gross profit margin, operating profit margin, asset turnover, liquidity measures, ROCE, and external economic/industry indicators.

2.6   The uses of analytical review procedures in the review of the financial statements

The auditor should carry out an overall review of the information in the financial statements and compare it with other available data. This should not reveal material unexpected variations as they should normally have been detected at an earlier stage of the audit. If, however, they are discovered, it may be necessary either to perform additional procedures or re-perform the original procedures.

2.7   SAS 410: Analytical procedures

The SAS lays down best practice for the techniques discussed above.

Auditing standards

410.1   Auditors should apply analytical procedures at the planning and overall review stages of the audit.

410.2   Auditors should apply analytical procedures at the planning stage to assist in understanding the entity's business, in identifying areas of potential audit risk and in planning the nature, timing and extent of other audit procedures.

410.3   When completing the audit, auditors should apply analytical procedures in forming an overall conclusion as to whether the financial statements as a whole are consistent with their knowledge of the entity's business.

410.4   When significant fluctuations or unexpected relationships are identified that are inconsistent with other relevant information or that deviate from predicted patterns, auditors should investigate and obtain adequate explanations and appropriate corroborative evidence.

3   CHAPTER SUMMARY

Substantive testing refers to the procedures used to obtain audit evidence required to satisfy the audit objectives.

Audit objectives can be categorised by reference to financial statement assertions.

Substantive testing may be by tests of details and/or analytical review. Analytical review procedures can provide conclusions on the reasonableness of the data.

4   SELF TEST QUESTIONS

4.1   What are the two broad categories of substantive testing? (1.1)

4.2   What are financial statement assertions? (1.1)

4.3   What are the seven categories of financial statement assertions? (1.2)

4.4   What is completeness a mirror image of? (1.3)

4.5   What is an accounting estimate? (1.6)

4.6   How are materiality and risk related? (1.7)

4.7   What are the three differences between analytical review and tests of details? (2.1)

4.8   What audit procedures does analytical review encompass? (2.3)

5   EXAMINATION TYPE QUESTION

5.1   Healthy Milk Ltd

Healthy Milk Ltd buys milk from dairy farmers, processes the milk and delivers it to retail outlets. You are currently auditing the debtors system and determine the following information:

(i)   The company employs 75 drivers who are each responsible for delivering milk to customers. Each driver delivers milk to between 20 and 30 shops on a daily basis. Debtors normally amount to approximately £450,000. Payments by customers are not normally made to the drivers but are sent directly to the head office of the company.

(ii)   The sales ledger is regularly reviewed by the office manager who prepares a list for each driver of accounts with 90 day balances or older. This list is used for the purpose of intensive collection by the drivers. Each driver has a delivery book which is used for recording deliveries of milk and those debtors with 90 day balances.

(iii)   The audit programme used in previous audits for the selection of debtor balances for direct confirmation stated: 'Select two accounts from each driver's customers, one to be chosen by opening each driver's delivery book at random and the other as the fourth item on the list of 90 day or older accounts.' Each page of the driver's delivery book deals with a single customer.

Having reviewed the debtors system, you conclude that statistical sampling techniques should be used to assist your audit work. On the completion of your review and testing of the 2,000 debtor balances, your statistical sample of 100 accounts disclosed 10 errors. You therefore conclude that there must be 200 accounts in the entire population which are in error as you are sure that the errors detected in the sample will be in exact proportion to the errors in the population.

You are required:

(a)   to explain the reasons why the audit procedure used in the previous audit for the selection of debtors for audit confirmation would not produce a valid statistical sample.   **(4 marks)**

(b)   to explain briefly the audit objectives in selecting a sample of 90 day accounts for direct confirmation.   **(3 marks)**

(c)   to discuss whether the application of statistical sampling techniques would help in the attainment of the audit objectives set out in (b) above.   **(5 marks)**

(d)   to discuss whether it is reasonable to assume that the errors detected in the sample of debtor balances tested are in exact proportion to the errors in the total population of debtors.

          (4 marks)

(e)   to discuss the view that since statistical sampling techniques do not relieve the auditor of his responsibilities in the exercise of his professional judgement, then they are of no benefit to the auditor.   **(4 marks)**

          (Total: 20 marks)

6   ANSWER TO EXAMINATION TYPE QUESTION

6.1   Healthy Milk Ltd

(Tutorial note: parts (b) and (c) are likely to provide the most problems in this question. By remembering the auditor objectives in examining financial statement assertions, the objectives of a debtors circularisation may be determined. This provides a framework for part (b) which can be used again in (c), along with some ideas on non-sampling risk.*)*

(a)   A basic principle of statistical sampling is that each item in the population must have an equal chance of being selected. If this is not the case then there is a possibility that the sample selected will be biased in some way, and valid statistical results will not be obtainable.

The method of selection being used for Healthy Milk Ltd does not allow random selection of items for two reasons:

(i)   each roundsman is likely to have a different number of customers on his round. Choosing one customer from each book from a 'random' page means that customers on the smaller rounds have a higher chance of being picked. Taking one item from each book also assumes that the population is homogeneous (ie, all items are the same). This may not be the case because each route is different and will have different drivers;

(ii)   taking the fourth item on each list of older debtors automatically precludes the picking of other debtors on that list; again the choice is not random.

(b)   Audit objectives in circularising old debtors.

Valuation   -   provide evidence on any provision for bad debts (if circularisation request answered by liquidator or administrator) and also provide evidence as to the completeness of the balance. This ensures the value of the debtor is correctly stated in the financial statements.

Existence   -   provide evidence that the debtor balance actually exists and is therefore a bona fide debt.

Ownership   -   provide evidence that the debt is due to Healthy Milk Ltd.

Disclosure   -   provide some evidence on the value to be included for debtors in the balance sheet and the amount of any bad debt provision - especially if material.

(c)   Statistical sampling techniques may help attain the audit objectives in (b) as noted below:

Valuation   -   evidence on the completeness of the debtor balance, and therefore the accuracy of the recording of the sales system can be gained by circularising some debtors. This audit objective would otherwise be met by depth testing a statistical sample of sales invoices;

-    evidence on the bad debt provision can again come from the circularisation, although an after-date cash review is likely to provide the auditor with his main evidence.

Existence, ownership and disclosure   -   statistical evidence will be of use here because the auditor has identified potentially risky debtor balances. If these debtors are shown to be in existence, owned by the company and correctly disclosed, then the auditor has some evidence that the less risky, less old debtor balance will also be correctly treated;

-    stratification of the sample chosen will also assist the auditor because he can then concentrate on the larger balances for audit testing. Similarly increasing the confidence level will provide additional assurance that these balances are correctly stated.

The statistical technique in this situation will assist the auditor in meeting his audit objectives, as noted above, although it will suffer from additional non-sampling risk problems as follows:

(i)   debtors may fill the circularisation request form in incorrectly giving the auditor incorrect audit evidence;

(ii)   the auditor could use an incorrect audit test, or an incorrect confidence level meaning that the wrong number of items are tested;

(iii)   the auditor could also make mistakes in interpreting the results of his testing, especially regarding the number of errors found.

These factors will detract from the attainment of the audit objectives.

(d)   It is unlikely that the percentage of errors found in the sample testing will apply automatically to the whole population. Allowance must be made here for the level of precision, or movement away from this error percentage found in the sample when it is applied to the whole population. For example, a precision level of 2% would indicate that the error rate found would apply to the population, plus or minus 2%. The population error would therefore be in the range 8% to 12% for the sample error of 10% given in the question.

It is therefore possible that the error rate in the population is 10%, although this is unlikely and should not be relied upon. If the auditor wishes to be more precise regarding the population error rate, then the sample size of debtor balances tested must be increased. This will decrease the precision level to give a better estimate of the population error rate. To be 100% certain of the population error rate then all the items in the population must be tested.

In performing a statistical sample, the auditor accepts the (sampling) risk that his results may be different from those obtained from testing the whole population. As long as the maximum expected error does not exceed the tolerable error for this test, then the auditor can accept the results of the test, that is the correct degree of assurance has been achieved.

(e)   Statistical sampling techniques do not relieve the auditor of his responsibilities in the exercise of his professional judgement because:

(i)   the auditor must still determine the confidence and precision levels, and the tolerable error to use in the statistical sample; and

(ii)   in evaluating the results of the test, the auditor must still decide what constitutes an error and decide how this potentially affects the whole population.

Statistical sampling techniques do provide the following benefits to the auditor:

(i)   results of the tests can be determined precisely using statistical techniques;

(ii)   they decrease potential liability to clients and third parties by providing a precise audit methodology that can be defended in court;

(iii)   it assists in audit planning and testing by making the auditor identify populations for testing and determining the testing method.

Statistical techniques do therefore provide some benefit to the auditor and do not completely relieve him of his professional judgement.

26 COMPUTER AUDITING

INTRODUCTION & LEARNING OBJECTIVES

Computers affect the work of the auditor in two main ways:

(a)   The client uses a computer to produce all or part of the financial accounting data

(b)   The auditor may be able to use a computer to assist in his audit, particularly when the client has a computer system.

The main types of questions you may be asked in the examination are

(a)   the problems associated with auditing a computer system and procedures to overcome the problems

(b)   how a client operates controls in a computer system

(c)   the extent to which the auditor can use Computer Assisted Audit Techniques (CAATs) in his audit.

(d)   the use by auditors of microcomputers to assist in audits.

When you have studied this chapter you should be able to do the following:

*   Discuss the use of computers in the audit process.
*   Describe the use of CAATs.
*   Explain the establishment of controls in systems development.

---

1   THE USE OF COMPUTERS IN THE AUDIT PROCESS

1.1   The impact of computers on the auditing process

Until fairly recently, computers were mainly used in the administrative running of the office rather than the actual conduct of the audit. Tasks such as time sheets and maintenance of the fees ledger (ie, a sales invoicing procedure) were computerised.

Large firms also developed Computer Assisted Audit Techniques (CAATs) to use on their clients' mainframe computers. Their use was mainly on large audits as a result. CAATs are discussed in detail later in this chapter.

The advent of the portable micro-computer in recent years has led to their increasing use on the audit due to the portability of the hardware. The ability to take a computer 'out on audit' greatly increases the opportunities of use. Software has developed as a result of this portability.

1.2   Uses of microcomputers

A microcomputer may be used by the auditor in the following ways to assist his audit work

(a)   Flowcharting a client's systems

Specialist flowcharting packages can assist the auditor in the production of clear, well presented flowcharts. Although the package cannot review the system for the auditor, they do produce legible output and can be easily updated when systems change, unlike manually produced flowcharts.

(b)   **Evaluation of audit risk**

The auditor can input into the computer his assessment of the audit risk for the various transactions and balances in the client's systems. The computer can record these assessments in a word processing package, and may also provide guidance to the level of testing required via an expert systems shell.

(c)   **Preparation of audit programmes**

Audit programmes can be typed into a word processor, which again will allow for easy updating in the following years. Some firms may also have standard audit tests kept on a database within the word processor. When the test is required, it is simply copied out of the database into the audit programme. This is far quicker than typing the whole test into a computer.

(d)   **Analytical review techniques**

A standard template can be set up on a spreadsheet package. Onto this template, the auditor inputs key details such as balance sheet totals from the financial statements. The spreadsheet then calculates key accounting ratios to assist the auditor with his analytical review.

(e)   **Preparation of audit working papers**

Where a computer is available to audit staff at the client's premises, it can be used to type up audit working papers. Audit documents with a lot of writing such as memos and summaries of tests will benefit from being produced more quickly on the computer and to a higher standard of legibility.

1.3   Software

(a)   **Commercially available packages**

Most audit firms will purchase at least one word processor package and one spreadsheet package. These programs will then be used as outlined above to assist the auditor in his audit work.

(b)   **Specialist programmes written in-house**

Larger audit firms will employ computer programmers in-house to write specialist software for use only by that audit firm. Examples of this type of software include databases of standard audit tests that can be copied into audit programmes, and expert systems that will assist the auditor in his determination of audit risk and setting of testing levels.

1.4   Controls

The controls that must be exercised by the auditor when microcomputers are used in his audit work will include the following:

(a)   **Backup of files**

Backup copies of all audit files kept on the computer should be made regularly (at least once per day). These backup copies should be kept in a separate location from the microcomputer. If then the microcomputer is lost or damaged, the copy files can be used to continue work on that client.

When an audit is finished, and the client files are taken off the computer to make room for the next client's files, at least two and preferably three backup copies should be made. This ensures that if one copy becomes corrupted or lost, then the files can be retrieved from the second copy of the files.

(b)   **Security of files**

Audit information on clients can be very sensitive. Adequate procedures must therefore be in force to ensure that only authorised audit staff can gain access to the audit information. All audit computers should therefore be protected by passwords, and disks with client data stored in safe locations eg, a fire proof safe.

Care must also be taken to ensure that computers holding client data are not stolen. If a computer is left at a client's premises overnight then it should either be locked in a safe, or securely chained and padlocked to a table.

(c)   **Adequacy of documentation**

There is a danger with computers that not all the data or reasoning used to reach a particular decision will be documented. This can arise due to lack of ability to use the system. Adequate documentation must therefore be kept, including print-outs of all major documents, for future reference, together with the reasons for the decisions made.

(d)   **Testing of programs**

Before any program is used on audits, it should be tested to ensure that it is as far as possible error free. This is particularly true of programs written by the audit firm itself. The auditor could be particularly exposed in court if he made a wrong decision due to faulty or inadequately tested software.

2   THE AUDIT IMPLICATIONS OF THE COMPUTERISATION OF A CLIENT'S RECORDS

2.1   Introduction

There are a number of distinguishing features of computer based systems which must be recognised and considered by the auditor. The main features are:

- Concentration of controls in the computer department

- Lack of primary records

- Encoded data

- Loss of audit trail

- Data needed for audit purposes may be overwritten

- Program controls may be important to ensure the completeness and accuracy of accounting records

- The need for specialist expertise

- Availability of computer time

2.2   Concentration of controls in the computer department

The need to standardise procedures and utilise the computer resources of a business has led to a concentration of controls in the computer department. You should recognise that such a concentration represents a potential weakness. There is a danger of inadvertent or deliberate corruption of data of which other departments are unaware.

Most computer users minimise this danger by adopting control procedures which apportion responsibilities within the computer department and allow other (user) departments to check the accuracy of processed data. The auditor's work, particularly at the planning stage, will involve identifying the extent of controls. Clearly if such controls are concentrated in the computer department the adequate functioning of the department will be fundamental to the audit.

The recent reduction in costs of computer hardware has led to the dispersal of both processing and controls in some systems. This enables the users to be more closely involved with the data processing function but may lead to an absence of standardisation of controls. It is a problem considered in more detail later.

2.3   Lack of primary records

In some systems conventional day books will not be maintained. In others an originating document may not be created. In an on-line system for example an operator may receive an order by telephone and use a terminal to key in the relevant data immediately. The system creates despatch and invoice documentation and updates stock and customer files. The auditor would be unable to trace these transactions back to an originating document.

Such problems are relevant to both management and auditors and should be considered at the time the system is designed. It would be essential for computer generated reports to be provided and reviewed carefully by management.

2.4   Encoded data

There is always a danger of transposition errors arising at the encoding stage. The auditor's procedures should take into account the existence of checking procedures (eg, check digits, data validation) particularly on amendments to standing data items and on the conversion from one system to another.

2.5   Loss of audit trail

Modern systems are usually designed to limit the volume of printed data. Control is implemented by exception reporting principles so that detailed print-outs of magnetically stored data are not available. The auditor is therefore unable to trace an individual transaction through the system from originating document to financial statements (or vice-versa) in the traditional way. There is said to be a loss of (visible) audit trail.

The auditor must assess the implications of this at the planning stage. It may result in a need to use computer-assisted techniques to obtain appropriate evidence that controls have functioned adequately.

2.6   Data needed for audit purposes may be overwritten

When data is stored on magnetic tape or disk it will eventually be overwritten with new data. The auditor will need to plan audit testing to ensure that the appropriate data is available to him. He may need to make frequent visits to his client's premises to ensure that he covers an adequate spread of transactions during the year.

2.7   Program controls

The auditor must test controls upon which he wishes to rely. This means that he will need to test programmed controls. To do this he will inevitably have to use computer-assisted auditing techniques.

A further complication which often arises is that the program controls are regularly amended by the client. Old programs may be overwritten and may be unavailable at the accounting year end. The implication is that once again the auditor must be prepared to review and test controls regularly during the year so that he can obtain adequate evidence regarding the functioning of controls during the whole period.

2.8   The need for specialist expertise

As computers become extensively used it is relevant for all auditors to become computer auditors in the sense that they are capable of auditing systems which are computerised. However, it is no longer realistic to expect all staff to have the competence to conduct all audits. There is an irrefutable case for the employment of computer specialists. Survey data shows that there is a swing in internal audit departments toward using DP specialists rather than accountants for such audit work. This trend may spread to external audits as audit competence is put together on a team basis.

There is a major problem for external auditors in that employing and training such staff is expensive. This may be a particular problem for smaller practices who do not at present have an extensive portfolio of clients with computer-based accounting systems. It should be impressed upon clients that the installation of a cheap computer system does not necessarily decrease audit costs and may well increase them.

2.9   Availability of computer time

The use of computer-assisted auditing techniques involves the use of the client's computer facilities. There may be a need to organise such facilities well ahead of the required dates.

2.10   Activity

List the eight special features of computer based systems.

2.11   Activity solution

Concentration of controls in the computer department

Lack of primary records

Encoded data

Loss of audit trail

Data needed for audit purposes may be overwritten

Program controls may be important to ensure the completeness and accuracy of accounting records

The need for specialist expertise

Availability of computer time

3   AUDITING GUIDELINE 'AUDITING IN A COMPUTER ENVIRONMENT'

In 1984, Auditing Guideline 407 **Auditing in a computer environment** was issued. In this Guideline, it is possible to identify the following major features:

(a)   The message is strongly conveyed that the principles of an audit in a computer environment are the same as in other circumstances.

(b)   The Guideline includes in the preface a clear 'health warning' that detailed practical guidance should be obtained by those who are unaccustomed to auditing in a computer environment.

(c)   Emphasis is laid on the knowledge and skills that an auditor will need when auditing in a computer environment. In particular, auditors are recommended that they should develop a basic understanding of the fundamentals of data processing, and attain a level of technical computer knowledge and skills commensurate with the particular circumstances of the audit.

(d)   Smaller computers are discussed near the beginning of the document. The basic message is that, with the introduction of smaller computers, there is a greater likelihood of weak internal controls, and this will normally lead to greater emphasis being placed on substantive testing of transactions and balances, and on other procedures such as analytical review, rather than on tests of controls.

(e)   An explanation is given of audit techniques performed by computer, but the point is made that, where there is a computer-based accounting system, many of the auditor's procedures may still be carried out manually.

(f)   Account is given of the two major types of controls over computer-based accounting systems ('general controls' and 'application controls'), and of the interrelationship between them.

(g)   Guidance is given on the situation where third party service organisations (such as computer service bureaux or software houses) are used for the purpose of maintaining part or all of an enterprise's accounting records and procedures. It is explained that the auditor may encounter practical obstacles, as the enterprise may be placing some reliance on the proper operation of internal controls exercised by the third party. It is recommended that, where the auditor finds it impracticable to obtain all the information and explanations that he requires from the enterprise itself, he should carry out other procedures. These may include taking steps he considers necessary to enable him to rely on the work performed by other auditors, or carrying out procedures at the premises of the third party.

The details of the guideline are incorporated into the following sections of this chapter.

4   SAS 480 : SERVICE ORGANISATIONS

4.1   Introduction

The APB issued SAS 480 'Service organisations' in January 1999. As outsourcing of non-core activities becomes more prevalent in business life, standards are needed to set out a framework for determining the effect of outsourced activities on the audit, and the procedures that may be followed to obtain audit evidence concerning outsourced activities.

4.2   Key auditing standards

480.1   Auditors should identify whether a reporting entity uses service organisations and assess the effect of any such use on the procedures necessary to obtain sufficient appropriate audit evidence to determine with reasonable assurance whether the user entity's financial statements are free of material misstatement'.

Examples of outsourced activities carried out by service organisations include information processing, facilities management and the maintenance of accounting records. An entity's use of a service organisation does not alter the auditor's responsibilities when reporting on financial statements, but may affect the procedures necessary to obtain sufficient appropriate audit evidence.

480.2   'In planning the audit, user entity auditors should determine whether activities undertaken by service organisations are relevant to the audit'.

480.3   'User entity auditors should obtain and document an understanding of

(a)   the contractual terms which apply to relevant activities undertaken by service organisations; and

(b)   the way that the user entity monitors those activities so as to ensure that it meets its fiduciary and other legal responsibilities.'

480.4   'User entity auditors should determine the effect of relevant activities on their assessment of inherent risk and the user entity's control environment'.

Following their assessment of inherent and control risk, auditors must design audit tests aimed at providing sufficient appropriate audit evidence of whether the financial statements are free from material misstatement.

In some cases, auditors will need to visit the service organisation themselves, or be issued with a satisfactory report on the organisation's system of controls.

If the auditors conclude that evidence from records held by a service organisation is necessary to form their audit opinion and they are unable to obtain such evidence, they should:

(a)   describe the lack of evidence in the basis of opinion section of their report: and

(b)   qualify their opinion or issue a disclaimer of opinion on the financial statements.

Effective date

Auditors must comply with SAS 480 in all audits of financial statements for periods beginning on or after 23 December 1998.

5   THE USE OF CAATs INCLUDING EXPERT SYSTEMS AND AUDIT ENQUIRY PROGRAMS

5.1   Utilisation of CAATs

There are two main groups of CAATs.

(a)   **Audit software**

Computer programs used for audit purposes to examine the contents of the enterprise's computer files;

(b)   **Test data**

Data used by the auditor for computer processing to test the operation of the enterprise's computer programs. A general name for this testing is audit enquiry programs.

There are other more complex techniques. Such techniques will be considered later in this section.

5.2   The advantages of CAATs to the auditor

(a)   In a computer-based system the large volume of transactions is likely to force the auditor to rely upon programmed controls. CAATs are likely to be the only effective way of testing programmed controls.

(b)   The use of CAATs will enable the auditor to test a much larger number of items quickly and accurately and therefore increase the confidence he has in his opinion.

(c)   CAATs enable the auditor to test the accounting system and its records (ie, the tapes and disk files) rather than relying upon testing printouts of what he believes to be a copy of those records.

(d)   Once set up CAATs are likely to be a cost effective way of obtaining audit evidence provided that the enterprise does not regularly change its systems.

(e)   Careful planning by the auditor should enable the results of his work using CAATs to be compared with results from the traditional clerical audit work to increase confidence.

5.3   Audit software

(a)   Audit software comprises computer programs used by the auditor to examine an enterprise's computer files. It may consist of generalised package programs, specially written programs or the client's own programs.

(i)   **Generalised package programs**

These are programs already written either by the auditor or a specialist software company which are designed to be used on different types of machine. They need to be tailored to each specific case by defining the format of the files to be interrogated and by specifying the parameters of output data required and the form of that output. In some cases supplementary program coding is required.

(ii)   **Specially written programs**

In some cases it is not possible to adapt a package program due to the type of machine, processing or file organisation used. In such cases a purpose-written program is required. It could be written by the auditor himself, by a software specialist or by the client acting on the instructions of the auditor. In all cases it should be fully tested before being used 'live'.

(iii)   **The client's own programs ('enquiry programs')**

These can often be useful to the auditor. For example, when using a terminal it is necessary to use the existing enquiry programs to refer to data held on files, or to obtain a print-out of parts of a file. In many cases, however, the client's own programs will not provide all the facilities needed by the auditor. It is likely that the team responsible for writing the enquiry programs produced the rest of the system and there is therefore a danger that the same defects apply to all such programs in the system.

(b)   **Use of audit software**

Audit software may be used during many compliance and substantive procedures. Its use is particularly appropriate during substantive testing of transactions and balances, as it may scrutinise large volumes of data and extract information leaving skilled manual resources to concentrate upon the investigation of the results.

Typical uses of such programs include:

(i)   **Calculation checks**

eg, the program adds the value of open items on a file to ensure that they agree with control records which are maintained.

(ii)   **Detecting violations of systems rules**

eg, the program checks all accounts on the sales ledger to ensure that no customer has a balance above a specified credit limit.

(iii)   **Detecting unreasonable items**

eg, a check that no customer is allowed trade discount of more than 50%, or that no sales ledger balance is more than total sales made to that customer.

(iv)   **Conducting new calculations and analyses**

eg, obtaining a statistical analysis of stock movements to identify slow-moving items.

(v)   **Selection of items for audit testing**

eg, obtaining a stratified sample of sales ledger balances to be used as a basis for a debtors circularisation.

(vi)   **Completeness checks**

eg, checking continuity of sales invoices to ensure they are all accounted for.

(c)   **Difficulties in using computer audit programs**

(i)   **Costs**

There will be substantial set-up costs even in using a generalised package. This is because the client's procedures and files need to be investigated thoroughly prior to identifying audit tests. The use of specially written programs will be even more expensive.

(ii) **Changes to client's systems**

These can mean costly alterations to the programs or at least require the programs to be run regularly during the year to test the system at different dates.

(iii) **Small installations**

There may be no suitable audit software package for use on mini-computer or micro-computer installations. Software documentation may be incomplete so that it is very difficult to identify all procedures. It may be impossible to justify and hence recover the cost of specially written audit software.

(iv) **Over-elaboration**

There may be a tendency to produce over-elaborate enquiry programs which are expensive to develop, take up considerable computer running time and extensive reviewing time. The auditor should be able to justify the costs of using the program to the benefit in audit terms of its use.

(v) **Quantities of output**

An enquiry program may produce huge quantities of output. This may be because the system is wrong or the enquiry program was badly designed. To avoid this problem some packages can be set to terminate after a given number of items have been included in the count. The auditor must distinguish between cases when he has merely misjudged the parameters and obtained too large a sample and cases where the print-out is long because lots of items are wrong. In the latter case he must follow the audit work through and consider the implications of the problems encountered.

(vi) **Version of files used in the test**

The audit software only tests the files against which it is run. It is therefore preferable to use the software on the actual files of the client. The permission of the client is needed and the software must be carefully tested prior to its use on 'live' data.

An alternative approach is to run the programs against copies of the data files. To be valid there must be adequate general controls to ensure that the client uses the same files. Provided this is so the use of copy files enables the auditor to be more flexible in deciding when to test and to retain the copy files for further testing.

5.4 Test data

(a) **Description**

Audit test data consists of data submitted by the auditor for processing by the client's computer-based accounting system. It may be processed during a normal production run (running test data 'live') or during a special run at a point in time outside the normal cycle (running the test data 'dead').

Test data could be held in the form of a batch of documents put through the system to test both manual and computer controls. It is more often meant to refer to data recorded on magnetic tape or cassette used to test programmed controls. Its primary use is in the compliance testing of application controls.

Note that the use of test data is not confined to the external auditor. It is a method used by programmers, analysts and internal auditors as part of systems development and monitoring procedures. There may be scope for co-operation between internal and external auditors in creating such test data.

(b)   **Use of test data**

There are three major approaches:

(i)   **Using live data**

At its simplest level the auditor could use real data that has been processed which involves the controls he wants to test. He should then predetermine the results which he would expect from the processing of the data. He later checks that the actual processing has been carried out in the expected way and investigates any differences.

This method is not usually feasible. The auditor will usually want to use a collection of normal, exceptional and even absurd data to test controls. He is unlikely to find all these conditions in a batch of data. The vast bulk of day-to-day items will contain few exceptions and no absurd data. It would take the auditor a long time to find a suitable range of data items to use.

(ii)   **Dummy data in a normal production run**

The auditor constructs a series of dummy transactions which contain the required conditions. These are processed along with normal data. Actual results are then compared with predetermined results.

This method has the advantage of producing a realistic test environment. The client's actual programs and data files are being used in the test.

The dangers of this method are, however, considerable. Computer-generated documentation may have to be intercepted before it is released. There may be a need to reverse the transactions after testing to eliminate the effects of test data. This may be time-consuming and require program amendments. It may distort management information by swelling the number of cancelled orders and credit notes. It would indeed be ironic if a client's accounting records were corrupted by the auditor's own test data. Therefore great care is needed in planning and controlling the test.

(iii)   **Dummy data in a special run**

In this method the auditor creates special data and uses it against copies of the client's data files. The dangers associated with 'live' testing are therefore largely eliminated although the interaction of one file with another must still be carefully considered.

It is still essential to obtain the client's permission which reduces the independence of the test. It is also necessary to obtain assurance that the program being used in the test run is identical to that used by the client for production runs and not a special program kept aside for the auditor's use!

(c)   **Difficulties in using audit test data**

(i)   **Costs**

There may be considerable costs involved in ascertaining the relevant controls and in constructing test data from scratch. It may be very difficult to identify all relevant conditions. The need to predetermine the results manually may be both time-consuming and tedious. These costs, however, are normally substantially less than for audit software.

(ii)   **Objectives of the test**

Test data is likely to be confined to tests of controls and therefore may be less valuable in audit terms than using audit software.

(iii)   **Dangers of live testing**

Careful planning and control is needed to expurgate the test data from the records.

(iv)   **Dangers of testing during a special run**

If special test runs are used, an artificial testing environment is created. Assurance is needed that the normal programs and files have been used.

(v)   **Recording**

The use of test data does not necessarily provide visible evidence of the audit work performed. Working papers should therefore include details of the controls to be tested, an explanation of how they are to be tested, details of the transactions and files used, details of the predicted results, the actual results and evidence of the predicted and actual results having being compared.

5.5   Other techniques

An examination question would be likely to concentrate on audit software and test data: however more sophisticated techniques do exist and they could be tested perhaps in part of a question. Try to grasp the main principles and don't spend too much time on this section. In many cases the techniques were first developed for internal purposes eg, during program development. They often require considerable DP expertise to be used accurately.

(a)   **Integrated test facilities (ITF)**

This is an extension of the test data technique. The system is designed at the output stage to handle audit test data without unwanted side effects. The auditor uses test data, input as part of a normal run, and applied to 'dummy' test records held on master files. The weakness of this is that there is a danger of test data being subject to special procedures which are not applied to normal transactions.

ITF allows test data to be left in the system to see what happens eg, a dummy sale record eventually creates an overdue sales ledger balance. The auditor can use ITF to carry out regular testing of the system without using a special test run and indeed without being present during processing.

ITF is used largely to compliance test application controls.

(b)   **Embedded audit facilities**

Embedded audit facilities can be described as an 'expert system'.

A wide variety of terms is used to describe this technique, including 'integrated audit monitors', 'resident audit software' and 'integrated audit modules'. It consists of a module of a computer program written by the auditor which is incorporated into the client's computer system either temporarily or permanently.

This technique allows tests to be made at the time the data is being processed. It is 'real time auditing'. It is useful where the audit trail is deficient so that historical audit work is difficult, or where files are constantly being updated eg, in a real time or database system. The facilities may allow results to be printed immediately or to be written onto tape or disk for later evaluation by the auditor.

This technique may achieve the following objectives:

(i)   To store information as it is processed for subsequent audit review.

(ii)   To check the integrity of files which are being processed.

(iii)   To spot and record items which are of some special audit interest, as previously defined by the auditor.

(c)   **Systems software data analysis**

Most systems software provides facilities for logging information relating to computer activity. For example, details may be kept of invalid passwords used, attempts to gain unauthorised access to data, operator interventions or keying errors.

The data from this software may be analysed to provide evidence during the compliance testing of general controls. It may be particularly useful in systems which allow easy access to data through terminals but which have sophisticated software available to provide such data.

(d)   **Application program examination**

This involves detailed examination of the program instructions within the client's system.

It can be done manually but there are also some specially written computer programs which can be used to assist in this task.

The auditor may wish to check that a program is operating in the way that it should be. For example, the program code which performs a complex discount calculation may be examined to ensure that the discounts are properly computed. This would be done as part of the compliance testing of the application controls.

Alternatively the auditor may examine programs as part of his compliance testing of general controls. For example, in testing the controls that ensure that all program changes are adequately tested and documented, he may use software to compare two versions of the program in the production library before and after the changes and check them against the program change documentation.

(e)   **Parallel simulation**

This is a technique whereby the auditor writes a program which is intended to perform the same operation as a client's program.

Identical data is submitted to each program and the results are compared. Obviously they should be identical: if they are not then it means that one of the programs is not operating correctly.

(f)   **Tracing**

Tracing involves following a transaction through its processing from start to finish to determine which program instructions are executed. This is a means of determining what the system is.

5.6   CAATs in database management systems (DBMS)

Unfortunately, generalised audit software may be of limited use in database systems because:

(a)   There are many different DBMS and a lack of standardisation in languages used.

(b)   The enquiry programs may be geared to conventional sequential files and it may be very troublesome to convert the database into this form.

(c)   Management may be reluctant to allow the auditor access to the database without restrictions on his actions which all other users must suffer.

A more effective approach may be to use some sort of embedded facility. The auditor can then maintain a regular check of the controls and operation of the database. This approach requires considerable expertise and the software costs may be extremely high.

5.7 Activity

(a) What do the initials CAAT stand for?

(b) How is the use of CAATs advantageous to the auditor?

(c) Describe two main types of CAAT.

5.8 Activity solution

(a) Computer Assisted Audit Technique.

(b) CAATs are of use to the auditor in the following ways:

(i) in a computer-based system the sheer volume of transactions is likely to force the auditor to rely upon programmed controls. CAATs are likely to be the only effective way of testing programmed controls;

(ii) the use of CAATs will enable the auditor to test a much larger number of items quickly and accurately and therefore increase the confidence he has in his opinion;

(iii) CAATs enable the auditor to test the accounting system and its records rather than relying upon testing print-outs of what he believes to be a copy of those records;

(iv) once set up, CAATs are likely to be a cost-effective way of obtaining audit evidence;

(v) careful planning by the auditor should enable the results of his work using CAATs to be compared with results from the traditional clerical audit work to increase confidence.

(c) (i) Audit software comprises computer programs used by the auditor to examine an enterprise's computer files. It may consist of generalised package programs, specially written programs or the client's own programs.

Audit software may be used during both compliance and substantive procedures, although it is particularly appropriate for use in the substantive testing of transactions and balances as it may scrutinise large volumes of data and extract information leaving skilled manual resources to concentrate upon investigation of the results.

(ii) Test data consists of data submitted by the auditor for processing by the enterprise's computer-based accounting system. It may be processed during a normal production run ('live' test data) or during a special run at a point in time outside the normal cycle ('dead' test data).

6 AUDIT PROCEDURES RELATING TO SYSTEMS DEVELOPMENT

6.1 Establishment of internal controls

A computer system is able to significantly increase the speed of processing of accounting data but with its increased power and the use of fewer personnel, there is a danger of errors unless strong controls are established. The auditor should have an input on the initial and any subsequent developments of the system to ensure that controls are designed in the system. It is far easier to ensure good controls at the development stage rather than later.

6.2 **Application controls**

Definition Application controls cover the transactions and master files which are specific to an individual application.

They are applicable to both computer and manual processing and will therefore consist of both manually-performed and computer-performed controls.

Their objective is to ensure the completeness and accuracy of all processing and the validity of the accounting entries made. They fall under the following six main headings and the control *objectives* for each are:

(a) **Completeness of input**

- To ensure that a document is raised for every transaction.
- To ensure that each document is input in timely fashion.

(b) **Accuracy of input**

To identify the accuracy of data fields on data transactions.

(c) **Authorisation of input**

- To ensure that each transaction is authorised.
- To ensure that the individual who authorised the transaction was empowered to do so.

(d) **Controls over processing (updating)**

- To ensure that all input data is processed.
- To ensure that the correct versions of master files and standing data files are used.
- To ensure that the processing of each transaction is accurate to produce accurately updated master files.

(e) **Control over output**

- To ensure that output is checked for completeness and accuracy.
- To ensure that output is properly distributed and actioned.

(f) **Controls over master files**

- To ensure that all data held on master files is accurate and up-to-date.
- To ensure that any amendment to standing data is properly authorised.

The control *techniques* for application controls under the six headings are shown below.

6.3   Control techniques for application controls

PROCESSING	OUTPUT	MASTERFILE
• Batch reconciliation	• Check batch control outputs to inputs	• Check amendments on a one to one basis
• Run to run totals to ensure no data lost	• Summary of totals	• Periodic printout and checks
• Summary processing eg, check total depreciation equal to summary of elements	• 'End of Report' message	• Record counts checked
• External file labels	• Checklist for distribution of output	• Independent control totals
• Internal file labels	• Follow up exception reports	

APPLICATION CONTROLS

INPUT

COMPLETENESS	ACCURACY	AUTHORISATION
• One for one check ie, each input checked to output	• Check digits	• Manual authorisation
• Batch control totals	• Reasonableness checks to ensure data within certain ranges	• Clerical review of transactions
• Hash totals	• Existence checks eg, to check that customer account exists	• One for one checking of amendments to standing data
• Document counts	• Manual controls eg, batch controls and arithmetic checks	• Programmed checks on authorisation limits
• Sequence checks		
• Matching each master file record to a transaction record		

It should be appreciated that techniques which control the accuracy of input and processing will help to control master file data. As master file standing data items are used many times over in processing they take on a greater importance than transaction data and more costly controls such as one-for-one checks may be justified.

6.4   General controls

Definition   These controls cover the general environment within which application controls operate. Such controls can be expected to be relevant to all applications.

The objective of such controls is to ensure the integrity of application development and implementation and to ensure that computer operations are properly administered to protect hardware, programs and data files.

The Auditing Guideline envisages controls in the following areas and the control objectives for each are:

(a)   **Controls over systems development (application development)**

- To ensure developments are fully authorised.
- To ensure proper standards are followed during development.
- To ensure changes are properly tested and documented.

(b)   **Controls to prevent/detect errors during program execution**

To ensure any errors arising are noted and resolved.

(c)   **Controls to prevent/detect changes to data files**

- To ensure changes are authorised.
- To ensure changes are made accurately.

(d)   **Controls to ensure continuity of operations**

To ensure the system can continue to function in the event of disaster or breakdown.

6.5   Control techniques for general controls

ERRORS DURING PROGRAM EXECUTION	CHANGES TO DATA FILES	CONTINUITY OF OPERATIONS
• Systems software should report errors eg, wrong file, hardware malfunction	• Prior authorisation	• Back up procedures
• Detailed operations	• Password protection	• Standby arrangements
• Job scheduling	• Back up files	• Testing back up procedures
	• Record of amendments for subsequent checking	• Protection against fire and theft
	• Physical protection of files	• Maintenance agreements
		• Insurance
		• Copy of files

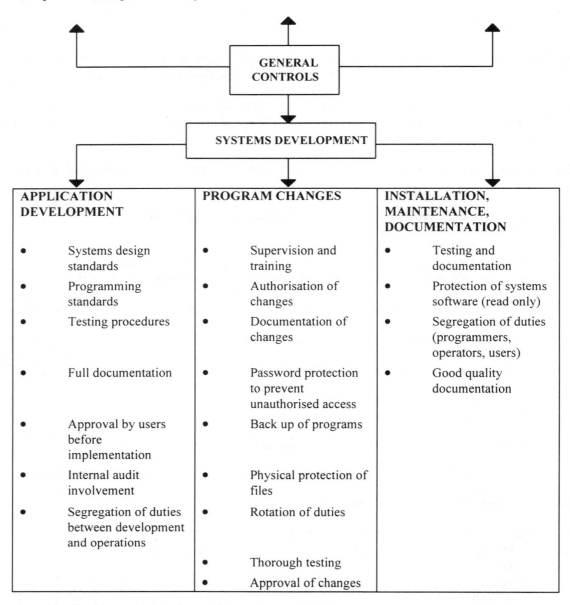

APPLICATION DEVELOPMENT	PROGRAM CHANGES	INSTALLATION, MAINTENANCE, DOCUMENTATION
• Systems design standards	• Supervision and training	• Testing and documentation
• Programming standards	• Authorisation of changes	• Protection of systems software (read only)
• Testing procedures	• Documentation of changes	• Segregation of duties (programmers, operators, users)
• Full documentation	• Password protection to prevent unauthorised access	• Good quality documentation
• Approval by users before implementation	• Back up of programs	
• Internal audit involvement	• Physical protection of files	
• Segregation of duties between development and operations	• Rotation of duties	
	• Thorough testing	
	• Approval of changes	

7 FURTHER EXAMPLES OF SELECTED CONTROLS

Some of the controls in the previous section may be unfamiliar to you. Further details are given here.

7.1 Manual controls

(a) Physical controls

Many of the more simple controls are largely a matter of common sense. To limit access to the computer room, by keeping it locked when not in use and allowing keys only to specified people, is an obvious ploy. It makes sense too to prevent smoking in the environs of the computers and disks since carefully stored data can be ruined by the practice.

Floppy disks can be damaged by direct sunlight, extremely cold temperatures and a damp atmosphere. It is important, therefore, to plan both the situation of the room to be used for electronic data processing and the positioning of computers and disks within the room with great care.

It need hardly be noted that fire precautions should be taken, and an arrangement made with, perhaps, another firm to utilise its equipment in an emergency. Service agreements with computer manufacturers frequently provide a useful emergency system. Such agreements enable machines to be exchanged, so that an operating machine remains in the department while the original one is repaired.

(b)   **Back-up disks**

One of the most fundamental aspects of a structure is the creation and updating of an identical back-up disk for every disk in the system (this means data files and program files). The back-up disks should be stored in an entirely separate place to where the main disks are kept. This covers not only local damage to one or a few disks, but also more drastic circumstances such as a fire in the computer room that destroys all the main disks kept there.

Having created a back-up copy of a disk, it is essential that it is altered every time any change is made to the main disk if the system is to function effectively.

(c)   **Data filing**

Having established a set of source and back-up disks, the need for a filing system is obvious. Each disk should be labelled clearly, following a set pattern so that the data stored on it can be identified immediately making it less likely that a disk full of vital information will be written over in mistake for a blank disk. It may be appropriate to print labels, thereby imposing a degree of control on how each disk is rendered identifiable.

The labelled disks should be filed in special disk boxes to provide a degree of protection against liquid being spilt on the disks or their being bent or folded (all of which is likely to damage them and ruin the data that they contain).

Since many disks will be collected over a period of time, it is important, as with any collection of material to which one will need to refer frequently, to file them efficiently so that any disk is easy to find at any given moment. (Naturally, this is applicable to the back-up disks too). The appointment of a disk librarian to control the filing and movement of disks is a useful precaution.

(d)   **Documentation**

This is as vital as any other of the system controls as it provides both a support system for work already stored on disk and file, and a progress report on data currently being processed or updated. A wall chart is often a workable means of charting the progress of data on, or being put onto disk. The chart should be clear and alterable, and, most importantly, kept up-to-date. It will then be possible to see at a glance the stage reached by any items of data.

Each process should also be documented and a job sheet, clearly explaining the tasks that are to be done, should pass to the person responsible for completing them.

As data is stored on disk, further useful documentation can be provided by creating an information file for each disk. A list of all the files on that disk and their contents, as well as the dates on which the files were originated and updated and the nature of the persons responsible for this, can be recorded on an information file, as well as any further notes likely to be of use later.

(e)   **Staff training**

In addition to these control structures, it is important that all staff involved with electronic data processing are adequately trained so that they understand the system and the reasoning behind the controls to which they must keep. They must be aware too of the need for careful handling of the disks themselves (a fingerprint on the floppy disk can spoil the data stored on it). They should follow instructions carefully concerning the reformatting of disks whose data has been updated and stored on another disk. It is essential that more than one version of the same material should not exist simultaneously where confusion could arise over which contains the more recent data.

(f)   **Proofing**

Finally, there is always room for manual checking or proofing to control data disks. This process should be carried out after data has been keyed onto the disk for the first time. Mistakes identified during proofing should be corrected and then the corrections proofed. If necessary, further corrections should then be completed, at which stage the data may usually be regarded as thoroughly checked and accurate.

7.2   Programmed controls

(a)   **Passwords**

The more sophisticated the program, the more in-built controls it is likely to have. This is particularly true of the control known as *data-hiding*. When a disk contains information that should not be widely available (for example, data concerning salaries on personnel files) it is possible to *hide it*, while making other information on the same disk less difficult to obtain. This may be done by *passwords*.

A program that operates through passwords will prevent access to either all or specific items of data to any user who is not aware of the relevant password.

Passwords can also be applied in such a way that Read-Only access to a file is available without the appropriate password. It is possible to impose a password on a disk drive (this is particularly relevant to computers with only one disk drive and hard disk storage). It is, however, not highly advisable, as to forget the password is to render access to the computer totally impossible.

(b)   **Date/time stamps**

A computer program can also contain a date and/or time stamp. This will ask the user to key in the date and time at which he/she loads the programs. It will continue then to stamp each file created or updated until the program is removed or the computer turned off with the date and time. This feature is very useful, especially when comparing two versions of the same data, as it will show immediately which is the more recent. Most computers now have their own internal clocks and calendars and will automatically fill in a program's requests concerning time and date.

(c)   **Prompts**

The deletion of any created file is often controlled by a stage at which the computer pauses and asks the user if he/she is sure that the deletion command was intentional. Similarly, any attempt to exit the program or retrieve another file without storing work done previously, is checked by a similar pause and query that provides the user with the opportunity to go back and save the data if it is required.

The same type of program prevents two files being created with identical names on the same disk and asks, when storing data, the name of the file on which it is to be stored.

(d)   **Check digits**

Check digits are a means of control in that they ascertain whether or not a number (for example, an International Standard Book Number) is valid. A formula is used to calculate the digit which is attached to the end of the number itself. Modulus 11 is a common system and works as follows:

Number say,	32153
Multiply by weightings (see below)	65432
Results	18/10/4/15/6
Results total	53
Results total ÷ modulus	53 ÷ 11 = 4, remainder 9
Modulus minus remainder	11 – 9 = 2
Check digit	2
Number now becomes	321532

The weightings to use are in ascending order starting on the right. The check digit will be assigned weighting 1 so start with weight 2 at the first stage above.

If there is no remainder the check digit is 0, if the remainder is 10 the check digit is X.

The check digit is initially calculated by the computer and then becomes an integral part of the number. The example above could be a customer account number.

The computer will then detect if the number is ever input incorrectly eg, a transposition error resulting in 231532. The computer performs the modulus 11 calculation and gets a check digit of 3 (check it yourself to confirm this) instead of 2. An error message will then be sent to the operator.

(e)   **Batch totals and hash totals**

These controls are often used in batch processing systems whereby documents are grouped (batched) together and processed in a single block.

A batch (or control) total is the sum of one of the numerical fields on the documents in the batch eg, total of the sales invoice values. This total is calculated manually and the documents are then input to the computer. The computer then calculates the batch total and this is compared with the manually calculated total. If they are different then an error has occurred: perhaps an invoice value has been mis-keyed or a document may have been omitted from input altogether. The input clerk is alerted to the error and can then investigate it.

A hash total works in exactly the same way as a batch total but a different type of field is used. A typical hash total would be the total of customer account numbers: unlike the batch total the value of the hash total is meaningless but it is still useful for control purposes to detect errors on input or omissions.

(f)   **Reasonable checks**

The program will check to ensure that the data input is reasonable given the type of input it is. An example on a payroll system would be to check that hours recorded for the week fall within the range 30 - 50.

(g)   **Existence checks**

The computer will check to ensure that the data input is valid by checking that the entity already exists on the system eg, check to ensure that an employee number input already exists on the system.

(h)   **Dependence checks**

In some cases, data input fields can be compared with other fields for reasonableness eg, when inputting a purchase invoice the operator keys in the net amount and the VAT amount and the computer will check that the VAT is a sensible amount as compared with the net amount.

8 RELIANCE BY THE AUDITOR ON INTERNAL CONTROLS

8.1 Introduction

Having considered in detail examples of both application controls and general controls, the question arises as to what extent the auditor should rely upon such controls. Inevitably there is no easy answer to such a question.

An auditor is required to obtain sufficient appropriate audit evidence for him to draw reasonable conclusions therefrom. The relationship between compliance and substantive testing holds in a computer-based accounting system: if the auditor obtains a reasonable assurance from testing the controls he can limit his substantive work.

8.2 The relationship between application and general controls

It may be appropriate for the auditor to concentrate upon application controls before deciding how far to proceed with examining general controls. The reasons for this are as follows:

(a) Application controls can be more easily related to a specific control objective, and therefore a specific audit objective, than can general controls.

(b) Application controls can be more easily tested by using specific transactions to act as a medium for the test which is then performed either clerically or by using computer-assisted audit techniques.

(c) As a result of (a) and (b) the testing of application controls may be more effective than general controls.

There are, however, certain reasons for still considering general controls to be highly relevant to the auditor:

(a) If application controls become concentrated in the computer department, the environment within which the application controls function will be fundamental.

(b) If certain application controls are lacking the auditor may attempt to limit his substantive testing by placing more reliance on general controls.

The Auditing Guideline sets out these basic rules relating to audit testing of controls:

(a) The auditor can test and rely on general controls alone without having to test application controls.

(b) The auditor can test and rely on manual application controls alone without having to test general controls.

(c) In order to rely on programmed application controls the auditor must first be satisfied with general controls. This is because if the controls covering the whole computer environment are poor, then the programmed application controls within it will be worthless.

8.3 Audit documentation

You have seen that the auditor is likely to wish to rely upon controls as a source of audit evidence. To do so he must obtain a record of the system and carry out a preliminary evaluation. His work will be assisted by the use of documentation to help identify the internal controls on which he may wish to place reliance.

The documentation may take a variety of forms but two particular methods will often form an important part of the audit documentation.

(a)   **An audit control file or systems file**

This file contains important details of both clerical and programmed procedures. It must be reviewed and updated regularly. The auditor should arrange to have his name on distribution lists to receive notification from the client of all procedural changes. The file might typically contain:

(i)   Copies of documents used in the system with details of checks performed on them.

(ii)   Description of how source documents are converted into input with control procedures.

(iii)   Detailed application controls in each area of the system.

(iv)   Flowcharts.

(v)   Details of all data files including storage media, organisation, labelling, storage arrangements, back-up facilities.

(vi)   Details and copies of output documents.

(vii)   The results of the auditor's review of the system and the effectiveness of the controls within it.

(b)   **Internal control questionnaire**

The ascertainment and evaluation of both application and general controls will be assisted by the use of specially designed ICQs. The ICQ would include questions covering both clerical and programmed controls as both types are likely to be relied upon by the auditor.

8.4   Activity

You are the auditor of Super Group plc, which operates a chain of garages through its fifteen subsidiaries. In the past each subsidiary has been responsible for its own accounting procedures and has had its own accounts department. Standards of accounting throughout the group are good. During 19X3 the holding company set up a centralised group computer department, using a mainframe computer, with responsibility for processing accounting information for all companies within the group. The new computer department will commence operations on 1 January 19X4 with a total staff of twenty, including the departmental manager, systems development staff, control staff and operational staff.

The finance director has asked you to report to him on controls within the computer department.

You are required to summarise the controls you would expect to find.

8.5   Activity solution

(a)   **Operational controls**

The objective of this aspect of general controls is to ensure that an acceptable standard of discipline and efficiency is maintained over the day-to-day running of the computer department.

The expected control techniques would involve ensuring:

(i)   an adequate segregation of duties between the 20 data processing personnel so that the work of different people is restricted to their defined functions. The department should therefore be organised so that the following functions are separated:

(1)   design and development of systems will be the responsibility of systems analysts and programmers

(2)   operation of the computer and ancillary equipment will be the responsibility of the operational staff

(3)   file security will be the responsibility of a specially designated librarian, whose duties would be confined to controlling the issue and return of files according to scheduled timetables, the maintenance of identification labels, and generally ensuring that files are maintained and stored in a suitable and secure environment to which access is restricted to authorised personnel only

(4)   data control will be the responsibility of control staff, whose duties would be confined to handling input data, to ensuring that data input is completely and accurately processed, and to distributing processed information to relevant user destinations.

If the above criteria are met a measure of internal control will be provided, as each section will check, either directly or indirectly, the work of the others.

(ii)   restricted access to the computer room. Use of the computer and access to data and program files are restricted to authorised persons at authorised times.

(iii)   continuity of operations. Protection is necessary against fire and other hazards, emergency and disaster recovery procedures (eg, the retention of copies of important files outside the installation and the establishment of standby arrangements so that the more essential accounting functions can be performed), maintenance agreements and adequate insurance.

(iv)   the establishment of procedures to prevent and detect unauthorised amendment of data files, examples of which would include authorisation of jobs prior to processing, password protection, software controls to record unauthorised access attempts, and regular periodic printouts of file contents for comparison by users, with manually maintained records and control totals

(v)   the establishment of procedures to prevent and detect errors during program execution, including operation manuals detailing set-up and execution procedures providing protection against errors such as incorrect data files, running programs in the wrong sequence, incorrect response to a program request and job control errors.

(b)   **System development controls**

The objectives of this aspect of general controls are to ensure a satisfactory standard of designing and testing authorised systems and programs, and of implementing and documenting them so that the system will operate as originally specified and that all the relevant documentation has been properly prepared and properly maintained. The same objectives will apply to all changes to systems and programs. To achieve these objectives the following controls would be expected:

(i)   the establishment of approval procedures by users and the computer manager over application development stages and the establishment of a framework of standards for systems design, programming, documentation, testing and internal audit involvement

(ii) the establishment of procedures designed to prevent or detect unauthorised changes to programs, examples of which would include physical protection of programs stored off-line (ie, under the supervision of the librarian), restrictions over access to programs during processing and regular periodic comparison of the contents of production programs to controlled copies (iii)	the authorisation, testing and documentation of all program changes prior to their becoming operational

(iv)	the establishment of procedures to ensure that system software is properly installed and maintained, such as authorisation and documentation of updates and amendments, and software exercised controls, such as the maintenance of files recording usage and access

(v)	the maintenance of adequate documentation recording the development and subsequent amendment of systems and programs, and the methods and results of testing prior to live operation

(vi)	the establishment of monitoring procedures to ensure that the new system is working according to original specifications and that its accuracy is determined.

9   EXAM QUESTIONS ON INFORMATION SYSTEMS DEVELOPMENT

9.1   Approach

Exam questions may be asked requiring you to advise on the installation of a computer system or the expansion/amendment of an existing system. This type of question does not require much more knowledge than is contained in sections 3 and 4 of this chapter. The main concern is the establishment of proper controls over the data within the system. In addition however you may need to cover the procedures necessary to control and properly record the development of the system.

Also you need to be responsive to the costs in terms of time and resources in developing systems. The client will obviously think this is important; it is his time and money. You should therefore not suggest systems/procedures which are out of all proportion to the size of the client's business. The key criterion should be whether the benefits of the changed system outweigh the costs.

An illustration of the approach to take and the procedures required is shown in a past exam question from the old syllabus Auditing and Investigations 'Plumtree Distributors' below. Attempt this before looking at the answer.

9.2   Activity

Plumtree Distributors plc is planning to develop a new integrated stock control, sales, purchases and nominal ledger system. You have been asked by the managing director to suggest controls which should be exercised over developing the computer system, setting it up and operating it. The company has been unable to find a software supplier who can provide either a standard system or a turnkey system which will meet their requirements. So, the company will use its own computer programmers to write the computer programs for the system. The new system will use the company's new computer and data will be input from remote terminals. The computer system can record details of the terminal being used to input data. In the system

(a)	details of purchase orders are entered by the buying department

(b)	details of goods received are entered by the goods received department

(c)	purchase invoice details are entered by the purchases accounting department

(d)	details of goods to be dispatched are entered by the sales department - the computer prints out the dispatch note and sales invoice from this data, and updates the stock records

(e)	the accounts department are responsible for posting journals to the nominal ledger and ensuring its accuracy. However, transactions in the sales and purchases systems (including cash) are automatically posted to the nominal ledger at the end of each month.

You are required:

(a)   to list and briefly describe the procedures which should be undertaken to authorise development of the system and to specify the input, processing and output requirements of the system.

(b)   to list and describe the controls which should be exercised over

(i)   testing the computer programs to ensure they operate satisfactorily, and correcting programming errors

(ii)   documentation of the system

(iii) training the staff, setting up the system and initial running of the system.

(c)   to list and briefly describe the controls which should be built into the new system to control and record access to the system from remote terminals.

9.3   Activity solution

(a)   Procedures to authorise the development of the computer system will include

(i)   initial approval by the board of directors of the decision to develop the system in-house, and agreement of the budget to produce the system

(ii)   agreement also by the board of the general system specification.   At the commencement of the project this will simply be that the system will cover stock, purchases, sales and general ledger.

Procedures to specify the input, processing and output of the new system will include

(i)   obtain details from the user departments concerning the outputs required from the system.   A list of detailed requirements would be expected with an indication of whether the outputs are essential or not to the department.

(ii)   from the list of outputs a list of inputs should be produced.   This list should be circulated to the departments generating the inputs to see if the required input is already available on the old system.   Existing documents can be amended rather than new ones produced if this is the case.   New forms will be produced where necessary

(iii) the lists of inputs and outputs will be given to the chief programmer and his team.   A summary of the steps necessary to turn the input into the output can then be produced

(iv)   an overview of the new system showing all proposed inputs, methods of processing and outputs should be circulated to all user departments.   Each department should be requested to suggest amendments to the proposal, or alternatively sign an authorisation sheet to confirm their acceptance of the project to date

(v)   in producing the above specification, the systems analysts should also have reviewed the systems already rejected by the company.   This will ensure that the company system includes all the good elements of these systems.

(b)   (i)   Controls over the testing of the computer programmes fall into three categories

Computer programmers

Firstly, the auditing programmers who wrote the programmes should test them.   This testing will attempt to ensure that the programmes meet the required specification, and that no errors occur in processing.   Dummy transaction data will be used for this purpose.

Independent computer programmers

The second test will be by programmers who were not involved in writing this particular part of the programme. (Most major programmes will be written in segments. The programmers here will not have been involved in writing this segment.)

This review will assist in identifying logic and other errors that the programmers writing the programme may have missed.

User review

Finally, the programme as it stands at present (the unfinished or 'beta test' version) should be given to a sample of users. This will ensure that it meets their expectations, and also assist in identifying errors.

Any errors noted in review stages two and three will be corrected by the original programmers as they have the detailed knowledge of the programme being written.

Again, the users should confirm in writing that the system meets their requirements, and therefore that work can continue.

(ii)　　The system documentation should include

Systems manual

This will be a draft manual initially to assist system testing.

After testing, a full manual will be required to completely explain how the system works. This manual may be summarised into a quick reference guide for users to give the basic information to use the system.

A detailed technical manual may be produced separately to assist advanced users and computer support staff. This will assist in identifying errors that may be found during the use of the system.

Programme documentation

Full listings of the finished programme, including flowcharts and any other system documentation, should be produced. This will serve as a permanent record of how the programme works should major problems occur, or detailed modification be required in the future.

(iii)　　**Training of staff**

Staff should be trained before the new system is implemented. Training should cover

(1)　　the transfer of data onto the new system

(2)　　normal use of the new system

(3)　　correction of errors, including how to use the system manual and any on-line help screens for this purpose

(4)　　where to obtain further assistance when required.

The latest version of the system should be available for demonstration so that staff can become familiar with the system. If possible, a few transactions should be entered into the system to demonstrate how the system is used.

Setting up the system

(1)   The system can be set up for use with all segments of the system commencing use at the same time. Alternatively, system segments can be brought on-line individually. The latter may be easier from a checking point of view.

(2)   The new software should be loaded onto the company's computers, and checks made that this has been correctly accomplished before the new software is used.

Basic checks on the software will include

(A)   ensure that the system works correctly with the remote terminals; and

(B)   checking that the printers work.

These and other checks will have already been carried out during development work. A recheck is required to ensure that the finished system is, as far as possible, error free.

(3)   The date that the new system 'goes live' will be widely published. Transaction data will be input to the new system from this date.

(4)   Balances on master files will be transferred at the end of the last day's processing on the old system. Detailed checking of the transfer using batch totals will be required to ensure that no errors occur.

(5)   It is possible not to transfer balances at this stage, but, for example, to enter all new sales on the new system, and cash received from debtors against the appropriate system balance. When the outstanding debtor balance on the old system is small, then these balances only are transferred to the new system.

Initial running of the system

The new system must be checked to ensure that it is processing the accounting data correctly. This can be carried out as follows

(1)   Parallel run

The old and new systems are run at the same time, processing the same accounting data. The outputs from both systems are compared. Any differences are investigated and changes made to the new system where errors are identified.

(2)   Piecemeal changeover

Where individual programme segments are brought on-line at different times, a parallel run of this segment only will be required.

(3)   Retrospective parallel run

Due to lack of staff time, the parallel run is performed, but the new system is processed in arrears of the old. The old system remains the primary system until the new has been proved as running correctly.

During this time with any changeover method, frequent copying of the programme, transaction and master files in the new system should be carried out. Should any major system error then occur, a recent processing position can be restored into the computer.

When the new system is working correctly, processing on the old system will be stopped. Frequent backups of the new system will still be taken to continue to guard against major system failures.

(c)   Controls to control and record access from the remote terminals are likely to include

(i)   **Passwords**

Each employee will be allocated a unique password or number. When an employee attempts to access the system, this password must be input. The computer programme will ensure that it is a valid password, and then give system access. As each transaction is recorded, the system will keep within the transaction record details of which terminal was used, and what employee input the transaction. It will therefore be possible at a later date to trace any transaction back to a particular individual.

Employees must be informed never to disclose their password to any other employee, or else incorrect data may be stored by the computer.

(ii)   **Access to system segments**

Individual employees should only be allowed to access that part of the computer system that they will use. To do this, each employee password file could have a field specifying the programme segments that particular employee can access. Sales staff will only be allowed access to the sales ledger, for example, and not the purchasing system.

(iii)   **Terminals**

Access may be restricted at terminals by either keeping the terminals in a secure room, or by only having the terminals 'live', that is on-line to the main computer, at certain times of the day. The main computer will control which terminals are live at any one time.

Individual terminals may only allow input of certain types of data. For example, terminals in the sales ledger department will only allow access to the sales system.

(iv)   **Unauthorised access**

Attempts to gain unauthorised access to the system, that is repeated attempts to input an incorrect password, should be monitored by the computer programme. If the terminal where access is attempted is also noted, detailed investigation at this terminal can take place to try and ascertain why the access was attempted.

(v)   **Input of transaction**

Any breaks in the sequence of transaction documents should be noted by the computer programme, and investigated later to ascertain the reasons for the missing documents. If batch controls are used then breaks in the batch sequence may also be investigated.

Breaks in the sequence of documents input could indicate control weaknesses at the terminal which requires investigation.

(vi)   **Screen countdown**

If a terminal is not used for a specified amount of time (say five minutes) it should be automatically logged off and the user required to gain fresh access to the computer.

(vii)   **Review of transaction and master files**

All transaction and master files should be periodically reviewed for unusual items like old debts and slow moving stock lines. These problems could indicate a lack of control over input. An investigation should be carried out to determine the exact cause of the problem.

10   TRENDS IN INFORMATION TECHNOLOGY AND THEIR IMPACT ON AUDITORS

10.1   Introduction

The main trends in information technology arise from the reduced size and the increased speed of hardware which allows the widespread use of micro-computers either as stand alone machines or linked into a network (including the Internet). There is now a widespread use of micro-computers by businesses of all sizes in the accounts function. In the larger clients which have large geographical divisions of sales outlets, on-line and real time computer systems continue to be installed. These two areas are considered in this section.

10.2   Problems associated with small computer systems

(a)   The reduction in the cost of small computers in recent years may lead the company to believe that controls are not needed or may be implemented at low cost. The auditor must encourage his client to appreciate that it is the value of the data not the cost of the computer that should dictate the time and money spent implementing control.

(b)   There is normally only a limited division of duties in a mini-computer system. The same person may be responsible for preparation of input data, computer operations and distribution of output. It is important to implement clerical application controls outside the computer department to counter the limited segregation of duties within it.

(c)   The client may be a first-time computer user and may not implement a wide range of application controls. In any case the system may not be fully documented and the supplier of a package may not be prepared to release full details. The auditor may need to rely largely on substantive testing to obtain adequate audit evidence.

(d)   There may be unrestricted access to terminals of data. This should be controlled by

(i)   nominating specified personnel to use terminals
(ii)   physical access restrictions
(iii)   password protection
(iv)   proper supervision by senior officials
(v)   user logs to record the use of terminals and attempts to gain unauthorised access.

(e)   Many small systems operate on a real-time basis. Controls may include detailed editing of transactions, the maintenance of transaction logs and control accounts and full review of output by officials outside the computer department. The auditor should check that editing and authorisation extend to changes in standing data as well as routine transactions.

(f)   There are dangers of errors or loss of data on the conversion to a new small computer system. The conversion process should be fully documented and controls such as maintaining record counts and control totals should be used. If possible the auditor should become involved prior to and during the conversion process.

(g)   There are dangers that program changes are made that are unauthorised or badly designed by the client's staff. In addition the client's staff may neglect other managerial duties in spending time attempting to program the computer.

The client should attempt to segregate operations staff from programmers. It is often cost-effective for the client to employ a consultant to design and amend programs. The existing software can be protected by being etched onto silicon chips to form 'read-only memory'. The object programs may be held in machine code only and so are much more difficult for staff to amend. Back-up versions of programs should be maintained.

(h)   There is finally a general problem that such systems may not provide visible audit trail. The auditor may wish to use audit interrogation packages but these were traditionally designed for mainframe systems and may not function on some small systems. The writing of a one-off program may not be cost-effective. The use of a manufacturer's own enquiry programs may not be cost-effective unless the portfolio of clients using that type of equipment is large.

The result is that a substantive-based approach is likely to dominate this type of audit until computer-assisted techniques which are reasonably priced and which can be applied to a wide range of small systems become available.

10.3   Problems associated with the audit of computer networks

The trend in recent years has been for companies to establish networks of computers, usually with a mainframe computer holding large quantities of data in storage and intelligent microcomputers (PCs) on each employee's desk which can download and manipulate the data from the mainframe. Local area networks (LANs) link together the computers in one site. Wide area networks (WANs) link together computers at different geographical sites using telecommunications technology including normal telephone lines and faster ISDN lines.

This networking of intelligent computers introduces new problems for the auditors:

(a)   The security risk will be greater if data is being transmitted by a public telephone line. The possibility of data being intercepted or eavesdropped on increases in a WAN.

(b)   Computer viruses can be spread quickly from computer to computer in a LAN environment, and may even corrupt the main storage data in the mainframe. Anti-virus checks should be made on all programs and data before they are input into any computer in the network.

(c)   If a network 'crashes', it can mean that all computers in a company are simultaneously unable to be used; proper back-up procedures are even more important.

(d)   Only authorised personnel should be able to access the system from any workstation. The auditor should determine the risk of unauthorised users gaining access to the networked functions.

10.4   On-line and real-time systems

The usual implication of an on-line system is that a user has access to the computer system and to some extent control of it through a terminal. These systems are sometimes called 'transaction-driven' systems in that a particular transaction may be input to be processed rather than a whole batch of transactions in a 'program-driven' system.

A large variety of types of terminals are available with differing facilities. 'Intelligent' terminals have some computer-type logic incorporated so that they can perform limited validation routines. There are a number of major variations in on-line systems notably:

(a)   **Interrogation systems**

Users can access data held on existing computer files.

(b)   **On-line data input**

Users may input transaction data which must pass validation tests. The system does not allow existing master-file data to be amended. The transactions are usually input in batches and master files may be updated centrally overnight.

(c)   **On-line updating**

Users may input transaction data which is validated and the master file is immediately updated. If the system maintains all of its master files on-line then a real-time system is created in which transactions are processed when received and files are kept permanently up-to-date.

You should appreciate that while all real-time systems are on-line, not all on-line systems are real-time.

(d)   **Remote job entry (RJE)**

In these systems other peripherals besides VDUs are physically located with the user, and not at the mainframe location. Card readers, line printers, etc, may be present at the user's location and they can load and run programs and receive output in their own departments.

The processing and usually the retention of files is done centrally but it enables the user to have effective control over powerful computer equipment.

10.5   Audit problems in such systems

The main problems associated with these systems are:

(a)   The fact that records are maintained within the system with the minimum of printouts and so a loss of visible audit trail.

(b)   The lack of transactional batch controls.

(c)   The sophistication of the software and filing systems needed for the system to function adequately.

10.6   Controls in such systems

(a)   **Control over development**

At the initial development stage rules should be established relating to who will be permitted to access, add, change or delete data. The system should be fully tested, and special software is available to assist such testing. It is clearly preferable for both internal and external auditors to be consulted fully at this development stage.

(b)   **Division of responsibilities**

The data processing and other administrative staff are likely to have clearly segregated functions. It is important however for adequate supervision in places where administrative staff have access to terminals.

(c)   **Serial numbering of documents**

When transactions are entered through terminals they should be recorded on prenumbered documents. Hence checks can be made of movements on records against the documentation. The system should report any missing documents or multiple use of the same document reference.

(d)   **Physical access restrictions**

Access to data should be physically restricted by the terminals being kept in rooms which are locked when the terminal is not in use. Operators may be issued with a terminal key and unauthorised personnel should have access to the terminal restricted. More stringent controls may be provided at the computer centre through the use of special keys, badges, closed circuit television, etc.

(e)   **Logical access restrictions**

Logical access to the data can be restricted by the use of passwords. Each operator has his or her own password which allows the use of certain terminals and allows access only to certain data held on the computer. Different passwords may be used to either read data from a file or write data onto a file. Clearly the distribution of passwords should be carefully controlled and any attempted violations should be recorded by the operating system, reported to management and thoroughly investigated.

(f)   **Transaction logs**

Although the traditional batch controls are lost, the system should keep a record of all transactions processed each day or shift. The total of transactions of each type then forms a basis for reconciliation to control accounts or movements on each file and for reconciliation periodically to the documentation in the system.

(g)   **Additional editing of input**

One great advantage of on-line processing is the extension of the editing (or validation) process. Since master files are on-line each item of transaction data can be checked for format and matched against data held on the master files.

(h)   **Back-up facilities**

The usual need to retain security copies of files by regular dumping routines applies in on-line systems. There should be emergency facilities to provide computer processing at another location if needed. If (unusually) it is considered feasible to have a manual back-up system, that too should be tested periodically.

There may be a good case for having standby terminals and power supplies. Reserve terminal operators should be properly trained.

(i)   **Computer log file**

A sophisticated on-line system will maintain a computer log file which is used to produce statistics of all activities in the system. This file can highlight down-time, operator efficiency, unauthorised attempts to gain access to data, and may be a powerful tool for management control.

(j)   **Internal audit involvement**

The client will have set up extensive test facilities himself in a sophisticated on-line system and it is likely that an organisation of a size, sufficient to support such a system will have a competent internal audit function, whose members should be involved with continual testing of procedures.

11   CHAPTER SUMMARY

Computers are increasingly used in the audit process due to their portability.

CAATs consist of audit software and test data.

The use by clients of computers can lead to loss of controls and loss of audit trail. Controls can be established at the development stage of a computerised system and can be classified as application controls and general controls. The auditor should look at application controls before general controls.

12   SELF TEST QUESTIONS

12.1   In what areas can a microcomputer assist in the auditor's work? (1.2)

12.2   What are the eight features of computer-based systems which are most relevant to auditors? (2.1)

12.3   What are the two types of CAATs? (5.1)

12.4   What are the three types of audit software available? (5.3)

12.5   What is a definition of application controls? (6.2)

12.6   What is a definition of general controls? (6.4)

12.7   What are the reasons for the auditor referring to application controls before deciding on general controls? (8.2)

13   EXAMINATION TYPE QUESTION

13.1   Lenton Manufacturing plc

The partner in charge of the audit of Lenton Manufacturing plc has asked your advice on the computer assisted audit techniques which can be used on the company's sales accounting system.

The company operates from a single site. Access to the computer system is controlled by the use of passwords for individuals and the computer identifying the terminal which is being used.   The computer only permits input of data into the sales system by authorised users from authorised terminals during the normal working hours of the business.

Transactions can be input from terminals in the individual departments, as follows

(a)   Customer orders are input into the system by the sales department.

(b)   When the goods are available for dispatch to the customer, the sales department raises a dispatch note on the computer. The credit controller confirms that the goods can be sent to the customer. The dispatch department prints the dispatch note on the terminal and sends the goods to the customer.

(c)   When the dispatch note has been printed, the computer automatically raises the sales invoice and posts it to the sales ledger.

(d)   When cash is received, the sales accounting department posts the cash to the sales ledger.

(e)   For issue of credit notes over £100 and posting of adjustments to the sales ledger, the clerk inputs these items and the computer system requires the sales director or chief accountant to give his authorisation by means of a password before they are posted to the sales ledger.

(f)   Addition, amendment and deletion of product details and prices are carried out by the sales department.   The list of these changes must be authorised by the sales director using a password before the standing data file on the computer is updated.

(g)   Authorisation by the credit controller, using a password, is required before any new customer can be added to the sales ledger, or credit limits of customers changed.

The company's sales ledger has about 3,000 live accounts with a total balance of about £2,500,000.

The company has said test files can be set up, for checking controls over access to the system, and the use of test data. You are satisfied that you will be able to audit these systems using test files.

You are required:

(a)   In relation to controls over access to the sales accounting system

    (i)   to give examples of the procedures you will carry out to check that the system allows authorised data to be processed and prevents unauthorised input of data.   **(6 marks)**

    (ii)   to describe the additional controls the company should carry out over passwords to prevent unauthorised access to the system.   **(3 marks)**

(b)   In relation to test data

    (i)   to briefly describe what you understand by the term, and the auditor's purpose in using test data. You should state why an auditor should use test data, and why it is not adequate to just 'audit round the computer'.   **(4 marks)**

    (ii)   to list and describe the tests you will carry out using test data on the standing data and transaction data files of the sales accounting system.   **(5 marks)**

(c)   To describe what you understand by computer audit programs, and give examples of their use in the audit of the sales accounting system.   **(7 marks)**

(Total: 25 marks)

14   ANSWER TO EXAMINATION TYPE QUESTION

14.1   Lenton Manufacturing plc

(a)   (i)   Procedures that the auditor will use to check that the sales system allows authorised data to be processed and prevents unauthorised input of data will include those noted below. The auditor should obtain a list of valid passwords before commencing these tests.

    (1)   Attempting to gain access to the computer in the sales department without the appropriate password. The computer would be expected to allow say three attempts at access, and then the terminal should close down. The auditor will ensure that this happens and check the amount of time that elapses before the terminal becomes live again.

    (2)   Attempting to print out a dispatch note without a customer order being entered onto the computer.

    (3)   Attempting to raise a dispatch note without the authorisation from the credit controller for the dispatch to be made.

    (4)   Attempting to gain access to the computer in a different department than the sales department, but using the sales department passwords. Access should be denied.

    (5)   Attempting to issue a credit note in excess of £100 without the password of the sales director or chief accountant.

    (6)   Attempting to add, delete or amend the product details file without using the sales director's password.

    (7)   Attempting to add a new customer to the sales ledger without using the credit controller's password.

    (8)   Attempting to process a transaction outside of normal office hours. Access to the computer should again be denied.

    (9)   Checking the processing of a valid transaction as follows

- access the computer in the sales department using a valid password

- entering a customer order onto the computer

- raising a dispatch note and obtaining authorisation from the credit controller

- checking that the sales invoice is raised by the computer, entered into the sales day book and posted to the correct sales ledger account

- entering cash received in payment of the invoice

- ensuring that the invoice is cleared from the customer's sales ledger account.

(ii)   The additional controls that the company should use in respect of computer passwords should include

(1)   Changing the password on a regular basis.

(2)   Ensuring that employees do not write their password on or near the computer monitor.

(3)   Checking that passwords are not related to factors that are easy to guess like names of employees or spouses, children, pets, birthdays and similar items.

(4)   Checking that passwords are not displayed on-screen when they are entered. A line of asterisks, or even a blank screen, should be displayed when the password is entered to ensure that other people cannot read the password as it is typed in.

(5)   Ensuring that the password file on the computer hard disk is encrypted; this means it cannot be read by simple DOS commands like 'type' and 'edlin'.

(b)   (i)   Test data is data prepared by the auditor ie, data generated by the company's accounting system, which is then input to the computer system by the auditor. The test data will include both valid and invalid transactions. The auditor will check the output from the computer for the test data after processing and compare this to the output he expected from manually processing the data. If the data agrees to the expected output then this provides the auditor with some confidence that the computer programmes are working correctly.

To use test data correctly, the auditor will set up 'dummy' files to ensure that the client's live data is not amended by the test data.

The auditor should use test data and not just audit 'around the computer' for a number of reasons which include

(1)   Test data checks the computer programmes directly. Auditing around the computer does not directly check the computer programmes; the auditor has to assume that because the output is correct then the computer programmes are also correct. This assumption may not be correct; for example, the computer could have updated a sales ledger account with the VAT net amount of an invoice but printed out the gross value on an output report of that ledger account.

(2)   Test data allows many potential error conditions to be tested quickly. Testing a small sample of items through the computer means that unusual or large items are unlikely to be tested regularly. By using test data, many unusual and large items are processed in a short space of time providing an effective test of the computer programmes' accuracy.

(ii)   To perform these tests, 'dummy' or test data files would first be set up, and the test data constructed.   The test data for transaction files will then include the following transactions in addition to normal data, which should be processed correctly.

(1)   Credit notes in excess of £100. These should not be processed without the sales director's or chief accountant's approval.

(2)   Invoices for negative amounts. The system should reject these or ask for authorisation for the 'credit note'.

(3)   Cash receipts for negative amounts. Again the system should reject these items.

(4)   Sales invoices with invalid stock references. Error messages should be given and the transaction not processed.

(5)   Sales invoices for which there is no customer ledger account. Again these transactions should not be processed.

(6)   Transactions with incorrect data in certain fields; for example, quantity fields on invoices with letters in them or date field with invalid dates (eg, March 32nd). Again these transactions should be rejected.

Tests on the standing data files will include

(1)   Attempting to delete customer ledger accounts that have positive balances on them.

(2)   Attempting to insert new customer accounts without the authorisation of the credit controller.

(3)   Attempting to add new stock lines or amend prices of stock without the authorisation of the sales director.

(4)   Attempting to delete stock lines where there is a stock balance.

All of the above transactions should not be allowed by the computer.   If the appropriate authorisation is given, then the transaction will proceed; this will also confirm that the system is working correctly.

(c)   Computer audit programmes are computer programmes that are written by firms of auditors to assist them in the audit of computer systems. The computer programme will access and examine a company's computer files and perform tests on the data contained within those files.

One of the normal uses of computer audit programmes is to re-perform some of the processing already carried out by the company's computer programmes. The output from both the company's and the audit's programmes will be compared; any differences are investigated by the auditor.

Computer audit programmes are particularly useful where the client has large data files that could not easily be reviewed manually. The computer audit programmes can quickly cast the whole file, and also highlight individual items that meet certain criteria eg, over a certain monetary limit, which the auditor will then investigate in more detail.

Typical uses of computer audit programmes in a sales accounting system will include

(i)   **Completeness checks**

The programme adds the value of individual transactions within a sales ledger account and ensures that they agree with the balance on that account. Similarly, the programme can add the balances on all the 3,000 sales ledger accounts and ensure that this agrees to the total on the sales ledger control account.

(ii)   **Detecting violation of systems rules**

The programme checks all the accounts on the sales ledger to ensure that no customer has a balance above their individual credit limit. Any items found not to meet the rule will be printed out for further analysis by the auditor.

(iii)   **Detecting unreasonable items**

Examples here would include checking that no sales ledger balance exceeded the total sales made to that customer, or that no customer is allowed a trade discount of more than, say, 50%. Exceptions found would be investigated by the auditor.

(iv)   **Conducting new calculations and analyses**

Examples here would include calculating the debtor/days ratio for the debtors balance as a whole, and credit period taken for each debtor individually. This information would be useful to the auditor for his analytical review of debtors.

(v)   **Selection of items for audit work**

Debtor balances over certain criteria (ie, 3 months and £1,000) could be listed for further investigation. Also, debtor accounts could be selected for other tests like circularisations. In fact the programme could extract the balances and insert the details into a standard confirmation letter and print these out. The letters would then only require checking, signing and posting manually.

*(**Tutorial note:** there is plenty of information in the question which can be used here to provide relevant examples in part (a). Try and give these examples as it will show the examiner that you have read the question and can identify the examples given; it will also assist in keeping your answer to the point of the question.)*

27 THE FINAL AUDIT

INTRODUCTION & LEARNING OBJECTIVES

This chapter considers the final audit and audit completion stage. This area can be tested as a full auditing question or as an 'integrated' accounting and audit question. The syllabus requirement to review financial statements for their compliance with GAAP is a prime area for an integrated question. In this regard, the audit problems that have been outlined in earlier chapters on accounting show the type of information required in an answer.

When you have studied this chapter you should be able to do the following:

- Explain the ways the auditor reviews the financial statements.
- Deal with final audit matters.
- Consider specific problems that arise in the completion of the audit.

1 CONTROL OF AUDIT

1.1 Quality control

The reporting partner of the audit firm needs to be satisfied that on each audit the work is being performed to an acceptable standard. The most important elements of control are the direction and supervision of the audit staff and the review of the work which they have performed.

1.2 Typical control procedures

(a) **Allocation of staff**

This is aided by allocating job titles to each member of the audit staff. It is assisted by audit staff at all levels clearly understanding their responsibilities and the objectives of the work which they are expected to perform. Thus, all audit staff should be adequately trained and versed in the procedures adopted by their firm. All members of the audit staff should be aware of the person to whom they are directly responsible.

(b) **Working papers**

The basic control requirement is that all audit work performed is properly recorded. If working papers are standardised this helps to ensure that the work is both performed and is recorded as it is performed.

(c) **Review**

Review of audit work takes a number of different forms:

(i) 'Hot' review. The working papers produced by a member of the audit staff are checked by a more experienced member of the staff. Such a review is usually evidenced by the reviewer initialing that particular working paper.

(ii) Post-audit review. At the end of the audit, but before the audit report is signed, the manager or partner should review the audit file and the final accounts.

(iii) Audit review department. Some firms use a small group of experienced employees to form a review team or department. This team has the job of reviewing in detail the work performed by an audit group and ensuring that the audit has been conducted in accordance with the firm's standard procedures.

(iv)   Peer review. A system where one firm of auditors reviews the working practices of another firm and reports to the partners of the investigated firm on the ways in which their procedures might be improved.

(d)   **Consultation**

Where matters of a contentious nature arise the auditor should consult his partners or even another practitioner. Some firms require that if a qualification is proposed in the audit report, another partner must be consulted and must review the situation.

1.3   The importance of the review of audit working papers

The reasons for preparing audit working papers include the following.

(a)   During his review, the reporting partner needs assurances that the work delegated by him has been properly completed. Working papers, therefore, assist the auditor in forming an opinion on the financial statements.

(b)   Working papers provide evidence that an effective audit has been carried out. Working papers set out difficulties encountered, evidence of work performed and conclusions drawn. This may be required for future reference, for example in a court of law.

(c)   Working papers increase the efficiency and effectiveness of the audit by ensuring that the members of the audit staff carry out their duties in a systematic way and understanding the significance of the tasks they are performing.

Working papers should achieve the following general objectives:

(a)   They should be sufficiently detailed and complete as to enable an auditor with no previous experience of the audit to establish the work completed and the reasons for the conclusions reached.

(b)   They should be up-to-date so that the progress of the audit at any point in time can be assessed.

(c)   They should indicate the facts available at a particular point in time and justify the reasonableness of the auditor's conclusions from those facts.

1.4   SAS 230: Working papers

SAS 230 contains extensive guidance in relation to the content of working papers and the retention of notes on queries arising from review (which can be discarded once the relevant matter has been cleared). Working papers should show the detailed reasoning on matters of judgement.

Auditing standards

230.1   Auditors should document in their working papers matters which are important in supporting their report.

230.2   Working papers should record the auditors' planning, the nature, timing and extent of the audit procedures performed, and the conclusions drawn from the audit evidence obtained.

230.3   Auditors should record in their working papers their reasoning on all significant matters which require the exercise of judgement, and their conclusions thereon.

230.4   Auditors should adopt appropriate procedures for maintaining the confidentiality and safe custody of their working papers.

1.5   SAS 240: Quality control for audit work

SAS 240 contains guidance on maintaining quality control over audit work generally.

240.1   Quality control policies and procedures should be implemented both at the level of the audit firm and on individual audits.

1.6   Quality control for the firm

240.2   A firm is required to:

1   establish and monitor quality control policies and procedures designed to ensure that all audits are conducted in accordance with SASs;

2   communicate these policies and procedures to all personnel in an appropriate manner.

1.7   Individual audit

For the individual audit the requirements are as follows:

240.3   The audit engagement partner should apply quality control procedures appropriate to the particular audit which ensure compliance with SASs.

240.4   Any work delegated to assistants should be directed, supervised and reviewed in a manner which provides reasonable assurance that such work is performed competently.

2   REVIEW OF FINANCIAL STATEMENTS

2.1   SAS 470: Overall review of financial statements

Auditing standards

470.1   Auditors should carry out such a review of the financial statements as is sufficient in conjunction with the conclusions drawn from the other audit evidence obtained, to give them a reasonable basis for their opinion on the financial statements.

470.2   Auditors should consider whether:

(a)   the information presented is in accordance with statutory requirements

(b)   the accounting policies employed are in accordance with accounting standards, properly disclosed, consistently applied and appropriate to the entity.

470.3   Auditors should consider whether:

(a)   the financial statements as a whole and the assertions contained therein are consistent with their knowledge of the entity's business and with the results of other audit procedures

(b)   the manner of disclosure is fair.

2.2   The need for skill and judgement

Throughout the review the auditor needs to take account of the materiality of the matters under review and the confidence which his other audit work has already given him in the accuracy and completeness of the information contained in the financial statements.

Skill and imagination are required to recognise the matters to be examined in carrying out an overall review and sound judgement is needed to interpret the information obtained. Accordingly the review should not be delegated to someone lacking the necessary experience and skill.

An overall review of the financial statements based on the auditor's knowledge of the business of the enterprise is not of itself a sufficient basis for the expression of an audit opinion on those statements. However, it provides valuable support for the conclusions arrived at as a result of the other audit work. In addition apparent inconsistencies could indicate areas in which material errors, omissions or irregularities may have occurred which have not been disclosed by other auditing procedures.

2.3   Ways in which the auditor reviews the financial statements

The table below identifies a number of 'review tasks' some of which have been considered in this chapter, and some which will be considered later.

	Review task	*Regulations or guidance available*
(a)	Confirm acceptability of accounting policies	CA85 Accounting standards Exposure drafts Industry practice Accounting standards in force in other countries, covering areas not yet covered by UK.
(b)	Confirm compliance with disclosure requirements	CA85 Accounting standards Stock Exchange requirements
(c)	Review credibility	SAS 410
(d)	Going concern review	SAS 130
(e)	Post balance sheet audit review of contingencies	SSAP 17 and FRS 12 SAS 150
(f)	Review of the directors' report to ensure consistency with financial statements, and general review of other financial information issued with financial statements	SAS 160
(g)	Review of corresponding figures, preceding financial statements, and corresponding figures	SAS 450
(h)	Review of related party transactions with directors	CA85 FRS 8 SAS 460

A point can be made which you may already have experience of in practice. It is not easy to 'read' a set of accounts and spot inconsistencies. Audit partners and managers are experienced at this and often spot some rather strange trends or problems. Less senior staff are generally involved in more mundane tasks, such as preparing ratios for the review of such partners, or perhaps checking that the accounts add up and notes are properly cross-referenced!

2.4   Procedures

The auditor should conduct a detailed review of the figures disclosed in the financial statements in order to determine whether

(a) **Individual amounts are compatible with each other and with comparative figures**

The auditor will, for example, check the relationship of cost of sales to turnover to ensure that the figures are reasonable by calculating the gross profit percentage and comparing it with that of previous years and those of other companies or businesses in the same field of operations. Likewise he will compare the figure for trade debtors with turnover, expressing debtors in terms of the number of days' sales outstanding to ensure that it appears reasonable in the light of previous results and his knowledge of the industry in which his client operates. (Local authorities, for example, are notorious for the long credit periods they negotiate with their contractors. If the client carries out a large percentage of local authority work, the number of debtor days will be a lot more than the ideal of 30).

(b) **Amounts appearing in the financial statements compare with internal data such as management accounts, budget statements and forecasts**

The auditor should obtain the above documents insofar as they are prepared by the management so that he can compare actual performance with expected performance. The inspection and comparison of monthly levels may highlight areas which were beyond the management's control - a particularly bad summer will depress ice-cream sales, or an internal dispute with employees will affect production.

(c) **Information disclosed is compatible with the auditor's knowledge of the enterprise**

As well as reviewing amounts disclosed, percentages and ratios with his knowledge of the industry in mind, the auditor should also remember all the evidence concerning his client's operations obtained during the course of the audit. It is important to realise that, just as planning an audit does not end once the audit proper has commenced; neither is the review stage confined to the very end audit. Audit staff should be trained to look for significant or unusual transactions during the course of audit testing so that any further audit work which might be considered necessary is planned at the earliest opportunity.

(d) **Presentation and disclosure is reasonable**

The auditor should not be influenced by management's desire to present facts in a more favourable (or unfavourable) form. The financial statements should reflect the substance of the underlying transactions and not merely the form, so that for instance the nature of each of the various types of liability is disclosed separately ie, they are not simply lumped together under one heading. Debtors too should be scrutinised to check for example that those debts recoverable more than a year after the balance sheet date are disclosed separately.

(e) **Regulations are complied with**

In reviewing the financial statements to ensure compliance with the requirements of statutes, accounting standards and other applicable regulations, the auditor may find it helpful to use a checklist or other aide mémoire.

Most firms use a standard checklist to be completed by the auditor in charge before the partner review.

3 REVIEWING FINANCIAL STATEMENTS FOR COMPLIANCE WITH GAAP

3.1 Introduction

This section is concerned with the final audit and the link between financial reporting and auditing. Remember that it is the auditor's responsibility to report on the truth and fairness of the financial statements. In doing this he will need to consider, inter alia, whether items have been fairly treated and fairly disclosed in the financial statements.

Questions on this area are likely to present you with a number of items in the context of a particular company.

Part (a) or parts (a) and (b) are likely to require you to compute some figures and/or comment on the proposed/actual accounting treatment.

Part (b) or (c) is likely to require you to discuss the audit implications of some of the items. The audit implications may be in the form of asking for the evidence needed in order to allow you, as an auditor, to reach a decision on the appropriate treatment and disclosure. Alternatively the question may ask you to summarise the auditing problems associated with a particular area. This also is very much concerned with the problems of obtaining sufficient evidence to support an accounting treatment.

3.2   Comments on treatment and disclosure

The secret of exam questions which require an 'audit' comment on an 'accounting' topic is to realise that in the details of the question there may be missing information which would require assumptions to be made in determining the treatment.

Instead of merely making the assumptions and stating one black and white conclusion, the various possibilities should be indicated and the possible alternative treatments and disclosures discussed.

The basic technical background would be a specific accounting standard, SSAP 2 (in the absence of a specific accounting standard) or the Companies Act, ie

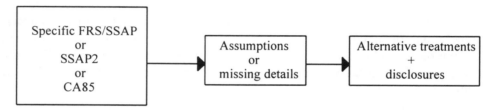

Note that the appropriate disclosure is almost as important as the treatment.

As an example, consider the treatment

'The directors do not provide depreciation on freehold buildings'.

Comments might include

FRS 15 -   required to depreciate all assets with finite life
CA85

but as an alternative

SSAP 2   -   it is industry practice in eg, retailing or brewery industries not to
Consistency   depreciate

and

FRS 15   -   it is justified in these cases since buildings are maintained such as to
have effectively infinite life (so that charge would be immaterial) and
annual impairment reviews are carried out

-     requires regular repairs etc to be carried out and charged to P&L

SSAP 2   -   the company should disclose the reasons for non-depreciation in the
accounting policy note.

Note: the missing information in the statement was the type of business, the regularity of repairs and whether the policy is disclosed.

3.3   The further evidence

This now becomes easier. It refers to the evidence required to clarify the final acceptability of the treatment. In the example above that might mean

(a)   confirm the industry practice

(b)   review regularity of repairs and the current state of freeholds

(c)   consider materiality of amounts involved

(d)   check with the directors the proposed disclosure.

3.4   Activity

Watson Homes Ltd is a housebuilding company in the Midlands and you are the manager in charge of the audit. The company's building sites typically comprise between 20 and 200 houses, when developed, and the larger sites can take several years to complete.

The company was formed in 19X3, and has enjoyed considerable growth during the late 19X0s. The financial statements for the year ended 28 February 19X10 disclosed turnover of £30 million and profit before taxation of £6 million.

However, due to the economic downturn in the housing market, the draft accounts for the year ended 28 February 19X11 show turnover of £16 million and profit before taxation of £2 million.

This result has caused the directors to review the company's accounting policies and the application of these policies to certain areas in the draft accounts. They now propose to make the following adjustments, all of which are material.

(1)   Land, both undeveloped sites and the unsold proportion of partially developed sites, has previously been included in the balance sheet at cost (the value of the land had exceeded cost each year since 19X3). Since land prices have now fallen dramatically, the directors believe it prudent to amend the accounting policy note to value all land at the lower of cost and net realisable value.

Net realisable value has been computed on the estimated market price per acre, on a site by site basis, at 28 February 19X11. The adjustment is a write down of £3.5 million.

(2)   Work in progress valuations include an appropriate proportion of attributable overheads, but this has not previously taken into account interest on the company's considerable borrowings.

The directors take the view that interest payable is now their main overhead, and propose to capitalise part of the total interest charge for the year, using the same proportion as for other overheads. The adjustment to work in progress is £1.5 million.

(3)   In 19X6, the company completed two substantial developments comprising units for warehousing or light industrial use, which have been let to commercial tenants. These developments have been accounted for as investment properties.

On the advice of professional surveyors, these investment properties have been valued annually by the directors at 10 times the current aggregate rental income. However, during March, April and May 19X11, the first rent reviews on most of the units were implemented.

The directors propose to use these higher rents in their valuations, on the basis that they would have been reflected in the market value at 28 February 19X11. The increase in valuation is £1 million.

> **You are required:**
>
> (a)   to prepare a memorandum for the partner in charge of the audit, commenting on the suitability or otherwise of each of the directors' proposals. Where you do not consider any of the proposals suitable, suggest alternative treatments which the directors may adopt.
>
> (b)   after considering your views, the partner decides to accept the adjustments as they stand. State what extra disclosures will be required to the accounting policies and notes to the financial statements.
>
> (c)   to draft the specific paragraphs, relating to the above matters, that you would wish the directors to include in their letter of representation.

3.5   Activity solution

(a)   **Memorandum re suitability or otherwise of proposals**

MEMORANDUM

To: A Jones (partner)

From: B Smith (manager)

Client: Watson Homes Ltd

Date: 23 July 19X11

Re: Draft accounts for the year ended 28 February 19X11 - adjustments proposed by directors

As you are aware the directors of this client have proposed three material adjustments, resulting from a review of the company's accounting policies following the serious downturn in the housing market which has led from last year to this to a decline in turnover of 47% and in profit before tax of 67%.

In addition to reduced materiality thresholds, two particular risks arise

(i)   that the directors may wish to improve the results for the year ended 28 February 19X11. Although shareholders are anticipating poorer results, they may be worse than expected.

(ii)   that the directors anticipate a further downturn in the year ended 29 February 19X12 and so may wish to pull this year's profits down (when shareholders' expectations are low) to minimise a fall next year.

(i)   **Land to be valued at the lower of cost and NRV**

Where such land is held as stock or WIP the proposed policy is prudent and follows both SSAP 9 and the CA85, and the principle of non-aggregation embodied in both (by valuation on a site by site basis).

However, a fall in land prices does not necessarily mean an adjustment is required. To comply with SSAP 9 the net realisable value of land needs to be found by deducting costs to completion and selling expenses from selling price of completed homes, on a site by site basis. The suggested basis of estimated market price per acre is unlikely to meet this SSAP 9 basis.

Any write down should be made through the profit and loss account for the year as an exceptional item.

(ii)   **Capitalisation of interest as part of WIP**

SSAP 9 states that in ascertaining the costs of long-term contracts it is not normally appropriate to include interest payable on borrowed money unless sums borrowed can be identified as financing specific contracts which may or may not be the case here. Otherwise the interest should be written off through the accounts for the year as an exceptional item on the basis of its size.

We should also consider what proportion of attributable profit has been included in this year's WIP and whether full provision for foreseeable losses has been made.

(iii)   **Investment properties - increase in valuation**

Investment properties should be shown in the balance sheet at their open market value.   10 times the current aggregate rental income will therefore only be acceptable if it approximates to open market value at the balance sheet date, regardless of whether the higher or lower current rental income is used as a starting point for calculations.

SSAP 19 also requires that where a substantial proportion of total assets is represented by investment properties, valuation should be made at least every five years by an external valuer. Since the developments were completed in 19X6 an external valuation is due, and simply to obtain the advice of professional surveyors is insufficient. This would resolve the difficulty outlined above.

(b)   **Extra disclosure as a result of the directors' adjustments**

(i)   **Land**

Disclosure of the write down as an exceptional item giving an adequate description

The accounting policy note should be amended to give the valuation basis as amended (there will be no prior year adjustment as in previous years value has always exceeded cost).

(ii)   **Work in progress**

The amount of interest capitalised as part of the work in progress note

The accounting policy note should be amended to refer to the inclusion of capitalised interest in costs

Subject to information being available a prior year adjustment should be made by restating the corresponding profit and loss account and balance sheet amounts for the preceding year and adjusting the opening balance of retained profits accordingly. The effect on the results for the preceding year should be disclosed where practicable.

(iii)   **Investment properties**

The £1 million transfer to the Investment Revaluation Reserve as a reserve movement and in the statement of total recognised gains and losses.

(c)   **Specific paragraphs for the letter of representation**

(i)   **Land**

Land has been prudently valued at £X at the lower of cost and net realisable value. This valuation has been carried out on a site by site basis. In arriving at net realisable value the estimated market price per acre is believed to be appropriate.

(ii)   **Work in progress**

Interest of £1.5 million has been fairly allocated to total work in progress of £X million. This is a change of accounting policy and gives a fairer presentation of the company's results and position.

(iii) **Investment properties**

Properties falling within the definition of investment properties per SSAP 19 have been included in the balance sheet at £X being 10 times the current aggregate rental income. This valuation is a fair approximation to open market value.

4 LETTERS OF REPRESENTATION AND OTHER FINAL AUDIT MATTERS

4.1 Introduction

This section summarises other matters which need to be cleared in the completion of the audit. Some of these matters are covered in later sections of this chapter such as contingencies, post balance sheet events, preceding year amounts, published unaudited information, and going concern evaluation.

4.2 Letters of representation

Representations by management are one source of audit evidence. They may be an important part of audit evidence in the audit of companies of all sizes. SAS 440 **Management representations** lays down rules on the procedures to adopt in collecting and using such evidence.

The advice given is important because there are certain dangers in relying too heavily upon representations by management, for example:

(a) The representations may not be properly recorded in the working papers.

(b) The representations may be misunderstood by the auditor. This is particularly likely if they are given by word of mouth rather than in a written form.

(c) The representations may be biased. It is therefore important for the auditor to get independent corroborative evidence whenever he can.

4.3 Procedures

(a) **Production of representation letter**

Where oral representations by management are uncorroborated by sufficient other audit evidence and where they relate to matters which are material to the financial statements, they should be summarised in the auditor's working papers. The auditor should ensure that these representations are either formally minuted as being approved by the board of directors or included in a signed letter, addressed to the auditor, known as a 'letter of representation', or else the auditor must write a letter outlining their understanding of management's representations, this letter being acknowledged and confirmed in writing by the management.

Because the representations are those of management, standard letters of representations may not be appropriate. In any event, management should be encouraged to participate in drafting any letter of representation or, after review and discussion, to make appropriate amendments to the auditor's draft, provided that the value of the audit evidence obtained is not thereby diminished.

(b) **Arrangements for signing letter**

A letter of representation should be signed by persons whose level of authority is appropriate to the significance of the representations made, normally by one or more of the executive directors (for example by the chief executive and the financial director), on behalf of the whole board. The signatories of the letter should be fully conversant with the matters contained in it. The auditor should request that the consideration of the letter and its approval by the board for signature be minuted. He may request that he be allowed to attend the meeting at which the board is due to approve the letter. Such attendance may also be desirable where the representations are to be formally minuted, rather than included in a letter.

(c)   **Actions if management refuse to sign letter**

Procedures regarding written representations should be agreed at an early stage in order to reduce the possibility of the auditor being faced with a refusal by management to co-operate in providing such representations. However, management may at the outset indicate that they are not willing to sign letters of representation or to pass minutes requested by the auditor. If they do so indicate, the auditor should inform management that he will himself prepare a statement in writing setting out his understanding of the principal representations that have been made to him during the course of the audit and he should send this statement to management with a request for confirmation that his understanding of the representations is correct.

If management disagrees with the auditor's statement of representations, discussions should be held to clarify the matters in doubt and, if necessary, a revised statement prepared and agreed. Should management fail to reply, the auditor should follow the matter up to try to ensure that his understanding of the position, as set out in his statement, is correct.

(d)   **Qualification**

There may, however, be circumstances where the auditor is unable to obtain the written representations which he requires. This may be because of a refusal by management to co-operate, or because management properly declines to give the representations required on the ground of its own uncertainty regarding the particular matter. In either case if the auditor is unable to satisfy himself, he may have to conclude that he has not received all the information and explanations that he requires, and consequently may need to consider qualifying his audit report.

4.4   Dating

The formal record of representations by management should be approved on a date as close as possible to the date of the audit report and after all other work, including the review of events after the balance sheet date, has been completed. It should never be approved after the audit report since it is part of the evidence on which the auditor's opinion, expressed in his report, is based.

If there is a substantial delay between the approval of the formal record of representations by management and the date of the audit report, the auditor should consider whether to obtain further representations in respect of the intervening period and also whether any additional audit procedures need to be carried out, as described in SAS 150 **Subsequent events.**

4.5   Contents and wording

The precise scope of the formal record of representations should be appropriate to the circumstances of each particular audit. The representations will be necessary where there are matters which are material to the financial statements, in respect of which the auditor cannot obtain independent corroborative evidence and could not reasonably expect it to be available.

4.6   SAS 440: Management representations

SAS 440's auditing standards set down best practice to be adopted.

Auditing standards

440.1   Auditors should obtain written confirmation of appropriate representations from management before their report is issued.

440.2   Auditors should obtain evidence that the directors acknowledge their collective responsibility for the preparation of the financial statements and have approved the financial statements.

440.3   Auditors should obtain written confirmation of representations from management on matters material to the financial statements when those representations are critical to obtaining sufficient appropriate audit evidence.

440.4   If a representation appears to be contradicted by other audit evidence, the auditors should investigate the circumstances to resolve the matter and consider whether it casts doubt on the reliability of other representations.

440.5   If management refuses to provide written confirmation of a representation that the auditors consider necessary, the auditors should consider the implications of this scope limitation for their report.

4.7   Audit completion checklists

These have already been referred to in the context of the review of financial statements as a means of ensuring that regulations are complied with. They can also be used to check that all material audit procedures have been carried out. There will probably be a section which is to be filled in by the manager and a section to be completed by the partner. As it is a standardised form, care should be taken that it is used as a tool and not as a crutch. The audit partner should not blindly rely on the fact that the checklist has been completed by the manager. He needs to ensure that the work has actually been done.

4.8   Management letters

It should be normal practice at the end of an audit to send a letter to the client setting out weaknesses in the system of internal control. Certain rules should be observed when preparing such a letter.

(a)   It should make clear that the object of the audit is not to discover fraud, but to report on the financial statements. The matters referred to have been discovered incidentally to the main objective.

(b)   The points should be listed logically.

(c)   There is no point in drawing attention to a weakness which is inherent in the nature or size of the business, or is totally trivial.

(d)   Only the weakness should be noted. It should not be implied that any fraud is taking place although the possible consequences of the weakness can be expanded upon.

(e)   Recommendations for improvements should be made in respect of each weakness.

The management letter is sometimes called the letter of weakness, the internal control memorandum, the letter of recommendations or the constructive service letter.

The management letter will normally be a natural by-product of the audit, and the auditor should incorporate the need to issue the letter in the planning of the audit.

To be effective, the letter should be sent as soon as possible after completion of the audit procedures giving rise to the need to comment. Where audit work is carried out in more than one stage it may be appropriate to issue a letter at the interim audit stage as well as the final audit stage.

It is preferable to discuss all the points in the letter with management before the letter is issued. It is essential that the contents of the letter are considered by the management. The auditor should therefore ask the management to reply to the letter. A copy of the letter with replies should be kept on the files. Points made in previous years should be reviewed by the auditor.

When a group of companies is involved, the management of the holding company may want to be informed of significant points arising in the reports to the management of the subsidiaries. The auditor must obtain permission from the management of the subsidiary before releasing such information.

Any report made to management should be regarded as a confidential communication. The auditor should therefore not normally reveal the contents of the report to any third party without the prior written consent of the management of the company.

In practice, the auditor has little control over what happens to the report once it has been despatched. Occasionally, management may provide third parties eg, their bankers, with copies of the report.

The auditor can use a disclaimer of liability against unforeseen liability to third parties, but this may not give full protection from liability where the auditor knows or ought to know that a report to management may be passed to a third party who would rely on it.

4.9   SAS 610: Reports to directors or management

SAS 610 contains guidance on how management letters should be sent to directors, including any audit committee, or to management.

Auditing standards

610.1   Auditors should consider the matters which have come to their attention during the audit and whether they should be included in a report to directors or management.

610.2   When material weaknesses in the accounting and internal control systems are identified during the audit, auditors should report them in writing to the directors, the audit committee or an appropriate level of management on a timely basis.

4.10   Summarising errors

As part of the final audit procedures a summary needs to be prepared of errors found as a result of substantive procedures in order to formally determine the effect of errors on audit risk and the overall conclusion of the audit. The recording of errors has already been referred to in a previous chapter in the context of formulating conclusions on substantive tests.

5   THE AUDIT RESPONSIBILITY FOR OPENING BALANCES AND COMPARATIVES

5.1   Amounts derived from the preceding financial statements

If the auditor himself issued an unqualified audit report on the preceding financial statements and nothing has arisen in the current audit to suggest any doubt as to the validity of those statements, then the auditor must ensure that:

(a)   amounts have been correctly brought forward;

(b)   corresponding amounts have been properly classified and disclosed;

(c)   accounting policies have been consistently applied.

5.2   Preceding period audited by another auditor or unaudited

In these circumstances the auditor will need to perform additional work in order to satisfy himself regarding the opening position. His work would include:

(a)   consulting the client's management;

(b)   reviewing records and accounting and control procedures in the preceding period; and

(c)   consulting with the previous auditor and reviewing his working papers and relevant management letters.

Some evidence of the opening position will also usually be gained from the audit work performed in the current period.

If the auditor is unable to satisfy himself with regard to the preceding period, he will have to consider qualifying his audit report.

5.3 SAS 450: Opening balances and comparatives

Auditing standards

450.1 Auditors should obtain sufficient appropriate audit evidence that amounts derived from the preceding period's financial statements are free from material misstatements and are appropriately incorporated in the financial statements for the current period.

450.2 Auditors should obtain sufficient appropriate audit evidence that:

(a) opening balances have been appropriately brought forward;

(b) opening balances do not contain errors or misstatements which materially affect the current period's financial statements; and

(c) appropriate accounting policies are consistently applied or changes in accounting policies have been properly accounted for and adequately disclosed.

In the event that the auditors are unable to obtain such audit evidence, they need to consider the implications for their report.

450.3 Auditors should obtain sufficient appropriate audit evidence that:

(a) the accounting policies used for the comparatives are consistent with those of the current period and appropriate adjustments and disclosures have been made where this is not the case;

(b) the comparatives agree with the amounts and other disclosures presented in the preceding period and are free from errors in the context of the financial statements of the current period; and

(c) where comparatives have been adjusted as required by relevant legislation and accounting standards, appropriate disclosures have been made.

In the event that the auditors are unable to obtain such audit evidence, they need to consider the implications for their report.

6 THE AUDIT IMPLICATIONS OF PUBLISHED UNAUDITED INFORMATION

6.1 Other information issued with audited financial statements

The annual report and accounts of a company will contain a number of unaudited financial statements. SAS 160 considers the responsibilities if any, of the auditor, for these unaudited statements. A distinction is drawn between the directors' report and other unaudited statements.

6.2 The directors' report

The auditor is not required to form an opinion on the directors' report itself. As a result, under normal circumstances, the auditor should confine his work to satisfying himself whether or not the directors' report contains any matters which are inconsistent with the audited financial statements to comply with S235 CA85.

Such matters may include the following

(a) an inconsistency between actual figures appearing in, respectively, the audited financial statements and the directors' report;

(b)   an inconsistency between the bases of preparation of related items appearing in the audited financial statements and the directors' report, where the figures themselves are not directly comparable;

(c)   an inconsistency between figures contained in the audited financial statements and a narrative interpretation of the effect of those figures in the directors' report.

The auditor should consider the implications of any inconsistency and should hold discussions with directors of the company, or other senior members of management, in order to achieve its elimination.

Where, after holding such discussions, the auditor is of the opinion that an inconsistency still exists, his course of action will depend on whether he believes that an amendment is required to the audited financial statements or to the directors' report.

If, in the auditor's opinion, it is the audited financial statements which require amendment, he should consider qualifying his report on those financial statements. In these circumstances, the auditor should make use of the SAS on Audit Reports.

If, in his opinion, it is the directors' report which requires amendment, the auditor should refer in his report to the inconsistency in order to comply with S235 CA85.

The auditor does not have a responsibility to search the directors' report for items which, while not inconsistent with the audited financial statements, are misleading in some other respect. Furthermore, counsel has advised that it is doubtful that he has a right to comment on misleading as opposed to inconsistent items in his report on the audited financial statements.

6.3   Other financial information

The auditor has no statutory responsibilities in respect of other financial information issued with audited financial statements. Nevertheless, it should be reviewed by the auditor as, where there is a material inconsistency with the audited financial statements or an item which is misleading in some other respect, the credibility of the audited financial statements may be undermined.

Where the auditor considers that a material inconsistency or an item which is misleading in some other respect exists, he should consider its implications and hold discussions with directors, or other senior members of management, and may also make his views known in writing to all the directors in order to achieve its elimination. Where communication with directors and their representatives does not result in the elimination of the problem, he should consider whether an amendment is required to the audited financial statements or the other financial information.

If, in the auditor's opinion, it is the audited financial statements which require amendment, he should follow the guidance as given above.

Counsel has advised that it is doubtful whether the auditor has a right to comment on other financial information in his report on the audited financial statements. In a serious case he could use his rights under S387 CA85 to be heard at any general meeting or any business of the meeting which concerns him as an auditor.

If information which forms part of the directors' report is contained in the other financial information (eg, the directors' report states that the review of the company's activities is given in the chairman's statement) then it would appear that the detail in the other financial statements should be covered by the auditor in his review under S235 CA85.

6.4   SAS 160: Other information in documents containing audited financial statements

Auditing standards

160.1   Auditors should read other information in documents containing audited financial statements. If as a result they become aware of any apparent misstatements therein, or identify any material inconsistencies with the audited financial statements, they should seek to resolve them.

160.2   If auditors identify an inconsistency between the financial statements and the other information, or a misstatement within the other information, they should consider whether an amendment is required to the financial statements or to the other information and should seek to resolve the matter through discussion with the directors.

160.3   If, after discussion with the directors, the auditors conclude that the financial statements require amendment and no such amendment is made, they should consider the implications for their report. If, after discussion with the directors, the auditors conclude that the other information requires amendment and no such amendment is made, they should consider appropriate action.

6.5   ED of SAS 160 (revised) 'Other information in documents containing audited financial statements'

A draft revised SAS 160 was issued by the APB in April 1999 to clarify two aspects of the original SAS 160:

(a)   the requirement to 'read' the other information;

(b)   the remedies at auditors' disposal should they identify a material misstatement or inconsistency.

These matters are clarified as follows:

(a)   the engagement partner (or other appropriate senior members of the audit team) should read the other information with a view to identifying significant misstatements therein or matters which are inconsistent with the financial statements.

(b)   a distinction may be drawn between a factual error and a qualitative statement. A factual error will be easier to take issue with than a qualitative statement, but auditors must consider the implications of both.

7   TESTS CONDUCTED TO INVESTIGATE POST BALANCE SHEET EVENTS

7.1   The audit of post balance sheet events

The advent of SSAP 17 led to the need for guidance to clarify the auditor's responsibilities with regard to examining and reporting upon events which occur after the date of the balance sheet. Best practice developed as follows:

(a)   The auditor dated his report, which could not be earlier than the date on which the directors approve the financial statements.

(b)   The auditor ensured that he was aware of all significant events up to the date of his report and that such events were accounted for or disclosed in the financial statements.

(c)   A 'post-balance sheet events' review took place which was adequately recorded in the working papers. This review consisted of discussions with management and examination of records of the following

       (i)   the accounting records and management accounts

       (ii)   profit forecasts and cash flow projections

       (iii)   known risk areas and contingencies

       (iv)   minutes, correspondence and memoranda relating to items therein

       (v)   relevant information from outside sources.

(d)   The letter of representation detailed post-balance sheet events or included a statement that no such events have occurred.

7.2 SAS 150: Subsequent events

SAS 150 now gives mandatory guidance in this area.

Definition A subsequent event is an event between the end of the accounting period and the date when the financial statements are laid before the members.

It is thus a longer period than the post balance sheet event period of SSAP 17.

SAS 150 considers the subsequent events period which is divided into three periods:

(a) up to the date of the audit report
(b) after the date of the audit report but before the financial statements are issued
(c) after the financial statements are issued but before they are laid before the members.

The date the audit report is signed is covered in SAS 600 (see later).

Auditing standards

General

150.1 Auditors should consider the effect of subsequent events on the financial statements and on their report.

Responsibilities to the date of the audit report

150.2 Auditors should perform procedures designed to obtain sufficient appropriate audit evidence that all material subsequent events up to the date of their report which require adjustment of, or disclosure in, the financial statements have been identified and properly reflected therein.

SSAP 17 contains the mandatory accounting guidance in this area.

Responsibilities after the date of the audit report, but before the financial statements are issued

150.3 When, after the date of their report but before the financial statements are issued, auditors become aware of subsequent events which may materially affect the financial statements, they should establish whether the financial statements need amendment, should discuss the matter with the directors and should consider the implications for their report, taking additional action as appropriate.

Responsibility after the financial statements have been issued, but before their laying before the members

150.4 In such circumstances the auditors should consider whether the financial statements need amendment, should discuss the matter with the directors, and should consider the implications for their report, taking additional action as appropriate.

8 THE AUDITORS' RESPONSIBILITIES FOR GOING CONCERN

8.1 The going concern concept

The preparation of accounts must follow the five fundamental accounting principles laid down in the Companies Act 1985. One of these, the going concern concept, is defined in SSAP 2 as the assumption that the enterprise will continue in operational existence for the foreseeable future. This means in particular that the profit and loss account and balance sheet assume no intention or necessity to liquidate or curtail significantly the scale of operations.

The auditors will need to satisfy themselves that the going concern assumption is reasonable. In the absence of a clear note to the contrary, there is a presumption that the fundamental concepts (of going concern, accruals, consistency and prudence) have been observed.

Auditors should not assume the going concern concept will continue to apply but need to conduct a specific examination of the relevant factors to reach a decision. This will involve an overall review of financial factors, preferably before the client's year end, in order to establish whether there are factors which cast doubt on the going concern basis. If there are, further investigation is required.

8.2   Investigations to be carried out

(a)   **Indicators of problems**

Possible reasons for non-applicability of a going concern basis could include a combination of

(i)   Declining profitability

(ii)   Inability to re-finance loans as they fall due.

The pointers to such situations, for which the auditor should watch, include

(i)   Rapidly increasing costs which cannot be matched by increasing sales prices.

(ii)   Shortages of supplies.

(iii)   Adverse movements in exchange rates.

(iv)   Business failures amongst customers or suppliers.

(v)   Loan repayments falling due in the near future.

(vi)   Higher gearing (fixed interest borrowing becoming a larger proportion of long-term finance).

(vii)   Long-term assets financed by short-term borrowing.

(viii)   Nearness to present borrowing limits with no sign of a reduction in borrowing requirements.

(ix)   Small companies financed by loans from directors. If these rank pari passu with other creditors they should be treated as current liabilities.

(b)   **Audit review**

Initial enquiries will be

(i)   General enquiries by partners/managers

(ii)   Observation by junior audit staff

(iii)   Examination of cash flow forecasts.

If any of these indicate potential problems, then a more detailed review of the points above will be needed.

(c)   **Cash flow forecasts**

Cash flow forecasts should normally be prepared by management as a matter of course. In situations where there is doubt about the applicability of the going concern basis, and such forecasts are not prepared, the auditors should request that they be prepared.

Where a cash forecast is prepared, the auditors will review it critically, and consider whether the cash requirements indicated will in fact be available.

(d)   **Availability of financial support**

Where the cash forecasts indicate borrowing requirements beyond those currently available, the auditors will need to satisfy themselves that such funds will be available. Assurances that such funds will be available should be in writing.

The auditor will also need to consider

(i)   The company's ability to maintain the financial viability of both itself and its pension fund.

(ii)   Limits on the company's borrowing powers imposed by trust deeds, Articles of Association, and so on.

(e)   **Evidence from directors**

In cases of doubt, the auditors may want the directors to

(i)   Give a full description of the situation in their confirmation that the business is a going concern (required for listed companies by the Stock Exchange Combined Code).

(ii)   Provide a certificate that there are no post-balance sheet events which significantly alter the balance sheet position.

These representations do not, however, relieve the auditor of any of his responsibility.

SAS 600 gives examples on possible qualified audit reports that may be considered appropriate (see later).

8.3   SAS 130: The going concern basis in financial statements

SAS 130 has introduced two main areas of change from previous best practice.

(a)   **More thorough assessment of the going concern basis**

The previous guideline only required the auditor to perform additional procedures if he became aware that the going concern basis may not be valid ie, there were specific procedures to test this presumption.

By contrast, SAS 130 requires auditors to perform procedures specifically designed to identify indications that the going concern basis may not be valid. Only if these specific procedures and the auditor's other work do not reveal such indications can the auditor conclude that the going concern basis is appropriate. The change is designed to reduce the possibility of auditors not detecting going concern problems.

(b)   **Fuller disclosures and effect on audit report**

(i)   **Inherent uncertainty**

It is considered that previous guidance has not been conducive to the full disclosure of uncertainties regarding a company's ability to continue as a going concern.

Under SAS 130, if an inherent uncertainty exists which could affect this ability the auditors should consider whether disclosure of the matters giving rise to the uncertainty is adequate to give a true and fair view.

(1)   **Adequate disclosure**

The auditors should draw attention to the matters in their report. This is consistent with the treatment of significant inherent uncertainties as outlined in the SAS on the audit report.

The added emphasis is required even if the recoverability and classification of recorded assets or the amount and classification of liabilities are not in question.

(2)   **Inadequate disclosure**

An 'except for' or 'adverse' qualification should be given in respect of the inadequate disclosure.

(ii)   **Disagreement**

If the auditors disagree with the presumption that the company is a going concern they should give an 'adverse' opinion and provide in their report such additional information as they consider necessary and are able to provide.

(iii)   **Limitation in scope**

A total disclaimer should be issued in this rare circumstance.

(iv)   **Financial statements prepared on a non-going concern basis**

If considered appropriate, and the financial statements contain the necessary disclosures, the auditors should not qualify but should draw attention to the basis of preparation and the notes concerning this basis.

9   CHAPTER SUMMARY

The auditor must review the financial statements sufficiently so that, in conjunction with other audit evidence obtained, he has a reasonable basis for coming to an opinion on the financial statements.

Matters such as accounting policies, disclosure requirements, going concern and post balance sheet events need to be considered.

10   SELF TEST QUESTIONS

10.1   What are typical control procedures in the conduct of an audit? (1.2)

10.2   What should a firm do to establish quality control in a firm? (1.6)

10.3   What things should an auditor do in his review of the financial statements? (2.1)

10.4   What are three dangers in relying on management representations? (4.2)

10.5   What other names are given to the management letter? (4.8)

10.6   What three things should an auditor do regarding amounts derived from preceding financial statements? (5.1)

10.7   What duties does an auditor have in regard to the Directors' Report? (6.2)

10.8   Define a subsequent event. (7.2)

10.9   What indicators should be looked for in considering the going concern status of a client? (8.2)

11   EXAMINATION TYPE QUESTION

11.1   Audit work

You have been asked to describe the audit work you will carry out on the following matters relating to a number of companies your firm is currently auditing, which have the same year-end of 31 March 19X2.

(a)   Newthorpe Manufacturing plc has reviewed its asset lives in accordance with FRS 15 *Tangible fixed assets*. Its review has resulted in an increase in asset lives and it is proposed to credit the profit and loss account with £1.1 million as an exceptional item. The total depreciation provision as shown in the notes to the accounts on tangible fixed assets has been reduced by the same amount, making an accumulated £12.3 million at the year-end. The cost of fixed assets at the year-end is £31.5 million.

You have been asked to verify that the change in the asset lives is reasonable and to consider whether the company's treatment of the depreciation charge for the year is in accordance with the Companies Acts and FRS 15 *Tangible fixed assets.*

(b)   Arnold Garages plc sells motor vehicles to the public and businesses from a number of retail outlets which it owns. During the year the company's land and buildings were revalued by a professional valuer. This resulted in an increase in their value from £14.3 million to £19.8 million, and this revaluation was credited to a capital reserve. The directors believe that this increase in the value is due entirely to an increase in land values, so they have not altered the depreciation charge on these properties. This remains at 2% on cost of the buildings.

You have been asked to check that the revaluation of the properties is accurate, and that it is acceptable to continue to depreciate the buildings at 2% on cost.

(c)   Forest Computing plc acquired Clifton Software Ltd on 1 April 19X1. Included in the purchase of Clifton Software were a number of computer programs which the company sells to businesses and individuals. Forest Computing plc has decided to include in the group accounts £6.4 million as an intangible fixed asset, which is the fair value of the software rights acquired. In Forest Computing's consolidated accounts, £0.9 million has been charged as amortisation on these software rights.

You are required to list and describe the audit work you will perform on the items described above to decide whether the company's treatment on the items in the accounts is correct

(a)   Newthorpe Manufacturing plc - increase in asset lives and credit of £1.1 million for depreciation for the year   **(8 marks)**

(b)   Arnold Garages plc - whether the increase in the value of the land and buildings is accurate, and whether the depreciation charged on the buildings is acceptable   **(9 marks)**

(c)   Forest Computing plc - whether the capitalised fair value of the software rights and the amortisation charge for the year are reasonable.   **(8 marks)**
(Total: 25 marks)

12   ANSWER TO EXAMINATION TYPE QUESTION

12.1   Audit work

(a)   Audit work on the increase in asset lives will include

(i)   Obtain a schedule from the directors showing the change in asset values for each individual asset summarised by asset category. Cast the schedule to ensure that there are no addition errors.

(ii)   Ascertain who revalued the assets. The directors could have revalued the assets, in which case justification for the revised values should be sought from the directors. Alternatively, the assets may have been revalued by a professional valuer. If this is the case, ask permission from the directors to contact the valuer directly and ask him to supply copies of his working papers. These should be reviewed to ensure that the revaluation has been correctly carried out.

(iii)   Obtain additional evidence to check the accuracy of the revaluation above.

(1)   Review disposals of assets over the last few years. If there were large profits on sale, then this indicates that depreciation rates were too high; the rate could therefore be decreased, as the company has done here, to more accurately match NBV with sale proceeds. If there are large losses on sale then this

indicates that the opposite is true, and therefore that depreciation rates should be increased.

(2) If Newthorpe has a policy of regularly replacing assets, then the accumulated depreciation should be about half of the asset costs. If accumulated depreciation is more than half of the asset cost then this indicates that assets are being depreciated too quickly, and that a decrease in the depreciation rate could be made.

(3) Review the schedules of fixed assets. If there are many assets that are still in use, but that are fully depreciated, then this again indicates that depreciation rates are high; a downward revision could therefore be made.

(4) A fall in the rate of depreciation effectively increases the asset lives. Consider whether this increase is justifiable from the nature of the client's business and also the assets making up the balance sheet values.

(iv) Reach a conclusion based on the above audit evidence. As long as the change in asset lives appears reasonable, then the auditor is likely to agree with the change. It is only if the new asset lives appear to be unrealistically long that the change will be queried, and consideration given to qualifying the audit report.

Note that the auditors generally prefer assets to be written off over too few years rather than too many, as this is prudent accounting treatment.

Audit work on the depreciation credit to the profit and loss account

(i) Obtain a schedule from the directors showing the calculation £1.1 million total; review and cast this to ensure that it is correct.

(ii) Consider whether the proposed accounting treatment is acceptable.

FRS 15 does not permit such a treatment (although it was permitted in certain circumstances by SSAP 12). FRS 15 now requires that, where asset lives have been revised, the carrying amount of the tangible fixed asset at the date of revision should be depreciated over the revised remaining useful economic life, so this is the treatment that should be adopted.

(b) Audit work on the revaluation of land and buildings

(i) Obtain a schedule of the land and buildings showing the values before and after the revaluation. Cast the schedule and agree it to the nominal ledger and financial statements (if these have been produced).

(ii) Check that the credit on revaluation has in fact been taken to the capital reserve; vouch this item from the revaluation schedule to the capital reserve in the nominal ledger and financial statements.

(iii) Review the work of the professional valuer to ensure that it is accurate and can be relied on.

(1) Ensure that the valuer has the appropriate professional qualifications, and experience to value this type of property. If there are a number of properties in different locations, check that appropriate local knowledge is used to value the properties accurately.

(2) Check that the valuer is independent of Arnold Garages. To maintain independence, the valuer should not be employed by Arnold, or by any director of Arnold, and also he should not own any shares in Arnold.

(3)   Ensure that the basis of valuation is appropriate - eg, existing use basis would be acceptable for Arnold.

(iv)   Ensure that the increase in property values appears reasonable.

      (1)   Review recent property sales in the books of Arnold. If properties are undervalued, then large profits should have been made on sale.

      (2)   Review sales of similar properties either from trade journals or similar audit clients. Compare these prices to those proposed by the valuer to ensure that the latter are reasonable.

(v)   Form an opinion on whether the revised values are reasonable. Unless there are significant differences (eg, recent property sales have shown a loss and the property market in general is falling), then the auditor is likely to concur with the re-valuation. If the revaluation appears excessive, then the directors will be asked to re-assess the proposed values, and a qualified report could be issued if the auditor believes that the new values are materially incorrect.

Audit work on the depreciation charge on land and buildings includes

(i)   Obtain reasons from the directors why the buildings have not been revalued. If necessary, ask the directors, and the professional valuer for a split of the revalued amounts between land and buildings.

(ii)   If the directors will not provide the information, consider approaching the valuer directly and ask him to provide the information. Alternatively, employ a second specialist to provide the information.

(iii)   Review the revaluation information supplied above and quantify the depreciation charge based on the potential revised buildings values.

(iv)   Compare the depreciation charge based on cost to that based on the potential revalued amount. If the difference is not material then no further action need be taken except to note the possibly incorrect accounting treatment in the management letter. In this case FRS 15 has not been complied with because buildings have not been depreciated on their revalued amounts - the buildings have not been revalued when they should have been.

(v)   If the difference between the two depreciation charges is material then the auditor will need to consider qualifying the audit report. Materiality in this case could be taken to mean that the net profit figure is overstated by a certain percentage to be decided by the audit firm.

(c)   Audit work to check the capitalised fair value of the software rights will include the following

(i)   Obtain a schedule of the rights acquired from the client; cast the schedule and agree the total to the nominal ledger account and the financial statements.

(ii)   Agree individual software packages back to the purchase agreement with Clifton to ensure that these items of software were, in fact, purchased from the company.

(iii)   Agree individual software packages to sales summaries of software sold. The amount of sales will give an indication of the relative value to be ascribed to the software in the rights schedule. The higher the value of the rights, then the higher should be the total expected sales over the year.

(iv)   Vouch the software itself (this will mean obtaining some of the software actually being sold); ensure that the programs appear on the software list, and ensure that the software packaging states that Forest actually owns the software.

(v)   Check that future sales are expected for the individual product lines. Obtain copies of the sales budgets from the client's staff. Review the budgets to ensure the software rights with higher value have a higher NRV.

(vi)   Ensure that future sales will exceed the capitalised value of the software.

(vii)   Check that the estimated useful life of the software is not excessive. Well known packages are likely to have a shorter life than small specialised packages. Well known packages are reviewed annually and new versions issued.

From the above work, the auditor will reach an opinion on whether the value placed on software rights is reasonable.

Audit work on the amortisation charge will include the following

(i)   From the schedule of software, test check the accuracy of the amortisation calculation for a number of lines of software. Cast the amortisation charge and agree this to the nominal ledger and final accounts.

(ii)   Ascertain from the directors what the policy for amortising software is. It would appear prudent to amortise software lines over the life of that individual piece of software. The average life implied in the question of 7.1 years may be excessive given that some items of software will already be a few years old. A more realistic timescale for many popular packages could be in the region of 2 or 3 years. The amortisation rate may therefore be unreasonable.

        Furthermore, it would also seem prudent to match the amortisation charge with the sales of the software, as they are made. This would therefore suggest that larger amortisation charges are made in earlier years as more copies of the software are reviewed - if it is found that many packages are recent, then again the amortisation charge would appear to be unreasonable; a higher charge would be expected in the earlier years to match the higher sales of each piece of software at this time.

(iii)   Reach a conclusion on whether the amortisation charge is correct. Given that the average useful life of the software is 7 years, and that the amortisation charge may not be being allocated to reflect the falling value of the software over time, then the amortisation charge may be too low.

The auditor will make his own estimate of the amortisation required on each software line, calculate the amortisation required and compare his total to that produced by the company.

If the difference between the two totals is material, then the company would be asked to change its depreciation policy. If a change is refused, then a qualification of the audit report would be required.

Note that software lives are difficult to determine; therefore the difference between the auditor's calculation, and the company's value for the amortisation of software must be fairly large before the auditor will consider a qualification.

(*Tutorial note:*

Ensure that audit work is given only for the objective requested in the question. Note also that qualifications are not always clear cut. It is appropriate to mention that some assets are difficult to value, and as long as the company's valuation is reasonably close to that expected by the auditor, then the auditor is likely to accept this.)

28 COMPLEX AUDIT SITUATIONS

INTRODUCTION & LEARNING OBJECTIVES

This chapter deals with the audit of groups and problematical audit situations. You should find the audit of groups fairly easy to deal with in an exam question. There is little new to learn and many of the situations given concern accounting rather than audit issues.

Related party transactions including transactions with directors requires careful study. Definitions need to be learned as an answer could depend on a detailed point of law.

Illegal acts by clients can give rise to complex ethical problems. The legal responsibilities of the auditor need to be clearly known.

When you have studied this chapter you should be able to do the following:

- Explain the organisation, planning and managing of complex audit situations
- Explain the special considerations of the planning and controlling of a group audit
- Discuss the auditor's duties regarding related party transactions including directors.
- Discuss the auditor's responsibility for detecting illegal acts by clients.

1 COMPLEX AUDIT SITUATIONS

1.1 The organisation, planning and managing of complex audit situations

An audit can be defined as 'complex' if it deviates, in whole or in part, from a normal audit. Examples include the following

(a) Group audit

   The complexity arises from the need to consider special statutory provisions, consolidation techniques and perhaps the need to rely on other auditors.

(b) Joint audit

   An audit is split between two reporting auditors and clearly, in this fairly rare event, there are problems of co-ordination of activities to overcome.

(c) Reliance on other specialists

   This affects part of the audit but in some audits of specialised businesses there may need to be considerable use made of specialists.

(d) Related party transactions

   In some situations there may be many related companies or individuals having dealings with the company being audited. These dealings may not be at an arm's length price because of these relationships.

The complexity of the above situations requires organisation and planning in order to control the expected complexities. Differences from the normal audit can be clarified and planned for accordingly.

Although the situations are complex, they are not unmanageable ie, an audit can still be validly undertaken.

1.2   The special considerations of the planning and controlling of a group audit

The auditors are required to report to the members of the holding company on the accounts examined by them including the group accounts as prepared in accordance with the Companies Act.

It should be noted that the auditors' responsibility for the group accounts is exactly the same as their responsibility for the accounts of an individual company which they audit.

The audit report will cover the relevant information for the individual holding company accounts and the group accounts.

At the planning stage, the holding company auditor will need to consider:

(a)   The client's procedures for preparing the group's financial statements including:

    (i)   The client's group accounting instructions.

    (ii)   The standard account forms - specifying layout of financial statements of each subsidiary so as to facilitate consolidation.

    (iii)   The client's timetable for production of financial statements of individual companies, sub-groups, etc.

(b)   The auditor's own timetable. This will involve:

    (i)   Audit staffing.

    (ii)   Liaison with other auditors of subsidiaries and associated companies (see below).

    (iii)   Anticipating problem areas: for example, certain overseas subsidiaries.

The relationship between the various accounting and audit stages is complex.

1.3   Other auditors

The various subsidiary and associated companies in the group may be audited by a combination of:

(a)   The firm which audits the holding company, although this may well involve other offices.

(b)   Other firms (secondary auditors) - see below.

In either case, there is the problem of obtaining information. The holding company auditor is responsible for the audit opinion on the financial statements of the group as a whole.

1.4   Statutory right to information

S389A CA85 gives the auditor of the holding company important additional rights relating to information about subsidiaries.

> A subsidiary undertaking which is a body corporate incorporated in Great Britain, and the auditors of such an undertaking, shall give to the auditors of any parent company of the undertaking such information and explanations as they may reasonably require for the purpose of their duties as auditors of that company.

> A parent company having a subsidiary undertaking which is not a body corporate incorporated in Great Britain shall, if required by its auditors to do so, take all such steps as are reasonably open to it to obtain from the subsidiary undertaking such information and explanations as they may reasonably require for the purposes of their duties as auditors of that company.

1.5   Duties of auditors

Auditors of the holding company (the primary or principal auditors) are not relieved of their responsibility under S235 CA85 for expressing an opinion on the group accounts where the accounts contain amounts, which may be material, relating to other companies of which they are not the auditors. Nor is this responsibility discharged by an uninformed acceptance of the accounts of those other companies, even if they have been independently audited (by the secondary auditors). The opinion is wholly the responsibility of the primary auditors.

Whilst entitled to take account of the work and the report of the secondary auditors, the primary auditors should nevertheless conduct such further enquiries as they consider necessary to satisfy themselves that, with the inclusion of figures which they themselves have not audited, the group accounts give a true and fair view.

This applies whether the results to be incorporated are those of subsidiary or associated companies.

1.6   Work of the primary auditor

The main matters that the primary auditors should examine before relying on accounts not audited by them are

(a)   Accounting policies. The primary auditors should try to ensure that there are uniform accounting policies throughout the group

(b)   Availability of information. The primary auditors should try to ensure that there is sufficient information available to enable the accounts to show a true and fair view.

(c)   Scope of the work of the secondary auditors. The primary auditors must consider:

    (i)   Whether all material aspects of the underlying accounts have been subjected to audit examination.

    (ii)   Are there any reasons why they cannot rely on the work of the secondary auditors?

The auditors must consider any qualifications in the secondary auditors' reports when drafting their own report.

(d)   Materiality. The primary auditors must consider the materiality of the amounts involved when deciding the extent of their enquiries.

1.7   Consolidation questionnaires

It is now normal practice for the auditors of the holding company to send to each of the subsidiaries' auditors a questionnaire. This will be designed to provide the following types of information

(a)   Accounting policies.

(b)   Accounting details needed for consolidation but not available from the published accounts.

(c)   Information relevant for group accounts but not for the subsidiaries' own accounts.

1.8   The problems of auditing a foreign subsidiary

The accounting techniques for the consolidation of a foreign subsidiary where the financial statements of the subsidiary are stated in another currency, are not in this syllabus. However, the problems of control are included.

The first problem arises due to the geographical location of the subsidiary. If the auditing firm has an office in the country in which the subsidiary operates, then the audit client will probably choose the holding company auditor as the auditor of the subsidiary company. However, this may not be the case if the holding company auditor does not have such representation. The client will not just be influenced by cost considerations here. You must appreciate that the subsidiary will require an audit to be carried out on it as a separate entity and complying with the audit requirements in that country. An auditor based in that country is likely to be in a better position to carry out the required audit.

The second problem concerns the consolidation of the subsidiary into the group accounts. In addition to the normal problems of, perhaps, the subsidiary being audited by another firm, the holding company will need to consider the following points.

(a)   Whether the local audit is different in scope to a UK audit. In such an event, the holding company auditor may require the local auditor to carry out further work.

(b)   Whether different accounting policies are being used to comply with local regulations.

(c)   Language problems may arise in both the examination of the financial statements of the foreign subsidiary and liaising with the local auditor. Provision should be made to anticipate and solve this problem.

(d)   Translation of the amounts in the foreign currency financial statements will be required.

1.9   SAS 510: The relationship between principal auditors and other auditors

This SAS sets out standards for principal auditors and other auditors regarding the use by the principal auditor of the other auditor's work. It extends the scope of the guidance beyond that set out in the previous guideline to circumstances other than involving group financial statements. Thus it covers for example, a situation where an auditor may use the services of an affiliated firm to audit a branch of a company. The affiliated firm is used because of their geographical closeness to the branch.

The other changes are as follows.

(a)   Auditors need to consider whether their own participation is sufficient to enable them to act as principal auditors. For example if they do not audit a material part of the transactions of the company themselves, are they in a position to act as principals?

(b)   Principal auditors need to consider the professional competence of the other auditors (not specifically stated in previous guidance).

(c)   Other aspects of work are covered in SAS 200 **Planning** and SAS 150 **Subsequent events** and therefore the level of detail in the SAS is less than in previous guidance.

Auditing standards

510.1   When using the work of other auditors, principal auditors should determine how that work will affect their audit.

510.2   Auditors should consider if their own participation is sufficient to enable them to act as principal auditors.

510.3   Consider the professional competence of the other auditors at the planning stage.

510.4   Obtain satisfactory evidence that the work of the other auditors is adequate.

510.5   Consider the significant findings of the other auditors.

510.6   There is a requirement for other auditors to co-operate with and actively assist the principal auditors.

2   THE REGULATORY REQUIREMENTS OF ACCOUNTING FOR GROUPS OF COMPANIES

2.1   Audit problems relating to the correct classification of investments

The auditor needs to examine investments held by the holding company to determine whether an investment constitutes an associated company or a subsidiary. In most cases the auditor will not have a problem in identifying subsidiaries as the company is not likely to try and hide the existence of subsidiaries from the auditor.

What is of more concern is the process by which the auditor obtains sufficient evidence to confirm the position taken by a client company as to whether or not the investment constitutes a subsidiary undertaking.

The precise shareholding can be ascertained from the register of members of the potential subsidiary undertaking. Examination is then required of the particular circumstances against the statutory definition.

Once the group members have been identified, the auditor will be particularly concerned with the following areas

(a)   accounting policies

(b)   consolidation adjustments

(c)   accounting periods

(d)   changes in the composition of the group

(e)   loss-making subsidiaries

(f)   foreign subsidiaries

(g)   restrictions on distributions

(h)   contingencies and post balance sheet events.

The above points are discussed below.

2.2   Accounting policies

In order for the group accounts to present a true and fair view, they should be based on consistent accounting policies. Wherever practicable, all group companies should adopt uniform policies.

However, there will be situations where this is not always possible; for example, an overseas subsidiary may follow different accounting policies because of local legal or accounting requirements. In such cases

(a)   Appropriate consolidation adjustments should be made, purely for the purpose of preparing group accounts. No comment will be needed in the group accounts, since the group accounts give a true and fair view of the position for the group.

(b)   In very exceptional cases, consolidation adjustments will be impracticable or undesirable, perhaps because of possible adverse consequences. In such cases, the following should be disclosed

(i)   the different accounting policies followed

(ii)   an indication of the amounts of assets and liabilities involved; if possible some indication of the effect on group profits and assets of using those different policies

(iii)   the reasons for the different treatment.

2.3   Consolidation adjustments

Certain types of adjustments are required purely for the purposes of preparing group accounts, (consolidation adjustments) and include

(a)   adjustments required because certain subsidiary companies have based their financial statements on accounting policies different from those of the rest of the group (see above)

(b)   adjustments for unrealised inter-company profits on the transfer of stock and fixed assets

(c)   adjustments for inter-company management charges

(d)   adjustments for in-transit items.

This is clearly an area which is of particular importance to the group auditor. He will need to make sure that he has the necessary information to ensure all such adjustments are reflected in the group accounts.

2.4   Accounting periods

Para 2(2) Sch 4A CA85 (introduced by the CA89) states

> If the financial year of a subsidiary undertaking included in the consolidation differs from that of the parent company, the group accounts shall be made up

(a)   from the accounts of the subsidiary undertaking for its financial year last ending before the end of the parent company's financial year, provided that year ended no more than three months before that of the parent company, or

(b)   from interim accounts prepared by the subsidiary undertaking as at the end of the parent company's financial year.

(a)   Thus if a group makes up its accounts to 31 December and one subsidiary makes its accounts to 31 August, interim accounts need to be prepared. The consolidated financial statements would include

(i)   1 January to 31 August based on audited accounts for the year to 31 August, and

(ii)   1 September to 31 December based on interim accounts. The auditor would need to audit these interim accounts to the extent necessary to ensure they were suitable for inclusion in the group accounts.

Note that the group balance sheet would include the interim balance sheet of the company at 31 December.

(b)   If the subsidiary makes up its accounts to 30 September or later the procedure in (a) above can still be followed or the subsidiary's accounts for the year would be included in the group accounts.

FRS 2 prefers the former approach ie, interim accounts prepared. If this is not practicable, the latter approach results in a consolidation of subsidiaries made up to different dates.

Particular care should be taken in the case of group companies where there are significant trading relationships between them. Their financial statements should relate to the same periods and be made up to the same date. If they were not, it is difficult to see how the group accounts could give a true and fair view unless all significant transactions were adjusted. Window-dressing between group companies could distort the view given by the group accounts.

2.5   Changes in the composition of the group

The auditor should ensure that the requirements of FRS 2 have been followed as regards

(a)   The effective date of acquisition or disposal.

(b)   The overriding rule that the consolidated financial statements should contain sufficient information regarding purchases or sales as to enable shareholders to appreciate the effect on the consolidated results.

In addition there are detailed disclosure requirements in FRS 6.

(c)   The treatment of goodwill on purchase of a subsidiary - it is important to consider the fair value of assets acquired.

2.6   Loss-making subsidiaries

This is a difficult area and the auditor may need to consider the following aspects

(a)   If a subsidiary company continues to make losses, the directors may consider there has been a permanent fall in value of the holding company's investment. This could involve

     (i)   in the separate accounts of the holding company - writing down the cost of investment in the subsidiary to below cost

     (ii)   in the group accounts - writing down goodwill on consolidation through the consolidated profit and loss account.

The auditor will need to satisfy himself that the write-down is adequate.

(b)   If a subsidiary company is making losses on such a scale that it is almost insolvent, the holding company may well be guaranteeing loans, overdrafts and normal trade credit. If the policy of the holding company is to continue to support (rather than abandon) the subsidiary, the subsidiary is likely to be included within the consolidation. The auditor will need to examine the extent of support of the holding company, the subsidiary's cash flow projections and the extent of disclosure of guarantees in the group financial statements.

2.7   Restrictions on distributions

There may be significant restrictions on the ability of the holding company to distribute group retained profits because of statutory, contractual or exchange control restrictions. FRS 2 requires the extent of these restrictions to be indicated.

The difficulty is that a group with subsidiaries operating in a large number of overseas countries is likely to be affected by a variety of restrictions, some of which may be relatively short-term in nature. For example, restrictions could relate to

(a)   profits which have been appropriated to statutory reserves because of legal requirements in a particular country

(b)   profits capitalised by a subsidiary

(c)   post-acquisition profits of a subsidiary applied against its pre-acquisition losses

(d)   local exchange control restrictions

(e)   exchange control restrictions preventing distribution of prior-year retained profits.

(a), (b) and (c) are likely to be permanent, whereas (d) and (e) may be temporary in nature. The auditor must ensure that the company's disclosure is consistent with a true and fair view.

2.8   Contingencies and post balance sheet events

(a)   Contingencies. It is common for a holding company to guarantee loans and overdrafts of subsidiary and associated companies. The auditor should ensure that there is appropriate disclosure in the financial statements.

(b)   Post balance sheet events. In a large group of companies, there may have been significant acquisitions and disposals of subsidiaries between the balance sheet date and the date on which the financial statements are approved by the directors.

The auditor should ensure that there is adequate disclosure of these non-adjusting events. An appropriate method of disclosure might be a memorandum proforma consolidation balance sheet indicating what the year-end balance sheet would have looked like had it reflected the post balance sheet acquisitions and disposals.

2.9   Activity

Your firm is the auditor of Keyworth Marketing plc which is the holding company of a group of companies with businesses in the marketing and advertising field. Some of the subsidiaries of Keyworth Marketing are audited by other firms of certified accountants and you have been asked by the partner in charge of the audit to describe the factors you will consider, to check the reliability of the work of the secondary auditors. Keyworth Marketing has expanded through the purchase of similar businesses. All these purchases have been treated as acquisitions (rather than mergers), and it is the company's policy to include the goodwill on consolidation in the group balance sheet and amortise it over its estimated useful life.

You are required:

(a)   to list and briefly describe the factors you will consider in deciding the extent to which you can rely on the work of the auditors of subsidiaries. Your answer should include consideration of the size of the subsidiary being audited by the secondary auditor.

(b)   to describe the matters you will consider in deciding whether you should qualify your audit report on the parent company's accounts, when you are aware that the audit report of a subsidiary's accounts is qualified.

(c)   to list and describe the work you will carry out and the factors you will consider to decide the period over which the goodwill on consolidation of subsidiaries should be amortised.

(d)   Tollerton Advertising Ltd, a wholly owned subsidiary of Keyworth Marketing plc, has made a large loss in the current year. Previously the subsidiary had been very profitable, and there was substantial goodwill in the consideration paid by Keyworth for Tollerton.

Describe the work you will carry out and the matters you will consider in deciding

(i)   whether the goodwill on consolidation in Keyworth's group accounts, which relates to Tollerton Advertising, should be written down or written off and

(ii)   whether it is necessary to write down the value of the investment in Tollerton, as shown in Keyworth's own balance sheet.

2.10   Activity solution

(Tutorial note: a bookwork question on SAS 510 and the treatment of goodwill where it has suffered a possible impairment. These are both areas in which students should have felt reasonably comfortable before attempting this question.*)*

(a)   In deciding on the extent to which primary auditors can rely on the work of secondary auditors in the context of the audit of group financial statements, the following matters should be taken into consideration.

(i)   **Subsidiary company**

The larger the subsidiary company, the greater its 'problems': the more inherently risky the business, the more audit work will be required to gain adequate comfort for group purposes and the more closely the primary auditors will need to examine the secondary auditors' work. This will also apply where material errors in the subsidiaries' financial statements have been discovered in the past, in particular where qualified audit reports have been given. A suspicion of errors in the current year will also warrant closer attention.

(ii)   **Secondary auditors**

If the secondary auditors are reputable and have proved reliable in the past, we can place more reliance on their work. We must ensure, however, that their work is to acceptable (ie, UK) standards - which may be a problem with foreign subsidiaries and their auditors - that it covers all the areas which should be covered and that they are properly independent of their clients. Problems in any of these areas may give rise to the need for additional work.

(b)   Qualification on consolidated accounts may be necessary where a material subsidiary's accounts are qualified or where many immaterial subsidiaries' accounts are qualified in the same respect which collectively would give rise to a material error in the group accounts (eg, where many small subsidiaries have individually understated stock to a material extent in respect of the individual subsidiary's accounts).

In order to form a judgement in this respect it will be necessary to obtain schedules from all subsidiaries of the following

(i)   details of matters in respect of which the audit report was qualified

(ii)   details of matters in respect of which no qualification was thought necessary

(iii)   details of all errors apart from minor errors.

Monetary limits will need to be set at a relatively low level.

(c)   In deciding on the period over which goodwill should be amortised in the consolidated accounts we should consider

(i)   The fact that CA85 does not permit goodwill be carried in the balance sheet permanently and FRS 10 requires amortisation over the goodwill's useful economic life when this is limited (the normal situation).

(ii)   How companies in similar businesses treat goodwill arising on consolidation.

This is obviously a very subjective area and the following should be borne in mind

(i)   marketing is a 'fashion'-led business; fashions are short-lived and as such it would be difficult to justify writing off goodwill over an extensive period of time in this case

(ii)   any group with profitability problems (which is highly likely to include marketing groups in recession) or gearing problems will be pressurised into amortising goodwill over as long a period as possible in order to avoid a sudden dent in reserves or profits.

(d)   (i)   FRS 11 states that goodwill should be immediately written down where it suffers an impairment in value. The value of goodwill if measured in terms of the ability to generate future profits will be judged to have suffered a diminution in value if its ability to generate future profits is impaired.

Our judgement in this area will be affected by the following

(1)   the reliability of profit and cash flow forecasts which will depend on some detailed review either by us or by Tollerton Ltd's auditors

(2)   the economic climate and the prospects for the recovery in the fortunes of this subsidiary

(3)   the price at which similar businesses are currently being sold: if they are close to or below net asset value, the goodwill is likely to be worthless and should therefore be written off.

(ii)   It will only be necessary to write down the investment in the parent company's individual accounts if the carrying value (whether it be cost or market value) has suffered an impairment in value. As it will be difficult to ascertain the market value of a subsidiary such as Tollerton, it is likely that the investment will be carried at cost. This should only be written down where the net asset value has fallen below cost, which may be the case where the purchase consideration included a considerable amount of goodwill.

3   THE IMPLICATIONS OF WORKING WITH OTHER AUDITORS

3.1   Joint audits

Other auditors will be worked with in two main situations: where a subsidiary is audited by a different firm to the holding company (covered above) and a joint audit.

It could be argued that reliance on the work of the internal auditor is another situation where auditors work together and thus SAS 500 is also briefly dealt with here.

The problem of joint audits is not directly related to the audit of group accounts. In practice, however, joint audits frequently arise when the holding company auditors are appointed jointly with the existing auditors of a subsidiary.

3.2   Advantages and disadvantages of joint audits

Advantages		*Disadvantages*	
(a)	Improved service through firms' different expertise.	(a)	Each joint auditor takes responsibility for the others' shortcomings.
(b)	Improved geographical coverage.	(b)	It may be more expensive.
(c)	Holding company and subsidiary's auditors can work closely together.	(c)	Audit methods of different firms may not be easily reconciled.
(d)	The use of two independent firms can give added assurance to the client.	(d)	Close control of the division of work is required.
(e)	Client firm may be so large as to require more than one firm of auditors			

3.3   Requirements for joint audits to work

The main requirement is that the division and scope of the audit work should be decided and clearly documented. The stages involved are

(a)   A preliminary meeting between the two audit firms should be held to decide on

(i)   Methods of work to be employed.
(ii)   Timing.
(iii)   Staff.
(iv)   Division of work.
(v)   Working papers to be kept.

Relevant factors in these decisions would be the relative size of the audit firms, their experience of the industry in general and the client in particular, geographical and linguistic factors, and internal staff availability.

(b)   The result of these discussions should be fully documented so that the audit staff are made fully aware of requirements.

(c)   During and after the audit there would need to be free interchange of information, and access to working papers.

(d)   At the conclusion of fieldwork, but before the issue of the first opinion, both audit firms would need to meet again. At this meeting, working papers would need to be available for review and discussions before preparing

  (i)   the joint opinion.
  (ii)   the letter of weakness.

(e)   It is appropriate for both firms to take an active part in audit work. This means allocating work not necessarily equally but avoiding the dominance of the work of one firm over the work of the other.

(f)   Both firms should ensure that they have suitable professional indemnity insurance.

3.4   SAS 500: Considering the work of internal audit

Internal auditors are established by the management of a company to benefit the organisation by reviewing and reporting on the accounting and internal control systems. SAS 500 gives guidance on how external auditors can tailor their work most effectively where an internal audit department exists.

Auditing standards

The external auditor is required to:

500.1   Consider the activities of the internal auditors

500.2   Obtain a sufficient understanding of internal audit to assist in planning an effective audit

500.3   Perform a preliminary assessment of internal audit during planning

500.4   Evaluate and confirm the adequacy of internal audit work if it is used to reduce the extent of other audit procedures.

3.5   Auditing Guideline on internal audit

In contrast to SAS 500 **Considering the work of internal audit**, which looks at how the external auditor places reliance on the internal audit function in a company, Auditing Guideline 308 **Guidance for internal auditors** gives guidance to internal auditors about how they should structure their work to make it effective. The aim of the Guideline is to give positive assistance to internal auditors.

The Guideline considers eight areas that are essential for the internal audit department to be effective. Many of these areas, and the explanations of procedures within them could equally apply to external auditors, which is not surprising given that the internal and external auditors' work is similar in many ways. Each of the sections of the Guideline will be considered in turn:

(a)   **Independence**

    The internal auditor should be independent in organisational status. That is the internal audit department should be involved in setting its own objectives, and the head of internal audit should have access to senior management for reporting purposes.

    The internal auditor should also be independent in terms of personal objectivity. He should therefore avoid any conflicts of interest that could impair his objectivity in the same way that the external auditor tries to avoid such conflicts. The situation is made more difficult for the internal auditor because he is employed by the company. He should always declare any conflicts of interest to management, and appropriate action should be decided on.

(b)   Staffing and training

The internal audit department should have sufficient suitably qualified staff to perform its work. Specialist staff will be recruited as required.

As with any other group of employees, the internal audit department staff require adequate training. This training will be divided into three main areas:

(i)   Basic training to give the common skills of internal auditing;

(ii)   Development training to give advanced auditing and inter-personal skills; and

(iii)   Specialist training where specialist skills are needed in the department.

(c)   Relationships

Relationships are important in a number of areas:

(i)   With management - to identify areas which the internal auditor needs to investigate, and give confidential reporting to later.

(ii)   With external audit - to achieve mutual recognition and respect, and to ensure that work is shared where possible to give cost and other benefits to the company.

(iii)   With review agencies and specialists - where the internal auditor's work could be used by external agencies (eg, management consultants), and where the work done by these agencies affects the internal control system of the company.

(d)   Due care

The internal auditor should ensure that his work is carried out with appropriate care. This will normally mean being able to demonstrate from working papers that work has been performed in accordance with the Guideline, and with any other regulatory requirements that he may face.

The internal auditor will also follow the ethical standards of the professional body to which he belongs, and the chief of the department will ensure that the quality of work is adequately monitored to show that it is of an acceptable standard.

(e)   Planning, controlling and recording

As with the external auditor, the internal auditor must adequately plan, control and record his work.

(i)   Planning

The methods of planning for the internal auditor differ from the external auditor in that the former should have a number of different work plans which will represent the greater degree of checking that he will be involved in within the company.

A *strategic* plan will cover a time period of between two and five years during which all major systems in the company will be scheduled for review.

A *periodic* plan will translate the strategic plan into a detailed work plan for one financial year.

An *operational* plan will show the objectives, scope, budget and procedures for one audit assignment within the periodic plan.

(ii)   **Controlling**

As with the external auditor, controlling for the internal auditor means ensuring that work done is carried out to an acceptable standard. The head of internal audit must ensure that individual audit assignments are correctly reviewed, and also that an annual review is given to management concerning the activities of the department along with the Head's comments as to its effectiveness.

(iii)   **Recording**

Recording of audit work is necessary to ensure that:

(1)   work delegated is properly performed;

(2)   there is evidence for future reference of the decisions made on an audit; and

(3)   to encourage a methodical approach to the audit.

In these respects there is no difference between internal and external auditors.

(f)   **Evaluation of the system of internal control**

The internal auditor will review the internal control system to ensure that:

(i)   management policies are adhered to;

(ii)   the assets are safeguarded;

(iii)   the records are as complete and accurate as possible; and

(iv)   legislation is complied with.

Again these are the same objectives that the external auditor will be checking.

(g)   **Evidence**

The internal auditor will collect sufficient appropriate audit evidence on which to base his reasonable conclusions. The only difference here between the collection of evidence for the internal auditor as compared to the external auditor, is that the sufficiency of evidence may be affected by the cost of obtaining it. Costs in excess of budget should be cleared with the Head of Internal audit, or from appropriate management before they are incurred.

(h)   **Reporting and follow-up**

The results of the work of internal auditors must be communicated to management within a suitable time, and the internal auditor must seek a response from management over any recommendations made. For reports not to be timely, or recommendations not to be followed would severely limit the effectiveness of the internal audit department.

| Conclusion | As can be seen, the Guideline to internal auditors includes a lot of information that external auditors will already be aware of and be following. In effect, the Guideline is suggesting that the two groups of auditors have similar work to do and similar standards to maintain, which on the whole is correct. |

4   **WORKING WITH SPECIALISTS**

4.1   **Reliance on other specialists**

An auditor has a general knowledge of business, but he cannot be expected to have a detailed knowledge in all disciplines. During the course of an audit, therefore, the auditor may need to consider audit evidence from specialists in arriving at an audit opinion.

4.2   Determining the need for specialist evidence

One element of the planning of an audit would be the consideration of whether specialist evidence (from lawyers, stockbrokers, geologists, actuaries, etc) may be necessary for the auditor to form his opinion. Factors affecting this decision would include the materiality of the item concerned and the possibility of alternative sources of evidence being available.

If it is decided that specialist evidence is needed, the specialist should be appointed either by the client, or by the auditor with the consent of the client. If the client refuses, for whatever reasons, and there is no other source of evidence for the item concerned, the auditor should qualify his audit report.

4.3   The work of the specialist

In order to be able to rely on the evidence provided by the specialist, the auditor must be satisfied that the specialist is competent and objective. If the auditor is in any doubt, he should discuss the problem with the client management.

Once a specialist is appointed, there should be a consultation between the auditor, client and specialist to determine the specialist's terms of reference. These should clarify the objectives of the specialist's work, sources of information available to him, the form and content of the report required, etc.

The auditor will need to evaluate the specialist's findings with respect to sufficiency, relevance and reliability. He should, therefore, examine the specialist's report and, as an informed layman, determine if it is acceptable. If the auditor is not satisfied that the specialist's evidence is relevant and reliable, he should discuss the problem with the client management and with the specialist. It may occasionally be necessary to obtain the opinion of a second specialist.

4.4   Auditors' reports

Where an auditor has relied on specialist evidence in forming his opinion he should not refer to that fact in his audit report as it may be misunderstood as a qualification or division of responsibility.

A qualified opinion should be given where

(a)   management is unable or unwilling to obtain specialist evidence

(b)   the relevance and reliability of the specialist's evidence remains uncertain

(c)   management refuses to accept and make use of specialist evidence which is relevant, reliable and material to the financial statements, and

(d)   management refuses to agree to the appointment of another specialist when the auditor considers that a second opinion is needed.

4.5   SAS 520: Using the work of an expert

Auditing standards

The auditor is required to:

520.1   Obtain appropriate evidence that the expert's work is adequate for the purposes of the audit

520.2   Assess the objectivity and competence of the expert

520.3   Assess the scope of the expert's work

520.4   Assess the appropriateness of the expert's work as audit evidence.

5   RELATED PARTY TRANSACTIONS

5.1   FRS 8: Related party disclosures

Related party transactions can cause considerable problems from an audit perspective. Before these are considered, the main elements of FRS 8 *Related party disclosures* are covered.

When transactions take place between related parties they may not be on arm's length terms. Disclosure of the existence of such transactions, and of the relationships underlying them, gives important information to users of financial statements.

One striking example of the need for disclosure is that related party transactions have been a feature of a number of financial scandals in recent years, many of which have had in common the dominance of the company by a powerful chief executive who was also involved with the related party.

More generally, transactions between related parties - eg, companies in the same group - are now a common feature of business operations. Disclosure of these transactions, some of which may not have been at arm's length, together with information about the underlying relationship, gives the user of accounts an important indication of their significance to the operating results and financial position of the reporting company. For the same reasons disclosure is called for where transactions take place with a wide range of other related parties - eg, directors, associates, pension funds and key management.

(Definition)   A related party transaction is the transfer of assets or liabilities or the performance of services by, to or for a related party irrespective of whether a price is charged.

FRS 8 requires the disclosure of:

(a)   all material related party transactions, and

(b)   the name of the party controlling the reporting entity and, if different, that of the ultimate controlling party whether or not any transactions between the reporting entity and those parties have taken place.

5.2   Definition of related parties

FRS 8 defines related parties as follows.

(Definition)   Two or more parties are related parties when for all or part of the financial period:

        (i)   one party has control over the other party; or
        (ii)   the parties are subject to common control from the same source; or
        (iii)   one party has significant influence over the other party; or
        (iv)   the parties are subject to influence from the same source to such an extent that one of the parties has subordinated its own separate interests.

5.3   Intragroup transactions

No disclosure is required in consolidated accounts of intragroup transactions and balances eliminated on consolidation.

5.4 Activity

Which of the following are related parties of a company?

(i)   its ultimate parent company;
(ii)   a fellow subsidiary;
(iii)   a subsidiary;
(iv)   an associated company;
(v)   a joint venture;
(vi)   directors of the company;
(vii)   a pension fund for the benefit of the company's employees.

5.5 Activity solution

All of them are related parties.

5.6 The audit implications of related party transactions

The APB issued SAS 460: **Related parties**, in November 1995 shortly after FRS 8 itself was issued. The implications of related party transactions for the auditor are explained below.

(a)   **General objectives**

The overriding objective of the audit is to express an opinion, backed up by sufficient audit evidence, as to whether or not financial statements present a true and fair view. As part of this process the auditor should endeavour to establish

(i)   the existence of related parties
(ii)   the nature and volume of transactions with those related parties
(iii)   whether those transactions have been fairly presented in the financial statements.

The auditor should gain evidence on these three points because

(i)   the ability of the company to recognise such related party transactions represents a control strength; conversely, if a company pays no attention to such transactions, a weakness is established which the auditor should report in his letter of weakness

(ii)   the recognition of such transactions helps the auditor to develop audit work and obtain evidence in these areas of risk

(iii)   in some cases the volume or nature of the transactions may cause financial statements to be misleading unless disclosure is made

(iv)   in some cases, such transactions are required under law to be disclosed: for example, under S237 CA85 the auditor should disclose in his report details of loans to directors, contracts etc, where those have not been disclosed in the accounts.

(b)   **Establishing the existence of related parties**

In the course of his audit work, the auditor will normally be aware of the existence of certain related parties. He will, however, need to make specific enquiries to be reasonably assured that all major related parties have been discovered. He may adopt some of the following procedures

(i)   make other members of his audit team aware of the importance of related parties and be on the watch and report the discovery of such parties

(ii)   ascertain whether the company has any established system for identifying related parties and reporting transactions with them to management, together with a review of the results of the system

(iii)   a review of the board minutes to establish whether directors have disclosed their interests in contracts in pursuance of S317 CA85

(iv)   a review of any statements giving 'conflict of interest' details which directors may be required to deposit with the company and which should be regularly reviewed by the board

(v)   a review of the directors' other directorships and of the list of shareholders contained in the statutory books

(vi)   a review of previous years' audit files or consultation with previous auditors

(vii)   a review of services or goods provided 'free-of-charge' either by or to the client company

(viii) a review of invoices and correspondence relating to professional fees, particularly relating to the purchase or sale of significant assets and interests in land and property

(ix)   a review of confirmations from third parties received during the audit, particularly regarding loans payable and receivable.

(c)   **Establishing the nature and volume of related party transactions**

The prime requirement here is for the auditor to understand the nature and functioning of his client's business. He will not wish to expend too much effort dealing with immaterial items.

He should, however, pay particular attention to

(i)   transactions involving the borrowing or lending of sums either being interest free or at rates appreciably below market rates, or where repayment terms have not been specified

(ii)   non-monetary transactions involving perhaps the exchange of assets without a valid identification of a fair value should be fully investigated

(iii)   unusual transactions should be considered individually, particularly those which have taken place near the end of the accounting year and which may indicate an attempt to manipulate the financial statements for the year

(iv)   it will normally be sufficient to test a small sample of related party transactions which occur within the normal course of business; such tests may be covered as part of other audit procedures

(v)   transactions outside the normal course of business should be examined individually; independent evidence such as agreements with third party documentation should be obtained to support any management representations and the auditor should examine minutes of board meetings to ensure that board approval has been obtained.

5.7   Reporting on the effects of related party transactions

(a)   **To the directors of the company**

It should be noted that if the auditor believes that the board as a whole are unaware of related party transactions (eg, approval of a transaction was not discovered in the board minutes) the auditor should formally notify the board of such transactions.

He should also obtain, as part of the letter of representation, a statement that no related party transactions, other than those already disclosed to him, have taken place.

(b) **To the members of the company**

If related party transactions have taken place within the normal course of business and the disclosure of them in the financial statements is fair, the auditor will be able to give an unqualified opinion. He may consider the transactions to be so significant to the understanding of the financial statements that specific reference to the matter should be made as an emphasis of matter paragraph. This might apply for instance where a subsidiary makes all its sales to its holding company.

If inadequate disclosure is made, the audit report will need to be qualified if the transactions involved are material to the adequate appreciation of the financial statements.

If related party transactions have taken place, full details of the transactions should be disclosed, including

(i) the relationship of the parties
(ii) the nature of the transactions
(iii) the amounts involved
(iv) the terms of settlement.

If such disclosure is not made, or the accounting treatment adopted does not conform to the commercial substance of the transaction, the auditor may need to qualify his report.

In addition the auditor must ensure that the financial statements comply with the disclosure requirements of the CA85 or any other relevant statutory obligation.

6 THE AUDITOR'S DUTIES REGARDING DIRECTORS

6.1 Loans to directors

Transactions between the company and its directors can cause special audit problems which come within the general coverage of related party transactions. The CA85 recognises the close relationship between the company and its directors by placing restrictions on the ability of a company to make a loan to a director and requiring detailed disclosures if a loan is made (whether legally or illegally).

6.2 Legality

(a) **Basic rule applying to all companies**

No company may make a loan to its directors or a director of its holding company.

The ban also includes entering into a guarantee or providing security in connection with a loan or third party loan. The prohibition is drafted widely enough to catch, for example, loans to directors of another independent company in return for similarly favoured treatment.

(b) **Additional rules applying to relevant companies**

Definition A relevant company is a public company or a private company in a group which contains a public company.

A relevant company may not

(i) make a quasi-loan to its director (or director of its holding company) unless

(1) it is to be reimbursed within 2 months, and
(2) the total of quasi-loans to that director does not exceed £5,000.

> **Definition** A quasi-loan is an indirect loan ie, the director buys the goods, the company pays for them and then the director reimburses the company eg, a company credit card

(ii) make a loan or quasi-loan to a connected person of its directors. Save that such a transaction is permitted in favour of another company within the group

(iii) guarantee or provide security for a third party loan or quasi-loan to its directors or connected person. Save that such a transaction is permitted in favour of another company within the group

(iv) enter into a credit transaction as creditor (or provide a guarantee or security) for its directors or connected person unless

    (1) the total credit transactions per director plus connected persons do not exceed £10,000, or

    (2) the transaction is made in the ordinary course of the company's business and on no more favourable terms than might have been offered to an outsider.

> **Definition** A credit transaction is where the company buys or leases the goods, and the director repays by instalments.

6.3 General exceptions

Notwithstanding the prohibitions outlined above the following are permitted.

(a) A company may make small loans up to and including £5,000 to its directors.

(b) A company may provide a director with funds to meet expenditure incurred (or to be incurred) for the purposes of the company or to enable the director to perform duties properly provided

(i) the company gives prior approval in general meeting of the purpose and amount, or

(ii) the provision is made on condition that if the company does not give approval at or before the next annual general meeting, it will be repaid within 6 months of that AGM, and

(iii) in the case of a relevant company the aggregate does not exceed £20,000 for any director.

6.4 Disclosure

Any loans, quasi-loans, guarantees and credit transactions with a director or his connected persons must be disclosed, irrespective of whether the transaction is legal or illegal.

There are exceptions from disclosure for credit transactions and guarantees related thereto which at no time during the period exceeded £5,000.

Under CA85 where officers who are not directors have been granted loans, guarantees, securities, quasi-loans, credit transactions or reciprocal arrangements, the amounts outstanding, grouped under appropriate headings, have to be disclosed. The number of officers involved, but not their names, has to be given.

6.5 Significant contracts involving directors

(a) Disclosure is required of any transaction or arrangement with the company involving a person who, at any time during the period, was a director of the company and had directly or indirectly a material interest.

(b)   What is 'material' is determined by the remaining directors who are not personally involved in the transaction.   Should they be unable to come to an opinion the auditor should decide whether the interest is material. Also, note that it is not materiality to the company which is the point but the materiality of the directors' interest to the transaction or arrangement.

(c)   There are exceptions from disclosure for transactions not exceeding the higher of

(i)   £1,000, or

(ii)   the lower of £5,000 or 1% of the net assets.

6.6   Directors' remuneration

Company law has precise rules regarding the disclosures required of directors' remuneration. These requirements have been dealt with earlier. The duty of the auditor is to ensure the calculations are correct and disclosures comply with the law. It is an area which is politically sensitive and even slight errors should be regarded as material.

Disclosure is required in the audit report if not complied with in the financial statements. This, of course, results in the correct disclosure being made.

Particular points to watch out for include the following.

(a)   Payments to former directors need to be included.

(b)   Directors' service contracts should be examined to ensure that all payments/benefits have been included.

(c)   If group accounts are being prepared, the disclosures required are the amounts paid to the holding company directors by **any** company within the group.

7   THE AUDITOR'S RESPONSIBILITY FOR DETECTING ILLEGAL ACTS BY CLIENTS

7.1   Introduction

For a time, the auditor's responsibility in this area was treated in the same way as the auditor's responsibility for detecting fraud and error within the business of the client. The APB regards these areas as separate and accordingly has issued two separate SASs. SAS 110 **Fraud and error** is dealt with in the next chapter in the context of the expectations gap. SAS 120 **Consideration of law and regulations** covers illegal acts by the client company and is thus dealt with here.

7.2   Responsibilities of the directors

It is the responsibility of the directors

(a)   to ensure that the entity complies with law and regulations applicable to its activities, and

(b)   to establish effective arrangements for preventing any non-compliance with law or regulations and detecting any that occurs.

Neither the assignment of particular responsibilities to management nor the audit process relieves the directors of these fundamental responsibilities.

7.3   Auditors' responsibilities

However, the APB recognises that the auditors have a role in relation to non-compliance with law and regulations.   Auditors plan, perform and evaluate their audit work with the aim of providing reasonable, though not absolute, assurance of detecting any material misstatement in the financial statements which arises from non-compliance with law or regulations (or from any other cause).

SAS 120 sets out responsibilities for auditors based on the distinction between two main categories of laws and regulations.

(a)   The auditors are required to obtain sufficient appropriate audit evidence about compliance with the laws and regulations that determine the form and content of the financial statements, such as prescribed formats or the measurement or disclosure requirements for individual items or amounts. It is recognised that auditors have a level of expertise in this area which they are not expected to have in other areas.

(b)   The second category of laws and regulations are those which provide a legal framework within which the entity conducts its business and where non-compliance may reasonably be expected to have a fundamental effect on the operations of the entity and hence on its financial statements.

To identify possible instances of non-compliance with these laws and regulations, the auditors need to obtain a general understanding of the applicable legal and regulatory framework and of the entity's compliance. They also need to enquire of management to identify the particular laws and regulations that may be expected to have a fundamental effect on the operations of the entity.

On the basis of this understanding, the auditors' procedures aim to identify possible instances of non-compliance. However, auditors cannot be expected to be experts in all the many different laws and regulations where non-compliance might have such an effect and their procedures - in addition to remaining alert for any possible instances of non-compliance with law or regulations which come to their attention while carrying out other audit procedures - are limited to enquiring of management as to the entity's compliance and inspecting any correspondence with relevant regulators or authorities. To require auditors to go further would be unreasonable as it would involve auditors entering the spheres of dedicated regulatory and inspecting agencies.

7.4   The auditors' consideration of compliance with law and regulations

Auditing standards

120.1   Auditors should plan and perform their audit procedures, and evaluate and report on the results thereof, recognising that non compliance by the entity with law or regulations may materially affect the financial statements.

120.2   The auditors should obtain sufficient appropriate audit evidence about compliance with those laws and regulations which relate directly to the preparation of, or the inclusion or disclosure of specific items in, the financial statements.

120.3   The auditors should perform procedures to help identify instances of non compliance with those laws and regulations which provide a legal framework within which the entity conducts its business by:

(a)   obtaining a general understanding of the legal and regulatory framework applicable to the entity and the industry, and of how the entity is complying with that framework;

(b)   inspecting correspondence with relevant licensing or regulatory authorities;

(c)   enquiring of the directors as to whether they are on notice of any such possible instance of non compliance with law or regulations; and

(d)   obtaining written confirmation from the directors that they have disclosed to the auditors all those events of which they are aware which involve possible non compliance, together with the actual or contingent consequences which may arise therefrom.

120.4   When carrying out their procedures for the purpose of forming an opinion on the financial statements, the auditors should in addition be alert for instances of possible or actual non compliance with law or regulations which might affect the financial statements.

7.5 Situations where non compliance may have occurred

The appendix to the SAS sets out examples of the types of information that may come to the auditors' attention and may indicate that non-compliance with law or regulations has occurred as listed below.

- Investigation by government department or payment of fines or penalties.

- Payments for unspecified services or loans to consultants, related parties, employees or government employees.

- Sales commissions or agents' fees that appear excessive in relation to those normally paid by the entity or in its industry or to the services actually received.

- Purchasing at prices significantly above or below market price.

- Unusual payments in cash, purchases in the form of cashiers' cheques payable to bearer or transfers to numbered bank accounts.

- Unusual transactions with companies registered in tax havens.

- Payments for goods or services made other than to the country from which the goods or services originated.

- Existence of an accounting system that fails, whether by design or by accident, to provide adequate audit trail or sufficient evidence.

- Unauthorised transactions or improperly recorded transactions.

- Media comment.

7.6 Procedures when possible non-compliance is discovered

120.5   When the auditors become aware of information concerning a possible instance of non compliance with law or regulations, they should obtain an understanding of the nature of the act and the circumstances in which it has occurred, and sufficient other information to evaluate the possible effect on the financial statements.

120.6   When the auditors believe there may be non compliance with law or regulations, they should document their findings and, subject to any requirement to report them direct to a third party, discuss them with the appropriate level of management.

120.7   The auditors should consider the implications of suspected or actual non compliance with law or regulations in relation to other aspects of the audit, particularly the reliability of management representations.

7.7 Reporting non-compliance

(a)   To management

120.8   The auditors should, as soon as practicable, either

(a)   communicate with management, the board of directors or the audit committee; or

(b)   obtain evidence that they are appropriately informed, regarding any suspected non compliance with law or regulations that comes to the auditors' attention.

120.9   If, in the auditor's judgement, the non compliance with law or regulations is material or is believed to be intentional, the auditors should communicate the finding without delay.

(b)   To shareholders

120.10 Where the auditors conclude that the non-compliance leads to a fundamental uncertainty in the financial statements, they should include an explanatory paragraph referring to the matter in their report.

120.11 Where the auditors conclude that a suspected instance of non compliance with law or regulation has a material effect on the financial statements and they disagree with the accounting treatment or with the extent, or the lack, of any disclosure in the financial statements of the instance or of its consequences they should issue an adverse or qualified opinion. If the auditors are unable to determine whether non compliance with law or regulations has occurred because of limitation in the scope of their work, they should issue a disclaimer or a qualified opinion.

(c)   To third parties

The SAS gives guidance to auditors on the circumstances in which to report to third parties who have a proper interest in receiving such information. In addition, auditors of financial institutions subject to statutory regulation, who are required to report certain information direct to the relevant regulator, have separate responsibilities. Guidance on these responsibilities is given in SAS 620 **The auditors' right and duty to report to regulators in the financial sector** and the associated Practice Notes.

Confidentiality is an implied term of the auditors' contract. The duty of confidentiality, however, is not absolute. In certain exceptional circumstances auditors are not bound by the duty of confidentiality and have the right to report matters to a proper authority in the public interest. Auditors need to weigh the public interest in maintaining confidential client relationships against the public interest in disclosure to a proper authority. Determination of where the balance of public interest lies requires careful consideration. Auditors whose suspicions have been aroused need to use their professional judgement to determine whether their misgivings justify them in carrying the matter further or are too insubstantial to deserve report.

8   CHAPTER SUMMARY

Any complex audit situation can be managed by planning for the situation. The audit of groups requires extra consideration of law, accounting and perhaps relying on the work of secondary auditors.

An auditor needs to establish whether any related parties exist and, if so, the nature of any transactions between the client and the related party.

Illegal acts by the client may materially affect the financial statements. Therefore, the auditors should perform procedures to help identify instances of non-compliance.

9   SELF TEST QUESTIONS

9.1   What is the holding company auditor responsible for? (1.3)

9.2   What rights does the holding company auditor have in relation to information about subsidiaries? (1.4)

9.3   What is the law regarding coterminous accounting periods? (2.4)

9.4   What are the disadvantages of joint audits? (3.2)

9.5   What types of experts are likely to fall within the scope of SAS 520? (4.2)

9.6   What is the definition of related parties? (5.2)

9.7   What are the three general objectives in the audit of related party transactions? (5.3)

9.8   What is a quasi-loan? (6.2)

9.9 What are the limits for non-disclosure of significant transactions with directors? (6.5)

9.10 What is the auditors' responsibility for detecting illegal acts by clients? (7.3)

10 EXAMINATION TYPE QUESTION

10.1 Plastic Engineering

You have recently been appointed the auditor of Plastic Engineering Ltd, a company with a turnover of £10 million owned by the two directors, Mr and Mrs Amery. During your first audit to 30 June 19X7 you are informed of the following

(a) Mortgage interest payments of £6,300 on the house owned by the Amerys have been made by the company and charged to interest paid.

(b) In December 19X6 expense advances totalling £4,300 were made to Mr Amery and his wife which were not cleared by expenses at the year end. The Amerys propose to clear this balance by voting themselves bonuses totalling £4,300 backdated to the year end.

(c) Mr Amery himself has majority shareholdings in the businesses of two customers, Alpha Plastics Ltd and Beta Mouldings Ltd, who between them account for 10% of the turnover of Plastic Engineering Ltd. When asked about these holdings Mr Amery indicates that they are his private interests and are kept confidential because news of them could harm Plastic Engineering's trade with other customers.

(d) In November 19X6, Mr Amery took out various cash sums which totalled £160,000. He repaid £160,000 early in June 19X7. When asked about these amounts he explained that the money was needed to purchase a property on behalf of the company but that the deal was not successfully completed. He informs you that no interest has been earned on the money while it was in his possession.

You are required in respect of each matter set out above, in order to reach a conclusion on the proper treatment and disclosure of those matters in the financial statements of Plastic Engineering Ltd, to state

(a) the factors you would consider **(10 marks)**
(b) the audit evidence you would seek. **(10 marks)**

(Total: 20 marks)

11 ANSWER TO EXAMINATION TYPE QUESTION

11.1 Plastic Engineering

Factors to consider

(a) **Mortgage interest payments £6,300**

The interest paid is not an expense of the company and should be reclassified as either

(i) Remuneration. To the extent the house is jointly owned by the Amerys the payments of £6,300 will be allocated equally to Mr and Mrs Amery. The amount would be included in the total directors' remuneration disclosure as part of the 'after charging' note and may need to be included as part of the highest paid director's emoluments. The total would also be included in staff costs since these include directors.

Since PAYE and NI have not been accounted for they should be accrued. The Inland Revenue may claim that the amount drawn is an interest-free loan and that the resultant benefit should be taxed accordingly if PAYE and NI are not accounted for properly.

or   (ii)   If the interest payments made by the company are reimbursable by the Amerys a quasi-loan arises. Quasi-loans are not illegal when made on behalf of the directors of a non-relevant company.   Details of the transaction would, however, require to be disclosed in the notes.

(b)   **Expense advances £4,300**

    (i)   Ordinary expense advances are not intended to be repaid by the recipient who should use the amount advanced in his capacity as agent for the company and for the benefit of the company. The position will not usually change if the amount advanced exceeds the subsequent expenditure, provided the recipient accounts promptly to the company for the difference.

        However, in circumstances where the amount advanced is clearly excessive or remains unspent for an unduly long time (as is the case here) then the recipient is likely to have derived some personal benefit.

        In these circumstances the transaction takes on the nature of a loan and, since they are both directors, it is disclosable but not illegal unless the expense advance to one of the directors is deemed to exceed £5,000.

        The disclosures in the notes to the financial statements for a loan would be as in (a) above.

    (ii)   If a director draws remuneration on account, the question arises as to whether the amount drawn is in fact a loan. If there is no intention that the amount drawn should be repaid no loan arises.

        However, as in (a) above, the payment should then be included in the directors' remuneration disclosure for that year. The same considerations would also apply as in (a) regarding PAYE and NIC.

(c)   **Transaction in which director has material interest**

Mr Amery has majority shareholdings in both companies and therefore meets the CA85 definition of holding 20% of the shares and the votes for the purposes of determining connected persons.

He has a material interest through a connected person and as such the transaction requires disclosure in the notes comprising the nature of the director's interest and the 'value' of the transactions during the year.

Mrs Amery (as the other director) should have formally minuted her view as to whether Mr Amery's interest was material. However this would not affect the auditor's consideration.

There would have been exemption from the above disclosure if all companies were part of the same group since the transactions appear to have been entered into in the ordinary course of business and on commercial terms (ie, at arm's length).

However, if this is not the case, disclosure must be made as set out above.

(d)   **£160,000 for property purchase**

The auditor would need to ascertain how the money was held by Mr Amery since it was held for a total of seven months, and apparently no interest had been earned on the money while it was in his possession.

There appears to have been therefore some personal benefit to Mr Amery with the possibility that the director has in fact made a secret profit which would be recoverable by the company and hence should be accrued as a debtor balance.

The advance appears in any case to constitute a loan. If this was the case, then the same disclosure would be made in the notes to the financial statements as for the quasi-loan in (a) above.

General consideration

If the company does not make the appropriate disclosures set out in (a) to (d) above, it is the responsibility of the auditors under S237 of the Companies Act 1985 to include the details in their report, so far as they are reasonably able to do so.

Audit evidence required

General evidence

(a)   Enquire into client's own procedures for ensuring all disclosable transactions are identified and recorded.

(b)   Inspect Board minutes and records of transactions with directors and connected persons and consider whether these appear to be up to date.

(c)   Inspect agreements and contracts involving directors and connected persons and check details of transactions to source documentation.

(d)   Check whether transactions disclosed are based on commercial terms.

(e)   Consider whether amounts due from directors or connected persons are recoverable.

(f)   Consider the legality of transactions disclosed. Illegal transactions should be notified to the directors promptly. The auditor should take legal advice before referring to illegality in the audit report.

(g)   Consider whether any subsequent events might have an effect on the matters requiring disclosure, for example, events after the year end may suggest that a loan due from a director is likely to be irrecoverable, in which case a provision should be made.

(h)   Obtain a statement from the directors confirming the details of disclosable transactions in a letter of representation.

Specific evidence

(a)   **Mortgage interest payments £6,300**

    (i)   agree amounts paid to bank/building society statement of mortgage.
    (ii)   examine returned paid cheques.
    (iii)   write to bank/building society to confirm amounts paid.
    (iv)   ensure appropriate disclosure is made as directors' remuneration or quasi-loan.

(b)   **Expense advances £4,300**

    (i)   examine expense vouchers to assess whether they support the nature of the original advance.

    (ii)   vouch to returned paid cheques.

    (iii)   examine directors'/members' minutes.

    (iv)   ensure appropriate disclosure is made as part of directors' remuneration.

(c)   **Transaction in which material interest**

 (i) review level of such transactions and form an opinion on the directors' estimate of their total value.

 (ii) compare prices charged to Alpha Plastics and Beta Mouldings with those to other customers to ascertain that such transactions are on arm's length terms.

 (iii) ensure appropriate disclosures have been made in the financial statements, setting out the nature of the directors' interest and the total value of such transactions for the year.

(d)   **Property purchase**

 (i) review minutes of members for evidence of approval in general meeting.

 (ii) examine any correspondence relating to proposed acquisition of property.

 (iii) vouch returned paid cheques and scrutinise for any unusual endorsements.

 (iv) vouch receipt of money back into company bank account and review the account after the year end to ensure monies not subsequently re-borrowed.

 (v) ensure appropriate disclosure made in the financial statements as a loan to a director, where this is considered to be the nature of the arrangement.

29 AUDIT REPORTING AND CURRENT ISSUES

INTRODUCTION & LEARNING OBJECTIVES

The audit report is the final act of the auditor. It is an important area for the exam which has been standardised by the issue of SAS 600.

You need to have an awareness of current issues of concern in auditing for the examination. This chapter summarises these issues.

When you have studied this chapter you should be able to do the following:

- Prepare audit reports to meet different specified situations.
- Describe the current position on the legal liability of the auditor.
- Discuss current issues and controversies relating to auditors.

1 THE CONTENT AND MEANING OF UNQUALIFIED AND QUALIFIED AUDIT REPORTS

1.1 Introduction

The audit report is usually the only channel of communication between the auditor and the shareholders of the company whose financial statements have been subject to audit. As such the report acts as a bridge taking the large volume of information possessed by the auditors and conveying it to the shareholders in a much abbreviated form.

In order to convey information in a succinct form the audit report has become an extremely formalised group of phrases, each of which has special significance. Any deviation from the standard format is regarded by accountants as being significant and may provide important extra data.

It is important for the auditor to know the following details

(a)   The form of an unqualified audit report and the meaning of the phrases used.

(b)   The situations where a qualified audit report is needed and how such a report should be phrased.

(c)   The situations where, although the opinion is unqualified, it may be relevant to include additional detail emphasising one particular aspect of the accounts.

The APC issued an Auditing Standard **The audit report** in order to reduce the differences which previously existed in the method of reporting so that shareholders and other users of financial statements could grasp more easily the message which the auditor wished to convey.

The Auditing Standard is generally held to have been successful in achieving this objective. However, criticism mounted over the sparse terminology used in the audit report. It was felt by many that the auditor needed to explain his function and opinion more to the shareholder ie, he should produce an 'expanded audit report'.

In 1993 the APB issued SAS 600 **Auditors' reports on financial statements** to replace the old Auditing Standard.

1.2 Reasons for change

Auditors cannot 'guarantee' or 'certify' that financial statements are correct, they can only express opinions on the two matters required by statute ie,

(a)   Truth and fairness

(b)   Proper preparation in accordance with CA85.

The previous 'short-form' report did not set out the respective responsibilities of directors and auditors and it was felt that clarification of the issue on the face of the audit report might help dispel public confusion (and criticism) in relation to the precise extent of auditors' responsibilities in particular. The standard unqualified report is therefore worded as follows.

AUDITORS' REPORT TO THE SHAREHOLDERS OF XYZ PLC

We have audited the financial statements on pages... to ... which have been prepared under the historical cost convention (as modified by the revaluation of certain fixed assets) and the accounting policies set out on page...

Respective responsibilities of directors and auditors

As described on page... the company's directors are responsible for the preparation of financial statements. It is our responsibility to form an independent opinion, based on our audit, on those statements and to report our opinion to you.

Basis of opinion

We conducted our audit in accordance with Auditing Standards issued by the Auditing Practices Board. An audit includes examination, on a test basis, of evidence relevant to the amounts and disclosures in the financial statements. It also includes an assessment of the significant estimates and judgements made by the directors in the preparation of the financial statements, and of whether the accounting policies are appropriate to the company's circumstances, consistently applied and adequately disclosed.

We planned and performed our audit so as to obtain all the information and explanations which we considered necessary in order to provide us with sufficient evidence to give reasonable assurance that the financial statements are free from material misstatement, whether caused by fraud or other irregularity or error. In forming our opinion we also evaluated the overall adequacy of the presentation of information in the financial statements.

Opinion

In our opinion the financial statements give a true and fair view of the state of the company's affairs as at 31 December 19... and of its profit (loss) for the year then ended and have been properly prepared in accordance with the Companies Act 1985.

Registered auditors   Address
Date

1.3   Basic elements

(a)   **Title**

Audit reports should be addressed to the members of the company (on whose behalf the audit is undertaken) in the absence of alternative statutory or contractual arrangements.

(b)   **Introductory paragraph**

This identifies the financial statements audited by the use of page numbers, to distinguish such information from other documents that have not been subject to audit. The primary financial statements and associated notes that are subject to audit comprise the following:

(i)   Balance sheet.
(ii)   Profit and loss account.

(iii)   Cash flow statement.

(iv)   Statement of total recognised gains and losses.

Items (i) and (ii) are required by CA85, item (iii) is required by FRS 1 and item (iv) is required by FRS 3. Note that the opinion paragraph in the example given above only refers to items (i) and (ii). This is because items (iii) and (iv) are deemed to be necessary in order that the 'financial statements' give a true and fair view. Therefore if they were omitted or defective a qualification may arise.

The introductory paragraph also refers to the accounting convention under which the financial statements have been prepared.

(c)   **Statement of responsibilities of directors and auditors**

The report refers to a note of directors' responsibilities. If that note is absent auditors should include details of directors' responsibilities on the face of the audit report.

Auditors are required to form an opinion as to whether

(i)   proper accounting records have been kept by the company

(ii)   proper returns adequate for their audit have been received from branches not visited by them (where applicable)

(iii)   the company's balance sheet and (if not consolidated) its profit and loss account are in agreement with the accounting records and returns

(iv)   such information and explanations as auditors think necessary for the performance of their duties have been received from the company's officers

(v)   the directors' report is consistent with the financial statements.

Auditors must report on these matters only if, in their opinion, these requirements have not been met. This is known as reporting by exception. The absence of any comment in the report is, therefore, equivalent to a positive statement that they have satisfied themselves on all these matters.

In addition, if the financial statements do not properly disclose the details of directors' remuneration, and particulars of transactions with directors and officers required by the CA85, auditors have a duty to include a statement in their report giving the required particulars. Auditors would also need to qualify their report as the financial statements would not have met the requirements of the CA85.

Note that a report by exception is not in itself a qualification. However it can lead to one. For example where the company has not kept proper accounting records the auditor may not have been able to gather sufficient evidence and this would lead to a limitation of scope uncertainty (see below).

(d)   **Basis of opinion**

If auditors have not conducted their audit in accordance with Auditing Standards they should explain their departure. Normally this will be as a result of client imposed restrictions and will give rise to a qualification (see below).

(e)   **Opinion**

This covers the four primary statements and associated notes referred to in (b) above (even though only the first two are referred to explicitly).

The opinion stated is on

(i) truth and fairness

(ii) preparation in accordance with CA85

(iii) by exception only - the matters referred to in (c) above. Items (ii) and (iii) of (c) above are almost unheard of. Items (i) and (iv) are more common and invariably give rise to a qualification.

Such a statement would be made at the end of the qualified opinion paragraph. Item (v) does not normally give rise to a qualification as the directors' report is not subject to audit. The statement would be made in this case at the end of an unqualified opinion paragraph, as a separate paragraph.

(f) **Auditor's signature**

This should include reference to the auditor's status as a Registered Auditor. The report may be signed by the firm, by the auditor individually or both. Normally the firm's signature is given as the firm as a whole assumes responsibility for the audit. The location of the relevant office is also normally given.

(g) **Date of report**

This must be after directors have approved the financial statements (as the statements do not legally exist before then) and preferably on the same day. The post balance sheet events review extends to the date on which the auditor signs his report. SSAP 17 on post balance sheet events however, only extends to the date on which the financial statements are approved by directors.

It is not necessary that the final typewritten copies of financial statements are available for signature - draft copies may be signed provided the draft documents are sufficiently clear to enable a proper overall assessment of presentation to be made.

1.4 Qualified opinions

All qualifications arise from either disagreements or uncertainties.

This qualification 'grid' is a useful summary of the decisions to be made in drafting a qualified audit report.

		Material	*Fundamental*
(a)	**Uncertainty**		
	ie, Scope limitations	'Except for'	'Unable to form an opinion' = Disclaimer of opinion
	- inability to carry out audit procedures (perhaps because of a lack of accounting records or information and explanations from officers)		
(b)	**Disagreements**		
		'Except for'	'Do not give a true and fair view' = Adverse opinion
	(i) Inappropriate accounting policies		
	(ii) Re facts or amounts (eg, failure to provide for a bad debt)		

(iii)   Re manner or extent of disclosure
of facts or amounts

(iv)   Re compliance with legislation or
other requirements

1.5   Preparing audit reports to meet different specified situations

An audit report should only be qualified as a last resort. Whenever the auditor is concerned about his opinion, he should consult with management in order to try and resolve the problem without the need to issue a qualification. Management generally want to avoid a qualification and are therefore often willing to change their position or provide more information if the auditor has given a firm view of the need to qualify unless something is done.

Where there is a disagreement it is within the control of the management to change their mind so as to agree with the auditor. Where the auditor has been unable to carry out the audit fully, then there may be nothing the management can do to remedy the situation. However if there is an **inherent uncertainty** as to whether the financial statements give a true and fair view, the audit report is not qualified.

All these circumstances are detailed below:

1.6   Disagreements

Extract from SAS (600.8)

Where the auditors disagree with the accounting treatment or disclosure of a matter in the financial statements, and in the auditors' opinion the effect of that disagreement is material to the financial statements:

(a)   The auditors should include in the opinion section of their report

(i)   ·   a description of all substantive factors giving rise to the disagreement
(ii)   their implications for the financial statements
(iii)   whenever practicable, a quantification of the effect on the financial statements

(b)   When the auditors conclude that the effect of the matter giving rise to disagreement is so material or pervasive that the financial statements are seriously misleading, they should issue an adverse opinion.

(c)   In the case of other material disagreements, the auditors should issue a qualified opinion indicating that it is expressed except for the effects of the matter giving rise to the disagreement.

Adverse opinions are very rare. An adverse opinion is expressed by stating that the financial statements do not give a true and fair view.

An example of an 'except for' opinion is

AUDITORS' REPORT TO THE SHAREHOLDERS OF XYZ PLC

Opening narrative - as normal

Qualified opinion arising from disagreement about accounting treatment

Included in the debtors shown on the balance sheet is an amount of £Y due from a company which has ceased trading. XYZ plc has no security for this debt. In our opinion the company is unlikely to receive any payment and full provision of £Y should have been made, reducing profit before tax and net assets by that amount.

Except for the absence of this provision, in our opinion the financial statements give a true and fair view of the state of the company's affairs as at 31 December 19.. and of its profit (loss) for the year then ended and have been properly prepared in accordance with the Companies Act 1985.

Registered auditors   Address
Date

1.7   Uncertainties

Auditors may be uncertain as to whether the financial statements give a true and fair view etc, for one of two reasons. Either

(a)   the matter is inherently uncertain (ie, insufficient evidence is available because the matter can only reasonably be expected to be resolved at some future date eg, going concern doubts or major liquidation).

or

(b)   some limitation has been imposed on the scope of the auditor's work and insufficient evidence is therefore available even though it does (or could reasonably be expected to) exist.

1.8   Inherent uncertainties

Important points to note are as follows.

(a)   Inherent uncertainties, provided they are adequately disclosed, do not give rise to qualified opinions.

(b)   Instead reference is made to the inherent uncertainty via an explanatory paragraph within the 'basis of opinion' section, where inherent uncertainties are fundamental.

An inherent uncertainty is fundamental when the magnitude of its potential impact is so great that, without clear disclosure of the nature and implications of the uncertainty, the view given by the financial statements would be seriously misleading.

The magnitude of an inherent uncertainty's potential impact is judged by reference to

(i)   the risk that the estimate included in financial statements may be subject to change
(ii)   the range of possible outcomes, and
(iii)   the consequences of those outcomes on the view shown in the financial statements.

(c)   Where inherent uncertainties are not fundamental, no reference is necessary.

(d)   Where inherent uncertainties are inadequately disclosed, a disagreement qualification will arise.

(e)   If an explanatory paragraph is included in the report, it should be made clear that the report is unqualified.

Example of unqualified opinion with explanatory paragraph describing a fundamental uncertainty

AUDITORS' REPORT TO THE SHAREHOLDERS OF XYZ PLC

Opening narrative as normal

Basis of opinion

First part as normal but with the following added

Fundamental uncertainty

In forming our opinion, we have considered the adequacy of the disclosures made in the financial statements concerning the possible outcome to litigation against B Ltd, a subsidiary undertaking of the company, for an alleged breach of environmental regulations. The future settlement of this litigation could result in additional liabilities and the closure of B Ltd's business, whose net assets included in the consolidated balance sheet total £ .... and whose profit before tax for the year is £... Details of the circumstances relating to this fundamental uncertainty are described in note... Our opinion is not qualified in this respect.

Opinion

As normal

1.9   Limitation in scope

Important points to note are as follows.

(a)   A disclaimer of opinion is expressed when the possible effect of a limitation on scope is so material or pervasive that the auditors have not been able to support, and accordingly are unable to express, an opinion on the financial statements (SAS 600.7). Total disclaimers of opinion are rare.

(b)   When the auditors conclude that the effect of a disagreement is not so significant as to require an adverse opinion, they express an opinion that is qualified. The term 'except for' is used in the opinion paragraph (ie, the same terminology as for a material disagreement).

(c)   The auditors' report should include a description of the factors leading to the limitation in the opinion section of their report. This enables the reader to understand the reasons for the limitation and to distinguish between

    (i)   limitations imposed on the auditors (for example, where not all the accounting records are made available to the auditors or where the directors prevent a particular procedure considered necessary by the auditors from being carried out); and

    (ii)   limitations outside the control of the auditors or the directors (for example, when the timing of the auditors' appointment is such that attendance at the entity's stock-take is not possible and there is no alternative form of evidence regarding the existence of stock).

Example of qualified opinion: limitation on the auditors' work

AUDITORS' REPORT TO THE SHAREHOLDERS OF XYZ PLC

Opening narrative as normal

Basis of opinion

First part as normal but with the following included

We planned our audit so as to obtain all the information and explanations which we considered necessary in order to provide us with sufficient evidence to give reasonable assurance that the financial statements are free from material misstatement, whether caused by fraud or other irregularity or error. However, the evidence available to us was limited because £... of the company's recorded turnover comprises cash sales, over which there was no system of control on which we could rely for the purpose of our audit. There were no other satisfactory audit procedures that we could adopt to confirm that cash sales were properly recorded.

In forming our opinion we also evaluated the overall adequacy of the presentation of information in the financial statements.

Qualified opinion arising from limitation in audit scope

Except for any adjustments that might have been found to be necessary had we been able to obtain sufficient evidence concerning cash sales, in our opinion the financial statements give a true and fair view of the state of the company's affairs as at 31 December 19.. and of its profit (loss) for the year then ended and have been properly prepared in accordance with the Companies Act 1985.

In respect alone of the limitation on our work relating to cash sales:

- we have not obtained all the information and explanations that we considered necessary for the purpose of our audit; and

- we were unable to determine whether proper accounting records had been maintained.

Registered auditors   Address
Date

1.10   Activity

Explain the meaning of **each** of the following terms which are used in connection with audit reports

(a)   circumstances of uncertainty
(b)   a disclaimer of opinion
(c)   circumstances of disagreement
(d)   an 'except for' opinion
(e)   limitations in the scope of the audit
(f)   inherent uncertainties.

1.11   Activity solution

(a)   **Circumstances of uncertainty**

Uncertainty can arise from

(i)   a limitation in the scope of the audit caused by a failure to obtain all the information and explanations considered necessary; or

(ii)   an inherent uncertainty resulting from circumstances in which it is not possible to reach an objective conclusion as to the outcome of a situation due to the circumstances themselves. Such uncertainties relate to matters where considerable judgement is required as regards the likely outcome and the probable outcome is not sufficiently capable of estimation.

Items under (i) may lead to qualification. Items under (ii) may lead to an explanatory paragraph in the audit report.

(b)   **A disclaimer of opinion**

This arises where there is a fundamental uncertainty relating to the scope of the auditor such that he is unable to form an opinion on whether a true and fair view is given by the financial statements. For a matter to be fundamental it should have an impact so great as to render the financial statements as a whole meaningless. It is, therefore, only used as a last resort.

(c)   **Circumstances of disagreement**

The circumstances giving rise to a disagreement will include

(i)   departure from acceptable accounting practices

(1)   failure to follow a SSAP or FRS

(2)   an unacceptable policy not covered by a SSAP or FRS

(3)   compliance with a SSAP or FRS where this does not in the circumstances give a true and fair view

(ii)   disagreement as to facts or amounts included in financial statements

(iii)   disagreement as to the manner or extent of disclosure of facts or amounts

(iv)   failure to comply with legislation

and may result in an 'except for' or an adverse opinion.

(d)   **An 'except for' opinion**

This arises on a particular matter which, while being material to the true and fair view given by the financial statements, is not so fundamental as to render them totally misleading. The 'except for' opinion, therefore, indicates that, with the exception of the particular matter, the financial statements do give a true and fair view.

(e)   **Limitations in the scope of the audit**

Limitations in the scope of an audit are an example of circumstances giving rise to uncertainty (see (a) for explanation) which prevent an auditor from forming an opinion or issuing an 'except for' report.

(f)   **Inherent uncertainties**

These arise where the circumstances giving rise to an uncertainty relate to an uncertain situation, not being an inability to carry out audit procedures to obtain audit evidence. An example would be the assessment of the likely outcome of major litigation where the outcome is contingent and the probability of its occurrence is not capable of reasonable estimation, even given the opportunity to examine the evidence.

1.12   SAS 601 : Imposed limitation of audit scope

(a)   **Introduction**

The APB issued SAS 601 'Imposed limitation of audit scope' in March 1999. The APB had become concerned that, when faced with a serious director-imposed limitation on the scope of their audit work, some auditors have not given sufficient consideration to whether it is proper for them to accept or continue such an engagement, but have simply issued a disclaimer of opinion on the financial statements.

The SAS therefore clarifies the standards that apply when auditors encounter serious limitations on the scope of their audit work, that are likely to prevent them from forming an opinion on the financial statements.

(b)   **Auditing standards**

601.1   If the auditors are aware, before accepting an audit engagement, that the directors of the entity, or those who appoints its auditors will impose a limitation on the scope of their work which they consider likely to result in the need to issue a disclaimer of opinion on the financial statements, they should not accept that engagement, unless required to do so by statute.

601.2   If the auditors become aware, after accepting an audit engagement, that the directors of the entity, or those who appointed them as its auditors, have imposed a limitation on the scope of their work which they consider likely to result in the need to issue a disclaimer of opinion on the financial statements, they should request the removal of the limitation. If the limitation is not removed, they should consider resigning from the audit engagement.

(c)   **Effective date**

Auditors must comply with SAS 601 in all audits of financial statements for periods beginning on or after 1 June 1999. In due course, the substance of SAS 601 will be incorporated into a revised version of SAS 600.

2   OTHER MATTERS

2.1   Directors' responsibilities

The SASs do not tell directors what to put in their statement about their responsibilities. It is, after all, their responsibility not the APB's.

The example below is from a recent Annual Report and it appeared on the same page as the Auditor's Report.

'Statement by the Directors in respect of the preparation of financial statements

The Directors are required by company law to prepare financial statements which give a true and fair view of the state of affairs of the Company and the Group at the end of the financial year and of the profit of the Group for the period to that date. The financial statements must be prepared in compliance with the required formats and disclosures of the Companies Act 1985 and with applicable accounting standards. In addition, the Directors are required

- to make judgements and estimates that are reasonable and prudent;

- to take account of expenses and income relating to the period being reported on, whether or not they have been paid or received in that period; and

- to prepare the financial statements on a going concern basis unless it is inappropriate to presume that the Company will continue in business.

The Directors confirm that the financial statements comply with the above requirements. The Directors are also responsible for maintaining adequate records so as to enable them to ensure that the financial statements comply with the requirements of the Companies Act 1985, for safeguarding the assets of the Group, and for preventing and detecting fraud and other irregularities.

KPMG Peat Marwick, the independent auditors appointed by the shareholders, have examined the financial statements and their report follows. They have full and unrestricted access to the Audit Committee to discuss any matters arising from their audit.'

Note the statement to an Audit Committee. Audit Committees are dealt with later in this chapter.

2.2   The extent to which users understand the audit report

Users of accounts have information needs, and the auditor's report as an independent attestation lends credibility to the accounting information. However there has been the tendency for users to place far more reliance on the audit report than its actual function merits.

Typical, and erroneous, beliefs of users have included the following.

(a)   Auditors are the persons responsible for ensuring the accounts show a true and fair view.
(b)   Auditors are responsible for preventing and/or detecting fraud.
(c)   Auditors guarantee that the company is a going concern.

Clearly the old form of audit report did little to clarify matters as it was very brief with a few highly formalised phrases. SAS 600 is an attempt to overcome this problem by explaining the conduct of an audit. In addition, and perhaps more importantly, the directors' statement details their responsibilities. It is however too early to conclude to what extent users understand the audit report now than formerly.

2.3   How qualifications may be avoided by negotiation with management

Management are generally keen to avoid qualifications in the audit report because:

(a)   Adverse publicity may arise from the media.

(b)   If the qualification concerns a matter of accounting policy, the powers of the Financial Reporting Review Panel may result in the preparation of revised accounts.

(c)   Loan/debenture deeds may refer to an audit qualification as giving rise to a breach of a covenant, thus giving loan stock holders an immediate right to repayment or the right to appoint a receiver.

Therefore if the auditors have a contentious issue, the directors will often reconsider their decision on a particular policy provided that the auditors raise the matter in a forceful way with management.

It should be appreciated however that in SAS 600, an unqualified report can be given if there is an inherent uncertainty provided that the notes in the financial statements give sufficient clarification of the uncertainty. If there is a fundamental uncertainty, there is still an unqualified report but the report must contain an explanatory paragraph.

2.4   Flowchart

This flowchart is taken from SAS 600 and should be helpful in problem type questions in deciding the action(s) an auditor should take in respect of his report.

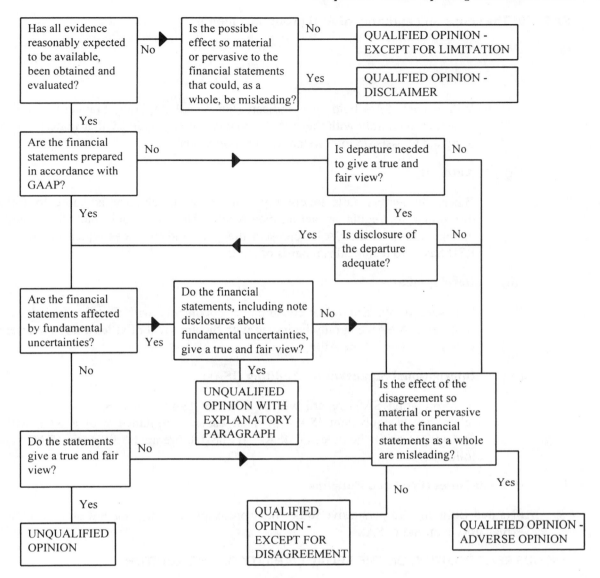

Questions concerning limitation and disagreement are presumed to involve matters considered to be material. GAAP = Generally accepted accounting practice.

3   THE ROLE OF THE APB IN ISSUING AUDITING STANDARDS

3.1   The Auditing Practices Board

The APB was established in 1991 by the CCAB, to replace the old APC. Its objectives are to advance standards of auditing, ensure public confidence in the auditing process and to meet the needs of users of financial statements.

In particular it takes an active role in the development of the regulation of the profession and publishes the principles and procedures with which auditors are required to comply, along with explanatory material to assist in interpretation. The main differences between it and its predecessor are that its non-practitioner members (academics, lawyers and industrialists) have voices on the board and that the board can issue standards in its own right (ie, CCAB members can no longer veto the issue of the standards).

The types of statements issued by the APB have been explained earlier.

3.2   SAS 010: The scope and authority of APB pronouncements

(a)   **SASs**

(i)   **Scope**

Within each SAS bold type indicates an actual Auditing Standard. Auditors are expected to comply with these in the conduct of any audit. Other material included is designed to assist in interpretation and application.

(ii)   **Authority**

Where a member fails to comply with SASs an enquiry is liable to follow and disciplinary or regulatory action may result. The latter could include the withdrawal of registration as the SASs represent the rules and practices which the ACCA as an RSB has as to technical standards of audit.

(iii)   **Development**

Exposure drafts and other consultative documents will first be issued for public comment. A SAS can only be issued with the approval of at least three quarters of the voting members of the APB.

(iv)   **International Standards on Auditing (ISAs)**

In formulating SASs regard will be taken of ISAs. Each SAS will explain how it relates to its equivalent ISA. In most cases compliance with a SAS will ensure compliance with the relevant ISA. If the requirements differ the SAS should be followed.

(b)   **Practice Notes (PNs) and Bulletins**

PNs and Bulletins are persuasive rather than prescriptive. They have a similar status to the explanatory material in SASs.

4   THE CURRENT POSITION ON THE LEGAL LIABILITY OF THE AUDITOR

4.1   Liability in contract

The company has a contract with the auditor and hence can sue the auditor for breach of contract if there is suspected negligence. Since the company rarely sues, the more important liability of the auditor is that to third parties in tort, which is discussed below.

Note that the shareholders do not have a contract with the auditor so shareholders cannot sue in contract (an important decision in the Caparo v Touche Ross case).

The auditor may also be liable to others who have relied on the financial statements upon which he expressed an opinion.

4.2   Duty of care of the auditor

When carrying out his duties the auditor must exercise care and skill. The degree of care and skill to be shown, in particular in relation to the depth of his investigation and the types of check to be made, is shown by judicial decision.

In general, the auditor must exercise a reasonable degree of care and skill. As stated in Re London and General Bank (No 2) (1895):

'It is the duty of an auditor to bring to bear on the work he has to perform that skill, care and caution which a reasonably careful and cautious auditor would use. What is reasonable skill, care and caution must depend on the particular circumstances of each case. An auditor ... is not bound to do more than exercise reasonable care and skill in making enquiries. He is not an insurer; he does not guarantee that the books do correctly show the true position of the company's affairs; he must be honest ie, he must not certify what he does not believe to be true, and he must take reasonable care and skill before he believes that what he certifies is true.'

The meaning of reasonable in this respect has been expanded and clarified by later decided cases. It should, however, be appreciated that decisions in older cases will tend to under-state rather than over-state the degree of care and skill required, since what is regarded as reasonable by the courts will necessarily be affected by current standards of auditing practice.

In the absence of suspicious circumstances, an auditor would not be liable for failing to uncover fraud and falsities which were not discoverable by the exercise of normal skill and care - Re City Equitable Fire Insurance (1925). Similarly, in the absence of suspicious circumstances, the auditor is entitled to accept the word of a responsible company official. But once an auditor's suspicions have been aroused there is a duty to probe the matter to the bottom. (Re Kingston Cotton Mill Co (1896)).

4.3   Liability in tort

A third party (ie, a person who has no contractual relationship with the auditor) may sue the auditor in the tort of negligence for damages.

In the tort of negligence, the plaintiff (ie, the third party) must prove that

(a)   the defendant (ie, the auditor) owes a duty of care, and

(b)   the defendant has breached the appropriate standard of care (ie, has been negligent), and

(c)   the plaintiff has suffered loss resulting from the defendant's breach.

To whom a person making a negligent mis-statement causing economic loss owes a duty of care has been the subject of litigation, viz Hedley Byrne v Heller (1963) and JEB Fasteners v Marks Bloom (1980-2), albeit in this case it was obiter dicta.

The principles were established in Hedley Byrne v Heller. A duty of care exists where there is a special relationship between the parties ie, where the auditors knew, or ought to have known, that the audited accounts would be made available to, and would be relied on by, a particular person (or class of person).

For example, suppose that X, a director of a company, said to the auditors: I am going to show the audited accounts to Mr John Brown and members of my Yacht Club as they are thinking of buying shares in the company.

The auditors would then owe a duty of care to Mr John Brown because they knew that he, a particular person, would rely on the accounts. Similarly the auditors would owe a duty of care to the members of the Yacht Club because the auditors knew that they, a particular class of persons would rely on the accounts.

The essence of Hedley Byrne is that the third parties must have been identified in some way to the auditors.

If, to continue the example, the directors, without telling or warning the auditors, showed the accounts to a prospective take-over bidder, then under Hedley Byrne there would appear to be no duty of care.

The principles of JEB Fasteners v Marks Bloom

At first instance, and obiter dicta, it was stated that a duty of care will exist where the defendant auditors

(i)   knew or reasonably should have foreseen at the time that the accounts were audited that a person might rely on those accounts for the particular purpose, and

(ii)   that in all the circumstances it would be reasonable for such reliance to be placed on those accounts for that particular purpose.

The question that therefore arises is the possible liability of an auditor to a member of the general public who reads the accounts and then buys shares in the company in reliance on those accounts. Does the auditor owe a duty of care to such an unknown person? It is likely that it would be held that an auditor should reasonably foresee that a member of the public might read the accounts since they are available for public inspection at Companies House. But whether it is reasonable for a member of the public to rely on the accounts in making an investment decision would depend on all the surrounding circumstances; for example, the length of time which has elapsed between preparation and auditing the accounts and reliance by the third party upon them.

One recent case in particular is indicative of the current trend towards limiting the circumstances in which a duty of care is owed. On 8 February 1990 the House of Lords gave its decision on the following case

Caparo Industries v Dickman and Touche Ross & Co (1989)

Fidelity plc was taken over by Caparo Industries. Fidelity's accounts had been audited by Touche Ross. Caparo alleged that the accounts overstated the profits of Fidelity plc and that its purchases of shares and take-over bid were all made in reliance on the audited accounts.

Held by the House of Lords, that a duty of care was not owed to potential investors in, or take-over bidders for, the company having regard to

(a)   the lack of proximity between auditor and potential investor and

(b)   the fact that it would not be just and reasonable to impose a duty on the auditor to such investors.

In the above case, the House of Lords identified the auditor's functions as being

(a)   to protect the company itself from errors and wrongdoing

(b)   to provide shareholders with information such that they can scrutinise the conduct of a company's affairs and remove or reward those responsible.

The auditor does not exist to aid investment decisions.

Since the Caparo case there have been no fundamental changes to the legal position with respect to auditors' liability. However, one case, Morgan Crucible Co plc v Hill Samuel & Co Ltd and others (1990) has established that duty of care may be owed to take-over bidders in some circumstances. In the court of appeal it was held that directors, auditors and financial advisers of a company which is the subject of a contested take-over bid can owe a duty to identified bidders to take reasonable care with regard to financial statements on which the bidders could foreseeably rely when deciding whether or not to make or increase their offer.

This does not contradict or amend the Caparo decision. However, it makes clear that accountants may owe a duty when producing financial information for the purposes of a take-over bid. The case is distinguished from Caparo because the financial information was additional to a Companies Act audit report.

Conclusion

To sum up, an auditor does not owe a duty of care to potential take-over bidders when auditing company accounts.

However, an auditor who produces other or additional information in the context of a contested take-over bid may owe a duty to the identified bidders not to mislead them.

4.4   The relationship with indemnity insurers

All registered auditors must have sufficient professional indemnity insurance to meet claims arising from audit work, before they are allowed to carry out company audits. This is a requirements of the CA 89 which is regulated by the ACCA for its members. Some people therefore argue that the auditor's liability is not a problem for the auditor; they believe that the insurance company will pick up the bill. This reasoning is flawed for the following reasons:

(a)   Indemnity insurance is unlikely to cover 100% of claims against the auditor

(b)   There is considerable bad publicity whenever an auditor is sued for negligence, which reflects badly on the auditor's reputation

(c)   The time taken up in contesting claims for negligence would much better be spent in chargeable time servicing clients.

5   CURRENT ISSUES AND CONTROVERSIES RELATING TO AUDITORS

5.1   The expectation gap

There has been considerable discussion in recent years on the role of the auditor, and the 'Expectation Gap'.

In general terms this can be described as the gap that exists between what the public, especially users of financial statements, believe auditors do (or ought to do) and what the auditors actually do. Such a gap usually surfaces on the unexpected failure of a company.

Various elements of this gap have been identified

(a)   **A standards gap**

Where the public perceive Auditing Standards as different from what they actually are.

(b)   **A performance gap**

Where auditors perform below existing standards.

(c)   **A liability gap**

Where the public does not know to whom an auditor is legally responsible. This has arisen particularly after the Caparo decision.

5.2   Potential ways of closing the gap

(a)   **Understanding financial statements and the audit report**

False or unrealistic expectations in users of financial statements are frequent. They may not appreciate the conventions on which accounts are prepared, the inevitable degree of estimation and judgement involved or the test nature of audit work.

Communication with these users to improve their understanding could be improved. The most significant work on this area has been the Statement of Auditing Standard (SAS) to 'expand' the old form of audit report.

(b)   **Fraud**

When questioned, a high proportion of the public believed the auditor has a responsibility to detect fraud of all kinds, or that he should actively search for fraud. However deep-seated fraud with wide collusion may be virtually impossible to identify, given the limitations of audit techniques. The auditor may not reasonably be expected to have discovered a particular fraud in particular circumstances.

Once again, the profession should attempt to explain these limitations to the users of accounts, so that they are aware the auditor's responsibility is to have only a 'reasonable expectation' of detecting material fraud.

Alternatively the auditor could be required to limit the opportunity for fraud in the first place. A requirement could be set for companies and their auditors to review the effectiveness of controls to prevent serious fraud, and to report serious deficiencies.

(c)   **Control of the auditing profession**

The Companies Act 1985 now requires the professional bodies to implement a regime of practice quality control inspection, the intention being to reassure the public.

Audit failures are sometimes due to poor performance. Education (keeping up to date) should remedy this. Legal action and disciplinary proceedings serve as a warning.

5.3   SAS 110: Fraud and error

Auditing standards

110.1   Auditors should plan and perform their audit procedures and evaluate and report the results thereof, recognising that fraud or error may materially affect the financial statements.

110.2   When planning the audit the auditors should assess the risk that fraud or error may cause the financial statements to contain material misstatements.

110.3   Based on their risk assessment the auditors should design audit procedures so as to have a reasonable expectation of detecting misstatements arising from fraud and error which are material to the financial statements.

6   THE CHANGING ROLE OF THE AUDITOR

6.1   Background

In November 1992 the APB issued a discussion paper **The future development of auditing** as a stimulus to debate. The proposals are set to mark a turning point for the UK auditing profession and focus on the needs of the listed or other public interest company. The following is a summary of the paper.

6.2   Present perceptions of the audit

(a)   A gap between the role expected of auditors and that performed by them, particularly with regard to the responsibilities of directors, fraud, internal controls, future prospects/risks and interim reporting.

(b)   A lack of independence, exacerbated by the commercial relationship between the auditor and the company with the result that auditors have not taken a sufficiently tough stand over accounting policies.

(c)   Insufficient disclosure of material concerns in the audit report.

(d)   A lowering of quality through increased competition amongst auditors for work and through pressure on directors to cut audit fees.

(e)   A barrier to pro-activity and change amongst auditors because of a fear of potential litigation.

(f)   Concern that the relatively new system of audit regulation is ineffective.

6.3   Redefining the role and scope of audit

Purpose of the audit to be redefined as being

To provide an independent opinion to those with an interest in a company that they have received from those responsible for its direction and management an adequate account of

(a)   the proper conduct of the company's affairs
(b)   the company's financial performance and position
(c)   future risks attaching to the company.

(a)   This is a role which is now widely expected of auditors but is not part of the conventional definition of an audit. This could extend current responsibilities with regard to reporting on internal controls, fraud and illegal acts.

Remember that the auditor has duties under the Financial Services Act 1986 to report to the Regulator where management are failing to act responsibly.

(b)   This is the traditional role of reporting on financial stewardship, and is considered insufficient in isolation to satisfy users' needs today.

(c)   This is a newly defined role, recognising that it is not the purpose of financial statements to predict the future. This would represent a cultural shift of the audit so that it looks forward as well as backward.

6.4   Enhancing the independence of auditors

A number of ways to enhance objectivity are suggested.

(a)   Instigating the Cadbury Committee proposals re audit committees (see next section).

(b)   The obligatory rotation of auditors either in terms of the auditing firm or in terms of the audit partner.

(c)   Strong internal controls within the audit firm over those involved in the audit.

(d)   Encouraging shareholders to take an active part in the audit and in other areas of corporate governance. Various methods are proposed.

6.5   The Audit Agenda

The APB received a large response to its 1992 discussion paper. After reviewing these responses a further discussion paper **The Audit Agenda** was published in December 1994.

This built on the work of **The future development of auditing** by putting forward proposals in four key areas.

(a)   The future role of auditors and scope of audit

•   the scope of audit for large and listed companies should be differentiated from that for unlisted, owner-managed businesses.

•   the scope of listed company audits should be extended while the APB will develop guidance on how auditing standards can be applied to the audit of owner-managed businesses.

•   the ASB should issue guidance on how going concern status can be verified.

•   auditors of listed companies should report to the board on the systems intended to combat fraud.

(b)   Objectivity

- auditors should sign their opinion by name, as well as with the name of the audit firm.

- the partner responsible for the audit of a listed company should not be responsible for marketing non-audit services to the company.

- audit committees of listed companies should be specifically responsible for the appointment and remuneration of auditors, as a proxy for shareholders.

(c)   Litigation

- the extended scope of the audit of listed companies and reporting to directors on governance issues should be capped with respect to the auditor's liability.

(d)   Other development and research

- the APB will review techniques of total quality management for enabling audit quality to be achieved at effective cost.

- the APB will keep in mind the implications of future changes in auditing in carrying out its work.

In February 1996 the APB published a further paper entitled *The Audit Agenda - Next Steps* setting out the steps that the APB intends to take in order to implement, or encourage others to implement, the proposals in *The Audit Agenda* in the light of comments received.

7   CORPORATE GOVERNANCE - THE CADBURY REPORT AND OTHER DEVELOPMENTS

7.1   Background

The Cadbury Committee was set up in 1991 by the FRC, the Stock Exchange and the accountancy profession to examine the reporting and control functions of boards of directors and the role of auditors and shareholders. Its full title was 'The Committee on the Financial Aspects of Corporate Governance', chaired by Sir Adrian Cadbury. In the wake of a number of large company disasters a better title might have been 'The Committee on How to Stop Fraud'.

The draft report entitled 'The Financial Aspects of Corporate Governance' was issued in May 1992. The final report followed in December. It contains two main areas of recommendation which are briefly summarised below.

7.2   The annual audit

Two central issues were considered with regard to this vital part of corporate governance.

(a)   How to ensure that a professional and objective relationship exists between auditors and management.

It was concluded that this would be helped by

(i)   The ASB's development of more effective accounting standards
(ii)   The formation of audit committees (see below)
(iii)   Full disclosure of fees paid to auditors for non-audit work
(iv)   Periodic change of audit partner.

(b)   How to increase the effectiveness and value of the audit.

The report contains a recommendation that reporting practice is extended in the areas of internal control and going concern. It also recommends that the Companies Act be amended to allow auditors the freedom to report a 'reasonable suspicion of fraud' without breaking their fiduciary duty to a client company.

7.3   Code of best practice for company directors

This is applicable to the boards of all listed companies in the UK from June 1993 and has been incorporated into the Stock Exchange's Combined Code on corporate governance. Annual reports have to carry a statement of compliance. Non-compliance will have to be explained.

Broadly the Cadbury proposals cover

- membership of the board with effective division of responsibility (combination of executive and non-executive directors)

- independence of the board (no financial connection with the company except fees and shareholdings)

- remuneration committees to be established and service contracts over three years approved by shareholders

- reporting and disclosure (including disclosure of directors' emoluments and reporting on internal control systems)

- establishment of audit committees (with at least three non-executive directors, at least two being independent).

7.4   Audit committees

In the US over 80% of large companies have audit committees and the Securities and Exchange Commission has made them compulsory for all companies listed on the New York Stock Exchange.

An audit committee can be defined as a committee of directors, usually without executive responsibility, or top-ranking managers, which considers both the external and internal plans and activity with a specific brief to review internal control arrangements.

(a)   **Objectives and advantages**

Three main objectives are usually associated with audit committees

(i)   Increasing public confidence in the credibility and objectivity of published financial information (including unaudited interim statements).

(ii)   Assisting directors (particularly non-executive directors) in meeting their responsibilities in respect of financial reporting.

(iii)   Strengthening the independent position of a company's external auditor by providing an additional channel of communication.

In addition

(iv)   They may improve the quality of management accounting, being better placed to criticise internal functions.

(v)   They should lead to better communication between the directors, external auditors and management.

(b)   **Disadvantages**

Audit committees may lead to

(i)   fear that their purpose is to catch management out
(ii)   non-executive directors being over-burdened with detail
(iii)   a 'two-tier' board of directors.

Finally, there is undoubtedly additional cost in terms of, at the least, time involved.

(c)   **The functions of an audit committee**

These could include the following

(i)   Review of a company's internal control procedures.

(ii)   Review of the internal audit function - the audit committee providing an independent reporting channel.

(iii)   Review of the company's current accounting policies and possible changes resulting from the introduction of new accounting standards.

(iv)   Review of regular management information (for example, monthly management accounts).

(v)   Review of the annual financial statements presented to shareholders.

(vi)   Review of the results of the external auditors' examination to ensure that the auditors have performed an effective, efficient and independent audit.

(vii)   Procedures for reviewing published interim (preliminary) statements, draft prospectus, profit forecasts, etc.

(viii)   Receiving and dealing with external auditors' criticisms of management, and ensuring that recommendations of internal and external auditors have been implemented.

(ix)   Recommending nomination and remuneration of the external auditors.

8   INTERNATIONAL ISSUES AFFECTING AUDITING

8.1   EC and European Directives

The European Community (EC) issues Directives, some of which (such as those on company law) have an impact on audit practice. For example, the 8th Company Law Directive was the Directive which resulted in the RSB system being introduced in the UK by the CA89.

More recently, the EC has proposed a voluntary Community environmental auditing scheme. This aims to improve the impact that a company has on the environment. Environmental auditing is covered below.

8.2   International auditing bodies

The International Federation of Accountants (IFAC) has about 130 member bodies from about 100 separate countries. One of its committees, the International Auditing Practices Committee (IAPC) publishes International Standards on Auditing (ISAs). The APB tries to ensure that its own national standards embrace the principles contained in the relevant ISAs.

In the EC, the FEE (Fédération des Experts Comptables Européens) attempts to co-ordinate the activities of European accountancy bodies, but does not publish standards.

8.3   Environmental audit

Definition   An audit which determines the degree of compliance with emission and pollution standards.

This type of audit is slowly increasing in importance due to the concern of the public, and hence governments with the effects that organisations, particularly industrial, can have on the environment.

The method of audit is straightforward. Predetermined targets are established either voluntarily by the organisation or set by government and actual outcomes are compared to the targets.

8.4   Eco-audit scheme

The EC has adopted a scheme for the establishment of a voluntary Community environmental auditing scheme - the **eco-audit scheme.** It is aimed at companies carrying on industrial activities.

A company would, under the scheme, have an environmental audit on each of its sites at regular intervals and set up a framework for acting on the audit findings. A statement would be prepared on the results of the audit which would be available for public inspection. The statement could be carried out by internal staff but would need to be validated by authorised environmental auditors.

8.5   Impact on annual reports

A recent report has been produced which suggests that companies should act in a number of areas to respond to the growing importance of 'green issues'.

The annual report should contain details of:

- the company's environmental policy and objectives
- the impact of the business on the environment
- the extent to which the company complies with external requirements
- identity of director with environmental responsibility.

External auditors need to be aware of contingent liabilities that may require disclosure because of the consequences of damage caused to the environment. The auditor may view many of these liabilities as too remote to be included within the financial statements under the FRS 12 criteria. Therefore it may be appropriate to have additional environmental reports.

9   PROSPECTIVE FINANCIAL INFORMATION

On certain occasions a company may issue financial information to its shareholders and others about the future eg, a profit forecast. An auditor may be appointed as a **reporting accountant** to make a report on the forecast.

Auditors may be called on to report on financial information relating to a future period (eg statements of cash flow and working capital requirements, profit forecasts in a prospectus).

In relation to procedures, the main point to note is that the auditor **cannot** audit the financial information itself as it relates to the **future**. His work is restricted to checking that the financial information has been properly prepared from stated management assumptions, which he can review for reasonableness.

It is thus misleading to refer to the report as an auditors' report and it is thus signed as an accountant.

The report should contain the following elements:

- identify prospective financial information under review;

- include a statement of management's responsibility for preparing the information and the underlying assumptions;

- indicate that any profit estimates are unaudited;

- include a caveat referring to the greater uncertainty of prospective information compared with historical information;

- include the opinion;

- state the date of the opinion.

10   CHAPTER SUMMARY

The audit report is the major channel of communication between the auditor and the user of the financial statements. The unqualified audit report consists of a number of elements which must follow the SAS.

Audit qualifications arise due to either disagreements or limitations in scope. Inherent uncertainties give rise to disclosures by management in the financial statements and do not normally give rise to a qualification.

Negligence under common law is the most important form of potential liability. A duty of care is owed to a third party where it is foreseen a statement will be relied upon, there is a relevant degree of proximity between the parties and it must be just and reasonable to impose a duty of care.

A number of ways have been suggested for closing the expectations gap by either widening the scope of the auditors' duties and/or ensuring the user has a better understanding of the auditors' role.

11   SELF TEST QUESTIONS

11.1   An exception report is required in the audit report in what circumstances? (1.3)

11.2   What should be included in the auditor's signature? (1.3)

11.3   What are examples of disagreements? (1.4)

11.4   A fundamental disagreement gives rise to what? (1.6)

11.5   What is an inherent uncertainty? (1.8)

11.6   What type of items are likely to be included in a statement of directors' responsibilities? (2.1)

11.7   Can shareholders sue the auditors under contract law? (4.1)

11.8   In the tort of negligence what three things must the plaintiff prove? (4.3)

11.9   What elements exist in an expectation gap? (5.1)

11.10   What are the two issues relating to the annual audit per the Cadbury Report? (7.2)

12   EXAMINATION TYPE QUESTION

12.1   Millers Villas Ltd

Millers Villas Ltd operate five holiday centres on freehold sites in the British Isles. The company's financial statements for the year ended 31 May 19X3 disclose total turnover for the year of £3,800,000 and net profit before taxation of £420,000. The following matters have arisen from your audit work on these financial statements.

(a)   Cost of brochures and advertising relating to the 19X3 summer season of £132,000 have been carried forward in the balance sheet as a prepayment.

(b)   Bar stocks at one site were not physically counted on 31 May 19X3 but were estimated by the bar manager at £7,000 based on the previous physical stocktaking at 30 April 19X3 which disclosed a value of £6,400 and sales during the month of May which amounted to £11,000. The subsequent physical stocktaking took place on 30 June 19X3. Using the estimated value on 31 May 19X3, a review of the trading results from the months of May and June disclosed a gross profit percentage of 60% and 39% respectively, compared with an average of 46% for the other months of the year.

(c)   The manager of each camp is responsible for paying casual labour taken on during the six peak holiday weeks in the summer and for shorter periods at other times of the year. These payments are made in cash and amount to approximately £40,000 per centre for the year, but no receipts or vouchers are available apart from the weekly lists of payments signed by each manager. However, all necessary PAYE and Social Security requirements have been complied with in respect of such payments.

(d)   Provisions for liabilities and charges include a provision for future maintenance of £200,000 representing one third of the estimated cost of totally renovating all camp buildings. During March each year one third of the properties on each site is fully renovated.

You are required:

(a)   to comment on the further considerations required of each of the above matters in order to conclude the audit and   **(14 marks)**

(b)   to indicate the possible effects on the audit report.   **(6 marks)**
                                                                        (Total: 20 marks)

13   ANSWER TO EXAMINATION TYPE QUESTION

13.1   Millers Villas Ltd

(a)   **Cost of brochures and advertising**

   (i)   **Accruals concept**

   The auditor should ascertain whether advance booking receipts are deferred until the time the holiday-maker actually takes the holiday or credited to the profit and loss account on a cash basis.

   If the company adopts the former policy, then the carrying forward of brochure costs and advertising to match the associated revenue would be appropriate and acceptable as it represents a material expense.

   It could, however, be argued that there is no real **future** benefit expected in the post year end period as the primary objective of printing brochures and advertising is to encourage advance bookings. If the brochures were printed before the end of May 19X3 to achieve this objective, both advance booking receipts and related brochure costs could justifiably be accounted for as they arise.

   (ii)   **Consistency**

   The auditor should also consider whether the above policy has been consistently applied. If the carrying forward of brochure costs represents a change in policy the auditor will hence be concerned with the appropriateness of the new policy **and** its current treatment and disclosure in compliance with SSAP 2 and FRS 3 (prior period adjustment).

   Effect on audit report

   The auditor would have to consider the need to qualify his report on the grounds of disagreement (material but not fundamental) if he is dissatisfied with:

      (i)   the policy itself, and/or

      (ii)   implementation and disclosure of the policy (particularly if it represents a change in policy where an FRS 3 prior period adjustment would be required).

(b)   **Bar stock at one site**

   Points to be considered

      (i)   This is not a material problem in terms of forming an audit opinion since the unexplained difference in contribution is only £1,500. However this could become a risk area if allowed to go unchecked.

The auditor would compare the average of 46% with the gross profit margin at other sites (this margin sounds reasonable for the type of business). He would also compare the estimated stock figure with the results of physical stocktakings at other dates (eg, April and June of 19X3 and of April, May and June of 19X2) making necessary adjustments for changes in turnover levels.

(ii)   Internal control implications.

The auditor would wish to identify whether this control breakdown is an isolated departure - the implication is that bar stocks were counted satisfactorily on 31 May at the other four centres.

He would consider reporting the control problem to management in his weakness letter.

Effect on audit report

This minor control breakdown would not, in isolation, warrant an audit report qualification.

(c)   **Casual labour**

Points to be considered in respect of each camp

(i)   The auditor would familiarise himself with the PAYE/Social Security regulations and test that the individual payments per the weekly lists are within the thresholds permitted by the authorities for sanctioning payments by cash and any non-deduction of income tax and national insurance contributions. Any correspondence from the authorities querying payments should be reviewed.

(ii)   As no statutory records are maintained in respect of the casual workers there is the possibility that dummy names have been entered on the weekly lists. It may be possible and advisable to carry out a test circularisation of the names on the lists - assuming addresses are available - to confirm existence. Non-replies would have to be followed up carefully and tactfully with the respective managers.

(iii)   The adequacy of the accounting records must be determined to ensure, for example, that the cash payments can be reconciled to the weekly lists. This will depend on whether these disbursements are made by formal withdrawal from petty cash and are hence identifiable in the petty cash book (or equivalent) or, less satisfactorily, made out of cash takings before such takings are recorded and subsequently banked.

(iv)   Analytical review procedures should be applied comparing one centre with another and with previous periods. The review would be particularly concerned with total cash receipts, gross profit percentages, total casual labour costs and the relationship between casual labour costs and cash receipts for each centre.

Effect on audit report

If, as a result of his investigations, the auditor is unable to substantiate the casual payments for any or all centres he will have to consider qualifying his report on the grounds of uncertainty as he has not obtained all the information and explanations he considers necessary (ie, a limitation in the scope of his audit).

Furthermore he should report that he has been unable to satisfy himself that proper accounting records, in respect of casual payments, have been kept in accordance with S221 Companies Act 1985.

(d)   **Provision for future maintenance**

Points to be considered

(i)   **Past experience**

The auditor should ascertain whether this is a new accounting policy.   If not, the provision last year and the actual costs of renovation incurred in the current year, against which the provision brought forward was presumably released, should be determined.   The amount transferred to and from the provision should be disallowed for tax purposes.

(ii)   **Classification**

FRS 12 only allows a provision to be recognised where there is an **obligation** to transfer economic benefits.   An intention to make a payment is not enough.   The auditor should therefore investigate whether an obligation for the expenditure exists (eg, a contract has been signed that cannot be withdrawn from), in which case setting up the provision would be acceptable).

The auditor should determine the audit evidence available to confirm provision of £200,000. This will include discussions with management and formal representations.   If possible, documentary evidence of external estimates of costs of renovation should be obtained, and a review made of past provisions compared with actual costs incurred.

Effect on audit report

If a provision can validly be established, it must be disclosed per the Companies Act 1985 under the heading 'provisions for liabilities and charges'.   It should be shown separately as the provision is material when assessing the company's state of affairs.   Such disclosure may be made either on the face of the balance sheet or in the notes to the financial statements. Assuming that the auditor is satisfied with the disclosure and the validity of the provision there will be no requirement for a qualification.

Student Questionnaire

Invoice number: . . . .

Because we believe in listening to our customers, this questionnaire has been designed to discover exactly what you think about us and our materials. We want to know how we can continue improving our customer support and how to make our top class books even better - how do you use our books, what do you like about them and what else would you like to see us do to make them better?

---

1 Where did you hear about AT Foulks Lynch ACCA Textbooks?

☐ Colleague or friend   ☐ Employer recommendation   ☐ Lecturer recommendation

☐ AT Foulks Lynch mailshot   ☐ Conference   ☐ ACCA literature

☐ Student Newsletter   ☐ Pass Magazine   ☐ Internet

☐ Other ....

---

2 Overall, do you think the AT Foulks Lynch ACCA Textbooks are:

☐ Excellent   ☐ Good   ☐ Average   ☐ Poor   ☐ No opinion

---

3 Please evaluate AT Foulks Lynch service using the following criteria:

	Excellent	Good	Average	Poor	No opinion
Professional	☐	☐	☐	☐	☐
Polite	☐	☐	☐	☐	☐
Informed	☐	☐	☐	☐	☐
Helpful	☐	☐	☐	☐	☐

---

4 How did you obtain this book?

☐ From a bookshop (name)   ☐ From your college (name)   ☐ From us by mail order

....

☐ From us by telephone   ☐ Internet   ☐ Other ....

---

5 How long did it take to receive your materials?   .... days.

☐ Very fast   ☐ Fast   ☐ Satisfactory   ☐ Slow   ☐ No opinion

---

6 How do you rate the value of these features of this Textbook?

Paper No ....   Title ....

		Excellent	Good	Average	Poor	No opinion
1	Syllabus referenced to chapters	☐	☐	☐	☐	☐
2	Teaching Guide referenced to chapters	☐	☐	☐	☐	☐
3	Step by step approach and solutions	☐	☐	☐	☐	☐
4	Activities throughout the chapters	☐	☐	☐	☐	☐
5	Self test questions	☐	☐	☐	☐	☐
6	Examination type questions	☐	☐	☐	☐	☐
7	Index	☐	☐	☐	☐	☐

Continued/...

7 Have you purchased any other AT Foulks Lynch ACCA titles?
If so, please specify title(s) and your rating of each below:

Title	Excellent	Good	Average	Poor	No opinion
....	☐	☐	☐	☐	☐
....	☐	☐	☐	☐	☐
....	☐	☐	☐	☐	☐
....	☐	☐	☐	☐	☐

8 Have you used publications other than AT Foulks Lynch ACCA titles?
If so, please specify title(s) and your rating of each below:

Title and Publisher	Excellent	Good	Average	Poor	No opinion
....	☐	☐	☐	☐	☐
....	☐	☐	☐	☐	☐
....	☐	☐	☐	☐	☐
....	☐	☐	☐	☐	☐

9 Will you buy the AT Foulks Lynch ACCA Textbooks again?

☐ Yes   ☐ No   ☐ Not sure

Why? ....

10 Please write here any additional comments you might have on any of the above areas or tell us what you would like us to do to make the books even better:

....

....

....

....

11 Your details: these are for the internal use of AT Foulks Lynch Ltd only and will not be supplied to any outside organisations.

Name
....

Address
....

....

Telephone
....

Do you have your own e-mail address?   ☐ Yes   ☐ No

Do you have access to the World Wide Web?   ☐ Yes   ☐ No   ....

Do you have access to a CD Rom Drive?   ☐ Yes   ☐ No

Please send to:

Quality Feedback Department
FREEPOST 2254
AT Foulks Lynch Ltd, 4 The Griffin Centre, Staines Road, Feltham, Middlesex, TW14 0BR.

Thank you for your time.

HOTLINES

Telephone: 00 44 (0)181 844 0667
Enquiries: 00 44 (0)181 831 9990
Fax: 00 44 (0)181 831 9991

AT FOULKS LYNCH LTD

Number 4, The Griffin Centre
Staines Road, Feltham
Middlesex TW14 0HS

Examination Date: □ December 99 □ June 2000	Publications				Distance Learning	Open Learning
	Textbooks	Revision Series	Lynchpins	Tracks	Include helpline & marking (except for overseas Open Learning)	
Module A – Foundation Stage						
1 Accounting Framework	£18.95 [UK] [IAS]	£10.95 [UK] [IAS]	£5.95 ☐	£10.95 ☐	£85 ☐	£89 ☐
2 Legal Framework	£18.95 ☐	£10.95 ☐	£5.95 ☐	£10.95 ☐	£85 ☐	£89 ☐
Module B						
3 Management Information	£18.95 ☐	£10.95 ☐	£5.95 ☐	£10.95 ☐	£85 ☐	£89 ☐
4 Organisational Framework	£18.95 ☐	£10.95 ☐	£5.95 ☐	£10.95 ☐	£85 ☐	£89 ☐
Module C – Certificate Stage						
5 Information Analysis	£18.95 ☐	£10.95 ☐	£5.95 ☐	£10.95 ☐	£85 ☐	£89 ☐
6 Audit Framework	£18.95 [UK] [IAS]	£10.95 [UK] [IAS]	£5.95 ☐	£10.95 ☐	£85 ☐	£89 ☐
Module D						
7 Tax Framework FA98 – D99	£17.95 ☐	£10.95 ☐	£5.95 ☐	£10.95 ☐	£85 ☐	£89 ☐
FA99 – J2000	£18.95 ☐	£10.95 ☐*	£5.95 ☐	£10.95 ☐*	£85 ☐	£89 ☐
8 Managerial Finance	£18.95 ☐	£10.95 ☐	£5.95 ☐	£10.95 ☐	£85 ☐	£89 ☐
Module E – Professional Stage						
9 ICDM	£18.95 ☐	£10.95 ☐	£5.95 ☐	£10.95 ☐	£85 ☐	£89 ☐
10 Accounting & Audit Practice	£22.95 [UK]	£10.95 [UK] [IAS]	£5.95 ☐	£10.95 ☐	£85 ☐	£89 ☐
10 Accounting & Audit Practice (IAS)	£23.95 [IAS]	£10.95 ☐				
11 Tax Planning FA98 – D99	£18.95 ☐	£10.95 ☐	£5.95 ☐	£10.95 ☐	£85 ☐	£89 ☐
FA99 – J2000	£18.95 ☐	£10.95 ☐*	£5.95 ☐	£10.95 ☐*	£85 ☐	£89 ☐
Module F						
12 Management & Strategy	£18.95 ☐	£10.95 ☐	£5.95 ☐	£10.95 ☐	£85 ☐	£89 ☐
13 Financial Rep Environment	£20.95 [IAS]	£10.95 [IAS]	£5.95 ☐	£10.95 ☐	£85 ☐	£89 ☐
14 Financial Strategy	£19.95 ☐	£10.95 ☐	£5.95 ☐	£10.95 ☐	£85 ☐	£89 ☐
		*Available Feb 2000		*Available Feb 2000		
P & P + Delivery UK Mainland	£2.00/book	£1.00/book	£1.00/book	£1.00/tape	£5.00/subject	£5.00/subject
NI, ROI & EU Countries	£5.00/book	£3.00/book	£3.00/book	£1.00/tape	£15.00/subject	£15.00/subject
Rest of world standard air service	£10.00/book	£8.00/book	£8.00/book	£2.00/tape	£25.00/subject	£25.00/subject
Rest of world courier service†	£22.00/book	£20.00/book	Not applicable	Not applicable	£47.00/subject	£47.00/subject

SINGLE ITEM SUPPLEMENT FOR TEXTBOOKS AND REVISION SERIES:

If you only order 1 item, INCREASE postage costs by £2.50 for UK, NI & EU Countries or by £15.00 for Rest of World Services

TOTAL	Sub Total £					
	Post & Packing £					
	Total £					

†*Telephone number essential for this service*   *Payments in Sterling in London* | Order Total   £ | |

DELIVERY DETAILS

☐ Mr ☐ Miss ☐ Mrs ☐ Ms Other

Initials   Surname

Address

                    Postcode

Telephone   Deliver to home ☐

Company name

Address

                    Postcode

Telephone   Fax

Monthly report to go to employer ☐   Deliver to work ☐

PAYMENT

1 I enclose Cheque/PO/Bankers Draft for £_____
   Please make cheques payable to AT Foulks Lynch Ltd.

2 Charge Mastercard/Visa/Switch A/C No:

   | | | | | | | | | | | | | | | | | | |

   Valid from: |__|__|__| Expiry Date: |__|__|__|
   Issue No: (Switch only) |__|__|

Signature   Date

DECLARATION

I agree to pay as indicated on this form and understand that
AT Foulks Lynch Terms and Conditions apply (available on
request). I understand that AT Foulks Lynch Ltd are not liable
for non-delivery if the rest of world standard air service is used.

Signature   Date

Please Allow:	UK mainland	- 5-10 w/days	**Notes:**	All delivery times subject to stock availability.
	NI, ROI & EU Countries	- *1-3 weeks		Signature required on receipt (except rest of world
	Rest of world standard air service	- 6 weeks		standard air service). Please give both addresses for
	Rest of world courier service	- 10 w/days		Distance Learning students where possible.

Form effective at June 99   *All details correct at time of printing*   *Source: ACCATXJ99*